The Oxford Dictionary of

Humorous
Quotations

The Oxford Dictionary of

Humorous Quotations

SECOND EDITION

edited by **Ned Sherrin**

OXFORD
UNIVERSITY PRESS

OXFORD
UNIVERSITY PRESS

Great Clarendon Street, Oxford OX2 6DP

Oxford University Press is a department of the University of Oxford.
It furthers the University's objective of excellence in research, scholarship,
and education by publishing worldwide in

Oxford New York

Athens Auckland Bangkok Bogotá Buenos Aires Cape Town
Chennai Dar es Salaam Delhi Florence Hong Kong Istanbul Karachi
Kolkata Kuala Lumpur Madrid Melbourne Mexico City Mumbai Nairobi
Paris São Paulo Shanghai Singapore Taipei Tokyo Toronto Warsaw

with associated companies in Berlin Ibadan

Oxford is a registered trade mark of Oxford University Press
in the UK and in certain other countries

Published in the United States
by Oxford University Press Inc., New York

Selection and arrangement © Ned Sherrin, Oxford University Press 1995, 2001
Introduction © Ned Sherrin 1995, 2001

The moral rights of the author have been asserted
Database right Oxford University Press (makers)

First published 1995
Second edition published 2001

British Library Cataloguing in Publication Data
Data available

Library of Congress Cataloging-in-Publication Data
The Oxford dictionary of humorous quotations /
edited by Ned Sherrin.—2nd ed.
p. cm.
Includes indexes.
ISBN 0-19-860289-8
1. Quotations, English.
2. Wit and humor. I. Sherrin, Ned.
PN6084.H8 O94 2001   082'.02'07—dc21   2001021062

10 9 8 7 6 5 4 3 2 1

Designed by Jane Stevenson
Typeset in Photina and Argo
by Interactive Sciences Ltd
Printed in Great Britain
on acid free paper by
T. J. International Ltd, Padstow, Cornwall

Project Team

Managing Editor	Elizabeth Knowles
Associate Editor	Susan Ratcliffe
Index Editor	Carolyn Garwes
Reading Programme	Jean Harker Verity Mason Helen Rappaport
Library Research	Ralph Bates Marie G. Diaz
Data Capture	Muriel Summersgill
Proof-reading	Fabia Claris Penny Trumble

Preface to Second Edition

This edition of the *Oxford Dictionary of Humorous Quotations*, like its predecessor, attempts to ensure that 'the liveliest effusions of wit and humour are conveyed to the world in the best chosen language' (Jane Austen, *Northanger Abbey*). In the pursuit of this aim, over 800 new quotations have been added, some material has (regretfully but firmly) been cut, and over 30 completely new themes (from **Baseball** to **Secrecy**) have been added.

Canvassing readers' opinions confirmed the importance of contemporary resonance, and underlined (as a critic of the first edition pointed out) that we are now so blest with living humorists. Among welcome new arrivals to the *Dictionary* are Dick Vosburgh ('I'm aghast! if there ever was one') and David Mamet ('They say the definition of ambivalence is watching your mother-in-law drive over a cliff in your new Cadillac'). Some older quotations have had to go, but earlier periods still make fresh contributions, as with Lady Mary Wortley Montagu's view of Queen Caroline and her maids-of-honour dressed in pink:

> Superior to her waiting nymphs,
> As lobster to attendant shrimps.

Inadvertent humour can also make an insistent claim, as with the rebuke to Zero Mostel when appearing before the House Un-American Activities Committee: 'If your interpretation of a butterfly at rest brought any money into the coffers of the Communist Party, you contributed directly to the propaganda effort of the Communist Party.'

In reviewing another dictionary, the same critic, Mr Bevis Hillier, took issue with the recycling of quotations: 'As a child I would politely decline the gobstopper that three other kids had already sucked.' The problem here is that a dictionary is a reference book, and if its proud purchaser wishing to check a famous quotation dimly recalled goes to his *Humorous Quotations* and does not find it there, he feels short changed. Again, some wiseacres opening the book will discover that a quotation the editor has rejected is absent, and conclude gleefully that ignorance is the explanation. And what if this Mr Know-All has less self-awareness than the character in Edward Albee's *Who's Afraid of Virginia Woolf*: 'I have a fine sense of the ridiculous but no sense of humour'?

Mr Hillier's advice is to 'buy a large hard-backed notebook, read books and newspapers for ten years, writing down the things that make you smile or laugh, then organize them into a book'. This is very much the method I have employed for both these editions, augmenting my own finds from the Oxford University Press's vast store of quotations. Items which I have been pleased to add range from Gore Vidal's response to his novel *Lincoln* being described as 'meretricious' ('Really? Well, meretricious and a happy New Year to you!') to Lord Runcie's comment after appearing on *Loose Ends* with Diana Rigg in the last months of his life: 'Being hugged by Diana Rigg is worth three sessions of chemotherapy.' Despite the risk of contagion from a second suck at the gobstopper, I have included those quotations which amused me from lists of omissions in reviews: two welcome additions of this kind are Mary Anne Disraeli's assessment of her husband ('I wish you could only see Dizzy in his bath, then you would know what a white skin is') and Else Mendl on her dislike of soup: 'I do not believe in building a meal on a lake.'

It is not only a fisherman who laments the one that got away. One quotation found just too late was Peter Nichols' comment on Harold Hobson's assessment of Tom Stoppard: 'Last time Hobson compared him favourably with Shakespeare. This time he puts him in the scales with God and finds the older man a bit lightweight.' And only as the *Dictionary* goes to press have I remembered that Arlington Stringham's jokes were filched (on Clovis's evidence) from Lady Isabel, 'who slept in a hammock and understood Yeats's poems'. Eleanor Stringham took an overdose on discovering this. When the story was first published in a Saki collection in 1912, the *New Age* complained, 'Why, oh why, can we see no humour in these stories?' John Lane published the criticism in the midst of universal raves to advertise the book, but the sole voice of dissent reminds us of the eternal problem of humour—its unassailable subjectivity.

Another wonderful item, which also surfaced just too late, was a couplet by H. F. Ellis, quoted by Miles Kington in his *Guardian* obituary of Ellis in December 2000:

> Mine eyes have missed the glory of the coming of the Lord
> Through searching through my pockets where my optic aids are stored . . .

Here I hope to have included 'the Quip Modest, the Reproof Valiant and the Countercheck Quarrelsome' in sufficient measure to satisfy the reader. At least the Quips, Reproofs and Counterchecks are offered without analysis. 'Humour can be dissected in the same way as a frog can—but the thing dies in the process' (E. B. White).

As a tiny envoi to this preface, here is a story that does not fit the main text. Sir Michael Gambon told me the other day that he had once played Oscar Wilde. A civilian had asked him, 'Was it hard playing a homosexual?'

'Oh, no,' said the great Gambon, whimsically leading him on. 'You see, I used to be one.'

'Why did you stop?'

'It made my eyes water.'

On reflection, I think 'It made my eyes water' might slip into the literature to do duty for a multitude of excuses.

NED SHERRIN

November 2000

Introduction to the First Edition

Wittgenstein claimed that his ambition to write a philosophical work constructed entirely of jokes was frustrated when he realized that he had no sense of humour. The editor of a dictionary of humorous quotations, looking back on his final selection, must wonder how many of his choices will convince the reader that he shares Wittgenstein's disability. For the philosopher there was comfort in the thought that no-one *completely* devoid of a sense of humour would be so aware of his limitations. There is also the suspicion, supported by diligent research, that many jokes are indeed fashioned by people who have no sense of humour.

These reassurances are denied to an editor. He is accountable for deciding that every one of roughly 5,000 quotations in this collection is likely to set the table on a roar. His paranoia is increased by the spectrum of attitudes to humour. 'Humour's a funny thing,' says a character in Terry Johnson's play *Dead Funny*. But an old lady coming out of one of Victoria Wood's shows complained within earshot of the star, 'I don't find humour funny.'

'The joy of simple laughter' is another of Terry Johnson's deftly deployed clichés. Laughter is not invariably joyous and what produces it is rarely simple. I make this disclaimer because I have been encouraged by the publishers to make a more personal selection than the compilers of the fourth edition of the *Oxford Dictionary of Quotations* and the *Oxford Dictionary of Modern Quotations*. These were assembled in the former case by recruiting 'a team of distinguished advisers, united by scholarship in particular literary periods and subject fields' who picked their way through 'the *embarras de richesses*' offered by earlier editions; and in the latter by reducing 'a collection of more than 200,000 citations assembled by combing books, magazines, and newspapers'. Both books are 'an objective selection of quotations which are most widely known and used'.

It is impossible to be objective about humour. Therefore although I have combed both dictionaries because they contain so many quotations which are humorous as well as well-known, I have also sought to admit many which gain entrance not because they are well-known but because they are amusing and deserve our better acquaintance.

Chronologically the spread is from the earliest quotations; but I have justified the inclusion of antique saws solely on the grounds that they raise a smile today. Paul Johnson recently suggested in the *Spectator* that the first recorded laughter occurred at the end of the Early Bronze Age, about 2000 BC:

> Significantly it was a woman who laughed. The Book of Genesis tells us (xviii. 10 ff.) that, when Sarah overheard the Lord inform her husband Abraham she was to have a son, 'Sarah laughed within herself, saying, after I am waxed old shall I have pleasure, my lord being old also?'

Johnson's conclusion is that the first joke was female and was about sex. Sarah tried to keep it to herself; but the men accused her of laughing. She denied it, 'for she was afraid'. It may have seemed a good joke to Sarah in 2000 BC but that does not justify its inclusion today. On the other hand some 3,600 years later, Shakespeare's stage direction 'Exit, pursued by a bear' in *The Winter's Tale*, now a mellow 400 years old, still makes me smile—whether he intended it or not. However, there is no room for all the smiles in Shakespeare. I mourn the passing of 'Nay, faith, let me not play a woman: I have a beard coming,' from the *Dream*, which is warm, funny, and well observed; however, it is preserved in the *Oxford Dictionary of Quotations*.

I have not thought it necessary to reopen the ever-raging debate fought over the boundaries between wit and humour. In introducing his *Anthology of Wit*, Guy Boas derives humour from the supposition that human nature was once held to be determined by the physical 'humours' and fluids which make up the body. Imbalance of these fluids produces (as in Ben Jonson's plays) conduct which was freakish, absurd, or whimsical—provoking laughter at the recognizably humorous situation. The word 'wit', however, stems from the Old English *witan* to know, which lent itself flatteringly to the Anglo-Saxon approximation to Parliament, and implied optimistically the exercise there of the intellect. So wit is associated with the mind's contribution to what is amusing. 'Humour', to Boas, 'is the funny situation or object; wit is the fun which a particular mind subjectively perceives on the situation or object.' There is room in this book for both. So what were the criteria for the quotations which survive?

No such book can afford to ignore perennials like Wilde, Mencken, Coward, Parker, Kaufman, and Shaw; Johnny Speight, the creator of *Till Death Do Us Part* (and therefore, in America, of *All in the Family*) grew up reading collections of quotations and concluded that Bernard Shaw was a gag-writer, which fuelled his own ambitions in the field of comedy. Among phrase-makers in recent years Gore Vidal, Tom Stoppard, Alan Bennett, Russell Baker, P. J. O'Rourke, Stephen Fry, and Craig Brown demand inclusion as new hardy annuals. Some writers are consistently witty, some have a happy inspiration. The former earn more entries that the latter. I did not consider it useful to operate a quota system.

The unintentionally humorous can be as diverting and must also be found a place. With its 'Colemanballs' feature *Private Eye* magazine spotlighted for our superior pleasure the pressure under which sports commentators try and sometimes fail to find the right word—though who can be sure whether 'the batsman's Holding, the bowler's Willey' was Brian Johnston's accidental comment or the result of a confrontation for which he had long been lying in wait. In America there is the famous Phil Rizzuto remark when his commentary was interrupted by the news of the Pope's death: 'that puts a damper, even on a Yankee win.' Dan Quayle and George Bush are modern political stars on the unconscious humour circuit. It is hard to do better than Quayle's alleged hesitation on visiting Latin America, 'not having studied Latin', or his insistence on the 'e' at the end of 'potato'.

Political correctness throws up a shoal of examples of unconscious humour, some of which have found a place. I might have found room for excerpts from the reported BBC *Woman's Hour* directive to new presenters in the early 1990s:

> 3. Do not be surprised that a woman has achieved something . . . 4. Do not be surprised that an older person has achieved something . . . 5. Do not be surprised that a black person has achieved something . . .

but there is a leaden mind behind that directive which does not deserve to be included.

The pronouncements of censors are another rich vein of unconscious humour. In the 1920s Nina Shortt, a daughter of a film censor and ex-Home Secretary, Sir Edward Shortt, refused a certificate to Jean Cocteau's avant-garde movie *The Seashell and the Clergyman*:

> [This film] is so cryptic as to be almost meaningless. If there is a meaning, it is doubtless objectionable.

Lord Tyrell, who succeeded Shortt, went one better in 1937:

> We take pride in observing that there is not a single film showing in London today that deals with any of the burning issues of the hour.

The sublimely named Major de Fonblanque Cox combined censorship with dogbreeding. On his appointment he declared:

> No, my boy, let us show clean films in the old country! I shall judge film stories as I would horseflesh, or a dog. I shall look for clean lines everywhere.

There may be less art in this than in the words which the Grossmiths put into Mr Pooter's mouth, 'I left the room with silent dignity but caught my foot in the mat,' but there is no less humour.

Another *Private Eye* feature, 'Pseud's Corner', is based on yet another sort of unconscious humour, I do not think Professor Karl Miller's verdict on the footballer Paul Gascoigne for *The London Review of Books* found its way there, but it deserved to:

> He was a highly charged spectacle on the field of play: fierce and comic, formidable and vulnerable, urchin-like and waiflike, a strong head and torso with comparatively breakable legs, strange-eyed, pink-faced, fair-haired, tense and upright, a priapic monolith in the Mediterranean sun . . . he is magic, and fairy-tale magic at that.

Of them all, the late Lord Massereene and Ferrard emerges as a new star provider of unintentional amusement, recommending the warning notice, 'Beware of the Agapanthus'.

Quotations are taken from novels, plays, poems, essays, letters, speeches, films, radio and television broadcasts, songs, popular jokes, graffiti, and advertisements, accurately attributed wherever possible. Some have had to fall by the wayside for reasons of space, or because I could not legitimize them. Under the firm but patient guidance of the Dictionary Department at Oxford University Press, I have endeavoured to help their devoted detectives to verify the quotations chosen in original or authoritative sources.

I have found space for some of the best-known catch-phrases which have sprung from radio and television programmes, but sources are so prolific that a general anthology can only hint at the richness—from the inventive conceits of Frank Muir and Denis Norden in *Take It From Here* to the anachronistic whimsies of Ben Elton and Richard Curtis in *Blackadder*. In *Take It From Here* the puns were elaborate, the plotting devious:

> [SILAS THE PURITAN] Thou art spending all the royal coffers on this female person [Nell Gwynne]. But yesterday you sold the Crown Jewels . . . to buy her a sedan chair with a sunshine roof!
> [KING CHARLES II] So I blued a couple of baubles? 'Tis of no account.
> [SILAS] (reproachfully) But you're forever blueing baubles.

In *Blackadder* the humour is starker:

> The Germans are a cruel race. Their operas last for six hours and they have no word for fluffy.

Some catch-phrases demand to be included, such as the Chief Whip's notorious response in Michael Dobbs' *House of Cards*:

> You might very well think that. I couldn't possibly comment.

Formula jokes are also generally too plentiful and often too unfunny to earn a place—sick jokes, light-bulb jokes, elephant jokes, and drummer jokes are excluded. I have also resisted the temptation to follow a 1994 trend with the latest fashionable American joke craze, 'Doing the Dozens', allegedly a venerable Afro-American habit of trading insults—preferably about the opponent's mother. For example, 'Your mother is so ugly, when she walks into the bank they turn off the camera,' or 'Your mother is so dumb, she went to the movies and the sign said, "Under 17 not admitted", so she came back with 18 friends.' 'Doing the Dozens' can wait for the slim paperback volume in which these ripostes will doubtless one day be collected by another publisher.

At the moment when I identified a mass-multiplying reproach, 'like turkeys voting for Christmas', a scholarly commentator in the *Independent Magazine* traced the birth of this death-wish simile to the late David Penhaligon who used it to highlight his distaste for the British Lib-Lab pact (1977–8). For Penhaligon it emphasized the Prime Minister's (James Callaghan's) certainty that the Liberals would never vote to bring him down. Callaghan himself plundered it the next year to slight the weak position of Scottish Nationalists. It crossed the Irish Sea when a Fianna Fáil member of the Dáil said that, 'a woman voting for divorce is like turkeys . . .' Both the Bruges Group of Conservative MPs and Michael Heseltine rented the phrase for their own ends in 1991. Paddy Ashdown, the leader of Penhaligon's old party, grabbed it to pour scorn on rebel Tories during the Maastricht debate. The Tory Party, he said, would not be defeated by its place-preserving backbenchers. From them to bring the Government down, 'would be like turkeys . . .' he said, 'etc.' The apotheosis of this witfest came when the French awarded a special 'foreign political humour prize' to the British MP Teresa Gorman for trotting out the same rubric, once again in the context of Maastricht. If anyone deserves to accept the prize it is the Widow Penhaligon.

Topicality admitted the inclusion of a borderline case, a version of another cliché-ridden humorous quip which is custom-made for hand-me-down insults. John Major was not being witty or original when he called some of his backbenchers, 'a few apples short of a picnic', but the phrase caught the public fancy. I can't remember whether the ex-chairman of Test Selectors, Ted Dexter, said of someone or was described by someone as being, 'a few roos loose in the top paddock'. 'One brick short of a load' and 'One slice short of a sandwich' are in the same vein: but none of them earns inclusion. Victor Lewis-Smith, describing Lord Rees-Mogg as 'two coupons short of a pop-up toaster', gets nearer with a vivid variation but is still disqualified by the curse of formula. Had he been Prime Minister he might have made it.

The files of the OUP Dictionary Department have inevitably provided a mass of material, all providentially sourced. Sadly many of the contributions derived from my own serendipitizing were lodged solely in the mind which failed to remember where I had found them. However, perhaps I should have let stand more of those remarks at whose birth I was present. One example is Anthony Quinton's impromptu comment as solemn music flooded a BBC studio when we were taken off the air for a news bulletin during the Falklands War. 'I know that tune,' he said, 'it's Sibelius' "You Can't Win 'Em All".' I can't think of a better authority.

In culling the new material the decision to organize the book thematically and not to arrange quotations under author headings was often revealing. In the section on Wealth, for example, some fun is to be had by the witty at the expense of the wealthy; but I relish the petulant note that invades the voices of the rich from Lord Durham (who in the nineteenth century was known as 'King Jog' because he could 'jog along' on £40,000 a year) through Lord Northcliffe (who said that when he wanted a peerage he would 'buy it like an honest man') and Chips Channon (who found it difficult in 1934 to go out shopping and spend less than £200) to Alan Clark (moaning in his diary in 1987 of the £700,000 in his Abbey National Crazy-High-Interest account, 'but what's the use?'). Sadly I could not confirm the Duke of Marlborough's bleat when urged to sack one of his many Viennese pastry-cooks, 'May not a man have a biscuit?'

Looking at other collections, I was frustrated by innumerable headings which yield very few quotations. Here we have a total of 149 classifications, some of which represent the combination of related headings. For example, Truth is linked with Lies rather than sitting unhappily in separate beds, while on the other hand the stage is such a productive source that I have separated Actors and Acting from The Theatre. Appropriate cross-reference entries are supplied, and keyword and author indexes further facilitate the chasing of references. (For a more detailed account, see 'How to Use the Dictionary'.)

I have introduced a large number of quotations from popular songs—so much wit is crammed into the discipline which a lyric writer observes. My selection cannot be comprehensive but it aims to point the road to a Samarkand of riches. Which do you choose from a Sondheim lyric? Look at 'Now', a song from *A Little Night Music*, in which a literary-minded middle-aged husband is trying to decide which gem will turn on his reluctant young wife. I sacrificed:

> The Brontes are grander
> But not very gay.
> Her taste is much blander
> I'm sorry to say,
> But is Hans Christian Ander-
> sen ever risqué?

in favour of:

> And Stendhal would ruin
> The plan of attack,
> As there isn't much blue in
> *The Red and the Black.*

But the whole score is laced with wit.

To backtrack, I was tempted to include the current Professor of Poetry at Oxford's review of Sondheim's *Sweeney Todd* in the *Sunday Times*, 'the worst rhymes in London', along with Dan Quayle's contributions to unconscious humour; but it got away. Coward, Porter, and Hart are dinosaurs in the field but other British and American lyric writers from E. Y. Harburg to Raymond Douglas Davis (The Kinks) deserve a more detailed examination than this book can afford. I hope enough creeps in to point the reader in the right direction.

Songs are easy to source, but an arrangement in themes prompted all sorts of quotations that dance tantalizingly in my magpie memory and have eluded our keenest detectives. Some of recollection's children I cannot legitimize. Some I have had to omit for others more favoured. Here are some of those I mourn:

Lord Thorneycroft's reply to Lord Houghton's letter, 'outlining his massive campaign to put animals into politics':

> Dear Douglas, Thank you for your letter about animals. I do think that the poor creatures have enough to put up with without being put into politics. Yours sincerely . . .

Nietzsche and Michael Frayn on books:

> Books for general reading always smell badly. The odour of the common people hangs about them. (Nietzsche)

> There is something about a blurb-writer paying his respects to a funny book which puts one in mind of a short-sighted Lord Mayor raising his hat to a hippopotamus. (Frayn)

Robert Altman on children:

> If you have a child who is seven feet tall, you don't cut off his head or his legs. You buy him a bigger bed and hope he plays basketball.

Evelyn Waugh on class:

> No writer before the middle of the nineteenth century wrote about the working-class other than as grotesques or as pastoral decorations. Then when they were given the vote, certain writers started to suck up to them.

Ronald Firbank on the country:

> I'd like to spank the white walls of (that shepherd's) cottage.

Antonia Fraser on death:

> Once there was a Drag Hunt Ball, just outside Oxford, to which I had unaccountably failed to be asked. I asked God to do something about it, and God recklessly killed poor King George, as a result of which the Hunt Ball was cancelled.

Mickey Rose on dress-sense:

> Nobody would wear beige to rob a bank.

Lord Rosebery's advice to Queen Victoria:

> There is much exaggeration about the attainments required for a speaker. All Speakers are highly successful, all Speakers are deeply regretted, and are generally announced to be irreplaceable. But a Speaker is soon found, and found, almost invariably, among the mediocrities of the House.

Bernard Levin on Barbara Cartland's grasp of history:

> Miss Cartland insists that Earl Mountbatten helped her with the writing . . .

All that expert help, however, has still not managed to correct her apparent belief that Trafalgar came very shortly after Waterloo; perhaps she has confused English history with the London Underground system.

Lily Tomlin on love:

If love is the answer, could you rephrase the question?

Chekhov on marriage:

If you're afraid of loneliness, don't marry.

Carl Sandburg on murder:

Papa loved Mamma
Mamma loved men
Mamma's in the graveyard
Papa's in the pen.

Thomas Beecham on a fellow-musician:

Sir Adrian Boult came to see me this morning—positively reeking of Horlicks.

J. G. Saxe on the newspaper world:

Who would not be an Editor? To write
The magic 'we' of such enormous might.
To be so great beyond the common span
It takes the plural to express the Man.

Senator Wyche Fowler on being asked whether, in 'those permissive sixties', he had smoked a marijuana cigarette:

Only when committing adultery.

Norman Douglas on Suffolk:

Land of uncomfortable beds, brown sherry, and Perpendicular Gothic.

The Duke of Devonshire on President Nasser and Anthony Eden:

The camel that broke the straw's back.

P. G. Wodehouse's Sir Roderick Glossop on religion:

A lay interest in matters to do with liturgical procedure is invariably a prelude to insanity.

Horace Walpole on Queen Charlotte in her later years:

I do think the *bloom* of her ugliness is going off.

The Prince of Conti, a noted rake, when he at last became aware of his failing sexual prowess:

It is time for me to retire. Formerly my civilities were taken for declarations of love. Now my declarations of love are taken for civilities.

W. G. Grace, apologizing for his bad fielding in old age:

It is the ground, it's too far away.

The President of Cornell University on a proposed sporting fixture:

I shall not permit thirty men to travel four hundred miles (to Michigan) to agitate a ball of wind.

William Faulkner on Henry James:

One of the nicest old ladies I ever met.

Edith Sitwell and Herman Mankiewicz on modern writers:

> A lot of people writing poetry today would be better employed keeping rabbits. (Sitwell)

> 'Tell me, do you know any 75 dollar-a-week writers?'
> 'Yes, I know lots of them. But they're all making 1500 dollars a week.' (Mankiewicz)

I found one aspect of the arrangement of previous dictionaries unsympathetic to humorous quotations. It has been customary to print the quote and follow it with the contextual explanation. This is often like giving the punchline of a joke and then adding the premise. Where appropriate I have put the explanation first, for example this quotation from Thomas Gainsborough:

> *On attempting to paint two actors, David Garrick and Samuel Foote:*
> Rot them for a couple of rogues, they have everybody's faces but their own.

The learned editor of the *Oxford Dictionary of Quotations* has wisely written, 'Ideally, a quotation should be able to float free from its moorings, remaining detached from its original context.' However, one could compare two extracts from a page opened at random in the fourth edition; while the Wolcott Gibbs quote 'Backward ran sentences until reeled the mind' is arresting enough to stand with the subsequent note ('satirizing the style of *Time* magazine'), André Gide's sigh, '*Hugo—hélas!*' would read more entertainingly if the explanation, 'When asked who was the greatest 19th-century poet' preceded it.

I have tried to resist the temptation to admit anecdote where quotation is the brief. Lord Albemarle might have found a place in the unconscious humour section, but the preamble to his striking sentence is too long and involved:

> *The dancer Maude Allen had been accused of lesbianism in an article entitled 'The Cult of the Clitoris', and Miss Allen sued for libel in a much publicized lawsuit which caught the puzzled attention of Lord Albemarle, who complained:*
> I've never heard of this Greek chap Clitoris they're talking about.

However vivid the phrase may be its context is overpoweringly anecdotal. While Lord Macaulay's riposte, aged four, having had hot coffee spilt over his legs, 'Thank you, Madam, the agony is abated,' is a splendid quote preceded to its advantage by a succinct explanation.

I hope that this collection gathers together a vast number of old friends whom it would be disloyal to exclude—conscious that they will still surprise some. I am often astonished at the way an audience can pounce on an over-familiar quip by Coward or Wilde and welcome it as new-minted. It proved particularly enjoyable to hunt for less well-known quotations from established wits. Noel Coward's chestnuts are included, but also his vivid vignette (in spite of Lord Byron's warning, 'Damn description, it is always disgusting'):

> Edith Sitwell, in that great Risorgimento cape of hers, looks as though she were covering a teapot or a telephone.

Less familiar Oscar Wilde contributions include his admonishment to a waiter:

> When I ask for a watercress sandwich, I do not mean a loaf with a field in the middle of it;

his judgement on publishers:

> I suppose all publishers are untrustworthy. They certainly always look it;

and his request to his examiners in his viva at Oxford when he was asked to stop his brilliant translation of the Greek version of the New Testament:

> Oh, do let me go on, I want to see how it ends.

Sydney Smith is sharp on the incongruity of oratorio, 'How absurd to see 500 people fiddling like madmen about Israelites in the Red Sea,' and playful on two Edinburgh women hurling insults at one another across an alleyway, 'Those two women will never agree; they are arguing from different premises.' There is Whistler on the picture of his mother, 'Yes, one does like to make one's mummy just as nice as possible', and Gore Vidal on ex-President Eisenhower, 'reading a speech with his usual sense of discovery'.

Among the modern phrase-makers I enjoy Jonathan Lynn and Antony Jay in *Yes Minister*:

> I think it will be a clash between the political will and the administrative won't.

Richard Curtis and Ben Elton in *Blackadder*:

> To you, Baldrick, the Renaissance was just something that happened to other people, wasn't it?

Keith Waterhouse in his play *Bookends*:

> Should not the Society of Indexers be known as Indexers, Society of, The?

Joseph O'Connor in his novel *Cowboys and Indians*:

> Buckingham Palace looked a vast doll's house that some bullying skinhead brother had kicked down the Mall.

Clive James writes of John McEnroe that he 'did his complete Krakatoa number', and John Osborne says of his American producer David Merrick that he 'liked writers in the way a snake likes live rabbits'.

Unlikely candidates include: Lord Tennyson's brother, introducing himself to Dante Gabriel Rossetti:

> I am Septimus, the most morbid of the Tennysons.

Rupert Murdoch, asked to explain Page 3:

> I don't know. The editor did it while I was away.

T. E. Lawrence on reading *Lady Chatterley's Lover*:

> Surely the sex business isn't worth all this damned fuss? I've met only a handful of people who cared a biscuit for it.

Samuel Beckett encouraging an actor who lamented, 'I'm failing':

> Go on failing. Only next time, try to fail better.

C. S. Lewis on desire:

> He that but looketh on a plate of ham and eggs to lust after it, hath already committed breakfast with it in his heart.

There are some new Royal quotes, often falling into the category of unconscious humour. 'Aren't we due a royalty statement?' (Charles, Prince of Wales), 'I know no person so perfectly disagreeable and even dangerous as an author' (William IV), and George V, asked which film he would like to see while convalescing, 'Anything except that damned Mouse,' which makes a change from 'Bugger Bognor.' Furthermore, I have tried to add to the files of the OUP some quotations which are less familiar. This has meant casting a wider net over, for instance, North American sources, and again I have tried to balance the quotations which demand inclusion on account of the fame of their authors—Dorothy Parker, Robert Benchley, Mark Twain, Sam Goldwyn, and S. J. Perelman ('God, whom you doubtless remember as that quaint old subordinate of General Douglas MacArthur'), with the words of modern masters. I have taken pleasure in adding:

Mary McGrory on Watergate:

> Haldeman is the only man in America in this generation who let his hair grow for a courtroom appearance.

P. J. O'Rourke on certainty:

> That happy sense of purpose people have when they are standing up for a principle they haven't really been knocked down for yet.

Bill Bryson on childhood:

> I had always thought that once you grew up you could do anything you wanted—stay up all night or eat ice-cream straight out of the container.

The film critic James Agee on *Tycoon*:

> Several tons of dynamite are set off in this picture: none of it under the right people.

Jackie Mason on the English:

> If an Englishman gets run down by a truck he apologizes to the truck.

Woody Allen, Neil Simon, Fran Lebowitz, and Russell Baker appear *passim*, and for a British angle on America, Anthony Burgess supplies, 'the US Presidency is a Tudor monarchy with telephones.' George Bush ('What's wrong with being a boring kind of guy?') and Dan Quayle supply generous helpings of unconscious humour, such as 'Space is almost infinite. As a matter of fact, we think it is infinite' (Quayle), and are convenient targets, as in 'Poor George [Bush], he can't help it—he was born with a silver foot in his mouth' (Ann Richards). Sports writers like Jimmy Cannon are rewarding on their own craft, 'Let's face it, sports writers, we're not hanging around with brain surgeons'; so, sometimes, can sportsmen be, 'If people don't want to come out to the ball park, nobody's going to stop 'em' (Yogi Berra). Canada supplies both the unconscious humour of Brian Mulroney's 'I am not denying anything I did not say,' and, at the other extreme, Robertson Davies:

> I see Canada as a country torn between a very northern, rather extraordinary, mystical spirit which it fears and its desire to present itself to the world as a Scotch banker.

Australia under Paul Keating has been developing a rich vein of humorous invective like the exchange between the Prime Minister and his opponent John Hewson. Keating's comment:

> [John Hewson] is simply a shiver looking for a spine to run up,

is countered by Hewson with:

> I decided the worst thing you can call Paul Keating, quite frankly, is Paul Keating.

Reflecting on the insularity of his homeland, Clive James has written:

> A broad school of Australian writing has based itself on the assumption that

Australia not only has a history worth bothering about, but that all the history worth bothering about happened in Australia.

To verify this range of information would not have been possible without the diligent and imaginative work of the Oxford Dictionary Department researchers. However, the responsibility for the taste and the accuracy must be mine, the only caveat being Simon Strunsky's, 'Famous remarks are very seldom quoted correctly.' Above all it is my sense of humour which conditions the final choice and my regret if your favourite humorous quotations is not recorded here or if you pass too many entries without amusement.

NED SHERRIN

August 1994

How to Use the Dictionary

The Oxford Dictionary of Humorous Quotations is organized by themes, such as **Actors**, **The Family**, **Food and Drink**, **Love**, **Travel and Exploration**, **The Weather**, and **Writing**. The themes are placed in alphabetical order, and within each theme the quotations are arranged alphabetically according to author.

The themes have been chosen to reflect as wide a range of subjects as possible. Themes such as **Death**, **Life and Living**, and **Success and Failure** emphasize the general rather than the particular, but categories such as **Description**, **Last Words**, **People and Personalities**, and **Towns and Cities** have a wider coverage of quotations relevant to specific people, places, and events.

Related topics may be covered by a single theme, such as **Behaviour and Etiquette** and **Crime and Punishment**, and linked opposites may also be grouped in a single antithetical theme, such as **Heaven and Hell** and **Trust and Treachery**. A cross-reference from the second element of the pair appears in the appropriate place in the alphabetic sequence both in the main text and in the List of Themes.

Where themes are closely related, 'See also' references are given at the head of a section, immediately following the theme title and preceding the quotations. The heading **The Family** is thus followed by See also **Children**, **Parents**.

Each quotation has a marginal note giving the name of the author to whom the quotation is attributed; dates of birth and death (where known) are given. In general, the authors' names are given in the form by which they are best known, so that we have **Saki** rather than 'H. H. Munro'. If the authorship is unknown, 'Anonymous' appears.

A source note, usually including the specific date of the quotation, follows the author information. Quotations which are in general currency but which are not at present traceable to a specific source are indicated by 'attributed' in the source note; quotations which are popularly attributed to an author but whose authenticity is doubted are indicated by a note such as 'perhaps apocryphal'.

Contextual information regarded as essential to a full appreciation of the quotation precedes the relevant text in an italicized note; information seen as providing helpful amplification follows in an italicized note.

Allocation of a quotation to an individual theme is inevitably subjective, but the keyword index makes provision for tracing specific items other than by theme titles. Citations by named authors may similarly be traced via the author index. In each case, references show the theme name, sometimes in a shortened form (**Satisfaction** for **Satisfaction and Discontent**; **Theatre** for **The Theatre**), followed by the number of the quotation within the theme: '**Science** 7' therefore means the seventh quotation within the theme **Science and Technology**.

List of Themes

Acting See also **Actors**, **The Theatre**

1 This Othello had the naturalness, and the dignity, and the mind of a highly educated Moor, and not of a cultivated English gentleman who wakes up one morning to find that his skin has unexpectedly turned black.
of Balliol Holloway's Othello in 1927

James Agate 1877–1947: *Brief Chronicles* (1943)

2 This Iago was obviously an intellectual, and refreshingly unlike the usual furtive dog-stealer who would not impose upon the most trustful old lady, not to mention an experienced man of affairs like Othello.
of Neil Porter's Iago in 1927

James Agate 1877–1947: *Brief Chronicles* (1943)

supposed advice to a young actor:
3 Try and look as if you had a younger brother in Shropshire.

J. M. Barrie 1860–1937: Lady Cynthia Asquith diary, 6 January 1918

4 One day they may tell you you will not go far,
That night you open and there you are.
Next day on your dressing room
They hang a star!
Let's go on with the show!

Irving Berlin 1888–1989: 'There's No Business Like Show Business' (1946)

Shakespeare is trying to make a start on Love's Labour Won, *but Burbage interrupts him:*
5 'I've been thinking,' he said, 'I'd like to play a Dane— young, intellectual—I see him pale, vacillating, but above everything sad and prone to soliloquy.' 'I know,' said Shakespeare. 'Introspective.'

Caryl Brahms 1901–82 and **S. J. Simon** 1904–48: *No Bed for Bacon* (1941)

6 This Thane of Cawdor would be unnerved by Banquo's valet, never mind Banquo's ghost.
of Michael Hordern in Macbeth *in 1959*

Alan Brien 1925– : Diana Rigg *No Turn Unstoned* (1982)

7 When I read 'Be real, don't get caught acting,' I thought, 'How the hell do you do that?'

Billy Connolly 1942– : John Miller *Judi Dench: With a Crack in Her Voice* (1998)

8 Don't put your daughter on the stage, Mrs Worthington,
Don't put your daughter on the stage,
One look at her bandy legs should prove
She hasn't got a chance,
In addition to which
The son of a bitch
Can neither sing nor dance.

Noël Coward 1899–1973: 'Mrs Worthington' (1935)

9 CLAUDETTE COLBERT: I knew these lines backwards last night.
NOËL COWARD: And that's just the way you're saying them this morning.

Noël Coward 1899–1973: Cole Lesley *The Life of Noel Coward* (1976)

10 Anna Neagle playing Queen Victoria always made me think that Albert must have married beneath him.

Noël Coward 1899–1973: Sheridan Morley *The Quotable Noël Coward* (1999)

11 She's the only sylph I ever saw, who could stand upon one leg, and play the tambourine on her other knee, like a sylph.

Charles Dickens 1812–70: *Nicholas Nickleby* (1839)

when asked to say something terrifying during rehearsals for Peter Brook's Oedipus *in 1968:*

12 We open in two weeks.

John Gielgud 1904-2000: Peter Hay *Theatrical Anecdotes* (1987)

13 I made a great hit in *Macbeth* as the messenger because I took the precaution of running three times round the playground before I made my entrance so that I could deliver the news in a state of exhaustion.
   on a school production

Alec Guinness 1914-2000: John Mortimer *Character Parts* (1986)

14 I acted so tragic the house rose like magic,
   The audience yelled 'You're sublime.'
   They made me a present of Mornington Crescent
   They threw it a brick at a time.

W. F. Hargreaves 1846-1919: 'The Night I Appeared as Macbeth' (1922)

15 Shakespeare is so tiring. You never get a chance to sit down unless you're a king.

Josephine Hull 1886-1957: in *Time* 16 November 1953

16 If your interpretation of a butterfly at rest brought any money into the coffers of the Communist Party, you contributed directly to the propaganda effort of the Communist Party.
   to Zero Mostel, appearing before the House Un-American Activities Committee (HUAC)

Donald L. Jackson: at a hearing of HUAC, 14 October 1955

watching Spencer Tracy on the set of Dr Jekyll and Mr Hyde *(1941):*

17 Which is he playing now?

W. Somerset Maugham 1874-1965: attributed; Leslie Halliwell *The Filmgoer's Book of Quotes* (1978 edn)

18 When you do Shakespeare they think you must be intelligent because they *think* you understand what you're saying.

Helen Mirren 1945- : interviewed on *Ruby Wax Meets . . .* ; in *Mail on Sunday* 16 February 1997 'Night and Day'

on the part of Lear:

19 When you've the strength for it, you're too young; when you've the age you're too old. It's a bugger, isn't it?

Laurence Olivier 1907-89: in *Sunday Telegraph* 4 May 1986

20 But I have a go, lady, don't I? I 'ave a go. I do.

John Osborne 1929- : *The Entertainer* (1957)

21 Let me know where you are next week! I'll come and see you.

John Osborne 1929- : *The Entertainer* (1957); last lines

22 Acting is merely the art of keeping a large group of people from coughing.

Ralph Richardson 1902-83: in *New York Herald Tribune* 19 May 1946

23 I don't care for Lady Macbeth in the streetwalking scene.

Edward Linley Sambourne 1844-1910: R. G. C. Price *A History of Punch* (1957)

24 The best actors in the world, either for tragedy, comedy, history, pastoral, pastoral-comical, historical-pastoral, tragical-historical, tragical-comical-historical-pastoral, scene individable, or poem unlimited.

William Shakespeare 1564-1616: *Hamlet* (1601)

25 I could play Ercles rarely, or a part to tear a cat in, to make all split.

William Shakespeare 1564-1616: *A Midsummer Night's Dream* (1595-6)

26 I wish sir, you would practise this without me. I can't stay dying here all night.

Richard Brinsley Sheridan 1751-1816: *The Critic* (1779)

27 I told Mad Frankie Fraser 'I'm doing Hamlet'—he said, 'I'll do him for you.'

Arthur Smith 1954- : *Arthur Smith's Hamlet*

to an over-genteel actress in an Egyptian drama:
28 Oh my God! Remember you're in Egypt. The *skay* is only seen in Kensington.

Herbert Beerbohm Tree 1852–1917: M. Peters *Mrs Pat* (1984)

to a motley collection of American females, assembled to play ladies-in-waiting to a queen:
29 Ladies, just a little more virginity, if you don't mind.

Herbert Beerbohm Tree 1852–1917: Alexander Woollcott *Shouts and Murmurs* (1923)

30 This Rosalind was a gay and giddy creature—loads of fun, game for any jape, rather like a popular head girl—but a tiring companion, I felt, after a long day.

Kenneth Tynan 1927–80: review of *As You Like It* in 1952; *Curtains* (1961)

Actors See also **Film Stars**

1 John Hannah has the high cheekbones and low spirits for Inspector Rebus, a man under a cloud. He could also play John Knox, the teenage years.

Nancy Banks-Smith: in *Guardian* 27 April 2000

2 For an actress to be a success, she must have the face of a Venus, the brains of a Minerva, the grace of Terpsichore, the memory of a Macaulay, the figure of Juno, and the hide of a rhinoceros.

Ethel Barrymore 1879–1959: George Jean Nathan *The Theatre in the Fifties* (1953)

3 My only regret in the theatre is that I could never sit out front and watch me.

John Barrymore 1882–1942: Eddie Cantor *The Way I See It* (1959)

4 Tallulah Bankhead barged down the Nile last night as Cleopatra—and sank.

John Mason Brown 1900–69: in *New York Post* 11 November 1937

5 Like acting with 210 pounds of condemned veal.
of a dull actor

Coral Browne 1913–91: attributed

6 Like a rat up a rope.
of an over-busy actor

Coral Browne 1913–91: attributed

7 Tallulah [Bankhead] is always skating on thin ice. Everyone wants to be there when it breaks.

Mrs Patrick Campbell 1865–1940: in *The Times* 13 December 1968

8 I'm out of a job. London wants flappers, and I can't flap.
of the theatre of 1927

Mrs Patrick Campbell 1865–1940: Margot Peters *Mrs Pat* (1984)

9 She's such a nice woman. If you knew her you'd even admire her acting.
of another actress

Mrs Patrick Campbell 1865–1940: James Agate diary, 6 May 1937

10 I thought he was elderly, a cautionary-tale-finger-wagging-oracular Hamlet; rather like a university extension lecturer; a Hamlet in invisible pince-nez.
of Forbes-Robertson as Hamlet

Neville Cardus 1889–1975: *Autobiography* (1947)

the daughter of Sybil Thorndike and Lewis Casson explaining to a telephone enquiry why neither of her charitably inclined parents was at home:
11 Daddy is reading Shakespeare Sonnets to the blind and Mummy's playing Shakespeare to the lepers.

Anne Casson: recounted by Emlyn Williams; James Harding *Emlyn Williams* (1987)

12 She [Edith Evans] took her curtain calls as though she had just been un-nailed from the cross.

Noël Coward 1899–1973: diary, 25 October 1964

seeing a poster for 'Michael Redgrave and Dirk Bogarde in The Sea Shall Not Have Them*':*

13 I fail to see why not; everyone else has.

Noël Coward 1899–1973: Sheridan Morley *The Quotable Noël Coward* (1999)

14 Richard Briers played Hamlet like a demented typewriter.

W. A. Darlington 1890–1979: review of a RADA production; Diana Rigg *No Turn Unstoned* (1982)

15 Language was not powerful enough to describe the infant phenomenon.

Charles Dickens 1812–70: *Nicholas Nickleby* (1839)

16 Is it Colman's smile
That makes life worth while
Or Crawford's significant form?
Is it Lombard's lips
Or Mae West's hips
That carry you through the storm?

Gavin Ewart 1916–95: 'Verse from an Opera' (1939)

of Creston Clarke as King Lear:

17 He played the King as though under momentary apprehension that someone else was about to play the ace.

Eugene Field 1850–95: review attributed to Field; in *Denver Tribune* c.1880

18 Dear Ingrid—speaks five languages and can't act in any of them.
   of Ingrid Bergman

John Gielgud 1904–2000: Ronald Harwood *The Ages of Gielgud* (1984); attributed

19 People like to hear me say 'shit' in my gorgeous voice.
   of his popularity in America

John Gielgud 1904–2000: in *New Yorker* 10 July 2000; attributed

20 My dear fellow, I never saw anything so funny in my life, and yet it was not in the least bit vulgar.
   of Beerbohm Tree's Hamlet (1892)

W. S. Gilbert 1836–1911: D. Bispham *A Quaker Singer's Recollections* (1920)

21 An actor is a kind of a guy who if you ain't talking about him ain't listening.

George Glass 1910–84: Bob Thomas *Brando* (1973); said to be quoted frequently by Marlon Brando

Gogarty's patient Michael Scott, then an actor, coming to on the operating table, tried weakly to indicate that he was conscious:

22 Nurse, kindly put your hand over that man's mouth; we are not interested in an actor's subconscious.

Oliver St John Gogarty 1878–1957: Ulick O'Connor *Oliver St John Gogarty* (1964)

23 On the stage he was natural, simple, affecting;
   'Twas only that when he was off he was acting.
   of David Garrick

Oliver Goldsmith 1730–74: *Retaliation* (1774)

of Irving as Mephistopheles in Goethe's Faust*:*

24 The actor, of course, at moments presents to the eye a remarkably sinister figure. He strikes us, however, as superficial—a terrible fault for an archfiend.

Henry James 1843–1916: *The Scenic Art* (1948)

25 Massey won't be satisfied until he's assassinated.
   on Raymond Massey's success in playing Lincoln

George S. Kaufman 1889–1961: Howard Teichmann *George S. Kaufman* (1973)

26 I have pale blue eyes and I was receding in my late twenties. And if you look like this and you're 28, you play rapists.

Patrick Malahide 1945– : in *Daily Telegraph* 20 July 1996

on being refused membership of an exclusive golf-club:
27 I'm *not* an actor, and I enclose my press cuttings to prove it.

Victor Mature 1915- : Ned Sherrin *Cutting Edge* (1984)

28 I have worked with more submarines than leading ladies.

John Mills 1908- : in *Times* 12 February 2000 'Quotes of the Week'

29 Are fans likely to confuse the real-life Barrymore with the big-headed, foul-mouthed, envious, ungrateful, petty-minded game show host he portrays so convincingly and effortlessly?
on Michael Barrymore's first straight acting role

Bob Monkhouse 1928- : in *The Mail on Sunday* 9 April 2000 'Quotes of the Week'

30 Miss (Maureen) Stapleton played the part as though she had not yet signed her contract with the producer.
review of The Emperor's Clothes *in 1953*

George Jean Nathan 1882–1958: Diana Rigg *No Turn Unstoned* (1982)

of Katherine Hepburn at the first night of The Lake (*1933*)
31 She ran the whole gamut of the emotions from A to B, and put some distance between herself and a more experienced colleague [Alison Skipworth] lest she catch acting from her.

Dorothy Parker 1893–1967: attributed

32 It is greatly to Mrs Patrick Campbell's credit that, bad as the play was, her acting was worse.
review of Sardou Fedora *1 June 1895*

George Bernard Shaw 1856–1950: *Our Theatre in the Nineties* (1932)

33 I must somewhat tardily acknowledge an invitation to witness a performance at the Royalty Theatre by a Miss Hope Booth, a young lady who cannot sing, dance or speak, but whose appearance suggests that she might profitably spend three or four years in learning these arts, which are useful on the stage.

George Bernard Shaw 1856–1950: *Our Theatre in the Nineties* (1932); review 23 March 1895

34 We're *actors*—we're the opposite of people! . . . Think, in your head, *now*, think of the most . . . *private . . . secret . . . intimate* thing you have ever done secure in the knowledge of its privacy . . . Are you thinking of it? . . . *Well, I saw you do it!*

Tom Stoppard 1937- : *Rosencrantz and Guildenstern Are Dead* (1967)

35 The key to Beatrice Lillie's success is that she ignores her audience. This is an act of daring that amounts to revolution.

Kenneth Tynan 1927–80: in *Holiday* September 1956

36 As Virgilia in *Coriolanus* she yearns so hungrily that I longed to throw her a fish.
of Claire Bloom in 1955

Kenneth Tynan 1927–80: *Curtains* (1961)

37 As Lavinia, Vivien Leigh receives the news that she is about to be ravished on her husband's corpse with little more than the mild annoyance of one who would have preferred Dunlopillo.
review of Titus Andronicus *in 1955*

Kenneth Tynan 1927–80: *Curtains* (1961)

38 ALISON SKIPWORTH: You forget I've been an actress for forty years.
MAE WEST: Don't worry, dear. I'll keep your secret.

Mae West 1892–1980: G. Eells and S. Musgrove *Mae West* (1989)

on the Burton-Taylor Private Lives *in 1964:*
39 He's miscast and she's Miss Taylor.

Emlyn Williams 1905–87: James Harding *Emlyn Williams* (1987)

40 They say an actor is only as good as his parts. Well, my parts have done me pretty well, darling.

Barbara Windsor 1937– : in *The Times* 13 February 1999

41 She was like a sinking ship firing on the rescuers.
of Mrs Patrick Campbell in her later years

Alexander Woollcott 1887–1943: *While Rome Burns* (1944) 'The First Mrs Tanqueray'

Advertising

1 While you were out your exterminator called.
heading of leaflet left in a New York letter-box

Anonymous: Sylvia Townsend Warner letter to David Garnett, 12 May 1967

2 The cheap contractions and revised spellings of the advertising world which have made the beauty of the written word almost unrecognizable—surely any society that permits the substitution of 'kwik' for 'quick' and 'e.z.' for 'easy' does not deserve Shakespeare, Eliot or Michener.

Russell Baker 1925– : column in *New York Times*; Ned Sherrin *Cutting Edge* (1984)

3 Blurbs that appear on the back cover and in the advertisements recommending the book in glowing terms . . . are written by friends of the author who haven't read the book but owe the poor guy a favour.

Art Buchwald 1925– : *I Never Danced at the White House* (1974)

4 Advertising is the most fun you can have with your clothes on.

Jerry Della Femina 1936– : *From Those Wonderful Folks Who Gave You Pearl Harbor* (1971)

on a consultant who had given a paper 'Advertising in Medicine':
5 It was like listening to a loudspeaker blaring out 'Mum's the word'.

Oliver St John Gogarty 1878–1957: Ulick O'Connor *Oliver St John Gogarty* (1964)

6 It is far easier to write ten passably effective sonnets, good enough to take in the not too enquiring critic, than one effective advertisement that will take in a few thousand of the uncritical buying public.

Aldous Huxley 1894–1963: *On the Margin* (1923) 'Advertisement'

7 Society drives people crazy with lust and calls it advertising.

John Lahr 1941– : in *Guardian* 2 August 1989

8 Advertising may be described as the science of arresting human intelligence long enough to get money from it.

Stephen Leacock 1869–1944: *Garden of Folly* (1924)

9 The explanation of intuition is the same as that of advertisement: tell a man ten thousand times that Pears Soap is good for the complexion and eventually he will have an intuitive certainty of the fact.

W. Somerset Maugham 1874–1965: *A Writer's Notebook* (1949) written in 1901

10 Good wine needs no bush,
And perhaps products that people really want need no
    hard-sell or soft-sell TV push.
Why not?
Look at pot.

Ogden Nash 1902–71: 'Most Doctors Recommend or Yours For Fast, Fast, Fast Relief' (1972)

11 I think that I shall never see
A billboard lovely as a tree.
Perhaps, unless the billboards fall,
I'll never see a tree at all.

Ogden Nash 1902–71: 'Song of the Open Road' (1933)

12 The consumer isn't a moron; she is your wife.

David Ogilvy 1911– : *Confessions of an Advertising Man* (1963)

13 Advertising is the rattling of a stick inside a swill bucket.

George Orwell 1903–50: attributed

asked why he had made a commercial for American Express:
14 To pay for my American Express.

Peter Ustinov 1921– : in *Ned Sherrin in his Anecdotage* (1993)

Alcohol See also **Food and Drink**

1 R-E-M-O-R-S-E!
Those dry Martinis did the work for me;
Last night at twelve I felt immense,
Today I feel like thirty cents.
My eyes are bleared, my coppers hot,
I'll try to eat, but I cannot.
It is no time for mirth and laughter,
The cold, grey dawn of the morning after.

George Ade 1866–1944: *The Sultan of Sulu* (1903)

2 Let's get out of these wet clothes and into a dry Martini.

Anonymous: line coined in the 1920s by Robert Benchley's press agent and adopted by Mae West in *Every Day's a Holiday* (1937 film)

3 Somewhere in the limbo which divides perfect sobriety from mild intoxication.

Cyril Asquith 1890–1954: J. A. Gere and John Sparrow (eds.) *Geoffrey Madan's Notebooks* (1981)

4 At Dirty Dick's and Sloppy Joe's
We drank our liquor straight,
Some went upstairs with Margery,
And some, alas, with Kate.

W. H. Auden 1907–73: 'The Sea and the Mirror' (1944)

5 There's also parsnip or dandelion but this seems to have a slightly better bouquet. The dandelion's all right but I lost the use of one side of my face for about half an hour after I drunk it.

Alan Ayckbourn 1939– : *Table Manners* (1975)

6 The teacher I most wanted to emulate, however, was single, drank wine and had been gassed in World War I. Of his three admirable traits, there was only one I wanted to copy, and sure enough, to this day, I love the sound of a popping cork.

Russell Baker 1925– : column in *New York Times*; Ned Sherrin *Cutting Edge* (1984)

7 I saw a notice which said 'Drink Canada Dry' and I've just started.

Brendan Behan 1923–64: attributed (probably not original); Nigel Rees *Cassell Dictionary of Humorous Quotations* (1999)

on being told that the particular drink he was consuming was slow poison:
8 So who's in a hurry?

Robert Benchley 1889–1945: Nathaniel Benchley *Robert Benchley* (1955)

9 Often Daddy sat up very late working on a case of Scotch.

Robert Benchley 1889–1945: *Pluck and Luck* (1925)

10 An admirable man, who puts down half a bottle of whisky a day and has two convictions for drunken driving, but otherwise a pillar of society.

Alan Bennett 1934– : *Getting On* (1972)

of claret:

11 It would be port if it could.

Richard Bentley 1662–1742: R. C. Jebb *Bentley* (1902)

12 One evening in October, when I was one-third sober,
An' taking home a 'load' with manly pride;
My poor feet began to stutter, so I lay down in the gutter,
And a pig came up an' lay down by my side;
Then we sang 'It's all fair weather when good fellows get together,'
Till a lady passing by was heard to say:
'You can tell a man who "boozes" by the company he chooses'
And the pig got up and slowly walked away.

Benjamin Hapgood Burt 1880–1950: 'The Pig Got Up and Slowly Walked Away' (1933)

13 And Noah he often said to his wife when he sat down to dine,
'I don't care where the water goes if it doesn't get into the wine.'

G. K. Chesterton 1874–1936: 'Wine and Water' (1914)

14 I have taken more out of alcohol than alcohol has taken out of me.

Winston Churchill 1874–1965: Quentin Reynolds *By Quentin Reynolds* (1964)

on being invited by a friend to dine at a Middle Eastern restaurant:
15 The aftertaste of foreign food spoils the clean, pure flavour of gin for hours.

Eddie Condon 1905–73: Bill Crow *Jazz Anecdotes* (1990)

when seriously ill and given a blood transfusion:
16 This must be Fats Waller's blood. I'm getting high.

Eddie Condon 1905–73: Bill Crow *Jazz Anecdotes* (1990)

17 A Mr Dewar from somewhere in the British Isles was also in the studio at the time, very welcome indeed, although exhausted at the end of the ceremony.

Eddie Condon 1905–73: record album note; Bill Crow *Jazz Anecdotes* (1990)

18 Take the juice of two quarts of whisky.
recommended hangover cure

Eddie Condon 1905–73: in *New York Sunday News* 10 June 1951

19 Sure I eat what I advertise. Sure I eat Wheaties for breakfast. A good bowl of Wheaties with Bourbon can't be beat.
a baseball star's comment

Dizzy Dean: in *Guardian* 23 December 1978 'Sports Quotes of the Year'

20 Therefore I *do* require it, which I makes confession, to be brought reg'lar and draw'd mild.

Charles Dickens 1812–70: *Martin Chuzzlewit* (1844)

21 'Mrs Harris,' I says, 'leave the bottle on the chimley-piece, and don't ask me to take none, but let me put my lips to it when I am so dispoged.'

Charles Dickens 1812–70: *Martin Chuzzlewit* (1844)

22 'I rather like bad wine,' said Mr Mountchesney; 'one gets so bored with good wine.'

Benjamin Disraeli 1804–81: *Sybil* (1845)

23 There is wan thing, an' on'y wan thing, to be said in favour iv dhrink, an' that is that it has caused manny a lady to be loved that otherwise might've died single.

Finley Peter Dunne 1867–1936: *Mr. Dooley Says* (1910)

when the Queen accepted a second glass of wine at lunch:
24 Do you think it's wise, darling? You know you've got to rule this afternoon.

Queen Elizabeth, the Queen Mother 1900– : Compton Miller *Who's Really Who* (1983)

25 A man shouldn't fool with booze until he's fifty; then he's a damn fool if he doesn't.

William Faulkner 1897–1962: James M. Webb and A. Wigfall Green *William Faulkner of Oxford* (1965)

26 Some weasel took the cork out of my lunch.

W. C. Fields 1880–1946: *You Can't Cheat an Honest Man* (1939 film)

27 I always keep a supply of stimulant handy in case I see a snake — which I also keep handy.

W. C. Fields 1880–1946: Corey Ford *Time of Laughter* (1970); attributed

28 A woman drove me to drink and I never even had the courtesy to thank her.

W. C. Fields 1880–1946: attributed

29 Best while you have it use your breath,
There is no drinking after death.

John Fletcher 1579–1625: *The Bloody Brother, or Rollo Duke of Normandy* (with Ben Jonson and others, performed c.1616)

30 And he that will go to bed sober,
Falls with the leaf still in October.

John Fletcher 1579–1625: *The Bloody Brother, or Rollo Duke of Normandy* (with Ben Jonson and others, performed c.1616)

31 There is no such thing as a small whisky.

Oliver St John Gogarty 1878–1957: attributed

32 From the bathing machine came a din
As of jollification within;
It was heard far and wide,
And the incoming tide
Had a definite flavour of gin.

Edward Gorey 1925– : *The Listing Attic* (1954)

33 Licker talks mighty loud w'en it git loose fum de jug.

Joel Chandler Harris 1848–1908: *Uncle Remus: His Songs and His Sayings* (1880) 'Plantation Proverbs'

34 I felt that the assortment of tablets that I had been given may have been mis-prescribed, since they seemed to interfere with the pleasant effects of alcohol. In the interests of my health, therefore, I stopped taking them.

Barry Humphries 1934– : *More Please* (1992)

35 We drink one another's healths, and spoil our own.

Jerome K. Jerome 1859–1927: *Idle Thoughts of an Idle Fellow* (1886)

36 Claret is the liquor for boys; port, for men; but he who aspires to be a hero (smiling) must drink brandy.

Samuel Johnson 1709–84: James Boswell *Life of Samuel Johnson* (1791) 7 April 1779

37 The Lord above made liquor for temptation
To see if man could turn away from sin.
The Lord above made liquor for temptation—but
With a little bit of luck,
With a little bit of luck,
When temptation comes you'll give right in!

Alan Jay Lerner 1918–86: 'With a Little Bit of Luck' (1956)

38 I don't drink liquor. I don't like it. It makes me feel good.

Oscar Levant 1906–72: in *Time* 5 May 1958

39 Heineken refreshes the parts other beers cannot reach.

Terry Lovelock: slogan for Heineken lager, 1975 onwards

40 Love makes the world go round? Not at all. Whisky makes it go round twice as fast.

Compton Mackenzie 1883–1972: *Whisky Galore* (1947)

41 Prohibition makes you want to cry into your beer and denies you the beer to cry into.

Don Marquis 1878–1937: *Sun Dial Time* (1936)

42 You're not drunk if you can lie on the floor without holding on.

Dean Martin 1917– : Paul Dickson *Official Rules* (1978)

43 Just a wee deoch-an-doris,
Just a wee yin, that's a'.
Just a wee deoch-an-doris,
Before we gang awa'.
There's a wee wifie waitin',
In a wee but-an-ben;
If you can say
'It's a braw bricht moonlicht nicht',
Ye're a' richt, ye ken.

R. F. Morrison: 'Just a Wee Deoch-an-Doris' (1911); popularized by Harry Lauder

44 If one glass of stout on a Sunday night is not enough, his spiritual home is the bodega.

J. B. Morton 1893–1975: M. Frayn *The Best of Beachcomber* (1963)

45 Candy
Is dandy
But liquor
Is quicker.

Ogden Nash 1902–71: 'Reflections on Ice-breaking' (1931)

on the water content of a glass of whiskey:
46 True, it is nearly impossible to avoid absorbing water in one form or another. But are you quite sane to be paying four shillings for a modest glasheen of it?

Flann O'Brien 1911–66: *Myles Away from Dublin* (1990)

47 Sometimes I have a sherry before dinner.
a notable understatement

Charlie Parker 1920–55: Bill Crow *Jazz Anecdotes* (1990)

48 You can always tell that the crash is coming when I start getting tender about Our Dumb Friends. Three highballs and I think I'm St Francis of Assisi.

Dorothy Parker 1893–1967: *Here Lies* (1939)

49 One more drink and I'd have been under the host.

Dorothy Parker 1893–1967: Howard Teichmann *George S. Kaufman* (1973)

50 When at dinner and supper, I drank, I know not how, of my own accord, so much wine, that I was even almost foxed and my head ached all night. So home.

Samuel Pepys 1633–1703: diary 29 September 1661

51 So make it another old-fashioned, please.
Leave out the cherry,
Leave out the orange,
Leave out the bitters,
Just make it a straight rye!

Cole Porter 1891–1964: 'Make it Another Old-Fashioned, Please' (1940)

52 A good general rule is to state that the bouquet is better than the taste, and vice versa.
on wine-tasting

Stephen Potter 1900–69: *One-Upmanship* (1952)

53 Doth it not show vilely in me to desire small beer?

William Shakespeare 1564–1616: *Henry IV, Part 2* (1597)

54 PORTER: Drink, sir, is a great provoker of three things.
MACDUFF: What three things does drink especially provoke?
PORTER: Marry, sir, nose-painting, sleep, and urine.
Lechery, sir, it provokes, and unprovokes; it provokes the desire, but it takes away the performance.

William Shakespeare 1564–1616: *Macbeth* (1606)

55 Alcohol . . . enables Parliament to do things at eleven at night that no sane person would do at eleven in the morning.

George Bernard Shaw 1856–1950: *Major Barbara* (1907)

56 I'm only a beer teetotaller, not a champagne teetotaller.

George Bernard Shaw 1856–1950: *Candida* (1898)

57 Gin was mother's milk to her.

George Bernard Shaw 1856–1950: *Pygmalion* (1916)

58 A bumper of good liquor
Will end a contest quicker
Than justice, judge, or vicar.

Richard Brinsley Sheridan 1751–1816: *The Duenna* (1775)

59 Was 1 a good year?

Burt Shevelove 1915–82 and **Larry Gelbart** ?1928– : *A Funny Thing Happened on the Way to the Forum* (1962)

60 But I'm not so think as you drunk I am.

J. C. Squire 1884–1958: 'Ballade of Soporific Absorption' (1931)

61 BRINDLEY: It does say Burgundy on the bottle.
MARKS: It's the old wine ramp, vicar! Cheapish, reddish and Spanish.

Tom Stoppard 1937– : *Where Are They Now?* (1973)

62 Champagne certainly gives one werry gentlemanly ideas, but for a continuance, I don't know but I should prefer mild hale.

R. S. Surtees 1805–64: *Jorrocks's Jaunts and Jollities* (1838)

63 There are two things that will be believed of any man whatsoever, and one of them is that he has taken to drink.

Booth Tarkington 1869–1946: *Penrod* (1914)

64 [An alcoholic:] A man you don't like who drinks as much as you do.

Dylan Thomas 1914–53: Constantine Fitzgibbon *Life of Dylan Thomas* (1965)

65 It's a naïve domestic Burgundy without any breeding, but I think you'll be amused by its presumption.

James Thurber 1894–1961: cartoon caption in *New Yorker* 27 March 1937

66 There is no such thing [as a Temperance Hotel], you might as well talk of a celibate brothel.

Robert Yelverton Tyrrell 1844–1914: Ulick O'Connor *Oliver St John Gogarty* (1964)

67 What have you been doing in my absinthe?

Dick Vosburgh: *A Saint She Ain't* (1999)

68 I have a rare intolerance to herbs which means I can only drink fermented liquids, such as gin.

Julie Walters 1950– : in *Observer* 14 March 1999 'Sayings of the Week'

69 It was my Uncle George who discovered that alcohol was a food well in advance of medical thought.

P. G. Wodehouse 1881–1975: *The Inimitable Jeeves* (1923)

70 At the present moment, the whole Fleet's lit up. When I say 'lit up', I mean lit up by fairy lamps.

Thomas Woodrooffe 1899–1978: engaged to make a live outside broadcast of the Spithead Review, 20 May 1937, Woodrooffe was so overcome by his reunion with many old Naval colleagues that the celebrations sabotaged his ability to commentate.

America and Americans See also Countries and Peoples, Places

1 Every American woman has two souls to call her own, the other being her husband's.

James Agate 1877–1947: diary, 15 May 1937

2 California is a fine place to live—if you happen to be an orange.

Fred Allen 1894–1956: in *American Magazine* December 1945

3 He held, too, in his enlightened way, that Americans have a perfect right to exist. But he did often find himself wishing Mr Rhodes had not enabled them to exercise that right in Oxford.

Max Beerbohm 1872–1956: *Zuleika Dobson* (1911)

4 They're the experts where personality is concerned, the Americans; they've got it down to a fine art.

Alan Bennett 1934– : *Talking Heads* (1988)

5 America is a model of force and freedom and moderation—with all the coarseness and rudeness of its people.

Lord Byron 1788–1824: letter, 12 October 1821

6 I would rather . . . have a nod from an American, than a snuff-box from an Emperor.

Lord Byron 1788–1824: letter, 8 June 1822

7 Your eyes are like the prairie flowers
When they're refreshed by sudden showers,
Next to Texas I love you.

Sammy Cahn 1913– : 'Next to Texas I Love You' (1947)

8 I have always liked Americans, and the sort of man that likes Americans is liable to like Russians.

Claud Cockburn 1904–81: *Crossing the Line* (1958)

9 Father's name was Hezikiah,
Mother's name was Anna Maria,
Yanks, through and through!
Red White and Blue.

George M. Cohan 1878–1942: 'Yankee Doodle Dandy' (1904)

10 I like America . . .
All delegates
From Southern States
Are nervy and distraught.
In New Orleans
The wrought-iron screens
Are dreadfully overwrought . . .
But—I like America,
Every scrap of it,
All the sentimental crap of it.

Noël Coward 1899–1973: 'I like America' (1949)

11 When I was a boy I was told that anybody could become President. I'm beginning to believe it.

Clarence Darrow 1857–1938: Irving Stone *Clarence Darrow for the Defence* (1941)

12 The thing that impresses me most about America is the way parents obey their children.

Edward VIII 1894–1972: in *Look* 5 March 1957

13 Molasses to
Rum to
Slaves!
'Tisn't morals, 'tis money that saves!
Shall we dance to the sound
Of the profitable pound, in
Molasses and
Rum and Slaves?

Sherman Edwards: 'Molasses to Rum' (1969)

14 When J. P. Morgan bows, I just nod;
Green Pastures wanted me to play God.
But you've got me down hearted
'Cause I can't get started with you.

Ira Gershwin 1896–1983: 'I Can't Get Started' (1936)

15 I'm as corny as Kansas in August
I'm as normal as blueberry pie . . .
. . . High as a flag on the fourth of July.

Oscar Hammerstein II 1895–1960: 'I'm in Love with a Wonderful Guy' (1949)

16 If I had to give a definition of capitalism I would say: the process whereby American girls turn into American women.

Christopher Hampton 1946– : *Savages* (1974)

17 Once we had a Roosevelt
Praise the Lord!
Now we're stuck with Nixon, Agnew, Ford
Brother, can you spare a rope!

E. Y. Harburg 1898–1981: parody of 'Brother Can You Spare a Dime?', written for the *New York Times* at the time of Watergate

Gilbert Harding, applying for a US visa, was irritated by having to fill in a long form with many questions, including 'Is it your intention to overthrow the Government of the United States by force?':
18 Sole purpose of visit.

Gilbert Harding 1907–60: W. Reyburn *Gilbert Harding* (1978)

19 I could come back to America . . . to die—but never, never to live.

Henry James 1843–1916: letter to Mrs William James, 1 April 1913

20 To Americans, English manners are far more frightening than none at all.

Randall Jarrell 1914–65: *Pictures from an Institution* (1954)

21 Never criticize Americans. They have the best taste that money can buy.

Miles Kington 1941– : *Welcome to Kington* (1989)

the universal philosophy of young America:
22 I can do that.

Ed Kleban: song-title (1975)

23 So I really think that American gentlemen are the best after all, because kissing your hand may make you feel very very good but a diamond and safire bracelet lasts forever.

Anita Loos 1893–1981: *Gentlemen Prefer Blondes* (1925)

24 I like to be in America!
O.K. by me in America!
Ev'rything free in America
For a small fee in America!

Stephen Sondheim 1930– : 'America' (1957)

25 In the United States there is more space where nobody is than where anybody is. That is what makes America what it is.

Gertrude Stein 1874–1946: *The Geographical History of America* (1936)

26 In America any boy may become President and I suppose it's just one of the risks he takes!

Adlai Stevenson 1900–65: speech in Detroit, 7 October 1952

27 America is a vast conspiracy to make you happy.

John Updike 1932– : *Problems* (1980) 'How to love America and Leave it at the Same Time'

28 The land of the dull and the home of the literal.

Gore Vidal 1925– : *Reflections upon a Sinking Ship* (1969)

29 MRS ALLONBY: They say, Lady Hunstanton, that when good Americans die they go to Paris.

LADY HUNSTANTON: Indeed? And when bad Americans die, where do they go to?

LORD ILLINGWORTH: Oh, they go to America.

Oscar Wilde 1854–1900: *A Woman of No Importance* (1893)

30 The youth of America is their oldest tradition. It has been going on now for three hundred years.

Oscar Wilde 1854–1900: *A Woman of No Importance* (1893)

Anger

1 At this present moment, I have a strong urge to go over there, wrap both his legs round his neck and stick his suede shoes in his mouth. But I suppose that would only be termed a temporary solution.

Alan Ayckbourn 1939– : *Sisterly Feelings* (1981)

2 Anger makes dull men witty, but it keeps them poor.

Francis Bacon 1561–1626: *Works* (1859) 'Baconiana'

3 I was angry with my friend;
I told my wrath, my wrath did end.
I was angry with my foe:
I told it not, my wrath did grow.

William Blake 1757–1827: 'A Poison Tree' (1794)

4 I expect to pass through this world but once and therefore if there is anybody that I want to kick in the crutch I had better kick them in the crutch *now*, for I do not expect to pass this way again.
while lunching at the Reform Club with a bishop at the next table

Maurice Bowra 1898–1971: Arthur Marshall *Life's Rich Pageant* (1984)

5 When you get angry, they tell you, count to five before you reply. Why should I count to five? It's what happens *before* you count to five which makes life interesting.

David Hare 1947– : *The Secret Rapture* (1988)

6 McEnroe . . . did his complete Krakatoa number.
of John McEnroe disputing a line call at Wimbledon

Clive James 1939– : in *Observer* 5 July 1981

7 It's my rule never to lose me temper till it would be dethrimental to keep it.

Sean O'Casey 1880–1964: *The Plough and the Stars* (1926)

8 Whereat, with blade, with bloody blameful blade,
He bravely broached his boiling bloody breast.

William Shakespeare 1564–1616: *A Midsummer Night's Dream* (1595–6)

9 He never let the sun go down on his wrath, though there were some colourful sunsets while it lasted.
of W. G. Grace

A. A. Thomson: Alan Gibson *The Cricket Captains of England* (1979)

10 When angry, count four; when very angry, swear.

Mark Twain 1835–1910: *Pudd'nhead Wilson* (1894)

11 The adjective 'cross' as a description of his Jovelike wrath . . . jarred upon Derek profoundly. It was as though Prometheus, with the vultures tearing his liver, had been asked if he were piqued.

P. G. Wodehouse 1881–1975: *Jill the Reckless* (1922)

Animals See also **Birds, Dogs**

1 The lion and the calf shall lie down together but the calf won't get much sleep.

Woody Allen 1935– : in *New Republic* 31 August 1974

during his time in the Lords the eighth Earl of Arran was
concerned with measures for homosexual reform and the protection
of badgers, interests concisely summed up by a fellow peer:

2 Teaching people not to bugger badgers and not to badger buggers.

Anonymous: in *Ned Sherrin in his Anecdotage* (1993)

3 The rabbit has a charming face:
Its private life is a disgrace.
I really dare not name to you
The awful things that rabbits do.

Anonymous: *The Week-End Book* (1925) 'The Rabbit'

4 *Puella Rigensis ridebat*
Quam tigris in tergo vehebat;
Externa profecta,
Interna revecta,
Risusque cum tigre manebat.

There was a young lady of Riga
Who went for a ride on a tiger;
They returned from the ride
With the lady inside,
And a smile on the face of the tiger.

Anonymous: R. L. Green (ed.) *A Century of Humorous Verse* (1959)

5 I shoot the Hippopotamus
With bullets made of platinum,
Because if I use leaden ones
His hide is sure to flatten 'em.

Hilaire Belloc 1870–1953: 'The Hippopotamus' (1896)

6 The Tiger, on the other hand, is kittenish and mild,
He makes a pretty play fellow for any little child;
And mothers of large families (who claim to common
   sense)
Will find a Tiger well repay the trouble and expense.

Hilaire Belloc 1870–1953: 'The Tiger' (1896)

7 I had an Aunt in Yucatan
Who bought a Python from a man
And kept it for a pet.
She died, because she never knew
These simple little rules and few;—
The Snake is living yet.

Hilaire Belloc 1870–1953: 'The Python' (1897)

8 It's awf'lly bad luck on Diana,
Her ponies have swallowed their bits;
She fished down their throats with a spanner
And frightened them all into fits.

John Betjeman 1906–84: 'Hunter Trials' (1954)

9 To my mind, the only possible pet is a cow. Cows love you
... They will listen to your problems and never ask a thing
in return. They will be your friends for ever. And when
you get tired of them, you can kill and eat them. Perfect.

Bill Bryson 1951– : *Neither Here Nor There* (1991)

10 He thought he saw an Elephant,
That practised on a fife:
He looked again, and found it was
A letter from his wife.
'At length I realize,' he said,
'The bitterness of life!'

Lewis Carroll 1832–98: *Sylvie and Bruno* (1889)

11 I am fond of pigs. Dogs look up to us. Cats look down on
us. Pigs treat us as equal.

Winston Churchill 1874–1965: M. Gilbert *Never Despair* (1988); attributed

after an operation to remove a fishbone stuck in her throat:

12 After all these years of fishing, the fish are having their revenge.

Queen Elizabeth, the Queen Mother 1900– : in November 1982, attributed; Christopher Dobson (ed.) *Queen Elizabeth the Queen Mother: Chronicle of a Remarkable Life* (2000)

13 The great thing about racehorses is you don't need to take them for walks.

Albert Finney 1936– : in *The Mail on Sunday* 9 April 2000

14 Commodus killed a camelopardalis or giraffe . . . the tallest, the most gentle, and the most useless of the large quadrupeds. This singular animal, a native only of the interior parts of Africa, has not been seen in Europe since the revival of letters, and though M. de Buffon . . . has endeavoured to describe, he has not ventured to delineate the giraffe.

Edward Gibbon 1737–94: *The Decline and Fall of the Roman Empire* (1776–88)

15 My God . . . The hero is a bee!

Sam Goldwyn 1882–1974: on reading the synopsis of a story by Maurice Maeterlinck in 1920; Michael Freedland *The Goldwyn Touch* (1986)

16 Even the rabbits
Inhibit their habits
On Sunday at Cicero Falls.

E. Y. Harburg 1898–1981: 'Sunday at Cicero Falls' (1944)

17 Tar-baby ain't sayin' nuthin', en Brer Fox, he lay low.

Joel Chandler Harris 1848–1908: *Uncle Remus and His Legends of the Old Plantation* (1881) 'The Wonderful Tar-Baby Story'

18 Bred en bawn in a brier-patch!

Joel Chandler Harris 1848–1908: *Uncle Remus and His Legends of the Old Plantation* (1881) 'How Mr Rabbit was too Sharp for Mr Fox'

19 [Arthur Platt] was a Fellow of the Zoological Society, frequented its Gardens, and inspired a romantic passion in their resident population. There was a leopard which at Platt's approach would almost ooze through the bars of its cage to establish contact with the beloved object.

A. E. Housman 1859–1936: preface to Arthur Platt *Nine Essays* (1927)

20 What the horse is to the Arab, or the dog is to the Greenlander, the pig is to the Irishman.

J. G. Kohl 1808–78: *Ireland, Scotland and England* (1844)

21 Spiders are the SAS of nature, and will spend hours flying through the air on their ropes, prior to landing and subjecting some hapless insect to savage interrogation. The question they usually ask is: 'Have you any last requests?'

Miles Kington 1941– : *Nature Made Ridiculously Simple* (1983)

22 Arabs of means rode none but she-camels, since they . . . were patient and would endure to march long after they were worn out, indeed until they tottered with exhaustion and fell in their tracks and died: whereas the coarser males grew angry, flung themselves down when tired, and from sheer rage would die there unnecessarily.

T. E. Lawrence 1888–1935: *Seven Pillars of Wisdom* (1926)

23 Its tail was a plume of such magnificence that it almost wore the cat.

Hugh Leonard 1926– : *Rover and Other Cats* (1992)

24 Where are you going
With your fetlocks blowing in the . . . wind
I want to shower you with sugar lumps
And ride you over . . . fences
I want to polish your hooves every single day
And bring you to the horse . . . dentist.
  'My Lovely Horse' as sung by Fathers Ted and Dougal

Graham Linehan and **Arthur Mathews**: 'A Song for Europe' (1996), episode from *Father Ted* (Channel 4 TV, 1994–)

25 A
 water bison
 is what
 yer wash
 yer face in.

Roger McGough 1937– : *An Imaginary Menagerie* (1988)

26 Rudolph, the Red-Nosed Reindeer
Had a very shiny nose,
And if you ever saw it,
You would even say it glows.

Johnny Marks 1909–85: 'Rudolph, the Red-Nosed Reindeer' (1949)

27 I have had some extremely endearing bulls. I had one
Ayrshire bull down in Kent who was extremely friendly.
One day he walked into a wedding reception in the village
hall. He was, of course, perfectly harmless but caused a bit
of a panic. I believe he also knocked over the wedding
cake.

Lord Massereene and Ferrard 1914–93: speech on the Wildlife and Countryside Bill, House of Lords 19 February 1981

28 Slow but sure the turtle
Enormously fert'le
Lays her eggs by the dozens,
Maybe some are her cousins,
Even the catamount is nonplussed by that amount
It's Spring, Spring, Spring!

Johnny Mercer 1909–76: 'Spring, Spring, Spring' (1954)

29 Eeyore, the old grey Donkey, stood by the side of the
stream, and looked at himself in the water. 'Pathetic,' he
said. 'That's what it is. Pathetic.'

A. A. Milne 1882–1956: *Winnie-the-Pooh* (1926)

30 Pooh began to feel a little more comfortable, because when
you are a Bear of Very Little Brain, and you Think of
Things, you find sometimes that a Thing which seemed
very Thingish inside you is quite different when it gets out
into the open and has other people looking at it.

A. A. Milne 1882–1956: *The House at Pooh Corner* (1928)

31 Diana gives a terrible account of your cat, such a wrecker?
Alas old animals are so much nicer I love my cat now, but
it took about 8 years.

Nancy Mitford 1904–73: letter to Lady Redesdale, 16 December 1959

32 One disadvantage of being a hog is that at any moment
some blundering fool may try to make a silk purse out of
your wife's ear.

J. B. Morton 1893–1975: *By the Way* (1931)

33 God in His wisdom made the fly
And then forgot to tell us why.

Ogden Nash 1902–71: 'The Fly' (1942)

34 The turtle lives 'twixt plated decks
Which practically conceal its sex.
I think it clever of the turtle
In such a fix to be so fertile.

Ogden Nash 1902–71: 'Autres Bêtes, Autres Moeurs' (1931)

35 The cow is of the bovine ilk;
One end is moo, the other, milk.

Ogden Nash 1902–71: 'The Cow' (1931)

36 Four legs good, two legs bad.

George Orwell 1903–50: *Animal Farm* (1945)

37 Your elephant seal . . . is not a natural self-starter. Start him, however, and he goes, not like a rocket, but a sort of turbo-charged mega-caterpillar.

Matthew Parris 1949– : in *Spectator* 17 June 2000

38 Don't go into Mr McGregor's garden: your father had an accident there, he was put into a pie by Mrs McGregor.

Beatrix Potter 1866–1943: *The Tale of Peter Rabbit* (1902)

39 There was one poor tiger that hadn't *got* a Christian.

Punch 1841–1992: vol. 68 (1875)

40 Oh how the family affections combat
Within this heart, and each hour flings a bomb at
My burning soul! Neither from owl or from bat
Can peace be gained until I clasp my wombat.

Dante Gabriel Rossetti 1828–82: on the loss of his pet wombat, and his other pets; 'The Wombat' (1849)

41 I know two things about the horse
And one of them is rather coarse.

Naomi Royde-Smith c.1875–1964: in *Weekend Book* (1928)

42 When a man wants to murder a tiger he calls it sport; when a tiger wants to murder him, he calls it ferocity.

George Bernard Shaw 1856–1950: *Man and Superman* (1903)

Appearance

1 My face looks like a wedding cake left out in the rain.

W. H. Auden 1907–73: Humphrey Carpenter *W. H. Auden* (1981)

2 In appearance Dior is like a bland country curate made out of pink marzipan.
of Christian Dior

Cecil Beaton 1904–80: *The Glass of Fashion* (1954)

3 He had a thin vague beard—or rather, he had a chin on which a large number of hairs weakly curled and clustered to cover its retreat.

Max Beerbohm 1872–1956: 'Enoch Soames' (1912)

4 Look at this dry pink plate of a face. Why didn't God give me a face on which the skin hangs in genial brown folds, the mouth is firm . . . but kindly . . . and with long large ears. Nearly every man of distinction has long ears.

Alan Bennett 1934– : *Getting On* (1972)

5 He had the sort of face that makes you realise God does have a sense of humour.

Bill Bryson 1951– : *Neither Here Nor There* (1991)

6 I look like an elderly *wasp* in an interesting condition.
of her appearance in her black and yellow costume for False Gods *in 1917*

Mrs Patrick Campbell 1865–1940: Margot Peters *Mrs Pat* (1984)

7 Glamour is on a life-support machine and not expected to live.

Joan Collins 1933– : in *Independent* 24 April 1999

8 Edith Sitwell, in that great Risorgimento cape of hers, looks as though she were covering a teapot or a telephone.

Noël Coward 1899–1973: William Marchant *The Pleasure of his Company* (1975)

9 I was very plain. My rich mouse hair was straight but my teeth were not. I wore tin-rimmed spectacles.
of himself in youth

Quentin Crisp 1908–99: in *Daily Telegraph* 22 November 1999; obituary

10 She looks like a big meringue.

Richard Curtis 1956– : *Four Weddings and a Funeral* (1994 film)

11 I guess a drag queen's like an oil painting: You gotta stand back from it to get the full effect.

Harvey Fierstein 1954– : *Torch Song Trilogy* (1979)

12 I sympathize with the Prescotts. Last week they took the car because of what the seaside air did to their hair. I don't blame them. Look what it did to mine.

William Hague 1961– : speech at Conservative Party Conference, 3 October 1999; see **Transport** 29

13 I kept thinking, if his face was that wrinkled, what did his balls look like?
after drawing W. H. Auden

David Hockney 1937– : attributed

14 I don't trust photographers. I'm now a relaxed, contented 60-year-old, but look at my pictures and you see a crazy, bug-eyed serial killer.
on a photograph accompanying an Independent *article to mark his 60th birthday*

Richard Ingrams 1937– : in *Observer* 24 August 1997

15 RICHARD: You look fabulous!
ALLY: I know, I just got fired for it.

David E. Kelley: *Ally McBeal* (US television series, 1998–) episode 1

16 I'm tired of all this nonsense about beauty being only skin-deep. That's deep enough. What do you want—an adorable pancreas?

Jean Kerr 1923– : *The Snake has all the Lines* (1958)

17 The most common error made in matters of appearance is the belief that one should disdain the superficial and let the true beauty of one's soul shine through. If there are places on one's body where this is a possibility, you are not attractive—you are leaking.

Fran Lebowitz 1946– : *Metropolitan Life* (1978)

18 You have a very odd manner . . . 'Tis that sneaky little Presbyterian smile.

Frank McCourt 1930– : *Angela's Ashes* (1996)

19 No power on earth, however, can abolish the merciless class distinction between those who are physically desirable and the lonely, pallid, spotted, silent, unfancied majority.

John Mortimer 1923– : *Clinging to the Wreckage* (1982)

20 Her ugliness was destined to bloom late, hidden first by the unformed gawkiness of youth, budding to plainness in young womanhood and now flowering to slow maturity in her early forties.

Brian Moore 1921– : *The Lonely Passion of Judith Hearne* (1955)

21 Sure, deck your lower limbs in pants;
Yours are the limbs, my sweeting.
You look divine as you advance—
Have you seen yourself retreating?

Ogden Nash 1902–71: 'What's the Use?' (1940)

22 My beauty am faded.

Rudolf Nureyev 1939–93: on being rejected by a young man he had tried to pick up; in *Ned Sherrin in his Anecdotage* (1993)

23 My general appearance, and especially my face, have always been a source of depression to me.

William Orpen 1878–1931: *Stories of Old Ireland and Myself* (1924)

24 I always say beauty is only sin deep.

Saki 1870–1916: *Reginald* (1904)

25 You're welcome to take a bath. You look like the second week of the garbage strike.

Neil Simon 1927– : *The Gingerbread Lady* (1970)

26 Women never look so well as when one comes in wet and dirty from hunting.

R. S. Surtees 1805–64: *Mr. Sponge's Sporting Tour* (1853) ch. 21

27 If beauty is truth, why don't women go to the library to have their hair done?

Lily Tomlin 1939– : Sally Feldman (ed.) *Woman's Hour Book of Humour* (1993)

28 His physiognomy: a great blotched moon emanating waves of self-regard.
   on C. P. Snow

George Walden 1939– : *Lucky George: Memoirs of an Anti-Politician* (1999)

29 It is better to be beautiful than to be good. But . . . it is better to be good than to be ugly.

Oscar Wilde 1854–1900: *The Picture of Dorian Gray* (1891)

30 I was so ugly when I was born, the doctor slapped my mother.

Henny Youngman 1906–98: in *Times* 26 February 1998; obituary

Architecture

1 The floozie in the jacuzzi.
   popular description of the monument in O'Connell Street, Dublin

Anonymous: comment, c.1988

of the cramped office he shared with Dorothy Parker:
2 One square foot less and it would be adulterous.

Robert Benchley 1889–1945: in *New Yorker* 5 January 1946

3 Sir Christopher Wren
   Said, 'I am going to dine with some men.
   If anybody calls
   Say I am designing St Paul's.'

Edmund Clerihew Bentley 1875–1956: 'Sir Christopher Wren' (1905)

4 Ghastly good taste, or a depressing story of the rise and fall of English architecture.

John Betjeman 1906–84: title of book (1933)

5 The existence of St Sophia is atmospheric; that of St Peter's, overpoweringly, imminently substantial. One is a church to God: the other a salon for his agents. One is consecrated to reality, the other, to illusion. St Sophia in fact is large, and St Peter's is vilely, tragically small.

Robert Byron 1905–41: *The Road to Oxiana* (1937)

6 A monstrous carbuncle on the face of a much-loved and elegant friend.

Charles, Prince of Wales 1948– : speech on the proposed extension to the National Gallery, London, 30 May 1984

7 The Pavilion
   Cost a million
   As a monument to Art,
   And the wits here
   Say it sits here
   Like an Oriental tart!

Noël Coward 1899–1973: on Brighton Pavilion; 'There was Once a Little Village' (1934)

8 Architecture offers quite extraordinary opportunities to serve the community, to enhance the landscape, refresh the environment and to advance mankind—the successful architect needs training to overcome these pitfalls however, and start earning some serious money.

Stephen Fry 1957– : *Paperweight* (1992)

9 O Dome gigantic, Dome immense
   Built in defiance of common sense.

P. D. James 1920– : attributed in *Daily Telegraph* 18 May 2000

10 Terence Conran's vast Bluebird complex on the King's Road is to New Labour what the Crystal Palace was to High Victorianism.

John Lahr 1941– : in *New Yorker* July 1997; *Observer* 6 July 1997 'Soundbites'

11 A taste for the grandiose, like a taste for morphia, is, once it has been fully acquired, difficult to keep within limits.

Osbert Lancaster 1908–80: *Homes Sweet Homes* (1939)

12 A lot of nuns in a rugger scrum.
   on the Sydney Opera House

George Molnar 1910–98: attributed

13 I am proud to be an Eskimo, but I think we can improve on the igloo as a permanent dwelling.

Abraham Okpik: in *Northern Affairs Bulletin* March 1960

14 A singularly dreary street. What I would term Victorian Varicose.

Peter Shaffer 1926– : *Lettice and Lovage* (rev. ed. 1989)

on Brighton Pavilion:
15 As if St Paul's had come down and littered.

Sydney Smith 1771–1845: Peter Virgin *Sydney Smith* (1994)

16 I *do* like the mullioned window between the Doric columns—that has a quality of coy desperation, like a spinster gatecrashing a costume ball in a flowered frock.

Tom Stoppard 1937– : *The Dog It Was That Died* (1983)

17 Whatever may be said in favour of the Victorians, it is pretty generally admitted that few of them were to be trusted within reach of a trowel and a pile of bricks.

P. G. Wodehouse 1881–1975: *Summer Moonshine* (1938)

18 The physician can bury his mistakes, but the architect can only advise his client to plant vines.

Frank Lloyd Wright 1867–1959: in *New York Times* 4 October 1953

Argument

1 Sir Roger told them, with the air of a man who would not give his judgement rashly, that much might be said on both sides.

Joseph Addison 1672–1719: *The Spectator* 20 July 1711

2 It won't upset her. She'll insist on being carried downstairs to be in at the kill. There's nothing she likes better than a good row.

Alan Ayckbourn 1939– : *Living Together* (1975)

3 I've never won an argument with her; and the only times I thought I had I found out the argument wasn't over yet.
   of his wife Rosalynn

Jimmy Carter 1924– : in *Reader's Digest* March 1979

4 You can't turn a thing upside down if there's no theory about it being the right way up.

G. K. Chesterton 1874–1936: attributed

5 'My idea of an agreeable person,' said Hugo Bohun, 'is a person who agrees with me.'

Benjamin Disraeli 1804–81: *Lothair* (1870)

6 I'll not listen to reason . . . Reason always means what someone else has got to say.

Elizabeth Gaskell 1810–65: *Cranford* (1853)

7 Those who in quarrels interpose,
   Must often wipe a bloody nose.

John Gay 1685–1732: *Fables* (1727) 'The Mastiffs'

8 There is no arguing with Johnson; for when his pistol misses fire, he knocks you down with the butt end of it.

Oliver Goldsmith 1730–74: James Boswell *Life of Samuel Johnson* (1934 ed.) 26 October 1769

9 Any stigma, as the old saying is, will serve to beat a dogma.

Philip Guedalla 1889–1944: *Masters and Men* (1923)

10 The concept of two people living together for 25 years without having a cross word suggests a lack of spirit only to be admired in sheep.

A. P. Herbert 1890–1971: in *News Chronicle*, 1940

11 Several excuses are always less convincing than one.

Aldous Huxley 1894–1963: *Point Counter Point* (1928)

12 [Logic] is neither a science nor an art, but a dodge.

Benjamin Jowett 1817–93: Lionel A. Tollemache *Benjamin Jowett* (1895)

13 I think it will be a clash between the political will and the administrative won't.

Jonathan Lynn 1943– and **Antony Jay** 1930– : *Yes Prime Minister* vol. 2 (1987)

14 The first obligation of the demonstrator is to be legible. Miss Manners cannot sympathize with a cause whose signs she cannot make out even with her glasses on.

Judith Martin 1938– : 'Advice from Miss Manners', column in *Washington Post* 1979–82

15 Casuistry has got a bad name in the world, mainly, I suppose, because of the dubious uses to which it was put during the Sixteenth and Seventeenth Centuries by some of its Jesuit practitioners. But it is really a very useful art.

H. L. Mencken 1880–1956: *Minority Report* (1956)

16 I had inherited what my father called the art of the advocate, or the irritating habit of looking for the flaw in any argument.

John Mortimer 1923– : *Clinging to the Wreckage* (1982)

17 Why, i'faith, I believe I am between *both*.
  when two royal dukes walking on either side of him told him that they were trying to decide if he was a greater fool or rogue

Richard Brinsley Sheridan 1751–1816: Walter Jerrold *Bon-Mots* (1893)

18 JUDGE: What do you suppose I am on the Bench for, Mr Smith?
  SMITH: It is not for me, Your Honour, to attempt to fathom the inscrutable workings of Providence.

F. E. Smith 1872–1930: Lord Birkenhead *F. E.* (1959 ed.)

on seeing two Edinburgh women hurling insults at one another across an alleyway:
19 Those two women will never agree; they are arguing from different premises.

Sydney Smith 1771–1845: Peter Virgin *Sydney Smith* (1994)

20 And who are you? said he.—Don't puzzle me, said I.

Laurence Sterne 1713–68: *Tristram Shandy* (1759–67)

21 My uncle Toby would never offer to answer this by any other kind of argument, than that of whistling half a dozen bars of Lillabullero.

Laurence Sterne 1713–68: *Tristram Shandy* (1759–67)

22 I don't take orders from you, you're just a figure-head and I've seen better ones on the sharp end of a dredger.

Tom Stoppard 1937– : *The Dog It Was That Died* (1983)

23 When two strong men stand face to face, each claiming to be Major Brabazon-Plank, it is inevitable that there will be a sense of strain, resulting in a momentary silence.

P. G. Wodehouse 1881–1975: *Uncle Dynamite* (1948)

The Aristocracy See also **Class**

1 The young Sahib shot divinely, but God was very merciful to the birds.

Anonymous: G. W. E. Russell *Collections and Recollections* (1898)

the much-married Duke of Westminster had died the previous day:
2 There was a bad fire next door; lots of smoke, but it turned out *not* to be the four bereaved Duchesses of Westminster committing suttee.

Chips Channon 1897–1958: diary, 21 July 1953

3 The Stately Homes of England,
How beautiful they stand,
To prove the upper classes
Have still the upper hand.

Noël Coward 1899–1973: 'The Stately Homes of England' (1938)

after Lord Dunsany's arrest in 1921 by the Black and Tans, Oliver St John Gogarty's attempt to console him diverged into a reminder of a peer's privilege of being hanged with a silken rope and speculation on the probable elasticity of silk, neither of which were well-received:

4 There are certain things which are not jokes, Gogarty, and one of them is my hanging.

Lord Dunsany 1878–1957: Ulick O'Connor *Oliver St John Gogarty* (1964)

5 Spurn not the nobly born
With love affected,
Nor treat with virtuous scorn
The well-connected.

W. S. Gilbert 1836–1911: *Iolanthe* (1882)

6 I can trace my ancestry back to a protoplasmal primordial atomic globule. Consequently, my family pride is something in-conceivable. I can't help it. I was born sneering.

W. S. Gilbert 1836–1911: *The Mikado* (1885)

7 Hearts just as pure and fair
May beat in Belgrave Square
As in the lowly air
Of Seven Dials.

W. S. Gilbert 1836–1911: *Iolanthe* (1882)

8 They are no members of the common throng;
They are all noblemen who have gone wrong!

W. S. Gilbert 1836–1911: *The Pirates of Penzance* (1879)

9 There never was a Churchill from John of Marlborough down that had either morals or principles.

W. E. Gladstone 1809–98: in conversation in 1882, recorded by Captain R. V. Briscoe; R. F. Foster *Lord Randolph Churchill* (1981)

10 I am a well-known élitist. I don't even own a pair of trainers. If I did, I am sure they would be very fragrant.

Lord Gowrie 1939– : in *Independent* 24 January 1998

11 We don't represent anybody, it's true,
But that's not a thing to regret;
We can say what we think—and I know one or two
Who've never said anything yet.
While the Commons must bray like an ass every day
To appease their electoral hordes,
We don't say a thing till we've something to say—
There's a lot to be said for the Lords.

A. P. Herbert 1890–1971: *Big Ben* (1946)

replying to Harold Wilson's remark (on Home's leading the Conservatives to victory in the 1963 election) that 'the whole [democratic] process has ground to a halt with a fourteenth Earl':

12 As far as the fourteenth earl is concerned, I suppose Mr Wilson, when you come to think of it, is the fourteenth Mr Wilson.

Lord Home 1903– : in *Daily Telegraph* 22 October 1963

13 I am an ancestor.
reply when taunted on his lack of ancestry, having been made Duke of Abrantes, 1807

Marshal Junot 1771–1813: attributed

14 The aristocracy and landed gentry, although Nationally Entrusted and sadly Thirkellized, are still, thank goodness, for all their constant complainings of extinction, visibly and abundantly there.

Osbert Lancaster 1908–80: *All Done From Memory* (1953)

15 We always feel kindly disposed towards noble authors.

Lord Macaulay 1800–59: in *Edinburgh Review* January 1833

16 An aristocracy in a republic is like a chicken whose head
has been cut off: it may run about in a lively way, but in
fact it is dead.

Nancy Mitford 1904–73: *Noblesse Oblige* (1956) 'The English Aristocracy'

17 This world consists of men, women, and Herveys.

Lady Mary Wortley Montagu 1689–1762: attributed by Lord Wharncliffe in *Letters and Works of Lady Mary Wortley Montagu* (1837), 'Herveys' being a reference to John Hervey, Baron Hervey of Ickworth, 1696–1743

18 I'll purge, and leave sack, and live cleanly, as a nobleman
should do.

William Shakespeare 1564–1616: *Henry IV, Part 1* (1597)

19 At the palace of the Duke of Ferrara,
Who was prematurely deaf but a dear,
At the palace of the Duke of Ferrara
I acquired some position
Plus a tiny Titian . . .
Liaisons! What's happened to them?

Stephen Sondheim 1930– : 'Liaisons' (1972)

20 LORD ILLINGWORTH: A title is really rather a nuisance in
these democratic days. As George Harford I had everything
I wanted. Now I have merely everything that other people
want.

Oscar Wilde 1854–1900: *A Woman of No Importance* (1893)

The Armed Forces See also **War**

1 We joined the Navy to see the world,
And what did we see? We saw the sea.

Irving Berlin 1888–1989: 'We Saw the Sea' in *Follow the Fleet* (1936)

2 I should like to take the opportunity to correct some
widespread misconceptions about the part played in the
global struggle by the Irish Navy—a force with whom no
one, except the patriots afloat, mucked in at all.

Patrick Campbell 1913–80: *The Campbell Companion* (1994) 'Sean Tar Joins Up'

3 Don't talk to me about naval tradition. It's nothing but
rum, sodomy, and the lash.

Winston Churchill 1874–1965: Peter Gretton *Former Naval Person* (1968)

4 I can always guarantee that the Irish Citizen Army will
fight, but I cannot guarantee that it will be on time.

James Connolly 1868–1916: Diana Norman *Terrible Beauty* (1987)

5 Have you had any word
Of that bloke in the 'Third',
Was it Southerby, Sedgwick or Sim?
They had him thrown out of the club in Bombay
For, apart from his mess bills exceeding his pay,
He took to pig-sticking in *quite* the wrong way.
I wonder what happened to him!

Noël Coward 1899–1973: 'I Wonder What Happened to Him' (1945)

6 Has anybody seen our ship?
The H.M.S. Peculiar
We've been on shore
For a month or more,
And when we see the Captain we shall get 'what for'.

Noël Coward 1899–1973: 'Has Anybody Seen Our Ship' (1935)

7 Admirals extolled for standing still,
Or doing nothing with a deal of skill.

William Cowper 1731–1800: 'Table Talk' (1782)

8 For a soldier I listed, to grow great in fame,
And be shot at for sixpence a-day.

Charles Dibdin 1745–1814: 'Charity' (1791)

to the Duke of Newcastle, who had complained that General Wolfe was a madman:

9 Mad, is he? Then I hope he will *bite* some of my other generals.

George II 1683–1760: Henry Beckles Willson *Life and Letters of James Wolfe* (1909)

10 Stick close to your desks and never go to sea, And you all may be Rulers of the Queen's Navee!

W. S. Gilbert 1836–1911: *HMS Pinafore* (1878)

11 I'm very good at integral and differential calculus, I know the scientific names of beings animalculous; In short, in matters vegetable, animal, and mineral, I am the very model of a modern Major-General.

W. S. Gilbert 1836–1911: *The Pirates of Penzance* (1879)

12 Fortunately, the army has had much practice at ignoring impossible instructions.

Michael Green 1927– : *The Boy Who Shot Down an Airship* (1988)

13 I had examined myself pretty thoroughly and discovered that I was unfit for military service.

Joseph Heller 1923–99: *Catch-22* (1961)

14 Ben Battle was a soldier bold, And used to war's alarms: But a cannon-ball took off his legs, So he laid down his arms!

Thomas Hood 1799–1845: 'Faithless Nelly Gray' (1826)

15 For here I leave my second leg, And the Forty-second Foot!

Thomas Hood 1799–1845: 'Faithless Nelly Gray' (1826)

16 My parents were very pleased that I was in the army. The fact that I hated it somehow pleased them even more.

Barry Humphries 1934– : *More Please* (1992)

17 No man will be a sailor who has contrivance enough to get himself into a jail; for being in a ship is being in a jail, with the chance of being drowned . . . A man in a jail has more room, better food, and commonly better company.

Samuel Johnson 1709–84: James Boswell *Life of Samuel Johnson* (1791) 16 March 1759

18 The uniform 'e wore Was nothin' much before, An' rather less than 'arf o' that be'ind.

Rudyard Kipling 1865–1936: 'Gunga Din' (1892)

19 Though I've belted you and flayed you, By the livin' Gawd that made you, You're a better man than I am, Gunga Din!

Rudyard Kipling 1865–1936: 'Gunga Din' (1892)

as young army musician, having composed a march for his regiment:

20 GENERAL: Isn't it a little fast, Korngold? The men can't march to that.
KORNGOLD: Ah yes, well, you see Sir, this was composed for the retreat!

Erich Korngold 1897–1957: Brendan G. Carroll *The Last Prodigy* (1997)

to a general who sent his dispatches from 'Headquarters in the Saddle':

21 The trouble with Hooker is that he's got his headquarters where his hindquarters ought to be.

Abraham Lincoln 1809–65: P. M. Zall *Abe Lincoln Laughing* (1982)

22 [Haig is] brilliant—to the top of his boots.

David Lloyd George 1863–1945: Paul Johnson (ed.) *The Oxford Book of Political Anecdotes* (1986); attributed

23 If these gentlemen had their way, they would soon be asking me to defend the moon against a possible attack from Mars.

    of his senior military advisers, and their tendency to see threats which did not exist

Lord Salisbury 1830–1903: Robert Taylor *Lord Salisbury* (1975)

24 I don't consider myself dovish and I certainly don't consider myself hawkish. Maybe I would describe myself as owlish—that is, wise enough to understand that you want to do everything possible to avoid war.

H. Norman Schwarzkopf III 1934– : in *New York Times* 28 January 1991

25 Napoleon's armies always used to march on their stomachs shouting: 'Vive l'Intérieur!'

W. C. Sellar 1898–1951 and **R. J. Yeatman** 1898–1968: *1066 and All That* (1930)

26 Your friend the British soldier can stand up to anything except the British War Office.

George Bernard Shaw 1856–1950: *The Devil's Disciple* (1901)

27 When the military man approaches, the world locks up its spoons and packs off its womankind.

George Bernard Shaw 1856–1950: *Man and Superman* (1903)

28 Oh, you are a very poor soldier—a chocolate cream soldier!

George Bernard Shaw 1856–1950: *Arms and the Man* (1898)

29 As for being a General, well at the age of four with paper hats and wooden swords we're all Generals. Only some of us never grow out of it.

Peter Ustinov 1921– : *Romanoff and Juliet* (1956)

30 The General was essentially a man of peace, except in his domestic life.

Oscar Wilde 1854–1900: *The Importance of Being Earnest* (1895)

Art and Artists

an old lady on Epstein's controversial Christ in Majesty:
1 I can never forgive Mr Epstein for his representation of Our Lord. So very un-English!

Anonymous: in *Ned Sherrin in his Anecdotage* (1993)

2 Oh, I wish I could draw. I've always wanted to draw. I'd give my right arm to be able to draw. It must be very relaxing.

Alan Ayckbourn 1939– : *Joking Apart* (1979)

3 All the arts in America are a gigantic racket run by unscrupulous men for unhealthy women.

Thomas Beecham 1879–1961: in *Observer* 5 May 1946

4 Of course he [William Morris] was a wonderful all-round man, but the act of walking round him has always tired me.

Max Beerbohm 1872–1956: letter to S. N. Behrman *c.*1953; *Conversations with Max* (1960)

5 The artistic temperament is a disease that afflicts amateurs. It is a disease which arises from men not having sufficient power of expression to utter and get rid of the element of art in their being.

G. K. Chesterton 1874–1936: *Heretics* (1905)

6 There are only two styles of portrait painting; the serious and the smirk.

Charles Dickens 1812–70: *Nicholas Nickleby* (1839)

to a lawyer who had asked him why he laid such stress on 'the painter's eye':
7 The painter's eye is to him what the lawyer's tongue is to you.

Thomas Gainsborough 1727–88: William Hazlitt *Conversations of James Northcote* (1830)

on attempting to paint two actors, David Garrick and Samuel Foote:

8 Rot them for a couple of rogues, they have everybody's faces but their own.

Thomas Gainsborough 1727–88: Allan Cunningham *The Lives of the Most Eminent Painters, Sculptors and Architects* (1829)

9 Then a sentimental passion of a vegetable fashion must
    excite your languid spleen,
An attachment à la Plato for a bashful young potato, or a
    not too French French bean!
Though the Philistines may jostle, you will rank as an
    apostle in the high aesthetic band,
If you walk down Piccadilly with a poppy or a lily in your
    medieval hand.

W. S. Gilbert 1836–1911: *Patience* (1881)

a few days after the funeral of Sir William Orpen:

10 Our painter! He never got under the surface till he got under the sod.

Oliver St John Gogarty 1878–1957: Ulick O'Connor *Oliver St John Gogarty* (1964)

11 Yes, Frances [his wife] has the most beautiful hands in the world—and someday I'm going to have a bust made of them.

Sam Goldwyn 1882–1974: Michael Freedland *The Goldwyn Touch* (1986)

12 As my poor father used to say
In 1863,
Once people start on all this Art
Goodbye, moralitee!

A. P. Herbert 1890–1971: 'Lines for a Worthy Person' (1930)

13 It's amazing what you can do with an E in A-level art, twisted imagination and a chainsaw

Damien Hirst 1965– : in *Observer* 3 December 1995 'Sayings of the Week'

14 There is, perhaps, no more dangerous man in the world than the man with the sensibilities of an artist but without creative talent. With luck such men make wonderful theatrical impresarios and interior decorators, or else they become mass murderers or critics.

Barry Humphries 1934– : *More Please* (1992)

15 It is a symbol of Irish art. The cracked lookingglass of a servant.

James Joyce 1882–1941: *Ulysses* (1922)

16 Little bits of porcelain,
Little sticks of Boule
Harmonize with Venuses
Of the Flemish school.

Osbert Lancaster 1908–80: *Homes Sweet Homes* (1939)

of Art Nouveau:

17 Certainly no style seems at first glance to provide a richer field for the investigations of Herr Freud.

Osbert Lancaster 1908–80: *Homes Sweet Homes* (1939)

18 Mr Landseer whose only merit as a painter was the tireless accuracy with which he recorded the more revoltingly sentimental aspects of the woollier mammals.

Osbert Lancaster 1908–80: *Homes Sweet Homes* (1939)

19 If a scientist were to cut his ear off, no one would take it as evidence of a heightened sensibility.

Peter Medawar 1915–87: 'J. B. S.' (1968)

20 The perfect aesthete logically feels that the artist is strictly a turkish bath attendant.

Flann O'Brien 1911–66: *The Best of Myles* (1968)

on a South African statue of the Voortrekkers:
21 Patriotism is the last refuge of the sculptor.

William Plomer 1903–73: Rupert Hart-Davis letter to George Lyttelton, 13 October 1956

22 My art belongs to Dada.

Cole Porter 1891–1964: attributed

23 If you want art to be like ovaltine, then clearly some art is not for you.

Peter Reading 1946– : in *Critics' Forum*, Radio 3, 22 November 1986; attributed

on the probable reaction to the painting of the subjects of Turner's Girls Surprised while Bathing:
24 I should think devilish surprised to see what Turner has made of them.

Dante Gabriel Rossetti 1828–82: O. Doughty *A Victorian Romantic* (1960)

25 I don't know what art is, but I do know what it isn't. And it isn't someone walking around with a salmon over his shoulder, or embroidering the name of everyone they have slept with on the inside of a tent.

Brian Sewell: in *Independent* 26 April 1999

26 I doubt that art needed Ruskin any more than a moving train needs one of its passengers to shove it.

Tom Stoppard 1937– : in *Times Literary Supplement* 3 June 1977

the ingredients for a successful exhibition:
27 You've got to have two out of death, sex and jewels.

Roy Strong 1935– : in *Sunday Times* 23 January 1994

28 There is only one position for an artist anywhere: and that is, upright.

Dylan Thomas 1914–53: *Quite Early One Morning* (1954)

29 If Botticelli were alive today he'd be working for *Vogue*.

Peter Ustinov 1921– : in *Observer* 21 October 1962

30 A genius with the IQ of a moron.
   of Andy Warhol

Gore Vidal 1925– : in *Observer* 18 June 1989

on a Constable painting of the Thames:
31 It is as though Constable had taken a long steady appraising stare at Canaletto and then charged straight through him.

Sylvia Townsend Warner 1893–1978: letter, 6 February 1969

32 Mrs Ballinger is one of the ladies who pursue Culture in bands, as though it were dangerous to meet it alone.

Edith Wharton 1862–1937: *Xingu and Other Stories* (1916)

33 Yes—one does like to make one's mummy just as nice as possible!
   on his portrait of his mother

James McNeill Whistler 1834–1903: E. R. and J. Pennell *The Life of James McNeill Whistler* (1908)

in his case against Ruskin, replying to the question: 'For two days' labour, you ask two hundred guineas?':
34 No, I ask it for the knowledge of a lifetime.

James McNeill Whistler 1834–1903: D. C. Seitz *Whistler Stories* (1913)

to a lady who had been reminded of his work by an 'exquisite haze in the atmosphere':
35 Yes madam, Nature is creeping up.

James McNeill Whistler 1834–1903: D. C. Seitz *Whistler Stories* (1913)

36 All that I desire to point out is the general principle that Life imitates Art far more than Art imitates Life.

Oscar Wilde 1854–1900: *Intentions* (1891) 'The Decay of Lying'

after the death of the outlaw Jesse James relics of his house were sold:

37 His sole work of art, a chromo-lithograph of the most dreadful kind, of course was sold at a price which in Europe only a Mantegna or an undoubted Titian can command!

Oscar Wilde 1854–1900: letter 25 April 1882

38 The Sheridan stands in the heart of New York's Bohemian and artistic quarter. If you threw a brick from any of its windows, you would be certain to brain some rising young interior decorator, some Vorticist sculptor or a writer of revolutionary *vers libre*.

P. G. Wodehouse 1881–1975: *The Small Bachelor* (1927)

Autobiography See also **Biography**

1 Every time somebody's Autobiography comes out I turn to the Index to see if my name occurs, and of course it never does.

James Agate 1877–1947: diary 16 September 1932

2 I used to think I was an interesting person, but I must tell you how sobering a thought it is to realize your life's story fills about thirty-five pages and you have, actually, not much to say.

Roseanne Arnold 1953– : *Roseanne* (1990)

on James Agate's autobiography:
3 I did so enjoy your book. Everything that everybody writes in it is so good.

Mrs Patrick Campbell 1865–1940: James Agate diary 6 May 1937

4 The reader need not become uneasy; I do not intend to write of the boy that made good.

Neville Cardus 1889–1975: *Autobiography* (1947)

5 Reformers are always finally neglected, while the memoirs of the frivolous will always eagerly be read.

Chips Channon 1897–1958: diary, 7 July 1936

6 An autobiography should give the reader opportunity to point out the author's follies and misconceptions.

Claud Cockburn 1904–81: *Crossing the Line* (1958)

7 I am really not motivated by revenge of any description . . . The book is rather gentle.
on her autobiography, describing the break up of her marriage to Robin Cook

Margaret Cook 1944– : in *Guardian* 11 January 1999

8 An autobiography is an obituary in serial form with the last instalment missing.

Quentin Crisp 1908–99: *The Naked Civil Servant* (1968)

Giles Gordon's father had criticized the length of his son's entry in Who's Who:
9 I've just measured it, with a ruler; it's exactly the same length as my male organ, which I've also just measured.

Giles Gordon 1940– : *Aren't We Due a Royalty Statement?* (1993)

10 Autobiography is now as common as adultery and hardly less reprehensible.

John Grigg 1924– : in *Sunday Times* 28 February 1962

11 Next to the writer of real estate advertisements, the autobiographer is the most suspect of prose artists.

Donal Henahan: in *New York Times* 1977

12 The purpose of the Presidential Office is not power, or leadership of the Western World, but reminiscence, best-selling reminiscence.

Roger Jellinek 1938– : in *New York Times Book Review* 1969

13 If a man is to write *A Panegyric* he may keep vices out of sight; but if he professes to write *A Life*, he must represent it as it really was.

Samuel Johnson 1709–84: James Boswell *Life of Samuel Johnson* (1791) 1777

14 The reminiscences of Mrs Humphrey Ward . . . convinced me that autobiography is a sin.

Harold Laski 1893–1950: letter to Oliver Wendell Holmes, 1 December 1918

on Margot Asquith's forthcoming memoirs:
15 As scandal is the second breath of life my name is down for an early copy.

Harold Laski 1893–1950: letter to Oliver Wendell Holmes, 6 March 1920

16 I write no memoirs. I'm a gentleman. I cannot bring myself to write nastily about persons whose hospitality I have enjoyed.

John Pentland Mahaffy 1839–1919: W. B. Stanford and R. B. McDowell *Mahaffy* (1971)

17 As a devoted reader of autobiographies, I have long since come to dread passages which begin with 'The family hailed originally, I believe, from Cleckheaton', and back we go to the middle of the eighteenth century where, before long, there surges up a frightful old 'Character' called 'Grumps', first cousin to the Starkadders, who becomes the Scourge of Bradford and extremely bad news all over Yorkshire.

Arthur Marshall 1910–89: *Life's Rich Pageant* (1984)

18 Like all good memoirs it has not been emasculated by considerations of good taste.

Peter Medawar 1915–87: review of James D. Watson *The Double Helix* (1968)

19 Every autobiography . . . becomes an absorbing work of fiction, with something of the charm of a cryptogram.

H. L. Mencken 1880–1956: *Minority Report* (1956)

20 Even when Micheál [MacLíammoir] took in later life to autobiographies, they were about as reliable as his hairpieces.

Sheridan Morley 1941– : in *Sunday Times* 6 February 1994

21 To write one's memoirs is to speak ill of everybody except oneself.

Henri Philippe Pétain 1856–1951: in *Observer* 26 May 1946

22 If you really want to hear about it, the first thing you'll probably want to know is where I was born, and what my lousy childhood was like, and how my parents were occupied and all before they had me, and all that David Copperfield kind of crap, but I don't feel like going into it.

J. D. Salinger 1919– : *The Catcher in the Rye* (1951)

23 My problem is that I am not frightfully interested in anything, except myself. And of all forms of fiction autobiography is the most gratuitous.

Tom Stoppard 1937– : *Lord Malquist and Mr Moon* (1966)

24 Only when one has lost all curiosity about the future has one reached the age to write an autobiography.

Evelyn Waugh 1903–66: *A Little Learning* (1964)

25 I shall not say why and how I became, at the age of fifteen, the mistress of the Earl of Craven.

Harriette Wilson 1789–1846: opening words of *Memoirs* (1825)

of political memoirists:
26 It is an exceptionally inadequate ex-minister who fails to secure a six-figure sum for his work, serialization included.

Hugo Young 1938– : in *Guardian* 20 September 1990

Awards and Prizes

1 Prizes are like sashes, you can wear them and be Miss World for a bit . . . I've been royally dissed by prizes.

Martin Amis 1949– : in *Observer* 10 March 1996 'Sayings of the Week'

2 My career must be slipping. This is the first time I've been
available to pick up an award.

Michael Caine 1933– : at the
Golden Globe awards, Beverly Hills,
California, 24 January 1999

3 Had they sent me ¼ lb of good tobacco, the addition to my
happiness had probably been suitabler and greater!
on being awarded the Prussian Order of Merit

Thomas Carlyle 1795–1881: letter to
his brother John Carlyle, 14 February
1874

*suggestion for a winning poem for the competition for Bard of
Humberside:*
4 I put my luncheon in the fridge
and go and look at Humber Bridge.

Philip Larkin 1922–85: in
conversation with Andrew Motion;
quoted in *Sunday Times* 23 May 1999

5 Awards are like piles. Sooner or later, every bum gets one.

Maureen Lipman 1946– : in
Independent 31 July 1999

6 In the end I accepted the honour, because during dinner
Venables told me, that, if I became Poet Laureate, I should
always when I dined out be offered the liver-wing of a
fowl.
on being made Poet Laureate in 1850

Alfred, Lord Tennyson 1809–92: in
*Alfred Lord Tennyson: A Memoir by his
Son* (1897) vol. 1

7 People fail you, children disappoint you, thieves break in,
moths corrupt, but an OBE goes on for ever.

Fay Weldon 1931– : *Praxis* (1978)

Baseball See also **Sports and Games**

1 One of the chief duties of the fan is to engage in arguments
with the man behind him. This department of the game
has been allowed to run down fearfully.

Robert Benchley 1889–1945: Ralph
S. Graben *The Baseball Reader* (1951)

2 Think! How the hell are you gonna think and hit at the
same time?

Yogi Berra 1925– : *Nice Guys Finish
Seventh* (1976)

3 If people don't want to come out to the ball park, nobody's
going to stop 'em.

Yogi Berra 1925– : attributed

4 For those of us who are baseball fans and agnostics, the
[Baseball] Hall of Fame is as close to a religious experience
as we may ever get.

Bill Bryson 1951– : *The Lost
Continent* (1989)

5 If baseball goes for pay television, shouldn't the viewers be
given a bonus for watching a ball game between Baltimore
and Kansas City?

Jimmy Cannon 1910–73: in *New York
Post* 1951–54 'Nobody Asked Me, But
. . .'

6 Baseball is very big with my people. It figures. It's the only
way we can get to shake a bat at a white man without
starting a riot.

Dick Gregory 1932– : D. H. Nathan
(ed.) *Baseball Quotations* (1991)

*after leaving his sick-bed in October 1935 to attend the World
Baseball Series in Detroit, and betting on the losers:*
7 I should of stood in bed.

Joe Jacobs 1896–1940: John Lardner
Strong Cigars (1951)

8 Although he is a bad fielder he is also a poor hitter.
of a baseball player

Ring Lardner 1885–1933: R. E.
Drennan *Wit's End* (1973)

9 Take me out to the ball game,
Take me out with the crowd.
Buy me some peanuts and cracker-jack—
I don't care if I never get back.

Jack Norworth 1879–1959: 'Take Me
Out to the Ball Game' (1908 song)

10 Don't look back. Something may be gaining on you.
a baseball pitcher's advice

Satchel Paige 1906–82: in *Collier's* 13 June 1953

11 All you have to do is keep the five players who hate your guts away from the five who are undecided.
a baseball manager's view in 1974

Casey Stengel 1891–1975: John Samuel (ed.) *The Guardian Book of Sports Quotes* (1985)

12 I don't think I can be expected to take seriously any game which takes less than three days to reach its conclusion.
a cricket enthusiast on baseball

Tom Stoppard 1937– : in *Guardian* 24 December 1984 'Sports Quotes of the Year'

13 Baseball, it is said, is only a game. True. And the Grand Canyon is only a hole in Arizona. Not all holes, or games, are created equal.

George F. Will 1941– : *Men At Work: The Craft of Baseball* (1990)

Behaviour and Etiquette

1 Thank you for the most *marvellous* interview, darling, you're quite the politest lesbian I've ever met.
calling out in a crowded lobby after a self-righteous reporter

Tallulah Bankhead 1903–68: Bryony Lavery *Tallulah Bankhead* (1999)

2 My grandmother took a bath every year, whether she was dirty or not.

Brendan Behan 1923–64: *Brendan Behan's Island* (1962)

3 It looked bad when the Duke of Fife
Left off using a knife;
But people began to talk
When he left off using a fork.

Edmund Clerihew Bentley 1875–1956: 'The Duke of Fife' (1905)

4 You know what charm is: a way of getting the answer yes without having asked any clear question.

Albert Camus 1913–60: *La Chute* (1956)

5 It isn't etiquette to cut any one you've been introduced to. Remove the joint.

Lewis Carroll 1832–98: *Through the Looking-Glass* (1872)

6 Curtsey while you're thinking what to say. It saves time.

Lewis Carroll 1832–98: *Through the Looking-Glass* (1872)

7 I always take blushing either for a sign of guilt, or of ill breeding.

William Congreve 1670–1729: *The Way of the World* (1700)

8 Don't let us be familiar or fond, nor kiss before folks, like my Lady Fadler and Sir Francis . . . Let us be very strange and well-bred: Let us be as strange as if we had been married a great while, and as well-bred as if we were not married at all.

William Congreve 1670–1729: *The Way of the World* (1700)

9 HECKLER: We expected a better play.
COWARD: I expected better manners.
to a heckler in the audience after Sirocco *(1927) was booed*

Noël Coward 1899–1973: Sheridan Morley *A Talent to Amuse* (1969)

10 How would I like to be remembered? By my charm, you silly bugger.

Noël Coward 1899–1973: Sheridan Morley *The Quotable Noël Coward* (1999)

11 I tried to keep in mind the essential rules of British conduct which the Major had carefully instilled in me:
1. The English never speak to anyone unless they have been properly introduced (except in case of shipwreck).
2. You must never talk about God or your stomach.

Pierre Daninos: *Major Thompson and I* (1957)

12 After a brief period of anguish over whether or not to sling out the fish-knives, everyone said, 'Oh, stuff it', and heaved a sigh of relief, and the haut-ton was gone for ever.

Alice Thomas Ellis 1932– : in *Independent on Sunday* 2 October 1993

13 He'd say 'Par'n my glove', politely
When he shook my hand.
And he'd pass me the evening paper
When his soup was fanned.
He only used four-letter words
I didn't understand.
He had refinement.

Dorothy Fields 1905–74: 'He Had Refinement' (in *A Tree Grows in Brooklyn*, 1951 musical)

14 You children must be extra polite to strangers because your father's an actor.

Mrs Fields: Dorothy Fields' mother; taped lecture in Caryl Brahms and Ned Sherrin *Song by Song* (1984)

15 Suspect all extraordinary and groundless civilities.

Thomas Fuller 1654–1734: *Gnomologia* (1734)

16 I get too hungry for dinner at eight.
I like the theatre, but never come late.
I never bother with people I hate.
That's why the lady is a tramp.

Lorenz Hart 1895–1943: 'The Lady is a Tramp' (1937)

on Harold Wilson's 'Lavender List' (the honours list he drew up on resigning the British premiership in 1976):
17 Such a graceful exit. And then he had to go and do this on the doorstep.

John Junor 1919–97: in *Observer* 23 December 1990

18 'What are you doing for dinner tonight?'
'Digesting it.'
    to a dinner invitation arriving at 8.30 pm

George S. Kaufman 1889–1961: Howard Teichmann *George S. Kaufman* (1973)

19 Eccentricity, to be socially acceptable, had still to have at least four or five generations of inbreeding behind it.

Osbert Lancaster 1908–80: *All Done From Memory* (1953)

20 The mayor gave no other answer than that deep guttural grunt which is technically known in municipal interviews as refusing to commit oneself.

Stephen Leacock 1869–1944: *Arcadian Adventures with the Idle Rich* (1914)

21 I have noticed that the people who are late are often so much jollier than the people who have to wait for them.

E. V. Lucas 1868–1938: *365 Days and One More* (1926)

aged four, having had hot coffee spilt over his legs:
22 Thank you, madam, the agony is abated.

Lord Macaulay 1800–59: G. O. Trevelyan *Life and Letters of Lord Macaulay* (1876)

23 Etiquette, sacred subject of, 1–389.

Judith Martin 1938– : *Miss Manners' Guide to Rearing Perfect Children* (1985); index entry

24 Good manners are a combination of intelligence, education, taste, and style mixed together so that you don't need any of those things.

P. J. O'Rourke 1947– : *Modern Manners* (1984)

25 Do you suppose I could buy back my introduction to you?

S. J. Perelman 1904–79 et al.: in *Monkey Business* (1931 film)

26 Miss Otis regrets she's unable to lunch today, Madam.

Cole Porter 1891–1964: 'Miss Otis Regrets' (1934)

27 In olden days, a glimpse of stocking
Was looked on as something shocking,
But now, God knows,
Anything goes.

Cole Porter 1891–1964: 'Anything Goes' (1934)

28 One of those telegrams of which M. de Guermantes had wittily fixed the formula: 'Cannot come, lie follows'.

Marcel Proust 1871–1922: *Le Temps retrouvé* (Time Regained, 1926)

29 I am a woman of the world, Hector; and I can assure you that if you will only take the trouble always to do the perfectly correct thing, and to say the perfectly correct thing, you can do just what you like.

George Bernard Shaw 1856–1950: *Heartbreak House* (1919)

30 These sort of boobies think that people come to balls to do nothing but dance; whereas everyone knows that the real business of a ball is either to look out for a wife, to look after a wife, or to look after somebody else's wife.

R. S. Surtees 1805–64: *Mr Facey Romford's Hounds* (1865)

Somerset Maugham excused his leaving early when dining with Lady Tree by saying, 'I must look after my youth':
31 Next time do bring him. We adore those sort of people.

Lady Tree 1863–1937: in *Ned Sherrin in his Anecdotage* (1993); a similar story is told of Maugham and Lady Cunard

32 This is a free country, madam. We have a right to share your privacy in a public place.

Peter Ustinov 1921– : *Romanoff and Juliet* (1956)

33 Orthodoxy is my doxy; heterodoxy is another man's doxy.

William Warburton 1698–1779: to Lord Sandwich; Joseph Priestley *Memoirs* (1807)

34 Manners are especially the need of the plain. The pretty can get away with anything.

Evelyn Waugh 1903–66: in *Observer* 15 April 1962

35 I am very sorry to hear that Duff [Cooper] was surprised and grieved to hear that I had detested him for 23 years. I must have nicer manners than people normally credit me with.

Evelyn Waugh 1903–66: letter to Lady Diana Cooper, 29 August 1953

hearing someone object that the good manners of the French were all on the surface:
36 Well, you know, a very good place to have them.

James McNeill Whistler 1834–1903: E. R. and J. Pennell *The Life of James McNeill Whistler* (1908)

37 It is very vulgar to talk like a dentist when one isn't a dentist. It produces a false impression.

Oscar Wilde 1854–1900: *The Importance of Being Earnest* (1895)

38 Duty is what one expects from others, it is not what one does oneself.

Oscar Wilde 1854–1900: *A Woman of No Importance* (1893)

39 It is a good rule in life never to apologize. The right sort of people do not want apologies, and the wrong sort take a mean advantage of them.

P. G. Wodehouse 1881–1975: *The Man Upstairs* (1914)

40 The confessions of error, as jocular as they are suspect, which the upper class have always associated with good manners.

Hugo Young 1938– : in *Guardian* 20 September 1990

Betting and Gambling

1 It's one thing to ask your bank manager for an overdraft to buy 500 begonias for the borders in Haslemere, but quite another to seek financial succour to avail oneself of some of the 5–2 they're offering on Isle de Bourbon for the St Leger.

Jeffrey Bernard 1932–97: in *Guardian* 23 December 1978 'Sports Quotes of the Year'

2 I have a notion that gamblers are as happy as most people—being always excited.

> **Lord Byron** 1788–1824: 'Detached Thoughts' 15 October 1821

3 Rowe's Rule: the odds are five to six that the light at the end of the tunnel is the headlight of an oncoming train.

> **Paul Dickson** 1939– : in *Washingtonian* November 1978

4 Never give a sucker an even break.

> **W. C. Fields** 1880–1946: title of a W. C. Fields film (1941); the catch-phrase (Fields's own) is said to have originated in the musical comedy *Poppy* (1923)

5 Horse sense is a good judgement which keeps horses from betting on people.

> **W. C. Fields** 1880–1946: attributed; Nigel Rees *Cassell Dictionary of Humorous Quotations* (1999)

6 GAMBLER: Say, is this a game of chance?
CUTHBERT J. TWILLIE: Not the way I play it.

> **W. C. Fields** 1880–1946: *My Little Chickadee* (1940 film), spoken by W. C. Fields

7 Two-up is Australia's very own way of parting a fool and his money.

> **Germaine Greer** 1939– : in *Observer* 1 August 1982

8 Don't let's go to the dogs tonight,
For mother will be there.

> **A. P. Herbert** 1890–1971: 'Don't Let's Go to the Dogs Tonight' (1926)

asked how his bridge-partner should have played a hand:
9 Under an assumed name.

> **George S. Kaufman** 1889–1961: Scott Meredith *George S. Kaufman and the Algonquin Round Table* (1974)

10 I got a horse right here,
The name is Paul Revere,
And here's a guy that says if the weather's clear,
Can do, can do, this guy says the horse can do.

> **Frank Loesser** 1910–69: 'Fugue for Tinhorns' (1950)

11 Not for good old reliable Nathan for it's always just a short walk,
To the oldest established permanent floating crap game in New York.

> **Frank Loesser** 1910–69: 'The Oldest Established' (1950)

12 'You are snatching a hard guy when you snatch Bookie Bob. A very hard guy, indeed. In fact,' I say, 'I hear the softest thing about him is his front teeth.'

> **Damon Runyon** 1884–1946: in *Collier's* 26 September 1931, 'The Snatching of Bookie Bob'

13 I long ago come to the conclusion that all life is 6 to 5 against.

> **Damon Runyon** 1884–1946: in *Collier's* 8 September 1934, 'A Nice Price'

14 My immediate reward for increasing the tax on bookmaking was major vilification. It was confidently asserted in the bookmakers' circles that my mother and father met only once and then for a very brief period.
in 1972, when Chairman of the British Betting Levy Board

> **George Wigg** 1900–83: Jonathon Green and Don Atyeo (eds.) *The Book of Sports Quotes* (1979)

The Bible

1 There's a great text in Galatians,
Once you trip on it, entails
Twenty-nine distinct damnations,
One sure, if another fails.

> **Robert Browning** 1812–89: 'Soliloquy of the Spanish Cloister' (1842)

on Moses and the reason why there are only ten commandments:

2 He probably said to himself, 'Must stop or I shall be getting silly.'

Mrs Patrick Campbell 1865–1940: James Agate diary, 6 May 1937

3 The Bible . . . is a lesson in how not to write for the movies.

Raymond Chandler 1888–1959: letter to Edgar Carter, 28 March 1947

4 A wonderful book, but there are some very queer things in it.

George V 1865–1936: K. Rose *King George V* (1983)

5 It ain't necessarily so,
It ain't necessarily so—
De t'ings that yo' li'ble
To read in de Bible—
It ain't necessarily so.

Ira Gershwin 1896–1983: 'It Ain't Necessarily So' (1935)

6 The number one book of the ages was written by a committee, and it was called the Bible.

Louis B. Mayer 1885–1957: attributed

7 LORD ILLINGWORTH: The Book of Life begins with a man and a woman in a garden.
MRS ALLONBY: It ends with Revelations.

Oscar Wilde 1854–1900: *A Woman of No Importance* (1893)

8 I read the book of Job last night. I don't think God comes well out of it.

Virginia Woolf 1882–1941: letter to Lady Robert Cecil, 12 November 1922

9 It's just called 'The Bible' now. We dropped the word 'Holy' to give it a more mass-market appeal.
a publisher's view

Judith Young: attributed, 1989

Biography   See also **Autobiography**

1 Biography should be written by an acute enemy.

Arthur James Balfour 1848–1930: in *Observer* 30 January 1927

2 Nobody likes being written about in their lifetime, it's as though the FBI and the CIA were suddenly to splash your files in the paper.
on his forthcoming biography

Saul Bellow 1915– : in *Guardian* 10 September 1997

3 The Art of Biography
Is different from Geography.
Geography is about Maps,
But Biography is about Chaps.

Edmund Clerihew Bentley 1875–1956: *Biography for Beginners* (1905) introduction

reason for shelving a planned biography of L. P. Hartley:
4 I was told I had to track one butler down to a male brothel in Norway.

Penelope Fitzgerald 1916–2000: in *Daily Telegraph* 6 May 2000; obituary

5 Biography, like big game hunting, is one of the recognized forms of sport, and it is as unfair as only sport can be.

Philip Guedalla 1889–1944: *Supers and Supermen* (1920)

6 Do not send me your manuscript. Worse than the practice of writing books about living men is the conduct of living men in supervising such books.
to his would-be biographer Houston Martin

A. E. Housman 1859–1936: letter, 22 March 1936

on hearing that Arthur Benson was to write the life of Rossetti:
7 No, no, no, it won't do. *Dear* Arthur, we know just what he can, so beautifully, do, but no, oh no, this is to have the story of a purple man written by a white, or at the most, a pale green man.

Henry James 1843–1916: George Lyttelton letter to Rupert Hart-Davis, 28 February 1957

8 Sir John Malcolm, whose love passes the love of biographers, and who can see nothing but wisdom and justice in the action of his idol.

Lord Macaulay 1800–59: 'Lord Clive' (1840)

9 I never read the life of any important person without discovering that he knew more and could do more than I could ever hope to know or to do in half a dozen lifetimes.

J. B. Priestley 1894–1984: *Apes and Angels* (1928)

10 I have done my best to die before this book is published. It now seems possible that I may not succeed . . . I shall try to keep my sense of humour and the perspective of eternity.
letter to his biographer, Humphrey Carpenter, shortly before publication

Robert Runcie 1921–2000: H. Carpenter *Robert Runcie* (1996)

11 He's written me a rather plaintive letter, saying will you at least read the typescript to correct any factual errors and I've replied no, I want it to be as inaccurate as possible.
of his response to a would-be and unwanted biographer

Tom Stoppard 1937– : in *Daily Telegraph* 27 February 1999

12 Discretion is not the better part of biography.

Lytton Strachey 1880–1932: Michael Holroyd *Lytton Strachey* (1967)

13 I have a good track record with larger-than-life iron ladies.
on writing the story of the liner QEII

Carol Thatcher 1953– : in *Sunday Times* 19 March 2000 'Talking Heads'

14 I have always liked reading biographies. It is the ideal literary genre for someone too prim, like me, to acknowledge a gossipy interest in the living—don't you *hate* gossips, aren't they *too* awful?—but avid for any nuggets from the private lives of the dead because that is perfectly respectable, an altogether worthy and informative way of spending one's time.

Jill Tweedie 1936–93: *It's Only Me* (1980)

15 Blamelessness runs riot through six hundred pages.
review of Kenneth Harris's biography of Attlee

John Vincent 1937– : in *Sunday Times* 26 September 1982

16 Then there is my noble and biographical friend who has added a new terror to death.

Charles Wetherell 1770–1846: on Lord Campbell's *Lives of the Lord Chancellors* being written without the consent of heirs or executors; also attributed to Lord Lyndhurst (1772–1863)

17 Every great man nowadays has his disciples, and it is always Judas who writes the biography.

Oscar Wilde 1854–1900: *Intentions* (1891) 'The Critic as Artist'

on being lent a hot-from-the-press copy of Lytton Strachey's Eminent Victorians in 1918:
18 We are in for a bad time.

G. M. Young 1882–1959: attributed

Birds See also **Animals**

1 A Heron flies in a slow leisurely manner, as if it was hoping to remember where it's going before it actually gets there.

Anthony Armstrong 1897–1976: *Good Egg!* (1944)

2 It's from one of those battery farms . . . A few hens who've earned privileges for good behaviour are allowed out in front of the sheds. Meanwhile the rest are bound and gagged inside.

Alan Bennett 1934– : *Getting On* (1972)

3 A hen is only an egg's way of making other eggs.

Samuel Butler 1835–1902: *Life and Habit* (1877)

4 Get out of town!
And he went, with a quack and a waddle and a quack,
In a flurry of eiderdown.

Frank Loesser 1910–69: 'The Ugly Duckling' (1952)

5 This woodcock, by a happy fluke,
Might have avoided either duke.
Had it the commoner preferred,
It would have been a wiser bird.
Alas, its fate became a cert,
Betwixt Duke Bobo and Duke Bert.

Harold Macmillan 1894–1986: 'Ode to a woodcock which, on emerging from the covert, was fired on simultaneously by the Dukes of Roxburghe and Marlborough'; collected by Peter Fleming from an unidentified gamebook, and quoted by Duff Hart-Davis in *Sunday Telegraph* 6 August 2000

6 Oh, a wondrous bird is the pelican!
His beak holds more than his belican.
He takes in his beak
Food enough for a week.
But I'll be darned if I know how the helican.

Dixon Lanier Merritt 1879–1972: in *Nashville Banner* 22 April 1913

7 Canaries, caged in the house, do it,
When they're out of season, grouse do it.

Cole Porter 1891–1964: 'Let's Do It, Let's Fall in Love' (1928)

8 If I were a cassowary
On the plains of Timbuctoo,
I would eat a missionary,
Cassock, band, and hymn-book too.

Samuel Wilberforce 1805–73: impromptu verse, attributed

The Body See also **Appearance, Description**

1 My brain? It's my second favourite organ.

Woody Allen 1935– and **Marshall Brickman** 1941– : *Sleeper* (1973 film)

2 Even thin people look fat there [New York], and fat women are always out with handsome men (not like in California, where everyone thinks fat is something you can catch, and therefore is to be avoided).

Roseanne Arnold 1953– : *Roseanne* (1990)

3 If I had the use of my body I would throw it out of the window.

Samuel Beckett 1906–89: *Malone Dies* (1988)

4 Hello boys, have a good night's rest? . . . I missed you.
Governor Le Petomane facing his secretary's cleavage

Andrew Bergman 1945– and **Mel Brooks** 1926– : *Blazing Saddles* (1974 film), spoken by Mel Brooks

5 People don't come in my size until they're old . . . I used to think people were born with big bones and large frames, but apparently these grow when you're about sixty-eight.

Maeve Binchy 1940– : *Circle of Friends* (1990)

6 And our carcases, which are to rise again, are they worth raising? I hope, if mine is, that I shall have a better pair of legs than I have moved on these two-and-twenty years, or I shall be sadly behind in the squeeze into Paradise.

Lord Byron 1788–1824: letter, 13 September 1811

7 I've got difficult feet. They're almost round, like an elephant's. Lengthways they're size ten and sideways size twelve.

Patrick Campbell 1913–80: *Gullible Travels* (1969)

8 I'm the female equivalent of a counterfeit $20 bill. Half of what you see is a pretty good reproduction, the rest is a fraud.

Cher 1946- : Doug McClelland *Star Speak: Hollywood on Everything* (1987)

9 Imprisoned in every fat man a thin one is wildly signalling to be let out.

Cyril Connolly 1903-74: *The Unquiet Grave* (1944)

10 I didn't pay three pounds fifty just to see half a dozen acorns and a chipolata.

Noël Coward 1899-1973: on David Storey's *The Changing Room*; attributed

11 He had but one eye, and the popular prejudice runs in favour of two.

Charles Dickens 1812-70: *Nicholas Nickleby* (1839)

12 If you could see my legs when I take my boots off, you'd form some idea of what unrequited affection is.

Charles Dickens 1812-70: *Dombey and Son* (1848)

13 What is man, when you come to think upon him, but a minutely set, ingenious machine for turning, with infinite artfulness, the red wine of Shiraz into urine?

Isak Dinesen 1885-1962: *Seven Gothic Tales* (1934) 'The Dreamers'

14 I wish you could only see Dizzy in his bath, then you would know what a white skin is.
of her husband

Mary Anne Disraeli d. 1872: attributed; William Gregory *An Autobiography* (1894)

to William Cecil, who suffered from gout:
15 My lord, we make use of you, not for your bad legs, but for your good head.

Elizabeth I 1533-1603: F. Chamberlin *Sayings of Queen Elizabeth* (1923)

16 Being a woman is worse than being a farmer—There is so much harvesting and crop spraying to be done: legs to be waxed, underarms shaved, eyebrows plucked, feet pumiced, skin exfoliated and moisturized, spots cleansed, roots dyed, eyelashes tinted, nails filed, cellulite massaged, stomach muscles exercised . . . Is it any wonder girls have no confidence?

Helen Fielding 1958- : *Bridget Jones's Diary* (1996)

17 I travel light; as light,
That is, as a man can travel who will
Still carry his body around because
Of its sentimental value.

Christopher Fry 1907- : *The Lady's not for Burning* (1949)

18 I have a left shoulder-blade that is a miracle of loveliness. People come miles to see it. My right elbow has a fascination that few can resist.

W. S. Gilbert 1836-1911: *The Mikado* (1885)

19 There is something between us.

Donald Hall 1928- : 'Breasts' (a one-line poem, 1971)

20 Lydia, oh Lydia—Say, have you met Lydia?
Oh, Lydia, the tattooed lady?
When she stands, her lap grows littler,
When she sits, she sits on Hitler!

E. Y. Harburg 1898-1981: 'Lydia, the Tattooed Lady' (*A Day at the Circus*, 1939 film)

21 [Alfred Hitchcock] thought of himself as looking like Cary Grant. That's tough, to think of yourself one way and look another.

Tippi Hedren 1935- : interview in California, 1982; P. F. Boller and R. L. Davis *Hollywood Anecdotes* (1988)

22 What they call 'heart' lies much lower than the fourth waistcoat button.

Georg Christoph Lichtenberg 1742-99: notebook (1776-79) in *Aphorisms* (1990)

23 If your mother had married a proper decent Limerickman
you wouldn't have this standing up, North of Ireland,
Presbyterian hair.

Frank McCourt 1930– : *Angela's Ashes* (1996)

seaside postcard showing a very fat man whose stomach obscures the small boy at his feet:
24 Can't see my little Willy.

Donald McGill 1875–1962: caption, c.1910; in 'Quote Unquote Newsletter', July 1994

25 I'd like to borrow his body for just 48 hours. There are
three guys I'd like to beat up and four women I'd like to
make love to.

Jim Murray: of Muhammad Ali; attributed

26 A bit of talcum
Is always walcum.

Ogden Nash 1902–71: 'The Baby' (1931)

27 In an advanced state of nudity.

Joe Orton 1933–67: *Up Against It*, screenplay written for the Beatles but never filmed

a gay friend, patting her bottom, had commented that it was flabby:
28 FRIEND: You should feel mine. It's all taut.
JENNIFER PATERSON: Oh really? And who taut it?

Jennifer Paterson 1928–99: in *Times* 11 August 1999, obituary

29 I'm deeply honoured, but a bit confused. I was only ever a
B-cup.
   on being voted the sexiest television star 'of all time' by Americans

Diana Rigg 1938– : in *The Times* 3 May 1999

30 I don't really like knees.

Yves Saint Laurent 1936– : in *Observer* 3 August 1958

31 Thou seest I have more flesh than another man, and
therefore more frailty.

William Shakespeare 1564–1616: *Henry IV, Part 1* (1597)

32 The body of a young woman is God's greatest achievement
. . . Of course, He could have built it to last longer but you
can't have everything.

Neil Simon 1927– : *The Gingerbread Lady* (1970)

33 Mrs Bennett . . . had but two back teeth in her head, but,
thank God, they still met.

Edith Œ. Somerville 1858–1949 and **Martin Ross** 1862–1915: *Some Experiences of an Irish R.M.* (1899)

34 Big breasts à la Pamela Anderson are one thing but ones
that look more like old socks with tangerines dropped in
the bottom are an entirely different kettle du poisson.

Arabella Weir: *Does My Bum Look Big in This?* (1997)

35 Bah! the thing is not a nose at all, but a bit of primordial
chaos clapped on to my face.

H. G. Wells 1866–1946: *Select Conversations with an Uncle* (1895) 'The Man with a Nose'

36 Let's forget the six feet and talk about the seven inches.

Mae West 1892–1980: G. Eells and S. Musgrove *Mae West* (1989)

37 How dare he tell me what to do when he has a
circumference to rival the Equator.
   on the advice of Health Minister Frank Dobson that a healthy diet should include more bran and fibre

Ann Widdecombe 1947– : in *Guardian* 8 July 1998

38 He was built on large lines, and seemed to fill the room to overflowing. In physique he was not unlike what Primo Carnera would have been if Carnera hadn't stunted his growth by smoking cigarettes when a boy.

P. G. Wodehouse 1881–1975: *Mulliner Nights* (1933)

39 You're a man, and that's a bonus
'Cause when you're swinging your cojones
You'll show 'em what testosterone is.

David Yazbek: 'Man' in *The Full Monty* (musical, 2000)

Books See also **Dictionaries, Indexes, Libraries, Literature, Poetry and Poets, Reading, Publishing, Writers and Writing**

1 If Kafka had been a bookseller, Foyles would have been the result.

comment on the famous bookshop quoted after the death of Christina Foyle

Anonymous: in *Mail on Sunday* 13 June 1999

2 One of those big, fat paperbacks, intended to while away a monsoon or two, which, if thrown with a good overarm action, will bring a water buffalo to its knees.

Nancy Banks-Smith: review of television adaptation of M. M. Kaye *The Far Pavilions*; in *Guardian* 4 January 1984

3 I am writing a book about the Crusades so *dull* that I can scarcely write it.

Hilaire Belloc 1870–1953: Rupert Hart-Davis letter to George Lyttelton, 25 March 1956

4 My desire is . . . that mine adversary had written a book.

Bible: *Job*

5 Take care not to understand editions and title-pages too well. It always smells of pedantry, and not always of learning . . . Beware of the *bibliomanie*.

Lord Chesterfield 1694–1773: *Letters to his Son* (1774)

on hearing that a fellow guest was 'writing a book':
6 Neither am I.

Peter Cook 1937–95: attributed (disclaimed as original by Cook); Nigel Rees *Cassell Dictionary of Humorous Quotations* (1999)

7 When the [Supreme] Court moved to Washington in 1800, it was provided with no books, which probably accounts for the high quality of early opinions.

Robert H. Jackson 1892–1954: *The Supreme Court in the American System of Government* (1955)

8 One man is as good as another until he has written a book.

Benjamin Jowett 1817–93: Evelyn Abbott and Lewis Campbell (eds.) *Life and Letters of Benjamin Jowett* (1897)

9 This is primarily a picture-book and the letterpress is intended to do no more than provide a small mass of information leavened by a large dose of personal prejudice.

Osbert Lancaster 1908–80: *Pillar to Post* (1938)

10 Synopsis of Previous Chapters: There are no Previous Chapters.

Stephen Leacock 1869–1944: *Nonsense Novels* (1911) 'Gertrude the Governess'

11 Having been unpopular in high school is not just cause for book publication.

Fran Lebowitz 1946– : *Metropolitan Life* (1978)

12 Book—what they make a movie out of for television.

Leonard Louis Levinson: Laurence J. Peter (ed.) *Quotations for our Time* (1977)

13 Things were easier for the old novelists who saw people all of a piece. Speaking generally, their heroes were good through and through, their villains wholly bad.

W. Somerset Maugham 1874–1965: *A Writer's Notebook* (1949) written in 1922

14 I opened it at page 96—the secret page on which I write my name to catch out borrowers and book-sharks.

Flann O'Brien 1911–66: *Myles Away from Dublin* (1990)

15 Some savage faculty for observation told him that most respectable and estimable people usually had a lot of books in their houses.

Flann O'Brien 1911–66: *The Best of Myles* (1968)

16 This is not a novel to be tossed aside lightly. It should be thrown with great force.

Dorothy Parker 1893–1967: R. E. Drennan *Wit's End* (1973)

17 I hate books; they only teach us to talk about things we know nothing about.

Jean-Jacques Rousseau 1712–78: *Émile* (1762)

18 A best-seller is the gilded tomb of a mediocre talent.

Logan Pearsall Smith 1865–1946: *Afterthoughts* (1931) 'Art and Letters'

19 No furniture so charming as books.

Sydney Smith 1771–1845: Lady Holland *Memoir* (1855)

20 A. L. ROWSE: You don't read my books, John. Do you know *Tudor Cornwall*?
JOHN SPARROW: Do you know Stuart Hampshire?

John Sparrow 1906–92: Noel Annan *The Dons* (1999)

21 Digressions, incontestably, are the sunshine;—they are the life, the soul of reading;—take them out of this book for instance,—you might as well take the book along with them.

Laurence Sterne 1713–68: *Tristram Shandy* (1759–67)

22 'Pilgrim's Progress', about a man that left his family it didn't say why . . . The statements was interesting, but tough.

Mark Twain 1835–1910: *The Adventures of Huckleberry Finn* (1884)

23 I haven't been so happy since the day Reader's Digest lost my address.

Dick Vosburgh: *A Saint She Ain't* (1999)

24 In every first novel the hero is the author as Christ or Faust.

Oscar Wilde 1854–1900: attributed

25 There is no such thing as a moral or an immoral book. Books are well written, or badly written.

Oscar Wilde 1854–1900: *The Picture of Dorian Gray* (1891)

26 The good ended happily, and the bad unhappily. That is what fiction means.

Oscar Wilde 1854–1900: *The Importance of Being Earnest* (1895)

27 The scratching of pimples on the body of the bootboy at Claridges.

Virginia Woolf 1882–1941: of James Joyce's *Ulysses*; letter to Lytton Strachey, 24 April 1922

Bores and Boredom

1 The chancellor is an anorak. He has the social skills of a whelk.
    unidentified Treasury official on Gordon Brown

Anonymous: in *Sunday Times* 31 January 1999

2 He really is terribly heavy going. Like running up hill in roller skates.

Alan Ayckbourn 1939– : *Living Together* (1975)

3 A person who talks when you wish him to listen.

Ambrose Bierce 1842–c.1914: definition of a bore; *Cynic's Word Book* (1906)

4 What's wrong with being a boring kind of guy?

George Bush 1924- : during the campaign for the Republican nomination; in *Daily Telegraph* 28 April 1988

5 Dullness is so much stronger than genius because there is so much more of it, and it is better organized and more naturally cohesive *inter se*. So the arctic volcano can do nothing against arctic ice.

Samuel Butler 1835-1902: *Notebooks* (1912)

6 He is not only dull in himself, but the cause of dullness in others.

Samuel Foote 1720-77: on a dull law lord; James Boswell *Life of Samuel Johnson* (1934 ed.) 1783

7 Across the table . . . loomed the benignant but deadly form of Lord Dunsany, who will bore you to sleep on the subject of rock-salt if you give him a glimpse of an opening.

Rupert Hart-Davis 1907-99: letter to George Lyttelton, 26 February 1956

8 Most of my contemporaries at school entered the World of Business, the logical destiny of bores.

Barry Humphries 1934- : *More Please* (1992)

9 He was dull in a new way, and that made many people think him *great.*

Samuel Johnson 1709-84: of Thomas Gray; James Boswell *Life of Samuel Johnson* (1791) 28 March 1775

10 The boredom occasioned by too much restraint is always preferable to that produced by an uncontrolled enthusiasm for a pointless variety.

Osbert Lancaster 1908-80: *Pillar to Post* (1938)

11 A bore is simply a nonentity who resents his humble lot in life, and seeks satisfaction for his wounded ego by forcing himself on his betters.

H. L. Mencken 1880-1956: *Minority Report* (1956)

12 The only rule I have found to have any validity in writing is not to bore yourself.

John Mortimer 1923- : *Clinging to the Wreckage* (1982)

13 He was not only a bore; he bored for England.

Malcolm Muggeridge 1903-90: of Anthony Eden; *Tread Softly* (1966)

14 It is to be noted that when any part of this paper appears dull there is a design in it.

Richard Steele 1672-1729: *The Tatler* 7 July 1709

15 A bore is a man who, when you ask him how he is, tells you.

Bert Leston Taylor 1866-1901: *The So-Called Human Race* (1922)

16 Dylan talked copiously, then stopped. 'Somebody's boring me,' he said, 'I think it's me.'

Dylan Thomas 1914-53: Rayner Heppenstall *Four Absentees* (1960)

17 He is an old bore. Even the grave yawns for him.
   of the actor Israel Zangwill

Herbert Beerbohm Tree 1852-1917: Max Beerbohm *Herbert Beerbohm Tree* (1920)

18 My boredom threshold is low at the best of times but I have spent more time being slowly and excruciatingly bored by children than any other section of the human race.

Jill Tweedie 1936-93: *It's Only Me* (1980)

to a bore at table:
19 Have some tongue, like cures like.

Robert Yelverton Tyrrell 1844-1914: Ulick O'Connor *Oliver St John Gogarty* (1964)

*a device used by Wavell, when Viceroy, 'to get him through the
tedium of Indian dinner parties':*

20 He turns to his female neighbour, when conversation
flags, and asks 'If you were not a woman—what animal
would you like to be?'

Lord Wavell 1883–1950: Chips
Channon diary, 7 January 1944

21 In England people actually try to be brilliant at breakfast.
That is so dreadful of them! Only dull people are brilliant
at breakfast.

Oscar Wilde 1854–1900: *An Ideal
Husband* (1895)

Boxing See also **Sports and Games**

1 I figure I'll be champ for about ten years and then I'll let
my brother take over—like the Kennedys down in
Washington.
   before becoming world heavyweight champion in 1964

Muhammad Ali 1942– : attributed,
1979

2 Boxing is show-business with blood.

David Belasco: in 1915; Michael
Parkinson *Sporting Lives* (1993); later
also used by Frank Bruno

3 And I want to say anything is possible. Comma. You
know.

Frank Bruno: in *Guardian* 24
December 1990 'Sports Quotes of
the Year'

4 Tall men come down to my height when I hit 'em in the
body.

Jack Dempsey 1895–1983: in 1920,
attributed

5 The bigger they are, the further they have to fall.

Robert Fitzsimmons 1862–1917:
prior to a fight, in *Brooklyn Daily
Eagle* 11 August 1900 (similar forms
found in proverbs since the 15th
century)

6 I want to keep fighting because it is the only thing that
keeps me out of the hamburger joints. If I don't fight, I'll
eat this planet.

George Foreman 1948– : in *Times*
17 January 1990

7 Putting a fighter in the business world is like putting silk
stockings on a pig.
   in 1961, a boxing promoter's view

Jack Hurley: attributed, 1979

*after Jack Sharkey beat Max Schmeling (of whom Jacobs was
manager) in the heavyweight title fight, 21 June 1932:*
8 We was robbed!

Joe Jacobs 1896–1940: Peter Heller
In This Corner (1975)

9 I miss the things like the cameraderie in the gym. I don't
miss being smacked in the mouth every day.
   on retirement from the ring

Barry McGuigan 1961– : in *Irish
Times* 18 April 1998 'This Week They
Said'

10 They're selling video cassettes of the Ali–Spinks fight for
$89.95. Hell, for that money Spinks will come to your
house.

Ferdie Pacheco: in *Guardian* 23
December 1978 'Sports Quotes of
the Year'

11 While Spider McCoy manages a number of fighters, he
never gets excited about anything but a heavyweight, and
this is the way all fight managers are. A fight manager
may have a lightweight champion of the world, but he will
get more heated up about some sausage who scarcely
knows how to hold his hands up if he is a heavyweight.

Damon Runyon 1884–1946: *Take It
Easy* (1938)

Broadcasting   See also **Television**

1 We hope to amuse the customers with music and with
   rhyme
   But ninety minutes is a long, long time.

Noël Coward 1899–1973: '90
Minutes is a Long, Long Time' (1955);
opening song for a CBS television
live special starring Noël Coward and
Mary Martin

2 IAN ST JOHN: Is he speaking to you yet?
   JIMMY GREAVES: Not yet, but I hope to be incommunicado
   with him in a very short space of time.

Jimmy Greaves 1940– : Barry
Fantoni (ed.) *Private Eye's
Colemanballs 2* (1984)

3 Every time I think that Ned Sherrin is dead I switch on the
   television and see him in some dreadful, off-colour
   programme which brings home all too painfully the fact
   that he is still alive.

Ian Hamilton 1938– : Ned Sherrin
Cutting Edge (1984); attributed

4 To goad the BBC is a rewarding sport in itself. It makes a
   tabloid feel like a heavyweight.

Clive James 1939– : *The Dreaming
Swimmer* (1992)

5 Perhaps one of the more noteworthy trends of our time is
   the occupation of buildings accompanied by the taking of
   hostages. The perpetrators of these deeds are generally
   motivated by political grievance, social injustice, and the
   deeply felt desire to see how they look on TV.

Fran Lebowitz 1946– : *Metropolitan
Life* (1978)

6 [Men] are happier with women who make their coffee
   than make their programmes.

Denise O'Donoghue: G. Kinnock
and F. Miller (eds.) *By Faith and
Daring* (1993)

7 The media. It sounds like a convention of spiritualists.

Tom Stoppard 1937– : *Night and
Day* (1978)

Bureaucracy   See also **Civil Servants**

1 A memorandum is written not to inform the reader but to
   protect the writer.

Dean Acheson 1893–1971: in *Wall
Street Journal* 8 September 1977

2 We trained hard . . . but it seemed that every time we were
   beginning to form up into teams we would be reorganized.
   I was to learn later in life that we tend to meet any new
   situation by reorganizing; and a wonderful method it can
   be for creating the illusion of progress while producing
   confusion, inefficiency, and demoralization.

Anonymous: modern saying,
frequently (and wrongly) attributed
to Petronius Arbiter

3 MAM: Opportunities calling for devoted self-sacrifice don't
   turn up every day of the week.
   MS CRAIG: Quite. Any really first-rate chance of improving
   the soul gets snapped up by the social services
   department.

Alan Bennett 1934– : *Enjoy* (1980)

4 This island is made mainly of coal and surrounded by fish.
   Only an organizing genius could produce a shortage of
   coal and fish at the same time.

Aneurin Bevan 1897–1960: speech
at Blackpool 24 May 1945

5 Whatever was required to be done, the Circumlocution
   Office was beforehand with all the public departments in
   the art of perceiving—HOW NOT TO DO IT.

Charles Dickens 1812–70: *Little Dorrit*
(1857)

6 The Arts Council doesn't believe in supporting amateurs,
   except in its own ranks.
   explaining his support for youth orchestras

John Drummond 1934– : in
Observer 29 March 1998

7 The Pentagon, that immense monument to modern man's subservience to the desk.

Oliver Franks 1905–92: in *Observer* 30 November 1952

his secretary had suggested throwing away out-of-date files:
8 A good idea, only be sure to make a copy of everything before getting rid of it.

Sam Goldwyn 1882–1974: Michael Freedland *The Goldwyn Touch* (1986)

9 Official dignity tends to increase in inverse ratio to the importance of the country in which the office is held.

Aldous Huxley 1894–1963: *Beyond the Mexique Bay* (1934)

on his dislike of working in teams:
10 A camel is a horse designed by a committee.

Alec Issigonis 1906–88: in *Guardian* 14 January 1991 'Notes and Queries' (attributed)

11 The truth in these matters may be stated as a scientific law: 'The persistence of public officials varies inversely with the importance of the matter on which they are persisting.'

Bernard Levin 1928– : *In These Times* (1986)

12 It is characteristic of committee discussions and decisions that every member has a vivid recollection of them and that every member's recollection differs violently from every other member's recollection.

Jonathan Lynn 1943– and **Antony Jay** 1930– : *Yes Prime Minister* vol. 2 (1987)

13 The man who is denied the opportunity of taking decisions of importance begins to regard as important the decisions he is allowed to take.

C. Northcote Parkinson 1909–93: *Parkinson's Law* (1958)

14 Perfection of planned layout is achieved only by institutions on the point of collapse.

C. Northcote Parkinson 1909–93: *Parkinson's Law* (1958)

15 Underneath runs the main current of preoccupation, which is keeping one's nose clean at all times. This means that when things go wrong you have to pass the blame along the line, like pass-the-parcel, till the music stops.

Tom Stoppard 1937– : *Neutral Ground* (1983)

Business and Commerce

1 GERALD: Is she not connected with Trade?
LADY D: Trade? Nonsense. Her father made a fortune by introducing the corset to the Eskimos. That is not trade. It is philanthropy.

Alan Bennett 1934– : *Forty Years On* (1969)

2 My first rule of consumerism is never to buy anything you can't make your children carry.

Bill Bryson 1951– : *The Lost Continent* (1989)

3 Some accountants are comedians, but comedians are never accountants.
defending Ken Dodd on the charge of tax evasion

George Carman 1930– : in *Times* 30 August 2000; attributed

4 Only the paranoid survive.
dictum on which he has long run his company, the Intel Corporation

Andrew Grove 1936– : in *New York Times* 18 December 1994

5 Accountants are the witch-doctors of the modern world and willing to turn their hands to any kind of magic.

Lord Justice Harman 1894–1970: speech, February 1964

6 The last stage of fitting the product to the market is fitting the market to the product.

Clive James 1939– : in *Observer* 16 October 1989

7 As a simple countryman, he distrusted the use of money and, finding barter cumbersome, preferred to steal.

Miles Kington 1941– : *Welcome to Kington* (1989)

8 Doing well by doing good.
  now the slogan of Monsanto

Tom Lehrer 1928– : 'The Old Dope Peddler' (1953 song)

9 A: I play it the company way
  Where the company puts me, there I'll stay.
  B: But what is your point of view?
  A: I have no point of view!
  Supposing the company thinks . . . I think so too!

Frank Loesser 1910–69: 'The Company Way' (1962)

10 Could Henry Ford produce the Book of Kells? Certainly not. He would quarrel initially with the advisability of such a project and then prove it was impossible.

Flann O'Brien 1911–66: *Myles Away from Dublin* (1990)

11 Jane Austen doesn't sell hi-tech cars. We do the past very well in this country but how can we compete from a high-tech point of view when the rest of the world sees us dressed up in top hats and crinolines all the time?

Roger Puttnam: in *Independent* 7 June 1997

12 We even sell a pair of earrings for under £1, which is cheaper than a prawn sandwich from Marks & Spencers. But I have to say the earrings probably won't last as long.

Gerald Ratner 1949– : speech to the Institute of Directors, Albert Hall, 23 April 1991

13 Running a company on market research is like driving while looking in the rear view mirror.

Anita Roddick 1942– : in *Independent* 22 August 1997

14 Whenever I feel in the least tempted to be methodical or business-like or even decently industrious, I go to Kensal Green and look at the graves of those who died in business.

Saki 1870–1916: *The Square Egg* (1924)

15 Breakages, Limited, the biggest industrial corporation in the country.

George Bernard Shaw 1856–1950: *The Apple Cart* (1930)

16 I long for the day when a new generation of Anita Roddicks can address the AGM in a bright pink dress and strappy sandals.

Alexandra Shulman 1957– : in *Sunday Times* 23 May 1999 'Talking Heads'

  definition of insider trading:
17 Stealing too fast.

Calvin Trillin 1935– : 'The Inside on Insider Trading' (1987)

18 It's a recession when your neighbour loses his job; it's a depression when you lose yours.

Harry S. Truman 1884–1972: in *Observer* 13 April 1958

19 Put all your eggs in one basket—and WATCH THAT BASKET.

Mark Twain 1835–1910: *Pudd'nhead Wilson* (1894)

20 The public be damned! I'm working for my stockholders.

William H. Vanderbilt 1821–85: comment to a news reporter, 2 October 1882

21 [Commercialism is] doing well that which should not be done at all.

Gore Vidal 1925– : in *Listener* 7 August 1975

22 Go to your business, I say, pleasure, whilst I go to my pleasure, business.

William Wycherley c.1640–1716: *The Country Wife* (1675)

23 Nothing is illegal if one hundred well-placed business men decide to do it.

Andrew Young 1932– : Morris K. Udall *Too Funny to be President* (1988)

Catchphrases See **Comedy Routines and Catchphrases**

Censorship

1 She insists on all these torrid romances . . . I have to wrap them round with copies of *Country Life* to carry them home.

Alan Ayckbourn 1939– : *Round and Round the Garden* (1975)

2 There are no alternatives to 'bastard' agreeable to me. Nevertheless I have offered them 'swine' in its place.
on changes to the text of Endgame *required by the Lord Chamberlain for the London production, summer 1958*

Samuel Beckett 1906–89: James Knowlson *Damned to Fame* (1996)

3 I'm all in favour of free expression provided it's kept rigidly under control.

Alan Bennett 1934– : *Forty Years On* (1969)

4 Everybody favours free speech in the slack moments when no axes are being ground.

Heywood Broun 1888–1939: in *New York World* 23 October 1926

5 It's because it's in English, you can get away with much more in French. Think what you could get away with in Japanese!
on the refusal of the Lord Chamberlain to grant a licence to Samuel Beckett's Endgame, *February 1958*

George Devine 1910–66: Irving Wardle *The Theatres of George Devine* (1978)

6 Free speech is not to be regulated like diseased cattle and impure butter. The audience . . . that hissed yesterday may applaud today, even for the same performance.

William O. Douglas 1898–1980: dissenting opinion in *Kingsley Books, Inc. v. Brown* 1957

7 I dislike censorship. Like an appendix it is useless when inert and dangerous when active.

Maurice Edelman 1911–75: Jonathon Green (ed.) *A Dictionary of Contemporary Quotations* (1982)

8 It's red hot, mate. I hate to think of this sort of book getting into the wrong hands. As soon as I've finished this, I shall recommend they ban it.

Ray Galton 1930– and **Alan Simpson** 1929– : *The Missing Page* (1960 BBC television programme) words spoken by Tony Hancock

of the tendency of the Classical Dictionary *to deprave and corrupt:*
9 The boys of Eton must not be encouraged to dress themselves as swans or wild beasts for the purpose of idle and illicit flirtation; but that can be the only effect of these deplorable anecdotes.

A. P. Herbert 1890–1971: *Misleading Cases* (1935)

10 No government ought to be without censors: and where the press is free, no one ever will.

Thomas Jefferson 1743–1826: letter to George Washington, 9 September 1792

11 No less than twenty-two publishers and printers read the manuscript of *Dubliners* and when at last it was printed some very kind person bought out the entire edition and had it burnt in Dublin.

James Joyce 1882–1941: letter, 2 April 1932

12 My desire to curtail undue freedom of speech extends only to such public areas as restaurants, airports, streets, hotel lobbies, parks, and department stores. Verbal exchanges between consenting adults in private are of as little interest to me as they probably are to them.

Fran Lebowitz 1946– : *Metropolitan Life* (1978)

13 Freedom of the press is guaranteed only to those who own one.

A. J. Liebling 1904–63: 'The Wayward Press: Do you belong in Journalism?' (1960)

14 Careful now!
placard alerting Craggy Island to a banned film

Graham Linehan and **Arthur Mathews**: 'The Passion of St Tibulus' (1994), episode from *Father Ted* (Channel 4 TV, 1994–8)

15 She sits among the cabbages and leeks.
substitution for 'she sits among the cabbages and peas', which was supposedly forbidden by a local watch committee

Marie Lloyd 1870–1922: attributed; Nigel Rees *Cassell Dictionary of Humorous Quotations* (1999)

16 Censorship, like charity, should begin at home, but, unlike charity, it should end there.

Clare Boothe Luce 1903–87: attributed, 1982

17 We have long passed the Victorian Era when asterisks were followed after a certain interval by a baby.

W. Somerset Maugham 1874–1965: *The Constant Wife* (1926)

On being appointed Irish film censor:
18 I am between the devil and the Holy See . . . [My task is to prevent] the Californication of Ireland.

James Montgomery: Ulick O'Connor *Oliver St John Gogarty* (1964)

19 I suppose that writers should, in a way, feel flattered by the censorship laws. They show a primitive fear and dread at the fearful magic of print.

John Mortimer 1923– : *Clinging to the Wreckage* (1982)

20 Mr de Valera, like Mr Cosgrave, regarded literary censorship as part of our freedom to achieve fuller freedom.

Brendan Ó hEithir 1930– : *The Begrudger's Guide to Irish Politics*

21 A censor is a man who knows more than he thinks you ought to.

Laurence J. Peter 1919– : Jonathon Green (ed.) *A Dictionary of Contemporary Quotations* (1982)

22 Assassination is the extreme form of censorship.

George Bernard Shaw 1856–1950: *The Showing-Up of Blanco Posnet* (1911) 'Limits to Toleration'

23 We are paid to have dirty minds.

John Trevelyan: when British Film Censor; in *Observer* 15 November 1959 'Sayings of the Week'

24 'This country [Ireland] . . . has already got a State Censorship of Films which is said to be the strictest in Europe.'
'It's not strict enough.'

Mervyn Wall 1908– : *Leaves for the Burning* (1952)

of Valentine Ackland's longing to enter the censor's department:
25 She has always been perfectly shameless about reading letters not meant for her, and, as she said, she was ideally suited for the work by never having much inclination to answer letters back.

Sylvia Townsend Warner 1893–1978: letter 17 November 1940

Certainty and Doubt See also **Religion**

1 He used to be fairly indecisive, but now he's not so certain.

Peter Alliss 1931– : Barry Fantoni (ed.) *Private Eye's Colemanballs 3* (1986)

2 Often undecided whether to desert a sinking ship for one that might not float, he would make up his mind to sit on the wharf for a day.
of Lord Curzon

Lord Beaverbrook 1879–1964: *Men and Power* (1956)

3 ESTRAGON: Charming spot. Inspiring prospects. Let's go.
VLADIMIR: We can't.

Samuel Beckett 1906–89: *Waiting for Godot* (1955)

VLADIMIR: We're waiting for Godot.

4 Oh! let us never, never doubt
   What nobody is sure about!

when asked whether he really believed a horseshoe hanging over his door would bring him luck:

5 Of course not, but I am told it works even if you don't believe in it.

6 There is something pagan in me that I cannot shake off. In short, I deny nothing, but doubt everything.

7 I don't believe in astrology; I'm a Sagittarius and we're sceptical.

of Thomas Arnold, son of Dr Arnold of Rugby, a notable and frequent nineteenth-century convert:

8 Poor Tom Arnold has lost his faith *again*.

9 I do not pretend to know where many ignorant men are sure—that is all that agnosticism means.

10 The archbishop [Archbishop Runcie] is usually to be found nailing his colours to the fence.

11 I'll give you a definite maybe.

12 PHILIP: I'm sorry. (Pause.) I suppose I'm indecisive. (Pause). My trouble is, I'm a man of no convictions. (Longish pause.) At least, I think I am.

13 At this moment in time I did not say them things.

14 Certitude is not the test of certainty. We have been cocksure of many things that were not so.

15 A young man who wishes to remain a sound atheist cannot be too careful of his reading.

W. H. Macaulay had been an atheist from his undergraduate days, but when he was dying his sister was pleased by his response to her mentioning 'God and a future life':

16 Well, there's nothing so rum it might not be true.

17 Like all weak men he laid an exaggerated stress on not changing one's mind.

18 I wish I was as cocksure of anything as Tom Macaulay is of everything.

19 I am not denying anything I did not say.

Hilaire Belloc 1870–1953: 'The Microbe' (1897)

Niels Bohr 1885–1962: A. Pais *Inward Bound* (1986)

Lord Byron 1788–1824: letter, 4 December 1811

Arthur C. Clarke 1917– : attributed; Nigel Rees *Cassell Dictionary of Humorous Quotations* (1999)

Eliza Conybeare 1820–1903: Rose Macaulay letter to Father Johnson, 8 April 1951

Clarence Darrow 1857–1938: speech at the trial of John Thomas Scopes, 15 July 1925; *The World's Most Famous Court Trial* (1925)

Frank Field 1942– : attributed in *Crockfords 1987/88* (1987); Geoffrey Madan records in his *Notebooks* that Harry Cust made a similar comment on A. J. Balfour, c.1904.

Sam Goldwyn 1882–1974: attributed

Christopher Hampton 1946– : *The Philanthropist* (1970)

Glenn Hoddle 1957– : in *Daily Telegraph* 2 February 1999

Oliver Wendell Holmes Jr. 1841–1935: 'Natural Law' (1918)

C. S. Lewis 1898–1963: *Surprised by Joy* (1955)

William Herrick Macaulay 1853–1936: Rose Macaulay letter to Father Johnson, 30 August 1950

W. Somerset Maugham 1874–1965: *Of Human Bondage* (1915)

Lord Melbourne 1779–1848: Lord Cowper *Preface to Lord Melbourne's Papers* (1889)

Brian Mulroney 1939– : in *The Globe and Mail* 18 September 1986

20 That happy sense of purpose people have when they are standing up for a principle they haven't really been knocked down for yet.

P. J. O'Rourke 1947- : *Give War a Chance* (1992)

21 Well, sir, you never can tell. That's a principle in life with me, sir, if you'll excuse my having such a thing, sir.

George Bernard Shaw 1856–1950: *You Never Can Tell* (1898)

22 All right, have it your own way—you heard a seal bark!

James Thurber 1894–1961: cartoon caption; in *New Yorker* 30 January 1932

23 I would earnestly warn you against trying to find out the reason for and explanation of everything . . . To try and find out the reason for everything is very dangerous and leads to nothing but disappointment and dissatisfaction, unsettling your mind and in the end making you miserable.

Queen Victoria 1819–1901: letter to Princess Victoria of Hesse, 22 August 1883

Character See also Self-Knowledge and Self-Deception

1 He never failed to seek a peaceful solution of a problem when all other possibilities had failed.

Anonymous: Cecil Roth 'Joseph Herman Hertz' (1959) in *The Dictionary of National Biography*

2 A thin, unkempt young man who gives the impression of having inner fires that have been damped by ceaseless disappointment.

Alan Ayckbourn 1939- : *Sisterly Feelings* (1981)

3 It was one of the deadliest and heaviest feelings of my life to feel that I was no longer a boy.—From that moment I began to grow old in my own esteem—and in my esteem age is not estimable.

Lord Byron 1788–1824: 'Detached Thoughts' 15 October 1821

4 Take care not to be the kind of person for whom the band is always playing in the other room.

Quentin Crisp 1908–99: in *Spectator* 20 November 1999

5 We never knows wot's hidden in each other's hearts; and if we had glass winders there, we'd need keep the shutters up, some on us, I do assure you!

Charles Dickens 1812–70: *Martin Chuzzlewit* (1844)

6 Claudia's the sort of person who goes through life holding on to the sides.

Alice Thomas Ellis 1932- : *The Other Side of the Fire* (1983)

7 Clevinger was one of those people with lots of intelligence and no brains, and everyone knew it except those who soon found it out. In short, he was a dope.

Joseph Heller 1923–99: *Catch-22* (1961)

8 Nice guys, when we turn nasty, can make a terrible mess of it, usually because we've had so little practice, and have bottled it up for too long.

Matthew Parris 1949- : in *The Spectator* 27 February 1993

9 He's so wet you could shoot snipe off him.

Anthony Powell 1905–2000: *A Question of Upbringing* (1951)

10 You can tell a lot about a fellow's character by his way of eating jellybeans.

Ronald Reagan 1911- : in *New York Times* 15 January 1981

11 My father named me Autolycus; who being, as I am, littered under Mercury, was likewise a snapper-up of unconsidered trifles.

William Shakespeare 1564–1616: *The Winter's Tale* (1610–11)

12 An unforgiving eye, and a damned disinheriting countenance!

Richard Brinsley Sheridan 1751–1816: *The School for Scandal* (1777)

13 He's too nervous to kill himself. He wears his seat belt in a drive-in movie.

Neil Simon 1927– : *The Odd Couple* (1966)

14 Felix? Playing around? Are you crazy? He wears a vest and galoshes.

Neil Simon 1927– : *The Odd Couple* (1966)

15 I'm told he's [a] decent sort when you get to know him, but no one ever has, so his decency is sort of secret.

Tom Stoppard 1937– : *Neutral Ground* (1983)

16 Then, with that faint fleeting smile playing about his lips, he faced the firing squad; erect and motionless, proud and disdainful, Walter Mitty, the undefeated, inscrutable to the last.

James Thurber 1894–1961: in *New Yorker* 18 March 1939 'The Secret Life of Walter Mitty'

17 Few things are harder to put up with than the annoyance of a good example.

Mark Twain 1835–1910: *Pudd'nhead Wilson* (1894)

18 There, standing at the piano, was the original good time who had been had by all.

Kenneth Tynan 1927–80: at an Oxford Union Debate, while an undergraduate; attributed (also attributed to Bette Davis of a passing starlet)

19 CECIL GRAHAM: What is a cynic?
LORD DARLINGTON: A man who knows the price of everything and the value of nothing.

Oscar Wilde 1854–1900: *Lady Windermere's Fan* (1892)

20 I am afraid that he has one of those terribly weak natures that are not susceptible to influence.

Oscar Wilde 1854–1900: *An Ideal Husband* (1895)

21 I've met a lot of hardboiled eggs in my time, but you're twenty minutes.

Billy Wilder 1906– : *Ace in the Hole* (1951 film, co-written with Lesser Samuels and Walter Newman)

22 Slice him where you like, a hellhound is always a hellhound.

P. G. Wodehouse 1881–1975: *The Code of the Woosters* (1938)

Children See also **The Family**, **Parents**, **Youth**

1 I was very relieved when the child was born at the Chelsea and Westminster hospital. I had thought he would be born in a manger.
on the birth of Leo Blair

Leo Abse 1917– : in *Observer* 28 May 2000 'They said what . . . ?'

2 A Trick that everyone abhors
In Little Girls is slamming Doors.

Hilaire Belloc 1870–1953: 'Rebecca' (1907)

3 And always keep a-hold of Nurse
For fear of finding something worse.

Hilaire Belloc 1870–1953: 'Jim' (1907)

4 Children always assume the sexual lives of their parents come to a grinding halt at their conception.

Alan Bennett 1934– : *Getting On* (1972)

5 I had always thought that once you grew up you could do anything you wanted—stay up all night or eat ice-cream straight out of the container.

Bill Bryson 1951– : *The Lost Continent* (1989)

6 If the literary offspring is not to die young, almost as much trouble must be taken with it as with the bringing up of a physical child. Still, the physical child is the harder work of the two.

Samuel Butler 1835–1902: *Notebooks* (1912)

7 I don't know what Scrope Davies meant by telling you I liked children, I abominate the sight of them so much that I have always had the greatest respect for the character of Herod.

Lord Byron 1788–1824: letter 30 August 1811

8 The place is very well and quiet and the children only scream in a low voice.

Lord Byron 1788–1824: letter 21 September 1813

9 Speak roughly to your little boy,
And beat him when he sneezes;
He only does it to annoy,
Because he knows it teases.

Lewis Carroll 1832–98: *Alice's Adventures in Wonderland* (1865)

10 Timothy Winters comes to school
With eyes as wide as a football-pool,
Ears like bombs and teeth like splinters:
A blitz of a boy is Timothy Winters.

Charles Causley 1917– : 'Timothy Winters' (1957)

on being asked what sort of child he was:
11 When paid constant attention, extremely lovable. When not, a pig.

Noël Coward 1899–1973: interview with David Frost in 1969

12 I'll thcream and thcream and thcream till I'm thick. And I *can.*
    Violet Elizabeth Bott's habitual threat

Richmal Crompton 1890–1969: *Still—William* (1925)

13 If men had to have babies, they would only ever have one each.
    while in late pregnancy

Diana, Princess of Wales 1961–97: in *Observer* 29 July 1984 'Sayings of the Week'

14 I only know two sorts of boys. Mealy boys, and beef-faced boys.

Charles Dickens 1812–70: *Oliver Twist* (1838)

15 There never was a child so lovely but his mother was glad to get asleep.

Ralph Waldo Emerson 1803–82: *Journal* 1836

16 O'er the rugged mountain's brow
Clara threw the twins she nursed,
And remarked, 'I wonder now
Which will reach the bottom first?'

Harry Graham 1874–1936: 'Calculating Clara' (1899)

at the first night of J. M. Barrie's Peter Pan*:*
17 Oh, for an hour of Herod!

Anthony Hope 1863–1933: Denis Mackail *The Story of JMB* (1941)

definition of a baby:
18 A loud noise at one end and no sense of responsibility at the other.

Ronald Knox 1888–1957: attributed

19 The parent who could see his boy as he really is, would shake his head and say: 'Willie is no good; I'll sell him.'

Stephen Leacock 1869–1944: *Essays and Literary Studies* (1916)

20 Ask your child what he wants for dinner only if he's buying.

Fran Lebowitz 1946– : *Social Studies* (1981)

21 Don't bother discussing sex with small children. They rarely have anything to add.

Fran Lebowitz 1946– : *Social Studies* (1981)

Jack Llewelyn-Davies, stuffing himself with cakes at tea, was warned by his mother Sylvia, 'You'll be sick tomorrow':
22 I'll be sick tonight.

Jack Llewelyn-Davies 1894–1959: Andrew Birkin *J. M. Barrie and the Lost Boys* (1979); Barrie used the line in *Little Mary* (1903)

23 Having a baby is like trying to push a grand piano through a transom.

Alice Roosevelt Longworth 1884–1980: Michael Teague *Mrs L* (1981)

a nurse, excusing her illegitimate baby:
24 If you please, ma'am, it was a very little one.

Frederick Marryat 1792–1848: *Mr Midshipman Easy* (1836)

25 With the birth of each child you lose two novels.

Candia McWilliam 1955– : in *Guardian* 5 May 1993

26 All bachelors love dogs, and we would love children just as much if they could be taught to retrieve.

P. J. O'Rourke 1947– : *The Bachelor Home Companion* (1987)

27 Every luxury was lavished on you—atheism, breast-feeding, circumcision.

Joe Orton 1933–67: *Loot* (1967)

28 As yet a child, nor yet a fool to fame,
I lisped in numbers, for the numbers came.

Alexander Pope 1688–1744: 'An Epistle to Dr Arbuthnot' (1735)

29 Parents—especially step-parents—are sometimes a bit of a disappointment to their children. They don't fulfil the promise of their early years.

Anthony Powell 1905–2000: *A Buyer's Market* (1952)

30 Go directly—see what she's doing, and tell her she mustn't.

Punch 1841–1992: vol. 63 (1872)

31 The fat greedy owl of the Remove.

Frank Richards 1876–1961: 'Billy Bunter' in *Magnet* (1909)

32 Children with Hyacinth's temperament don't know better as they grow older; they merely know more.

Saki 1870–1916: *Toys of Peace and Other Papers* (1919)

33 Children are given us to discourage our better emotions.

Saki 1870–1916: *Reginald* (1904)

34 Childhood is Last Chance Gulch for happiness. After that, you know too much.

Tom Stoppard 1937– : *Where Are They Now?* (1973)

35 I s'pect I growed. Don't think nobody never made me.

Harriet Beecher Stowe 1811–96: *Uncle Tom's Cabin* (1852)

36 Children can be awe-inspiringly horrible; manipulative, aggressive, rude, and unfeeling to a point where I often think that, if armed, they would make up the most terrifying fighting force the world has ever seen.

Jill Tweedie 1936–93: *It's Only Me* (1980)

37 Any child with sense knew you didn't involve yourself with the adult world if you weren't absolutely forced to. We lived on our side of a great divide and we crossed it at our peril.

Jill Tweedie 1936–93: *Eating Children* (1993)

38 You will find as the children grow up that as a rule children are a bitter disappointment—their greatest object being to do precisely what their parents do not wish and have anxiously tried to prevent.

Queen Victoria 1819–1901: letter to the Crown Princess of Prussia, 5 January 1876

39 I fear the seventh granddaughter and fourteenth grandchild becomes a very uninteresting thing—for it seems to me to go on like the rabbits in Windsor Park!

Queen Victoria 1819–1901: letter to the Crown Princess of Prussia, 10 July 1868

40 [The baby] romped on my lap like a short stout salmon.

Sylvia Townsend Warner 1893–1978: diary, 13 October 1929

41 Children begin by loving their parents; after a time they judge them; rarely, if ever, do they forgive them.

Oscar Wilde 1854–1900: *A Woman of No Importance* (1893)

Choice

1 More than any other time in history, mankind faces a crossroads. One path leads to despair and utter hopelessness. The other, to total extinction. Let us pray we have the wisdom to choose correctly.

Woody Allen 1935– : *Side Effects* (1980)

2 That's a bit like asking a man crawling across the Sahara whether he would prefer Perrier or Malvern Water.
replying to a question by Ian McKellen on his sexual orientation

Alan Bennett 1934– : attributed

3 I'll have what she's having.
woman to waiter, seeing Sally acting an orgasm

Nora Ephron 1941– : *When Harry Met Sally* (1989 film)

4 He had polyester sheets and I wanted to get cotton sheets. He discussed it with his shrink many times before he made the switch.

Mia Farrow 1945– : in *Independent* 8 February 1997 'Quote Unquote'

on the contrast between Alec Douglas-Home and Harold Wilson:
5 Dull Alec versus Smart Alec.

David Frost 1939– : in *That Was The Week That Was* in 1963

George V was asked which film he would like to see while convalescing:
6 Anything except that damned Mouse.

George V 1865–1936: George Lyttelton letter to Rupert Hart-Davis, 12 November 1959

7 Why does he [Tony Blair] not split the job of mayor of London? The former health secretary [Frank Dobson] can run as his 'day mayor' and Ken Livingstone can run as his 'night mayor'.

William Hague 1961– : speech, House of Commons, 17 November 1999

8 On Monday you gave the French the third way and today they gave you the two fingers.
to the Prime Minister on the government's handling of the beef war

William Hague 1961– : in *Sunday Times* 14 November 1999

9 'You oughtn't to yield to temptation.' 'Well, somebody must, or the thing becomes absurd,' said I.

Anthony Hope 1863–1933: *The Dolly Dialogues* (1894)

10 Economy is going without something you do want in case you should, some day, want something you probably won't want.

Anthony Hope 1863–1933: *The Dolly Dialogues* (1894)

11 Still raise for good the supplicating voice,
But leave to heaven the measure and the choice.

Samuel Johnson 1709–84: *The Vanity of Human Wishes* (1749)

12 So here I am the victim of my own choices, and I'm just starting.
Ally's view of herself

David E. Kelley: *Ally McBeal* (US television series, 1998–) episode 1

13 A compromise in the sense that being bitten in half by a shark is a compromise with being swallowed whole.

P. J. O'Rourke 1947– : *Parliament of Whores*

14 Place the following in order of importance:
(a) Food (b) World peace (c) A Lanceolated Warbler.

Bill Oddie 1941– : *Bill Oddie's Little Black Bird Book* (1980)

on the presidential contest between Gerald Ford and Jimmy Carter:
15 No longer a choice between the lesser of two weevils, you now know that you can't win.

S. J. Perelman 1904–79: letter 18 October 1976

a restaurateur asked for his most unusual request from a customer:

16 The table next to Michael Winner, please.

Simon Slater: in *Evening Standard* 27 May 1999

in the post office, pointing at the centre of a sheet of stamps:

17 I'll take that one.

Herbert Beerbohm Tree 1852–1917: Hesketh Pearson *Beerbohm Tree* (1956)

Christmas

1 I have often thought, says Sir Roger, it happens very well that Christmas should fall out in the Middle of Winter.

Joseph Addison 1672–1719: *The Spectator* 8 January 1712

2 There are six evacuated children in our house. My wife and I hate them so much that we have decided to *take away* something from them for Christmas!

Anonymous: letter from a friend in the country; James Agate diary 22 December 1939

3 And girls in slacks remember Dad,
And oafish louts remember Mum,
And sleepless children's hearts are glad,
And Christmas-morning bells say 'Come!'
Even to shining ones who dwell
Safe in the Dorchester Hotel.

And is it true? And is it true,
This most tremendous tale of all,
Seen in a stained-glass window's hue,
A Baby in an ox's stall?
The Maker of the stars and sea
Become a Child on earth for me?

John Betjeman 1906–84: 'Christmas' (1954)

4 Christmas Eve can be hell on earth . . . Everyone running round doing their last-minute shopping. It's as if Christmas comes on people by surprise, as it they hadn't known for weeks it was on its way.

Maeve Binchy 1940– : *The Glass Lake* (1994)

5 If the Three Wise Men arrived here tonight, the likelihood is that they would be deported.
advocating an amnesty for asylum-seekers

Proinsias de Rossa: in *Irish Times* 20 December 1997 'This Week They Said'

6 A Merry Christmas to all my friends except two.

W. C. Fields 1880–1946: attributed

7 I am a poor man, but I would gladly give ten shillings to find out who sent me the insulting Christmas card I received this morning.

George Grossmith 1847–1912 and **Weedon Grossmith** 1854–1919: *The Diary of a Nobody* (1894)

8 DRIFTWOOD (Groucho Marx): It's all right. That's—that's in every contract. That's—that's what they call a sanity clause.
FIORELLO (Chico Marx): You can't fool me. There ain't no Sanity Claus.

George S. Kaufman 1889–1961 and **Morrie Ryskind** 1895–1985: *Night at the Opera* (1935 film)

9 I'm walking backwards for Christmas
Across the Irish Sea.

Spike Milligan 1918– : 'I'm Walking Backwards for Christmas' (1956)

10 Christmas begins about the first of December with an office party and ends when you finally realize what you spent, around April fifteenth of the next year.

P. J. O'Rourke 1947– : *Modern Manners* (1984)

11 Christmas, that time of year when people descend into the bunker of the family.

Byron Rogers: in *Daily Telegraph* 27 December 1993

The Cinema See also **Acting, Actors, Films, Film Stars**

1 Hollywood is a place where people from Iowa mistake each other for stars.

Fred Allen 1894–1956: Maurice Zolotow *No People like Show People* (1951)

2 Cecil B. de Mille
Rather against his will,
Was persuaded to leave Moses
Out of 'The Wars of the Roses'.

Anonymous: J. W. Carter (ed.) *Clerihews* (1938); attributed to Nicolas Bentley

an assistant director trying to encourage some uninspired extras during the filming of Julius Caesar *(1953):*
3 All right, kids. It's Rome, it's hot and here comes Julius!

Anonymous: recounted by John Gielgud; in *Ned Sherrin in his Anecdotage* (1993)

4 There are no rules in filmmaking. Only sins. And the cardinal sin is dullness.

Frank Capra 1897–1991: in *People* 16 September 1991

5 Bring on the empty horses!

Michael Curtiz 1888–1962: said while directing the 1936 film *The Charge of the Light Brigade*; David Niven *Bring on the Empty Horses* (1975)

6 It might be a fight like you see on the screen
A swain getting slain for the love of a Queen,
Some great Shakespearean scene
Where a ghost and a prince meet
And everyone ends as mince-meat . . .

Howard Dietz 1896–1983: 'That's Entertainment' (1953)

7 Hollywood is bounded on the north, south, east, and west by agents.

William Fadiman: *Hollywood Now* (1972)

8 Ah don't believe Ah know which pictures are yours. Do you make the Mickey Mouse brand?
to Irving Thalberg

William Faulkner 1897–1962: Max Wilk *The Wit and Wisdom of Hollywood* (1972)

9 'She reads at such a pace,' she complained, 'and when I asked her *where* she had learnt to read so quickly, she replied "On the screens at cinemas."'

Ronald Firbank 1886–1926: *The Flower Beneath the Foot* (1923)

10 The movies are the only court where the judge goes to the lawyer for advice.

F. Scott Fitzgerald 1896–1940: *The Crack-up* (1945)

11 Will Hays is my shepherd, I shall not want, He maketh me to lie down in clean postures.
on the establishment of the 'Hays Office' in 1922 to monitor the Hollywood film industry

Gene Fowler: Clive Marsh and Gaye Ortiz (eds.) *Explorations in Theology and Film* (1997)

12 GEORGES FRANJU: Movies should have a beginning, a middle and an end.
JEAN-LUC GODARD: Certainly. But not necessarily in that order.

Jean-Luc Godard 1930– : in *Time* 14 September 1981

resigning from the Motion Picture Producers and Distributors of America in 1933:

13 Gentlemen, include me out.

> **Sam Goldwyn** 1882–1974: Michael Freedland *The Goldwyn Touch* (1986)

14 PRODUCTION ASSISTANT: But Mr Goldwyn, you said you wanted a spectacle.
GOLDWYN: Yes, but goddam it, I wanted an intimate spectacle!

> **Sam Goldwyn** 1882–1974: attributed, perhaps apocryphal

15 The trouble with this business is the dearth of bad pictures.

> **Sam Goldwyn** 1882–1974: after making *The Goldwyn Follies* in 1937; Michael Freedland *The Goldwyn Touch* (1986)

16 Our comedies are not to be laughed at.

> **Sam Goldwyn** 1882–1974: N. Zierold *Hollywood Tycoons* (1969)

17 Pictures are for entertainment, messages should be delivered by Western Union.

> **Sam Goldwyn** 1882–1974: Arthur Marx *Goldwyn* (1976)

18 This business is dog eat dog and nobody is gonna eat me.

> **Sam Goldwyn** 1882–1974: Michael Freedland *The Goldwyn Touch* (1986)

19 Let's have some new clichés.

> **Sam Goldwyn** 1882–1974: attributed, perhaps apocryphal

20 That's the way with these directors, they're always biting the hand that lays the golden egg.

> **Sam Goldwyn** 1882–1974: Alva Johnston *The Great Goldwyn* (1937)

21 A verbal contract isn't worth the paper it is written on.

> **Sam Goldwyn** 1882–1974: Alva Johnston *The Great Goldwyn* (1937)

22 What we need is a story that starts with an earthquake and works its way up to a climax.

> **Sam Goldwyn** 1882–1974: attributed, perhaps apocryphal

23 The trouble with this business is that the stars keep 90% of the money.

> **Lew Grade** 1906–98: attributed; Nigel Rees *Cassell Dictionary of Humorous Quotations* (1999)

24 'Do you have a leading lady for your film?'
'We're trying for the Queen, she sells.'

> **George Harrison** 1943– : at a press conference in the 1960s; Ned Sherrin *Cutting Edge* (1984)

on Hollywood:

25 The most beautiful slave-quarters in the world.

> **Moss Hart** 1904–61: attributed

26 If I made Cinderella, the audience would immediately be looking for a body in the coach.

> **Alfred Hitchcock** 1899–1980: in *Newsweek* 11 June 1956

27 I can't tell you [the perfect ending to a script] . . . I thought of the answer after 5.30.
to Jack Warner, who imposed a strict nine-to-five-thirty schedule on his scriptwriters

> **Norman Krasna** 1909–84: M. Freedland *Warner Brothers* (1983)

28 Behind the phoney tinsel of Hollywood lies the real tinsel.

> **Oscar Levant** 1906–72: Laurence J. Peter (ed.) *Quotations for our Time* (1977)

29 Porn? That's films where the plot doesn't thicken.

> **Sean Lock**: *No Flatley! I am Lord of the Dance* (Edinburgh Festival, August 2000)

30 Life in the movies is like the beginning of a love affair. It's full of surprises and you're constantly getting —ed.

> **David Mamet** 1947– : *Speed-the-Plow* (1988)

31 Hooray for Hollywood,
Where you're terrific if you're even good!

Johnny Mercer 1909–76: 'Hooray for Hollywood' (*Hollywood Hotel*, 1938 musical)

32 Jack Warner has oilcloth pockets so he can steal soup.

Wilson Mizner 1876–1933: Max Wilk *The Wit and Wisdom of Hollywood* (1972)

of Hollywood:
33 A trip through a sewer in a glass-bottomed boat.

Wilson Mizner 1876–1933: Alva Johnston *The Legendary Mizners* (1953), reworked by Mayor Jimmy Walker into 'A reformer is a guy who rides through a sewer in a glass-bottomed boat'

34 This might have been good for a picture—except it has too many characters in it.
to Jack Warner, on the LA telephone directory

Wilson Mizner 1876–1933: Max Wilk *The Wit and Wisdom of Hollywood* (1972)

35 The writer, in the eyes of many film producers, still seems to occupy a position of importance somewhere between the wardrobe lady and the tea boy, with this difference: it's often quite difficult to replace the wardrobe lady.

John Mortimer 1923– : *Clinging to the Wreckage* (1982)

36 The only 'ism' in Hollywood is plagiarism.

Dorothy Parker 1893–1967: attributed

37 Oh, it's all right. You make a little money and get caught up on your debts. We're up to 1912 now . . .
on Hollywood

Dorothy Parker 1893–1967: Max Wilk *The Wit and Wisdom of Hollywood* (1972)

38 Hollywood money isn't money. It's congealed snow, melts in your hand, and there you are.

Dorothy Parker 1893–1967: Malcolm Cowley (ed.) *Writers at Work* 1st Series (1958)

39 Oh come, my love, and join with me
The oldest infant industry.
Come seek the bourne of palm and pearl
The lovely land of Boy-Meets-Girl.
Come grace this lotus-laden shore,
This Isle of Do-What's-Done-Before.
Come, curb the new, and watch the old win,
Out where the streets are paved with Goldwyn.

Dorothy Parker 1893–1967: 'The Passionate Screen Writer to His Love' (1937)

on the take-over of United Artists by Charles Chaplin, Mary Pickford, Douglas Fairbanks and D. W. Griffith:
40 The lunatics have taken charge of the asylum.

Richard Rowland c.1881–1947: Terry Ramsaye *A Million and One Nights* (1926)

41 Tsar of all the rushes.
of Louis B. Mayer

B. P. Schulberg d. 1957: Norman Zierold *The Hollywood Tycoons* (1969)

42 The trouble, Mr Goldwyn, is that you are only interested in art and I am only interested in money.
telegraphed version of the outcome of a conversation between Shaw and Sam Goldwyn

George Bernard Shaw 1856–1950: Alva Johnson *The Great Goldwyn* (1937)

43 Hollywood: They know only one word of more than one syllable here, and that is fillum.

Louis Sherwin: Laurence J. Peter (ed.) *Quotations for our Time* (1977)

44 Once a month the sky falls on my head, I come to, and I see another movie I want to make.

Steven Spielberg 1947– : in *Time* 8 June 1998

45 To Raoul Walsh a tender love scene is burning down a whorehouse.

Jack Warner 1892–1978: P. F. Boller and R. L. Davis *Hollywood Anecdotes* (1988)

46 This is the biggest electric train any boy ever had!
of Hollywood

Orson Welles 1915–85: Leo Rosten *Hollywood* (1941)

47 I like the old masters, by which I mean John Ford, John Ford, and John Ford.

Orson Welles 1915–85: P. F. Boller and R. L. Davis *Hollywood Anecdotes* (1988)

48 I wouldn't say when you've seen one Western you've seen the lot; but when you've seen the lot you get the feeling you've seen one.

Katharine Whitehorn 1926– : *Sunday Best* (1976) 'Decoding the West'

49 Johnny, it's the usual slashed-wrist shot . . . Keep it out of focus. I want to win the foreign picture award.

Billy Wilder 1906– : to his lighting cameraman, John Seitz, when filming *Sunset Boulevard* (1950); P. F. Boller and R. L. Davis *Hollywood Anecdotes* (1988)

50 He could do more with a closed door than other directors could do with an open fly.
of Ernst Lubitsch

Billy Wilder 1906– : attributed

51 The first nine commandments for a director are 'Thou shalt not bore.' The tenth is 'Thou shalt have the right of final cut.'

Billy Wilder 1906– : attributed, perhaps apocryphal

Cities See **Towns and Cities**

Civil Servants

1 A mechanism that prides itself on being a Rolls-Royce appeared more like an old banger.
of the Foreign Office's handling of the arms-to-Africa affair

Donald Anderson 1939– : in *Guardian* 10 February 1999

2 Going about persecuting civil servants.
assessment by one unidentified senator of how politicians spend their time

Anonymous: R. F. Foster *Modern Ireland* (1988)

3 I confidently expect that we [civil servants] shall continue to be grouped with mothers-in-law and Wigan Pier as one of the recognized objects of ridicule.

Edward Bridges 1892–1969: *Portrait of a Profession* (1950)

4 Give a civil servant a good case and he'll wreck it with clichés, bad punctuation, double negatives and convoluted apology.

Alan Clark 1928–99: diary 22 July 1983

5 A civil servant doesn't make jokes.

Eugène Ionesco 1912–94: *Tueur sans gages* (The Killer, 1958)

6 May I hasten to support Mrs McGurgle's contention that civil servants are human beings, and must be treated as such?

J. B. Morton 1893–1975: M. Frayn (ed.) *The Best of Beachcomber* (1963)

7 By the time the civil service has finished drafting a document to give effect to a principle, there may be little of the principle left.

Lord Reith 1889–1971: *Into the Wind* (1949)

8 Here lies a civil servant. He was civil
To everyone, and servant to the devil.

C. H. Sisson 1914– : *The London Zoo* (1961)

Class See also **The Aristocracy**, **Snobbery**

1 A gentleman never eats. He breakfasts, he lunches, he dines, but he *never* eats!

Anonymous: Cole Porter's headmaster, *c*.1910; Caryl Brahms and Ned Sherrin *Song by Song* (1984)

2 His lordship may compel us to be equal upstairs, but there will never be equality in the servants' hall.

J. M. Barrie 1860–1937: *The Admirable Crichton* (performed 1902)

3 Mankind is divisible into two great classes: hosts and guests.

Max Beerbohm 1872–1956: *And Even Now* (1920)

4 Like many of the Upper Class
He liked the Sound of Broken Glass.

Hilaire Belloc 1870–1953: 'About John' (1930)

5 If you bed people of below-stairs class, they will go to the papers.

Jane Clark: in *Daily Telegraph* 31 May 1994

6 A branch of one of your antediluvian families, fellows that the flood could not wash away.

William Congreve 1670–1729: *Love for Love* (1695)

7 I came upstairs into the world; for I was born in a cellar.

William Congreve 1670–1729: *Love for Love* (1695)

8 Today it may be three white feathers,
But yesterday it was three brass balls.

Noël Coward 1899–1973: 'Three White Feathers' (1932)

9 Dear me, I never knew that the lower classes had such white skins.

Lord Curzon 1859–1925: K. Rose *Superior Person* (1969)

10 Gentlemen do not take soup at luncheon.

Lord Curzon 1859–1925: E. L. Woodward *Short Journey* (1942)

11 All men fall into two main divisions: those who value human relationships, and those who value social or financial advancement. The first division are gentlemen; the second division are cads.

Norman Douglas 1868–1952: *An Almanac* (1941)

12 He [Lord Home] is used to dealing with estate workers. I cannot see how anyone can say he is out of touch.
comment on her father's becoming Prime Minister

Caroline Douglas-Home 1937– : in *Daily Herald* 21 October 1963

13 If they could see me now,
My little dusty group,
Traipsing 'round this
Million-dollar chicken coop!
I'd hear those thrift shop cats say:
'Brother! Get her!'
Draped on a bedspread made from
Three kinds of fur.

Dorothy Fields 1905–74: 'If my Friends could See Me Now' (1966)

14 We are all Adam's children but silk makes the difference.

Thomas Fuller 1654–1734: *Gnomologia* (1732)

15 Boston social zones
Are changing social habits,
And I hear the Cohns
Are taking up the Cabots.

Ira Gershwin 1896–1983: 'Love is Sweeping the Country' (1931)

16 The Earl, the Marquis, and the Dook,
The Groom, the Butler, and the Cook— . . .
The Aristocrat who banks with Coutts . . .
The Aristocrat who cleans our boots—
They all shall equal be.

W. S. Gilbert 1836–1911: *The Gondoliers* (1889)

17 Bow, bow, ye lower middle classes!
Bow, bow, ye tradesmen, bow, ye masses.

W. S. Gilbert 1836–1911: *Iolanthe* (1882)

18 When every one is somebodee,
Then no one's anybody.

W. S. Gilbert 1836–1911: *The Gondoliers* (1889)

on a social climber who was becoming notorious for the number of times he had fallen off his horse:
19 Acquired concussion won't open the doors of country houses. The better classes are born concussed.

Oliver St John Gogarty 1878–1957: Ulick O'Connor *Oliver St John Gogarty* (1964)

20 When the idle poor become the idle rich
You'll never know just who is who or who is which.

E. Y. Harburg 1898–1981: 'When the Idle Poor become the Idle Rich' (1947)

21 Finer things are for the finer folk
Thus society began
Caviar for peasants is a joke
It's too good for the average man.

Lorenz Hart 1895–1943: 'Too Good for the Average Man' (1936)

22 There are those who think that Britain is a class-ridden society, and those who think it doesn't matter either way as long as you know your place in the set-up.

Miles Kington 1941– : *Welcome to Kington* (1989)

23 Of all the hokum with which this country [America] is riddled the most odd is the common notion that it is free of class distinctions.

W. Somerset Maugham 1874–1965: *A Writer's Notebook* (1949) written in 1941

24 The ancient native order [of Irish society] was patriarchal and aristocratic, the people knew their place (i.e. the scullery).

Flann O'Brien 1911–66: *The Hair of the Dogma* (1977)

25 I no longer keep the coal in the bath. I keep it in the bidet.

John Prescott 1938– : in *Independent* 3 July 1999

26 'She's leaving her present house and going to Lower Seymour Street.' 'I dare say she will, if she stays there long enough.'

Saki 1870–1916: *The Toys of Peace* (1919)

27 I don't want to talk grammar, I want to talk like a lady.

George Bernard Shaw 1856–1950: *Pygmalion* (1916)

28 He's a gentleman: look at his boots.

George Bernard Shaw 1856–1950: preface to *Pygmalion* (1916)

29 Mr Knox . . . was a fair, spare young man, who looked like a stableboy among gentlemen, and a gentleman among stableboys.

Edith Œ. Somerville 1858–1949 and **Martin Ross** 1862–1915: *Some Experiences of an Irish R.M.* (1899)

30 She sits
At The Ritz
With her splits
Of Mum's
And starts to pine
For a Stein
With her Village chums.
But with a Schlitz
In her mitts
Down in Fitz—
Roy's Bar,
She thinks of the Ritz—oh,

Stephen Sondheim 1930– : 'Uptown Downtown', song rejected from *Follies* (1971); composer's archive

It's so
Schizo.

31 The only infallible rule we know is, that the man who is always talking about being a gentleman never is one.

R. S. Surtees 1805–64: *Ask Mamma* (1858)

32 The so called immorality of the lower classes is not to be named on the same day with that of the higher and highest. This is a thing which makes my blood boil, and they will pay for it.

Queen Victoria 1819–1901: letter to the Crown Princess of Prussia, 26 June 1872

33 Impotence and sodomy are socially O.K. but birth control is flagrantly middle-class.

Evelyn Waugh 1903–66: 'An Open Letter'; Nancy Mitford *Noblesse Oblige* (1956)

34 I expect you'll be becoming a schoolmaster, sir. That's what most of the gentlemen does, sir, that gets sent down for indecent behaviour.

Evelyn Waugh 1903–66: *Decline and Fall* (1928)

35 Really, if the lower orders don't set us a good example, what on earth is the use of them?

Oscar Wilde 1854–1900: *The Importance of Being Earnest* (1895)

The Clergy See also **Religion**

1 A priest is a man who is called Father by everyone except his own children who are obliged to call him Uncle.

Anonymous: said to be an Italian saying found in a French novel; Rupert Hart-Davis letter to George Lyttelton, 15 July 1956

2 As for the British churchman, he goes to church as he goes to the bathroom, with the minimum of fuss and with no explanation if he can help it.

Ronald Blythe 1922– : *The Age of Illusion* (1963)

3 Don't like bishops. Fishy lot. Blessed are the meek my foot! They're all on the climb. Ever heard of meekness stopping a bishop from becoming a bishop? Nor have I.

Maurice Bowra 1898–1971: in conversation while lunching at the Reform Club with a bishop at the next table; Arthur Marshall *Life's Rich Pageant* (1984)

on 23 March 1936, The Dean and Chapter of Liverpool had refused to say prayers for the Cabinet during Evensong, as a protest against British support for the French occupation of the Rhineland:

4 The attitude of some of these clerics [to the army] . . . makes me feel some sympathy with Henry II, who in a moment of haste expressed an opinion which led to an unexpected vacancy at Canterbury.

Duff Cooper 1890–1954: Artemis Cooper *Mr Wu and Mrs Stitch* (1991)

5 Poor Uncle Harry
Having become a missionary
Found the natives' morals rather crude.
He and Aunt Mary
Quickly imposed an arbitrary
Ban upon them shopping in the nude.
They all considered this silly and they didn't take it well,
They burnt his boots and several suits and wrecked the
   Mission Hotel,
They also burnt his mackintosh, which made a disgusting
   smell . . .
Uncle Harry's not a missionary now.

Noël Coward 1899–1973: 'Uncle Harry' (1946)

6 The parson knows enough who knows a duke.

William Cowper 1731–1800: 'Tirocinium' (1785)

7   As a priest,
A piece of mere church furniture at best.

William Cowper 1731–1800: 'Tirocinium' (1785)

8 Mr Doctor, that loose gown becomes you so well I wonder your notions should be so narrow.
> to the Puritan Dr Humphreys, as he was about to kiss her hand on her visit to Oxford in 1566

Elizabeth I 1533–1603: F. Chamberlin *Sayings of Queen Elizabeth* (1923)

9 I remember the average curate at home as something between a eunuch and a snigger.

Ronald Firbank 1886–1926: *The Flower Beneath the Foot* (1923)

10 I was a pale young curate then.

W. S. Gilbert 1836–1911: *The Sorcerer* (1877)

11 As I take my shoes from the shoemaker, and my coat from the tailor, so I take my religion from the priest.

Oliver Goldsmith 1730–74: James Boswell *Life of Samuel Johnson* (1934 ed.) 9 April 1773

12 The Bishops [in the House of Lords] treat everyone like patient peasants waiting to be told which way to vote.

Lord Hailsham 1907– : in an interview; John Mortimer *Character Parts* (1986)

13 Having the chaplain around Headquarters all the time made the other officers uncomfortable. It was one thing to maintain liaison with the Lord, and they were all in favour of that; it was something else, though, to have Him hanging around twenty-four hours a day.

Joseph Heller 1923–99: *Catch-22* (1961)

14 The crisis of the Church of England is that too many of its bishops, and some would say of its archbishops, don't quite realise that they are atheists, but have begun to suspect it.

Clive James 1939– : *The Dreaming Swimmer* (1992)

15 This merriment of parsons is mighty offensive.

Samuel Johnson 1709–84: James Boswell *Life of Samuel Johnson* (1791) March 1781

16 Evangelical vicar, in want of a portable, second-hand font, would dispose, for the same, of a portrait, in frame, of the Bishop, elect, of Vermont.
> advertisement placed in a newspaper

Ronald Knox 1888–1957: W. S. Baring-Gould *The Lure of the Limerick* (1968)

17 It's great being a priest, isn't it, Ted?

Graham Linehan and **Arthur Mathews**: 'Good Luck, Father Ted' (1994), episode from *Father Ted* (Channel 4 TV, 1994–8)

18 I rather wish the rising generation of clergy were more intellectual; so many seem rather chumps.

Rose Macaulay 1881–1958: letter to Father Johnson, 30 August 1950

19 They were good and bad. Those who were good were very good. Those who were bad were mental, to tell you the truth.
> a former pupil's view of the Christian Brothers

Martin McGuinness: in *Irish Times* 4 April 1998 'This Week They Said'

on the appointment of Michael Ramsey to succeed Geoffrey Fisher as Archbishop of Canterbury:
20 We have had enough of Martha and it is time for some Mary.

Harold Macmillan 1894–1986: attributed

to a clergyman who thanked him for the enjoyment he'd given the world:

21 And I want to thank you for all the enjoyment you've taken out of it.

Groucho Marx 1895–1977: Joe Adamson *Groucho, Harpo, Chico and sometimes Zeppo* (1973)

22 As the French say, there are three sexes—men, women, and clergymen.

Sydney Smith 1771–1845: Lady Holland *Memoir* (1855)

23 I have seen nobody since I saw you, but persons in orders. My only varieties are vicars, rectors, curates, and every now and then (by way of turbot) an archdeacon.

Sydney Smith 1771–1845: letter to Miss Berry, 28 January 1843

24 A Curate—there is something which excites compassion in the very name of a Curate!!!

Sydney Smith 1771–1845: *Edinburgh Review* (1822) 'Persecuting Bishops'

25 There is a species of person called a 'Modern Churchman' who draws the full salary of a beneficed clergyman and need not commit himself to any religious belief.

Evelyn Waugh 1903–66: *Decline and Fall* (1928)

26 *Merit*, indeed! . . . We are come to a pretty pass if they talk of *merit* for a bishopric.

Lord Westmorland 1759–1841: Lady Salisbury, diary, 9 December 1835

27 The Bishop . . . was talking to the local Master of Hounds about the difficulty he had in keeping his vicars off the incense.

P. G. Wodehouse 1881–1975: *Mr. Mulliner Speaking* (1929)

Colours

1 I was shown round Tutankhamun's tomb in the 1920s. I saw all this wonderful pink on the walls and the artefacts. I was so impressed that I vowed to wear it for the rest of my life.

Barbara Cartland 1901–2000: in *Irish Times* 28 March 1998 'This Week They Said'

2 I cannot pretend to feel impartial about the colours. I rejoice with the brilliant ones, and am genuinely sorry for the poor browns.

Winston Churchill 1874–1965: *Thoughts and Adventures* (1932)

3 Gentlemen never wear brown in London.

Lord Curzon 1859–1925: attributed; Nigel Rees *Cassell Dictionary of Humorous Quotations* (1999)

on the choice of colour for the Model T Ford:
4 Any colour—so long as it's black.

Henry Ford 1863–1947: Allan Nevins *Ford* (1957)

5 It's just my colour: it's *beige!*
   a fashionable interior decorator's first view of the Parthenon

Elsie Mendl 1865–1950: Osbert Sitwell *Rat Week: An Essay on the Abdication* (1986)

6 A brilliant blue garment that was an offence alike to her convictions and her complexion.

Edith Œ. Somerville 1858–1949 and **Martin Ross** 1862–1915: *Further Experiences of an Irish R.M.* (1908)

7 If I could find anything blacker than black, I'd use it.

J. M. W. Turner 1775–1851: remark, 1844

8 Pink is the navy blue of India.

Diana Vreeland 1903–89: attributed, 1977

9 I think it pisses God off if you walk by the colour purple in a field somewhere and don't notice it.

Alice Walker 1944– : *The Colour Purple* (1982)

Comedy Routines and Catchphrases

1 CECIL: After you, Claude.
CLAUDE: No, after you, Cecil.

Ted Kavanagh 1892–1958: catchphrase in *ITMA* (BBC radio programme, 1939-49)

2 Can I do you now, sir?

Ted Kavanagh 1892–1958: catchphrase spoken by 'Mrs Mopp' in *ITMA* (BBC radio programme, 1939-49)

3 Collapse of Stout Party.
supposed standard dénouement in Victorian humour

Anonymous: R. Pearsall *Collapse of Stout Party* (1975) introduction

4 Don't forget the diver.

Ted Kavanagh 1892–1958: catchphrase spoken by 'The Diver' in *ITMA* (BBC radio programme, 1939-49)

5 Don't have a cow, man.

Matt Groening 1954- : catchphrase associated with Bart Simpson; *The Simpsons* (American TV series, 1990-)

6 Drink! Drink!
habitual cry of Father Jack

Graham Linehan and **Arthur Mathews**: 'New Jack City' (1996), episode from *Father Ted* (Channel 4 TV, 1994-8)

7 Eat my shorts!

Matt Groening 1954- : catchphrase associated with Bart Simpson; *The Simpsons* (American TV series, 1990-), created by Matt Groening

8 Ee, it was agony, Ivy.

Ted Ray 1906-77: catchphrase in *Ray's a Laugh* (BBC radio programme, 1949-61)

9 'Er indoors.

Leon Griffiths 1928-92: used in ITV television series *Minder* (1979 onwards) by Arthur Daley (played by George Cole) to refer to his wife

10 A good idea—son.

Eric Sykes and **Max Bygraves** 1922- : *Educating Archie*, 1950-3 BBC radio comedy series

11 Good morning, sir—was there something?

Richard Murdoch 1907-90 and **Kenneth Horne** 1900-69: catchphrase used by Sam Costa in radio comedy series *Much-Binding-in-the-Marsh* (started 2 January 1947)

12 BURNS: Say goodnight, Gracie.
ALLEN: Goodnight, Gracie.

George Burns 1896-1996: said to be customary conclusion to *The George Burns and Gracie Allen Show* (1950-58), although Burns in *Gracie: a Love Story* (1990) described this as a showbusiness myth

13 *Grazie, grazie*, you have-a brought great joy to this old Italian stereotype.

Matt Groening 1954- : Springfield's local Mafia leader, Don Vittorio; *The Simpsons* (American TV series, 1990-)

14 Have you read any good books lately?

Richard Murdoch 1907–90 and **Kenneth Horne** 1900–69: catchphrase used by Richard Murdoch in radio comedy series *Much-Binding-in-the-Marsh* (started 2 January 1947)

15 Hello, I'm Julian and this is my friend, Sandy.

Barry Took and **Marty Feldman** 1933–83: catchphrase in *Round the Horne* (BBC radio series, 1965–8)

16 Hello possums!

Barry Humphries 1934– : Dame Edna's habitual greeting to her fans; *The Barry Humphries Show: Dame Edna Everage*

17 He's loo-vely, Mrs Hoskin . . . he's loo-ooo-vely!

Ted Ray 1906–77: catchphrase in *Ray's a Laugh* (BBC radio programme, 1949–61)

18 I didn't get where I am today without —.

David Nobbs 1935– : habitual boast of Reggie Perrin's boss CJ in BBC television series *The Fall and Rise of Reginald Perrin*, 1976–80

19 I don't mind if I do.

Ted Kavanagh 1892–1958: catchphrase spoken by 'Colonel Chinstrap' in *ITMA* (BBC radio programme, 1939–49)

20 If you've got it, flaunt it!

Mel Brooks 1926– : *The Producers* (1967 film)

21 I go—I come back.

Ted Kavanagh 1892–1958: catchphrase spoken by 'Ali Oop' in *ITMA* (BBC radio programme, 1939–49)

22 I have a cunning plan.

Richard Curtis 1956– and **Ben Elton** 1959– : *Blackadder II* (1987) television series; Baldrick's habitual overoptimistic promise

23 It's being so cheerful as keeps me going.

Ted Kavanagh 1892–1958: catchphrase spoken by 'Mona Lott' in *ITMA* (BBC radio programme, 1939–49)

24 It's *sooo* unfair!

Harry Enfield 1961– : habitual plaint of Kevin the Teenager; *Harry Enfield and Chums* (BBC TV, 1994)

25 I've arrived and to prove it I'm here!

Eric Sykes and **Max Bygraves** 1922– : *Educating Archie*, 1950–3 BBC radio comedy series

26 Just like that!

Tommy Cooper 1921–84: catchphrase associated with Tommy Cooper

27 Meredith, we're in!

Fred Kitchen 1872–1950: catchphrase originating in *The Bailiff* (1907 stage sketch)

28 Mind my bike!

Jack Warner 1895–1981: catchphrase used in the BBC radio series *Garrison Theatre*, 1939 onwards

29 Nobody expects the Spanish Inquisition! Our chief weapon is surprise—surprise and fear . . . fear and surprise . . . our two weapons are fear and surprise—and ruthless efficiency . . . our *three* weapons are fear and surprise and ruthless efficiency and an almost fanatical devotion to the Pope . . . our *four* . . . no . . . *Amongst* our weapons—amongst our weaponry—are such elements as fear, surprise . . . I'll come in again.

Graham Chapman 1941–89, **John Cleese** 1939– , et al.: *Monty Python's Flying Circus* (BBC TV programme, 1970)

30 No sex, please—we're British.

Anthony Marriott 1931– and **Alistair Foot**: title of play (1971)

31 Oh, calamity!

Robertson Hare 1891–1979: catchphrase in *Yours Indubitably* (1956)

32 Ohhh, I don't *believe* it!

David Renwick 1951– : Victor Meldrew in *One Foot in the Grave* (BBC television series, 1989–)

33 Pass the sick bag, Alice.

John Junor 1919–97: referring to a canteen lady at the old *Express* building in Fleet Street, who conveyed plates of egg and chips to journalists at their desks; in *Sunday Express* 28 December 1980

34 So Harry says, 'You don't like me any more. Why not?' And he says, 'Because you've got so terribly pretentious.' And Harry says, 'Pretentious? *Moi?*'

John Cleese 1939– and **Connie Booth**: *Fawlty Towers* (BBC TV programme, 1979)

35 Seriously, though, he's doing a grand job!

David Frost 1939– : catchphrase written by Waterhouse and Hall for Roy Kinnear's sketch 'The Safe Comedian', and adopted by David Frost for 'That Was The Week That Was', on BBC Television, 1962–3

36 Shome mishtake, shurely?

Anonymous: catchphrase in *Private Eye* magazine, 1980s

37 STRIKER: Surely you can't be serious.
   DR RUMACK: I am serious. And don't call me Shirley.

Jim Abrahams, David Zucker, and **Jerry Zucker**: *Airplane!* (1980 film)

38 Take my wife—please!

Henny Youngman 1906–98: in *Times* 26 February 1998; obituary

39 Very interesting . . . but stupid.

Dan Rowan 1922–87 and **Dick Martin** 1923– : catchphrase in *Rowan and Martin's Laugh-In* (American television series, 1967–73)

40 ABBOTT: Now, on the St Louis team we have Who's on first, What's on second, I Don't Know is on third.
   COSTELLO: That's what I want to find out.

Bud Abbott 1895–1974 and **Lou Costello** 1906–59: *Naughty Nineties* (1945)

41 SEAGOON: Ying tong iddle I po.

Spike Milligan 1918– : *The Dreaded Batter Pudding Hurler* in *The Goon Show* (BBC radio series) 12 October 1954; catchphrase also used in *The Ying Tong Song* (1956)

42 You can't get the wood, you know.

Spike Milligan 1918– : *The Goon Show* (BBC radio, 1951–61)

43 You might very well think that. I couldn't possibly comment.

Michael Dobbs 1948– : *House of Cards* (televised 1990); the Chief Whip's habitual response to questioning

Commerce See **Business and Commerce**

Computers See also **Science, Technology**

1 To err is human but to really foul things up requires a computer.

Anonymous: in *Farmers' Almanac for 1978*

2 A modern computer hovers between the obsolescent and the nonexistent.

Sydney Brenner 1927– : in *Science* 5 January 1990; attributed

3 I am afraid it is a non-starter. I cannot even use a bicycle pump.
when asked whether she uses e-mail

Judi Dench 1934– : in *The Times* 13 February 1999

4 This Ken Starr report is now posted on the Internet. I'll bet Clinton's glad he put a computer in every classroom.

Jay Leno 1950– : in *Sunday Times* 20 September 1998

5 We've all heard that a million monkeys banging on a million typewriters will eventually reproduce the entire works of Shakespeare. Now, thanks to the Internet, we know this is not true.

Robert Wilensky 1951– : in *Mail on Sunday* 16 February 1997 'Quotes of the Week'

6 I should prefer to have a politician who regularly went to a massage parlour than one who promised a laptop computer for every teacher.

A. N. Wilson 1950– : in *Observer* 21 March 1999

Conversation See also **Speeches and Speechmaking**

1 Nothing comes amiss to her but speaking commendably of anybody but herself without some tokens of reserve.

Anonymous: in *The Female Tatler* September 1709

2 We don't discuss anything anyway. Unless it appears on Patrick's official breakfast-time agenda. And that consists mainly of food. Minutes of the last meal and proposals for the next.

Alan Ayckbourn 1939– : *Sisterly Feelings* (1981)

3 Although there exist many thousand subjects for elegant conversation, there are persons who cannot meet a cripple without talking about feet.

Ernest Bramah 1868–1942: *The Wallet of Kai Lung* (1900)

4 When you were quite a little boy somebody ought to have said 'hush' just once!

Mrs Patrick Campbell 1865–1940: letter to George Bernard Shaw, 1 November 1912

5 'Then you should say what you mean,' the March Hare went on. 'I do,' Alice hastily replied; 'at least—at least I mean what I say—that's the same thing, you know.' 'Not

Lewis Carroll 1832–98: *Alice's Adventures in Wonderland* (1865)

the same thing a bit!' said the Hatter. 'Why, you might just as well say that "I see what I eat" is the same thing as "I eat what I see!" '

on visiting Lord Alfred Douglas:

6 We had resolved not to mention Oscar Wilde, prison, Winston, Robbie Ross or Frank Harris, but we were soon well embarked on all five subjects, though not at once.

Chips Channon 1897–1958: diary, 10 October 1942

7 It makes a change from talking to plants.
   being photographed with penguins in the Falklands

Charles, Prince of Wales 1948– : in *Sunday Times* 21 March 1999 'Talking Heads'

8 Too much agreement kills a chat.

Eldridge Cleaver 1935– : *Soul on Ice* (1968)

9 Is it possible to cultivate the art of conversation when living in the country all the year round?

E. M. Delafield 1890–1943: *The Diary of a Provincial Lady* (1930)

10 The fun of talk is to find what a man really thinks, and then contrast it with the enormous lies he has been telling all dinner, and, perhaps, all his life.

Benjamin Disraeli 1804–81: *Lothair* (1870)

11 How time flies when you's doin' all the talking.

Harvey Fierstein 1954– : *Torch Song Trilogy* (1979)

12 If you are ever at a loss to support a flagging conversation, introduce the subject of eating.

Leigh Hunt 1784–1859: J. A. Gere and John Sparrow (eds.) *Geoffrey Madan's Notebooks* (1981); attributed

13 I hate historic talk, and when Charles Fox said something to me once about Catiline's Conspiracy, I withdrew my attention, and thought about Tom Thumb.

Samuel Johnson 1709–84: Hester Lynch Piozzi letter 21 August 1819

14 I've just spent an hour talking to Tallulah for a few minutes.

Fred Keating: Denis Brian *Tallulah, Darling* (1980)

15 There are two things in ordinary conversation which ordinary people dislike—information and wit.

Stephen Leacock 1869–1944: *The Boy I Left Behind Me* (1947)

16 The opposite of talking isn't listening. The opposite of talking is waiting.

Fran Lebowitz 1946– : *Social Studies* (1981)

17 The conversational overachiever is someone whose grasp exceeds his reach. This is possible but not attractive.

Fran Lebowitz 1946– : *Social Studies* (1981)

18 She . . . couldn't take a phone call without getting into a seminar on the meaning of life with the caller.

Mary Maher: 'Lucy's Story' (1997)

19 Considering how foolishly people act and how pleasantly they prattle, perhaps it would be better for the world if they talked more and did less.

W. Somerset Maugham 1874–1965: *A Writer's Notebook* (1949) written in 1892

20 She plunged into a sea of platitudes, and with the powerful breast stroke of a channel swimmer made her confident way towards the white cliffs of the obvious.

W. Somerset Maugham 1874–1965: *A Writer's Notebook* (1949) written in 1919

21 It is clear enough that you are making some distinction in what you said, that there is some nicety of terminology in your words. I can't quite follow you.

Flann O'Brien 1911–66: *The Dalkey Archive* (1964)

22 With first-rate sherry flowing into second-rate whores, And third-rate conversation without one single pause: Just like a young couple

William Plomer 1903–73: 'Father and Son: 1939' (1945)

Between the wars.

23 If you have nothing to say, or, rather, something
extremely stupid and obvious, say it, but in a 'plonking'
tone of voice—i.e. roundly, but hollowly and dogmatically.

Stephen Potter 1900-69:
Lifemanship (1950)

commenting that George Bernard Shaw's wife was a good listener:
24 God knows she had plenty of practice.

J. B. Priestley 1894-1984: *Margin Released* (1962)

25 [Macaulay] has occasional flashes of silence, that make his
conversation perfectly delightful.

Sydney Smith 1771-1845: Lady Holland *Memoir* (1855)

26 —d! said my mother, 'what is all this story about?'— 'A
Cock and a Bull,' said Yorick.

Laurence Sterne 1713-68: *Tristram Shandy* (1759-67)

27 *You* talked animatedly for some time about language being
the aniseed trail that draws the hounds of heaven when
the metaphysical fox has gone to earth; he must have
thought you were barmy.

Tom Stoppard 1937- : *Jumpers* (rev. ed. 1986)

28 Faith, that's as well said, as if I had said it myself.

Jonathan Swift 1667-1745: *Polite Conversation* (1738)

29 I re-iterate. You remember, I iterated before.

Dick Vosburgh: *A Saint She Ain't* (1999)

30 If one plays good music, people don't listen and if one
plays bad music people don't talk.

Oscar Wilde 1854-1900: *The Importance of Being Earnest* (1895)

31 If one could only teach the English how to talk, and the
Irish how to listen, society here would be quite civilized.

Oscar Wilde 1854-1900: *An Ideal Husband* (1895)

32 'What ho!' I said.
'What ho!' said Motty.
'What ho! What ho!'
'What ho! What ho! What ho!'
After that it seemed rather difficult to go on with the
conversation.

P. G. Wodehouse 1881-1975: *My Man Jeeves* (1919)

Cookery See also **Food and Drink**

1 Cook my own lunch—a thing I have not done for twenty
years. Pork Chop. Looking for guidance in my Electrical
Cookery Book, I turn up the letter 'P', and find any
amount of instruction about Peach Gâteau, Petits Fours,
Pineapple Soufflée, Pound Cake, and Prairie Oysters, but
not a word about Pork Chops.

James Agate 1877-1947: diary, 18 April 1943

2 You know that really was quite the most appalling meal
I've ever tasted. I'd forgotten how bad she was. Burnt Earl
Grey omelettes. It's almost an art form to mistreat food in
that way.

Alan Ayckbourn 1939- : *Woman in Mind* (1986)

3 Anyone who tells a lie has not a pure heart, and cannot
make a good soup.

Ludwig van Beethoven 1770-1827: Ludwig Nohl *Beethoven Depicted by his Contemporaries* (1880)

4 Be content to remember that those who can make
omelettes properly can do nothing else.

Hilaire Belloc 1870-1953: *A Conversation with a Cat* (1931)

5 My mother tells me she's worn out pouring tinned sauce over the frozen chicken.

Maeve Binchy 1940– : *Evening Class* (1996)

6 The discovery of a new dish does more for the happiness of mankind than the discovery of a new star.

Anthelme Brillat-Savarin 1755–1826: *Physiologie du Goût* (1826)

7 The restaurant is like a theatre: we do two shows a day and when you are doing Shakespeare you don't want to throw in something out of Walt Disney.
   on tomato ketchup

Philip Britten 1957– : in *Evening Standard* 4 February 1999

8 He said, 'I look for butterflies
That sleep among the wheat:
I make them into mutton-pies,
And sell them in the street.'

Lewis Carroll 1832–98: *Through the Looking-Glass* (1872)

9 Heaven sends us good meat, but the Devil sends cooks.

David Garrick 1717–79: 'On Doctor Goldsmith's Characteristical Cookery' (1777)

10 The difference between a chef and a cook is the difference between a wife and a prostitute. Cooks do meals for people they know and love. Chefs do it anonymously for anyone who's got the price.

A. A. Gill 1954– : in *Independent* 4 November 1998

11 We could not have had a better dinner had there been a *Synod of Cooks*.

Samuel Johnson 1709–84: James Boswell *Life of Samuel Johnson* (1791) 5 August 1763

12 A cucumber should be well sliced, and dressed with pepper and vinegar, and then thrown out, as good for nothing.

Samuel Johnson 1709–84: James Boswell *Journal of a Tour to the Hebrides* (1785) 5 October 1773

watching the TV chef Michael Barry prepare a venison dish:
13 Bambi—see the movie! Eat the cast!

Henry Kelly: in *Daily Telegraph* 26 February 1994

14 The test of a cook is how she boils an egg. My boiled eggs are FANTASTIC, FABULOUS. Sometimes as hard as a 100 carat diamond, or again soft as a feather bed, or running like a cooling stream, they can also burst like fireworks from their shells and take on the look and rubbery texture of a baby octopus. Never a dull egg, with me.

Nancy Mitford 1904–73: letter, 3 October 1963

15 The tragedy of English cooking is that 'plain' cooking cannot be entrusted to 'plain' cooks.

Countess Morphy fl. 1930–50: *English Recipes* (1935)

16 The vulgar boil, the learned roast, an egg.

Alexander Pope 1688–1744: *Imitations of Horace* (1738)

17 Her cooking is the missionary position of cooking. That is how everybody starts.
   defending Delia Smith, whose new series was accused of being insulting to the public

Egon Ronay: in *Independent on Sunday* 1 November 1998

18 The cook was a good cook, as cooks go; and as cooks go, she went.

Saki 1870–1916: *Reginald* (1904)

19 'But why should you want to shield him?' cried Egbert; 'the man is a common murderer.' 'A common murderer, possibly, but a very uncommon cook.'

Saki 1870–1916: *Beasts and Super-Beasts* (1914)

20 You won't be surprised that diseases are innumerable—count the cooks.

Seneca c.4 BC–AD 65: *Epistles*

21 The most remarkable thing about my mother is that for 30 years she served nothing but leftovers. The original meal was never found.

Tracey Ullman 1959– : in *Observer* 23 May 1999 'Sayings of the Week'

22 And now with some pleasure I find that it's seven; and must cook dinner. Haddock and sausage meat. I think it is true that one gains a certain hold on sausage and haddock by writing them down.

Virginia Woolf 1882–1941: diary, 8 March 1941

Countries and Peoples See also **Places**

1 That Britain was no part of Europe was his conviction.
of Lord Milner

Lord Beaverbrook 1879–1964: *Men and Power* (1956)

2 It's like Bob Benchley's remark on India—'India, what does the name *not* suggest?' To which Benchley himself gives the answer—'a hell of a lot of things.'

Robert Benchley 1889–1945: Stephen Leacock *The Boy I Left Behind Me* (1947); attributed

3 Canada is a country so square that even the female impersonators are women.

Richard Benner: *Outrageous* (1977)

4 It's where they commit suicide and the king rides a bicycle, Sweden.

Alan Bennett 1934– : *Enjoy* (1980)

5 Germans are flummoxed by humour, the Swiss have no concept of fun, the Spanish think there is nothing at all ridiculous about eating dinner at midnight, and the Italians should never, ever have been let in on the invention of the motor car.

Bill Bryson 1951– : *Neither Here Nor There* (1991)

6 The perpetual lamentations after beef and beer, the stupid bigoted contempt for every thing foreign, and insurmountable incapacity of acquiring even a few words of any language, rendered him like all other English servants, an encumbrance.

Lord Byron 1788–1824: letter, 14 January 1811

7 France is the only place where you can make love in the afternoon without people hammering on your door.

Barbara Cartland 1901–2000: in *Guardian* 24 December 1984

8 I gather it has now been decided not to embrace the Russian bear, but to hold out a hand and accept its paw gingerly. No more. The worst of both worlds.

Chips Channon 1897–1958: diary, 16 May 1939

9 I like my 'abroad' to be Catholic and sensual.

Chips Channon 1897–1958: diary 18 January 1924

10 Belgium has only one real claim to fame. Thanks to all the wars that have been fought on its soil, there are more dead people there than anywhere else in the world. So, while there's no quality of life in Belgium, there is a simply wonderful quality of death.

Jeremy Clarkson 1960– : in *Sunday Times* 18 July 1999

11 They're Germans. Don't mention the war.

John Cleese 1939– and **Connie Booth**: *Fawlty Towers* (BBC TV programme, 1975)

the French jazz critic Hugues Panassie had given Condon a
generally favourable notice:

12 I don't see why we need a Frenchman to come over here
    and tell us how to play American music. I wouldn't think
    of going to France and telling him how to jump on a
    grape.

Eddie Condon 1905–73: Bill Crow
Jazz Anecdotes (1990)

13 To speak with your mouth full
    And swallow with greed
    Are national traits
    Of the travelling Swede.

Duff Cooper 1890–1954: Philip
Ziegler *Diana Cooper* (1981)

14 In a bar on the Piccola Marina
    Life called to Mrs Wentworth-Brewster,
    Fate beckoned her and introduced her
    Into a rather queer
    Unfamiliar atmosphere . . .
    Just for fun three young sailors from Messina
    Bowed low to Mrs Wentworth-Brewster,
    Said 'Scusi' and politely goosed her.
    Then there was quite a scena.
    Her family, in floods of tears, cried,
    'Leave these men, Mama.'
    She said, 'They're just high-spirited, like all Italians are
    And most of them have a great deal more to offer than
        Papa,
    In a bar on the Piccola Marina.'

Noël Coward 1899–1973: 'A Bar on
the Piccola Marina' (1954)

15 Don't let's be beastly to the Germans
    When our Victory is ultimately won.
    It was just those nasty Nazis who persuaded them to fight
    And their Beethoven and Bach are really far worse than
        their bite,
    Let's be meek to them—
    And turn the other cheek to them
    And try to bring out their latent sense of fun.

Noël Coward 1899–1973: 'Don't
Let's Be Beastly to the Germans'
(1943)

16 Every wise and thoroughly worldly wench
    Knows there's always something fishy about the French!

Noël Coward 1899–1973: 'There's
Always Something Fishy about the
French' (1933)

17 I see Canada as a country torn between a very northern,
    rather extraordinary, mystical spirit which it fears and its
    desire to present itself to the world as a Scotch banker.

Robertson Davies 1913–95: *The
Enthusiasms of Robertson Davies*
(1990)

18 How can you govern a country which has 246 varieties of
    cheese?

Charles de Gaulle 1890–1970: Ernest
Mignon *Les Mots du Général* (1962)

19 Some people . . . may be Rooshans, and others may be
    Prooshans; they are born so, and will please themselves.
    Them which is of other naturs thinks different.

Charles Dickens 1812–70: *Martin
Chuzzlewit* (1844)

20 When you enter a house you take your shoes off
    It's better with your shoes off! . . .
    Get yourself a Geisha. The flower of Asia,
    She's one with whom to take up.
    At night your bed she'll make up,
    And she'll be there when you wake up.

Howard Dietz 1896–1983: 'Get
Yourself a Geisha' (1935)

21 The Arabs are only Jews upon horseback.

Benjamin Disraeli 1804–81: *Tancred* (1847)

to a Boer who had told her that he could never quite forgive the British for having conquered his country:
22 I understand that perfectly. We feel very much the same in Scotland.

Queen Elizabeth, the Queen Mother 1900– : Elizabeth Longford (ed.) *The Oxford Book of Royal Anecdotes* (1989)

23 I'm not Jewish. I only look intelligent.
German cabaret artist to Nazis in his audience, 1931

Werner Finck 1902– : Humphrey Carpenter *That Was Satire That Was* (2000)

24 We sing you the Song of the Rhineland—
Europe's beauty spot . . .
That wonderful pretzel-and-stein land
Can never be forgot!

Ira Gershwin 1896–1983: 'Song of the Rhineland' (1945)

25 What cleanliness everywhere! You dare not throw your cigarette into the lake. No graffiti in the urinals. Switzerland is proud of this; but I believe this is just what she lacks: manure.

André Gide 1869–1951: diary, Lucerne, 10 August 1917

26 For he might have been a Roosian,
A French, or Turk, or Proosian,
Or perhaps Ital-ian!
But in spite of all temptations
To belong to other nations,
He remains an Englishman!

W. S. Gilbert 1836–1911: *HMS Pinafore* (1878)

27 I hate the French, I hate them all,
From Toulouse Lafucking Trec to Charles de Gaulle.

Paul Scott Goodman: 'I Hate the French' (*Bright Lights, Big City*, 1988 musical, from the book by Jay McInerney)

28 We did have a form of Afro-Asian studies which consisted of colouring bits of the map red to show the British Empire.

Michael Green 1927– : *The Boy Who Shot Down an Airship* (1988)

29 Australia is a huge rest home, where no unwelcome news is ever wafted on to the pages of the worst newspapers in the world.

Germaine Greer 1939– : in *Observer* 1 August 1982

30 Holland . . . lies so low they're only saved by being dammed.

Thomas Hood 1799–1845: *Up the Rhine* (1840) 'Letter from Martha Penny to Rebecca Page'

31 Just as America had, in Bernard Shaw's perception, moved from barbarism to decadence without an intervening period of civilization, Australian humour had somehow skipped the ironic and gone from folksy to camp.

Barry Humphries 1934– : *More Please* (1992)

32 Then brim the bowl with atrabilious liquor!
We'll pledge our Empire vast across the flood:
For Blood, as all men know, than Water's thicker,
But Water's wider, thank the Lord, than Blood.

Aldous Huxley 1894–1963: 'Ninth Philosopher's Song' (1920)

33 The best thing I know between France and England is—the sea.

Douglas Jerrold 1803–57: *The Wit and Opinions of Douglas Jerrold* (1859) 'The Anglo-French Alliance'

34 Earth is here so kind, that just tickle her with a hoe and she laughs with a harvest.

Douglas Jerrold 1803-57: *The Wit and Opinions of Douglas Jerrold* (1859) 'A Land of Plenty' (Australia)

35 If one had to be foreign it was far better to be German, preferably a Prussian . . . Indeed, had the Germans only possessed a sense of humour they might almost have qualified as honorary Englishmen.

Osbert Lancaster 1908-80: *All Done From Memory* (1953)

36 No matter how politely or distinctly you ask a Parisian a question he will persist in answering you in French.

Fran Lebowitz 1946- : *Metropolitan Life* (1978)

37 And we will all go together when we go—
Every Hottentot and every Eskimo.

Tom Lehrer 1928- : 'We Will All Go Together When We Go' (1953)

38 ELIZA: The Rain in Spain stays mainly in the plain.
HIGGINS: By George, she's got it!

Alan Jay Lerner 1918-86: 'The Rain in Spain' (1956)

39 I'd love to get you
On a slow boat to China,
All to myself, alone.

Frank Loesser 1910-69: 'On a Slow Boat to China' (1948)

40 'We went in [to the European Community],' he said, 'to screw the French by splitting them off from the Germans. The French went in to protect their inefficient farmers from commercial competition. The Germans went in to cleanse themselves of genocide and apply for readmission to the human race.'

Jonathan Lynn 1943- and **Antony Jay** 1930- : *Yes, Minister* vol. 2 (1982)

41 Canadians are Americans with no Disneyland.

Margaret Mahy 1937- : *The Changeover* (1984)

42 In fact, I'm not really a *Jew*. Just Jew-*ish*. Not the whole hog, you know.

Jonathan Miller 1934- : *Beyond the Fringe* (1960 review) 'Real Class'

43 Frogs . . . are slightly better than Huns or Wops, but abroad is unutterably bloody and foreigners are fiends.

Nancy Mitford 1904-73: *The Pursuit of Love* (1945)

44 Yet, who can help loving the land that has taught us
Six hundred and eighty-five ways to dress eggs?

Thomas Moore 1779-1852: *The Fudge Family in Paris* (1818)

45 I have to spend so much time explaining to Americans that I am not English and to Englishmen that I am not American that I have little time left to be Canadian . . . (On second thought, I am a true cosmopolitan—unhappy anywhere.)

Laurence J. Peter 1919- : *Quotations for our Time* (1977)

46 The Dutch in old Amsterdam do it,
Not to mention the Finns,
Folks in Siam do it,
Think of Siamese twins.
Some Argentines, without means, do it,
People say, in Boston, even beans do it
Let's do it, let's fall in love.

Cole Porter 1891-1964: 'Let's Do It, Let's Fall in Love' (1928)

47 If you come on a camel, you can park it,
So come to the supermarket
And see
Pe-
king.

Cole Porter 1891-1964: 'Come to the Supermarket in Old Peking' (1958)

48 In Australia,
Inter alia,
Mediocrities
Think they're Socrates.

Peter Porter 1929– : unpublished clerihew; Stephen Murray-Smith (ed.) *The Dictionary of Australian Quotations* (1984)

49 I'm world famous, Dr Parks said, all over Canada.

Mordecai Richler 1931– : *The Incomparable Atuk* (1963)

50 The people of Crete unfortunately make more history than they can consume locally.

Saki 1870–1916: *Chronicles of Clovis* (1911)

51 All my wife has ever taken from the Mediterranean—from that whole vast intuitive culture—are four bottles of Chianti to make into lamps.

Peter Shaffer 1926– : *Equus* (1973)

52 That's the main trouble with the two nations: bad Brits are snobs, bad Americans are slobs.

Peter Shaffer 1926– : *Whom Do I Have the Honour of Addressing?* (1990)

53 I think he bought his doublet in Italy, his round hose in France, his bonnet in Germany, and his behaviour everywhere.

William Shakespeare 1564–1616: *The Merchant of Venice* (1596–8)

54 I was early taught to regard Germany as a very serious place because I was a little Irish Protestant and knew that Martin Luther was a German. I therefore concluded that all Germans went to heaven, an opinion which I no longer hold with any conviction.

George Bernard Shaw 1856–1950: 'What I Owe to German Culture' (1911)

55 England and America are two countries divided by a common language.

George Bernard Shaw 1856–1950: attributed in this and other forms, but not found in Shaw's published writings

56 I look upon Switzerland as an inferior sort of Scotland.

Sydney Smith 1771–1845: letter to Lord Holland, 1815

57 They order, said I, this matter better in France.

Laurence Sterne 1713–68: opening words of *A Sentimental Journey* (1768)

58 Paris last year. Wonderful town but the French are awful, the waiters and so on, they're tip mad.

Tom Stoppard 1937– : *Neutral Ground* (1983)

59 Lump the whole thing! say that the Creator made Italy from designs by Michael Angelo!

Mark Twain 1835–1910: *The Innocents Abroad* (1869)

60 I don't like Norwegians at all. The sun never sets, the bar never opens, and the whole country smells of kippers.

Evelyn Waugh 1903–66: letter to Lady Diana Cooper, 13 July 1934

61 In Italy for thirty years under the Borgias they had warfare, terror, murder, bloodshed—they produced Michelangelo, Leonardo da Vinci and the Renaissance. In Switzerland they had brotherly love, five hundred years of democracy and peace and what did that produce . . . ? The cuckoo clock.

Orson Welles 1915–85: *The Third Man* (1949 film); words added by Welles to Graham Greene's script

of art and the Swiss:

62 The sons of patriots are left with the clock that turns the mill, and the sudden cuckoo, with difficulty restrained in its box!
For this was Tell a hero! For this did Gessler die!

James McNeill Whistler 1834–1903: lecture in London, 20 February 1885; in *Mr Whistler's 'Ten O'Clock'* (1888)

63 I don't like Switzerland: it has produced nothing but theologians and waiters.

Oscar Wilde 1854–1900: letter from Switzerland, 20 March 1899

64 France is a country where the money falls apart in your hands and you can't tear the toilet paper.

Billy Wilder 1906– : Leslie Halliwell *The Filmgoer's Book of Quotes* (1973)

The Country

1 He likes the country, but in truth must own,
Most likes it, when he studies it in town.

William Cowper 1731–1800: 'Retirement' (1782)

2 God made the country, and man made the town.

William Cowper 1731–1800: *The Task* (1785)

3 Having always been told that living at Crowborough was 'living in the country' I wrongly identified English country life with interminable calls on elderly ladies whose favourite topic was the servant problem.

Tom Driberg 1905–76: *The Best of Both Worlds* (1953)

4 'You are a pretty urban sort of person though, wouldn't you say?'
'Only nor'nor'east,' I said. 'I know a fox from a fax-machine.'

Stephen Fry 1957– : *The Hippopotamus* (1994)

5 A weekend in the country—
Trees in the orchard call.
When you've examined one tree,
Then you've examined them all.

Ira Gershwin 1896–1983: 'A Weekend in the Country' (*The Barkleys of Broadway*, 1949 film)

6 June is bustin' out all over
The sheep aren't sleepin' any more!
All the rams that chase the ewe sheep
Are determined there'll be new sheep
And the ewe sheep aren't even keepin' score!

Oscar Hammerstein II 1895–1960: 'June is Bustin' Out All Over' (1945)

7 In a mountain greenery
Where God paints the scenery—.

Lorenz Hart 1895–1943: 'Mountain Greenery' (1926)

8 There is nothing good to be had in the country, or if there is, they will not let you have it.

William Hazlitt 1778–1830: *The Round Table* (1817)

9 The Farmer will never be happy again;
He carries his heart in his boots;
For either the rain is destroying his grain
Or the drought is destroying his roots.

A. P. Herbert 1890–1971: 'The Farmer' (1922)

10 Hey, buds below, up is where to grow,
Up with which below can't compare with.
Hurry! It's lovely up here! *Hurry*!

Alan Jay Lerner 1918–86: 'It's Lovely Up Here' (1965)

11 So *that's* what hay looks like.
said at Badminton House, where she was evacuated during the Second World War

Queen Mary 1867–1953: James Pope-Hennessy *Life of Queen Mary* (1959)

12 It is no good putting up notices saying 'Beware of the bull' because very rude things are sometimes written on them. I have found that one of the most effective notices is 'Beware of the Agapanthus'.

Lord Massereene and Ferrard 1914–93: speech on the Wildlife and Countryside Bill, House of Lords 16 December 1980

13 Very few people have settled entirely in the country but have grown at length weary of one another. The lady's conversation generally falls into a thousand impertinent effects of idleness, and the gentleman falls in love with his dogs and horses, and out of love with every thing else.

Lady Mary Wortley Montagu 1689–1762: letter to Edward Wortley Montagu, 12 August 1712

14 Whose woods are whose everybody knows exactly, and everybody knows who got them rezoned for a shopping mall and who couldn't get the financing to begin construction and why it was he couldn't get it.
   on a traditional New England community, with reference to Robert Frost's 'Whose woods these are I think I know'

P. J. O'Rourke 1947- : *Parliament of Whores* (1991)

15 A farm is an irregular patch of nettles bounded by short-term notes, containing a fool and his wife who didn't know enough to stay in the city.

S. J. Perelman 1904-79: *The Most of S. J. Perelman* (1959) 'Acres and Pains'

16 Farming, that's the fashion,
Farming, that's the passion
Of our great celebrities of today.
Kit Cornell is shellin' peas,
Lady Mendl's climbin' trees,
Dear Mae West is at her best in the hay . . .

The natives think it's utterly utter
When Margie Hart starts churning her butter . . .

Miss Elsa Maxwell, so the folks tattle,
Got well-goosed while dehorning her cattle . . .

Liz Whitney has, on her bin of manure, a
Clip designed by the Duke of Verdura,
Farming is so charming, they all say.

Cole Porter 1891-1964: 'Farming' (1941)

17 Sylvia . . . was accustomed to nothing much more sylvan than 'leafy Kensington'. She looked on the country as something excellent and wholesome in its way, which was apt to become troublesome if you encouraged it overmuch.

Saki 1870-1916: *The Chronicles of Clovis* (1911)

18 I have no relish for the country; it is a kind of healthy grave.

Sydney Smith 1771-1845: letter to Miss G. Harcourt, 1838

19 You don't get nice trees in other places, not the variety. Nice trees are taken for granted in England. Yes, awfully fond of trees, damned fond . . . Carol's got a tree, you know—her own. I actually *bought* her a tree for her birthday.

Tom Stoppard 1937- : *Neutral Ground* (1983)

20 Anybody can be good in the country.

Oscar Wilde 1854-1900: *The Picture of Dorian Gray* (1891)

21 What do we see at once but a little robin! There is no need to burst into tears fotherington-tomas swete tho he be. Nor to buzz a brick at it, molesworth 2.

Geoffrey Willans 1911-58 and **Ronald Searle** 1920- : a nature walk at St Custards; *Down with Skool!* (1953)

Cricket See also **Sports and Games**

when playing in a Lancashire league game, Dennis Lillee's ball hit the batsman on the leg. Although given out, the batsman remained at the crease, and Lillee insisted forcefully that he must go:
1 I'd love to go Dennis but I daren't move. I think you've broken my bloody leg.

Anonymous: Michael Parkinson *Sporting Lives* (1993)

in Australian cricket, traditional line of wicket-keeper to new batsman:
2 How's the wife and my kids?

Anonymous: Simon Hughes *Yakking Around the World* (2000)

3 Life as we know it is over.

an unnamed member of the Marylebone Cricket Club, after the MCC voted to admit women members

Anonymous: in *Irish Times* 3 October 1998 'This Week They Said'

the umpire had called 'not out' after W. G. Grace was unexpectedly bowled first ball:

4 They have paid to see Dr Grace bat, not to see you bowl.

to the bowler

Anonymous: Harry Furniss *A Century of Grace* (1985); perhaps apocryphal

on being approached for a contribution to W. G. Grace's testimonial:

5 It's not in support of cricket but as an earnest protest against golf.

Max Beerbohm 1872–1956: attributed

6 Broken marriages, conflicts of loyalty, the problems of everyday life fall away as one faces up to Thomson.

on Jeff Thomson's bowling

Mike Brearley 1942– : Ned Sherrin *Cutting Edge* (1984)

reflecting on the cricketer Billy Barnes who had made a century at Lord's while tipsy:

7 The modern professional cricketer does not get drunk at Lord's or often get a century there, or anywhere else, before lunch.

Neville Cardus 1889–1975: *Autobiography* (1947)

8 I couldn't bat for the length of time required to score 500. I'd get bored and fall over.

Denis Compton 1918– : to Brian Lara; in *Daily Telegraph* 27 June 1994

9 That's the trouble with these West Country teams. They bowl and field beautifully for an hour, and then—They begin to think of apples.

C. B. Fry 1872–1956: Iain Wilton *C. B. Fry* (1999)

10 Never read print, it spoils one's eye for the ball.

habitual advice to his players

W. G. Grace 1848–1915: Harry Furniss *A Century of Grace* (1985)

11 Cricket—a game which the English, not being a spiritual people, have invented in order to give themselves some conception of eternity.

Lord Mancroft 1914– : *Bees in Some Bonnets* (1979)

12 He is also too daring for the majority of the black-beards, the brown-beards and the no-beards, and the all-beards, who sit in judgement on batsmen; in short, too daring for those who have never known what it is to dare in cricket. Only for those who have not yet grown to the tyranny of the razor is Gimblett possibly not daring enough.

on Harold Gimblett, sometimes accused of being 'too daring for the greybeards'

R. C. Robertson-Glasgow 1901–65: *Cricket Prints* (1943)

13 He loved to walk sideways towards them, like a grimly playful crab.

of George Gunn's approach to faster bowlers

R. C. Robertson-Glasgow 1901–65: *Cricket Prints* (1943)

14 He mistrusts anyone who reads past the sports pages of the tabloids.

of Michael Stewart, the former English Test team manager

Peter Roebuck 1956– : in *Ned Sherrin in his Anecdotage* (1993)

15 Personally, I have always looked upon cricket as organized loafing.

view of a future archbishop of Canterbury in 1925

William Temple 1881–1944: Michael Parkinson *Sporting Lives* (1993)

16 I need nine wickets from this match, and you buggers had better start drawing straws to see who I don't get.

to an opposing team

Freddie Trueman 1931– : in *Ned Sherrin in his Anecdotage* (1993)

17 It's a well-known fact that, when I'm on 99, I'm the best judge of a run in all the bloody world.
   to Cyril Washbrook

Alan Wharton 1923- : Freddie Trueman *You Nearly Had Me That Time* (1978)

18 Cricket is basically baseball on valium.

Robin Williams 1952- : attributed

Crime and Punishment See also **The Law, Judges**

1 When their lordships asked Bacon
How many bribes he had taken
He had at least the grace
To get very red in the face.

Edmund Clerihew Bentley 1875–1956: 'Bacon' (1939)

to a prison visitor who asked if he were sewing:
2 No, reaping.

Horatio Bottomley 1860–1933: S. T. Felstead *Horatio Bottomley* (1936)

3 Since it is probable that any book flying a bullet in its title is going to produce a corpse sooner or later—here it is.

Caryl Brahms 1901-82 and **S. J. Simon** 1904-48: *A Bullet in the Ballet* (1937)

4 What is robbing a bank compared with founding a bank?

Bertolt Brecht 1898–1956: *Die Dreigroschenoper* (1928)

5 Thieves respect property. They merely wish the property to become their property that they may more perfectly respect it.

G. K. Chesterton 1874–1936: *The Man who was Thursday* (1908)

6 Thou shalt not steal; an empty feat,
When it's so lucrative to cheat.

Arthur Hugh Clough 1819-61: 'The Latest Decalogue' (1862)

7 Here in our city
We're all of us pretty
Well sure that vice
Will in a trice
Be bundled out of sight,
Old men in lobbies
With dubious hobbies
Can still get the deuce of a fright
In London at night.

Noël Coward 1899–1973: 'London at Night' (1953)

8 Three juvenile delinquents,
Juvenile delinquents,
Happy as can be—we
Waste no time
On the wherefores and whys of it;
We like crime
And that's about the size of it.

Noël Coward 1899–1973: 'Three Juvenile Delinquents' (1949)

of a burglar:
9 He found it inconvenient to be poor.

William Cowper 1731–1800: 'Charity' (1782)

a prisoner before Mr Justice Darling objected to being called 'a professional crook':
10 PRISONER: I've only done two jobs, and each time I've been nabbed.
   LORD DARLING: It has never been suggested that you are successful in your profession.

Lord Darling 1849–1936: Edward Maltby *Secrets of a Solicitor* (1929)

11 It's over, and can't be helped, and that's one consolation, as they always says in Turkey, ven they cuts the wrong man's head off.

Charles Dickens 1812–70: *Pickwick Papers* (1837)

12 It is quite a three-pipe problem, and I beg that you won't speak to me for fifty minutes.

Arthur Conan Doyle 1859–1930: *The Adventures of Sherlock Holmes* (1892) 'The Red-Headed League'

13 'Excellent,' I cried. 'Elementary,' said he.

Arthur Conan Doyle 1859–1930: *The Memoirs of Sherlock Holmes* (1894) 'The Crooked Man'. 'Elementary, my dear Watson' is not found in any book by Conan Doyle

14 Major Strasser has been shot. Round up the usual suspects.

Julius J. Epstein 1909–2001 et al.: *Casablanca* (1942 film)

15 Thwackum was for doing justice, and leaving mercy to heaven.

Henry Fielding 1707–54: *Tom Jones* (1749)

16 Hanging is too good for him. He must be posted to the infantry.
  on being asked to endorse the execution of a cavalryman who sodomized his horse

Frederick the Great 1712–86: Giles MacDonogh *Frederick the Great: a Life in Deed and Letters* (1999)

17 Awaiting the sensation of a short, sharp shock,
From a cheap and chippy chopper on a big black block.

W. S. Gilbert 1836–1911: *The Mikado* (1885)

18 As some day it may happen that a victim must be found,
I've got a little list—I've got a little list
Of society offenders who might well be under ground
And who never would be missed—who never would be missed!

W. S. Gilbert 1836–1911: *The Mikado* (1885)

19 Something lingering, with boiling oil in it, I fancy.

W. S. Gilbert 1836–1911: *The Mikado* (1885)

20 It was beautiful and simple as all truly great swindles are.

O. Henry 1862–1910: *Gentle Grafter* (1908) 'Octopus Marooned'

21 But when our neighbours do wrong, we sometimes feel the fitness of making them smart for it, whether they have repented or not.

Oliver Wendell Holmes Jr. 1841–1935: *The Common Law* (1881)

22 The Warden threw a party at the county jail,
The prison band was there an' they began to wail.
The brass band was jumpin' an' the joint began to swing
You should have heard those knocked out jail birds sing.

Jerry Leiber 1933– and **Mike Stoller** 1933– : 'Jailhouse Rock' (1957)

23 If you import cannabis you get 25 years—is importation of cannabis four times as bad as rape?

Lord McCluskey 1914– : speech, Edinburgh, 12 July 1999

24 He would be astounded if you told him he was a crook. He honestly looks upon a fifty-fifty proposition as seventy-five for himself and twenty-five for the other fellow.

W. Somerset Maugham 1874–1965: *A Writer's Notebook* (1949) written in 1941

25 Let it appear in a criminal trial that the accused is a Sunday-school superintendent, and the jury says guilty almost automatically.

H. L. Mencken 1880–1956: *Minority Report* (1956)

26 When I heard the words criminal investigation my mindset changed considerably.

Oliver North 1943– : in *New York Times* 10 July 1987 'Quotation of the Day'

27 If I ever hear you accuse the police of using violence on a prisoner in custody again, I'll take you down to the station and beat the eyes out of your head.

Joe Orton 1933–67: *Loot* (1966)

28 The most peaceable way for you, if you do take a thief, is, to let him show himself what he is and steal out of your company.

William Shakespeare 1564–1616: *Much Ado About Nothing* (1598–9)

29 She starts to tell me how she's . . . married to an Italian with four restaurants on Long Island and right away I dig he's in with the mob. I mean one restaurant, you're in business, four restaurants it's the Mafia.

Neil Simon 1927– : *The Gingerbread Lady* (1970)

30 In sentencing a man for one crime, we may well be putting him beyond the reach of the law in respect of those crimes which he has not yet had an opportunity to commit. The law, however, is not to be cheated in this way. I shall therefore discharge you.

N. F. Simpson 1919– : *One Way Pendulum* (1960)

Critics and Criticism

1 About one thing I am determined. This is not to be afraid of saying No to pretentious rubbish because fifty years ago Clement Scott made a fool of himself over Ibsen.

James Agate 1877–1947: diary, 24 December 1939

2 The *Times* critic said that the author was entitled to telescope history and re-interpret it. I think I must now write a play to prove that Nero went behind the scenes at circuses for intellectual conversation, and another to show that fire descended upon Sodom because the inhabitants refused to pay poll-tax.

James Agate 1877–1947: diary, 11 September 1934

3 A bad review may spoil your breakfast but you shouldn't allow it to spoil your lunch.

Kingsley Amis 1922–95: Giles Gordon *Aren't We Due a Royalty Statement?* (1993); attributed

4 Full many a gallant man lies slain
On Waterloo's ensanguined plain,
But none by bullet or by shot
Fell half so flat as Walter Scott.
   comment on Scott's poem 'The Field of Waterloo' (1815),
   sometimes attributed to Thomas Erskine

Anonymous: Una Pope-Hennessy *The Laird of Abbotsford* (1932)

5 I have always thought it was a sound impulse by which he [Kipling] was driven to put his 'Recessional' into the waste-paper basket, and a great pity that Mrs Kipling fished it out and made him send it to *The Times*.

Max Beerbohm 1872–1956: letter 30 October 1913

apparent reassurance to a leading lady after a particularly bad first night:
6 My dear, good is not the word.

Max Beerbohm 1872–1956: attributed; Nigel Rees *Cassell Dictionary of Humorous Quotations* (1999)

7 Critics are like eunuchs in a harem; they know how it's done, they've seen it done every day, but they're unable to do it themselves.

Brendan Behan 1923–64: Jonathon Green (ed.) *A Dictionary of Contemporary Quotations* (1982)

8 Hebrews 13.8. [Jesus Christ, the same yesterday, and today, and forever.]
   summing up the long-running 1920s Broadway hit Abie's Irish Rose

Robert Benchley 1889–1945: Peter Hay *Theatrical Anecdotes* (1987)

9 Listen, dear, you couldn't write 'fuck' in the dust on a Venetian blind.
   to a Hollywood writer who had criticized Alan Bennett's 'An Englishman Abroad'

Coral Browne 1913–91: attributed

10 Send me no more reviews of any kind.—I will read no more of evil or good in that line.—Walter Scott has not read a review of *himself* for *thirteen years*.

Lord Byron 1788–1824: letter to his publisher John Murray, 3 November 1821

11 Like all good dramatic critics, we retired to the pub across the road.

Eric Cross 1905–80: *The Tailor and Ansty* (1942)

12 You know who the critics are? The men who have failed in literature and art.

Benjamin Disraeli 1804–81: *Lothair* (1870)

13 One of the most characteristic sounds of the English Sunday is the sound of Harold Hobson barking up the wrong tree.

Penelope Gilliatt 1933–93: in *Encore* November–December 1959

explaining why Vikram Seth's A Suitable Boy had not been shortlisted for the 1993 Booker Prize:
14 All the wrong bits are in and the right bits are out.

Lord Gowrie 1939– : in *Guardian* 9 March 1994

15 Dr Leavis believed he could identify a woman writer by her style, even though necessarily all that she wrote must have been a parody of some man's superior achievement. After all, there was not much wrong with Virginia Woolf except that she was a woman.

Germaine Greer 1939– : *The Female Eunuch* (1970)

16 Asking a working writer what he thinks about critics is like asking a lamp-post how it feels about dogs.

Christopher Hampton 1946– : in *Sunday Times Magazine* 16 October 1977

17 When I read something saying I've not done anything as good as *Catch-22* I'm tempted to reply, Who has?'

Joseph Heller 1923–99: in *The Times* 9 June 1993

18 This method answers the purpose for which it was devised; it saves lazy editors from working and stupid editors from thinking.

A. E. Housman 1859–1936: 'The Editing of Manilius' (1903)

19 There is a sort of savage nobility about his firm reliance on his own bad taste.
   of Richard Bentley's edition of Paradise Lost

A. E. Housman 1859–1936: 'Introductory Lecture' (1892)

20 Criticism is a study by which men grow important and formidable at very small expense.

Samuel Johnson 1709–84: *The Idler* 9 June 1759

21 He took the praise as a greedy boy takes apple pie, and the criticism as a good dutiful boy takes senna-tea.
   of Bulwer Lytton, whose novels he had criticized

Lord Macaulay 1800–59: letter, 5 August 1831

22 He takes the long review of things;
   He asks and gives no quarter.
   And you can sail with him on wings
   Or read the book. It's shorter.

David McCord 1897– : 'To A Certain Most Certainly Certain Critic' (1945)

23 Reviewing here [in Baltimore] is a hazardous occupation. Once I spoke harshly of an eminent American novelist, and he retaliated by telling a very charming woman that I was non compos penis. In time she came to laugh at him as a liar.

H. L. Mencken 1880–1956: letter to Hugh Walpole, 1922

24 The lot of critics is to be remembered by what they failed to understand.

George Moore 1852–1933: *Impressions and Opinions* (1891) 'Balzac'

25 [Jeanne Aubert's] husband, if you can believe the papers, recently pled through the French courts that he be allowed to restrain his wife from appearing on the stage. Professional or not, the man is a dramatic critic.

Dorothy Parker 1893–1967: in *New Yorker* February 1931; Dorothy Hart *Thou Swell, Thou Witty* (1976)

26 And it is that word 'hummy', my darlings, that marks the first place in 'The House at Pooh Corner' at which Tonstant Weader fwowed up.

Dorothy Parker 1893–1967: review in *New Yorker* 20 October 1928

27 At ev'ry word a reputation dies.

Alexander Pope 1688–1744: *The Rape of the Lock* (1714)

28 For 18 years he *started the day* by reading a French novel (in preparation for his history of them) an act so unnatural to man as to amount almost to genius.

Stephen Potter 1900–69: of the critic G. E. B. Saintsbury; *The Muse in Chains* (1937)

29 GLAND: I would say it's somehow redolent, and full of vitality.
HILDA: Well, I would say it's got about as much life in it as a potted shrimp.
GLAND: Well, I think we're probably both trying to say the same thing in different words.

Henry Reed 1914–86: *The Primal Scene, as it were* (1958 radio play)

30 Let my people go!
at a viewing of Exodus

Mort Sahl 1926– : attributed, 1961; Nigel Rees *Cassell Dictionary of Humorous Quotations* (1999)

31 Last year I gave several lectures on 'Intelligence and the Appreciation of Music Among Animals'. Today I am going to speak to you about 'Intelligence and the Appreciation of Music Among Critics'. The subject is very similar.

Erik Satie 1866–1925: Nat Shapiro (ed.) *An Encyclopedia of Quotations about Music* (1978)

32 Criticism is not only medicinally salutary: it has positive popular attractions in its cruelty, its gladiatorship, and the gratification given to envy by its attacks on the great, and to enthusiasm by its praises.

George Bernard Shaw 1856–1950: preface to *Plays Unpleasant* (1898)

33 Never pay any attention to what critics say . . . A statue has never been set up in honour of a critic!

Jean Sibelius 1865–1957: Bengt de Törne *Sibelius: A Close-Up* (1937)

34 I never read a book before reviewing it; it prejudices a man so.

Sydney Smith 1771–1845: H. Pearson *The Smith of Smiths* (1934)

35 As learned commentators view
In Homer more than Homer knew.

Jonathan Swift 1667–1745: 'On Poetry' (1733)

John Churton Collins, a rival of Edmund Gosse, launched a bitter critical attack on him. When Gosse took tea with Tennyson he found an ally who defined Collins as:

36 A louse in the locks of literature.

Alfred, Lord Tennyson 1809–92: Evan Charteris *Life and Letters of Sir Edmund Gosse* (1931)

37 My dear Sir: I have read your play. Oh, my dear Sir!
Yours faithfully.
   rejecting a play

Herbert Beerbohm Tree 1852–1917:
Peter Hay *Theatrical Anecdotes* (1987)

38 A critic is a man who knows the way but can't drive the
car.

Kenneth Tynan 1927–80: in *New
York Times Magazine* 9 January 1966

39 The original Greek is of great use in elucidating
Browning's translation of the *Agamemnon*.

Robert Yelverton Tyrrell
1844–1914: habitual remark to
students; Ulick O'Connor *Oliver St
John Gogarty* (1964)

40 Critics search for ages for the wrong word which, to give
them credit, they eventually find.

Peter Ustinov 1921– : Ned Sherrin
Cutting Edge (1984)

41 She also writes with the authority and easy confidence of
someone who knows that she is very well known indeed to
those few who know her.

Gore Vidal 1925– : of Midge Decter;
Pink Triangle and Yellow Star (1984)

*Norman Mailer, annoyed at Vidal's literary style of criticism, hit
him over the head with a glass tumbler:*
42 Ah, Mailer is, as usual, lost for words.

Gore Vidal 1925– : attributed; in
Guardian 27 February 1999

43 WILDE: I shall always regard you as the best critic of my
   plays.
TREE: But I have never criticized your plays.
WILDE: That's why.

Oscar Wilde 1854–1900:
conversation with Beerbohm Tree
after the first-night success of *A
Woman of No Importance*; Hesketh
Pearson *Beerbohm Tree* (1956)

44 One must have a heart of stone to read the death of Little
Nell without laughing.

Oscar Wilde 1854–1900: Ada
Leverson *Letters to the Sphinx* (1930)

Dance

1 I made the little buggers hop.

Thomas Beecham 1879–1961: on
conducting the Diaghilev Ballet;
attributed

2 We are told that her supporting company are all relations,
and I dare say they do better than yours or mine would
under the circumstances.
   *of Carmen Armaya's Spanish Gypsy Dancers at the Prince's
Theatre*

Caryl Brahms 1901–82: in *Evening
Standard* 1948

The ballet designer Benois:
3 Benois . . . If 'e come.

Caryl Brahms 1901–82 and **S. J.
Simon** 1904–48: *A Bullet in the Ballet*
(1937)

4 Will you, won't you, will you, won't you, will you join the
dance?

Lewis Carroll 1832–98: *Alice's
Adventures in Wonderland* (1865)

5 Though no one ever could be keener
Than little Nina
On quite a number
Of very eligible men who did the Rhumba
When they proposed to her she simply left them flat.
She said that love should be impulsive
But not compulsive
And syncopation

Noël Coward 1899–1973: 'Nina'
(1945)

Has a discouraging effect on procreation
And that she'd rather read a book—and that was that!

6 We simply can't give roasted swans to the public this
season.
*forbidding dancers at the English National Ballet booked to
appear in* Swan Lake *to acquire a suntan*

Derek Deane 1953- : in *Daily
Telegraph* 23 August 1997 'They Said
It'

7 Do you want the whole countryside to be laughing at
us?—women of our years?—mature women, *dancing*?

Brian Friel 1929- : *Dancing at
Lughnasa* (1990)

8 Stately as a galleon, I sail across the floor,
Doing the Military Two-step, as in the days of yore . . .
So gay the band,
So giddy the sight,
Full evening dress is a must,
But the zest goes out of a beautiful waltz
When you dance it bust to bust.

Joyce Grenfell 1910-79: 'Stately as a
Galleon' (1978)

9 Miles of cornfields, and ballet in the evening.

Alan Hackney: of Russia; *Private Life*
(1958) (later filmed as *I'm All Right
Jack*, 1959)

10 No. You see there are portions of the human anatomy
which would keep swinging after the music had finished.
*reply to question on whether the fashion for nudity would
extend to dance*

Robert Helpmann 1909-86:
Elizabeth Salter *Helpmann* (1978)

11 Cheek to Cheek
Toes to Toes
Here's a dance you can do on a dime
Knees to Knees
Nose to Nose
Slowly move, and you're doin' 'The Slime'.

Jerry Leiber 1933- : 'The Slime'
(1942)

12 He waltzes like a Protestant curate.

Kate O'Brien 1897-1974: *The Last of
Summer* (1943)

13 Everyone else at the table had got up to dance, except him
and me. There I was, trapped. Trapped like a trap in a
trap.

Dorothy Parker 1893-1967: *After
Such Pleasures* (1933)

14 I wish I could shimmy like my sister Kate,
She shivers like the jelly on a plate.

Armand J. Piron: 'Shimmy like Kate'
(1919)

15 If the Louvre custodian can,
If the Guard Republican can,
If Van Gogh and Matisse and Cézanne can,
Baby, you can can-can too . . .
Lovely Duse in Milan can,
Lucien Guitry and Réjane can,
Sarah Bernhardt upon a divan can,
Baby, you can can-can too.

Cole Porter 1891-1964: 'Can-Can'
(1953)

16 [Dancing is] a perpendicular expression of a horizontal
desire.

George Bernard Shaw 1856-1950:
in *New Statesman* 23 March 1962

17 On the church gate a hand-painted notice with two
spelling mistakes announced that owing to the welcome
presence of the Redemptorist Fathers in the town there
would be no dance on Sunday.

Honor Tracy 1915- : *Mind You, I've
Said Nothing* (1953)

Death See also Epitaphs, Last Words, Murder

1 It's not that I'm afraid to die. I just don't want to be there when it happens.

Woody Allen 1935– : *Death* (1975)

2 I don't want to achieve immortality through my work . . . I want to achieve it through not dying.

Woody Allen 1935– : Eric Lax *Woody Allen and his Comedy* (1975)

3 Death has got something to be said for it:
There's no need to get out of bed for it;
Wherever you may be,
They bring it to you, free.

Kingsley Amis 1922–95: 'Delivery Guaranteed' (1979)

4 Regret to inform you Hand that rocked the cradle kicked the bucket.

Anonymous: reported telegram; in *Ned Sherrin in his Anecdotage* (1993)

5 [Death is] nature's way of telling you to slow down.

Anonymous: American life insurance proverb, in *Newsweek* 25 April 1960

on spiritualism:
6 I always knew the living talked rot, but it's nothing to the rot the dead talk.

Margot Asquith 1864–1945: Chips Channon diary, 20 December 1937

7 We met . . . Dr Hall in such very deep mourning that either his mother, his wife, or himself must be dead.

Jane Austen 1775–1817: letter to Cassandra Austen, 17 May 1799

8 Even death is unreliable: instead of zero it may be some ghastly hallucination, such as the square root of minus one.

Samuel Beckett 1906–89: attributed

9 When I came back to Dublin, I was courtmartialled in my absence and sentenced to death in my absence, so I said they could shoot me in my absence.

Brendan Behan 1923–64: *Hostage* (1958)

10 Lord Finchley tried to mend the Electric Light
Himself. It struck him dead: And serve him right!
It is the business of the wealthy man
To give employment to the artisan.

Hilaire Belloc 1870–1953: 'Lord Finchley' (1911)

11 When I am dead, I hope it may be said:
'His sins were scarlet, but his books were read.'

Hilaire Belloc 1870–1953: 'On His Books' (1923)

12 What I like about Clive
Is that he is no longer alive.
There is a great deal to be said
For being dead.

Edmund Clerihew Bentley 1875–1956: 'Clive' (1905)

13 Thou shalt not kill; but need'st not strive
Officiously to keep alive.

Arthur Hugh Clough 1819–61: 'The Latest Decalogue' (1862)

14 Swans sing before they die: 'twere no bad thing
Should certain persons die before they sing.

Samuel Taylor Coleridge 1772–1834: 'On a Volunteer Singer' (1834)

15 The only thing that really saddens me over my demise is that I shall not be here to read the nonsense that will be written about me . . . There will be lists of apocryphal jokes I never made and gleeful misquotations of words I never said. *What* a pity I shan't be here to enjoy them!

Noël Coward 1899–1973: diary, 19 March 1955

16 I'm amazed he was such a good shot.
on being told that his accountant had blown his brains out

Noël Coward 1899–1973: in *Ned Sherrin's Theatrical Anecdotes* (1991)

17 I read the *Times* and if my name is not in the obits I proceed to enjoy the day.

Noël Coward 1899–1973: attributed

before his death, Lord Curzon had informed his second wife of his arrangements for her burial in the family vault at Kedleston, when he 'placing his hand on one of the niches, said "This, Gracie dearest, is reserved for you."' In fact he had already placed in the niche 'a large Foreign Office envelope on which he had scrawled in blue pencil':

18 Reserved for the second Lady Curzon.

Lord Curzon 1859–1925: Harold Nicolson diary, 13 January 1934

19 He'd make a lovely corpse.

Charles Dickens 1812–70: *Martin Chuzzlewit* (1844)

20 Take away that emblem of mortality.
   on being offered an air cushion to sit on, 1881

Benjamin Disraeli 1804–81: Robert Blake *Disraeli* (1966)

21 When I die I want to decompose in a barrel of porter and have it served in all the pubs in Dublin. I wonder would they know it was me?

J. P. Donleavy 1926– : *Ginger Man* (1955)

22 In this world nothing can be said to be certain, except death and taxes.

Benjamin Franklin 1706–90: letter to Jean Baptiste Le Roy, 13 November 1789

23 Bombazine would have shown a deeper sense of her loss.

Elizabeth Gaskell 1810–65: *Cranford* (1853)

24 He makes a very handsome corpse and becomes his coffin prodigiously.

Oliver Goldsmith 1730–74: *The Good-Natured Man* (1768)

25 The babe with a cry brief and dismal,
   Fell into the water baptismal;
   Ere they gathered its plight,
   It had sunk out of sight,
   For the depth of the font was abysmal.

Edward Gorey 1925– : *The Listing Attic* (1954)

26 'There's been an accident,' they said,
   'Your servant's cut in half; he's dead!'
   'Indeed!' said Mr Jones, 'and please,
   Send me the half that's got my keys.'

Harry Graham 1874–1936: 'Mr Jones' (1899)

27 Billy, in one of his nice new sashes,
   Fell in the fire and was burnt to ashes;
   Now, although the room grows chilly,
   I haven't the heart to poke poor Billy.

Harry Graham 1874–1936: 'Tender-Heartedness' (1899)

28 The best of us being unfit to die, what an inexpressible absurdity to put the worst to death!

Nathaniel Hawthorne 1804–64: diary, 13 October 1851

during his last illness:
29 If Mr Selwyn calls again, show him up: if I am alive I shall be delighted to see him; and if I am dead he would like to see me.

Lord Holland 1705–74: J. H. Jesse *George Selwyn and his Contemporaries* (1844)

30 His death, which happened in his berth,
   At forty-odd befell:
   They went and told the sexton, and
   The sexton tolled the bell.

Thomas Hood 1799–1845: 'Faithless Sally Brown' (1826)

31 I still go up my 44 stairs two at a time, but that is in hopes of dropping dead at the top.

A. E. Housman 1859–1936: letter to Laurence Housman, 9 June 1935

32 At his funeral in Omaha he filled the church to capacity. He was a draw right to the finish.
   after the death of the boxer Vince Foster in 1949

Jack Hurley: Jonathon Green and Don Atyeo (eds.) *The Book of Sports Quotes* (1979)

33 But there, everything has its drawbacks, as the man said when his mother-in-law died, and they came down upon him for the funeral expenses.

Jerome K. Jerome 1859–1927: *Three Men in a Boat* (1889)

34 Depend upon it, Sir, when a man knows he is to be hanged in a fortnight, it concentrates his mind wonderfully.

Samuel Johnson 1709–84: James Boswell *Life of Samuel Johnson* (1791) 19 September 1777

ex-President Eisenhower's death prevented her photograph appearing on the cover of Newsweek:
35 Fourteen heart attacks and he had to die in my week. In MY week.

Janis Joplin 1943–70: in *New Musical Express* 12 April 1969

on how he would kill himself:
36 With kindness.

George S. Kaufman 1889–1961: Howard Teichmann *George S. Kaufman* (1973)

37 I detest life-insurance agents; they always argue that I shall some day die, which is not so.

Stephen Leacock 1869–1944: *Literary Lapses* (1910)

38 Death is the most convenient time to tax rich people.

David Lloyd George 1863–1945: in *Lord Riddell's Intimate Diary of the Peace Conference and After, 1918–23* (1933)

39 Alas! Lord and Lady Dalhousie are dead, and buried at last,
Which causes many people to feel a little downcast.

William McGonagall c.1825–1902: 'The Death of Lord and Lady Dalhousie'

40 Beautiful Railway Bridge of the Silv'ry Tay!
Alas, I am very sorry to say
That ninety lives have been taken away
On the last Sabbath day of 1879,
Which will be remembered for a very long time.

William McGonagall c.1825–1902: 'The Tay Bridge Disaster'

41 There is nothing like a morning funeral for sharpening the appetite for lunch.

Arthur Marshall 1910–89: *Life's Rich Pageant* (1984)

42 Either he's dead, or my watch has stopped.

Groucho Marx 1895–1977: in *A Day at the Races* (1937 film; script by Robert Pirosh, George Seaton, and George Oppenheimer)

43 BLUEBOTTLE: You rotten swines. I told you I'd be deaded.

Spike Milligan 1918– : *The Hastings Flyer* in *The Goon Show* (BBC radio series) 3 January 1956

44 Death and taxes and childbirth! There's never any convenient time for any of them.

Margaret Mitchell 1900–49: *Gone with the Wind* (1936)

45 V. hard on my poor old dad that he died too soon—if murder had been allowed when he was in his prime our home would have been like the last act of *Othello* almost daily.

Nancy Mitford 1904–73: letter 17 December 1969

46 I have nothing against undertakers personally. It's just that I wouldn't want one to bury my sister.

Jessica Mitford 1917–96: in *Saturday Review* 1 February 1964

47 Jimmy Hoffa's most valuable contribution to the American labour movement came at the moment he stopped breathing—on July 30th, 1975.

Don E. Moldea: *The Hoffa Wars* (1978)

48 One dies only once, and it's for such a long time!

Molière 1622–73: *Le Dépit amoureux* (performed 1656, published 1662)

on his deathbed, asked by an acquaintance how he was:
49 Hovering between wife and death.

James Montgomery: Ulick O'Connor *Oliver St John Gogarty* (1964)

during the Boxer rising it was erroneously reported that those besieged in the Legation quarter of Peking, including the Times *correspondent Dr Morrison, had been massacred. Morrison cabled the paper:*
50 Have just read obituary in the Times. Kindly adjust pay to suit.

George Ernest Morrison 1862–1920: Claud Cockburn *In Time of Trouble* (1956); attributed

51 Drink and dance and laugh and lie
Love, the reeling midnight through
For tomorrow we shall die!
(But, alas, we never do.)

Dorothy Parker 1893–1967: 'The Flaw in Paganism' (1937)

on being told by Robert Benchley that Calvin Coolidge had died:
52 DOROTHY PARKER: How can they tell?
ROBERT BENCHLEY: He had an erection.

Dorothy Parker 1893–1967: Ned Sherrin in *The Listener* 8 January 1987; Benchley's final remark vouched for by his grandson Peter on the authority of Benchley's widow.

53 Guns aren't lawful;
Nooses give;
Gas smells awful;
You might as well live.

Dorothy Parker 1893–1967: 'Résumé' (1937)

54 Here am I, dying of a hundred good symptoms.

Alexander Pope 1688–1744: to George, Lord Lyttelton, 15 May 1744

55 Not louder shrieks to pitying heav'n are cast,
When husbands or when lapdogs breathe their last.

Alexander Pope 1688–1744: *The Rape of the Lock* (1714)

56 But thousands die, without or this or that,
Die, and endow a college, or a cat.

Alexander Pope 1688–1744: *Epistles to Several Persons* 'To Lord Bathurst' (1733)

57 Once you're dead, you're made for life.

Jimi Hendrix 1942–70: c.1968, attributed; Nigel Rees *Cassell Dictionary of Humorous Quotations* (1999)

58 [Memorial services are the] cocktail parties of the geriatric set.

Ralph Richardson 1902–83: Ruth Dudley Edwards *Harold Macmillan* (1983)

59 The cemetery is a sort of Mayfair of the dead, the most expensive real estate in Buenos Aires.
   of the Recoleta Cemetery in Buenos Aires

Robert Robinson 1927– : in *The Times* 22 July 1978

the aged President of Magdalen was told of a Fellow's suicide by two colleagues anxious that the news would distress him:
60 Don't tell me. Let me guess.

Martin Routh 1755–1854: Dacre Balsdon *Oxford Life* (1957)

61 Waldo is one of those people who would be enormously improved by death.

Saki 1870–1916: *Beasts and Super-Beasts* (1914)

62 Ain't it grand to be blooming well dead?

Leslie Sarony 1897–1985: title of song (1932)

63 The thought of death has now become a part of my life. I read the obituaries every day just for the satisfaction of not seeing my name there.

Neil Simon 1927– : *Last of the Red Hot Lovers* (1970)

64 Well, it only proves what they always say—give the public something they want to see, and they'll come out for it.
on the crowds attending the funeral of the movie tycoon Harry Cohn, 2 March 1958

Red Skelton 1913– : attributed

65 Death is always a great pity of course but it's not as though the alternative were immortality.

Tom Stoppard 1937– : *Jumpers* (rev. ed. 1986)

66 Early to rise and early to bed makes a male healthy and wealthy and dead.

James Thurber 1894–1961: 'The Shrike and the Chipmunks'; in *New Yorker* 18 February 1939

67 He was just teaching me my death duties.
on her deathbed, having been visited by her solicitor to put her affairs in order

Lady Tree 1863–1937: in *Ned Sherrin in his Anecdotage* (1993)

68 The report of my death was an exaggeration.
usually quoted as, 'Reports of my death have been greatly exaggerated'

Mark Twain 1835–1910: in *New York Journal* 2 June 1897

69 I refused to attend his funeral, but I wrote a very nice letter explaining that I approved of it.

Mark Twain 1835–1910: on hearing of the death of a corrupt politician; James Munson (ed.) *The Sayings of Mark Twain* (1992)

of Truman Capote's death:
70 Good career move.

Gore Vidal 1925– : attributed

71 You're here to stay until the rustle in your dying throat relieves you!

H. M. Walker: addressed to Laurel and Hardy in *Beau Hunks* (1931 film; re-named *Beau Chumps* for British audiences)

72 Just think who we'd have been seen dead with!
on discovery that her name, with Noël Coward's, had been on the Nazi blacklist for arrest and probable execution

Rebecca West 1892–1983: postcard to Noël Coward, 1945

at the mention of a huge fee for a surgical operation:
73 Ah, well, then, I suppose that I shall have to die beyond my means.

Oscar Wilde 1854–1900: R. H. Sherard *Life of Oscar Wilde* (1906)

of the wallpaper in the room where he was dying:
74 One of us must go.

Oscar Wilde 1854–1900: attributed, probably apocryphal

Debt See also **Money, Poverty**

1 Cohen owes me ninety-seven dollars.

Irving Berlin 1888–1989: song-title (1913)

on Allied war debts:
2 They hired the money, didn't they?

Calvin Coolidge 1872–1933: John H. McKee *Coolidge: Wit and Wisdom* (1933)

3 Any further letters and I shall remove my overdraft.
telegram, c.1959, to his bankers, who had become alarmed at his expensive undergraduate lifestyle

Bobby Corbett 1940–99: in his obituary, *Daily Telegraph* 13 March 1999

4 My feet want to dance in the sun.
My head wants to rest in the shade.
The Lord says, 'Go out and have fun'.
But the Landlord says,
'Your rent ain't paid.'

E. Y. Harburg 1898–1981: 'Necessity' (1947)

5 [My father] taught me two things about bills; always query them and never pay till you have no alternative.

Miles Kington 1941– : *Welcome to Kington* (1989)

6 If the spoken word is repeated often enough, it is eventually written and thus made permanent . . . Many a decent man who has written a bad cheque knows the truth of that.

Flann O'Brien 1911–66: *Myles Away from Dublin* (1990)

7 I feel these days like a very large flamingo. No matter what way I turn, there is always a very large bill.

Joseph O'Connor 1963– : *The Secret World of the Irish Male* (1994)

8 The National Debt is a very Good Thing and it would be dangerous to pay it off, for fear of Political Economy.

W. C. Sellar 1898–1951 and **R. J. Yeatman** 1898–1968: *1066 and All That* (1930)

9 When creditors press you for debts that you cannot pay . . . remember that the position of a destitute person is impregnable: the County Court judge will not commit you under a judgment summons unless the creditor can prove that you have the means to pay. Maintain an insouciant dignity, and announce your condition frankly.

George Bernard Shaw 1856–1950: letter to Kerree Collins, 1938

10 One must have some sort of occupation nowadays. If I hadn't my debts I shouldn't have anything to think about.

Oscar Wilde 1854–1900: *A Woman of No Importance* (1893)

Democracy   See also **Government, Politics**

1 Elections are won by men and women chiefly because most people vote against somebody rather than for somebody.

Franklin P. Adams 1881–1960: *Nods and Becks* (1944)

2 If the Archangel Gabriel had stood with the name of Winston Churchill, Ken would still have won.
of Ken Livingstone's candidacy as Mayor of London

Jeffrey Archer 1940– : in *Independent on Sunday* 7 May 2000

3 Democracy means government by discussion, but it is only effective if you can stop people talking.

Clement Attlee 1883–1967: speech at Oxford, 14 June 1957

4 The worst thing I can say about democracy is that it has tolerated the Right Honourable Gentleman [Neville Chamberlain] for four and a half years.

Aneurin Bevan 1897–1960: speech in the House of Commons 23 July 1929

5 A majority is always the best repartee.

Benjamin Disraeli 1804–81: *Tancred* (1847)

6 Hell, I never vote *for* anybody. I always vote *against*.

W. C. Fields 1880–1946: Robert Lewis Taylor *W. C. Fields* (1950)

7 Democracy is the name we give the people whenever we need them.

Robert, Marquis de Flers 1872–1927 and **Armand de Caillavet** 1869–1915: *L'habit vert* (1913)

8 I always voted at my party's call,
And I never thought of thinking for myself at all.

W. S. Gilbert 1836–1911: *HMS Pinafore* (1878)

on John F. Kennedy's electoral victory:
9 I must say the Senator's victory in Wisconsin was a triumph for democracy. It proves that a millionaire has just as good a chance as anybody else.

Bob Hope 1903– : TV programme (1960); William Robert Faith *Bob Hope* (1983)

10 Democracy is the theory that the common people know what they want, and deserve to get it good and hard.

H. L. Mencken 1880–1956: *A Little Book in C major* (1916)

11 Under democracy one party always devotes its energies to trying to prove that the other party is unfit to rule—and both commonly succeed and are right.

H. L. Mencken 1880–1956: *Minority Report* (1956)

12 Every government is a parliament of whores. The trouble is, in a democracy the whores are us.

P. J. O'Rourke 1947– : *Parliament of Whores* (1991)

13 All animals are equal but some animals are more equal than others.

George Orwell 1903–50: *Animal Farm* (1945)

on the death of a supporter of Proportional Representation:
14 He has joined what even he would admit to be the majority.

John Sparrow 1906–92: J. A. Gere and John Sparrow (eds.) *Geoffrey Madan's Notebooks* (1981)

15 It's not the voting that's democracy, it's the counting.

Tom Stoppard 1937– : *Jumpers* (1972)

16 Democracy is the recurrent suspicion that more than half of the people are right more than half of the time.

E. B. White 1899–1985: in *New Yorker* 3 July 1944

17 Democracy means simply the bludgeoning of the people by the people for the people.

Oscar Wilde 1854–1900: *Sebastian Melmoth* (1891)

a voter canvassed by Wilkes had declared that he would sooner vote for the devil:
18 And if your friend is not standing?

John Wilkes 1727–97: Raymond Postgate 'That Devil Wilkes' (1956 rev. ed.)

Description

1 Though I yield to no one in my admiration for Mr Coolidge, I do wish he did not look as if he had been weaned on a pickle.

Anonymous: remark recorded in Alice Roosevelt Longworth *Crowded Hours* (1933)

2 Diana Manners has no heart but her brains are in the right place.

Cyril Asquith 1890–1954: J. A. Gere and John Sparrow (eds.) *Geoffrey Madan's Notebooks* (1981)

after a party given by Dorothy Parker:
3 The less I behave like Whistler's Mother the night before, the more I look like her the morning after.

Tallulah Bankhead 1903–68: R. E. Drennan *Wit's End* (1973)

4 Housman's cap, like a damp bun or pad of waste which engine-drivers clean their hands on.

A. C. Benson 1862–1925: J. A. Gere and John Sparrow (eds.) *Geoffrey Madan's Notebooks* (1981)

5 His smile bathed us like warm custard.

Basil Boothroyd 1910–88: *Let's Move House* (1977)

6 A high altar on the move.
of Edith Sitwell

Elizabeth Bowen 1899–1973: V. Glendinning *Edith Sitwell* (1981)

7 Damn description, it is always disgusting.

Lord Byron 1788–1824: letter 6 August 1809

8 What can you do with a man who looks like a female llama surprised when bathing?
of Charles de Gaulle

Winston Churchill 1874–1965: in conversation, c.1944; David Fraser Alanbrooke (1982)

9 The effect is of a Womble taking Cerberus for a walk.
of Roy Hattersley and his dog Buster

Will Cohn: interview in *Daily Telegraph* 19 September 1998

10 Two bursts in a sofa.
of a lady spectator at Wimbledon with pronouncedly hirsute armpits

Bobby Corbett 1940–99: in his obituary, *Daily Telegraph* 13 March 1999

11 The Henry Fondas lay on the evening like a damp mackintosh.

Noël Coward 1899–1973: diary, 8 May 1960

12 Like the silver plate on a coffin.
describing Robert Peel's smile

John Philpot Curran 1750–1817: quoted by Daniel O'Connell, House of Commons 26 February 1835

13 A day away from Tallulah is like a month in the country.

Howard Dietz 1896–1983: *Dancing in the Dark* (1974)

14 The ministers [on the Treasury Bench] reminded me of one of those marine landscapes not very uncommon on the coast of South America. You behold a range of exhausted volcanoes. Not a flame flickers on a single pallid crest.

Benjamin Disraeli 1804–81: speech at Manchester, 3 April 1872

15 Monsignor was forty-four then, and bustling—a trifle too stout for symmetry, with hair the colour of spun gold, and a brilliant, enveloping personality. When he came into a room clad in his full purple regalia from thatch to toe, he resembled a Turner sunset.

F. Scott Fitzgerald 1896–1940: *This Side of Paradise* (1921)

16 You are so graceful, have you wings?
You have a faceful of nice things
You have no speaking voice, dear . . .
With every word it sings.

Lorenz Hart 1895–1943: 'Thou Swell' (1927)

17 *Minder* . . . has been particularly nutritious lately, with George Cole's portrayal of Arthur Daley attaining such depths of seediness that a flock of starlings could feed off him.

Clive James 1939– : in *Observer* 28 February 1982

18 A man who so much resembled a Baked Alaska—sweet, warm and gungy on the outside, hard and cold within.
of C. P. Snow

Francis King 1923– : *Yesterday Came Suddenly* (1993)

19 His appearance with his large features and rich mane of hair suggested the attempt of some archaic sculptor only acquainted with sheep to achieve a lion by hearsay.

Osbert Lancaster 1908–80: *All Done From Memory* (1953)

20 Springing from the grassroots of the country clubs of America.
of Wendell Willkie

Alice Roosevelt Longworth 1884–1980: Michael Teague *Mrs L* (1981)

21 [He looks like] an explosion in a pubic hair factory.
of Paul Johnson

Jonathan Miller 1934– : Alan Watkins *Brief Lives* (1982)

22 Her face showed the kind of ferocious disbelief with which Goneril must have taken the news that her difficult old father King Lear had decided to retire and move in with her.

Frank Muir 1920–98: *The Walpole Orange* (1993)

23 Rudyard Kipling's eyebrows are very odd indeed! They curl up black and furious like the moustache of a Neapolitan tenor.

Harold Nicolson 1886–1968: diary 8 January 1930

24 The beach was almost deserted. The tide was out. Turnstones were turning stones. Oystercatchers were catching oysters. In the marshalling yards, shunting engines were shunting and marshalling.

David Nobbs 1935– : *Going Gently* (2000)

25 The place smelt of apple-scented air freshener, not like apples, but like a committee's idea of what apples smell like.

Joseph O'Connor 1963– : *Cowboys and Indians* (1992)

26 Buckingham Palace looked a vast doll's house that some bullying skinhead big brother had kicked down the Mall.

Joseph O'Connor 1963– : *Cowboys and Indians* (1992)

27 The butler who answered the door—and he took his time about it—looked like a Road Company Robert Morley at the Paper Mill Playhouse.

S. J. Perelman 1904–79: 'Call Me Monty and Grovel Freely'

28 A rose-red sissy half as old as time.

William Plomer 1903–73: 'Playboy of the Demi-World: 1938' (1945)

29 The Cavaliers (Wrong but Wromantic) and the Roundheads (Right but Repulsive).

W. C. Sellar 1898–1951 and **R. J. Yeatman** 1898–1968: *1066 and All That* (1930)

30 Hotter than Uncle Bud's pants on lesbian mud-wrestling night.

Mark Steyn: in *Spectator* 2 October 1999

31 'It's no good your saying a *word*,' his face tells us, 'I will *not* be eaten with a plastic spoon.'
    of Stanley Parker's resemblance to strawberry ice-cream

Kenneth Tynan 1927–80: in *Cherwell* 14 June 1948

32 We also saw Haworth, which surpassed even my appetite for gloomy churchyards. Glutted, is the only word for it.

Sylvia Townsend Warner 1893–1978: letter, 26 September 1935

33 I don't think I have ever seen a Silver Band so nonplussed. It was as though a bevy of expectant wolves had overtaken a sleigh and found no Russian peasant on board.

P. G. Wodehouse 1881–1975: *Uncle Dynamite* (1948)

34 I turned to Aunt Agatha, whose demeanour was now rather like that of one who, picking daisies on the railway, has just caught the down express in the small of the back.

P. G. Wodehouse 1881–1975: *The Inimitable Jeeves* (1923)

35 She fitted into my biggest armchair as if it had been built round her by someone who knew they were wearing armchairs tight about the hips that season.

P. G. Wodehouse 1881–1975: *My Man Jeeves* (1919)

36 Roderick Spode? Big chap with a small moustache and the sort of eye that can open an oyster at sixty paces?

P. G. Wodehouse 1881–1975: *The Code of the Woosters* (1938)

Despair See **Hope and Despair**

Diaries

1 Now that I am finishing the damned thing I realise that diary-writing isn't wholly good for one, that too much of it leads to living for one's diary instead of living for the fun of living as ordinary people do.

James Agate 1877–1947: letter, 7 December 1946

2 A page of my Journal is like a cake of portable soup. A little may be diffused into a considerable portion.

James Boswell 1740–95: *Journal of a Tour to the Hebrides* (1785)

3 What is more dull than a discreet diary? One might just as well have a discreet soul.

Chips Channon 1897–1958: diary, 26 July 1935

4 I regret, dear journal, this unworthy, sordid preoccupation with money, but I have worked hard all my life, I am £15,000 overdrawn in London, I am fifty-five years old and I fully intend to end my curious days in as much comfort, peace and luxury as I can get.

Noël Coward 1899–1973: diary, 15 April 1955

5 It is a fair proposition, I think, that the diaries of men who enjoy their own nudity ought not to be published unless they are as interesting as Pepys. Otherwise it is really too distressing for the observer.

Harold Laski 1893–1950: letter to Oliver Wendell Holmes, 23 October 1927

6 To write a diary every day is like returning to one's own vomit.

Enoch Powell 1912–98: interview in *Sunday Times* 6 November 1977

7 I have decided to keep a full journal, in the hope that my life will perhaps seem more interesting when it is written down.

Sue Townsend 1946– : *Adrian Mole: The Wilderness Years* (1993)

8 I always say, keep a diary and some day it'll keep you.

Mae West 1892–1980: *Every Day's a Holiday* (1937 film)

9 I never travel without my diary. One should always have something sensational to read in the train.

Oscar Wilde 1854–1900: *The Importance of Being Earnest* (1895)

Dictionaries

1 Big dictionaries are nothing but storerooms with infrequently visited and dusty corners.

Richard W. Bailey 1939– : *Images of English* (1991)

2 They are strange beings, these lexicographers.

John Brown 1810–82: *Horae Subsecivae* (rev. ed. 1884)

3 Like Webster's Dictionary, we're Morocco bound.

Johnny Burke 1908–64: *The Road to Morocco* (1942 film), title song

4 I hope you're not getting that deplorable habit of picking phrases out of newspapers and using them without knowing what they mean. A good thing to do is to read two pages of the *New Oxford Dictionary* every day. You get the exact derivations of all words and their differing shades of meaning at different periods. An excellent habit.

Henry Cockburn: advice to his son Claud; Claud Cockburn *In Time of Trouble* (1956)

5 The greatest masterpiece in literature is only a dictionary out of order.

Jean Cocteau 1889–1963: attributed

6 The Dictionary has not attempted to rival some of its predecessors in deliberate humour . . . Such rare occasions for a smile as may be found in it are unintentional.

W. A. Craigie 1867–1967: of the *New English Dictionary*; in *The Periodical* 15 February 1928

7 Short dictionaries should be improved because they are intended for people who actually need help.

William Empson 1906–84: attributed

8 *Lexicographer*. A writer of dictionaries, a harmless drudge.

Samuel Johnson 1709–84: *A Dictionary of the English Language* (1755)

9 I'm too weary going from one word to another in this heavy dictionary which leads me on a wild goose chase from this word to that word and all because the people who wrote the dictionary don't want the likes of me to know anything.

Frank McCourt 1930– : *Angela's Ashes* (1996)

of his coinage of the phrase 'life's rich pageant':

10 As far as I know, I didn't borrow the words from anywhere else and no less a body than the compilers of *The Oxford Dictionary of Quotations* have since taken an interest in the matter. They have finally decided that the phrase, such as it is, was my own invention and it is to be credited to me. Let me assure you that this small feather in my cap has not gone, so to speak, to my head.

Arthur Marshall 1910–89: *Life's Rich Pageant* (1984)

11 A bad business, opening dictionaries; a thing I very rarely do. I try to make it a rule never to open my mouth, dictionaries, or hucksters' shops.

Flann O'Brien 1911–66: *The Best of Myles* (1968)

12 I suppose that so long as there are people in the world, they will publish dictionaries defining what is unknown in terms of something equally unknown.

Flann O'Brien 1911–66: *Myles Away from Dublin* (1990)

Henry Liddell (1811–98) and Robert Scott (1811–87) were co-authors of the Greek Lexicon *(1843), Liddell being in the habit of ascribing to his co-author usages which he criticized in his pupils, and which they said that they had culled from the* Lexicon:

13 Two men wrote a lexicon, Liddell and Scott;
Some parts were clever, but some parts were not.
Hear, all ye learned, and read me this riddle,
How the wrong part wrote Scott, and the right part wrote
    Liddell.

Edward Waterfield: L. E. Tanner *Westminster School: A History* (1934)

14 I've been in *Who's Who*, and I know what's what, but it'll be the first time I ever made the dictionary.

Mae West 1892–1980: letter to the RAF, early 1940s, on having an inflatable life jacket named after her

Diplomacy See also **Politics**

1 The Prime Minister rather enjoyed being led up the garden path by the Taoiseach, but she didn't much like the garden when she got there.

Anonymous: unnamed civil servant on negotiations between Margaret Thatcher and Charles Haughey; in *Daily Telegraph* 14 August 1993

on the Council of Europe:

2 If you open that Pandora's Box, you never know what Trojan 'orses will jump out.

Ernest Bevin 1881–1951: Roderick Barclay *Ernest Bevin and the Foreign Office* (1975)

of a meeting with the Russians, when Vyshinsky began 'I have my instructions':

3 Well, I have no instructions other than those which I give myself. Clearly therefore we are not discussing on the same level and I had better turn you over to my deputy.

Ernest Bevin 1881–1951: at the Peace Conference in Paris, 1946; Harold Nicolson *Diaries* (1980)

R. A. Butler had asked whether he and Maisky could use Channon's house in Belgrave Square for a secret meeting:

4 I never thought that the Russian Ambassador would ever cross my threshold; I checked up on the snuff-boxes on my return but did not notice anything missing.

Chips Channon 1897–1958: diary 28 November 1939

5 We exchanged many frank words in our respective languages.

Peter Cook 1937–95: *Beyond the Fringe* (1961 revue)

6 American *diplomacy*. It's like watching somebody trying to do joinery with a chainsaw.

James Hamilton-Paterson 1941– : *Griefwork* (1993)

7 Diplomacy—lying in state.

Oliver Herford 1863–1935: Laurence J. Peter (ed.) *Quotations for Our Time* (1977)

8 There cannot be a crisis next week. My schedule is already full.

Henry Kissinger 1923– : in *New York Times Magazine* 1 June 1969

on the life of a Foreign Secretary:
9 Forever poised between a cliché and an indiscretion.

Harold Macmillan 1894–1986: in *Newsweek* 30 April 1956

On the Hoare-Laval pact:
10 Sam Hoare was certified by his doctors as unfit for public business, and on his way to the sanatorium he stops off in Paris and allows Laval to do him down.

Harold Nicolson 1886–1968: diary 12 December 1935

11 The French are masters of 'the dog ate my homework' school of diplomatic relations.

P. J. O'Rourke 1947– : *Holidays in Hell* (1988)

12 Lord Palmerston, with characteristic levity had once said that only three men in Europe had ever understood [the Schleswig-Holstein question], and of these the Prince Consort was dead, a Danish statesman (unnamed) was in an asylum, and he himself had forgotten it.

Lord Palmerston 1784–1865: R. W. Seton-Watson *Britain in Europe 1789–1914* (1937)

13 I was wisely seen as unsuitable.
admitting he was once rejected by the Diplomatic Corps

Jeremy Paxman 1950– : in *Observer* 2 May 1999 'Sayings of the Week'

14 The chief distinction of a diplomat is that he can say no in such a way that it sounds like yes.

Lester Bowles Pearson 1897–1972: a Canadian Prime Minister's view; Geoffrey Pearson *Seize the Day* (1993)

15 In return for a handsomely bound facsimile of Palestrina's music, the Vicar of God was rewarded with a signed photograph of the Grocer and a gramophone record of himself conducting an orchestra.
of a meeting between the Pope and Edward Heath

Nicholas Shakespeare 1957– : in *The Spectator* 19/26 December 1992

16 There is a story that when Mrs Thatcher first met Gorbachev he gave her a ball-point and she offered him Labour-voting Scotland.

Nicholas Shakespeare 1957– : in *The Spectator* 19/26 December 1992

17 A diplomat these days is nothing but a head-waiter who's allowed to sit down occasionally.

Peter Ustinov 1921– : *Romanoff and Juliet* (1956)

18 An ambassador is an honest man sent to lie abroad for the good of his country.

Henry Wotton 1568–1639: written in the album of Christopher Fleckmore in 1604

Discontent See **Satisfaction and Discontent**

Dogs

1 I look like a young wolf—cuddly in a frightening sort of way.
Buster's view of himself

Roy Hattersley 1932– : *Buster's Diaries* (1998)

2 Dogs who earn their living by appearing in television commercials in which they constantly and aggressively demand meat should remember that in at least one Far Eastern country they *are* meat.

Fran Lebowitz 1946– : *Social Studies* (1981)

of a dog belonging to the headmaster of Eton:

3 Do you recollect the Alington poodle—exactly like a typhoid germ magnified.

George Lyttelton 1883–1962: letter to Rupert Hart-Davis, 11 April 1957

4 A door is what a dog is perpetually on the wrong side of.

Ogden Nash 1902–71: 'A Dog's Best Friend is his Illiteracy' (1953)

the Lindbergh's fierce guard dog, Thor, had shown signs of not caring for Harold Nicolson:

5 By the time you get this I shall either be front-page news or Thor's chum.

Harold Nicolson 1886–1968: letter to his wife Vita Sackville-West, 30 September 1934

6 I think Crab my dog be the sourest-natured dog that lives.

William Shakespeare 1564–1616: *The Two Gentlemen of Verona* (1592–3)

7 That indefatigable and unsavoury engine of pollution, the dog.

John Sparrow 1906–92: letter to *The Times* 30 September 1975

8 The more one gets to know of men, the more one values dogs.

A. Toussenel 1803–85: *L'Esprit des bêtes* (1847); attributed to Mme Roland in the form 'The more I see of men, the more I like dogs'

9 They say a reasonable amount o' fleas is good fer a dog— keeps him from broodin' over bein' a dog, mebbe.

Edward Noyes Westcott 1846–98: *David Harum* (1898)

Doubt See **Certainty and Doubt**

Dreams See **Sleep and Dreams**

Dress See **Fashion and Dress**

Drink See **Food and Drink**

Drugs

1 LSD? Nothing much happened, but I did get the distinct impression that some birds were trying to communicate with me.

W. H. Auden 1907–73: George Plimpton (ed.) *The Writer's Chapbook* (1989)

2 I'll die young, but it's like kissing God.
   on his drug addiction

Lenny Bruce 1925–66: attributed

3 I experimented with marijuana a time or two. And I didn't like it, and I didn't inhale.

Bill Clinton 1946– : in *Washington Post* 30 March 1992

4 Drugs is like getting up and having a cup of tea in the morning.

Noel Gallagher 1967– : radio interview, 28 January 1997

5 In 1979 the way to tell an English gentleman is by the quality of his drugs.

Lord Hesketh 1950– : Alexander Chancellor *Some Times in America* (1999); attributed, perhaps apocryphal

6 Drugs have taught an entire generation of English kids the metric system.

P. J. O'Rourke 1947– : *Modern Manners* (1984, UK ed.)

7 Sure thing, man. I used to be a laboratory myself once.
   on being asked to autograph a fan's school chemistry book

Keith Richards 1943– : in *Independent on Sunday* 7 August 1994

8 It's not because ageing wrinklies have tried to stop people having fun.
   asserting his opposition to the legalization of cannabis

Jack Straw 1946– : on *Breakfast with Frost*, BBC1 TV, 4 January 1998

9 Reality is a crutch for people who can't cope with drugs.

Lily Tomlin 1939- : attributed; Phil Hammond and Michael Mosley *Trust Me (I'm a Doctor)* 1999

10 A drug is neither moral or immoral—it's a chemical compound. The compound itself is not a menace to society until a human being treats it as if consumption bestowed a temporary licence to act like an asshole.

Frank Zappa 1940-93: *The Real Frank Zappa Book* (1989)

Economics See also **Money**

1 No real English gentleman, in his secret soul, was ever sorry for the death of a political economist.

Walter Bagehot 1826-77: *Estimates of some Englishmen and Scotchmen* (1858) 'The First Edinburgh Reviewers'

2 John Stuart Mill,
By a mighty effort of will,
Overcame his natural *bonhomie*
And wrote 'Principles of Political Economy'.

Edmund Clerihew Bentley 1875-1956: 'John Stuart Mill' (1905)

3 I never could make out what those damned dots meant.
as Chancellor, on decimal points

Lord Randolph Churchill 1849-94: W. S. Churchill *Lord Randolph Churchill* (1906)

4 Trickle-down theory—the less than elegant metaphor that if one feeds the horse enough oats, some will pass through to the road for the sparrows.

J. K. Galbraith 1908- : *The Culture of Contentment* (1992)

5 I could seek to ease his pain, but only by giving him an aspirin.
the Governor of the Bank of England on economic problems of the small businessman

Eddie George 1938- : interview on *The Money Programme* BBC2 TV, 28 February 1999

6 Balancing the budget is like going to heaven. Everybody wants to do it, but nobody wants to do what you have to do to get there.

Phil Gramm 1942- : in a television interview, 16 September 1990

7 In '29 when the banks went bust,
Our coins still read 'In God We Trust'.

E. Y. Harburg 1898-1981: 'Federal Reserve' (1965)

8 If economists could manage to get themselves thought of as humble, competent people, on a level with dentists, that would be splendid!

John Maynard Keynes 1883-1946: 'Economic Possibilities for our Grandchildren'; David Howell *Blind Victory* (1986)

9 Political Economy has, quite obviously, turned out to be the Idiot Boy of the Scientific Family; all the more pitiful, as having been so bright at first; put up on a chair to recite by old Dr Adam Smith and Mr Ricardo—and then somehow went wrong.

Stephen Leacock 1869-1944: *The Boy I Left Behind Me* (1947)

10 People don't realize that the Victorian age was simply an interruption in British history . . . It's exciting living on the edge of bankruptcy.

Harold Macmillan 1894-1986: in conversation in 1961; Anthony Sampson *Macmillan* (1967)

11 Expenditure rises to meet income.

C. Northcote Parkinson 1909-93: *The Law and the Profits* (1960)

12 Nothink for nothink 'ere, and precious little for sixpence.

Punch 1841-1992: vol. 57 (1869)

13 Greed—for lack of a better word—is good. Greed is right. Greed works.

Stanley Weiser and **Oliver Stone** 1946- : *Wall Street* (1987 film)

Education   See also **Examinations**

1 I think Patrick plans to wean our child straight on to calculators.

Alan Ayckbourn 1939– : *Sisterly Feelings* (1981)

2 I read Shakespeare and the Bible and I can shoot dice. That's what I call a liberal education.

Tallulah Bankhead 1903–68: attributed

3 Exeter is the second oldest college in Oxford—unless you count lodging houses, in which case it is the fourth.

Eric Arthur Barber 1888–1965: the Rector of Exeter's welcoming speech to undergraduates in 1951

4 I was not unpopular [at school] . . . It is Oxford that has made me insufferable.

Max Beerbohm 1872–1956: *More* (1899) 'Going Back to School'

5 Someone once said, Rumbold, that education is what is left when you have forgotten all you have ever learned. You appear to be trying to circumvent the process by learning as little as possible.

Alan Bennett 1934– : *Forty Years On* (1969)

6 Education with socialists, it's like sex, all right so long as you don't have to pay for it.

Alan Bennett 1934– : *Getting On* (1972)

7 I went to public school, of course. But looking back on it, I think it may have been Borstal.

Alan Bennett 1934– : *Getting On* (1972)

8 Mother Bernard thought that Brother Healy had life easy. Boys were so simple and straightforward. They weren't devious like girls. Brother Healy thought it must be a very easy number just to have little girls in a uniform. They didn't write terrible words on the bicycle shed and beat each other black and blue in the yard.

Maeve Binchy 1940– : *The Glass Lake* (1994)

9 Gentlemen: I have not had your advantages. What poor education I have received has been gained in the University of Life.

Horatio Bottomley 1860–1933: speech at the Oxford Union, 2 December 1920

10 In my day, the principal concerns of university students were sex, smoking dope, rioting and learning. Learning was something you did only when the first three weren't available.

Bill Bryson 1951– : *The Lost Continent* (1989)

of Cambridge University:
11 This place is the Devil, or at least his principal residence, they call it the University, but any other appellation would have suited it much better, for study is the last pursuit of the society; the Master eats, drinks, and sleeps, the Fellows drink, dispute and pun, the employments of the undergraduates you will probably conjecture without my description.

Lord Byron 1788–1824: letter, 23 November 1805

12 I think I should feel considerably less rotten than I do this morning had I not learned all my anatomy from Arthur Mee's *Children's Encyclopaedia*. Never mind Ignatius Loyola, is my view: give a child to Arthur Mee until it is seven years old, and it will be his forever.

Alan Coren 1938– : *Seems Like Old Times* (1989)

13 No academic person is ever voted into the chair until he has reached an age at which he has forgotten the meaning of the word 'irrelevant'.

Francis M. Cornford 1874–1943: *Microcosmographia Academica* (1908)

14 C-l-e-a-n, clean, verb active, to make bright, to scour.
W-i-n, win, d-e-r, der, winder, a casement. When the boy
knows this out of the book, he goes and does it.

Charles Dickens 1812–70: *Nicholas Nickleby* (1839)

15 EDUCATION.—At Mr Wackford Squeers's Academy,
Dotheboys Hall, at the delightful village of Dotheboys, near
Greta Bridge in Yorkshire, Youth are boarded, clothed,
booked, furnished with pocket-money, provided with all
necessaries, instructed in all languages living and dead,
mathematics, orthography, geometry, astronomy,
trigonometry, the use of the globes, algebra, single stick (if
required), writing, arithmetic, fortification, and every
other branch of classical literature. Terms, twenty guineas
per annum. No extras, no vacations, and diet unparalleled.

Charles Dickens 1812–70: *Nicholas Nickleby* (1839)

16 Ev'ry pedagogue
Goes to bed agog at night—
Doing Collegiana . . . .

Dorothy Fields 1905–74: 'Collegiana' (1924)

17 The clever men at Oxford
Know all that there is to be knowed.
But they none of them know one half as much
As intelligent Mr Toad!

Kenneth Grahame 1859–1932: *The Wind in the Willows* (1908)

18 Common to all staff was a conviction that they could have
done better outside education. The teachers believed in a
mysterious world outside the school called 'business'
where money was handed out freely.

Michael Green 1927– : *The Boy Who Shot Down an Airship* (1988)

19 Education in those elementary subjects which are
ordinarily taught to our defenceless children, as reading,
writing, and arithmetic.

A. P. Herbert 1890–1971: *Misleading Cases* (1935)

20 At the University, I saw many men I knew doing courses
only to gratify their parents or, as the phrase went, 'to get
something solid behind them.' There was a moral virtue in
suppressing all real talent; in flying in the face of impulse
and vocation and doing something, instead, which was
completely repugnant. That made parents happy.

Barry Humphries 1934– : *More Please* (1992)

21 Beauty school report
No graduation day for you
Beauty school dropout
Mixed your mid-terms and flunked shampoo.

Jim Jacobs and **Warren Casey**: 'Beauty School Dropout' (1972)

22 [JOHNSON:] I had no notion that I was wrong or irreverent
to my tutor.
[BOSWELL:] That, Sir, was great fortitude of mind.
[JOHNSON:] No, Sir; stark insensibility.

Samuel Johnson 1709–84: James Boswell *Life of Samuel Johnson* (1791) 31 October 1728

23 That state of resentful coma that . . . dons dignify by the
name of research.

Harold Laski 1893–1950: letter to Oliver Wendell Holmes, 10 October 1922

24 Most people tire of a lecture in ten minutes; clever people
can do it in five. Sensible people never go to lectures at all.

Stephen Leacock 1869–1944: *My Discovery of England* (1922)

25 If you are truly serious about preparing your child for the
future, don't teach him to subtract—teach him to deduct.

Fran Lebowitz 1946– : *Social Studies* (1981)

26 Stand firm in your refusal to remain conscious during algebra. In real life, I assure you, there is no such thing as algebra.

Fran Lebowitz 1946– : *Social Studies* (1981)

27 Who walks in the classroom cool and slow?
Who calls his English teacher Daddy-O?

Jerry Leiber 1933– and **Mike Stoller** 1933– : 'Charlie Brown' (1959)

28 One master will hit you if you don't know that Eamon de Valera is the greatest man that ever lived. Another master will hit you if you don't know that Michael Collins was the greatest man that ever lived . . .
    If you ever say anything good about Oliver Cromwell they'll all hit you.

Frank McCourt 1930– : *Angela's Ashes* (1996)

29 At school I never minded the lessons. I just resented having to work terribly hard at playing.

John Mortimer 1923– : *A Voyage Round My Father* (1971)

30 The Socratic method is a game at which only one (the professor) can play.

Ralph Nader 1934– : Joel Seligman *The High Citadel* (1978)

31 It was then that Mr Furriskey surprised and, indeed, delighted his companions, not to mention our two friends, by a little act which at once demonstrated his resource and his generous urge to spread enlightenment. With the end of his costly malacca cane, he cleared away the dead leaves at his feet and drew the outline of three dials or clock faces on the fertile soil . . . How to read the gas-meter, he announced.

Flann O'Brien 1911–66: *At Swim-Two-Birds* (1939)

32 Liberals have invented whole college majors—psychology, sociology, women's studies— to prove that nothing is anybody's fault.

P. J. O'Rourke 1947– : *Give War a Chance* (1992)

33 The schoolteacher is certainly underpaid as a childminder, but ludicrously overpaid as an educator.

John Osborne 1929– : in *Observer* 21 July 1985 'Sayings of the Week'

34 I don't think one 'comes down' from Jimmy's university. According to him, it's not even red brick, but white tile.

John Osborne 1929– : *Look Back in Anger* (1956)

35 Oxford's instinctive hatred of any branch of education which is directly useful, superficially easy, or attractive, which above all has connections with universities younger than itself.

Stephen Potter 1900–69: *The Muse in Chains* (1937)

36 Good gracious, you've got to educate him first. You can't expect a boy to be vicious till he's been to a good school.

Saki 1870–1916: *Reginald in Russia* (1910)

37 For every person who wants to teach there are approximately thirty who don't want to learn—much.

W. C. Sellar 1898–1951 and **R. J. Yeatman** 1898–1968: *And Now All This* (1932) introduction

38 Very nice sort of place, Oxford, I should think, for people that like that sort of place. They teach you to be a gentleman there. In the Polytechnic they teach you to be an engineer or such like.

George Bernard Shaw 1856–1950: *Man and Superman* (1903)

39 He who can, does. He who cannot, teaches.

George Bernard Shaw 1856–1950: *Man and Superman* (1903) 'Maxims: Education'

40 *Educ*: during the holidays from Eton.

Osbert Sitwell 1892–1969: entry in *Who's Who* (1929)

replying to Woodrow Wilson's 'And what in your opinion is the trend of the modern English undergraduate?':

41 Steadily towards drink and women, Mr President.

F. E. Smith 1872–1930: attributed

42 To me education is a leading out of what is already there in the pupil's soul. To Miss Mackay it is a putting in of something that is not there, and that is not what I call education, I call it intrusion.

Muriel Spark 1918– : *The Prime of Miss Jean Brodie* (1961)

43 I am putting old heads on your young shoulders . . . all my pupils are the crème de la crème.

Muriel Spark 1918– : *The Prime of Miss Jean Brodie* (1961)

44 Soap and education are not as sudden as a massacre, but they are more deadly in the long run.

Mark Twain 1835–1910: *A Curious Dream* (1872) 'Facts concerning the Recent Resignation'

45 'We class schools, you see, into four grades: Leading School, First-rate School, Good School, and School. Frankly,' said Mr Levy, 'School is pretty bad.'

Evelyn Waugh 1903–66: *Decline and Fall* (1928)

46 Assistant masters came and went . . . Some liked little boys too little and some too much.

Evelyn Waugh 1903–66: *A Little Learning* (1964)

47 Any one who has been to an English public school will always feel comparatively at home in prison. It is the people brought up in the gay intimacy of the slums, Paul learned, who find prison so soul-destroying.

Evelyn Waugh 1903–66: *Decline and Fall* (1928)

48 MRS CHEVELEY: The higher education of men is what I should like to see. Men need it so sadly.
LADY MARKBY: They do, dear. But I am afraid such a scheme would be quite unpractical. I don't think man has much capacity for development. He has got as far as he can, and that is not far, is it?

Oscar Wilde 1854–1900: *An Ideal Husband* (1895)

49 In England, at any rate, education produces no effect whatsoever. If it did, it would prove a serious danger to the upper classes, and probably lead to acts of violence in Grosvenor Square.

Oscar Wilde 1854–1900: *The Importance of Being Earnest* (1895)

50 'Didn't Frankenstein get married?'
'Did he?' said Eggy. 'I don't know. I never met him. Harrow man, I expect.'

P. G. Wodehouse 1881–1975: *Laughing Gas* (1936)

51 A pretty example he sets to this Infants' Bible Class of which he speaks! A few years of sitting at the feet of Harold Pinker and imbibing his extraordinary views on morality and ethics, and every bally child on the list will be serving a long stretch at Wormwood Scrubs for blackmail.

P. G. Wodehouse 1881–1975: *The Code of the Woosters* (1938)

Enemies See **Friends and Enemies**

England and the English See also **Countries and Peoples**, **Places**

1 Boasting about modesty is typical of the English.

Anonymous: unattributed; in *Mail on Sunday* 21 February 1999 'Quotes of the Week'

2 An Englishman considers himself a self-made man, and thereby relieves the Almighty of a dreadful responsibility.

Anonymous: unattributed; in *Times* 23 February 1999

3 The English may not like music, but they absolutely love the noise it makes.

Thomas Beecham 1879–1961: in *New York Herald Tribune* 9 March 1961

4 He was born an Englishman and remained one for years.

Brendan Behan 1923–64: *Hostage* (1958)

5 We English are of course the chosen race; but we should be none the worse for a little intellectual apprehension.

A. C. Benson 1862–1925: *From a College Window* (1906)

6 Think of what our Nation stands for,
Books from Boots' and country lanes,
Free speech, free passes, class distinction,
Democracy and proper drains.
Lord, put beneath Thy special care
One-eighty-nine Cadogan Square.

John Betjeman 1906–84: 'In Westminster Abbey' (1940)

7 For 'tis a low, newspaper, humdrum, lawsuit
Country.

Lord Byron 1788–1824: *Don Juan* (1819–24)

8 Mad dogs and Englishmen
Go out in the midday sun.
The Japanese don't care to,
The Chinese wouldn't dare to,
The Hindus and Argentines sleep firmly from twelve to
one,
But Englishmen detest a siesta.
In the Philippines, there are lovely screens
To protect you from the glare;
In the Malay states, they have hats like plates
Which the Britishers won't wear.
At twelve noon, the natives swoon,
And no further work is done;
But mad dogs and Englishmen go out in the midday sun.

Noël Coward 1899–1973: 'Mad Dogs and Englishmen' (1931)

9 The English can be explained by their Anglo-Saxon heritage and the influence of the Methodists. But I prefer to explain them in terms of tea, roast beef and rain. A people is first what it eats, drinks and gets pelted with.

Pierre Daninos: *Major Thompson and I* (1957)

10 There is in the Englishman a combination of qualities, a modesty, an independence, a responsibility, a repose, combined with an absence of everything calculated to call a blush into the cheek of a young person, which one would seek in vain among the Nations of the Earth.

Charles Dickens 1812–70: *Our Mutual Friend* (1865)

11 But 'tis the talent of our English nation,
Still to be plotting some new reformation.

John Dryden 1631–1700: 'The Prologue at Oxford, 1680'

12 Stiff upper lip! Stout fella!
Carry on, old fluff!
Chin up! Keep muddling through!
Stiff upper lip! Stout fella!
When the going's rough—
Pip-pip to Old Man Trouble—and a toodle-oo, too!

Ira Gershwin 1896–1983: 'Stiff Upper Lip' (1937)

13 He is an Englishman!
For he himself has said it,
And it's greatly to his credit,
That he is an Englishman!

W. S. Gilbert 1836–1911: *HMS Pinafore* (1878)

14 Contrary to popular belief, English women do not wear tweed nightgowns.

Hermione Gingold 1897–1987: in *Saturday Review* 16 April 1955

15 The truth is that every Englishman's house is his hospital, particularly the bathroom. Patent medicine is the English patent.

Oliver St John Gogarty 1878–1957: *As I Was Going Down Sackville Street* (1937)

16 Even crushed against his brother in the Tube, the average Englishman pretends desperately that he is alone.

Germaine Greer 1939– : *The Female Eunuch* (1970)

17 Larkin was so English that he didn't even care much about Britain, and he rarely mentioned it.

Clive James 1939– : *The Dreaming Swimmer* (1992)

18 Not to be English was for my family so terrible a handicap as almost to place the sufferer in the permanent invalid class.

Osbert Lancaster 1908–80: *All Done From Memory* (1953)

19 The old English belief that if a thing is unpleasant it is automatically good for you.

Osbert Lancaster 1908–80: *Homes Sweet Homes* (1939)

20 In England it is very dangerous to have a sense of humour.

E. V. Lucas 1868–1938: *365 Days and One More* (1926)

21 If an Englishman gets run down by a truck he apologizes to the truck.

Jackie Mason 1931– : in *Independent* 20 September 1990

22 An Englishman, even if he is alone, forms an orderly queue of one.

George Mikes 1912– : *How to be an Alien* (1946)

23 The English are busy; they don't have time to be polite.

Montesquieu 1689–1755: *Pensées et fragments inédits . . .* (1901)

24 Let us pause to consider the English,
Who when they pause to consider themselves they get all
   reticently thrilled and tinglish,
Because every Englishman is convinced of one thing, viz.:
That to be an Englishman is to belong to the most
   exclusive club there is.

Ogden Nash 1902–71: 'England Expects' (1938)

25 But we, brave Britons, foreign laws despised,
And kept unconquered, and uncivilized.

Alexander Pope 1688–1744: *An Essay on Criticism* (1711)

26 Good evening, England. This is Gillie Potter speaking to you in English.

Gillie Potter 1887–1975: *Heard at Hogsnorton* (opening words of broadcasts, 6 June 1946 and 11 November 1947)

27 It is hard to tell where the MCC ends and the Church of England begins.

J. B. Priestley 1894–1984: in *New Statesman* 20 July 1962

28 The Roman Conquest was, however, a *Good Thing*, since the Britons were only natives at the time.

W. C. Sellar 1898–1951 and **R. J. Yeatman** 1898–1968: *1066 and All That* (1930)

29 We really *like* dowdiness in England. It's absolutely incurable in us, I believe.

Peter Shaffer 1926– : *Whom Do I Have the Honour of Addressing?* (1990)

30 An Englishman thinks he is moral when he is only uncomfortable.

George Bernard Shaw 1856–1950: *Man and Superman* (1903)

31 Englishmen never will be slaves: they are free to do whatever the Government and public opinion allow them to do.

George Bernard Shaw 1856–1950: *Man and Superman* (1903)

32 This Englishwoman is so refined
She has no bosom and no behind.

Stevie Smith 1902–71: 'This Englishwoman' (1937)

33 What two ideas are more inseparable than Beer and Britannia?

Sydney Smith 1771–1845: Hesketh Pearson *The Smith of Smiths* (1934)

34 What a pity it is that we have no amusements in England but vice and religion!

Sydney Smith 1771–1845: Hesketh Pearson *The Smith of Smiths* (1934)

35 I think for my part one half of the nation is mad—and the other not very sound.

Tobias Smollett 1721–71: *The Adventures of Sir Launcelot Greaves* (1762)

36 As an Englishman does not travel to see Englishmen, I retired to my room.

Laurence Sterne 1713–68: *A Sentimental Journey* (1768)

37 Now hang it! quoth I, as I looked towards the French coast—a man should know something of his own country too, before he goes abroad.

Laurence Sterne 1713–68: *Tristram Shandy* (1759–67)

38 No little lily-handed baronet he,
A great broad-shouldered genial Englishman,
A lord of fat prize-oxen and of sheep,
A raiser of huge melons and of pine,
A patron of some thirty charities,
A pamphleteer on guano and on grain.

Alfred, Lord Tennyson 1809–92: *The Princess* (1847)

on the suggestion that, in his books, washing has some symbolic significance:
39 I've noticed that the British are not given to it.

Gore Vidal 1925– : attributed; in *Guardian* 27 February 1999

40 You never find an Englishman among the under-dogs—except in England, of course.

Evelyn Waugh 1903–66: *The Loved One* (1948)

41 Any who have heard that sound will shrink at the recollection of it; it is the sound of English county families baying for broken glass.

Evelyn Waugh 1903–66: *Decline and Fall* (1928)

42 Other nations use 'force'; we Britons alone use 'Might'.

Evelyn Waugh 1903–66: *Scoop* (1938)

43 He is a typical Englishman, always dull and usually violent.

Oscar Wilde 1854–1900: *An Ideal Husband* (1895)

44 You should study the Peerage, Gerald . . . It is the best thing in fiction the English have ever done.

Oscar Wilde 1854–1900: *A Woman of No Importance* (1893)

45 I like a man to be a clean, strong, upstanding Englishman who can look his gnu in the face and put an ounce of lead in it.

P. G. Wodehouse 1881–1975: *Mr. Mulliner Speaking* (1929)

Environment See Nature and the Environment

Epitaphs See also Death

1 Whoever treadeth on this stone
I pray you tread most neatly
For underneath this stone do lie
Your honest friend
WILL WHEATLEY.

Anonymous: gravestone at Stepney, London, 10 November 1683; Fritz Spiegl (ed.) *A Small Book of Grave Humour* (1971)

2 In bloom of life
She's snatched from hence
She had not room
To make defence;

Anonymous: gravestone in Malmesbury churchyard to Hannah Twynnoy, who had been attacked by an escaped tiger from a travelling circus in 1703

For Tiger fierce
Took life away,
And here she lies
In a bed of clay
Until the Resurrection Day.

3 Here lies a poor woman who always was tired,
For she lived in a place where help wasn't hired.
Her last words on earth were, Dear friends I am going
Where washing ain't done nor sweeping nor sewing,
And everything there is exact to my wishes,
For there they don't eat and there's no washing of dishes
    . . .
Don't mourn for me now, don't mourn for me never,
For I'm going to do nothing for ever and ever.

Anonymous: epitaph in Bushey churchyard, before 1860; destroyed by 1916

4 Here lies Fred,
Who was alive and is dead:
Had it been his father,
I had much rather;
Had it been his brother,
Still better than another;
Had it been his sister,
No one would have missed her;
Had it been the whole generation,
Still better for the nation:
But since 'tis only Fred,
Who was alive and is dead,—
There's no more to be said.

Anonymous: epitaph for Frederick, Prince of Wales, killed by a cricket ball in 1751; Horace Walpole *Memoirs of George II* (1847)

5 I should like my epitaph to say, 'He helped people see God in the ordinary things of life, and he made children laugh.'

Revd W. Awdry 1911–97: in *Independent* 22 March 1997

suggested epitaph for an unnamed movie queen whose love-life had been notorious:
6 She sleeps alone at last.

Robert Benchley 1889–1945: attributed

7 John Adams lies here, of the parish of Southwell,
A carrier who carried his can to his mouth well;
He carried so much, and he carried so fast,
He could carry no more—so was carried at last;
For the liquor he drank, being too much for one,
He could not carry off—so he's now carri-on.

Lord Byron 1788–1824: 'Epitaph on John Adams of Southwell, a Carrier who Died of Drunkenness' (1807)

8 Alan died suddenly at Saltwood on Sunday 5th September. He said he would like it to be stated that he regarded himself as having gone to join Tom and the other dogs.

Alan Clark 1928–99: announcement in *The Times* 8 September 1999

9 Believing that his hate for queers
Proclaimed his love for God,
He now (of all queer things, my dears)
Lies under his first sod.
    on John Gordon (1890–1974), editor of the Sunday Express

Paul Dehn 1912–76: Nigel Rees *Cassell Dictionary of Humorous Quotations* (1999)

10 Under this stone, Reader, survey
Dead Sir John Vanbrugh's house of clay.
Lie heavy on him, Earth! for he
Laid many heavy loads on thee!

Abel Evans 1679–1737: 'Epitaph on Sir John Vanbrugh, Architect of Blenheim Palace'

11 Here lies W. C. Fields. I would rather be living in Philadelphia.

W. C. Fields 1880–1946: suggested epitaph for himself; in *Vanity Fair* June 1925

12 Here Skugg
Lies snug
As a bug
In a rug.

Benjamin Franklin 1706–90: letter to Georgiana Shipley on the death of her squirrel, 26 September 1772

13 Here lies Nolly Goldsmith, for shortness called Noll,
Who wrote like an angel, but talked like poor Poll.

David Garrick 1717–79: 'Impromptu Epitaph' (written 1773/4)

14 John Le Mesurier wishes it to be known that he conked out on November 15th. He sadly misses family and friends.

John Le Mesurier 1912–83: obituary notice in *The Times* 16 November 1983

15 Poor G.K.C., his day is past—
Now God will know the truth at last.

E. V. Lucas 1868–1938: mock epitaph for G. K. Chesterton; Dudley Barker *G. K. Chesterton* (1973)

16 Here lie I, Martin Elginbrodde:
Hae mercy o' my soul, Lord God;
As I wad do, were I Lord God,
And ye were Martin Elginbrodde.

George MacDonald 1824–1905: *David Elginbrod* (1863)

epitaph for a waiter:
17 By and by
God caught his eye.

David McCord 1897– : 'Remainders' (1935)

18 Beneath this slab
John Brown is stowed.
He watched the ads,
And not the road.

Ogden Nash 1902–71: 'Lather as You Go' (1942)

19 Excuse My Dust.

Dorothy Parker 1893–1967: suggested epitaph for herself; Alexander Woollcott *While Rome Burns* (1934) 'Our Mrs Parker'

epitaph for Maurice Bowra:
20 Without you, Heaven would be too dull to bear,
And Hell would not be Hell if you are there.

John Sparrow 1906–92: in *Times Literary Supplement* 30 May 1975

21 He gave the little wealth he had
To build a house for fools and mad;
And showed, by one satiric touch,
No nation wanted it so much.

Jonathan Swift 1667–1745: 'Verses on the Death of Dr Swift' (1731)

22 Poor Pope will grieve a month, and Gay
A week, and Arbuthnot a day.
St John himself will scarce forbear
To bite his pen, and drop a tear.
The rest will give a shrug, and cry,
'I'm sorry—but we all must die!'

Jonathan Swift 1667–1745: 'Verses on the Death of Dr Swift' (1731)

23 There was a poor poet named Clough,
Whom his friends all united to puff,
But the public, though dull,
Had not such a skull

Algernon Charles Swinburne 1837–1909: *Essays and Studies* (1875)

As belonged to believers in Clough.

24 I always thought I'd like my tombstone to be blank. No
epitaph, and no name. Well, actually I'd like it to say
'figment'.

Andy Warhol 1927-87: *America*
(1985)

25 His friends he loved. His direst earthly foes—
Cats—I believe he did but feign to hate.
My hand will miss the insinuated nose,
Mine eyes the tail that wagged contempt at Fate.

William Watson 1858-1936: 'An
Epitaph'

26 Here lies Mr Chesterton,
who to heaven might have gone,
but didn't, when he heard the news
that the place was run by Jews.

Humbert Wolfe 1886-1940: 'G. K.
Chesterton' (1925)

on the death of US President Warren G. Harding:
27 The only man, woman or child who wrote a simple
declarative sentence with seven grammatical errors is
dead.

e. e. cummings 1894-1962:
attributed

Etiquette See **Behaviour and Etiquette**

Examinations

1 I wrote my name at the top of the page. I wrote down the
number of the question '1'. After much reflection I put a
bracket round it thus '(1)'. But thereafter I could not think
of anything connected with it that was either relevant or
true. . . . It was from these slender indications of
scholarship that Mr Welldon drew the conclusion that I
was worthy to pass into Harrow. It is very much to his
credit.

Winston Churchill 1874-1965: *My
Early Life* (1930)

2 He had ambitions, at one time, to become a sex maniac,
but he failed his practical.

Les Dawson 1934-93: attributed;
Fred Metcalf (ed.) *Penguin Dictionary
of Modern Humorous Quotations*
(1987)

*explaining why he performed badly in the Civil Service
examinations:*
3 I evidently knew more about economics than my
examiners.

John Maynard Keynes 1883-1946:
Roy Harrod *Life of John Maynard
Keynes* (1951)

4 In examinations those who do not wish to know ask
questions of those who cannot tell.

Walter Raleigh 1861-1922: *Laughter
from a Cloud* (1923) 'Some Thoughts
on Examinations'

5 Do not on any account attempt to write on both sides of
the paper at once.

W. C. Sellar 1898-1951 and **R. J.
Yeatman** 1898-1968: *1066 and All
That* (1930) 'Test Paper 5'

*Whistler had been found 'deficient in chemistry' in a West Point
examination:*
6 Had silicon been a gas, I would have been a major-general
by now.

James McNeill Whistler 1834-1903:
E. R. and J. Pennell *The Life of James
McNeill Whistler* (1908)

*in his viva at Oxford Wilde was required to translate a passage
from the Greek version of the New Testament. Having acquitted
himself well, he was stopped:*

7 Oh, do let me go on, I want to see how it ends.

Oscar Wilde 1854–1900: James
Sutherland (ed.) *The Oxford Book of
Literary Anecdotes* (1975)

Exploration See **Travel and Exploration**

Failure See **Success and Failure**

Fame

1 A celebrity is a person who works hard all his life to
become well known, and then wears dark glasses to avoid
being recognized.

Fred Allen 1894–1956: Laurence J.
Peter (ed.) *Quotations for our Time*
(1977)

2 He may be a minister of the British Government but we
are the Walt Disney Corporation and we don't roll over for
anyone.
   *a Disneyland executive commenting on reports that Peter
   Mandelson might use the theme park's ideas in the Millennium
   Dome without authorization*

Anonymous: in *Sunday Telegraph* 18
January 1998

3 I go in and out of fashion like a double-breasted suit.

Alan Ayckbourn 1939– : in *Observer*
13 August 2000 'They said
what . . . ?'

4 He is remembered chiefly as the man about whom all is
forgotten.
   *of the British Liberal stateman Henry Campbell-Bannerman
   (1836–1908)*

Nicolas Bentley 1907–78: *An
Edwardian Album* (1974)

5 Oh, the self-importance of fading stars. Never mind, they
will be black holes one day.

Jeffrey Bernard 1932–97: in *The
Spectator* 18 July 1992

6 Oblivion . . . fame's eternal dumping ground.

Ambrose Bierce 1842–c.1914: *The
Enlarged Devil's Dictionary* (1967)

7 It must be unnerving to be so famous that you know they
are going to come in the moment you croak and hang
velvet cords across all the doorways and treat everything
with reverence. Think of the embarrassment if you left a
copy of *Reader's Digest Condensed Books* on the bedside
table.

Bill Bryson 1951– : *The Lost
Continent* (1989)

8 A legend in his own lunchtime.
   of Dennis Main Wilson

David Climie: Ned Sherrin *Theatrical
Anecdotes* (1991); also attributed to
Christopher Wordsworth of Clifford
Makins

9 I was unwise enough to be photographed in bed wearing a
Chinese dressing-gown and an expression of advanced
degeneracy.
   on being photographed everywhere after the success of The
   Vortex *in 1924*

Noël Coward 1899–1973: *Present
Indicative* (1937)

refusing to allow his biographer Sheridan Morley to out him as a
homosexual, despite the example of the theatre critic T. C.
Worsley:

10 You forget that the great British public would not care if
Cuthbert Worsley had slept with mice.

Noël Coward 1899–1973: in
Independent on Sunday Magazine 12
November 1995

11 Fancy being remembered around the world for the
invention of a mouse!

Walt Disney 1901–66: during his
last illness; Leonard Mosley *Disney's
World* (1985)

12 The best fame is a writer's fame: it's enough to get a table
at a good restaurant, but not enough that you get
interrupted when you eat.

Fran Lebowitz 1946– : in *Observer*
30 May 1993 'Sayings of the Week'

on being asked what it was like to be famous:
13 It's like having a string of pearls given you. It's nice, but
after a while, if you think of it at all, it's only to wonder if
they're real or cultured.

W. Somerset Maugham 1874–1965:
A Writer's Notebook (1949) written in
1941

14 You can't shame or humiliate modern celebrities. What
used to be called shame and humiliation is now called
publicity.

P. J. O'Rourke 1947– : *Give War a
Chance* (1992)

autographing a book for a dissatisfied customer:
15 CUSTOMER: But usen't you to be J. B. Priestley?
PRIESTLAND: That was a long time ago.

Gerald Priestland 1927–91:
Something Understood (1986)

16 The people, they need to adore me,
So Christian Dior me.

Tim Rice 1944– : *Evita* (1979)

17 Well, not exactly a big star . . . But I once had a sandwich
named after me at the Stage Delicatessen.

Neil Simon 1927– : *The Gingerbread
Lady* (1970)

18 Celebrity is good for kick-starting ideas, but often celebrity
is a lead weight around your neck. It's like you pointing at
the moon, but people are looking at your finger.
on campaigning

Sting 1951– : in *Mojo* February 1995

The Family See also **Children, Parents**

1 What is wrong with a little incest? It is both handy and
cheap.

James Agate 1877–1947: on *The
Barretts of Wimpole Street*;
attributed, perhaps apocryphal

2 And my parents finally realize that I'm kidnapped and
they snap into action immediately: They rent out my
room.

Woody Allen 1935– : Eric Lax
Woody Allen and his Comedy (1975)

3 Could you possibly whistle your father and put him back
on his lead, please.

Alan Ayckbourn 1939– : *Sisterly
Feelings* (1981)

4 NORMAN: She's stuck here, all on her own, day after day
    looking after that old sabre-toothed bat upstairs . . .
SARAH: Will you not refer to Mother like that.

Alan Ayckbourn 1939– : *Living
Together* (1975)

5 Daughters are best. They don't migrate.

Alan Bennett 1934– : *Talking Heads*
(1988)

6 My mother-in-law broke up my marriage. My wife came
home from work one day and found us in bed together.

Lenny Bruce 1925–66: attributed;
Fred Metcalf (ed.) *The Penguin
Dictionary of Modern Humorous
Quotations*

7 I should, many a good day, have blown my brains out, but for the recollection that it would have given pleasure to my mother-in-law; and, even *then*, if I could have been certain to haunt her . . .

Lord Byron 1788–1824: letter, 28 January 1817

8 We must all be very kind to Auntie Jessie,
For she's never been a Mother or a Wife,
You mustn't throw your toys at her
Or make a vulgar noise at her,
She hasn't led a very happy life.

Noël Coward 1899–1973: 'We Must All be Very Kind to Auntie Jessie' (c.1924)

9 My sister and my sister's child,
Myself and children three,
Will fill the chaise; so you must ride
On horseback after we.

William Cowper 1731–1800: 'John Gilpin' (1785)

10 If you must go flopping yourself down, flop in favour of your husband and child, and not in opposition to 'em.

Charles Dickens 1812–70: *A Tale of Two Cities* (1859)

11 Your sister is given to government.

Charles Dickens 1812–70: *Great Expectations* (1861)

12 Accidents will occur in the best-regulated families.

Charles Dickens 1812–70: *David Copperfield* (1850)

13 We do everything alike
We look alike, we dress alike,
We walk alike, we talk alike,
and what is more we hate each other very much.

Howard Dietz 1896–1983: 'Triplets' (1937)

14 John Donne, Anne Donne, Un-done.
in a letter to his wife, on being dismissed from the service of his father-in-law, Sir George More

John Donne 1572–1631: Izaak Walton *The Life of Dr Donne* (first printed in *LXXX Sermons*, 1640)

15 You know what they say, if at first you don't succeed, you're not the eldest son.

Stephen Fry 1957– : *Paperweight* (1992)

16 A man . . . is *so* in the way in the house!

Elizabeth Gaskell 1810–65: *Cranford* (1853)

17 He will be six foot two,
My son-in-law;
His haircut will be crew,
My son-in-law.

Ira Gershwin 1896–1983: 'My Son-in-Law' (1946)

18 And so do his sisters, and his cousins and his aunts!
His sisters and his cousins,
Whom he reckons up by dozens,
And his aunts!

W. S. Gilbert 1836–1911: *HMS Pinafore* (1878)

19 T'Morra, t'morra,
Lookin' for t'morra,
My aunt became a spinster that way.

E. Y. Harburg 1898–1981: 'T'Morra' (1944)

20 I'm also told that the latest popular game in America is called Incest—all the family can join in!

Rupert Hart-Davis 1907–99: letter to George Lyttelton, 14 November 1959

21 If Gloria hadn't divorced me she might never have become her own daughter-in-law.
of his ex-wife, Gloria Grahame, who had married her former stepson

Cy Howard: in *Ned Sherrin in his Anecdotage* (1993)

22 'It wouldn't hurt us to be nice, would it?'
'That depends on your threshold of pain.'
  on being told his aunt was coming to visit

George S. Kaufman 1889–1961: Howard Teichmann *George S. Kaufman* (1973)

  of his appointment of his brother Robert:
23 I see nothing wrong with giving Robert some legal experience as Attorney General before he goes out to practice law.

John F. Kennedy 1917–63: Bill Adler *The Complete Kennedy Wit* (1967)

24 BARBARA WALTERS: What would be your first act on becoming President?
JOHN F. KENNEDY JNR: Call Uncle Teddy and gloat.

John F. Kennedy Jnr. 1960–99: in *Sunday Telegraph* 25 July 1999; recalled by Ted Kennedy at his nephew's memorial service on 23 July 1999

25 My grandfather had displayed that Jovelike side to his character of which his family were always nervously aware.

Osbert Lancaster 1908–80: *All Done From Memory* (1953)

26 The black dog was the only intelligent member of the family. He died a few years later. He was poisoned, and no one will convince me it wasn't suicide.

Hugh Leonard 1926– : *Da* (1973)

27 There is usually something pretty odd about sisters that come in triplicate. Consider pretty little Cinderella and her ugly and dance-mad relations. Consider Chekhov's trio, high and dry in the provinces and longing gloomily for Moscow. Consider Macbeth's friends, bent keenly over the cauldron and intent on passing that Culinary Test for the Advanced Student.

Arthur Marshall 1910–89: *Life's Rich Pageant* (1984)

28 Few misfortunes can befall a boy which bring worse consequences than to have a really affectionate mother.

W. Somerset Maugham 1874–1965: *A Writer's Notebook* (1949), written in 1896

29 One would be in less danger
From the wiles of the stranger
If one's own kin and kith
Were more fun to be with.

Ogden Nash 1902–71: 'Family Court' (1931)

30 Uncle Carl Laemmle,
Has a very large faemmle.
  of a Hollywood mogul much given to nepotism

Ogden Nash 1902–71: Philip French *The Movie Moguls* (1969)

31 A home keeps you from living with your parents.

P. J. O'Rourke 1947– : *The Bachelor Home Companion* (1987)

32 Bury her naked? My own mum? It's a Freudian nightmare.

Joe Orton 1933–67: *Loot* (1967)

33 To your tents, O Israel!
  to his wife's Rothschild relations one evening at Mentmore

Lord Rosebery 1847–1929: Robert Rhodes James *Rosebery* (1963); perhaps apocryphal

34 I find it difficult to take much interest in a man whose father was a dragon.
  apologizing for his inability to appreciate William Morris's epic poem Sigurd the Volsung *(1876)*

Dante Gabriel Rossetti 1828–82: Osbert Sitwell *Noble Essences* (1950)

35 *Chutzpa* is that quality enshrined in a man who, having killed his mother and father, throws himself on the mercy of the court as an orphan.

Leo Rosten 1908– : *The Joys of Yiddish* (1968)

questionnaire for would-be Kings in the Wars of the Roses:

36 What have you done with your mother? (If *Nun*, write *None*.)

W. C. Sellar 1898–1951 and **R. J. Yeatman** 1898–1968: *1066 and All That* (1930)

37 It is a wise father that knows his own child.

William Shakespeare 1564–1616: *The Merchant of Venice* (1596–8)

38 Parentage is a very important profession, but no test of fitness for it is ever imposed in the interest of the children.

George Bernard Shaw 1856–1950: *Everybody's Political What's What?* (1944)

39 My father is a bastard
My Ma's an S.O.B.
My Grandpa's always plastered
My Grandma pushes tea
My sister wears a moustache
My brother wears a dress
Goodness gracious, that's why I'm a mess.

Stephen Sondheim 1930– : 'Gee, Officer Krupke' (1957)

40 'Never was born!' persisted Topsy . . . 'never had no father, nor mother, nor nothin'. I was raised by a speculator, with lots of others.'

Harriet Beecher Stowe 1811–96: *Uncle Tom's Cabin* (1852)

41 The young ladies entered the drawing-room in the full fervour of sisterly animosity.

R. S. Surtees 1805–64: *Mr Sponge's Sporting Tour* (1853)

42 I am Septimus, the most morbid of the Tennysons.
introducing himself to Dante Gabriel Rossetti

Septimus Tennyson 1815–66: Peter Levi *Tennyson* (1993)

43 If a man's character is to be abused, say what you will, there's nobody like a relation to do the business.

William Makepeace Thackeray 1811–63: *Vanity Fair* (1847–8)

44 We have become a grandmother.

Margaret Thatcher 1925– : in *The Times* 4 March 1989

45 I'm off to see if X Mansions is really razed to the ground, as I have an uncle who lives there and I know I'm in his will!

Ernest Thesiger 1879–1961: during the war; in *Ned Sherrin in his Anecdotage* (1993)

46 I'm Charley's aunt from Brazil—where the nuts come from.

Brandon Thomas 1856–1914: *Charley's Aunt* (1892)

47 I suppose that the high-water mark of my youth in Columbus, Ohio, was the night the bed fell on my father.

James Thurber 1894–1961: *My Life and Hard Times* (1933)

48 All happy families resemble one another, but each unhappy family is unhappy in its own way.

Leo Tolstoy 1828–1910: *Anna Karenina* (1875–7)

49 Familiarity breeds contempt—and children.

Mark Twain 1835–1910: *Notebooks* (1935)

explaining why he would support Ralph Nader for the presidency in preference to his own cousin Al Gore:

50 In the long run Gore is thicker than Nader.

Gore Vidal 1925– : in *Daily Telegraph* 18 August 2000

51 To lose one parent, Mr Worthing, may be regarded as a misfortune; to lose both looks like carelessness.

Oscar Wilde 1854–1900: *The Importance of Being Earnest* (1895)

52 To be born, or at any rate bred, in a hand-bag, whether it had handles or not, seems to me to display a contempt for the ordinary decencies of family life that reminds one of the worst excesses of the French Revolution.

Oscar Wilde 1854–1900: *The Importance of Being Earnest* (1895)

53 It is no use telling me that there are bad aunts and good aunts. At the core, they are all alike. Sooner or later, out pops the cloven hoof.

P. G. Wodehouse 1881–1975: *The Code of the Woosters* (1938)

54 To my daughter Leonora without whose never-failing sympathy and encouragement this book would have been finished in half the time.

P. G. Wodehouse 1881–1975: dedication to *The Heart of a Goof* (1926)

55 As a rule, you see, I'm not lugged into Family Rows. On the occasions when Aunt is calling to Aunt like mastodons bellowing across primeval swamps and Uncle James's letter about Cousin Mabel's peculiar behaviour is being shot round the family circle . . . the clan has a tendency to ignore me.

P. G. Wodehouse 1881–1975: *The Inimitable Jeeves* (1923)

56 It was that strange, almost unearthly light which comes into the eyes of wronged uncles when they see a chance of getting a bit of their own back from erring nephews.

P. G. Wodehouse 1881–1975: *Uncle Dynamite* (1948)

Fashion and Dress

1 It is totally impossible to be well dressed in cheap shoes.

Hardy Amies 1909– : *The Englishman's Suit* (1994)

of Asquith's first wife:
2 She lived in Hampstead and had no clothes.

Margot Asquith 1864–1945: Chips Channon diary, 31 October 1937

3 I never cared for fashion much. Amusing little seams and witty little pleats. It was the girls I liked.

David Bailey 1938– : in *Independent* 5 November 1990

4 I've no regrets other than a really awful haircut in the mid-Eighties—a haircut that launched a thousand third division soccer players.

Bono 1960– : in *Daily Telegraph* 1 February 1997 'They Said It'

5 I had spent the whole of my savings . . . on a suit for the wedding—a remarkable piece of apparel with lapels that had been modelled on the tail fins of a 1957 Coupe de Ville and trousers so copiously flared that when I walked you didn't see my legs move.

Bill Bryson 1951– : *Neither Here Nor There* (1991)

of Dior's New Look:
6 Clothes by a man who doesn't know women, never had one, and dreams of being one!

Coco Chanel 1883–1971: in *Vanity Fair* June 1994

on being told that several of his fly-buttons were undone:
7 No matter. The dead bird does not leave the nest.

Winston Churchill 1874–1965: Rupert Hart-Davis letter to George Lyttelton, 5 January 1957

8 You've got so much ice on your hands I could skate on them.
   to Liberace

John Curry 1949–94: Ned Sherrin *Cutting Edge* (1984)

9 He thinks he is a flower to be looked at
And when he pulls his frilly nylon pants right up tight
He feels a dedicated follower of fashion.

Raymond Douglas Davies: 'A Dedicated Follower of Fashion' (1966)

10 I guess I'll have to change my plan
I should have realized there'd be another man
Why did I buy those blue pyjamas
Before the big affair began?

Howard Dietz 1896–1983: 'I Guess I'll Have to Change My Plan' (1929)

I guess I'll have to change my plan.

to Sir Frederick Ponsonby, who had proposed accompanying him in a tail-coat:

11 I thought everyone must know that a *short* jacket is always worn with a silk hat at a private view in the morning.

Edward VII 1841–1910: Philip Magnus *Edward VII* (1964)

when Lord Harris appeared at Ascot in a brown bowler:
12 Goin' rattin', 'Arris?

Edward VII 1841–1910: Michael Hill 'Right Royal Remarks' (unpublished compilation); in *Ned Sherrin in his Anecdotage* (1993)

13 Uncool people never hurt anybody—all they do is collect stamps, read science-fiction books and stand on the end of railway platforms staring at trains.

Ben Elton 1959– : in *Radio Times* 18/24 April 1998

14 There are easier things in this life than being a drag queen. But, I ain't got no choice. Try as I may, I just can't walk in flats.

Harvey Fierstein 1954– : *Torch Song Trilogy* (1979)

15 When he buys his ties he has to ask if gin will make them run.

F. Scott Fitzgerald 1896–1940: *Notebooks* (1978)

Lord Charles Russell had appeared incorrectly dressed at a Court Ball:
16 Good evening, sir, I suppose you are the regimental doctor.

George IV 1762–1830: Michael Hill (ed.) 'Right Royal Remarks' (unpublished compilation); in *Ned Sherrin in his Anecdotage* (1993)

Dame Edna to Judy Steel:
17 Tell me the history of that frock, Judy. It's obviously an old favourite. You were wise to remove the curtain rings.

Barry Humphries 1934– : *Another Audience with Dame Edna* (TV, 1984); Nigel Rees (ed.) *Cassell Dictionary of Humorous Quotations* (1999)

18 You should never have your best trousers on when you go out to fight for freedom and truth.

Henrik Ibsen 1828–1906: *An Enemy of the People* (1882)

19 Satan himself can't save a woman who wears thirty-shilling corsets under a thirty-guinea costume.

Rudyard Kipling 1865–1936: *Debits and Credits* (1926)

20 A silk dress in four sections, and shoes with high heels that would have broken the heart of John Calvin.

Stephen Leacock 1869–1944: *Arcadian Adventures with the Idle Rich* (1914)

21 I am not . . . totally unreceptive to colour providing it makes its appearance quietly, deferentially, and without undue fanfare.

Fran Lebowitz 1946– : *Metropolitan Life* (1978)

when a waiter at Buckingham Palace spilled soup on her dress:
22 Never darken my Dior again!

Beatrice Lillie 1894–1989: *Every Other Inch a Lady* (1973)

23 Isn't it great that they have things like that to talk about? I think that I have three trouser suits to my name, but people think that when you wear them that that's all you ever wear.
    responding to reports that she had been criticized for wearing trouser suits on formal occasions

Mary McAleese 1951– : in *Irish Times* 28 February 1998

of the appearance of Princess Margaret at Princess Alexandra's wedding:

24 Unspeakable, like a hedgehog all in primroses.

Nancy Mitford 1904–73: letter 28 April 1963

25 The hats were nearly all as though made by somebody who had once heard about flowers but never seen one— huge muffs of horror.

Nancy Mitford 1904–73: of Princess Alexandra's wedding; letter 28 April 1963

on being asked what she wore in bed:

26 Chanel No. 5.

Marilyn Monroe 1926–62: Pete Martin *Marilyn Monroe* (1956)

27 The officers of this branch of the Force [the Obscene Publications Squad at Scotland Yard] have a discouraging club tie, on which a book is depicted being cut in half by a larger pair of scissors.

John Mortimer 1923– : *Clinging to the Wreckage* (1982)

28 The only really firm rule of taste about cross dressing is that neither sex should ever wear anything they haven't yet figured out how to go to the bathroom in.

P. J. O'Rourke 1947– : *Modern Manners* (1984)

29 Fur is a subject that makes sensitive toes curl in their leather shoes.
   introducing a discussion on fur coats

Jeremy Paxman 1950– : in *The Mail on Sunday* 13 February 2000 'Quotes of the Week'

30 I like curious clothes. Back in Dublin I stayed in my riding breeches, bought at a cheap shop in Dublin, and wore them for weeks after, as an enjoyable symbol of the Irish habit of life, until someone tactfully suggested I looked like a stable boy.

V. S. Pritchett 1900–97: *Midnight Oil* (1971)

31 Elizabeth Taylor is wearing Orson Welles designer jeans.

Joan Rivers 1937– : attributed; Ned Sherrin *Cutting Edge* (1984)

32 I wish I had invented blue jeans.
   on his only regret

Yves Saint Laurent 1936– : interview in *Harper's & Queen*; in *Independent on Sunday* 29 November 1998

33 His socks compelled one's attention without losing one's respect.

Saki 1870–1916: *Chronicles of Clovis* (1911)

34 Her frocks are built in Paris, but she wears them with a strong English accent.

Saki 1870–1916: *Reginald* (1904)

35 She wears her clothes, as if they were thrown on her with a pitchfork.

Jonathan Swift 1667–1745: *Polite Conversation* (1738)

36 If Botticelli were alive today he'd be working for *Vogue*.

Peter Ustinov 1921– : in *Observer* 21 October 1962 'Sayings of the Week'

37 I like to dress egos. If you haven't got an ego today, you can forget it.

Gianni Versace 1949–96: in *Guardian* 16 July 1997; obituary

38 It is charming to totter into vogue.

Horace Walpole 1717–97: letter to George Selwyn, 2 December 1765

to Ada Leverson, who with her husband visited Wilde on the morning he left Pentonville:

39 How marvellous of you to know exactly the right hat to wear at seven o'clock in the morning to meet a friend who has been away.

Oscar Wilde 1854–1900: Rupert Hart-Davis (ed.) *Selected Letters of Oscar Wilde* (1979)

40 She wore far too much rouge last night, and not quite enough clothes. That is always a sign of despair in a woman.

Oscar Wilde 1854-1900: *An Ideal Husband* (1895)

Films See also **The Cinema**

1 Disappointed with Edward G. Robinson in *The Sea Wolf*, a psychological film about a rascally captain with a split mind, whereas I had been looking forward to two hundred lashes in Technicolor.

James Agate 1877-1947: diary, 27 January 1942

2 Several tons of dynamite are set off in this picture [*Tycoon*]; none of it under the right people.

James Agee 1909-55: in *The Nation* 14 February 1948

Adolph Zukor had protested at the escalating costs of The Ten Commandments:

3 What do you want me to do? Stop shooting now and release it as *The Five Commandments*?

Cecil B. De Mille 1881-1959: M. LeRoy *Take One* (1974)

4 A movie so good they named a country after it.
on his film Brazil

Terry Gilliam 1940- : in *Mail on Sunday* 22 August 1999, attributed

of one of his own films:
5 It's more than magnificent, it's mediocre.

Sam Goldwyn 1882-1974: attributed, perhaps apocryphal

6 GOLDWYN: I hope you didn't think it was too blood and thirsty.
THURBER: Not only did I think so but I was horror and struck.
of The Secret Life of Walter Mitty, *Goldwyn's 1947 film of Thurber's story*

Sam Goldwyn 1882-1974: Michael Freedland *The Goldwyn Touch* (1986)

7 It would have been cheaper to lower the Atlantic!
of the disaster movie Raise the Titanic

Lew Grade 1906-98: *Still Dancing: My Story* (1987)

8 Do you have any idea how bad the picture is? I'll tell you. Stay away from the neighbourhood where it's playing— don't even go near that street! It might rain—you could get caught in the downpour, and to keep dry you'd have to go inside the theatre.

Herman J. Mankiewicz 1897-1953: attributed

9 I'm not [biting my fingernails]. I'm biting my knuckles. I finished the fingernails months ago.

Joseph L. Mankiewicz 1909- : while directing *Cleopatra* (1963); Dick Sheppard *Elizabeth* (1975)

10 The slaves . . . are so cordial and upbeat about having their lives and property gentrified in 1776 that you fear for the entire future of the blues.
of The Patriot

Wesley Morris: in *San Francisco Examiner* 28 June 2000

11 It was a cute picture. They used the basic story of *Wuthering Heights* and worked in surfriders.

Neil Simon 1927- : *Last of the Red Hot Lovers* (1970)

12 Anything but Beethoven. Nobody wants to see a movie about a blind composer.

Jack Warner 1892-1978: J. Lawrence *Actor* (1975)

13 I didn't have to act in 'Tarzan, the Ape Man'—just said, 'Me Tarzan, you Jane.'

Johnny Weissmuller 1904-84: in *Photoplay Magazine* June 1932 (the words 'Me Tarzan, you Jane' do not occur in the 1932 film)

asking Graham Greene to give a final polish to a rewrite of the last part of the screenplay for Ben Hur:

14 You see, we find a kind of anticlimax after the Crucifixion.

Sam Zimbalist: Graham Greene *Ways of Escape* (1980)

Film Stars

1 Can't act. Slightly bald. Also dances.
   studio official's comment on Fred Astaire

Anonymous: Bob Thomas *Astaire* (1985)

2 They used to shoot her through gauze. You should shoot me through linoleum.
   on Shirley Temple

Tallulah Bankhead 1903–68: attributed

3 JOE GILLIS: You used to be in pictures. You used to be big.
   NORMA DESMOND: I am big. It's the pictures that got small.

Charles Brackett 1892–1969 and **Billy Wilder** 1906– : *Sunset Boulevard* (1950 film)

4 When he meets Garbo in a suit of corduroy,
   He gives a little frown
   And knocks her down.
   Oh dear, oh dear, I'm mad about the boy.

Noël Coward 1899–1973: 'Mad About the Boy' (1932)

asked what it was like to kiss Marilyn Monroe:
5 It's like kissing Hitler.

Tony Curtis 1925– : A. Hunter *Tony Curtis* (1985)

6 Nowadays Mitchum doesn't so much act as point his suit at people.

Russell Davies 1946– : in *Sunday Times* 18 September 1983

during the making of Lifeboat *in 1944, Mary Anderson asked Hitchcock what he thought her 'best side' for photography was:*
7 My dear, you're sitting on it.

Alfred Hitchcock 1899–1980: D. Spoto *Life of Alfred Hitchcock* (1983)

8 That man's ears make him look like a taxi-cab with both doors open.
   of Clark Gable

Howard Hughes Jr. 1905–76: Charles Higham and Joel Greenberg *Celluloid Muse* (1969)

9 She is a phenomenon of nature, like Niagara Falls or the Grand Canyon. You can't talk to it. It can't talk to you. All you can do is stand back and be awed by it.
   of Marilyn Monroe

Nunnally Johnson 1897–1977: Peter Harry Brown and Patte B. Barham *Marilyn, the Last Take* (1990)

10 To work as hard as I've worked to accomplish anything and then have some yo-yo come up and say 'Take off those dark glasses and let's have a look at those blue eyes' is really discouraging.

Paul Newman 1925– : in *Observer* 5 October 1986 'Sayings of the Week'

11 Elizabeth [Taylor] is a wonderful movie actress: she has a deal with the film lab—she gets better in the bath overnight.

Mike Nichols 1931–: in *Vanity Fair* June 1994

12 Wet, she was a star—dry she ain't.
   of the swimmer Esther Williams and her 1940s film career

Joe Pasternak 1901–91: attributed

13 There are times when Richard Gere has the warm effect of a wind tunnel at dawn, waiting for work, all sheen, inner curve, and posed emptiness.

David Thomson 1941– : *A Biographical Dictionary of Film* (1994)

14 All Americans born between 1890 and 1945 wanted to be movie stars.

Gore Vidal 1925– : *Pink Triangle and Yellow Star* (1982)

on hearing that Ronald Reagan was seeking nomination as Governor of California:

15 No, *no. Jimmy Stewart* for governor—Reagan for his best friend.

Jack Warner 1892–1978: Max Wilk *The Wit and Wisdom of Hollywood* (1972)

16 It's not what I do, but the way I do it. It's not what I say, but the way I say it.

Mae West 1892–1980: G. Eells and S. Musgrove *Mae West* (1989)

on Marilyn Monroe's unpunctuality:

17 My Aunt Minnie would always be punctual and never hold up production, but who would pay to see my Aunt Minnie?

Billy Wilder 1906– : P. F. Boller and R. L. Davis *Hollywood Anecdotes* (1988)

18 The question is whether Marilyn [Monroe] is a person at all or one of the greatest Dupont products ever invented. She has breasts like granite and a brain like Swiss cheese, full of holes.

Billy Wilder 1906– : E. Goodman *The Fifty-Year Decline and Fall of Hollywood* (1961)

Flattery See **Praise and Flattery**

Food and Drink See also **Alcohol**

1 In Lent she ate onion soup and gave up drink; but otherwise she must have drunk the maximum compatible with survival and sanity.

of the television cook, Jennifer Paterson

Anonymous: obituary of Jennifer Paterson, in *Daily Telegraph* 11 August 1999

2 Shake and shake
The catsup bottle,
None will come,
And then a lot'll.

Richard Armour: Laurence J. Peter (ed.) *Quotations for our Time* (1977)

3 I had left home (like all Jewish girls) in order to eat pork and take birth control pills. When I first shared an intimate evening with my husband, I was swept away by the passion (so dormant inside myself) of a long and tortured existence. The physical cravings I had tried so hard to deny, finally and ultimately sated . . . But enough about the pork.

Roseanne Arnold 1953– : *Roseanne* (1990)

4 Salad. I can't bear salad. It grows while you're eating it, you know. Have you noticed? You start one side of your plate and by the time you've got to the other, there's a fresh crop of lettuce taken root and sprouted up.

Alan Ayckbourn 1939– : *Living Together* (1975)

5 I'm afraid I'm addicted to fat and love British beef. BSE holds no terror for me because . . . I am as likely to get it as win the National Lottery.

on her main difficulty in following a healthy diet

Joan Bakewell 1933– : in *Independent* 30 August 1997 'Quote Unquote'

6 A gourmet can tell from the flavour whether a woodcock's leg is the one on which the bird is accustomed to roost.

Lucius Beebe 1902– : Laurence J. Peter (ed.) *Quotations for our Time* (1977)

7 Good to eat, and wholesome to digest, as a worm to a toad, a toad to a snake, a snake to a pig, a pig to a man, and a man to a worm.

on the cycle of digestion

Ambrose Bierce 1842–c.1914: *The Enlarged Devil's Dictionary* (1967)

8 One of the sauces which serve the French in place of a state religion.
on mayonnaise

Ambrose Bierce 1842–c.1914: ;*The Enlarged Devil's Dictionary* (1967)

9 Sir Walter Raleigh gripped his seat under the table. He had sailed halfway round the world to find this root, he had faced great perils to bring it back, he had withstood the blandishments of the most expert cajolers at Court, and had not even hinted at the secret of its flavour, he had changed his chef six times, and now Elizabeth of England was tasting it.
He looked at her.
Elizabeth of England spat.
'Not enough salt,' she said.

Caryl Brahms 1901–82 and **S. J. Simon** 1904–48: *No Bed for Bacon* (1941)

10 Where else can you see, at a table for six, six grey suits?

Seymour Britchky: of the men at '21'; *The Restaurants of New York* (1974 ed.)

11 Some of the waiters discuss the menu with you as if they were sharing wisdom picked up in the Himalayas.

Seymour Britchky: *The Restaurants of New York* (1981 ed.)

12 The burger was horrid, thin and bitty like a Pekingese's tongue.

Craig Brown 1957– : *Craig Brown's Greatest Hits* (1993)

13 Mashed figs—a foodstuff that only your grandmother would eat, and only then because she couldn't find her dentures.

Bill Bryson 1951– : *Neither Here Nor There* (1991)

14 I'm President of the United States, and I'm not going to eat any more broccoli!

George Bush 1924– : in *New York Times* 23 March 1990

15 The healthy stomach is nothing if not conservative. Few radicals have good digestions.

Samuel Butler 1835–1902: *Notebooks* (1912)

16 Day will break and you'll awake and start to bake a sugar cake for all the boys to see.

Irving Caesar 1895– : 'Tea for Two' (1925)

17 'Take some more tea,' the March Hare said to Alice, very earnestly. 'I've had nothing yet,' Alice replied in an offended tone, 'so I can't take more.' 'You mean you can't take *less*,' said the Hatter: 'it's very easy to take *more* than nothing.'

Lewis Carroll 1832–98: *Alice's Adventures in Wonderland* (1865)

18 'There's nothing like eating hay when you're faint' . . . 'I didn't say there was nothing *better*,' the King replied, 'I said there was nothing *like* it.'

Lewis Carroll 1832–98: *Through the Looking-Glass* (1872)

19 Tea, although an Oriental,
Is a gentleman at least.
Cocoa is a cad and coward
Cocoa is a vulgar beast.

G. K. Chesterton 1874–1936: 'A Song of Right and Wrong' (1914)

20 Take away that pudding—it has no theme.

Winston Churchill 1874–1965: Lord Home *The Way the Wind Blows* (1976)

21 Open up the caviare
And say Thank God.

Noël Coward 1899–1973: 'Alice is At It Again' (1954)

22 I never see an egg brought on my table but I feel penetrated with the wonderful change it would have undergone but for my gluttony; it might have been a

St John de Crévècoeur 1735–1813: *Letters from an American Farmer* (1782)

gentle useful hen, leading her chickens with a care and vigilance which speaks shame to many women.

23 'It's very easy to talk,' said Mrs Mantalini. 'Not so easy when one is eating a demnition egg,' replied Mr Mantalini; 'for the yolk runs down the waistcoat, and yolk of egg does not match any waistcoat but a yellow waistcoat, demmit.'

Charles Dickens 1812–70: *Nicholas Nickleby* (1839)

24 It's a wery remarkable circumstance . . . that poverty and oysters always seem to go together.

Charles Dickens 1812–70: *Pickwick Papers* (1837)

25 Please, sir, I want some more.

Charles Dickens 1812–70: *Oliver Twist* (1838)

26 [Cheese is] milk's leap toward immortality.

Clifton Fadiman 1904– : *Any Number Can Play* (1957)

27 Roast Beef, Medium, is not only a food. It is a philosophy.

Edna Ferber 1887–1968: foreword to *Roast Beef, Medium* (1911)

28 Ask for heron's eggs whipped with wine into an amber foam.
   when asked by a friend what to order in a Lyons teashop

Ronald Firbank 1886–1926: Mervyn Horder *Ronald Firbank: Memoirs and Critiques* (1977)

29 Last night we went to a Chinese dinner at six and a French dinner at nine, and I can feel the sharks' fins navigating unhappily in the Burgundy.

Peter Fleming 1907–71: letter from Yunnanfu, 20 March 1938

30 Of soup and love, the first is the best.

Thomas Fuller 1654–1734: *Gnomologia* (1732)

31 You like potato and I like po-tah-to,
   You like tomato and I like to-mah-to;
   Potato, po-tah-to, tomato, to-mah-to—
   Let's call the whole thing off!

Ira Gershwin 1896–1983: 'Let's Call the Whole Thing Off' (1937)

32 The best number for a dinner party is two—myself and a dam' good head waiter.

Nubar Gulbenkian 1896–1972: in *Daily Telegraph* 14 January 1965

33 'For what we are about to receive,
   Oh Lord, 'tis Thee we thank,'
   Said the cannibal as he cut a slice
   Of the missionary's shank.

E. Y. Harburg 1898–1981: 'The Realist' (1965)

34 I ate his liver with some fava beans and a nice chianti.

Thomas Harris 1940– and **Ted Tally** 1952– : *The Silence of the Lambs* (1991 film)

35 Oh, I was down by Manly Pier
   Drinking tubes of ice-cold beer
   With a bucket full of prawns upon me knee.
   But when I'd swallowed the last prawn
   I had a technicolour yawn
   And I chundered in the old Pacific sea.

Barry Humphries 1934– : 'Chunder Down Under' (1964)

36 What proper man would plump for bints
   Ahead of After-Eight thin mints?
   True pleasure for a man of parts
   Is tarts in him, not him in tarts.

Clive James 1939– : Ned Sherrin *Cutting Edge* (1984)

37 Mr Leopold Bloom ate with relish the inner organs of beasts and fowls. He liked thick giblet soup, nutty gizzards, a stuffed roast heart, liverslices fried with crustcrumbs,

James Joyce 1882–1941: *Ulysses* (1922)

fried hencod's roes. Most of all he liked grilled mutton kidneys which gave to his palate a fine tang of faintly scented urine.

38 When I makes tea I makes tea, as old mother Grogan said. And when I makes water I makes water . . . *Begob, ma'am*, says Mrs Cahill, *God send you don't make them in the one pot*.

James Joyce 1882–1941: *Ulysses* (1922)

39 I feel about airplanes the way I feel about diets. It seems to me that they are wonderful things for other people to go on.

Jean Kerr 1923– : *The Snake Has All the Lines* (1958)

40 Lunch Hollywood-style—a hot dog and vintage wine.

Harry Kurnitz 1907–68: Max Wilk *The Wit and Wisdom of Hollywood* (1971)

41 Cannibalism went right out as soon as the American canned food came in.

Stephen Leacock 1869–1944: *The Boy I Left Behind Me* (1947)

42 Large, naked, raw carrots are acceptable as food only to those who live in hutches eagerly awaiting Easter.

Fran Lebowitz 1946– : *Metropolitan Life* (1978)

43 The piece of cod passeth all understanding.

Edwin Lutyens 1869–1944: Robert Lutyens *Sir Edwin Lutyens* (1942)

44 You are offered a piece of bread and butter that feels like a damp handkerchief and sometimes, when cucumber is added to it, like a wet one.

Compton Mackenzie 1883–1972: *Vestal Fire* (1927)

45 Sushi, crab claws, caviar, little heaps of pink glop . . . A taste of dank rock pools fills my mouth.

Liz McManus 1947– : 'Dwelling Below the Skies' (1997)

46 It's all right, the white wine came up with the fish.
   at a formal dinner at the home of the producer Arthur Hornblow Jr., having left the dinner table to be sick

Herman J. Mankiewicz 1897–1953: Max Wilk *The Wit and Wisdom of Hollywood* (1972); also claimed by Howard Dietz

47 'Can I have a table near the floor?'
   'Certainly, I'll have the waiter saw the legs off.'

Groucho Marx 1895–1977: attributed

48 [England] is the only country in the world where the food is more dangerous than sex. I mean, a hard cheese will kill you, but a soft cheese will kill you in *seconds*.

Jackie Mason 1931– : in *Independent* 17 February 1989

49 People often feed the hungry so that nothing may disturb their own enjoyment of a good meal.

W. Somerset Maugham 1874–1965: *A Writer's Notebook* (1949) written in 1896

to a friend who had said that he hated English food:
50 All you have to do is eat breakfast three times a day.

W. Somerset Maugham 1874–1965: Ted Morgan *Somerset Maugham* (1980)

explaining her dislike of soup:
51 I do not believe in building a meal on a lake.

Elsie Mendl 1865–1950: Elsie de Wolfe *After All* (1935)

52 Sue wants a barbecue, Sam wants to boil a ham,
   Grace votes for bouillabaisse stew,
   Jake wants a weeny-bake, steak and a layer cake,
   He'll get a tummy ache too.

Johnny Mercer 1909–76: 'In the Cool, Cool, Cool of the Evening' (1951)

53 Long as there is chicken and gravy on your rice
Ev'rything is nice.

Johnny Mercer 1909–76:
'Lazybones' (1932)

54 Parsley
Is gharsley.

Ogden Nash 1902–71: 'Further
Reflections on Parsley' (1942)

55 Never serve oysters in a month that has no paycheck in it.

P. J. O'Rourke 1947– : The Bachelor
Home Companion (1987)

56 I'll take a lemonade! . . . In a dirty glass!

Norman Panama 1914– and
Melvin Frank 1913–88: in Road to
Utopia (1946 film; words spoken by
Bob Hope)

57 I had never had a piece of toast
Particularly long and wide,
But fell upon the sanded floor,
And always on the buttered side.

James Payn 1830–98: in Chambers's
Journal 2 February 1884

58 The mountain sheep are sweeter,
But the valley sheep are fatter;
We therefore deemed it meeter
To carry off the latter.

Thomas Love Peacock 1785–1866:
'The War-Song of Dinas Vawr' (1823)

59 The divine took his seat at the breakfast-table, and began
to compose his spirits by the gentle sedative of a large cup
of tea, the demulcent of a well-buttered muffin, and the
tonic of a small lobster.

Thomas Love Peacock 1785–1866:
Crotchet Castle (1831)

60 There is no danger of my getting scurvy [while in
England], as I have to consume at least two gin-and-limes
every evening to keep the cold out.

S. J. Perelman 1904–79: letter, 13
December 1953

61 I've had a taste of society
And society has had a taste of me.
*the oyster ending up back in the sea after a day of social
climbing*

Cole Porter 1891–1964: 'The Tale of
the Oyster' (1929)

62 It just proves that fifty million Frenchmen can't be wrong.
They eat horses instead of ride them.
having been crippled in a riding accident in 1937

Cole Porter 1891–1964: G. Eells The
Life that Late He Led (1967)

63 It is said that the effect of eating too much lettuce is
'soporific'.

Beatrix Potter 1866–1943: The Tale
of the Flopsy Bunnies (1909)

64 Dinner at the Huntercombes' possessed 'only two dramatic
features—the wine was a farce and the food a tragedy'.

Anthony Powell 1905–2000: The
Acceptance World (1955)

65 Botticelli isn't a wine, you Juggins! Botticelli's a *cheese*!

Punch 1841–1992: vol. 106 (1894)

66 BISHOP: I'm afraid you've got a bad egg, Mr Jones.
CURATE: Oh no, my Lord, I assure you! Parts of it are
excellent!

Punch 1841–1992: vol. 109 (1895)

67 Look here, Steward, if this is coffee, I want tea; but if this
is tea, then I wish for coffee.

Punch 1841–1992: vol. 123 (1902)

68 Cheese it is a peevish elf
It digests all things but itself.

John Ray 1627–1705: English Proverbs
(1670)

69 And the sooner the tea's out of the way, the sooner we
can get out the gin, eh?

Henry Reed 1914–86: Private Life of
Hilda Tablet (1954 radio play)

70 Does the spearmint lose its flavour on the bedpost overnight?

Billy Rose 1899–1966 and **Marty Bloom**: title of song (1924); revived in 1959 by Lonnie Donegan with the title 'Does your chewing-gum lose its flavour on the bedpost overnight?'

71 The boy flew at the oranges with the enthusiasm of a ferret finding the rabbit family at home after a long day of fruitless subterranean research.

Saki 1870–1916: *The Toys of Peace* (1919)

72 Like a purée of white kid gloves.
   of a dish of lobster Newburg

Philip Sassoon 1888–1939: Chips Channon, diary, 3 June 1939

73 Methinks I have a great desire to a bottle of hay: good hay, sweet hay, hath no fellow.

William Shakespeare 1564–1616: *A Midsummer Night's Dream* (1595–6)

74 A plague o' these pickle herring!

William Shakespeare 1564–1616: *Twelfth Night* (1601)

75 Then my stomach must digest its waistcoat.
   when told that drinking would ruin the coat of his stomach

Richard Brinsley Sheridan 1751–1816: in *Sheridaniana* (1826)

76 OSCAR: I got brown sandwiches and green sandwiches . . .
   Well, what do you say?
   MURRAY: What's the green?
   OSCAR: It's either very new cheese or very old meat.

Neil Simon 1927– : *The Odd Couple* (1966)

77 Serenely full, the epicure would say,
   Fate cannot harm me, I have dined to-day.

Sydney Smith 1771–1845: Lady Holland *Memoir* (1855) 'Receipt for a Salad'

78 If there is a pure and elevated pleasure in this world it is a roast pheasant with bread sauce. Barn door fowls for dissenters but for the real Churchman, the thirty-nine times articled clerk—the pheasant, the pheasant.

Sydney Smith 1771–1845: letter to R. H. Barham, 15 November 1841

79 Shepherd's pie peppered with actual shepherd on top.
   one of Mrs Lovett's variations on Sweeney Todd's human meat pies

Stephen Sondheim 1930– : 'A Little Priest' (1979)

80 Have an egg roll, Mr Goldstone,
   Have a napkin, have a chopstick, have a chair!
   Have a sparerib, Mr Goldstone—
   Any sparerib that I can spare, I'd be glad to share!

Stephen Sondheim 1930– : 'Mr Goldstone, I Love You' (1959)

81 For the edible and the readable we give thanks to God, the Author of Life.

Mervyn Stockwood 1913–95: grace for a literary lunch, in Ned Sherrin *Cutting Edge* (1984)

82 I'll fill hup the chinks wi' cheese.

R. S. Surtees 1805–64: *Handley Cross* (1843)

83 Cauliflower is nothing but cabbage with a college education.

Mark Twain 1835–1910: *Pudd'nhead Wilson* (1894)

84 One cannot imagine Mr Jenkins sending a task force anywhere except to a good restaurant.
   on Roy Jenkins at the time of the Falklands War

Alan Watkins 1933– : in *Observer* 20 June 1982

85 'Turbot, Sir,' said the waiter, placing before me two fishbones, two eyeballs, and a bit of black mackintosh.

Thomas Earle Welby 1881–1933: *The Dinner Knell* (1932) 'Birmingham or Crewe?'

86 Beulah, peel me a grape.

Mae West 1892–1980: in *I'm No Angel* (1933 film)

87 MOTHER: It's broccoli, dear.
CHILD: I say it's spinach, and I say the hell with it.

E. B. White 1899–1985: cartoon caption in *New Yorker* 8 December 1928

88 When I ask for a watercress sandwich, I do not mean a loaf with a field in the middle of it.

Oscar Wilde 1854–1900: Max Beerbohm letter to Reggie Turner, 15 April 1893

89 I was so darned sorry for poor old Corky that I hadn't the heart to touch my breakfast. I told Jeeves to drink it himself.

P. G. Wodehouse 1881–1975: *My Man Jeeves* (1919)

90 The lunches of fifty-seven years had caused his chest to slip down into the mezzanine floor.

P. G. Wodehouse 1881–1975: *The Heart of a Goof* (1926)

91 What with excellent browsing and sluicing and cheery conversation and what-not, the afternoon passed quite happily.

P. G. Wodehouse 1881–1975: *My Man Jeeves* (1919)

92 JACKIE: Pity there's no such thing as Sugar Replacement Therapy.
VICTORIA: There is. It's called chocolate.

Victoria Wood 1953– : *Mens Sana in Thingummy Doodah* (1990)

93 If you dine out of tins, you should have the labels served up with the grub.

Jack B. Yeats 1871–1957: *The Charmed Life* (1938)

Foolishness and Ignorance

1 *New Year Resolutions*
  1. To refrain from saying witty, unkind things, unless they are really witty and irreparably damaging.
  2. To tolerate fools more gladly, provided this does not encourage them to take up more of my time.

James Agate 1877–1947: diary 2 January 1942

2 Fools have this happiness—to be easy with themselves, and let other people blush for 'em.

Anonymous: in *The Female Tatler* July–August 1709

3 Had your forefathers, Wigglesworth, been as stupid as you are, the human race would never have succeeded in procreating itself.

Alan Bennett 1934– : *Forty Years On* (1969)

4 The Cardinal [at Ravenna] is at his wit's end—it is true—that he had not far to go.

Lord Byron 1788–1824: letter, 22 July 1820

5 I sometimes wonder if the manufacturers of foolproof items keep a fool or two on their payroll to test things.

Alan Coren 1938– : *Seems Like Old Times* (1989)

6 How much a dunce that has been sent to roam
Excels a dunce that has been kept at home?

William Cowper 1731–1800: 'The Progress of Error' (1782)

7 Mr Kremlin himself was distinguished for ignorance, for he had only one idea,—and that was wrong.

Benjamin Disraeli 1804–81: *Sybil* (1845)

8 I believe they talked of me, for they laughed consumedly.

George Farquhar 1678–1707: *The Beaux' Stratagem* (1707)

9 The idiot who praises, with enthusiastic tone,
All centuries but this, and every country but his own.

W. S. Gilbert 1836–1911: *The Mikado* (1885)

10 Oh, innocent victims of Cupid,
Remember this terse little verse;
To let a fool kiss you is stupid,

E. Y. Harburg 1898–1981: 'Inscriptions on a Lipstick' (1965)

To let a kiss fool you is worse.

11 The Lord made Adam,
The Lord made Eve,
He made 'em both a little naïve.

E. Y. Harburg 1898–1981: 'The Begat' (1947)

12 The public is soon disarmed. This planet is largely inhabited by parrots, and it is easy to disguise folly by giving it a fine name.

A. E. Housman 1859–1936: 'The Editing of Manilius' (1903)

on the suggestion that Ellen Terry had rejected a play by James 'because she did not think the part suited her':
13 Think? Think? How should the poor, toothless, chattering hag THINK?

Henry James 1843–1916: Edmund Gosse letter 14 April 1920

on being asked why he had defined pastern *as the 'knee' of a horse:*
14 Ignorance, madam, pure ignorance.

Samuel Johnson 1709–84: James Boswell *Life of Samuel Johnson* (1791) 1755

15 You've heard of people living in a fool's paradise? Well, Leonora has a duplex there.
of Leonora Corbett

George S. Kaufman 1889–1961: Howard Teichmann *George S. Kaufman* (1973)

16 McIlwain asked a student the other day what he knew of St Petersburg and got for an answer that it was founded in the winter by St Peter. Do you wonder that Bolshevism triumphs?

Harold Laski 1893–1950: letter to Oliver Wendell Holmes, 1 December 1918

in response to the comment on another lawyer, 'It may be doubted whether any man of our generation has plunged more deeply into the sacred fount of learning':
17 Or come up drier.

Abraham Lincoln 1809–65: Leon Harris *The Fine Art of Political Wit* (1965)

18 When a line of action is said to be supported 'by all responsible men' it is nearly always dangerous or foolish.

Harold Macmillan 1894–1986: *The Past Masters* (1975)

19 I could name eight people—half of those eight are barmy. How many apples short of a picnic?
on Tory critics

John Major 1943– : comment, 19 September 1993

20 A bishop wrote gravely to the *Times* inviting all nations to destroy 'the formula' of the atomic bomb. There is no simple remedy for ignorance so abysmal.

Peter Medawar 1915–87: *The Hope of Progress* (1972)

21 A man may be a fool and not know it, but not if he is married.

H. L. Mencken 1880–1956: Laurence J. Peter (ed.) *Quotations for our Time* (1977)

22 Seriousness is stupidity sent to college.

P. J. O'Rourke 1947– : *Give War a Chance* (1992)

23 What a waste it is to lose one's mind, or not to have a mind. How true that is.

Dan Quayle 1947– : speech to the United Negro College Fund, whose slogan is 'a mind is a terrible thing to waste'; in *The Times* 26 May 1989

24 You know everybody is ignorant, only on different subjects.

Will Rogers 1879–1935: in *New York Times* 31 August 1924

25 He does it with a better grace, but I do it more natural.

William Shakespeare 1564–1616: *Twelfth Night* (1601)

Sheridan's son Tom announced that when he became an MP he would proclaim his independence of party by writing 'To Let' on his forehead:

26 And, under that, Tom, write 'unfurnished'.

Richard Brinsley Sheridan
1751–1816: Walter Jerrold *Bon-Mots* (1893)

27 'A soldier,' cried my Uncle Toby, interrupting the corporal, 'is no more exempt from saying a foolish thing, Trim, than a man of letters.'—'But not so often, an' please your honour,' replied the corporal.

Laurence Sterne 1713–68: *Tristram Shandy* (1759–67)

28 Major Yammerton was rather a peculiar man, inasmuch as he was an ass, without being a fool.

R. S. Surtees 1805–64: *Ask Mamma* (1858)

29 How haughtily he lifts his nose,
To tell what every schoolboy knows.

Jonathan Swift 1667–1745: 'The Journal' (1727)

30 Hain't we got all the fools in town on our side? and ain't that a big enough majority in any town?

Mark Twain 1835–1910: *The Adventures of Huckleberry Finn* (1884)

31 Man is without any doubt the most interesting fool there is. Also the most eccentric. He hasn't a single written law, in his Bible or out of it, which has any but one purpose and intention—to *limit or defeat a law of God.*

Mark Twain 1835–1910: *Letters from the Earth* (1905–09)

32 Better to keep your mouth shut and appear stupid than to open it and remove all doubt.

Mark Twain 1835–1910: James Munson (ed.) *The Sayings of Mark Twain* (1992); attributed, perhaps apocryphal

33 Ignorance is like a delicate exotic fruit; touch it and the bloom is gone.

Oscar Wilde 1854–1900: *The Importance of Being Earnest* (1895)

34 As any fule kno.

Geoffrey Willans 1911–58 and **Ronald Searle** 1920– : *Down with Skool!* (1953)

Football See also Sports and Games

1 Why is there only one ball for 22 players? If you gave a ball to each of them, they'd stop fighting for it.
  comment of a football widow, posted on an anti-World Cup website

Anonymous: in *Daily Telegraph* 28 December 1998 'Sporting Quotes of the Year'

2 If I had the wings of a sparrow
If I had the arse of a crow
I'd fly over Tottenham tomorrow
And shit on the bastards below.

Anonymous: frequently sung on the Chelsea terraces; Ned Sherrin *Cutting Edge* (1984)

3 I hate manly men. Four men in a car talking about football is my idea of hell.

David Bailey 1938– : in *Observer* 2 May 1999 'Sayings of the Week'

George Best was often told by Matt Busby not to bother to turn up for Busby's team talks to Manchester United:

4 It wasn't worth his coming. It was a very simple team talk. All I used to say was: 'Whenever possible, give the ball to George.'

Matt Busby 1909–94: Michael Parkinson *Sporting Lives* (1993)

5 Football's football; if that weren't the case, it wouldn't be the game it is.

Garth Crooks 1958– : Barry Fantoni (ed.) *Private Eye's Colemanballs 2* (1984)

6 United will no longer be a football club, it will be a giant Old Trafford fruit machine.

Tommy Docherty 1928– : in *Mail on Sunday* 13 September 1998 'Quotes of the Week'

7 One is not amused at that.
reported comment when the disallowing of a goal put England out of the World Cup

Elizabeth II 1926– : in *Daily Telegraph* 28 December 1998 'Sporting Quotes of the Year'

8 Football, wherein is nothing but beastly fury, and extreme violence, whereof proceedeth hurt, and consequently rancour and malice do remain with them that be wounded.

Thomas Elyot 1499–1546: *Book of the Governor* (1531)

9 The only thing that Norwich didn't get was the goal that they finally got.

Jimmy Greaves 1940– : Barry Fantoni (ed.) *Private Eye's Colemanballs 2* (1984)

10 The natural state of the football fan is bitter disappointment, no matter what the score.

Nick Hornby 1957– : *Fever Pitch* (1992)

11 The nice aspect about football is that, if things go wrong, it's the manager who gets the blame.
before his first match as captain of England

Gary Lineker 1960– : in *Independent* 12 September 1990

12 You can't buy talent like that. And even if you could, it would cost you a lot of money.
comment of the Republic of Ireland manager on the prodigiously talented Robbie Keane

Mick McCarthy: in *Daily Telegraph* 28 December 1998 'Sporting Quotes of the Year'

13 Oh, he's football crazy, he's football mad
And the football it has robbed him o' the wee bit sense he had.
And it would take a dozen skivvies, his clothes to wash and scrub,
Since our Jock became a member of that terrible football club.

Jimmy McGregor: 'Football Crazy' (1960)

14 Nobody cares if Le Saux is gay or not. It is the fact that he openly admits to reading *The Guardian* that makes him the most reviled man in football.

Piers Morgan 1965– : letter to *Guardian*, 5 March 1999

15 When you are two stone overweight and 44 years of age, winning one as a manager isn't bad either.
on the victory in the All-Ireland football championship of the Kerry team trained by him

Páidi O'Sé: in *Irish Post* 3 October 1997

16 At least he'll get a game now.
of Gianluca Vialli as replacement for Ruud Gullit as Chelsea's player-manager, referring to Vialli's frequent presence on the substitutes' bench during Gullit's management

Peter Osgood 1947– : on Sky TV, 12 February 1998; in *Daily Telegraph* 13 February 1998

17 To say that these men paid their shillings to watch twenty-two hirelings kick a ball is merely to say that a violin is wood and catgut, that *Hamlet* is so much paper and ink. For a shilling the Bruddersford United AFC offered you Conflict and Art.

J. B. Priestley 1894–1984: *Good Companions* (1929)

18 We didn't underestimate them. They were a lot better than we thought.
on Cameroon's football team

Bobby Robson 1933– : in *Guardian* 24 December 1990 'Sports Quotes of the Year'

19 I don't drop players. I make changes.
a football manager's view

Bill Shankly 1914–81: in *Guardian* 24 December 1973 'Sports Quotes of the Year'

20 Some people think football is a matter of life and death . . . I can assure them it is much more serious than that.

Bill Shankly 1914–81: in *Guardian* 24 December 1973 'Sports Quotes of the Year'

21 [Gary Lineker is] the Queen Mother of football.

Arthur Smith 1954– and **Chris England**: *An Evening with Gary Lineker* (1990)

22 The English football team—brilliant on paper, shit on grass.

Arthur Smith 1954– and **Chris England**: *An Evening with Gary Lineker* (1990)

23 Football and cookery are the two most important subjects in the country.
having been appointed a director of Norwich City football club

Delia Smith 1941– : in *Observer* 23 February 1997 'Said and Done'

24 We're having a philosophical discussion about the yob ethics of professional footballers.

Tom Stoppard 1937– : *Professional Foul* (1978)

25 Me and the wife are breeding our own team. When I get home tonight it'll be 'c'mon hen, we need a centre-back.'
comment by the manager of Coventry, whose son is a Sky Blues youth-team player

Gordon Strachan: in *Daily Telegraph* 28 December 1998 'Sporting Quotes of the Year'

Friends and Enemies

1 I may be wrong, but I have never found deserting friends conciliates enemies.

Margot Asquith 1864–1945: *Lay Sermons* (1927)

2 It may be more difficult to make new friends as you get older but it is some consolation to know how easy it is to lose them when you are young.

Jeffrey Bernard 1932–97: in *The Spectator* 17 August 1985

3 A person whom we know well enough to borrow from, but not well enough to lend to. A degree of friendship called slight when its object is poor or obscure, and intimate when he is rich or famous.

Ambrose Bierce 1842–c.1914: definition of an acquaintance; *The Cynic's Word Book* (1906)

4 I do not love thee, Dr Fell.
The reason why I cannot tell;
But this I know, and know full well,
I do not love thee, Dr Fell.

Thomas Brown 1663–1704: written while an undergraduate at Christ Church, Oxford, of which Dr Fell was Dean

of a rival:
5 Such a clever actress. Pity she does her hair with Bovril.

Mrs Patrick Campbell 1865–1940: in *Ned Sherrin in his Anecdotage* (1993); attributed

during an audience with the Pope:
6 I expect you know my friend Evelyn Waugh, who, like your holiness, is a Roman Catholic.

Randolph Churchill 1911–68: attributed; in *Penguin Dictionary of Modern Quotations* (1971)

7 To find a friend one must close one eye. To keep him—two.

Norman Douglas 1868–1952: *Almanac* (1941)

8 Rejoice, rejoice, rejoice.
telephone call to his office on hearing of Margaret Thatcher's fall from power in 1990

Edward Heath 1916– : attributed; in *Daily Telegraph* 24 September 1998 (online edition)

9 Greater love than this, he said, no man hath that a man lay down his wife for his friend. Go thou and do likewise. Thus, or words to that effect, saith Zarathustra, sometime regius professor of French letters to the university of Oxtail.

James Joyce 1882–1941: *Ulysses* (1922)

10 [Friends are] God's apology for relations.

Hugh Kingsmill 1889–1949: Michael Holroyd *The Best of Hugh Kingsmill* (1970)

11 I detest him more than cold boiled veal.

Lord Macaulay 1800–59: of the Tory essayist and politician John Wilson Croker; letter 5 August 1831

12 Money couldn't buy friends but you got a better class of enemy.

Spike Milligan 1918– : *Puckoon* (1963)

13 People wish their enemies dead—but I do not; I say give them the gout, give them the stone!

Lady Mary Wortley Montagu 1689–1762: W. S. Lewis et al. (eds.) *Horace Walpole's Correspondence* (1973)

14 There is nothing like sexual frustration to give warmth to friendship, which flourishes in prisons, armies, on Arctic expeditions and did well in wartime Oxford.

John Mortimer 1923– : *Clinging to the Wreckage* (1982)

15 Any kiddie in school can love like a fool,
But hating, my boy, is an art.

Ogden Nash 1902–71: 'Plea for Less Malice Toward None' (1933)

16 Scratch a lover, and find a foe.

Dorothy Parker 1893–1967: 'Ballade of a Great Weariness' (1937)

17 If it is abuse,—why one is always sure to hear of it from one damned goodnatured friend or another!

Richard Brinsley Sheridan 1751–1816: *The Critic* (1779)

18 I am a hoarder of two things: documents and trusted friends.

Muriel Spark 1918– : *Curriculum Vitae* (1992)

19 We were in some little time fixed in our seats, and sat with that dislike which people not too good-natured usually conceive of each other at first sight.

Richard Steele 1672–1729: *The Spectator* 1 August 1711

20 You had only two friends in the world, and having killed one you can't afford to irritate the other.

Tom Stoppard 1937– : *Artist Descending a Staircase* (1973)

on Harold Macmillan's sacking seven of his Cabinet on 13 July 1962:
21 Greater love hath no man than this, that he lay down his friends for his life.

Jeremy Thorpe 1929– : D. E. Butler and Anthony King *The General Election of 1964* (1965)

22 It takes your enemy and your friend, working together, to hurt you to the heart: the one to slander you and the other to get the news to you.

Mark Twain 1835–1910: *Following the Equator* (1897)

23 Unfortunately we have little in common except a mutual knowledge of a story by Charlotte Yonge in which the hero is an albino curate with eyes like rubies. This is cordial, but not enough.

Sylvia Townsend Warner 1893–1978: letter, 31 October 1967

24 He [Bernard Shaw] hasn't an enemy in the world, and none of his friends like him.

Oscar Wilde 1854–1900: George Bernard Shaw *Sixteen Self Sketches* (1949)

25 *I* go to the OP club [a theatrical society where he would have faced a hostile audience]? I should be like a poor lion in a den of Daniels.

Oscar Wilde 1854–1900: Ford Madox Ford *Return to Yesterday* (1931)

26 I find that forgiving one's enemies is a most curious morbid pleasure; perhaps I should check it.

Oscar Wilde 1854–1900: letter ?20 April 1894

27 A man cannot be too careful in the choice of his enemies.

Oscar Wilde 1854–1900: *The Picture of Dorian Gray* (1891)

28 We remain bestest of friends.
in the week of her divorce, on her relations with her former husband

Sarah, Duchess of York 1959– : in *Observer* 21 April 1996 'Sayings of the Week'

The Future See also **Past and Present**

1 Fascism is not in itself a new order of society. It is the future refusing to be born.

Aneurin Bevan 1897–1960: Leon Harris *The Fine Art of Political Wit* (1965)

2 That period of time in which our affairs prosper, our friends are true, and our happiness is assured.

Ambrose Bierce 1842–c.1914: *The Cynic's Word Book* (1906)

3 Posterity is as likely to be wrong as anybody else.

Heywood Broun 1888–1939: *Sitting on the World* (1924)

4 In our little house, the question was whether the war would break out first, or the revolution. This was around 1910.

Claud Cockburn 1904–81: *In Time of Trouble* (1956)

5 I never think of the future. It comes soon enough.

Albert Einstein 1879–1955: interview given on the *Belgenland*, December 1930

6 Why should I write for posterity?
What, if I may be free
To ask a ridiculous question,
Has posterity done for me?

E. Y. Harburg 1898–1981: 'Posterity is Right Around the Corner' (1976)

7 This very remarkable man
Commends a most practical plan:
You can do what you want
If you don't think you can't,
So don't think you can't think you can.

Charles Inge 1868–1957: 'On Monsieur Coué' (1928)

8 You can only predict things after they have happened.

Eugène Ionesco 1912–94: *Le Rhinocéros* (1959)

9 Cheer up! the worst is yet to come!

Philander Chase Johnson 1866–1939: in *Everybody's Magazine* May 1920

10 The bridge to the future is the phallus.

D. H. Lawrence 1885–1930: *Sex, Literature and Censorship* (1955)

11 Lord Kelvin presently ratified this. Being Scotch, he didn't mind damnation and he gave the sun and the whole solar system only ninety million years more to live.

Stephen Leacock 1869–1944: *The Boy I Left Behind Me* (1947)

announcing that he had abandoned his plan to have his head preserved by the cryonics movement:
12 They have no sense of humour. I was worried I would wake up in 50 years surrounded by people with clipboards.

Timothy Leary 1920–96: in *Daily Telegraph* 10 May 1996

13 Soon we'll be sliding down the razor-blade of life.

Tom Lehrer 1928– : 'Bright College Days' (c.1960)

14 ANDERSON: Tomorrow is another day, McKendrick.
MCKENDRICK: Tomorrow, in my experience, is usually the same day.

Tom Stoppard 1937– : *Professional Foul* (1978)

Gambling See **Betting and Gambling**

Games See **Sports and Games**

Gardens and Gardening

1 I'm not a dirt gardener. I sit with my walking stick and point things out that need to be done. After many years, the garden is now totally obedient.

Hardy Amies 1909– : in *Sunday Times* 11 July 1999

2 One thimbleful of water every blue moon does not constitute expertise. Otherwise we should all be fellows of the Royal Horticultural Society.

Alan Bennett 1934– : *Getting On* (1972)

3 Laid to lawn? This is laid to adventure playground.

Basil Boothroyd 1910–88: *Let's Move House* (1977)

4 A delectable sward, shaved as close as a bridegroom and looking just as green.

Basil Boothroyd 1910–88: *Let's Move House* (1977)

5 Gr-r-r—there go, my heart's abhorrence!
Water your damned flower-pots, do!
If hate killed men, Brother Lawrence,
God's blood, would not mine kill you!

Robert Browning 1812–89: 'Soliloquy of the Spanish Cloister' (1842)

6 I will keep returning to the virtues of sharp and swift drainage, whether a plant prefers to be wet or dry . . . I would have called this book Better Drains, but you would never have bought it or borrowed it for bedtime.

Robin Lane Fox 1946– : *Better Gardening* (1982)

7 Everyone had a Japanese maple, although after Pearl Harbour most of these were patriotically poisoned, ringbarked and extirpated.

Barry Humphries 1934– : *More Please* (1992)

8 I was dosing the greenfly . . . with that frightfully good aerosol defoliant that Picarda got the recipe for from some boffin on the run from Porton Down.

Richard Ingrams 1937– and **John Wells** 1936– : *The Other Half* (1981); 'Dear Bill' letters

9 Mad fools of gardeners go out in the pouring rain
To prove they're Anglo-Saxon
They rarely put their macks on;
Each puts on rubber boots and squelches through moist terrain,
Then leaves the mud and silt on
The Wilton.

Alan Melville 1910–83: *Gnomes and Gardens* (1983)

10 When you get down to it, as sooner or later you must, gardening is a long-drawn-out war of attrition against the elements, a tripartite agreement involving the animal, insect and bird worlds, and the occasional sheer perversity of Nature.

Alan Melville 1910–83: *Gnomes and Gardens* (1983)

11 Irish gardens beat *all* for horror. With 19 gardeners, Lord Talbot of Malahide has produced an affair exactly like a suburban golf course.

Nancy Mitford 1904–73: letter 24 May 1965

12 'I distinguish the picturesque and the beautiful, and I add to them, in the laying out of the grounds, a third and distinct character, which I call *unexpectedness*.'
'Pray, Sir,' said Mr Milestone, 'by what name do you distinguish this character, when a person walks round the grounds for a second time?'

Thomas Love Peacock 1785–1866: *Headlong Hall* (1816)

13 'All really grim gardeners possess a keen sense of humus.' Capt. W. D. Pontoon.

W. C. Sellar 1898–1951 and **R. J. Yeatman** 1898–1968: *Garden Rubbish* (1930); chapter heading

14 'A garden is a loathsome thing—so what? Capt. W. D. Pontoon.

W. C. Sellar 1898–1951 and **R. J. Yeatman** 1898–1968: *Garden Rubbish* (1930); chapter heading

15 'I want to be a lawn.' Greta Garbo.

W. C. Sellar 1898–1951 and **R. J. Yeatman** 1898–1968: *Garden Rubbish* (1930); chapter heading

16 There will be old ladies and their dogs lying in front of the bulldozers.
on the proposals to establish a memorial garden to Diana, Princess of Wales, in Kensington Garden, a plan opposed by many local residents

Brian Sewell: in *Daily Telegraph* 10 July 1998

17 Perennials are the ones that grow like weeds, biennials are the ones that die this year instead of next and hardy annuals are the ones that never come up at all.

Katharine Whitehorn 1926– : *Observations* (1970)

The Generation Gap See also **Children, Parents**

1 Time is the one thing you have got. If there's one thing I envy you for, it's not your cool and your easy birds . . . it's time.

Alan Bennett 1934– : *Getting On* (1972)

2 It is the one war in which everyone changes sides.

Cyril Connolly 1903–74: Tom Driberg, speech in House of Commons, 30 October 1959

3 Grown-ups never understand anything for themselves, and it is tiresome for children to be always and forever explaining things to them.

Antoine de Saint-Exupéry 1900–44: *Le Petit Prince* (1943)

4 When I was young, the old regarded me as an outrageous young fellow, and now that I'm old the young regard me as an outrageous old fellow.

Fred Hoyle 1915– : in *Scientific American* March 1995

5 What is a teenager in San Francisco to rebel against, for pity's sake? Their parents are all so busy trying to be non-judgemental, it's no wonder they take to dyeing their hair green.

Molly Ivins 1944– : in *Dallas Times Herald* 3 February 1987

6 I . . . remember how I regarded adults when I was small. They seemed a grey crew to me, too fond of sitting down, too keen on small talk, too accustomed to having nothing to look forward to.

Ian McEwan 1948– : *Enduring Love* (1998)

7 So what are we going to do with our pricey ancestors? I really can't think of anything. Except maybe we could hunt them down and kill them. The government could sell licenses and old-bat stamps.

P. J. O'Rourke 1947– : *Parliament of Whores* (1991)

8 Remember the battle between the generations twenty-some years ago . . . Well, our parents won. They're out there living the American dream on some damned golf course, and we're stuck with the jobs and haircuts.

P. J. O'Rourke 1947- : *Parliament of Whores* (1991)

9 The young have aspirations that never come to pass, the old have reminiscences of what never happened.

Saki 1870–1916: *Reginald* (1904)

10 The denunciation of the young is a necessary part of the hygiene of older people, and greatly assists the circulation of their blood.

Logan Pearsall Smith 1865–1946: *Afterthoughts* (1931) 'Age and Death'

11 There is more felicity on the far side of baldness than young men can possibly imagine.

Logan Pearsall Smith 1865–1946: *Afterthoughts* (1931) 'Age and Death'

12 When I was a boy of 14, my father was so ignorant I could hardly stand to have the old man around. But when I got to be 21, I was astonished at how much the old man had learned in seven years.

Mark Twain 1835–1910: attributed in *Reader's Digest* September 1939, but not traced in his works

13 Two things my parents did for me as a child stand head and shoulders above what parents usually do for their children. They had me in Egypt and they set me a vivid example of everything I didn't want to be when I grew up.

Jill Tweedie 1936–93: *Eating Children* (1993)

14 When I was your age . . . I had been an inconsolable widower for three months, and was already paying my addresses to your admirable mother.

Oscar Wilde 1854–1900: *An Ideal Husband* (1895)

God See also **Religion**

1 If it turns out that there is a God, I don't think that he's evil. But the worst that you can say about him is that basically he's an underachiever.

Woody Allen 1935- : *Love and Death* (1975 film)

2 If only God would give me some clear sign! Like making a large deposit in my name at a Swiss bank.

Woody Allen 1935- : 'Selections from the Allen Notebooks' in *New Yorker* 5 November 1973

3 God is silent, now if only we can get Man to shut up.

Woody Allen 1935- : 'Remembering Needleman' (1976)

4 God is not dead but alive and working on a much less ambitious project.

Anonymous: graffito quoted in *Guardian* 26 November 1975

5 Dear Sir,
Your astonishment's odd:
I am always about in the Quad.
And that's why the tree
Will continue to be,
Since observed by
Yours faithfully,
God.

Anonymous: reply to verse by Ronald Knox (see **God** 29); Langford Reed *Complete Limerick Book* (1924)

6 Not odd
Of God:
Goyim
Annoy 'im.

Anonymous: in *Leo Rosten's Book of Laughter* (1986); see **God** 13, 21

7 If I were Her what would really piss me off the worst is that they cannot even get My gender right for Christsakes.

Roseanne Arnold 1953- : *Roseanne* (1990)

8 CLAIRE: How do you know you're . . . God?
EARL OF GURNEY: Simple. When I pray to Him I find I'm
talking to myself.

Peter Barnes 1931– : *The Ruling Class* (1969)

9 Let us pray to God . . . the bastard! He doesn't exist!

Samuel Beckett 1906–89: *Endgame* (1958)

replying to the Master of Trinity College Cambridge, H. M. Butler, who in proposing the health of the College had said that 'it was well to remember that, at this moment, both the Sovereign and the Prime Minister are Trinity men':
10 The Master should have added that he can go further, for it is obvious that the affairs of the world are built upon the momentous fact that God also is a Trinity man.

Augustine Birrell 1850–1933: Harold Laski, letter to Oliver Wendell Holmes, 4 December 1926

Birrell once saw a man treat George Eliot rudely:
11 I sat down in a corner and prayed to God to blast him. God did nothing, and ever since I have been an agnostic.

Augustine Birrell 1850–1933: Harold Laski, letter to Oliver Wendell Holmes, 21 January 1928

Boswell's daughter had concluded that God did not exist:
12 I looked into Cambrai's *Education of a Daughter*, hoping to have found some simple argument for the being of God. But it is taken for granted.

James Boswell 1740–95: diary, 20 December 1779

13 But not so odd
As those who choose
A Jewish God,
But spurn the Jews.

Cecil Browne 1932– : reply to verse by William Norman Ewer; see **God** 6, 21

14 An apology for the Devil: It must be remembered that we have only heard one side of the case. God has written all the books.

Samuel Butler 1835–1902: *Notebooks* (1912)

15 God will not always be a Tory.

Lord Byron 1788–1824: letter, 2 February 1821

16 Isn't God a shit?
while reading the Bible straight through for a bet

Randolph Churchill 1911–68: Evelyn Waugh, diary 11 November 1944

17 Thou shalt have one God only; who
Would be at the expense of two?

Arthur Hugh Clough 1819–61: 'The Latest Decalogue' (1862)

18 Do I believe in God? Let's say we have a working relationship.

Noël Coward 1899–1973: Sheridan Morley *The Quotable Noël Coward* (1999)

19 I don't believe in God because I don't believe in Mother Goose.

Clarence Darrow 1857–1938: speech in Toronto in 1930

20 Our only hope rests on the off-chance that God does exist.

Alice Thomas Ellis 1932– : *Unexplained Laughter* (1985)

21 How odd
Of God
To choose
The Jews.

William Norman Ewer 1885–1976: *Week-End Book* (1924); see **God** 6, 13

22 Forgive, O Lord, my little jokes on Thee
And I'll forgive Thy great big one on me.

Robert Frost 1874–1963: 'Cluster of Faith' (1962)

23 Did God who gave us flowers and trees,
Also provide the allergies?

E. Y. Harburg 1898–1981: 'A Nose is a Nose is a Nose' (1965)

24 God will pardon me, it is His trade.

Heinrich Heine 1797–1856: on his deathbed, in Alfred Meissner *Heinrich Heine. Erinnerungen* (1856)

25 The great act of faith is when a man decides he is not God.

Oliver Wendell Holmes Jr. 1841–1935: letter to William James, 24 March 1907

to an undergraduate trying to excuse himself from attendance at early morning chapel on the plea of loss of faith:
26 You will find God by tomorrow morning, or leave this college.

Benjamin Jowett 1817–93: Kenneth Rose *Superior Person* (1969)

27 Zeus, 'the God of wine and whoopee'.

Garrison Keillor 1942– : *The Book of Guys* (1994)

28 The peculiar, even unsatisfactory system whereby God never communicated direct with his chosen people but preferred to give the Israelite leaders an off-the-record briefing.

Miles Kington 1941– : *Welcome to Kington* (1989)

29 There once was a man who said, 'God
Must think it exceedingly odd
If he finds that this tree
Continues to be
When there's no one about in the Quad.'

Ronald Knox 1888–1957: Langford Reed *Complete Limerick Book* (1924); see **God** 5

30 I do not have the ear of the Almighty, and I shrink from guessing His plans for this world; but there must be a file somewhere in the heavenly archives marked 'Total destruction by Fire/Brimstone/Plague/Flood/Great Beast/ Other', and I have an uneasy feeling He may be about to blow the dust off it.

Bernard Levin 1928– : *If You Want My Opinion* (1992)

on readings in the school chapel:
31 Why was almost everybody in the Old Testament permanently ratty and disagreeable, with God (whom we were constantly thanking for this or that) by far the rattiest of the lot? It didn't make sense then and, by golly, it makes a great deal less now.

Arthur Marshall 1910–89: *Life's Rich Pageant* (1984)

32 I don't know why it is that the religious never ascribe common sense to God.

W. Somerset Maugham 1874–1965: *A Writer's Notebook* (1949) written in 1941

33 The chief contribution of Protestantism to human thought is its massive proof that God is a bore.

H. L. Mencken 1880–1956: *Minority Report* (1956)

34 It is impossible to imagine the universe run by a wise, just and omnipotent God, but it is quite easy to imagine it run by a board of gods. If such a board actually exists it operates precisely like the board of a corporation that is losing money.

H. L. Mencken 1880–1956: *Minority Report* (1956)

35 God, to whom, if he existed, I felt I should have nothing very polite to say.

John Mortimer 1923– : *Clinging to the Wreckage* (1982)

36 Satan probably wouldn't have talked so big if God had been his wife.

P. J. O'Rourke 1947– : *Modern Manners* (1984)

37 God is an elderly or, at any rate, middle-aged male, a stern fellow, patriarchal rather than paternal and a great believer in rules and regulations.

P. J. O'Rourke 1947– : *Parliament of Whores* (1991)

38 God, whom you doubtless remember as that quaint old subordinate of General Douglas MacArthur.

S. J. Perelman 1904–79: letter to Mel Elliott, 24 April 1951

39 God can stand being told by Professor Ayer and Marghanita Laski that He doesn't exist.

J. B. Priestley 1894–1984: in *Listener* 1 July 1965

40 Those who set out to serve both God and Mammon soon discover that there is no God.

Logan Pearsall Smith 1865–1946: *Afterthoughts* (1931) 'Other People'

41 For ten years of my life, three times a day, I thanked the Lord for what I was about to receive and thanked him again for what I had just received, and then we lost touch—and I suddenly thought, *where is He now?*

Tom Stoppard 1937– : *Where Are They Now?* (1973)

42 Only one thing, is impossible for God: to find any sense in any copyright law on the planet.

Mark Twain 1835–1910: Notebook 23 May 1903

43 God was left out of the Constitution but was furnished a front seat on the coins of the country.

Mark Twain 1835–1910: *Mark Twain in Eruption* (1940)

44 Even God has become female. God is no longer the bearded patriarch in the sky. He has had a sex change and turned into Mother Nature.

Fay Weldon 1931– : in *The Times* 29 August 1998

Golf See also **Sports and Games**

1 His drive has gone to pieces, largely through having more hinges in it than a sardine tin. But he could always play his iron shots, and his never-ending chatter must be worth at least two holes to his side.

on the golf course, on being asked by Nancy Cunard, 'What is your handicap?'

James Agate 1877–1947: diary, 7 August 1938

2 Drink and debauchery.

Lord Castlerosse 1891–1943: Philip Ziegler *Diana Cooper* (1981)

3 QUESTION: What is your handicap?
ANSWER: I'm a colored, one-eyed Jew—do I need anything else?

Sammy Davis Jnr. 1925–90: *Yes I Can* (1965)

4 Of course I want to win it . . . I'm not here to have a good time, nor to keep warm and dry.
while leading the field, in wet weather, during the 1996 PGA Championship

Nick Faldo 1957– : in *Guardian* 25 May 1996

5 One who has to shout 'Fore' when he putts.
definition of a Coarse Golfer

Michael Green 1927– : *The Art of Coarse Golf* (1967)

6 Men who would face torture without a word become blasphemous at the short fourteenth. It is clear that the game of golf may well be included in that category of intolerable provocations which may legally excuse or mitigate behaviour not otherwise excusable.

A. P. Herbert 1890–1971: *Misleading Cases* (1935)

7 If you watch a game, it's fun. If you play it, it's recreation. If you work at it, it's golf.

Bob Hope 1903– : in *Reader's Digest* October 1958

8 At least our relationship lasted longer than either of Nick's two marriages.
on being sacked as Nick Faldo's coach after 13 years

David Leadbetter: in *Sunday Telegraph* 28 December 1998 'Sporting Quotes of the Year'

9 While tearing off
A game of golf
I may make a play for the caddy.

Cole Porter 1891–1964: 'My Heart belongs to Daddy' (1938)

But when I do
I don't follow through
'Cause my heart belongs to Daddy.

10 I'm playing like Tarzan and scoring like Jane.

Chi Chi Rodrigues 1935- : attributed, 1982

11 Golf is a good walk spoiled.

Mark Twain 1835–1910: Alex Ayres *Greatly Exaggerated: the Wit and Wisdom of Mark Twain* (1988); attributed

12 The uglier a man's legs are, the better he plays golf—it's almost a law.

H. G. Wells 1866–1946: *Bealby* (1915)

13 The least thing upset him on the links. He missed short putts because of the uproar of the butterflies in the adjoining meadows.

P. G. Wodehouse 1881–1975: *The Clicking of Cuthbert* (1922)

14 Golf . . . is the infallible test. The man who can go into a patch of rough alone, with the knowledge that only God is watching him, and play his ball where it lies, is the man who will serve you faithfully and well.

P. G. Wodehouse 1881–1975: *The Clicking of Cuthbert* (1922)

Gossip

1 I know that's a secret, for it's whispered every where.

William Congreve 1670–1729: *Love for Love* (1695)

2 They come together like the Coroner's Inquest, to sit upon the murdered reputations of the week.

William Congreve 1670–1729: *The Way of the World* (1700)

3 A secret in the Oxford sense: you may tell it to only one person at a time.

Oliver Franks 1905–92: in *Sunday Telegraph* 30 January 1977

4 It's the gossip columnist's business to write about what is none of his business.

Louis Kronenberger 1904- : *The Cart and the Horse* (1964)

5 I hate to spread rumours, but what else can one do with them?

Amanda Lear: in an interview in 1978; Jonathon Green (ed.) *A Dictionary of Contemporary Quotations* (1978)

6 If you haven't got anything good to say about anyone come and sit by me.

Alice Roosevelt Longworth 1884–1980: maxim embroidered on a cushion; Michael Teague *Mrs L: Conversations with Alice Roosevelt Longworth* (1981)

7 She proceeds to dip her little fountain-pen filler into pots of oily venom and to squirt this mixture at all her friends.
   of the society hostess Mrs Ronnie Greville

Harold Nicolson 1886–1968: diary, 20 July 1937

8 Gossip is what you say about the objects of flattery when they aren't present.

P. J. O'Rourke 1947- : *Modern Manners* (1984)

9 You have dished me up, like a savoury omelette, to gratify the appetite of the reading rabble for gossip.

Thomas Love Peacock 1785–1866: *Crotchet Castle* (1831)

10 I hope there's a tinge of disgrace about me. Hopefully, there's one good scandal left in me yet.

Diana Rigg 1938- : in *The Times* 3 May 1999

11 I'm called away by particular business—but I leave my character behind me.

Richard Brinsley Sheridan 1751–1816: *The School for Scandal* (1777)

12 Here is the whole set! a character dead at every word.

Richard Brinsley Sheridan
1751–1816: *The School for Scandal*
(1777)

13 It is perfectly monstrous the way people go about, nowadays, saying things against one behind one's back that are absolutely and entirely true.

Oscar Wilde 1854–1900: *A Woman of No Importance* (1893)

14 There is only one thing in the world worse than being talked about, and that is not being talked about.

Oscar Wilde 1854–1900: *The Picture of Dorian Gray* (1891)

Government See also **Democracy, Politics**

1 The first requirement of a statesman is that he be dull.

Dean Acheson 1893–1971: in *Observer* 21 June 1970

2 There is, in fact, no law or government at all [in Italy]; and it is wonderful how well things go on without them.

Lord Byron 1788–1824: letter, 2 January 1821

3 Democracy means government by the uneducated, while aristocracy means government by the badly educated.

G. K. Chesterton 1874–1936: in *New York Times* 1 February 1931

4 And they that rule in England,
In stately conclaves met,
Alas, alas for England
They have no graves as yet.

G. K. Chesterton 1874–1936: 'Elegy in a Country Churchyard' (1922)

5 Like most Chief Whips he [Michael Jopling] knew who the shits were.

Alan Clark 1928–99: diary, 17 June 1987

6 A wartime Minister of Information is compelled, in the national interest, to such continuous acts of duplicity that even his natural hair must grow to resemble a wig.
of Brendan Bracken

Claud Cockburn 1904–81: *Crossing the Line* (1958)

7 MRS THATCHER: I do not create peers to have them vote against me in the House of Lords.
LORD DENHAM: Prime Minister, even you should know better than to expect me to find you a majority during Gold Cup week.
exchange between the Prime Minister and the Leader of the House of Lords

Lord Denham 1927– : Peter Hennessy *The Prime Minister* (2000)

8 Distrust of authority should be the first civic duty.

Norman Douglas 1868–1952: *An Almanac* October (1941)

9 No patent medicine was ever put to wider and more varied use than the Fourteenth Amendment.

William O. Douglas 1898–1980: Hugo Black Jr. *My Father: A Remembrance* (1975)

10 Ambassadors cropped up like hay,
Prime Ministers and such as they
Grew like asparagus in May,
And dukes were three a penny.

W. S. Gilbert 1836–1911: *The Gondoliers* (1889)

11 But the privilege and pleasure
That we treasure beyond measure
Is to run on little errands for the Ministers of State.

W. S. Gilbert 1836–1911: *The Gondoliers* (1889)

12 The House of Peers, throughout the war,
Did nothing in particular,
And did it very well.

W. S. Gilbert 1836–1911: *Iolanthe* (1882)

13 'Do you pray for the senators, Dr Hale?' 'No, I look at the senators and I pray for the country.'

Edward Everett Hale 1822–1909: Van Wyck Brooks *New England Indian Summer* (1940)

14 This we learn from Watergate
That almost any creep'll
Be glad to help the Government
Overthrow the people.

E. Y. Harburg 1898–1981: 'History Lesson' (1976)

15 This high official, all allow,
Is grossly overpaid;
There wasn't any Board, and now
There isn't any Trade.

A. P. Herbert 1890–1971: 'The President of the Board of Trade' (1922)

16 People must not do things for fun. We are not here for fun. There is no reference to fun in any Act of Parliament.

A. P. Herbert 1890–1971: *Uncommon Law* (1935) 'Is it a Free Country?'

Alan Clark, then a Parliamentary Under-Secretary at the Department of Employment, asked Douglas Hogg, then a junior Whip, how he was 'keeping all the new boys in order':
17 By offering them your job.

Douglas Hogg 1945– : Alan Clark, diary, 28 July 1983

18 Many journalists have fallen for the conspiracy theory of government. I do assure you that they would produce more accurate work if they adhered to the cock-up theory.

Bernard Ingham 1932– : in *Observer* 17 March 1985

19 What an augmentation of the field for jobbing, speculating, plundering, office-building and office-hunting would be produced by an assumption of all the state powers into the hands of the general government.

Thomas Jefferson 1743–1826: letter, 13 August 1800

20 Office hours are from 12 to 1 with an hour off for lunch.
of the US Senate

George S. Kaufman 1889–1961: Howard Teichmann *George S. Kaufman* (1973)

21 We are a government of laws. Any laws some government hack can find to louse up a man who's down.

Murray Kempton 1917– : in *New York Post* 21 December 1955

22 I work for a Government I despise for ends I think criminal.

John Maynard Keynes 1883–1946: letter to Duncan Grant, 15 December 1917

23 Like Odysseus, the President [Woodrow Wilson] looked wiser when he was seated.

John Maynard Keynes 1883–1946: *The Economic Consequences of the Peace* (1919)

24 How is the world ruled and how do wars start? Diplomats tell lies to journalists and then believe what they read.

Karl Kraus 1874–1936: *Aphorisms and More Aphorisms* (1909)

25 We already have a sabbatical system. It's called opposition, and I've had enough of it.
on being told by an American professor of politics that he needed a sabbatical

Nigel Lawson 1932– : Greg Knight *Parliamentary Sauce* (1993); attributed

26 Office tends to confer a dreadful plausibility on even the most negligible of those who hold it.

Mark Lawson: Joe Queenan *Imperial Caddy* (1992); introduction

27 One of these days the people of Louisiana are going to get good government—and they aren't going to like it.

Huey Long 1893–1935: attributed

28 He [Calvin Coolidge] slept more than any other President, whether by day or by night. Nero fiddled, but Coolidge only snored.

H. L. Mencken 1880–1956: in *American Mercury* April 1933

29 The worst government is often the most moral. One composed of cynics is often very tolerant and humane. But when fanatics are on top there is no limit to oppression.

H. L. Mencken 1880–1956: *Minority Report* (1956)

30 There are two reasons for making an appointment. Either there was nobody else; or there *was* somebody else.

Lord Normanbrook 1902–67: Anthony Sampson *The Changing Anatomy of Britain* (1982)

criticism of an opposition motion to declare general warrants illegal, 17 February 1764:
31 If I was a Judge, I should pay no more regard to this resolution than to that of a drunken porter.

Fletcher Norton 1716–1789: Horace Walpole *Memoirs of the Reign of George III* (1845)

32 Whatever it is that the government does, sensible Americans would prefer that the government does it to somebody else. This is the idea behind foreign policy.

P. J. O'Rourke 1947– : *Parliament of Whores* (1991)

33 Feeling good about government is like looking on the bright side of any catastrophe. When you quit looking on the bright side, the catastrophe is still there.

P. J. O'Rourke 1947– : *Parliament of Whores* (1991)

34 Are you labouring under the impression that I read these memoranda of yours? I can't even lift them.
   to Leon Henderson

Franklin D. Roosevelt 1882–1945: J. K. Galbraith *Ambassador's Journal* (1969)

35 We all know that Prime Ministers are wedded to the truth, but like other married couples they sometimes live apart.

Saki 1870–1916: *The Unbearable Bassington* (1912)

36 Members [of civil service orders] rise from CMG (known sometimes in Whitehall as 'Call Me God') to the KCMG ('Kindly Call Me God') to—for a select few governors and super-ambassadors—the GCMG ('God Calls Me God').

Anthony Sampson 1926– : *Anatomy of Britain* (1962)

37 The art of government is the organization of idolatry.

George Bernard Shaw 1856–1950: *Man and Superman* (1903) 'Maxims: Idolatry'

38 A government which robs Peter to pay Paul can always depend on the support of Paul.

George Bernard Shaw 1856–1950: *Everybody's Political What's What?* (1944)

39 Back in the East you can't do much without the right papers, but *with* the right papers you can do *anything*. They *believe* in papers. Papers are power.

Tom Stoppard 1937– : *Neutral Ground* (1983)

40 The House of Lords, an illusion to which I have never been able to subscribe—responsibility without power, the prerogative of the eunuch throughout the ages.

Tom Stoppard 1937– : *Lord Malquist and Mr Moon* (1966)

41 I don't mind how much my Ministers talk, so long as they do what I say.

Margaret Thatcher 1925– : in *Observer* 27 January 1980

42 Those who want the Government to regulate matters of the mind and spirit are like men who are so afraid of being murdered that they commit suicide to avoid assassination.

Harry S. Truman 1884–1972: address at the National Archives, Washington, D.C., 15 December 1952

43 That loyal retainer of the Chase Manhattan Bank, the American president.

Gore Vidal 1925– : in *Esquire* August 1980

of his first Cabinet meeting as Prime Minister:
44 An extraordinary affair. I gave them their orders and they wanted to stay and discuss them.

Duke of Wellington 1769–1852: Peter Hennessy *Whitehall* (1990)

45 It was in dealing with the early feminist that the Government acquired the tact and skilfulness with which it is now handling Ireland.

Rebecca West 1892–1983: in *Daily News* 7 August 1916

46 I accept that anomalies exist but I would not wish to remove them by taking something from people who already have it.
  on the television license fee

William Whitelaw 1918–99: in House of Commons, 1 December 1981

47 Now that the House of Commons is trying to become useful, it does a great deal of harm.

Oscar Wilde 1854–1900: *An Ideal Husband* (1895)

the White House in the time of President Eisenhower:
48 The Tomb of the Well-Known Soldier.

Emlyn Williams 1905–87: James Harding *Emlyn Williams* (1987)

Handwriting

1 That exquisite handwriting like a fly which has been trained at the Russian ballet.
  of George Bernard Shaw's handwriting

James Agate 1877–1947: diary, 22 September 1944

2 I never saw Monty James's writing but doubt whether he can have been more illegible than Lady Colefax: the only hope of deciphering *her* invitations, someone said, was to pin them up on the wall and *run* past them!

Rupert Hart-Davis 1907–99: letter to George Lyttelton, 13 November 1955

3 The dawn of legibility in his handwriting has revealed his utter inability to spell.

Ian Hay 1876–1952: attributed; perhaps used in a dramatization of *The Housemaster* (1938)

4 Did you ever get a letter from Monty James? I once had a note from him inviting us to dinner—we guessed that the time was 8 and not 3, as it appeared to be, but all we could tell about the day was that it was not Wednesday.

George Lyttelton 1883–1962: letter to Rupert Hart-Davis, 9 November 1955

of Foreign Office handwriting:
5 Iron railings leaning out of the perpendicular.

Lord Palmerston 1784–1865: J. A. Gere and John Sparrow (eds.) *Geoffrey Madan's Notebooks* (1981)

6 No individual word was decipherable, but, with a bold reader, groups could be made to conform to a scheme based on probabilities.

Edith Œ. Somerville 1858–1949 and **Martin Ross** 1862–1915: *In Mr Knox's Country* (1915)

7 I do apologise for writing by hand—and so badly. I shall soon be like Helen Thomas, notoriously illegible. In her last letter only two words stood out plain: 'Blood pressure'. Subsequent research demonstrated that what she had actually written was 'Beloved friends'.

Sylvia Townsend Warner 1893–1978: letter, 21 June 1963

8 I know that handwriting . . . I remember it perfectly. The ten commandments in every stroke of the pen, and the moral law all over the page.

Oscar Wilde 1854–1900: *An Ideal Husband* (1895)

9 As regards the mode of copying: of course it is too long for any amanuensis to attempt: and your own handwriting, dear Robbie, in your last letter seems specially designed to remind me that the task is not to be yours.

Oscar Wilde 1854–1900: letter to Robert Ross from Reading Prison, 1 April 1897

Happiness and Unhappiness See also Hope and Despair, Satisfaction and Discontent

1 No pleasure is worth giving up for the sake of two more years in a geriatric home in Weston-super-Mare.

Kingsley Amis 1922–95: in *The Times* 21 June 1994; attributed

2 You have flair . . . It's handed out at birth . . . And as always happens in these cases, it's always given to the very people who in my opinion do least to earn it. It's taken me forty-two years to think of that and I'm very depressed.

Alan Ayckbourn 1939– : *Joking Apart* (1979)

3 When people say, 'You're breaking my heart,' they do in fact usually mean that you're breaking their genitals.

Jeffrey Bernard 1932–97: in *Spectator* 31 May 1986

4 Let us have wine and women, mirth and laughter, Sermons and soda-water the day after.

Lord Byron 1788–1824: *Don Juan* (1819–24)

5 MEDVEDENKO: Why do you wear black all the time? MASHA: I'm in mourning for my life, I'm unhappy.

Anton Chekhov 1860–1904: *The Seagull* (1896)

6 When constabulary duty's to be done, A policeman's lot is not a happy one.

W. S. Gilbert 1836–1911: *The Pirates of Penzance* (1879)

7 From the standpoint of pure reason, there are no good grounds to support the claim that one should sacrifice one's own happiness to that of others.

W. Somerset Maugham 1874–1965: *A Writer's Notebook* (1949) written in 1896

8 I can imagine no more comfortable frame of mind for the conduct of life than a humorous resignation.

W. Somerset Maugham 1874–1965: *A Writer's Notebook* (1949) written in 1903

9 The fact that I have no remedy for the sorrows of the world is no reason for my accepting yours. It simply supports the strong probability that yours is a fake.

H. L. Mencken 1880–1956: *Minority Report* (1956)

10 I told him that if somebody liked to dress up in chamois leather and be stung by wasps, I really couldn't see why one should stop him.
recalling a conversation with Lord Longford on pornography

Robert Morley 1908–92: Kenneth Tynan diary, 31 March 1975

11 He's simply got the instinct for being unhappy highly developed.

Saki 1870–1916: *Chronicles of Clovis* (1911)

12 But a lifetime of happiness! No man alive could bear it: it would be hell on earth.

George Bernard Shaw 1856–1950: *Man and Superman* (1903)

13 There are two tragedies in life. One is not to get your heart's desire. The other is to get it.

George Bernard Shaw 1856–1950: *Man and Superman* (1903)

14 MRS BAKER is a woman who has managed to find a little misery in the best of things. Sorrow and trouble are the only things that can make her happy.

Neil Simon 1927– : *Come Blow Your Horn* (1961)

15 Life would be very pleasant if it were not for its enjoyments.

R. S. Surtees 1805–64: *Mr Facey Romford's Hounds* (1865)

16 I feel like I'm floating on a cloud . . . Never in a million years did I think I would be a recipient of a Dameship. It just never was in my computer.
on being appointed a DBE

Elizabeth Taylor 1932– : in *Daily Telegraph* 17 May 2000

17 Let us all be happy, and live within our means, even if we have to borrer the money to do it with.

Artemus Ward 1834–67: *Artemus Ward in London* (1867)

18 A cigarette is the perfect type of a perfect pleasure. It is exquisite, and it leaves one unsatisfied. What more can one want?

Oscar Wilde 1854–1900: *The Picture of Dorian Gray* (1891)

19 All the things I really like to do are either illegal, immoral, or fattening.

Alexander Woollcott 1887–1943: R. E. Drennan *Wit's End* (1973)

Health See also **Medicine, Sickness**

1 I feel as young as I ever did, apart from the occasional heart attack.

Robert Benchley 1889–1945: attributed

2 The two best exercises in the world are making love and dancing but a simple one is to stand on tiptoe.

Barbara Cartland 1901–2000: in 1972, attributed; in *Guardian* 22 May 2000

3 In the face of such overwhelming statistical possibilities, hypochondria has always seemed to me to be the only rational position to take on life.

John Diamond: *C: Because Cowards Get Cancer Too* (1998)

4 Exercise is the yuppie version of bulimia.

Barbara Ehrenreich 1941– : *The Worst Years of Our Lives* (1991) 'Food Worship'

on Warren Clarke's portrayal of Hill's Superintendent Dalziel:
5 REGINALD HILL: For the sake of my art you should be seven stones heavier.
WARREN CLARKE: For the sake of my heart, I shouldn't.

Reginald Hill 1936– : in *Mail on Sunday* 30 July 2000

6 Aromatherapy is like going into the countryside and smelling flowers. It should be available in Parliament. They already have it in some mental hospitals.

Simon Hughes 1951– : in *Independent* 24 January 1998

7 My uterine contractions have been bogus for sometime.

Joe Orton 1933–67: *What the Butler Saw* (1969)

8 The only exercise I take is walking behind the coffins of friends who took exercise.

Peter O'Toole 1932– : in *Mail on Sunday* 27 December 1998 'Quotes of the Year'

9 At 70, I'm in fine fettle for my age, sleep like a babe and feel around 12. The secret? Lots of meat, drink and cigarettes and not giving in to things.

Jennifer Paterson 1928–99: in *Daily Mail* 18 August 1998

10 I try to keep fit. I've got these parallel bars at home. I run at them and try to buy a drink from both of them.

Arthur Smith 1954– : attributed

11 When people discussed tonics, pick-me-ups after a severe illness, she kept to herself the prescription of a quick dip in bed with someone you liked but were not in love with. A shock of sexual astonishment which could make you feel astonishingly well and high spirited.

Mary Wesley 1912– : *Not That Sort of Girl* (1987)

Heaven and Hell

of Lord Curzon, who at the age of thirty-nine had been created Viceroy of India:
1 For all the rest of his life Curzon was influenced by his sudden journey to heaven at the age of thirty-nine, and then by his return seven years later to earth, for the remainder of his mortal existence.

Lord Beaverbrook 1879–1964: *Men and Power* (1956)

2 All are inclined to believe what they covet, from a lottery-ticket up to a passport to Paradise,—in which, from description, I see nothing very tempting.

Lord Byron 1788–1824: diary 27 November 1813

3 I always say, as you know, that if my fellow citizens want to go to Hell I will help them. It's my job.

Oliver Wendell Holmes Jr. 1841–1935: letter to Harold Laski, 4 March 1920

4 The Devil himself had probably re-designed Hell in the light of information he had gained from observing airport layouts.

Anthony Price 1928– : *The Memory Trap* (1989)

5 My idea of heaven is, eating *pâté de foie gras* to the sound of trumpets.

Sydney Smith 1771–1845: view ascribed by Smith to his friend Henry Luttrell; Peter Virgin *Sydney Smith* (1994)

6 I have friends in both places.

Mark Twain 1835–1910: Archibald Henderson *Mark Twain* (1911)

7 If Max [Beaverbrook] gets to Heaven he won't last long. He will be chucked out for trying to pull off a merger between Heaven and Hell . . . after having secured a controlling interest in key subsidiary companies in both places, of course.

H. G. Wells 1866–1946: A. J. P. Taylor *Beaverbrook* (1972)

History

1 To give an accurate and exhaustive account of the period would need a far less brilliant pen than mine.

Max Beerbohm 1872–1956: in *Yellow Book* (1895)

2 An account, mostly false, of events, mostly unimportant, which are brought about by rulers, mostly knaves, and soldiers, mostly fools.
definition of history

Ambrose Bierce 1842–c.1914: *The Cynic's Word Book* (1906)

3 History repeats itself; historians repeat one other.

Rupert Brooke 1887–1915: letter to Geoffrey Keynes, 4 June 1906

4 People who make history know nothing about history. You can see that in the sort of history they make.

G. K. Chesterton 1874–1936: J. A. Gere and John Sparrow (eds.) *Geoffrey Madan's Notebooks* (1981)

5 History teaches us that men and nations behave wisely once they have exhausted all other alternatives.

Abba Eban 1915– : speech in London 16 December 1970

6 History is more or less bunk.

Henry Ford 1863–1947: in *Chicago Tribune* 25 May 1916

7 It is a fair summary of history to say that the safeguards of liberty have been forged in controversies involving not very nice people.

Felix Frankfurter 1882–1965: dissenting opinion in *United States v. Rabinowitz* 1950

8 History is not what you thought. *It is what you can remember.*

W. C. Sellar 1898–1951 and **R. J. Yeatman** 1898–1968: *1066 and All That* (1930) 'Compulsory Preface'

9 AMERICA was thus clearly top nation, and History came to a .

W. C. Sellar 1898–1951 and **R. J. Yeatman** 1898–1968: *1066 and All That* (1930)

10 SWINDON: What will history say?
BURGOYNE: History, sir, will tell lies as usual.

George Bernard Shaw 1856–1950: *The Devil's Disciple* (1901)

11 Like most of those who study history, he [Napoleon III] learned from the mistakes of the past how to make new ones.

A. J. P. Taylor 1906–90: in *Listener* 6 June 1963

12 History gets thicker as it approaches recent times.

A. J. P. Taylor 1906–90: *English History 1914–45* (1965), bibliography

on being asked what would have happened in 1963, had Khrushchev and not Kennedy been assassinated:

13 With history one can never be certain, but I think I can safely say that Aristotle Onassis would not have married Mrs Khrushchev.

Gore Vidal 1925– : in *Sunday Times* 4 June 1989

14 Thanks to modern technology . . . history now comes equipped with a fast-forward button.

Gore Vidal 1925– : *Screening History* (1992)

the accession of Elizabeth II had been greeted with numerous articles on 'the new Elizabethan Age':

15 We are in for the undoing of all the work of recent historians who have exposed the wickedness of Elizabeth Tudor. It has begun today in all weekly papers. Rebunking.

Evelyn Waugh 1903–66: letter to Lady Diana Cooper, February 1952

16 Human history becomes more and more a race between education and catastrophe.

H. G. Wells 1866–1946: *Outline of History* (1920)

17 The one duty we owe to history is to rewrite it.

Oscar Wilde 1854–1900: *Intentions* (1891) 'The Critic as Artist' pt. 1

18 History started badly and hav been geting steadily worse.

Geoffrey Willans 1911–58 and **Ronald Searle** 1920– : *Down with Skool!* (1953)

Holidays

1 The sort of place to send your mother-in-law for a month, all expenses paid.
of Pakistan, in a BBC Radio interview, 17 March 1984; in April 1984 he was fined £1000 for making the remark by the Test and County Cricket Board

Ian Botham 1955– : in *Times* 20 March 1984

2 I would love . . . a one-year break doing absolutely nothing. Now whether, as I say to my friends, I will take to the gin bottle at 11 o'clock in the morning, and drink myself or smoke myself to death, I don't know—but I'd love to find out.

Gay Byrne 1934– : in *Irish Post* 16 May 1998

4 What kind of holiday can you take when you live in almost continual sunshine in an olive grove in the mountains, which is only twenty minutes away from the beaches and the sea?

Patrick Campbell 1913–80: *Gullible Travels* (1969)

5 There's sand in the porridge and sand in the bed, And if this is pleasure we'd rather be dead.

Noël Coward 1899–1973: 'The English Lido' (1928)

6 Cannot avoid contrasting deliriously rapid flight of time when on a holiday with very much slower passage of days, and even hours, in other and more familiar surroundings.

E. M. Delafield 1890–1943: *The Diary of a Provincial Lady* (1930)

7 It will give the public a rest as much it will reward his family.
on the question of Tony Blair's taking paternity leave

Frank Field 1942– : in *Observer* 14 May 2000 'They said what . . . ?'

8 I don't think we can do better than 'Good old Broadstairs'.

George Grossmith 1847–1912 and **Weedon Grossmith** 1854–1919: *The Diary of a Nobody* (1894)

9 I suppose we all have our recollections of our earlier holidays, all bristling with horror.

Flann O'Brien 1911–66: *Myles Away from Dublin* (1990)

10 I like to have exciting evenings on holiday, because after you've spent 8 hours reading on the beach you don't feel like turning in early with a good book.

Arthur Smith 1954– : *The Live Bed Show* (1995)

11 A weekend in the country
With the panting
And the yawns
With the crickets and the pheasants
And the orchards and the hay,
With the servants and the peasants,
We'll be laying our plans
While we're playing croquet
For a weekend in the country
So inactive one has to lie down.
A weekend in the country
Where we're twice as upset
As in town.

Stephen Sondheim 1930– : 'A Weekend in the Country' (1972)

12 The Victorians had not been anxious to go away for the weekend. The Edwardians, on the contrary, were nomadic.

T. H. White 1906–64: *Farewell Victoria* (1933)

13 I wish I'd given Spain a miss this year—I nearly plumped for a crochet week in Rhyl. I was going to have a stab at a batwing blouson.

Victoria Wood 1953– : *Mens Sana in Thingummy Doodah* (1990)

The Home and Housework

1 Curtains in orange nylon and no place mats, there's not even the veneer of civilization.

Alan Bennett 1934– : *Talking Heads* (1988)

2 All the house-parlourmaids have evaporated into thin air! without a word. Ethics and manners have vanished in this particular pursuit.

Violet Bonham Carter 1887–1969: *Diaries and Letters, 1946–1969* (2000)

3 On moving house, the first candidates for the dustbin are your rose-coloured glasses with special hindsight attachment.

Basil Boothroyd 1910–88: *Let's Move House* (1977)

4 The premises are so delightfully extensive, that two people might live together without ever seeing, hearing, or meeting.
  of Newstead Abbey

Lord Byron 1788–1824: letter 30 (31?) August 1811

5 They tell me there is no more toilet paper in the house. How can I be expected to act a romantic part and remember to order TOILET PAPER!

Mrs Patrick Campbell 1865–1940: Margot Peters *Mrs Pat* (1984)

6 My old man said, 'Follow the van,
Don't dilly-dally on the way!'
Off went the cart with the home packed in it,
I walked behind with my old cock linnet.
But I dillied and dallied, dallied and dillied,
Lost the van and don't know where to roam.

Charles Collins: 'Don't Dilly-Dally on the Way' (1919, with Fred Leigh); popularized by Marie Lloyd

7 Love and a cottage! Eh, Fanny! Ah, give me indifference and a coach and six!

George Colman, the Elder 1732–94 and **David Garrick** 1717–79: *The Clandestine Marriage* (1766)

8 Conran's Law of Housework—it expands to fill the time available plus half an hour.

Shirley Conran 1932– : *Superwoman 2* (1977)

9 Tho' the pipes that supply the bathroom burst
And the lavatory makes you fear the worst,
It was used by Charles the First
Quite informally,
And later by George the Fourth
On a journey North.

Noël Coward 1899–1973: 'The Stately Homes of England' (1938)

10 Though the fact that they have to be rebuilt
And frequently mortgaged to the hilt
Is inclined to take the gilt
Off the gingerbread,
And certainly damps the fun
Of the eldest son.

Noël Coward 1899–1973: 'The Stately Homes of England' (1938)

11 Thus first necessity invented stools,
Convenience next suggested elbow-chairs,
And luxury the accomplished sofa last.

William Cowper 1731–1800: *The Task* (1785)

12 There was no need to do any housework at all. After the first four years the dirt doesn't get any worse.

Quentin Crisp 1908–99: *The Naked Civil Servant* (1968)

13 Mrs Crupp had indignantly assured him that there wasn't room to swing a cat there; but, as Mr Dick justly observed to me, sitting down on the foot of the bed, nursing his leg, 'You know, Trotwood, I don't want to swing a cat. I never do swing a cat. Therefore, what does that signify to *me*!'

Charles Dickens 1812–70: *David Copperfield* (1850)

14 There's no greater bliss in life than when the plumber eventually comes to unblock your drains. No writer can give that sort of pleasure.

Victoria Glendinning 1937– : in *Observer* 3 January 1993

15 What's the good of a home if you are never in it?

George Grossmith 1847–1912 and **Weedon Grossmith** 1854–1919: *The Diary of a Nobody* (1894)

16 I want a house that has got over all its troubles; I don't want to spend the rest of my life bringing up a young and inexperienced house.

Jerome K. Jerome 1859–1927: *They and I* (1909)

17 Although very few people are actually called upon to live in palaces a very large number are unwilling to admit the fact.

Osbert Lancaster 1908–80: *Homes Sweet Homes* (1939)

18 All I need is room enough to lay a hat and a few friends.

Dorothy Parker 1893–1967: R. E. Drennan *Wit's End* (1973)

on a guest who had outstayed his welcome:
19 There is a mad artist named Inchbold,
With whom you must be at a pinch bold:
Or you may as well score
The brass plate on your door
With the name of J. W. Inchbold.

Dante Gabriel Rossetti 1828–82: limerick written c.1870

20 Home life as we understand it is no more natural to us than a cage is natural to a cockatoo.

George Bernard Shaw 1856–1950: *Getting Married* (1911) preface 'Hearth and Home'

*on being encountered drinking a glass of wine in the street, while
watching his theatre, the Drury Lane, burn down, on 24 February
1809:*

21 A man may surely be allowed to take a glass of wine by
his own fireside.

Richard Brinsley Sheridan
1751–1816: T. Moore *Life of Sheridan*
(1825)

22 Is that bottle just going to sit up there or are you going to
turn it into a lamp?

Neil Simon 1927– : *Last of the Red
Hot Lovers* (1970)

23 It looks different when you're sober. I thought I had twice
as much furniture.

Neil Simon 1927– : *The Gingerbread
Lady* (1970)

24 I have heard of a man who had a mind to sell his house,
and therefore carried a piece of brick in his pocket, which
he shewed as a pattern to encourage purchasers.

Jonathan Swift 1667–1745: *The
Drapier's Letters* (1724)

25 The national sport of England is obstacle racing. People fill
their rooms with useless and cumbersome furniture, and
spend the rest of their lives in trying to dodge it.

Herbert Beerbohm Tree 1852–1917:
Hesketh Pearson *Beerbohm Tree*
(1956)

26 Hatred of domestic work is a natural and admirable result
of civilization.

Rebecca West 1892–1983: in *The
Freewoman* 6 June 1912

27 Everything's getting on top of me. I can't switch off. I've
got a self-cleaning oven—I have to get up in the night to
see if it's doing it.

Victoria Wood 1953– : *Mens Sana in
Thingummy Doodah* (1990)

Hope and Despair   See also **Happiness and Unhappiness**, **Satisfaction and Discontent**

1 A minor form of despair, disguised as a virtue.
  definition of patience

Ambrose Bierce 1842–c.1914: *The
Devil's Dictionary* (1911)

2 We seek to find peace of mind in the word, the formula,
the ritual. The hope is an illusion.

Benjamin N. Cardozo 1870–1938:
The Growth of the Law (1924)

3 There are bad times just around the corner,
There are dark clouds travelling through the sky
And it's no good whining
About a silver lining
For we know from experience that they won't roll by,
With a scowl and a frown
We'll keep our peckers down
And prepare for depression and doom and dread,
We're going to unpack our troubles from our old kitbag
And wait until we drop down dead.

Noël Coward 1899–1973: 'There are
Bad Times Just Around the Corner'
(1953)

4 I have known him come home to supper with a flood of
tears, and a declaration that nothing was now left but a
jail; and go to bed making a calculation of the expense of
putting bow-windows to the house, 'in case anything
turned up,' which was his favourite expression.

Charles Dickens 1812–70: *David
Copperfield* (1850)

5 but wotthehell
archy wotthehell
it s cheerio
my deario that
pulls a lady through.

Don Marquis 1878–1937: *archy and
mehitabel* (1927) 'cheerio my deario'

6 but wotthehell archy wotthehell
   jamais triste archy jamais triste
   that is my motto.

Don Marquis 1878–1937: *archy and mehitabel* (1927) 'mehitabel sees paris'

7 When I am sad and weary
   When I think all hope has gone
   When I walk along High Holborn
   I think of you with nothing on.

Adrian Mitchell 1932– : 'Celia, Celia'

8 'Blessed is the man who expects nothing, for he shall never be disappointed' was the ninth beatitude.

Alexander Pope 1688–1744: letter to Fortescue, 23 September 1725

9 Why, even the janitor's wife
   Has a perfectly good love life
   And here am I
   Facing tomorrow
   Alone with my sorrow
   Down in the depths on the ninetieth floor.

Cole Porter 1891–1964: 'Down in the Depths' (1936)

10 'Do you know what a pessimist is?' 'A man who thinks everybody is as nasty as himself, and hates them for it.'

George Bernard Shaw 1856–1950: *An Unsocial Socialist* (1887)

Hotels

1 All through the night there's a friendly receptionist Welcome to Holiday Inn.

Dorothy Fields 1905–74: 'Welcome to Holiday Inn' (1973)

2 The cushions had cushions, the curtains looked like duvets.
   of a typical English country house hotel

A. A. Gill 1954– : *Starcrossed* (1999)

3 The chambermaid is very kind,
   She always thinks we're so refined.
   Of course, she's deaf and dumb and blind—
   No fools we—
   In our little den of iniquity.

Lorenz Hart 1895–1943: 'In Our Little Den of Iniquity' (*Pal Joey*, 1940 musical)

supposedly quoting a letter from a Tyrolean landlord:
4 Standing among savage scenery, the hotel offers stupendous revelations. There is a French widow in every bedroom, affording delightful prospects.

Gerard Hoffnung 1925–59: speech at the Oxford Union, 4 December 1958

5 The great advantage of a hotel is that it's a refuge from home life.

George Bernard Shaw 1856–1950: *You Never Can Tell* (1898)

Housework See **The Home and Housework**

The Human Race

1 We used to build civilizations. Now we build shopping malls.

Bill Bryson 1951– : *Neither Here Nor There* (1991)

2 Well, of course, people are only human . . . But it really does not seem much for them to be.

Ivy Compton-Burnett 1884–1969: *A Family and a Fortune* (1939)

3 They are usually a mistake.
   of other people

Quentin Crisp 1908–99: in *Spectator* 20 November 1999

4 I got disappointed in human nature as well and gave it up because I found it too much like my own.

J. P. Donleavy 1926– : *A Fairy Tale of New York* (1973)

5 Certainty generally is illusion, and repose is not the destiny of man.

Oliver Wendell Holmes Jr. 1841–1935: 'The Path of the Law' (1897)

6 That habit of treading in ruts and trooping in companies which men share with sheep.

A. E. Housman 1859–1936: 'The Editing of Juvenal' (1905)

7 Men have an extraordinarily erroneous opinion of their position in nature; and the error is ineradicable.

W. Somerset Maugham 1874–1965: *A Writer's Notebook* (1949) written in 1896

8 Man is one of the toughest of animated creatures. Only the anthrax bacillus can stand so unfavourable an environment for so long a time.

H. L. Mencken 1880–1956: *Minority Report* (1956)

9 I wish I loved the Human Race;
I wish I loved its silly face;
I wish I liked the way it walks;
I wish I liked the way it talks;
And when I'm introduced to one
I wish I thought *What Jolly Fun!*

Walter Raleigh 1861–1922: 'Wishes of an Elderly Man' (1923)

10 I'm dealing in rock'n'roll. I'm, like, I'm not a bona fide human being.

Phil Spector 1940– : attributed

11 He's an animal lover . . . People he don't like so much.

Tom Stoppard 1937– : *Neutral Ground* (1983)

12 The only man who wasn't spoilt by being lionized was Daniel.

Herbert Beerbohm Tree 1852–1917: Hesketh Pearson *Beerbohm Tree* (1956)

13 Man is the Only Animal that Blushes. Or needs to.

Mark Twain 1835–1910: *Following the Equator* (1897)

14 Reality is something the human race doesn't handle very well.

Gore Vidal 1925– : in *Radio Times* 3 January 1990

15 This world is a comedy to those that think, a tragedy to those that feel.

Horace Walpole 1717–97: letter to Anne, Countess of Upper Ossory, 16 August 1776

16 'Have you ever seen Spode eat asparagus?'
'No.'
'Revolting. It alters one's whole conception of Man as Nature's last word.'

P. G. Wodehouse 1881–1975: *The Code of the Woosters* (1938)

Humility See **Pride and Humility**

Humour See also **Wit and Wordplay**

1 Among all kinds of writing, there is none in which authors are more apt to miscarry than in works of humour, as there is none in which they are more ambitious to excel.

Joseph Addison 1672–1719: *The Spectator* 10 April 1711

2 The end of satire is reformation, and this would be of more force than your societies for that purpose, were it duly observed and hearkened to, without being misconstrued defamation.

Anonymous: in *The Female Tatler* October 1709

3 The marvellous thing about a joke with a double meaning is that it can only mean one thing.

Ronnie Barker 1929– : *Sauce* (1977)

4 In Milwaukee last month a man died laughing over one of his own jokes. That's what makes it so tough for us outsiders. We have to fight home competition.

Robert Benchley 1889–1945: R. E. Drennan *Wit's End* (1973)

5 Mark my words, when a society has to resort to the lavatory for its humour, the writing is on the wall.

Alan Bennett 1934– : *Forty Years On* (1969)

6 The world dwindles daily for the humorist . . . Jokes are fast running out, for a joke must transform real life in some perverse way, and real life has begun to perform the same operation perfectly professionally upon itself.

Craig Brown 1957- : *Craig Brown's Greatest Hits* (1993)

7 When you tell an Iowan a joke, you can see a kind of race going on between his brain and his expression.

Bill Bryson 1951- : *The Lost Continent* (1989)

8 Without humour you cannot run a sweetie-shop, let alone a nation.

John Buchan 1875–1940: *Castle Gay* (1930)

to a tiresome dinner partner:
9 Do you know why God withheld the sense of humour from women? . . . That we may love you instead of laughing at you.

Mrs Patrick Campbell 1865–1940: Margot Peters *Mrs Pat* (1984)

10 A joke's a very serious thing.

Charles Churchill 1731–64: *The Ghost* (1763)

11 Reality goes bounding past the satirist like a cheetah laughing as it lopes ahead of the greyhound.

Claud Cockburn 1904–81: *Crossing the Line* (1958)

12 The role of humour is to make people fall down and writhe on the Axminster, and that is the top and bottom of it.

Alan Coren 1938- : *Seems Like Old Times* (1989)

13 Freud's theory was that when a joke opens a window and all those bats and bogeymen fly out, you get a marvellous feeling of relief and elation. The trouble with Freud is that he never had to play the old Glasgow Empire on a Saturday night after Rangers and Celtic had both lost.

Ken Dodd 1931- : in *Guardian* 30 April 1991 (quoted in many, usually much contracted, forms since the mid-1960s)

14 A difference of taste in jokes is a great strain on the affections.

George Eliot 1819–80: *Daniel Deronda* (1876)

15 Comedy, like sodomy, is an unnatural act.

Marty Feldman 1933–83: in *The Times* 9 June 1969

16 The funniest thing about comedy is that you never know why people laugh. I know *what* makes them laugh but trying to get your hands on the *why* of it is like trying to pick an eel out of a tub of water.

W. C. Fields 1880–1946: Richard J. Anobile *A Flask of Fields* (1972)

17 It is easy to forget that the most important aspect of comedy, after all, its great saving grace, is its ambiguity. You can simultaneously laugh at a situation, *and* take it seriously.

Stephen Fry 1957- : *Paperweight* (1992)

18 'Tis ever thus with simple folk—an accepted wit has but to say 'Pass the mustard', and they roar their ribs out!

W. S. Gilbert 1836–1911: *The Yeoman of the Guard* (1888)

19 The Irish have wit but little humour. They cannot laugh at the battle while they are involved in the broil of life.

Oliver St John Gogarty 1878–1957: *Tumbling in the Hay* (1939)

20 What do you mean, funny? Funny-peculiar or funny ha-ha?

Ian Hay 1876–1952: *The Housemaster* (1938)

21 A sober God-fearing man whose idea of a good joke was to lie about his age.

Joseph Heller 1923–99: *Catch-22* (1961)

22 I did not intend to write a funny book, at first. I did not know I was a humorist. I have never been sure about it. In the middle ages, I should probably have gone about preaching and got myself burnt or hanged.

Jerome K. Jerome 1859–1927: *My Life and Times* (1926)

23 By good rights, great humorists ought to be gentle, agreeable people to meet, with a breadth of view and a kindly tolerance of trifles—such as they show in print. Mostly they are not.

Stephen Leacock 1869–1944: *The Boy I Left Behind Me* (1947)

24 If 'tis a thing I ever find out you were telling jokes to Jesuits I'll tear the bloody kidneys outa you.

Frank McCourt 1930– : *Angela's Ashes* (1996)

25 My idea of an ideal programme would be a show where I would have all the questions and some other bastard would have to figure out the funny answers.

Groucho Marx 1895–1977: letter, 10 October 1940

26 It's an odd job, making decent people laugh.

Molière 1622–73: *La Critique de l'école des femmes* (1663)

27 I knew nothing about farce until I read [Feydeau's] *Puce à l'Oreille*, and had no idea what a deadly serious business it is.

John Mortimer 1923– : *Clinging to the Wreckage* (1982)

28 Good taste and humour . . . are a contradiction in terms, like a chaste whore.

Malcolm Muggeridge 1903–90: in *Time* 14 September 1953

29 Another day gone and no jokes.

Flann O'Brien 1911–66: *The Best of Myles* (1968)

30 That's the Irish people all over—they treat a joke as a serious thing and a serious thing as a joke.

Sean O'Casey 1880–1964: *The Shadow of a Gunman* (1923)

31 Humour is, by its nature, more truthful than factual.

P. J. O'Rourke 1947– : *Parliament of Whores* (1991)

32 There are those who, in their pride and their innocence, dedicate their careers to writing humorous pieces. Poor dears, the world is stacked against them from the start, for everybody in it has the right to look at their work and say, 'I don't think that's funny.'

Dorothy Parker 1893–1967: introduction to *The Most of S. J. Perelman* (1959)

33 Laughter is pleasant, but the exertion is too much for me.

Thomas Love Peacock 1785–1866: *Nightmare Abbey* (1818)

34 Everything is funny as long as it is happening to Somebody Else.

Will Rogers 1879–1935: *The Illiterate Digest* (1924) 'Warning to Jokers: lay off the prince'

35 All humour is based on hostility—that's why World War Two was funny.

Neil Simon 1927– : *Laughter on the 23rd Floor* (1993)

36 There are three basic rules for great comedy. Unfortunately no-one can remember what they are.

Arthur Smith 1954– : attributed

37 We often laughed at others in our house, and I picked up the craft of being polite while people were present and laughing later if there was anything to laugh about.

Muriel Spark 1918– : *Curriculum Vitae* (1992)

38 For every ten jokes, thou hast got an hundred enemies.

Laurence Sterne 1713–68: *Tristram Shandy* (1769)

39 Humour is emotional chaos remembered in tranquillity.

James Thurber 1894–1961: in *New York Post* 29 February 1960

40 That joke was lost on the foreigner—guides cannot master the subtleties of the American joke.

Mark Twain 1835–1910: *The Innocents Abroad* (1869)

41 Laughter would be bereaved if snobbery died.

Peter Ustinov 1921– : in *Observer* 13 March 1955

42 Life is a campus: in a Greenwich Village bookstore, looking for a New Yorker collection, I asked of an earnest-looking assistant where I might find the humour section. Peering over her granny glasses, she enquired, 'Humour studies would that be, sir?'

Keith Waterhouse 1929- : in *The Spectator* 15 January 1994

43 Mucky jokes. Obscenity—it's all the go nowadays. By law, you see. You're allowed to do it. You can say bum, you can say po, you can say anything . . . Well, he said it! The thin one! He said bum one night. I heard him! Satire!

Keith Waterhouse 1929- and **Willis Hall**: 'Close Down' in David Frost and Ned Sherrin *That Was The Week That Was* (1963)

44 Madeleine Bassett laughed the tinkling, silvery laugh that had got her so disliked by the better element.

P. G. Wodehouse 1881–1975: *The Code of the Woosters* (1938)

45 She had a penetrating sort of laugh. Rather like a train going into a tunnel.

P. G. Wodehouse 1881–1975: *The Inimitable Jeeves* (1923)

Hypocrisy

1 There are moments when we in the British press can show extraordinary sensitivity; these moments usually coincide with the death of a proprietor, or a proprietor's wife.

Craig Brown 1957- : *Craig Brown's Greatest Hits* (1993)

2 In England the only homage which they pay to Virtue—is hypocrisy.

Lord Byron 1788–1824: letter, 11 May 1821

speaking against the Welsh Disestablishment Bill, F. E. Smith had called it 'a Bill which has shocked the conscience of every Christian community in Europe':

3 Talk about the pews and steeples
and the Cash that goes therewith!
But the souls of Christian people . . .
Chuck it, Smith!

G. K. Chesterton 1874–1936: 'Antichrist, or the Reunion of Christendom: An Ode' (1912)

4 We are so very 'umble.

Charles Dickens 1812–70: *David Copperfield* (1850)

5 He combines the manners of a Marquis with the morals of a Methodist.

W. S. Gilbert 1836–1911: *Ruddigore* (1887)

6 Hypocrisy is not generally a social sin, but a virtue.

Judith Martin 1938- : *Miss Manners' Guide to Rearing Perfect Children* (1985)

the hypocritical Quaker, Ephraim Smooth, hears violin music:

7 I must shut my ears. The man of sin rubbeth the hair of the horse to the bowels of the cat.

John O'Keeffe 1747–1833: *Wild Oats* (1791)

8 Most people sell their souls, and live with a good conscience on the proceeds.

Logan Pearsall Smith 1865–1946: *Afterthoughts* (1931) 'Other People'

9 Of all the cants which are canted in this canting world,— though the cant of hypocrites may be the worst,—the cant of criticism is the most tormenting!

Laurence Sterne 1713–68: *Tristram Shandy* (1759–67)

10 I hope you have not been leading a double life, pretending to be wicked and being really good all the time. That would be hypocrisy.

Oscar Wilde 1854–1900: *The Importance of Being Earnest* (1895)

Ideas

1 I ran into Isosceles. He has a great idea for a new triangle!

Woody Allen 1935- : *If the Impressionists had been Dentists*

2 An original idea. That can't be too hard. The library must be full of them.

Stephen Fry 1957– : *The Liar* (1991)

3 I had a monumental idea this morning, but I didn't like it.

Sam Goldwyn 1882–1974: N. Zierold *Hollywood Tycoons* (1969)

4 The chief end of man is to frame general ideas—and . . . no general idea is worth a damn.

Oliver Wendell Holmes Jr. 1841–1935: letter to Morris R. Cohen, 12 April 1915

5 It is better to entertain an idea than to take it home to live with you for the rest of your life.

Randall Jarrell 1914–65: *Pictures from an Institution* (1954)

6 A household where a total unawareness of the world of ideas not only existed but was regarded as a matter for congratulation.

Osbert Lancaster 1908–80: *All Done From Memory* (1953)

7 He can compress the most words into the smallest ideas better than any man I ever met.
   of another Illinois lawyer

Abraham Lincoln 1809–65: Leon Harris *The Fine Art of Political Wit* (1965)

8 There are some ideas so wrong that only a very intelligent person could believe in them.

George Orwell 1903–50: attributed

9 The English approach to ideas is not to kill them, but to let them die of neglect.

Jeremy Paxman 1950– : *The English: a portrait of a people* (1998)

Ignorance See **Foolishness and Ignorance**

Indexes See also **Books**

1 If you don't find it in the Index, look very carefully through the entire catalogue.

Anonymous: in *Consumer's Guide, Sears, Roebuck and Co.* (1897); Donald E. Knuth *Sorting and Searching* (1973)

2 Whenever I am sent a new book on the lively arts, the first thing I do is look for myself in the index.

Julie Burchill 1960– : *The Spectator* 16 January 1992

   the Editors' acknowledgements:
3 Their thanks are also due to their wife for not preparing the index wrong. There is no index.

W. C. Sellar 1898–1951 and **R. J. Yeatman** 1898–1968: *1066 and All That* (1930)

4 An index is a great leveller.

George Bernard Shaw 1856–1950: G. N. Knight *Indexing* (1979); attributed, perhaps apocryphal

5 Should not the Society of Indexers be known as Indexers, Society of, The?

Keith Waterhouse 1929– : *Bookends* (1990)

Insults and Invective

1 Frazier is so ugly that he should donate his face to the US Bureau of Wild Life.

Muhammad Ali 1942– : in *Guardian* 23 December 1972 'Sports Quotes of the Year'

2 Lord Birkenhead is very clever but sometimes his brains go to his head.

Margot Asquith 1864–1945: in *Listener* 11 June 1953 'Margot Oxford' by Lady Violet Bonham Carter

3 Ettie [Lady Desborough] is an ox: she will be made into Bovril when she dies.

Margot Asquith 1864–1945: Jeanne Mackenzie *Children of the Souls* (1986)

4 The *t* is silent, as in *Harlow*.
to Jean Harlow, who had been mispronouncing her first name

Margot Asquith 1864–1945: T. S. Matthews *Great Tom* (1973)

5 I married beneath me, all women do.

Nancy Astor 1879–1964: in *Dictionary of National Biography 1961–1970* (1981)

6 NANCY ASTOR: If I were your wife I would put poison in your coffee!
WINSTON CHURCHILL: And if I were your husband I would drink it.

Nancy Astor 1879–1964: Consuelo Vanderbilt Balsan *Glitter and Gold* (1952)

7 I didn't know he'd been knighted. I knew he'd been doctored.

Thomas Beecham 1879–1961: on Malcolm Sargent's knighthood; attributed

8 The 'g' is silent—the only thing about her that is.
of Camille Paglia

Julie Burchill 1960– : in *The Spectator* 16 January 1992

9 Lillian Gish may be a charming person, but she is not Ophelia. She comes on stage as if she had been sent for to sew rings on the new curtains.

Mrs Patrick Campbell 1865–1940: Margot Peters *Mrs Pat* (1984)

10 [Clement Attlee is] a modest man who has a good deal to be modest about.

Winston Churchill 1874–1965: in *Chicago Sunday Tribune Magazine of Books* 27 June 1954

11 A sheep in sheep's clothing.
of Clement Attlee

Winston Churchill 1874–1965: Lord Home *The Way the Wind Blows* (1976)

12 BESSIE BRADDOCK: Winston, you're drunk.
CHURCHILL: Bessie, you're ugly. But tomorrow I shall be sober.

Winston Churchill 1874–1965: an exchange with the Labour MP Bessie Braddock; J. L. Lane (ed.) *Sayings of Churchill* (1992)

Henry Clay of Virginia unexpectedly moved out of the way of his political rival, John Randolph of Roanoke:
13 JOHN RANDOLPH: I never sidestep skunks.
HENRY CLAY: I always do.

Henry Clay 1777–1852: Robert V. Remini *Henry Clay* (1991)

14 A sophistical rhetorician, inebriated with the exuberance of his own verbosity.
of Gladstone

Benjamin Disraeli 1804–81: in *The Times* 29 July 1878

15 [*The Sun Also Rises* is about] bullfighting, bullslinging, and bull—.

Zelda Fitzgerald 1900–47: Marion Meade *What Fresh Hell Is This?* (1988)

16 The Deputy Prime Minister [John Prescott] will present a bill that is rambling, over-inflated, illogical and ridiculously cumbersome—funny coincidence, that.

William Hague 1961– : in *Sunday Times* 21 November 1999; attributed

17 A very weak-minded fellow I am afraid, and, like the feather pillow, bears the marks of the last person who has sat on him!
of Lord Derby

Earl Haig 1861–1928: letter to Lady Haig, 14 January 1918

18 His thoughts are seldom consecutive.
He just can write.
I know a movie executive
Who's twice as bright.

Lorenz Hart 1895–1943: 'Take Him' (*Pal Joey*, 1940 musical)

on being criticized by Geoffrey Howe:

19 Like being savaged by a dead sheep.

Denis Healey 1917– : speech, House of Commons 14 June 1978

20 Some men are born mediocre, some men achieve mediocrity, and some men have mediocrity thrust upon them. With Major Major it had been all three.

Joseph Heller 1923–99: *Catch-22* (1961)

21 Had your father spent more of your mother's immoral earnings on your education you would not even then have been a gentleman.

Seymour Hicks 1871–1949: *Vintage Years* (1943)

22 Such cruel glasses.
  of Robin Day

Frankie Howerd 1922–92: in *That Was The Week That Was* (BBC television series, from 1963)

23 So dumb he can't fart and chew gum at the same time.
  of Gerald Ford

Lyndon Baines Johnson 1908–73: Richard Reeves *A Ford, not a Lincoln* (1975)

24 Is not a Patron, my Lord, one who looks with unconcern on a man struggling for life in the water, and, when he has reached ground, encumbers him with help? The notice which you have been pleased to take of my labours, had it been early, had been kind; but it has been delayed till I am indifferent, and cannot enjoy it; till I am solitary, and cannot impart it; till I am known, and do not want it.

Samuel Johnson 1709–84: letter to Lord Chesterfield, 7 February 1755; James Boswell *Life of Samuel Johnson* (1791)

25 This man [Lord Chesterfield] I thought had been a Lord among wits; but, I find, he is only a wit among Lords.

Samuel Johnson 1709–84: James Boswell *Life of Samuel Johnson* (1791) (1754)

26 This little flower, this delicate little beauty, this cream puff, is supposed to be beyond personal criticism . . . He is simply a shiver looking for a spine to run up.
  of John Hewson, the Australian Liberal leader

Paul Keating 1944– : in *Ned Sherrin in his Anecdotage* (1993)

27 They were rude about my mother, the poor woman, who is from Florence. But I do think they could leave my father alone. He died six years ago.
  Juventus coach after receiving abuse from Fiorentina fans

Marcello Lippi: in *Daily Telegraph* 28 December 1998 'Sporting Quotes of the Year'

28 The truckman, the trashman and the policeman on the block may call me Alice but you may not.
  to Senator Joseph McCarthy

Alice Roosevelt Longworth 1884–1980: Michael Teague *Mrs. L* (1981)

on hearing that a Hollywood agent had swum safely in shark-infested waters:

29 I think that's what they call professional courtesy.

Herman J. Mankievicz 1897–1953: attributed; Nigel Rees *Cassell Dictionary of Humorous Quotations* (1999)

30 I never forget a face, but in your case I'll be glad to make an exception.

Groucho Marx 1895–1977: Leo Rosten *People I have Loved, Known or Admired* (1970) 'Groucho'

31 The majority of the members of the Irish parliament are professional politicians, in the sense that otherwise they would not be given jobs minding mice at crossroads.

Flann O'Brien 1911–66: *The Hair of the Dogma* (1977)

32 If you say a modern celebrity is an adulterer, a pervert and a drug addict, all it means is that you've read his autobiography.

P. J. O'Rourke 1947- : *Give War a Chance* (1992)

to Clare Boothe Luce, who had stood aside for her saying, 'Age before Beauty':
33 Pearls before swine.

Dorothy Parker 1893–1967: R. E. Drennan *Wit's End* (1973)

34 The affair between Margot Asquith and Margot Asquith will live as one of the prettiest love stories in all literature.

Dorothy Parker 1893–1967: review of Margot Asquith's *Lay Sermons*; in *New Yorker* 22 October 1927

35 Let Sporus tremble—'What? that thing of silk,
Sporus, that mere white curd of ass's milk?
Satire or sense, alas! can Sporus feel?
Who breaks a butterfly upon a wheel?'

Alexander Pope 1688–1744: of Lord Hervey; 'An Epistle to Dr Arbuthnot' (1735)

36 A cherub's face, a reptile all the rest.

Alexander Pope 1688–1744: of Lord Hervey; 'An Epistle to Dr Arbuthnot' (1735)

37 A wit with dunces, and a dunce with wits.

Alexander Pope 1688–1744: *The Dunciad* (1742)

38 Don't look at me, Sir, with—ah—in that tone of voice.

Punch 1841–1992: vol. 87 (1884)

39 Whenever I see his finger nails, I thank God I don't have to look at his feet.
of the journalist Hannen Swaffer

Athene Seyler 1889–1990: Bryan Forbes *Ned's Girl* (1977)

40 BEATRICE: I wonder that you will still be talking, Signior Benedick: nobody marks you.
BENEDICK: What! my dear Lady Disdain, are you yet living?

William Shakespeare 1564–1616: *Much Ado About Nothing* (1598–9)

41 Diana Rigg is built like a brick mausoleum with insufficient flying buttresses.
review of Abelard and Heloise *in 1970*

John Simon 1925- : Diana Rigg *No Turn Unstoned* (1982)

on being approached by the secretary of the Athenaeum, which he had been in the habit of using as a convenience on the way to his office:
42 Good God, do you mean to say this place is a club?

F. E. Smith 1872–1930: attributed

43 JUDGE: You are extremely offensive, young man.
SMITH: As a matter of fact, we both are, and the only difference between us is that I am trying to be, and you can't help it.

F. E. Smith 1872–1930: Lord Birkenhead *Earl of Birkenhead* (1933)

on a proposal to surround St Paul's with a wooden pavement:
44 Let the Dean and Canons lay their heads together and the thing will be done.

Sydney Smith 1771–1845: H. Pearson *The Smith of Smiths* (1934)

45 Science is his forte, and omniscience his foible.

Sydney Smith 1771–1845: of William Whewell, master of Trinity College, Cambridge; Isaac Todhunter *William Whewell* (1876)

46 I used to think it a pity that her mother rather than she had not thought of birth control.
of Marie Stopes

Muriel Spark 1918- : *Curriculum Vitae* (1992)

47 I regard you with an indifference closely bordering on aversion.

Robert Louis Stevenson 1850–94: *New Arabian Nights* (1882)

48 What time he can spare from the adornment of his person he devotes to the neglect of his duties.
of Richard Jebb, later Professor of Greek at Cambridge

William Hepworth Thompson 1810–86: M. R. Bobbit *With Dearest Love to All* (1960)

when pressed by a gramophone company for a written testimonial:
49 Sirs, I have tested your machine. It adds a new terror to life and makes death a long-felt want.

Herbert Beerbohm Tree 1852–1917: Hesketh Pearson *Beerbohm Tree* (1956)

to Richard Adams, who had described Vidal's novel on Lincoln as 'meretricious'
50 Really? Well, meretricious and a happy New Year to you too!
earlier uses of the response are attributed to Franklin P. Adams in the 1930s, and the NBC radio show starring the Marx Brothers, Flywheel, Shyster and Flywheel, *in 1933*

Gore Vidal 1925– : on *Start the Week*, BBC radio, 1970s

51 Every other inch a gentleman.

Rebecca West 1892–1983: of Michael Arlen; Victoria Glendinning *Rebecca West* (1987)

52 CECILY: When I see a spade I call it a spade.
GWENDOLEN: I am glad to say that I have never seen a spade.

Oscar Wilde 1854–1900: *The Importance of Being Earnest* (1895)

53 [EARL OF SANDWICH:] 'Pon my soul, Wilkes, I don't know whether you'll die upon the gallows or of the pox.
[WILKES:] That depends, my Lord, whether I first embrace your Lordship's principles, or your Lordship's mistresses.

John Wilkes 1727–97: Charles Petrie *The Four Georges* (1935); probably apocryphal

Intelligence and Intellectuals See also **The Mind**

1 To the man-in-the-street, who, I'm sorry to say,
Is a keen observer of life,
The word 'Intellectual' suggests straight away
A man who's untrue to his wife.

W. H. Auden 1907–73: *New Year Letter* (1941)

2 Men of genius are so few that they ought to atone for their fewness by being at any rate ubiquitous.

Max Beerbohm 1872–1956: letter to W. B. Yeats, 11 July 1911

3 But—Oh! ye lords of ladies intellectual,
Inform us truly, have they not hen-pecked you all?

Lord Byron 1788–1824: *Don Juan* (1819–24)

4 [He] behaved like an ostrich and put his head in the sand, thereby exposing his thinking parts.
of David Mellor

George Carman 1930– : in *Times* 30 August 2000; attributed

5 Genius is one per cent inspiration, ninety-nine per cent perspiration.

Thomas Alva Edison 1847–1931: said c.1903; in *Harper's Monthly Magazine* September 1932

6 With the thoughts I'd be thinkin'
I could be another Lincoln,
If I only had a brain.

E. Y. Harburg 1898–1981: 'If I Only Had a Brain' (1939)

7 Zip! Walter Lippman wasn't brilliant today,
Zip! Will Saroyan ever write a great play?
Zip! I was reading Schopenhauer last night.
Zip! And I think that Schopenhauer was right!
   satirizing the intellectual pretensions of Gypsy Rose Lee

Lorenz Hart 1895–1943: 'Zip' (1940)

8 Probably the greatest concentration of talent and genius in this house except for perhaps those times when Thomas Jefferson ate alone.
   of a dinner for Nobel Prizewinners at the White House

John F. Kennedy 1917–63: in *New York Times* 30 April 1962

9 *I think, therefore I am* is the statement of an intellectual who underrates toothaches.

Milan Kundera 1929– : *Immortality* (1991)

10 Cleverness is a quality that, in architecture no less than in life, we have always been notorious for regarding with ill-concealed dislike.

Osbert Lancaster 1908–80: *Pillar to Post* (1938)

11 Throughout my career I've been described as 'cerebral'. But I had to look up that word in a dictionary.

Graeme Le Saux 1968– : in *Independent on Sunday* 14 March 1999

12 No one in this world, so far as I know—and I have searched the records for years, and employed agents to help me—has ever lost money by underestimating the intelligence of the great masses of the plain people.

H. L. Mencken 1880–1956: in *Chicago Tribune* 19 September 1926

replying to Oliver St John Gogarty's suggestion that to recognize their own immortality during their lifetime was an attribute of great artists:
13 What about Marie Corelli gliding down the Avon in a gondola with her parasol?

George Bernard Shaw 1856–1950: Ulick O'Connor *Oliver St John Gogarty* (1964)

14 A genius. An I.Q. of 170. Same as her weight.

Neil Simon 1927– : *Come Blow Your Horn* (1961)

15 You can persuade a man to believe almost anything provided he is clever enough, but it is much more difficult to persuade someone less clever.

Tom Stoppard 1937– : *Professional Foul* (1978)

16 What is a highbrow? He is a man who has found something more interesting than women.

Edgar Wallace 1875–1932: in *New York Times* 24 January 1932

17 I have nothing to declare except my genius.

Oscar Wilde 1854–1900: at the New York Custom House; Frank Harris *Oscar Wilde* (1918)

18 'Jeeves is a wonder.'
'A marvel.'
'What a brain.'
'Size nine-and-a-quarter, I should say.'
'He eats a lot of fish.'

P. G. Wodehouse 1881–1975: *Thank You, Jeeves* (1934)

19 'Well, I think you're a pig.'
'A pig, maybe, but a shrewd, levelheaded pig. I wouldn't touch the project with a bargepole.'

P. G. Wodehouse 1881–1975: *The Code of the Woosters* (1938)

20 I know I've got a degree. Why does that mean I have to spend my life with intellectuals? I've got a life-saving certificate but I don't spend my evenings diving for a rubber brick with my pyjamas on.

Victoria Wood 1953– : *Mens Sana in Thingummy Doodah* (1990)

Invective See **Insults and Invective**

Ireland and the Irish See also **Countries and Peoples**, **Places**

1 PAT: He was an Anglo-Irishman.
MEG: In the blessed name of God what's that?
PAT: A Protestant with a horse.

Brendan Behan 1923–64: *Hostage* (1958)

2 Where would the Irish be without someone to be Irish at?

Elizabeth Bowen 1899–1973: *The House in Paris* (1935)

3 We rose to bring about Eutopia,
But all we got was Dev's myopia.

Oliver St John Gogarty 1878–1957: letter to James Montgomery; Ulick O'Connor *Oliver St John Gogarty* (1964)

4 Ireland is a small but insuppressible island half an hour nearer the sunset than Great Britain.

Thomas Kettle 1880–1916: 'On Crossing the Irish Sea'

5 The Irish, he says, don't care for clean government; they want Irish government.

Stephen Leacock 1869–1944: *Arcadian Adventures with the Idle Rich* (1914)

6 [In Ireland] they're working hard to restore the old Gaelic. If they're not careful, they'll learn to speak it and then they'll be sorry.

Stephen Leacock 1869–1944: *The Boy I Left Behind Me* (1947)

7 I'm Irish. We think sideways.

Spike Milligan 1918– : in *Independent on Sunday* 20 June 1999

8 I founded the Rathmines branch of the Gaelic League. Having nothing to say, I thought at that time that it was important to revive a distant language in which absolutely nothing could be said.

Flann O'Brien 1911–66: *The Best of Myles* (1968)

9 Our ancestors believed in magic, prayers, trickery, browbeating and bullying: I think it would be fair to sum that list up as 'Irish politics'.

Flann O'Brien 1911–66: *The Hair of the Dogma* (1977)

10 He'd . . . settled into a life of Guinness, sarcasm and late late nights, the kind of life that American academics think real Dubliners lead.

Joseph O'Connor 1963– : *Cowboys and Indians* (1991)

11 Gladstone . . . spent his declining years trying to guess the answer to the Irish Question; unfortunately whenever he was getting warm, the Irish secretly changed the Question.

W. C. Sellar 1898–1951 and **R. J. Yeatman** 1898–1968: *1066 and All That* (1930)

12 An Irishman's heart is nothing but his imagination.

George Bernard Shaw 1856–1950: *John Bull's Other Island* (1907)

denying that he was Irish:
13 Because a man is born in a stable, that does not make him a horse.

Duke of Wellington 1769–1852: Paul Johnson (ed.) *The Oxford Book of Political Anecdotes* (1986)

Journalism See also **Newspapers**

1 At certain times each year, we journalists do almost nothing except apply for the Pulitzers and several dozen other major prizes. During these times you could walk right into most newsrooms and commit a multiple axe

Dave Barry 1948– : in *Miami Herald* 29 March 1987

murder naked, and it wouldn't get reported in the paper because the reporters and editors would all be too busy filling out prize applications.

2 When a dog bites a man, that is not news, because it happens so often. But if a man bites a dog, that is news.

John B. Bogart 1848–1921: F. M. O'Brien *The Story of the* [New York] *Sun* (1918); often attributed to Charles A. Dana

on being asked whether George Mair had been a fastidious journalist:
3 He once telephoned a semicolon from Moscow.

James Bone: James Agate diary, 31 October 1935

4 A would-be satirist, a hired buffoon,
A monthly scribbler of some low lampoon,
Condemned to drudge, the meanest of the mean,
And furbish falsehoods for a magazine.
of journalists

Lord Byron 1788–1824: 'English Bards and Scotch Reviewers' (1809)

5 Let's face it, sports writers, we're not hanging around with brain surgeons.

Jimmy Cannon 1910–73: attributed

explaining the craft of sports writers:
6 We work in the toy department.

Jimmy Cannon 1910–73: Michael Parkinson *Sporting Lives* (1993)

7 When seagulls follow a trawler, it is because they think sardines will be thrown into the sea.

Eric Cantona 1966– : at the end of a press conference, 31 March 1995

8 Journalism largely consists in saying 'Lord Jones Dead' to people who never knew that Lord Jones was alive.

G. K. Chesterton 1874–1936: *Wisdom of Father Brown* (1914)

9 You are misunderstood, maligned, viewed by the press as a Pulitzer Prize ready to be won.
on the problems of investigative journalism for politicians

Lawton Chiles 1930– : in *St Petersburg (Florida) Times* 6 March 1991

10 The first law of journalism—to confirm existing prejudice rather than contradict it.

Alexander Cockburn 1941– : in 1974; Jonathon Green *Says Who?* (1988)

11 Thou god of our idolatry, the press . . .
Thou fountain, at which drink the good and wise;
Thou ever-bubbling spring of endless lies;
Like Eden's dread probationary tree,
Knowledge of good and evil is from thee.

William Cowper 1731–1800: 'The Progress of Error' (1782)

12 If you lose your temper at a newspaper columnist, he'll be rich, or famous, or both.

James Hagerty 1936– : the view of President Eisenhower's press secretary; Jonathon Green *Says Who?* (1988)

13 Power without responsibility: the prerogative of the harlot throughout the ages.
summing up the view of Lord Beaverbrook, who had said to Kipling: 'What I want is power. Kiss 'em one day and kick 'em the next'; Stanley Baldwin, Kipling's cousin, subsequently obtained permission to use the phrase in a speech in London on 18 March 1931

Rudyard Kipling 1865–1936: in *Kipling Journal* December 1971

14 I think it well to remember that, when writing for the newspapers, we are writing for an elderly lady in Hastings who has two cats of which she is passionately fond. Unless

Willmott Lewis 1877–1950: Claud Cockburn *In Time of Trouble* (1957)

our stuff can successfully compete for her interest with those cats, it is no good.

15　I like to do my principal research in bars, where people are more likely to tell the truth or, at least, lie less convincingly than they do in briefings and books.

P. J. O'Rourke 1947– : *Holidays in Hell* (1988)

16　No government in history has been as obsessed with public relations as this one . . . Speaking for myself, if there is a message I want to be off it.

Jeremy Paxman 1950– : in *Daily Telegraph* 3 July 1998

17　More like a gentleman than a journalist.

J. B. Priestley 1894–1984: of Bruce Richmond, editor of *The Times Literary Supplement*; letter to Edward Davison, 23 June 1924

18　I have no problem with cheque-book journalism, as long as some of the cheque goes to me.
　　on interviewing Monica Lewinsky

Jon Snow 1947– : in *Independent* 6 March 1999

19　Comment is free but facts are on expenses.

Tom Stoppard 1937– : *Night and Day* (1978)

20　A foreign correspondent is someone who lives in foreign parts and corresponds, usually in the form of essays containing no new facts. Otherwise he's someone who flies around from hotel to hotel and thinks the most interesting thing about any story is the fact that he has arrived to cover it.

Tom Stoppard 1937– : *Night and Day* (1978)

21　For a slashing article, sir, there's nobody like the Capting.

William Makepeace Thackeray 1811–63: *Pendennis* (1848–50)

22　Up to a point, Lord Copper.

Evelyn Waugh 1903–66: *Scoop* (1938)

23　A journalist is somebody who possesses himself of a fantasy and lures the truth towards it.

Arnold Wesker 1932– : *Journey into Journalism* (1977)

24　There is a journalistic curse of Eve. The woman who writes is always given anti-feminist books to review.

Rebecca West 1892–1983: in *The Clarion* 21 November 1913

the difference between journalism and literature:
25　Journalism is unreadable, and literature is not read.

Oscar Wilde 1854–1900: 'The Critic as Artist' (1891)

26　You cannot hope
　　to bribe or twist,
　　thank God! the
　　British journalist.
　　But, seeing what
　　the man will do
　　unbribed, there's
　　no occasion to.

Humbert Wolfe 1886–1940: 'Over the Fire' (1930)

27　Rock journalism is people who can't write interviewing people who can't talk for people who can't read.

Frank Zappa 1940–93: Linda Botts *Loose Talk* (1980)

Judges　See also **Crime and Punishment, The Law**

1　Reform! Reform! Aren't things bad enough already?

Mr Justice Astbury 1860–1939: attributed

affecting not to recognize Lord Campbell, the newly appointed Lord Chancellor, whom he encountered enveloped in a huge fur coat:

2 I beg your pardon, My Lord. I mistook you for the Great Seal.

Richard Bethell 1800–73: J. B. Atlay *Victorian Chancellors* (1908)

3 CONVICTED CRIMINAL: As God is my judge—I am innocent. LORD BIRKETT: He isn't; I am, and you're not!

Lord Birkett 1883–1962: attributed; Matthew Parris *Scorn* (1994)

4 I always approach Judge [Lemuel] Shaw as a savage approaches his fetish, knowing that he is ugly but feeling that he is great.

Rufus Choate 1799–1859: Van Wyck Brooks *The Flowering of New England* (1936)

5 I don't want to know what the law is, I want to know who the judge is.

Roy M. Cohn 1927–86: in *New York Times Book Review* 3 April 1988

6 Did you mail that cheque to the Judge?

Roy M. Cohn 1927–86: spoken to an aide, at breakfast with Ned Sherrin, 1978

7 Yes, I could have been a judge but I never had the Latin, never had the Latin for the judging, I just never had sufficient of it to get through the rigorous judging exams. They're noted for their rigour. People come staggering out saying, 'My God, what a rigorous exam'—and so I became a miner instead.

Peter Cook 1937–95: *Beyond the Fringe* (1961 revue)

the judge Sir James Mansfield had suggested that the Court might sit on Good Friday:

8 If your Lordship pleases. But your Lordship will be the first judge who has done so since Pontius Pilate.

William Davy d. 1780: Edward Parry *The Seven Lamps of Advocacy* (1923); the Court did *not* sit

9 Judges commonly are elderly men, and are more likely to hate at sight any analysis to which they are not accustomed, and which disturbs repose of mind, than to fall in love with novelties.

Oliver Wendell Holmes Jr. 1841–1935: in *Harvard Law Review* 1899

10 There are a lot of mediocre judges and people and lawyers, and they are entitled to a little representation [on the Supreme Court], aren't they? We can't have all Brandeises, Frankfurters, and Cardozos.

Roman L. Hruska 1904– : in *New York Times* 17 March 1970

of Judges Learned and Augustus Hand:

11 Quote Learned, and follow 'Gus'.

Robert H. Jackson 1892–1954: Hershel Shanks *The Art and Craft of Judging* (1968)

12 I always feel that there should be some comfort derived from any question from the bench. It is clear proof that the inquiring Justice is not asleep.

Robert H. Jackson 1892–1954: 'Advocacy before the Supreme Court: Suggestions for Effective Presentation' (1951)

13 Mr Justice Cocklecarrot began the hearing of a very curious case yesterday. A Mrs Tasker is accused of continually ringing the doorbell of a Mrs Renton, and then, when the door is opened, pushing a dozen red-bearded dwarfs into the hall and leaving them there.

J. B. Morton 1893–1975: *Diet of Thistles* (1938)

14 Poor fellow, I suppose he fancied he was on the bench. *on hearing that a judge had slept through his play* Pizarro

Richard Brinsley Sheridan 1751–1816: Walter Jerrold *Bon-Mots* (1893)

15 JUDGE: I have read your case, Mr Smith, and I am no wiser now than I was when I started.

SMITH: Possibly not, My Lord, but far better informed.

F. E. Smith 1872–1930: Lord Birkenhead *F. E.* (1959)

16 JUDGE WILLIS: Mr Smith, have you ever heard of a saying by Bacon—the great Bacon—that youth and discretion are ill-wed companions?

SMITH: Indeed I have, your Honour; and has your Honour ever heard of a saying by Bacon—the great Bacon— that a much talking Judge is like an ill-tuned cymbal?

F. E. Smith 1872–1930: Lord Birkenhead *F. E.* (1959)

17 At last we have a woolsack on the Woolsack.
on Lord Dilhorne's appointment as Lord Chancellor

Norman St John Stevas 1929– : attributed

Language See also **Languages**, **Words**

1 Sentence structure is innate but whining is acquired.

Woody Allen 1935– : 'Remembering Needleman' (1976)

2 I did spend a lot of time making sure his sentences always had verbs . . . I'm sorry to see he's slipped in recent years.
on teaching English to the young Tony Blair

Eric Anderson 1936– : in *Daily Telegraph* 25 October 1997

3 Don't swear, boy. It shows a lack of vocabulary.

Alan Bennett 1934– : *Forty Years On* (1969)

4 Would you convey my compliments to the purist who reads your proofs and tell him or her that I write in a sort of broken-down patois which is something like the way a Swiss waiter talks, and that when I split an infinitive, God damn it, I split it so it will stay split.

Raymond Chandler 1888–1959: letter to Edward Weeks, 18 January 1947

5 This is the sort of English up with which I will not put.

Winston Churchill 1874–1965: Ernest Gowers *Plain Words* (1948) 'Troubles with Prepositions'

6 Stars, Charlie had noticed before, always spoke slowly. Listening to Warren Beatty being interviewed was like waiting for speech to finish being invented.

Ray Connally: *Shadows on a Wall* (1994)

7 Where in this small-talking world can I find
A longitude with no platitude?

Christopher Fry 1907– : *The Lady's not for Burning* (1949)

8 Backward ran sentences until reeled the mind.

Wolcott Gibbs 1902–58: in *New Yorker* 28 November 1936 'Time . . . Fortune . . . Life . . . Luce' (satirizing the style of *Time* magazine)

9 When you're lying awake with a dismal headache, and repose is taboo'd by anxiety,
I conceive you may use any language you choose to indulge in, without impropriety.

W. S. Gilbert 1836–1911: *Iolanthe* (1882)

10 Though 'Bother it' I may
Occasionally say,
I never use a big, big D—

W. S. Gilbert 1836–1911: *HMS Pinafore* (1878)

11 The minute a phrase becomes current it becomes an apology for not thinking accurately to the end of the sentence.

Oliver Wendell Holmes Jr. 1841–1935: letter to Harold Laski, 2 July 1917

12 Every sentence he [George Bush] manages to utter scatters its component parts like pond water from a verb chasing its own tail.

Clive James 1939– : *The Dreaming Swimmer* (1992)

13 The subjunctive mood is in its death throes, and the best thing to do is to put it out of its misery as soon as possible.

W. Somerset Maugham 1874–1965: *A Writer's Notebook* (1949) written in 1941

14 My spelling is Wobbly. It's good spelling but it Wobbles, and the letters get in the wrong places.

A. A. Milne 1882–1956: *Winnie-the-Pooh* (1926)

15 Save the gerund and screw the whale.

Tom Stoppard 1937– : *The Real Thing* (1988 rev. ed.)

16 Linguistic analysis. A lot of chaps pointing out that we don't always mean what we say, even when we manage to say what we meant.

Tom Stoppard 1937– : *Professional Foul* (1978)

on the first-person plural pronoun:
17 Only presidents, editors, and people with tapeworms have the right to use the editorial 'we'.

Mark Twain 1835–1910: attributed

18 'Feather-footed through the plashy fen passes the questing vole' . . . 'Yes,' said the Managing Editor. 'That must be good style.'

Evelyn Waugh 1903–66: *Scoop* (1938)

19 Enormous romping vitality and a love for the beauty of language in which one would believe more thoroughly if she did not so frequently split her infinitives neatly down the middle.

Rebecca West 1892–1983: of the novelist Marjorie Bowen in 1915; *The Young Rebecca* (1982)

20 Good intentions are invariably ungrammatical.

Oscar Wilde 1854–1900: attributed

Languages See also **Language, Words**

1 The Norwegian language has been described as German spoken underwater.

Anonymous: Nigel Rees *Cassell Dictionary of Humorous Quotations* (1999)

2 If you understand English, press 1. If you do not understand English, press 2.
recorded message on Australian tax helpline

Anonymous: in *Mail on Sunday* 30 July 2000 'Quotes of the Week'

3 The letter is written in the tongue of the Think Tanks, a language more difficult to master than Basque or Navaho and spoken only where strategic thinkers clump together in Institutes.

Russell Baker 1925– : in *New York Times* 8 April 1981

4 Albanian . . . a language that sounded comic with all its pffts, pees, wees, pings and fitts.

Cecil Beaton 1904–80: diary, August 1940

5 Is there no Latin word for Tea? Upon my soul, if I had known that I would have let the vulgar stuff alone.

Hilaire Belloc 1870–1953: 'On Tea' (1908)

6 JOSEPHINE BAKER: Donnez-moi une tasse de café, s'il vous plait.
MARY CAMPBELL: Honey, talk out of the mouth you was born with.
exchange between Josephine Baker, who had moved to France from America, and who was staying with Lorenz Hart's parents, and Mary Campbell, who was the Harts' cook

Mary Campbell: Samuel Marx and Jan Clayton *Rodgers and Hart* (1975)

7 Speak in French when you can't think of the English for a thing.

Lewis Carroll 1832–98: *Through the Looking-Glass* (1872) *on speaking French fluently rather than correctly:*

8 It's nerve and brass, *audace* and disrespect, and leaping-before-you-look and what-the-hellism, that must be developed.

Diana Cooper 1892–1986: Philip Ziegler *Diana Cooper* (1981)

9 Anglish is what we don' know
Spanglish is langlish we know.

Dorothy Fields 1905–74: 'Spanglish' (1973)

10 I hear it's the Hebrew in Heaven, sir. Spanish is seldom spoken.

Ronald Firbank 1886–1926: *Concerning the Eccentricities of Cardinal Pirelli* (1926)

11 'Basta!' his master replied, with all the brilliant glibness of the Berlitz-school.

Ronald Firbank 1886–1926: *The Flower Beneath the Foot* (1923)

Dennis Wheatley had told Humbert Wolfe that his novels had been translated into 'every European language except one':

12 HUMBERT WOLFE: I can't think which.
PAMELA FRANKAU: English!

Pamela Frankau 1908–67: James Agate diary 10 April 1938

13 Weep not for little Léonie
Abducted by a French Marquis!
Though loss of honour was a wrench
Just think how it's improved her French.

Harry Graham 1874–1936: 'Compensation' (1930)

14 There even are places where English completely
disappears.
In America, they haven't used it for years!
Why can't the English teach their children how to speak?

Alan Jay Lerner 1918–86: 'Why Can't the English?' (1956)

when Khrushchev began banging his shoe on the desk:

15 Perhaps we could have a translation, I could not quite follow.

Harold Macmillan 1894–1986: during his speech to the United Nations, 29 September 1960

16 Soundbite and slogan, strapline and headline, at every turn we meet hyperbole. The soaring inflation of the English language is more urgently in need of control than the economic variety.

Trevor Nunn 1940– : in *Evening Standard* 3 June 1999

17 Waiting for the German verb is surely the ultimate thrill.

Flann O'Brien 1911–66: *The Hair of the Dogma* (1977)

on being told there was no English word equivalent to sensibilité:

18 Yes we have. Humbug.

Lord Palmerston 1784–1865: attributed

19 KENNETH: If you're so hot, you'd better tell me how to say she has ideas above her station.
BRIAN: Oh, yes, I forgot. It's fairly easy, old boy. *Elle a des idées au-dessus de sa gare.*
KENNETH: You can't do it like that. You can't say *au-dessus de sa gare.* It isn't that sort of station.

Terence Rattigan 1911–77: *French without Tears* (1937)

20 Remember that you are a human being with a soul and the divine gift of articulate speech: that your native language is the language of Shakespeare and Milton and The Bible; and don't sit there crooning like a bilious pigeon.

George Bernard Shaw 1856–1950: *Pygmalion* (1916)

21 Egad I think the interpreter is the hardest to be understood of the two!

Richard Brinsley Sheridan 1751–1816: *The Critic* (1779)

22 They spell it Vinci and pronounce it Vinchy; foreigners always spell better than they pronounce.

Mark Twain 1835–1910: *The Innocents Abroad* (1869)

23 I once heard a Californian student in Heidelberg say, in one of his calmest moods, that he would rather decline two drinks than one German adjective.

Mark Twain 1835–1910: *A Tramp Abroad* (1880)

24 An unalterable and unquestioned law of the musical world required that the German text of French operas sung by Swedish artists should be translated into Italian for the clearer understanding of English-speaking audiences.

Edith Wharton 1862–1937: *The Age of Innocence* (1920)

Last Words See also **Death**

1 I will not go down to posterity talking bad grammar.

Benjamin Disraeli 1804–81: while correcting proofs of his last Parliamentary speech, 31 March 1881; Robert Blake *Disraeli* (1966)

2 No it is better not. She would only ask me to take a message to Albert.
near death, declining a proposed visit from Queen Victoria

Benjamin Disraeli 1804–81: Robert Blake *Disraeli* (1966)

on his deathbed in 1936, when someone remarked 'Cheer up, your Majesty, you will soon be at Bognor again':
3 Bugger Bognor.

George V 1865–1936: Kenneth Rose *King George V* (1983); attributed

Lady Eldon had suggested that she should read to him from his own New Testament:
4 No . . . Awfully jolly of you to suggest it, though.

Ronald Knox 1888–1957: Evelyn Waugh *Life of Ronald Knox*

5 Die, my dear Doctor, that's the last thing I shall do!

Lord Palmerston 1784–1865: E. Latham *Famous Sayings and their Authors* (1904)

6 Put that bloody cigarette out!
before being shot by a sniper in World War One

Saki 1870–1916: attributed, perhaps apocryphal

7 They couldn't hit an elephant at this distance.
immediately prior to being killed by enemy fire at the battle of Spotsylvania in the American Civil War, May 1864

John Sedgwick d. 1864: Robert E. Denney *The Civil War Years* (1992)

8 If this is dying, then I don't think much of it.

Lytton Strachey 1880–1932: Michael Holroyd *Lytton Strachey* (1967)

9 I find, then, I am but a bad anatomist.
cutting his throat in prison, he severed his windpipe instead of his jugular, and lingered for several days

Wolfe Tone 1763–98: Oliver Knox *Rebels and Informers* (1998)

10 This is no time for making new enemies.
on being asked to renounce the Devil, on his deathbed

Voltaire 1694–1778: attributed

The Law See also **Crime and Punishment**, **Judges**

1 I get paid for seeing that my clients have every break the law allows. I have knowingly defended a number of guilty men. But the guilty never escape unscathed. My fees are sufficient punishment for anyone.

F. Lee Bailey 1933– : in *Los Angeles Times* 9 January 1972

2 Laws and institutions are constantly tending to gravitate. Like clocks, they must be occasionally cleansed, and wound up, and set to true time.

Henry Ward Beecher 1813–87: *Life Thoughts* (1858)

3 Equity does not demand that its suitors shall have led blameless lives.

Louis Brandeis 1856–1941: in *Loughran v. Loughran* 1934

4 Lawyers charge a fortune to handle a bond offering. You know what it takes to handle a bond offering? The mental capacities of a filing cabinet.

Jimmy Breslin 1929– : in *Legal Times* 17 January 1983

5 As a moth is drawn to the light, so is a litigant drawn to the United States. If he can only get his case into their courts, he stands to win a fortune. At no cost to himself; and at no risk of having to pay anything to the other side.

Lord Denning 1899–1999: *Smith Kline & French Laboratories Ltd. v. Bloch* 1983

6 'Little to do, and plenty to get, I suppose?' said Sergeant Buzfuz, with jocularity. 'Oh, quite enough to get, sir, as the soldier said ven they ordered him three hundred and fifty lashes,' replied Sam. 'You must not tell us what the soldier, or any other man, said, sir,' interposed the judge; 'it's not evidence.'

Charles Dickens 1812–70: *Pickwick Papers* (1837)

7 'If the law supposes that,' said Mr Bumble . . . 'the law is a ass—a idiot.'

Charles Dickens 1812–70: *Oliver Twist* (1838)

8 The one great principle of the English law is, to make business for itself.

Charles Dickens 1812–70: *Bleak House* (1853)

9 This contract is so one-sided that I am surprised to find it written on both sides of the paper.

Lord Evershed 1899–1966: Lord Denning *Closing Chapter* (1983)

10 When I was a lad I served a term
As office boy to an Attorney's firm.
I cleaned the windows and I swept the floor,
And I polished up the handle of the big front door.
I polished up that handle so carefullee
That now I am the Ruler of the Queen's Navee!

W. S. Gilbert 1836–1911: *HMS Pinafore* (1878)

11 The Law is the true embodiment
Of everything that's excellent.
It has no kind of fault or flaw,
And I, my Lords, embody the Law.

W. S. Gilbert 1836–1911: *Iolanthe* (1882)

12 Let's find out what everyone is doing,
And then stop everyone from doing it.

A. P. Herbert 1890–1971: 'Let's Stop Somebody from Doing Something' (1930)

an attempt is made to write a cheque on a cow:
13 'Was the cow crossed?'
'No, your worship, it was an open cow.'

A. P. Herbert 1890–1971: *Uncommon Law* (1935) 'The Negotiable Cow'

on the award of £600,000 libel damages to Sonia Sutcliffe against Private Eye:
14 If this is justice, I am a banana.

Ian Hislop 1960– : in *Guardian* 25 May 1989

15 Legal writing is one of those rare creatures, like the rat and the cockroach, that would attract little sympathy even as an endangered species.

Richard Hyland 1949– : 'A Defense of Legal Writing' (1986)

16 Johnson observed, that 'he did not care to speak ill of any man behind his back, but he believed the gentleman was an *attorney*.'

Samuel Johnson 1709–84: James Boswell *Life of Samuel Johnson* (1791) 1770

when Knox was Attorney General Theodore Roosevelt requested a legal justification for his acquisition of the Panama Canal:

17 Oh, Mr President, do not let so great an achievement suffer from any taint of legality.

Philander C. Knox 1853–1921: Tyler Dennett *John Hay: From Poetry to Politics*

18 If you want to get ahead in this world get a lawyer—not a book.

Fran Lebowitz 1946– : on self-help books; *Social Studies* (1981)

19 Whatever fees we [Judge Logan and I] earn at a distance, if not paid *before*, we notice we never hear of after the work is done. We therefore, are growing a little sensitive on the point.

Abraham Lincoln 1809–65: letter 2 November 1842

20 Sue me, sue me
Shoot bullets through me
I love you.

Frank Loesser 1910–69: 'Sue Me' (1950)

21 However harmless a thing is, if the law forbids it most people will think it wrong.

W. Somerset Maugham 1874–1965: *A Writer's Notebook* (1949) written in 1896

22 Haldeman is the only man in America in this generation who let his hair grow for a courtroom appearance.
on the Watergate hearings

Mary McGrory 1918– : in *Washington Star* 12 November 1974

23 Injustice is relatively easy to bear; what stings is justice.

H. L. Mencken 1880–1956: *Prejudices, Third Series* (1922)

24 Here [in Paris] they hang a man first, and try him afterwards.

Molière 1622–73: *Monsieur de Pourceaugnac* (1670)

25 I don't know as I want a lawyer to tell me what I cannot do. I hire him to tell me how to do what I want to do.

J. P. Morgan 1837–1913: Ida M. Tarbell *The Life of Elbert H. Gary* (1925)

26 A British criminal trial is not primarily an investigation to discover the truth, although truth may sometimes be disinterred by chance.

John Mortimer 1923– : *Clinging to the Wreckage* (1982)

27 No brilliance is needed in the law. Nothing but common sense, and relatively clean finger nails.

John Mortimer 1923– : *A Voyage Round My Father* (1971)

28 As it was once put to me, always remember that [as a barrister] you are in the position of a cabman on the rank, bound to answer the first hail.

Ralph Neville: in *The Times* 16 June 1913

29 The Polis as Polis, in this city, is Null an' Void!

Sean O'Casey 1880–1964: *Juno and the Paycock* (1925)

30 Policemen, like red squirrels, must be protected.

Joe Orton 1933–67: *Loot* (1967)

31 The Court's opinion will accomplish the seemingly impossible feat of leaving this area of the law more confused than it found it.

William H. Rehnquist 1924– : dissenting opinion in *Roe v. Wade* 1973

32 I have always noticed that any time a man can't come and settle with you without bringing his lawyer, why, look out for him.

Will Rogers 1879–1935: 'Slipping the Lariat Over' 14 January 1923

33 Went down and spoke at some lawyers' meeting last night. They didn't think much of my little squib yesterday about driving the shysters out of their profession. They seemed to kinder doubt just who would have to leave.

Will Rogers 1879–1935: 'Mr. Rogers is Hob Nobbing With Leaders of the Bar'

34 The first thing we do, let's kill all the lawyers.

William Shakespeare 1564–1616: *Henry VI, Part 2* (1592)

35 The sound of tireless voices is the price we pay for the right to hear the music of our own opinions.

Adlai Stevenson 1900–65: *The Guide to American Law* (1984)

36 Some circumstantial evidence is very strong, as when you find a trout in the milk.

Henry David Thoreau 1817–62: diary, 11 November 1850

37 What chance has the ignorant, uncultivated liar against the educated expert? What chance have I . . . against a lawyer?

Mark Twain 1835–1910: 'On the Decay of the Art of Lying' (1882)

38 Whenever a copyright law is to be made or altered, then the idiots assemble.

Mark Twain 1835–1910: *Notebook* 23 May 1903

39 The only regret she [Queen Victoria] feels about the decision is that so wicked a woman should escape by a mere legal quibble! The law is not a moral profession she must say.

Queen Victoria 1819–1901: on the commutation of Mrs Maybrick's death sentence; letter to Sir Henry Ponsonby, 22 August 1889

40 There's a lot of law at the end of a nightstick.

Grover A. Whalen 1886–1962: Quentin Reynolds *Courtroom* (1950)

41 There is a little shilling book—ninepence for cash—called *Every Man his own Lawyer*. If my friends had only sent it to me, or even read it themselves, all this trouble, expense, and worry would have been saved.
on the settlement to be made with his wife

Oscar Wilde 1854–1900: letter to Robert Ross from Reading Prison, 1 April 1897

42 Asking the ignorant to use the incomprehensible to decide the unknowable.

Hiller B. Zobel 1932– : 'The Jury on Trial' in *American Heritage* July–August 1995; see **Sports and Games** 36

Leisure See **Work and Leisure**

Letters and Letter-writing

formula with which to return unsolicited manuscripts:
1 Mr James Agate regrets that he has no time to bother about the enclosed in which he has been greatly interested.

James Agate 1877–1947: diary, 3 January 1936

2 It would have been less heterodox
If he had put the letter in the letter-o-box.

Brian Brindley: the Babes-in-the-Wood discovering a letter pinned to a tree by Robin Hood, in an Oxford pantomime in 1953; Ned Sherrin *Cutting Edge* (1984)

3 I am not a cautious letter-writer and generally say what comes uppermost at the moment.

Lord Byron 1788–1824: letter to Mary Shelley, 9 October 1822

4 WITWOUD: Madam, do you pin up your hair with all your letters?
MILLAMANT: Only with those in verse, Mr Witwoud. I never pin up my hair with prose.

William Congreve 1670–1729: *The Way of the World* (1700)

5 Regarding yours, dear Mrs Worthington, of Wednesday the 23rd.

Noël Coward 1899–1973: 'Mrs Worthington' (1935)

6 Dear 338171 (May I call you 338?).

Noël Coward 1899–1973: letter to T. E. Lawrence, 25 August 1930

7 Sir, My pa requests me to write to you, the doctors considering it doubtful whether he will ever recuvver the use of his legs which prevents his holding a pen.

Charles Dickens 1812–70: *Nicholas Nickleby* (1839)

8 It is wonderful how much news there is when people write every other day; if they wait for a month, there is nothing that seems worth telling.

O. Douglas 1877–1948: *Penny Plain* (1920)

9 [Charles Lamb's] sayings are generally like women's letters; all the pith is in the postscript.

William Hazlitt 1778–1830: *Conversations of James Northcote* (1826–7)

10 The applicant may publish the songs so far as I am concerned, but I had rather you should tell her so, as I do not want to write letters to a lady whose name is Birdie.

A. E. Housman 1859–1936: letter to his publisher Grant Richards, 1 March 1904

11 A man seldom puts his authentic self into a letter. He writes it to amuse a friend or to get rid of a social or business obligation, which is to say, a nuisance.

H. L. Mencken 1880–1956: *Minority Report* (1956)

12 I have made this [letter] longer than usual, only because I have not had the time to make it shorter.

Blaise Pascal 1623–62: *Lettres Provinciales* (1657)

13 Laura's repeated assurances to me that she had both replied to your letter and that she was about to do so are, I think, characteristic of a mind at bay.

S. J. Perelman 1904–79: letter 17 October 1948

responding to a savage review by Rudolph Louis in Münchener Neueste Nachrich *7 February 1906:*
14 I am sitting in the smallest room of my house. I have your review before me. In a moment it will be behind me.

Max Reger 1873–1916: Nicolas Slonimsky *Lexicon of Musical Invective* (1953)

circular sent out to forestall unwanted visitors:
15 Mr J. Ruskin is about to begin a work of great importance and therefore begs that in reference to calls and correspondence you will consider him dead for the next two months.

John Ruskin 1819–1900: attributed

Wilde had sent a letter on 'Fashion in Dress' to the Daily Telegraph, *but explained in a covering letter to the proprietor:*
16 I don't wish to sign my name, though I am afraid everybody will know who the writer is: one's style is one's signature always.

Oscar Wilde 1854–1900: letter, 2 February 1891

17 I have no need of your God-damned sympathy. I only wish to be entertained by some of your grosser reminiscences.

Alexander Woollcott 1887–1943: letter to Rex O'Malley, 1942

Libraries See also Books

1 RUTH: They'll sack you.
NORMAN: They daren't. I reorganized the Main Index. When I die, the secret dies with me.

Alan Ayckbourn 1939– : *Round and Round the Garden* (1975)

2 If you file your waste-paper basket for 50 years, you have a public library.

Tony Benn 1925– : in *Daily Telegraph* 5 March 1994

3 What a sad want I am in of libraries, of books to gather facts from! Why is there not a Majesty's library in every county town? There is a Majesty's jail and gallows in every one.

Thomas Carlyle 1795–1881: diary, 18 May 1832

4 There is nowhere in the world where sleep is so deep as in the libraries of the House of Commons.

Chips Channon 1897–1958: diary, 16 December 1937

5 Th' first thing to have in a libry is a shelf. Fr'm time to time this can be decorated with lithrachure. But th' shelf is th' main thing.

Finley Peter Dunne 1867–1936: *Mr Dooley Says* (1910)

6 I've been drunk for about a week now, and I thought it might sober me up to sit in a library.

F. Scott Fitzgerald 1896–1940: *The Great Gatsby* (1925)

7 Mr Cobb took me into his library and showed me his books, of which he had a complete set.

Ring Lardner 1885–1933: R. E. Drennan *Wit's End* (1973)

8 'Our library,' said the president, 'two hundred thousand volumes!' 'Aye,' said the minister, 'a powerful heap of rubbish, I'll be bound!'

Stephen Leacock 1869–1944: *Arcadian Adventures with the Idle Rich* (1914)

9 E. W. B. Nicholson [Bodley's Librarian] spending three days at the London Docks, watching outgoing ships, after losing a book from Bodley, which was afterwards discovered slightly out of place on the shelf.

Falconer Madan 1851–1935: J. A. Gere and John Sparrow (eds.) *Geoffrey Madan's Notebooks* (1981)

10 Those dreadful detective stories. Another corpse in the library this evening. Really, you know, too much of a good thing. Fourth this week. No doubt trouble is shortage of libraries.

Flann O'Brien 1911–66: *The Best of Myles* (1968)

11 The Librarian was, of course, very much in favour of reading in general, but readers in particular got on his nerves . . . He liked people who loved and respected books, and the best way to do that, in the Librarian's opinion, was to leave them on the shelves where Nature intended them to be.

Terry Pratchett 1948– : *Men at Arms* (1993)

Lies See also **Truth**

1 It reminds me of the small boy who jumbled his biblical quotations and said: 'A lie is an abomination unto the Lord, and a very present help in trouble.'

Anonymous: recalled by Adlai Stevenson; Bill Adler *The Stevenson Wit* (1966)

2 She [Lady Desborough] tells enough white lies to ice a wedding cake.

Margot Asquith 1864–1945: Lady Violet Bonham Carter 'Margot Oxford' in *Listener* 11 June 1953

3 Matilda told such Dreadful Lies,
It made one Gasp and Stretch one's Eyes;
Her Aunt, who, from her Earliest Youth,
Had kept a Strict Regard for Truth,
Attempted to Believe Matilda:
The effort very nearly killed her.

Hilaire Belloc 1870–1953: 'Matilda' (1907)

4 For every time She shouted 'Fire!'
They only answered 'Little Liar!'
And therefore when her Aunt returned,
Matilda, and the House, were Burned.

Hilaire Belloc 1870–1953: 'Matilda' (1907)

5 That branch of the art of lying which consists in very nearly deceiving your friends without quite deceiving your enemies.
of propaganda

Francis M. Cornford 1874–1943: *Microcosmographia Academica* (1922 ed.)

6 There are three kinds of lies: lies, damned lies and statistics.

Benjamin Disraeli 1804–81: attributed to Disraeli in Mark Twain *Autobiography* (1924)

7 What you take for lying in an Irishman is only his attempt to put an herbaceous border on stark reality.

Oliver St John Gogarty 1878–1957: *Going Native* (1940)

8 By the time you say you're his,
Shivering and sighing
And he vows his passion is
Infinite, undying—
Lady, make a note of this:
One of you is lying.

Dorothy Parker 1893–1967: 'Unfortunate Coincidence' (1937)

on being told that Lord Astor claimed that her allegations, concerning himself and his house parties at Cliveden, were untrue:
9 He would, wouldn't he?

Mandy Rice-Davies 1944– : in *Guardian* 1 July 1963

10 A little inaccuracy sometimes saves tons of explanation.

Saki 1870–1916: *The Square Egg* (1924)

11 I don't think the son of a bitch knows the difference between telling the truth and lying.
of Richard Nixon

Harry S. Truman 1884–1972: Merle Miller *Plain Speaking* (1974)

12 In exceptional circumstances it is necessary to say something that is untrue in the House of Commons.

William Waldegrave 1946– : in *Guardian* 9 March 1994

13 I am suing Lord Beaverbrook for libel and hope for some lovely tax-free money in damages. He has very conveniently told some lies about me.

Evelyn Waugh 1903–66: letter to Lady Diana Cooper, March 1956

14 Untruthful! My nephew Algernon? Impossible! He is an Oxonian.

Oscar Wilde 1854–1900: *The Importance of Being Earnest* (1895)

Life and Living

1 Alun's life was coming to consist more and more exclusively of being told at dictation speed what he knew.

Kingsley Amis 1922–95: *The Old Devils* (1986)

2 Life is a sexually transmitted disease.

Anonymous: graffito found on the London Underground

3 The only thing I regret about my life is the length of it. If I had to live my life again I'd make all the same mistakes—only sooner.

Tallulah Bankhead 1903–68: Laurence J. Peter (ed.) *Quotations for our Time* (1977)

4 Cocaine habit-forming? Of course not. I ought to know. I've been using it for years.

Tallulah Bankhead 1903–68: *Tallulah* (1952)

5 Brought up in the provinces in the forties and fifties one learned early the valuable lesson that life is generally something that happens elsewhere.

Alan Bennett 1934– : introduction to *Talking Heads* (1988)

6 E. F. Benson never lived his life at all; only stayed with it and lunched with it.

A. C. Benson 1862–1925: J. A. Gere and John Sparrow (eds.) *Geoffrey Madan's Notebooks* (1981)

7 It's as large as life, and twice as natural!

Lewis Carroll 1832–98: *Through the Looking-Glass* (1872)

8 Life is the funny thing that happens to you on the way to the grave.

Quentin Crisp 1908–99: in *Spectator* 20 November 1999

9 Never try to keep up with the Joneses. Drag them down to your level. It's cheaper that way.

Quentin Crisp 1908–99: in *The Times* 22 November 1999

10 It's a funny old world—a man's lucky if he gets out of it alive.

Walter de Leon and **Paul M. Jones**: *You're Telling Me* (1934 film); spoken by W. C. Fields

11 'Sairey,' says Mrs Harris, 'sech is life. Vich likeways is the hend of all things!'

Charles Dickens 1812–70: *Martin Chuzzlewit* (1844)

12 Life is a Cabaret, old chum
Come to the Cabaret.

Fred Ebb: 'Cabaret' (1965)

13 If *A* is a success in life, then *A* equals *x* plus *y* plus *z*. Work is *x*; *y* is play; and *z* is keeping your mouth shut.

Albert Einstein 1879–1955: in *Observer* 15 January 1950

14 There's nothing in the middle of the road but yellow stripes and dead armadillos.

Jim Hightower: attributed, 1984

15 Life is just one damned thing after another.

Elbert Hubbard 1859–1915: in *Philistine* December 1909, (often attributed to Frank Ward O'Malley)

16 Life is something to do when you can't get to sleep.

Fran Lebowitz 1946– : *Metropolitan Life* (1978)

17 Life, if you're fat, is a minefield—you have to pick your way, otherwise you blow up.

Miriam Margolyes 1941– : in *Observer* 9 June 1991

18 Laugh it off, laugh it off; it's all part of life's rich pageant.

Arthur Marshall 1910–89: *The Games Mistress* (recorded monologue, 1937)

19 Moderation in all things. Not too much of life. It often lasts too long.

H. L. Mencken 1880–1956: *Minority Report* (1956)

20 Life is a shit sandwich and every day you take another bite.

Joe Schmidt: a pro football player's view; Jonathon Green and Don Atyeo (eds.) *The Book of Sports Quotes* (1979)

21 I *love* living. I have some problems with my *life*, but living is the best thing they've come up with so far.

Neil Simon 1927– : *Last of the Red Hot Lovers* (1970)

22 Life is a gamble at terrible odds—if it was a bet, you wouldn't take it.

Tom Stoppard 1937– : *Rosencrantz and Guildenstern are Dead* (1967)

23 Above all, gentlemen, not the slightest zeal.

Charles-Maurice de Talleyrand 1754–1838: P. Chasles *Voyages d'un critique à travers la vie et les livres* (1868)

24 Oh, isn't life a terrible thing, thank God?

Dylan Thomas 1914–53: *Under Milk Wood* (1954)

25 What a queer thing Life is! So unlike anything else, don't you know, if you see what I mean.

P. G. Wodehouse 1881–1975: *My Man Jeeves* (1919)

26 As life goes on, don't you find that all you need is about two real friends, a regular supply of books, and a Peke?

P. G. Wodehouse 1881–1975: letter 28 October 1930

Literature See also **Books, Poetry and Poets, Writers and Writing**

1 All I want is a modest place in Mr X's *Good Reading*, Miss Y's *Good Writing*, and that new edition of *One Thousand Best Bits of Recent Prose*.

James Agate 1877–1947: diary 21 August 1941

on literature as taught in school:

2 Schoolteachers seemed determined to persuade me that 'classic' is a synonym for 'narcotic'.

Russell Baker 1925– : in *New York Times* 14 April 1982

3 A swear-word in a rustic slum
A simple swear-word is to some,
To Masefield something more.

Max Beerbohm 1872–1956: *Fifty Caricatures* (1912)

4 The literary gift is a mere accident—is as often bestowed on idiots who have nothing to say worth hearing as it is denied to strenuous sages.

Max Beerbohm 1872–1956: letter to George Bernard Shaw, 21 September 1903

5 Remote and ineffectual Don
That dared attack my Chesterton.

Hilaire Belloc 1870–1953: 'Lines to a Don' (1910)

6 We were put to Dickens as children but it never quite took. That unremitting humanity soon had me cheesed off.

Alan Bennett 1934– : *The Old Country* (1978)

7 Literature's always a good card to play for Honours. It makes people think that Cabinet ministers are educated.

Arnold Bennett 1867–1931: *The Title* (1918)

8 Dr Weiss, at forty, knew that her life had been ruined by literature.

Anita Brookner 1938– : *A Start in Life* (1981)

9 'The whole of this unfortunate business,' said Dr Lyster, 'has been the result of PRIDE AND PREJUDICE.'

Fanny Burney 1752–1840: *Cecilia* (1782)

10 I hate things all fiction . . . there should always be some foundation of fact for the most airy fabric—and pure invention is but the talent of a liar.

Lord Byron 1788–1824: letter to his publisher John Murray, 2 April 1817

11 We learn from Horace, Homer sometimes sleeps;
We feel without him: Wordsworth sometimes wakes.

Lord Byron 1788–1824: *Don Juan* (1819–24)

12 You praise the firm restraint with which they write—
I'm with you there, of course:
They use the snaffle and the curb all right,
But where's the bloody horse?

Roy Campbell 1901–57: 'On Some South African Novelists' (1930)

13 'What is the use of a book', thought Alice, 'without pictures or conversations?'

Lewis Carroll 1832–98: *Alice's Adventures in Wonderland* (1865)

14 If my books had been any worse, I should not have been invited to Hollywood, and if they had been any better, I should not have come.

Raymond Chandler 1888–1959: letter to Charles W. Morton, 12 December 1945

15 A literary man—*with* a wooden leg.

Charles Dickens 1812–70: *Our Mutual Friend* (1865)

16 When I want to read a novel, I write one.

Benjamin Disraeli 1804–81: W. Monypenny and G. Buckle *Life of Benjamin Disraeli* (1920)

17 The mama of dada.
of Gertrude Stein

Clifton Fadiman 1904– : *Party of One* (1955)

18 How rare, how precious is frivolity! How few writers can prostitute all their powers! They are always implying, 'I am capable of higher things.'

E. M. Forster 1879–1970: *Abinger Harvest* (1936)

19 The work of Henry James has always seemed divisible by a simple dynastic arrangement into three reigns: James I, James II, and the Old Pretender.

Philip Guedalla 1889–1944: *Supers and Supermen* (1920) 'Some Critics'

20 The cheerful clatter of Sir James Barrie's cans as he went round with the milk of human kindness.

Philip Guedalla 1889–1944: *Supers and Supermen* (1920) 'Some Critics'

21 He knew everything about literature except how to enjoy it.

Joseph Heller 1923–99: *Catch-22* (1961)

22 It takes a great deal of history to produce a little literature.

Henry James 1843–1916: *Hawthorne* (1879)

23 A beginning, a muddle, and an end.
  on the 'classic formula' for a novel

Philip Larkin 1922–85: in *New Fiction* January 1978

24 He has one eminent merit—that of being an enthusiastic admirer of mine—so that I may be the Hero of a novel yet, under the name of Delamere or Mortimer. Only think what an honour.
  of Bulwer Lytton

Lord Macaulay 1800–59: letter, 5 August 1831

25 From the moment I picked up your book until I laid it down, I was convulsed with laughter. Some day I intend reading it.

Groucho Marx 1895–1977: a blurb written for S. J. Perelman's 1928 book *Dawn Ginsberg's Revenge*

26 A novelist must preserve a childlike belief in the importance of things which common sense considers of no great consequence.

W. Somerset Maugham 1874–1965: *A Writer's Notebook* (1949) written in 1933

27 I have only ever read one book in my life, and that is *White Fang*. It's so frightfully good I've never bothered to read another.
  Uncle Matthew's view of literature

Nancy Mitford 1904–73: *Love in a Cold Climate* (1949)

28 The play was consumed in wholesome fashion by large masses in places of public resort; the novel was self-administered in private.

Flann O'Brien 1911–66: *At Swim-Two-Birds* (1939)

29 And I'll stay off Verlaine too; he was always chasing Rimbauds.

Dorothy Parker 1893–1967: 'The Little Hours' (1939)

30 If, with the literate, I am
Impelled to try an epigram,
I never seek to take the credit;
We all assume that Oscar said it.

Dorothy Parker 1893–1967: 'A Pig's-Eye View of Literature' (1937)

31 Nearly all our best men are dead! Carlyle, Tennyson, Browning, George Eliot!—I'm not feeling very well myself.

Punch 1841–1992: vol. 104 (1893)

32 I have known her pass the whole evening without mentioning a single book, or *in fact anything unpleasant*, at all.

Henry Reed 1914–86: *A Very Great Man Indeed* (1953)

33 In view of her penchant
For something romantic,
De Sade is too trenchant
And Dickens too frantic,
And Stendhal would ruin
The plan of attack
As there isn't much blue in
The Red and the Black.

Stephen Sondheim 1930– : 'Now' (1972)

34 I should have no objection to this method, but that I think it must smell too strong of the lamp.

Laurence Sterne 1713–68: *Tristram Shandy* (1759–67)

35 You're familiar with the tragedies of antiquity, are you? The great homicidal classics?

Tom Stoppard 1937– : *Rosencrantz and Guildenstern are Dead* (1967)

36 Every quarter century, like clockwork, there is a Peacock revival. The great tail feathers unfurl in all their Pavonian splendor, and like-minded folk delight in the display; and that's the end of that for the next twenty-five years.

Gore Vidal 1925– : *Pink Triangle and Yellow Star* (1982)

37 I don't give a toss about writing really. It's a bit ironic that the things I'm really into are music and football, and I have never really been good at either.

Irvine Welsh 1957– : in *Times* 1999, attributed

38 Any writer worth his salt knows that only a small proportion of literature does more than partly compensate people for the damage they have suffered in learning to read.

Rebecca West 1892–1983: Peter Vansittart *Path from a White Horse* (1985), author's note

39 Meredith's a prose Browning, and so is Browning.

Oscar Wilde 1854–1900: *Intentions* (1891) 'The Critic as Artist'

Living See **Life and Living**

Love See also **Marriage**, **Sex**

1 We men have got love well weighed up; our stuff
Can get by without it.
Women don't seem to think that's good enough;
They write about it.

Kingsley Amis 1922–95: 'A Bookshop Idyll' (1956)

2 Even logical positivists are capable of love.

A. J. Ayer 1910–89: Kenneth Tynan *Profiles* (1989)

3 Women who love the same man have a kind of bitter freemasonry.

Max Beerbohm 1872–1956: *Zuleika Dobson* (1911)

4 Make love to every woman you meet. If you get five percent on your outlays it's a good investment.

Arnold Bennett 1867–1931: attributed

5 Miss Joan Hunter Dunn, Miss Joan Hunter Dunn,
How mad I am, sad I am, glad that you won.
The warm-handled racket is back in its press,
But my shock-headed victor, she loves me no less.

John Betjeman 1906–84: 'A Subaltern's Love-Song' (1945)

6 The ability to make love frivolously is the chief characteristic which distinguishes human beings from beasts.

Heywood Broun 1888–1939: Howard Teichmann *George S. Kaufman* (1973)

7 Would I were free from this restraint,
Or else had hopes to win her;
Would she could make of me a saint,
Or I of her a sinner.

William Congreve 1670–1729: 'Pious Selinda Goes to Prayers' (song)

8 If this be not love, it is madness, and then it is pardonable.

William Congreve 1670–1729: *The Old Bachelor* (1693)

9 An affair between a mad rocking horse and a rawhide suitcase.
on Jeanette MacDonald and Nelson Eddy

Noël Coward 1899–1973: diary, 1 July 1946

10 They made love as though they were an endangered species.

Peter de Vries 1910–93: Laurence J. Peter (ed.) *Quotations for our Time* (1977)

11 Did you ever hear of Captain Wattle?
He was all for love, and a little for the bottle.

Charles Dibdin 1745–1814: 'Captain Wattle and Miss Roe' (1797)

12 Barkis is willin'.

Charles Dickens 1812–70: *David Copperfield* (1850)

13 Oh, Mrs Corney, what a prospect this opens! What a opportunity for a jining of hearts and house-keepings!

Charles Dickens 1812–70: *Oliver Twist* (1838)

14 The magic of first love is our ignorance that it can ever end.

Benjamin Disraeli 1804–81: *Henrietta Temple* (1837)

15 What is commonly called love, namely the desire of satisfying a voracious appetite with a certain quantity of delicate white human flesh.

Henry Fielding 1707–54: *Tom Jones* (1749)

16 I'm afraid I was very much the traditionalist. I went down on one knee and dictated a proposal which my secretary faxed over straight away.

Stephen Fry 1957– and **Hugh Laurie**: *A Bit More Fry and Laurie* (1991)

17 How happy could I be with either,
Were t'other dear charmer away!

John Gay 1685–1732: *The Beggar's Opera* (1728)

18 Holding hands at midnight
'Neath a starry sky . . .
Nice work if you can get it,
And you can get it if you try.

Ira Gershwin 1896–1983: 'Nice Work If You Can Get It' (1937)

19 With love to lead the way,
I've found more clouds of grey
Than any Russian play
Could guarantee . . .
. . . When ev'ry happy plot
Ends with the marriage knot—
And there's no knot for me.

Ira Gershwin 1896–1983: 'But Not For Me' (1930)

20 Love is sweeping the country;
Waves are hugging the shore;
All the sexes
From Maine to Texas
Have never known such love before.

Ira Gershwin 1896–1983: 'Love is Sweeping the Country' (1931)

21 So I fell in love with a rich attorney's
Elderly ugly daughter.

W. S. Gilbert 1836–1911: *Trial by Jury* (1875)

22 In the spring a young man's fancy lightly turns to thoughts of love;
And in summer,
and in autumn,
and in winter—
See above.

E. Y. Harburg 1898–1981: 'Tennyson Anyone?' (1965)

23 When I'm not near the girl I love,
I love the girl I'm near.
. . . When I can't fondle the hand I'm fond of
I fondle the hand at hand.

E. Y. Harburg 1898–1981: 'When I'm Not Near the Girl I Love' (1947)

24 The broken dates,
The endless waits,
The lovely loving and the hateful hates,
The conversation and the flying plates—
I wish I were in love again.

Lorenz Hart 1895–1943: 'I Wish I Were in Love Again' (1937)

25 When love congeals
It soon reveals
The faint aroma of performing seals,
The double crossing of a pair of heels.
I wish I were in love again!

Lorenz Hart 1895–1943: 'I Wish I Were in Love Again' (1937)

26 Love's like the measles—all the worse when it comes late in life.

Douglas Jerrold 1803–57: *The Wit and Opinions of Douglas Jerrold* (1859) 'Love'

27 Another bride, another June,
Another sunny honeymoon,
Another season, another reason,
For makin' whoopee!

Gus Kahn 1886–1941: 'Makin' Whoopee' (1928)

28 Snug as two baboons—in a bamboo tree
I'll bamboozle you
And you'll bamboozle me
By a goona goona goona,
by a goona goona goona lagoon.

John Latouche 1917–56: 'The Goona Goona Goona Lagoon' (*The Golden Apple*, 1954 musical)

29 You ain't nothin' but a hound dog,
Quit snoopin' round my door
You can wag your tail but I ain't gonna feed you no more.

Jerry Leiber 1933– and **Mike Stoller** 1933– : 'Hound Dog' (1956)

30 Tell me, George, if you had to do it all over would you fall in love with yourself again.
to George Gershwin

Oscar Levant 1906–72: David Ewen *The Story of George Gershwin* (1943)

31 Love's a disease. But curable.

Rose Macaulay 1881–1958: *Crewe Train* (1926)

advising someone rejected in love to be cheerful, forgiving, and unavailable:
32 Such behaviour will have two rewards. First, it will take the sufferer's mind off suffering and begin the recovery. Second, it will make the former lover worry that this supposed act of cruelty was actually a relief to the person it should have hurt. That hurts.

Judith Martin 1938– : 'Advice from Miss Manners', column in *Washington Post* 1979–82

33 Bed. No woman is worth more than a fiver unless you're in love with her. Then she's worth all she costs you.

W. Somerset Maugham 1874–1965: *A Writer's Notebook* (1949) written in 1903

34 Love is the delusion that one woman differs from another.

H. L. Mencken 1880–1956: *Chrestomathy* (1949)

35 Oh, life is a glorious cycle of song,
A medley of extemporanea;
And love is a thing that can never go wrong;
And I am Marie of Roumania.

Dorothy Parker 1893–1967: 'Comment' (1937)

36 Four be the things I'd been better without:
Love, curiosity, freckles, and doubt.

Dorothy Parker 1893–1967: 'Inventory' (1937)

37 Most gentlemen don't like love,
They just like to kick it around.

Cole Porter 1891–1964: 'Most Gentlemen don't like Love' (1938)

38 I get no kick from champagne,
Mere alcohol doesn't thrill me at all,
So tell me why should it be true
That I get a kick out of you?

Cole Porter 1891–1964: 'I Get a Kick Out of You' (1934)

39 There are various ways of mending a broken heart, but perhaps going to a learned conference is one of the more unusual.

Barbara Pym 1913–80: *No Fond Return of Love* (1961)

40 I was adored once too.

William Shakespeare 1564–1616: *Twelfth Night* (1601)

41 ELAINE: *Romantic?* In your mother's clean apartment with two glasses from Bloomingdale's and your rubbers dripping on the newspaper?
BARNEY: It was my belief that romance is inspired by the participants and not the accoutrements.

Neil Simon 1927– : *Last of the Red Hot Lovers* (1970)

42 Loving you
Is not a choice
And not much reason
To rejoice.

Stephen Sondheim 1930– : *Passion* (1994) 'Loving You'

43 Out upon it, I have loved
Three whole days together;
And am like to love three more,
If it prove fair weather.

Time shall moult away his wings,
Ere he shall discover
In the whole wide world again
Such a constant lover.

John Suckling 1609–42: 'A Poem with the Answer' (1659)

44 Love is the fart
Of every heart:
It pains a man when 'tis kept close,
And others doth offend, when 'tis let loose.

John Suckling 1609–42: 'Love's Offence' (1646)

45 If love is the answer, could you rephrase the question?

Lily Tomlin 1939– : attributed; David Housham and John Frank-Keyes *Funny Business* (1992)

46 My father was a man as unacquainted with love as a Scots pine tree and what's wrong with that? It makes a change, these days, when love slops out all over the place from any old bucket.

Jill Tweedie 1936–93: *Eating Children* (1993)

47 Love conquers all things—except poverty and toothache.

Mae West 1892–1980: attributed

48 To love oneself is the beginning of a lifelong romance.

Oscar Wilde 1854–1900: *An Ideal Husband* (1895)

49 LILL: He loves me. He's just waiting till the children are settled.
VICTORIA: What in—sheltered housing?

Victoria Wood 1953– : *Mens Sana in Thingummy Doodah* (1990)

Marriage See also **Love, Sex**

1 If it were not for the presents, an elopement would be preferable.

George Ade 1866–1944: *Forty Modern Fables* (1901)

2 It was partially my fault that we got divorced . . . I tended to place my wife under a pedestal.

Woody Allen 1935– : 'I Had a Rough Marriage' (monologue, 1964)

3 My wife was an immature woman . . . I would be home in the bathroom, taking a bath, and my wife would walk in whenever she felt like it and sink my boats.

Woody Allen 1935– : 'I Had a Rough Marriage' (monologue, 1964)

4 Your experience will be a lesson to all us men to be careful not to marry ladies in very high positions.
to Lord Snowdon on the break-up of his marriage to Princess Margaret

Idi Amin 1925- : attributed; Nigel Rees *Cassell Dictionary of Humorous Quotations* (1999)

5 Egghead weds hourglass.
on the marriage of Arthur Miller and Marilyn Monroe

Anonymous: headline in *Variety* 1956; attributed

6 [Marriage is] the only war where one sleeps with the enemy.

Anonymous: Mexican saying; Ned Sherrin *Cutting Edge* (1984)

7 Bigamy is having one husband too many. Monogamy is the same.

Anonymous: Erica Jong *Fear of Flying* (1973)

8 It is a truth universally acknowledged, that a single man in possession of a good fortune, must be in want of a wife.

Jane Austen 1775-1817: *Pride and Prejudice* (1813)

9 A fate worse than marriage. A sort of eternal engagement.

Alan Ayckbourn 1939- : *Living Together* (1975)

10 Marriage is very difficult if you're a woman and a writer. No wonder Virginia Woolf committed suicide.

Beryl Bainbridge 1933- : attributed

11 A man cannot marry before he has studied anatomy and has dissected at the least one woman.

Honoré de Balzac 1799-1850: *Physiology of Marriage* (1904)

12 Opposites, opposites,
Where Momma won't sit Poppa sits.

Lionel Bart 1930- : *Blitz!* (1962)

13 I've known for years our marriage has been a mockery. My body lying there night after night in the wasted moonlight. I know now how the Taj Mahal must feel.

Alan Bennett 1934- : *Habeas Corpus* (1973)

14 Being a husband is a whole-time job. That is why so many husbands fail. They cannot give their entire attention to it.

Arnold Bennett 1867-1931: *The Title* (1918)

15 Never marry a man who hates his mother, because he'll end up hating you.

Jill Bennett 1931-90: in *Observer* 12 September 1982 'Sayings of the Week'

16 My wife's gone to the country
Hooray! Hooray!
She thought it best, I need a rest,
That's why she's gone away.

Irving Berlin 1888-1989 and **George Whiting**: 'My Wife's Gone To The Country' (1910)

17 Another woman has said that I ruined her marriage, which is quite simply not true. No woman in her right mind would jeopardize a happy marriage by going to bed with me, but have any women got a right mind?

Jeffrey Bernard 1932-97: in *The Spectator* 18 July 1992

18 They stood before the altar and supplied
The fire themselves in which their fat was fried.

Ambrose Bierce 1842-c.1914: *The Enlarged Devil's Dictionary* (1967)

19 Love matches are formed by people who pay for a month of honey with a life of vinegar.

Countess of Blessington 1789-1849: *Desultory Thoughts and Reflections* (1839)

20 Even quarrels with one's husband are preferable to the ennui of a solitary existence.
view of the estranged American wife of Napoleon Bonaparte's brother Jerome

Elizabeth Patterson Bonaparte 1785-1879: Eugene L. Didier *The Life and Letters of Madame Bonaparte* (1879)

21 'Husband and dog missing . . . reward for dog.'
sign outside her home after her husband Grant left her for Anthea Turner

Della Bovey: in *Mail on Sunday* 27 December 1998 'Quotes of the Year'

22 'Vladimir,' said Natasha, 'do you love me?' 'Toujours,' said Stroganoff, with wariness. An unusual emotion for a honeymooning husband when this particular question crops up. But Stroganoff was lying in the upper berth of a railway compartment and Natasha was in the lower berth so the question could not be an overture to a delightful interlude but merely the prelude to some less delightful demand.

Caryl Brahms 1901–82 and **S. J. Simon** 1904–48: *Six Curtains for Stroganova* (1945)

23 It was very good of God to let Carlyle and Mrs Carlyle marry one another and so make only two people miserable instead of four.

Samuel Butler 1835–1902: letter, 21 November 1884

24 Think you, if Laura had been Petrarch's wife, He would have written sonnets all his life?

Lord Byron 1788–1824: *Don Juan* (1819–24)

25 I am about to be married—and am of course in all the misery of a man in pursuit of happiness.

Lord Byron 1788–1824: letter, 15 October 1814

26 I have great hopes that we shall love each other all our lives as much as if we had never married at all.

Lord Byron 1788–1824: letter to Annabella Milbanke, 5 December 1814

27 Love and marriage, love and marriage, Go together like a horse and carriage.

Sammy Cahn 1913– : 'Love and Marriage' (1955)

28 I certainly didn't go down on one knee. I think she said it's about time we got married.
    on his diamond wedding day, remembering his proposal

James Callaghan 1912– : in *Daily Telegraph* 29 July 1998

29 The deep, deep peace of the double-bed after the hurly-burly of the chaise-longue.

Mrs Patrick Campbell 1865–1940: Alexander Woollcott *While Rome Burns* (1934) 'The First Mrs Tanqueray'

30 Translations (like wives) are seldom strictly faithful if they are in the least attractive.

Roy Campbell 1901–57: in *Poetry Review* June–July 1949

31 I am not at all the sort of person you and I took me for.

Jane Carlyle 1801–66: letter to Thomas Carlyle, 7 May 1822

32 Yblessed be god that I have wedded fyve! Welcome the sixte, whan that evere he shal.

Geoffrey Chaucer c.1343–1400: *The Canterbury Tales* 'The Wife of Bath's Prologue'

33 Every woman should marry an archaeologist because she grows increasingly attractive to him as she grows increasingly to resemble a ruin.

Agatha Christie 1890–1976: Russell H. Fitzgibbon *The Agatha Christie Companion* (1980); attributed, perhaps apocryphal

34 The most happy marriage I can picture or imagine to myself would be the union of a deaf man to a blind woman.

Samuel Taylor Coleridge 1772–1834: Thomas Allsop *Letters, Conversations, and Recollections of S. T. Coleridge* (1836)

35 Marriage is a feast where the grace is sometimes better than the dinner.

Charles Caleb Colton 1780–1832: *Lacon* (1822)

36 Courtship to marriage, as a very witty prologue to a very dull play.

William Congreve 1670–1729: *The Old Bachelor* (1693)

37 Nay, for my part I always despised Mr Tattle of all things; nothing but his being my husband could have made me like him less.

William Congreve 1670–1729: *Love for Love* (1695)

38 Tho' marriage makes man and wife one flesh, it leaves 'em still two fools.

William Congreve 1670–1729: *The Double Dealer* (1694)

39 SHARPER: Thus grief still treads upon the heels of pleasure: Married in haste, we may repent at leisure.
SETTER: Some by experience find those words mis-placed: At leisure married, they repent in haste.

William Congreve 1670–1729: *The Old Bachelor* (1693)

40 The figure is unbelievable—just because she cooked a few meals now and again and wrote a few books.
on the £10 million divorce settlement awarded to Caroline Conran

Terence Conran 1931– : in *Mail on Sunday* 6 July 1997 'Quotes of the Week'

41 Marriage is a wonderful invention; but, then again, so is a bicycle repair kit.

Billy Connolly 1942– : Duncan Campbell *Billy Connolly* (1976)

42 There is no more sombre enemy of good art than the pram in the hall.

Cyril Connolly 1903–74: *Enemies of Promise* (1938)

43 One of those looks which only a quarter-century of wedlock can adequately marinate.

Alan Coren 1938– : *Seems Like Old Times* (1989)

44 'What are your views on marriage?'
'Rather garbled.'

Noël Coward 1899–1973: in *Ned Sherrin's Theatrical Anecdotes* (1991); attributed

45 She very soon married this short young man
Who talked about soldiers all day
But who wasn't above
Making passionate love
In a coarse, rather Corsican way.

Noël Coward 1899–1973: 'Josephine' (1946)

46 How was the wedding?
Brief, to the point and not unduly musical.

Noël Coward 1899–1973: *Shadow Play*

47 So basically you're saying marriage is just a way of getting out of an embarrassing pause in conversation.

Richard Curtis 1956– : *Four Weddings and a Funeral* (1994 film)

48 All these years we've been single and proud of it—never noticed that two of us were to all intents and purposes married all this time.

Richard Curtis 1956– : *Four Weddings and a Funeral* (1994 film)

49 It's my old girl that advises. She has the head. But I never own to it before her. Discipline must be maintained.

Charles Dickens 1812–70: *Bleak House* (1853)

50 I revere the memory of Mr F. as an estimable man and most indulgent husband, only necessary to mention Asparagus and it appeared or to hint at any little delicate thing to drink and it came like magic in a pint bottle it was not ecstasy but it was comfort.

Charles Dickens 1812–70: *Little Dorrit* (1857)

51 I have always thought that every woman should marry, and no man.

Benjamin Disraeli 1804–81: *Lothair* (1870)

52 No man is regular in his attendance at the House of Commons until he is married.

Benjamin Disraeli 1804–81: Hesketh Pearson *Dizzy* (1951)

53 Here lies my wife; here let her lie!
Now she's at peace and so am I.

John Dryden 1631–1700: epitaph; attributed but not traced in his works

54 I don't think matrimony consistent with the liberty of the subject.

George Farquhar 1678–1707: *The Twin Rivals* (1703)

55 His designs were strictly honourable, as the phrase is; that is, to rob a lady of her fortune by way of marriage.

Henry Fielding 1707–54: *Tom Jones* (1749)

56 I love to cry at weddings, anybody's weddings anytime! . . . anybody's weddings just so long as it's not mine!

Dorothy Fields 1905–74: 'I Love to Cry at Weddings' (1966)

57 The awe and dread with which the untutored savage contemplates his mother-in-law are amongst the most familiar facts of anthropology.

James George Frazer 1854–1941: *The Golden Bough* (2nd ed., 1900)

58 He taught me housekeeping; when I divorce I keep the house.

Zsa Zsa Gabor 1919– : of her fifth husband; Ned Sherrin *Cutting Edge* (1984)

59 A man in love is incomplete until he has married. Then he's finished.

Zsa Zsa Gabor 1919– : in *Newsweek* 28 March 1960

when asked how many husbands she had had:
60 You mean apart from my own?

Zsa Zsa Gabor 1919– : K. Edwards *I Wish I'd Said That* (1976)

61 The comfortable estate of widowhood, is the only hope that keeps up a wife's spirits.

John Gay 1685–1732: *The Beggar's Opera* (1728)

62 Do you think your mother and I should have lived comfortably so long together, if ever we had been married?

John Gay 1685–1732: *The Beggar's Opera* (1728)

63 POLLY: Then all my sorrows are at an end.
MRS PEACHUM: A mighty likely speech, in troth, for a wench who is just married!

John Gay 1685–1732: *The Beggar's Opera* (1728)

64 Imagine signing a lease together;
And hanging a Matisse together;
Being alone and baking bread together.
Reading the *New Yorker* in bed together!
Starting a family tree together!
Voting for the GOP together!

Ira Gershwin 1896–1983: 'There's Nothing Like Marriage for People' (1946)

65 By god, D. H. Lawrence was right when he had said there must be a dumb, dark, dull, bitter belly-tension between a man and a woman, and how else could this be achieved save in the long monotony of marriage?

Stella Gibbons 1902–89: *Cold Comfort Farm* (1932)

66 I . . . chose my wife, as she did her wedding gown, not for a fine glossy surface, but such qualities as would wear well.

Oliver Goldsmith 1730–74: *The Vicar of Wakefield* (1766)

67 It seemed to me pretty plain, that they had more of love than matrimony in them.

Oliver Goldsmith 1730–74: *The Vicar of Wakefield* (1766)

68 My mother said it was simple to keep a man, you must be a maid in the living room, a cook in the kitchen and a whore in the bedroom. I said I'd hire the other two and take care of the bedroom bit.

Jerry Hall 1956– : in *Observer* 6 October 1985 'Sayings of the Week'

69 I married many men,
A ton of them,
And yet I was untrue to none of them
Because I bumped off ev'ry one of them
To keep my love alive.
Sir Paul was frail,
He looked a wreck to me.
At night he was a horse's neck to me.
So I performed an appendectomy
To keep my love alive.

Lorenz Hart 1895–1943: 'To Keep My Love Alive' (1943)

70 It was not totally inconceivable that she could have joined me as my wife at No. 10.
on the TV starlet Jayne Mansfield

Edward Heath 1916– : in *Sunday Times* 6 February 2000

71 The critical period in matrimony is breakfast-time.

A. P. Herbert 1890–1971: *Uncommon Law* (1935) 'Is Marriage Lawful?'

72 Holy deadlock.

A. P. Herbert 1890–1971: title of novel (1934)

73 A TV host asked my wife, 'Have you ever considered divorce?' She replied: 'Divorce never, murder often.'

Charlton Heston 1924– : in *Independent* 21 July 1999

74 Who weddeth or he be wise shall die ere he thrive.

John Heywood c.1497–c.1580: *A Dialogue of Proverbs* (1546)

75 Death and marriage are raging through this College with such fury that I ought to be grateful for having escaped both.

A. E. Housman 1859–1936: letter 29 May 1925

76 Hogamus, higamus
Man is polygamous
Higamus, hogamus
Woman monogamous.

William James 1842–1910: in *Oxford Book of Marriage* (1990)

of a man who remarried immediately after the death of a wife with whom he had been unhappy:
77 The triumph of hope over experience.

Samuel Johnson 1709–84: James Boswell *Life of Samuel Johnson* (1791) 1770

78 I want you to assist me in forcing her on board the lugger; once there, I'll frighten her into marriage.

John Benn Johnstone 1803–91: *The Gipsy Farmer* (performed 1845); since quoted as 'Once aboard the lugger and the maid is mine'

79 [Izaak Walton] seems to have borne married life easily as a basis (as with some among us now) from which to go fishing.

Stephen Leacock 1869–1944: *The Boy I Left Behind Me* (1947)

80 I'm getting married in the morning!
Ding dong! The bells are gonna chime.
Pull out the stopper!
Let's have a whopper!
But get me to the church on time!

Alan Jay Lerner 1918–86: 'Get Me to the Church on Time' (1956)

81 I've been married six months. She looks like a million dollars, but she only knows a hundred and twenty words and she's only got two ideas in her head.

Eric Linklater 1899–1974: *Juan in America* (1931)

82 I went back to the study hall where I met my husband at a debating competition and where, I am pleased to put it on record, I beat him.

Mary McAleese 1951– : in *Irish Times* 6 December 1997 'This Week They Said'

83 Did you ever look through a microscope at a drop of pond water? You see plenty of love there. All the amoebae getting married. I presume they think it very exciting and important. We don't.

Rose Macaulay 1881–1958: *Crewe Train* (1926)

to her husband, who had asked the age of a flirtatious starlet with noticeably thick legs:
84 For God's sake, Walter, why don't you chop off her legs and read the rings?

Carol Matthau: Truman Capote *Answered Prayers* (1986)

85 No matter how happily a woman may be married, it always pleases her to discover that there is a nice man who wishes she were not.

H. L. Mencken 1880–1956: *Chrestomathy* (1949)

86 Kissing don't last: cookery do!

George Meredith 1828–1909: *The Ordeal of Richard Feverel* (1859)

87 It was an absolute mésalliance, the Barking Labour Party and Tom [Driberg, the constituency's MP]—it was like Zsa Zsa Gabor marrying Freddie Ayer.

Ian Mikardo: Francis Wheen *Tom Driberg* (1990)

88 There once was an old man of Lyme
Who married three wives at a time,
When asked 'Why a third?'
He replied, 'One's absurd!
And bigamy, Sir, is a crime!'

William Cosmo Monkhouse 1840–1901: *Nonsense Rhymes* (1902)

89 One doesn't have to get anywhere in a marriage. It's not a public conveyance.

Iris Murdoch 1919–99: *A Severed Head* (1961)

90 I'm Henery the Eighth, I am!
Henery the Eighth, I am, I am!
I got married to the widow next door,
She's been married seven times before.
Every one was a Henery,
She wouldn't have a Willie or a Sam.
I'm her eighth old man named Henery
I'm Henery the Eighth, I am!

Fred Murray: 'I'm Henery the Eighth, I Am!' (1911)

91 To keep your marriage brimming
With love in the loving cup,
Whenever you're wrong, admit it,
Whenever you're right, shut up.

Ogden Nash 1902–71: 'A Word to Husbands' (1957)

92 To Wanda, the only item of essential equipment—apart from a Rolex watch (boiled in a stew by Afghans to test its waterproof qualities)—not lost, stolen or simply worn out in the course of some thirty years of travel together.

Eric Newby 1919– : *On the Shores of the Mediterranean* (1984); dedication to his wife

to his wife Vita Sackville-West:
93 A crushed life is what I lead, similar to that of the hen you ran over the other day.

Harold Nicolson 1886–1968: diary, 8 October 1958

94 'It was she as set her bonnet at him!' cried Mrs Williams, who had never yet let her husband finish a sentence since his 'I will' at Trinity Church, Plymouth Dock, in 1782 [eighteen years before].

Patrick O'Brian 1914–2000: *Master and Commander* (1970)

agreeing with the comment, at her remarriage to Alan Campbell in 1950, that some of those present had not spoken to each other for years:
95 Including the bride and groom.

Dorothy Parker 1893–1967: Marion Meade *What Fresh Hell Is This?* (1988)

96 Marriage may often be a stormy lake, but celibacy is almost always a muddy horsepond.

Thomas Love Peacock 1785–1866: *Melincourt* (1817)

97 Strange to say what delight we married people have to see these poor fools decoyed into our condition.

Samuel Pepys 1633–1703: diary, 25 December 1665

98 My wife, who, poor wretch, is troubled with her lonely life.

Samuel Pepys 1633–1703: diary, 19 December 1662

99 Tolerance is the one essential ingredient . . . You can take it from me that the Queen has the quality of tolerance in abundance.

   his recipe for a successful marriage, 19 November 1997, marking their golden wedding anniversary

Prince Philip, Duke of Edinburgh 1921– : in *Times* 20 November 1997

100 They dream in courtship, but in wedlock wake.

Alexander Pope 1688–1744: *Translations from Chaucer* (1714)

101 HE: Have you heard Professor Munch
Ate his wife and divorced his lunch?
SHE: Well, did you evah!
What a swell party this is.

Cole Porter 1891–1964: 'Well, Did You Evah!' (1939)

102 It feels so fine to be a bride,
And how's the groom? Why, he's slightly fried,
It's delightful, it's delicious, it's de-lovely.

Cole Porter 1891–1964: 'It's De-lovely' (1936)

103 I'm a maid who would marry
And will take with no qualm
Any Tom, Dick or Harry,
Any Harry, Dick or Tom.

Cole Porter 1891–1964: 'Tom, Dick or Harry' (1948)

104 WIFE OF TWO YEARS' STANDING: Oh yes! I'm sure he's not so fond of me as at first. He's away so much, neglects me dreadfully, and he's so cross when he comes home. What *shall* I do?
WIDOW: Feed the brute!

Punch 1841–1992: vol. 89 (1885)

105 Advice to persons about to marry.—'Don't.'

Punch 1841–1992: vol. 8 (1845)

106 BISHOP: Who is it that sees and hears all we do, and before whom even I am but as a crushed worm?
PAGE: The Missus, my Lord.

Punch 1841–1992: vol. 79 (1880)

107 A husband is what is left of a lover, after the nerve has been extracted.

Helen Rowland 1875–1950: *A Guide to Men* (1922)

the Lord Chief Justice was once asked by a lady what was the maximum punishment for bigamy:
108 Two mothers-in-law.

Lord Russell of Killowen 1832–1900: Edward Abinger *Forty Years at the Bar* (1930)

109 But for marriage 'tis good for nothing, but to make friends fall out.

Thomas Shadwell c.1642–92: *The Sullen Lovers* (1668)

110 A young man married is a man that's marred.

William Shakespeare 1564–1616: *All's Well that Ends Well* (1603-4)

111 Many a good hanging prevents a bad marriage.

William Shakespeare 1564–1616: *Twelfth Night* (1601)

112 It is a woman's business to get married as soon as possible, and a man's to keep unmarried as long as he can.

George Bernard Shaw 1856–1950: *Man and Superman* (1903)

113 Marriage is popular because it combines the maximum of temptation with the maximum of opportunity.

George Bernard Shaw 1856–1950: *Man and Superman* (1903) 'Maxims: Marriage'

114 'Tis safest in matrimony to begin with a little aversion.

Richard Brinsley Sheridan 1751–1816: *The Rivals* (1775)

115 Take care of him. And make him feel important. And if you can do that, you'll have a happy and wonderful marriage. Like two out of every ten couples.

Neil Simon 1927– : *Barefoot in the Park* (1964)

116 PAUL: You want me to be rich and famous, don't you? CORRIE: During the day. At night I want you to be here and sexy.

Neil Simon 1927– : *Barefoot in the Park* (1964)

117 My definition of marriage . . . it resembles a pair of shears, so joined that they cannot be separated; often moving in opposite directions, yet always punishing anyone who comes between them.

Sydney Smith 1771–1845: Lady Holland *Memoir* (1855)

118 The concerts you enjoy together
Neighbours you annoy together
Children you destroy together,
That keep marriage intact.

Stephen Sondheim 1930– : 'The Little Things You Do Together' (1970)

119 My brother Toby, quoth she, is going to be married to Mrs Wadman. Then he will never, quoth my father, lie *diagonally* in his bed again as long as he lives.

Laurence Sterne 1713–68: *Tristram Shandy* (1759–67)

120 Even if we take matrimony at its lowest, even if we regard it as no more than a sort of friendship recognised by the police.

Robert Louis Stevenson 1850–94: *Virginibus Puerisque* (1881)

121 A woman with fair opportunities and without a positive hump, may marry whom she likes.

William Makepeace Thackeray 1811–63: *Vanity Fair* (1847–8)

explaining that when making an official visit to Paris he would not take his wife:
122 You don't take a ham sandwich to the Lord Mayor's banquet, do you?

J. H. Thomas 1874–1949: attributed; Nigel Rees (ed.) *Cassell Companion to Quotations* (1997)

123 A husband should not insult his wife publicly, at parties. He should insult her in the privacy of the home.

James Thurber 1894–1961: *Thurber Country* (1953)

124 That's my first wife up there and this is the *present* Mrs Harris.

James Thurber 1894–1961: cartoon caption in *New Yorker* 16 March 1933

125 LADY BRUTE: 'Tis a hard fate I should not be believed. SIR JOHN: 'Tis a damned atheistical age, wife.

John Vanbrugh 1664–1726: *The Provoked Wife* (1697)

126 Marriage isn't a word . . . it's a *sentence*!

King Vidor 1895–1982: in *The Crowd* (1928 film)

127 He is dreadfully married. He's the most married man I ever saw in my life.

Artemus Ward 1834–67: *Artemus Ward's Lecture* (1869) 'Brigham Young's Palace'

telegram supposedly sent to Tom Driberg on the occasion of Driberg's wedding:
128 I pray that the church is not struck by lightning.

Evelyn Waugh 1903–66: attributed; Nigel Rees (ed.) *Cassell Dictionary of Humorous Quotations* (1999)

129 Marriage is a great institution, but I'm not ready for an institution yet.

Mae West 1892–1980: Laurence J. Peter (ed.) *Quotations for our Time* (1977); attributed

130 An engagement should come on a young girl as a surprise, pleasant or unpleasant, as the case may be.

Oscar Wilde 1854–1900: *The Importance of Being Earnest* (1895)

131 Twenty years of romance make a woman look like a ruin; but twenty years of marriage make her something like a public building.

Oscar Wilde 1854–1900: *A Woman of No Importance* (1893)

132 *Once Upon a Time* was dreadful. Since the appearance of Tree in pyjamas there has been the greatest sympathy for Mrs Tree. It throws a lurid light on the difficulties of their married life.

Oscar Wilde 1854–1900: letter, ?April 1894

133 GERRY: We can't get married at all . . . I'm a man.
OSGOOD: Well, nobody's perfect.

Billy Wilder 1906– and **I. A. L. Diamond** 1915–88: *Some Like It Hot* (1959 film; closing words)

when courting his future wife (whom he married in 1949):
134 I would worship the ground you walk on, Audrey, if you only lived in a better neighbourhood.

Billy Wilder 1906– : M. Zolotow *Billy Wilder in Hollywood* (1977)

135 Marriage is a bribe to make a housekeeper think she's a householder.

Thornton Wilder 1897–1975: *The Merchant of Yonkers* (1939)

136 Chumps always make the best husbands. When you marry, Sally, grab a chump. Tap his forehead first, and if it rings solid, don't hesitate. All the unhappy marriages come from the husbands having brains.

P. G. Wodehouse 1881–1975: *The Adventures of Sally* (1920)

137 There are men who fear repartee in a wife more keenly than a sword.

P. G. Wodehouse 1881–1975: *Jill the Reckless* (1922)

138 'Tis my maxim, he's a fool that marries, but he's a greater that does not marry a fool.

William Wycherley c.1640–1716: *The Country Wife* (1675)

Medicine See also **Sickness and Health**

on a trip to Thorpe Bay Agate realized that he had left his 'asthma stuff' behind:
1 I just can't bear to run short of Acetylmethyldimethyloxamidphenylhydrazine.

James Agate 1877–1947: diary, 9 April 1937

2 She has her high days and low days, a bit like the church. It depends what miracle drug the doctor's currently got her on.

Alan Ayckbourn 1939– : *Joking Apart* (1979)

3 Medicinal discovery,
It moves in mighty leaps,
It leapt straight past the common cold
And gave it us for keeps.

Pam Ayres 1947– : 'Oh no, I got a cold' (1976)

4 Hark! the herald angels sing!
Beecham's Pills are just the thing,
Two for a woman, one for a child . . .
Peace on earth and mercy mild!

Thomas Beecham 1879–1961: advertising jingle devised for his father, but not used; Neville Cardus *Sir Thomas Beecham* (1961)

5 Physicians of the Utmost Fame
Were called at once; but when they came
They answered, as they took their Fees,
'There is no Cure for this Disease.'

Hilaire Belloc 1870–1953: 'Henry King' (1907)

6 Dr Sillitoes's got him on tablets for depression. It's not mental, in fact it's quite widespread. A lot of better-class people get it apparently.

Alan Bennett 1934– : *Enjoy* (1980)

7 I do wish the more suspicious of our GPs would stop feeling nervously for their wallets every time I mention the word reform.

Kenneth Clarke 1940– : after-dinner speech, when Minister of Health, to the Royal College of General Practitioners, 9 March 1989

8 I don't believe in vitamin pills. I swear by men, darling—and as many as possible.

Joan Collins 1933– : in *Independent* 10 June 2000 'Quotes of the Week'

9 And, on the label of the stuff,
He wrote this verse;
Which one would think was clear enough,
And terse:—
When taken,
To be well shaken.

George Colman the Younger 1762–1836: 'The Newcastle Apothecary' (1797)

10 Meaty jelly, too, especially when a little salt, which is the case when there's ham, is mellering to the organ.

Charles Dickens 1812–70: *Our Mutual Friend* (1865)

epigram on Dr John Lettsom, who would sign his prescriptions 'I. Lettsom':
11 Whenever patients come to I,
I physics, bleeds, and sweats 'em;
If after that they choose to die,
What's that to me!—*I letts 'em.*

Thomas Erskine 1750–1823: *Poetical Works* (1823)

12 A cousin of mine who was a casualty surgeon in Manhattan tells me that he and his colleagues had a one-word nickname for bikers: Donors. Rather chilling.

Stephen Fry 1957– : *Paperweight* (1992)

13 I came in here in all good faith to help my country. I don't mind giving a reasonable amount [of blood], but a pint . . . why that's very nearly an armful. I'm sorry. I'm not walking around with an empty arm for anybody.

Ray Galton 1930– and **Alan Simpson** 1929– : *The Blood Donor* (1961 television programme, words spoken by Tony Hancock)

14 Any man who goes to a psychiatrist should have his head examined.

Sam Goldwyn 1882–1974: Norman Zierold *Moguls* (1969)

15 If you have a stomach ache, in France you get a suppository, in Germany a health spa, in the United States they cut your stomach open and in Britain they put you on a waiting list.

Phil Hammond 1955– and **Michael Mosley**: *Trust Me (I'm a Doctor)* (1999)

16 Hungry Joe collected lists of fatal diseases and arranged them in alphabetical order so that he could put his finger without delay on any one he wanted to worry about.

Joseph Heller 1923–99: *Catch-22* (1961)

17 Jesus was a normal, run-of-the-mill sort of guy who had a genuine gift, just as Eileen has.
giving the view that his biggest mistake at the World Cup was to leave his faith-healer at home

Glenn Hoddle 1957– : in *Daily Telegraph* 28 December 1998 'Sporting Quotes of the Year'

18 The kind of doctor I want is one who, when he's not examining me, is home studying medicine.

George S. Kaufman 1889–1961: Howard Teichmann *George S. Kaufman* (1973)

19 In disease Medical Men guess: if they cannot ascertain a disease, they call it nervous.

John Keats 1795–1821: J. A. Gere and John Sparrow (eds.) *Geoffrey Madan's Notebooks* (1981); attributed

20 No herb ever cures anything, it is only *said* to cure something. This is always based on the testimony of somebody called Cuthbert who died in 1678. No one ever says what he died of.

Miles Kington 1941– : *Nature Made Ridiculously Simple* (1983)

21 Dr Milton's really lost it . . . Since he started fucking his secretary and going to Aspen his brow lifts are getting scary. He cuts way too much and makes everybody look either frightened or surprised.

Jay McInerney 1955- : *How It Ended* (2000)

22 The medics can now stretch your life out an additional dozen years but they don't tell you that most of these years are going to be spent flat on your back while some ghoul with thick glasses and a matted skull peers at you through a machine that's hot out of 'Space Patrol'.

Groucho Marx 1895–1977: letter 23 December 1954

23 All the errors that lead to burst appendixes are made by family doctors. The patient usually is sick enough to call for help, but by the time he gets to the specialist he is too far gone for it.

H. L. Mencken 1880–1956: *Minority Report* (1956)

24 GÉRONTE: It seems to me you are locating them wrongly: the heart is on the left and the liver is on the right.
SGANARELLE: Yes, in the old days that was so, but we have changed all that, and we now practise medicine by a completely new method.

Molière 1622–73: *Le Médecin malgré lui* (1667)

25 I fear that being a patient in any hospital in Ireland calls for two things—holy resignation and an iron constitution.

Flann O'Brien 1911–66: *Myles Away from Dublin* (1990)

26 The desire to take medicine is perhaps the greatest feature which distinguishes man from animals.

William Osler 1849–1919: H. Cushing *Life of Sir William Osler* (1925)

27 As for consulting a dentist regularly, my punctuality practically amounted to a fetish. Every twelve years I would drop whatever I was doing and allow wild Caucasian ponies to drag me to a reputable orthodontist.

S. J. Perelman 1904–79: *The Most of S. J. Perelman* (1959) 'Dental or Mental, I Say It's Spinach'

28 He said my bronchial tubes were entrancing,
My epiglottis filled him with glee,
He simply loved my larynx
And went wild about my pharynx,
But he never said he loved me.

Cole Porter 1891–1964: 'The Physician' (1933)

29 Cured yesterday of my disease,
I died last night of my physician.

Matthew Prior 1664–1721: 'The Remedy Worse than the Disease' (1727)

30 Being hugged by Diana Rigg is worth three sessions of chemotherapy.
after his appearance on Loose Ends *with Diana Rigg, 15 April 2000*

Robert Runcie 1921–2000: letter to the Editor, April 2000

31 There would never be any public agreement among doctors if they did not agree to agree on the main point of the doctor being always in the right.

George Bernard Shaw 1856–1950: preface to *The Doctor's Dilemma* (1911)

32 There is at bottom only one genuinely scientific treatment for all diseases, and that is to stimulate the phagocytes.

George Bernard Shaw 1856–1950: *The Doctor's Dilemma* (1911)

33 I can't stand whispering. Every time a doctor whispers in the hospital, next day there's a funeral.

Neil Simon 1927- : *The Gingerbread Lady* (1970)

34 A psychiatrist is a man who goes to the Folies-Bergère and looks at the audience.

Mervyn Stockwood 1913–95: in *Observer* 15 October 1961

35 Take anything that is either nasty, expensive or difficult to obtain, wrap it up in mystery and you have a cure.

Richard Totman: Phil Hammond and Michael Mosley *Trust Me (I'm a Doctor)* (1999)

36 Randolph Churchill went into hospital . . . to have a lung removed. It was announced that the trouble was not 'malignant' . . . it was a typical triumph of modern science to find the only part of Randolph that was not malignant and remove it.

Evelyn Waugh 1903–66: 'Irregular Notes 1960–65'; diary March 1964

37 Sir Roderick Glossop . . . is always called a nerve specialist, because it sounds better, but everybody knows that he's really a sort of janitor to the looney-bin.

P. G. Wodehouse 1881–1975: *The Inimitable Jeeves* (1923)

on being given aspirin from a small tin box by Jeeves:
38 Thank you, Jeeves. Don't slam the lid.

P. G. Wodehouse 1881–1975: *Ring for Jeeves* (1953) ch. 18

Men See also **Men and Women**

1 Nobody ever, unless he is very wicked, deliberately tries to hurt anybody. It's just that men cannot help not loving you or behaving badly.

Beryl Bainbridge 1933– : interview in *Daily Telegraph* 10 September 1996

2 Women were brought up to believe that men were the answer. They weren't. They weren't even one of the questions.

Julian Barnes 1946– : *Staring at the Sun* (1986)

3 You cannot make a man by standing a sheep on its hind-legs. But by standing a flock of sheep in that position you can make a crowd of men.

Max Beerbohm 1872–1956: *Zuleika Dobson* (1911)

4 My mother wanted me to be a nice boy. I didn't let her down. I don't smoke, drink or mess around with women.

Julian Clary 1959– : in *Independent* 2 March 1996 'Quote Unquote'

5 Faded boys, jaded boys, come what may,
Art is our inspiration,
And as we are the reason for the 'Nineties' being gay,
We all wear a green carnation.

Noël Coward 1899–1973: 'Green Carnation' (1929)

6 We are lads. We have burgled houses and nicked car stereos, and we like girls and swear and go to the football and take the piss.

Noel Gallagher 1967– : interview in *Melody Maker* 30 March 1996

7 Francesca di Rimini, miminy, piminy,
Je-ne-sais-quoi young man!

W. S. Gilbert 1836–1911: *Patience* (1881)

8 A greenery-yallery, Grosvenor Gallery,
Foot-in-the-grave young man!

W. S. Gilbert 1836–1911: *Patience* (1881)

9 Men are animals and as such are entitled to humane treatment and should not be trapped or shot or bred for food or fur.

Germaine Greer 1939– : in *Mail on Sunday* 7 March 1999 'Quotes of the Week'

10 Years ago, manhood was an opportunity for achievement, and now it is a problem to be overcome.

Garrison Keillor 1942– : *The Book of Guys* (1994)

11 There is nothing about which men lie so much as about their sexual powers. In this at least every man is, what in his heart he would like to be, a Casanova.

W. Somerset Maugham 1874–1965: *A Writer's Notebook* (1949) written in 1941

12 He's an oul' butty o' mine—oh, he's a darlin' man, a daarlin' man.

Sean O'Casey 1880–1964: *Juno and the Paycock* (1925)

13 The follies which a man regrets most, in his life, are those which he didn't commit when he had the opportunity.

Helen Rowland 1875–1950: *A Guide to Men* (1922)

14 God made him, and therefore let him pass for a man.

William Shakespeare 1564–1616: *The Merchant of Venice* (1596–8)

15 To be a well-favoured man is the gift of fortune; but to write and read comes by nature.

William Shakespeare 1564–1616: *Much Ado About Nothing* (1598–9)

16 You men are unaccountable things; mad till you have your mistresses, and then stark mad till you are rid of 'em again.

John Vanbrugh 1664–1726: *The Provoked Wife* (1697)

17 A hard man is good to find.

Mae West 1892–1980: attributed

18 There is something positively brutal about the good temper of most modern men.

Oscar Wilde 1854–1900: *A Woman of No Importance* (1893)

Men and Women See also **Men**, **Women** and **Woman's Role**

1 Women love scallywags, but some marry them and then try to make them wear a blazer.

David Bailey 1938– : in *Mail on Sunday* 16 February 1997 'Quotes of the Week'

2 All women dress like their mothers, that is their tragedy. No man ever does. That is his.

Alan Bennett 1934– : *Forty Years On* (1969)

3 We sat in the car park till twenty to one
And now I'm engaged to Miss Joan Hunter Dunn.

John Betjeman 1906–84: 'A Subaltern's Love-Song' (1945)

4 Women tend not to dress up in leather aprons and nail each other to coffee tables in their spare time.

Julie Burchill 1960– : in *The Spectator* 16 January 1992

5 Too many rings around Rosie
Never got Rosie a ring.

Irving Caesar 1895– : 'Too Many Rings around Rosie' (1925)

6 AMANDA: I've been brought up to believe that it's beyond the pale, for a man to strike a woman.
ELYOT: A very poor tradition. Certain women should be struck regularly, like gongs.

Noël Coward 1899–1973: *Private Lives* (1930)

7 ''Cos a coachman's a privileged indiwidual,' replied Mr Weller, looking fixedly at his son. ''Cos a coachman may do vithout suspicion wot other men may not; 'cos a coachman may be on the wery amicablest terms with eighty mile o' females, and yet nobody think that he ever means to marry any vun among them.'

Charles Dickens 1812–70: *Pickwick Papers* (1837)

8 The feminist movement seems to have beaten the manners out of men, but I didn't see them put up a lot of resistance.

Clarissa Dickson Wright: in *Mail on Sunday* 24 September 2000 'Quotes of the Week'

a fellow Congressman attacked a piece of women's rights legislation with the words, 'I've always thought of women as kissable, cuddly, and smelling good':
9 That's what I feel about men. I only hope you haven't been disappointed as often as I have.

Millicent Fenwick 1910– : in *Ned Sherrin in his Anecdotage* (1993)

10 I will not . . . sulk about having no boyfriend, but develop inner poise and authority and sense of self as woman of substance, complete *without* boyfriend, as best way to obtain boyfriend.

Helen Fielding 1958– : *Bridget Jones's Diary* (1996)

11 The minute you walked in the joint,
I could see you were a man of distinction,
A real big spender.
Good looking, so refined,
Say, wouldn't you like to know what's going on in my
 mind?
So let me get right to the point.
I don't pop my cork for every guy I see.
Hey! big spender, spend a little time with me.

Dorothy Fields 1905–74: 'Big Spender' (1966)

12 A fine romance with no kisses.
A fine romance, my friend, this is.
We should be like a couple of hot tomatoes,
But you're as cold as yesterday's mashed potatoes.

Dorothy Fields 1905–74: 'A Fine Romance' (1936)

13 If they ever invent a vibrator that can open pickle jars,
we've had it.
 on the bleak future facing men

Jeff Green: in *Mail on Sunday* 21 March 1999 'Quotes of the Week'

14 Our days will be so ecstatic
Our nights will be so exotic
For I'm a neurotic erratic
And you're an erratic erotic.

E. Y. Harburg 1898–1981: 'Courtship in Greenwich Village' (1965)

15 I'm wild again,
Beguiled again,
A simpering, whimpering child again—
Bewitched, bothered and bewildered am I.
Couldn't sleep
And wouldn't sleep
Until I could sleep where I shouldn't sleep—
Bewitched, bothered and bewildered am I.

Lorenz Hart 1895–1943: 'Bewitched, Bothered and Bewildered' (1940)

16 Take him, I won't put a price on him
Take him, he's yours
Take him, pyjamas look nice on him
But how he snores!

Lorenz Hart 1895–1943: 'Take Him' (1940)

17 A woman's mind is cleaner than a man's; she changes it
more often.

Oliver Herford 1863–1935: attributed; Evan Esar and Nicolas Bentley (eds.) *Treasury of Humorous Quotations* (1951)

18 Brought up in an epoch when ladies apparently rolled
along on wheels, Mr Quarles was peculiarly susceptible to
calves.

Aldous Huxley 1894–1963: *Point Counter Point* (1928)

19 If men could get pregnant, abortion would be a sacrament.

Florynce Kennedy 1916– : 'The Verbal Karate of Florynce R. Kennedy' (1973)

20 Being kissed by a man who *didn't* wax his moustache
was—like eating an egg without salt.

Rudyard Kipling 1865–1936: *The Story of the Gadsbys* (1889) 'Poor Dear Mamma'

21 The female sex has no greater fan than I, and I have the
bills to prove it.

Alan Jay Lerner 1918–86: *The Street Where I Live* (1978)

22 Yes, why can't a woman be more like a man?
Men are so honest, so thoroughly square;
Eternally noble, historically fair;

Alan Jay Lerner 1918–86: 'A Hymn to Him' (1956)

Who when you win will always give your back a pat—
Why can't a woman be like that?

23 But let a woman in your life
And your serenity is through!
She'll redecorate your home
From the cellar to the dome;
Then get on to the enthralling
Fun of overhauling
You.

Alan Jay Lerner 1918-86: 'I'm an
Ordinary Man' (1956)

24 Brother, do you know a nicer occupation,
Matter of fact, neither do I,
Than standing on the corner
Watching all the girls go by?

Frank Loesser 1910-69: 'Standing
on the Corner' (1956)

25 Oh! to be loved by a man I respect,
To bask in the glow of his perfectly understandable
neglect.

Frank Loesser 1910-69: 'Happy to
Keep his Dinner Warm' (1961)

26 When you meet a gent paying all sorts of rent
For a flat that would flatten the Taj Mahal,
Call it sad, call it funny
But it's better than even money
That the guy's only doing it for some doll.

Frank Loesser 1910-69: 'Guys and
Dolls' (1950)

27 So then he said that he used to be a member of the choir
himself, so who was he to cast the first rock at a girl like I.

Anita Loos 1893-1981: *Gentlemen
Prefer Blondes* (1925)

*approaching an unwelcoming Greta Garbo and peering up under
the brim of her floppy hat:*
28 Pardon me, Ma'am . . . I thought you were a guy I knew
in Pittsburgh.

Groucho Marx 1895-1977: David
Niven *Bring on the Empty Horses*
(1975)

29 I suppose true sexual equality will come when a general
called Anthea is found having an unwise lunch with a
young, unreliable male model from Spain.

John Mortimer 1923- : in *The
Spectator* 26 March 1994

30 He tells you when you've got on too much lipstick,
And helps you with your girdle when your hips stick.

Ogden Nash 1902-71: 'The Perfect
Husband' (1949)

31 A little incompatibility is the spice of life, particularly if he
has income and she is pattable.

Ogden Nash 1902-71: *Versus* (1949)

32 Twenty years ago when we had no respect for women
they just used to say, 'You're chucked.' And now we do
respect them we have to lie to them sensitively.

Simon Nye 1958- : *Men Behaving
Badly* (ITV, series 1, 1992) 'Intruders'

33 I killin' meself workin', an' he sthruttin' about from
mornin' till night like a paycock!

Sean O'Casey 1880-1964: *Juno and
the Paycock* (1925)

34 Men seldom make passes
At girls who wear glasses.

Dorothy Parker 1893-1967: 'News
Item' (1937)

35 Woman lives but in her lord;
Count to ten, and man is bored.
With this the gist and sum of it,
What earthly good can come of it?

Dorothy Parker 1893-1967: 'General
Review of the Sex Situation' (1937)

36 Some get a kick from cocaine.
I'm sure that if I took even one sniff

Cole Porter 1891-1964: 'I Get a Kick
out of You' (1934)

That would bore me terrific'ly too,
Yet I get a kick out of you.

37 Of course, I'm awfly glad that Mother had to marry
    Father,
But I hate men.

Cole Porter 1891–1964: 'I Hate Men' (1948)

38 The breeze is chasing the zephyr,
The moon is chasing the sea,
The bull is chasing the heifer,
But nobody's chasing me.

Cole Porter 1891–1964: 'Nobody's Chasing Me' (1950)

39 You're the Nile,
You're the Tow'r of Pisa,
You're the smile
On the Mona Lisa.
I'm a worthless check, a total wreck, a flop,
But if, baby, I'm the bottom
You're the top!

Cole Porter 1891–1964: 'You're the Top' (1934)

40 Only the male intellect, clouded by sexual impulse, could call the undersized, narrow-shouldered, broad-hipped, and short-legged sex the fair sex.

Arthur Schopenhauer 1788–1860: 'On Women' (1851), tr. E. Belfort Bax

41 A bunch of the boys were whooping it up in the Malamute saloon;
The kid that handles the music-box was hitting a jag-time tune;
Back of the bar, in a solo game, sat Dangerous Dan McGrew,
And watching his luck was his light-o'-love, the lady that's known as Lou.

Robert W. Service 1874–1958: 'The Shooting of Dan McGrew' (1907)

42 Say that she rail; why then I'll tell her plain
She sings as sweetly as a nightingale:
Say that she frown; I'll say she looks as clear
As morning roses newly washed with dew:
Say she be mute and will not speak a word;
Then I'll commend her volubility,
And say she uttereth piercing eloquence.

William Shakespeare 1564–1616: *The Taming of the Shrew* (1592)

an unknown woman wrote to Shaw suggesting that as he had the greatest brain in the world, and she the most beautiful body, they ought to produce the most perfect child:
43 What if the child inherits my body and your brains?

George Bernard Shaw 1856–1950: Hesketh Pearson *Bernard Shaw* (1942)

44 You think that you are Ann's suitor; that you are the pursuer and she the pursued . . . Fool: it is you who are the pursued, the marked down quarry, the destined prey.

George Bernard Shaw 1856–1950: *Man and Superman* (1903)

45 Won't you come into the garden? I would like my roses to see you.

Richard Brinsley Sheridan 1751–1816: to a young lady; attributed

46 You've got to understand, in a way a thirty-three-year-old guy is a lot younger than a twenty-four-year-old girl. That is, he may not be ready for marriage yet.

Neil Simon 1927– : *Come Blow Your Horn* (1961)

47 From my experience of life I believe my personal motto should be 'Beware of men bearing flowers.'

Muriel Spark 1918– : *Curriculum Vitae* (1992)

48 Yes, I am a fatal man, Madame Fribsbi. To inspire hopeless passion is my destiny.

William Makepeace Thackeray 1811–63: *Pendennis* (1848–50)

49 Werther had a love for Charlotte
Such as words could never utter;
Would you know how first he met her?
She was cutting bread and butter.

William Makepeace Thackeray 1811–63: 'Sorrows of Werther' (1855)

50 Always suspect any job men willingly vacate for women.

Jill Tweedie 1936–93: *It's Only Me* (1980)

51 In Europe, when a rich woman has an affair with a conductor, they have a baby. In America, she endows an orchestra for him.

Edgar Varèse 1885–1965: Herman G. Weinberg *Saint Cinema* (1970)

52 I don't want anyone to notice that I've been chucked, well, not even chucked, to be chucked you have to have been going out with someone, I've been . . . sort of sampled.

Arabella Weir: *Does My Bum Look Big in This?* (1997)

53 A man has one hundred dollars and you leave him with two dollars, that's subtraction.

Mae West 1892–1980: Joseph Weintraub *Peel Me a Grape* (1975)

54 Is that a gun in your pocket, or are you just glad to see me?

Mae West 1892–1980: Joseph Weintraub *Peel Me a Grape* (1975), usually quoted as 'Is that a pistol in your pocket . . . '

55 When women go wrong, men go right after them.

Mae West 1892–1980: in *She Done Him Wrong* (1933 film)

asked by the gossip columnist Hedda Hopper how she knew so much about men:
56 Baby, I went to night school.

Mae West 1892–1980: Max Wilk *The Wit and Wisdom of Hollywood* (1972)

57 Whatever women do they must do twice as well as men to be thought half as good. Luckily, this is not difficult.

Charlotte Whitton 1896–1975: in *Canada Month* June 1963

58 A man can be happy with any woman as long as he does not love her.

Oscar Wilde 1854–1900: *The Picture of Dorian Gray* (1891)

59 All women become like their mothers. That is their tragedy. No man does. That's his.

Oscar Wilde 1854–1900: *The Importance of Being Earnest* (1895); the same words occur in dialogue form in *A Woman of No Importance* (1893)

60 Girls are just friends who give you erections.
reporting his teenage son's words

Nigel Williams 1948– : *Fortysomething* (1999)

61 A mistress should be like a little country retreat near the town, not to dwell in constantly, but only for a night and away.

William Wycherley c.1640–1716: *The Country Wife* (1675)

62 What an odd thing to do. You might give an old girlfriend a Cartier brooch, but you don't make her prime minister.
commenting on Edith Cresson's appointment by François Mitterrand

Stani Yassukovich: in *Spectator* 20 March 1999; attributed

Middle Age See also Old Age, Youth

1 Years ago we discovered the exact point, the dead centre of middle age. It occurs when you are too young to take up golf and too old to rush up to the net.

Franklin P. Adams 1881–1960: *Nods and Becks* (1944)

2 I recently turned 60. Practically a third of my life is over.

Woody Allen 1935– : in *Observer* 'Sayings of the Week' 10 March 1996

3 You are thirty-two. You are rapidly approaching the age when your body, whether it embarrasses you or not, begins to embarrass other people.

Alan Bennett 1934– : *Getting On* (1972)

4 Whenever the talk turns to age, I say I am 49 plus VAT.

Lionel Blair 1936– : in *Mail on Sunday* 6 June 1999

5 After forty a woman has to choose between losing her figure or her face. My advice is to keep your face, and stay sitting down.

Barbara Cartland 1901–2000: Libby Purves 'Luncheon à la Cartland'; in *The Times* 6 October 1993

6 Nobody loves a fairy when she's forty.

Arthur W. D. Henley: title of song (1934)

7 When grown-ups pretend they are in playschool they are either trying to cheat you or are terrified to death.

P. J. Kavanagh 1931– : in *The Spectator* 5 December 1992

8 I have a bone to pick with Fate.
Come here and tell me, girlie,
Do you think my mind is maturing late,
Or simply rotted early?

Ogden Nash 1902–71: 'Lines on Facing Forty' (1942)

9 As invariably happens after one passes 40, the paper sagged open to the obituary page.

S. J. Perelman 1904–79: 'Swindle Sheet with Blueblood Engrailed Arrant Fibs Rampant'

10 When I was cuter,
Each night meant another suitor,
I sleep easier now.

Cole Porter 1891–1964: 'I Sleep Easier Now' (1950)

11 As we get older we do not get any younger.
Seasons return, and today I am fifty-five,
And this time last year I was fifty-four,
And this time next year I shall be sixty-two.

Henry Reed 1914–86: 'Chard Whitlow (Mr Eliot's Sunday Evening Postscript)' (1946)

12 It is one of the consolations of middle-aged reformers that the good they inculcate must live after them if it is to live at all.

Saki 1870–1916: *Beasts and Super-Beasts* (1914)

13 Maturity is a high price to pay for growing up.

Tom Stoppard 1937– : *Where Are They Now?* (1973)

14 From birth to 18 a girl needs good parents. From 18 to 35, she needs good looks. From 35 to 55, good personality. From 55 on, she needs good cash.

Sophie Tucker 1884–1966: Michael Freedland *Sophie* (1978)

15 Thirty-five is a very attractive age. London society is full of women of the very highest birth who have, of their own free choice, remained thirty-five for years.

Oscar Wilde 1854–1900: *The Importance of Being Earnest* (1895)

The Mind See also Intelligence and Intellectuals

1 If I am out of my mind, it's all right with me, thought Moses Herzog.

Saul Bellow 1915– : *Herzog* (1961) opening sentence

2 The asylums of this country are full of the sound of mind disinherited by the out of pocket.

Alan Bennett 1934– : *The Madness of George III* (performed 1991)

3 An apparatus with which we think that we think.
definition of the brain

Ambrose Bierce 1842–c.1914: *Cynic's Word Book* (1906)

4 'I am inclined to think—' said I [Dr Watson]. 'I should do so,' Sherlock Holmes remarked, impatiently.

Arthur Conan Doyle 1859–1930: *The Valley of Fear* (1915)

5 There was only one catch and that was Catch-22, which specified that a concern for one's own safety in the face of dangers that were real and immediate was the process of a rational mind . . . Orr would be crazy to fly more missions and sane if he didn't, but if he was sane he had to fly them. If he flew them he was crazy and didn't have to; but if he didn't want to he was sane and had to.

Joseph Heller 1923–99: *Catch-22* (1961)

6 If the nineteenth century was the age of the editorial chair, ours is the century of the psychiatrist's couch.

Marshall McLuhan 1911–80: *Understanding Media* (1964)

7 'Do you know if there was any insanity in her family?' 'Insanity? No, I never heard of any. Her father lives in West Kensington, but I believe he's sane on all other subjects.'

Saki 1870–1916: *Beasts and Super-Beasts* (1914)

8 O Lord, Sir—when a heroine goes mad she always goes into white satin.

Richard Brinsley Sheridan 1751–1816: *The Critic* (1779)

9 Not body enough to cover his mind decently with; his intellect is improperly exposed.

Sydney Smith 1771–1845: Lady Holland *Memoir* (1855)

10 I must have a prodigious quantity of mind; it takes me as much as a week, sometimes, to make it up.

Mark Twain 1835–1910: *The Innocents Abroad* (1869)

11 A neurosis is a secret you don't know you're keeping.

Kenneth Tynan 1927–80: Kathleen Tynan *Life of Kenneth Tynan* (1987)

12 Dr Tayler's thoughts are very white and pure, recalling in their disorder a draper's shop on the last day of a great white sale.

Rebecca West 1892–1983: in *The Clarion* 7 March 1913

Mistakes and Misfortunes

1 Instead of being arrested, as we stated, for kicking his wife down a flight of stairs and hurling a lighted kerosene lamp after her, the Revd James P. Wellman died unmarried four years ago.

Anonymous: from an American newspaper, quoted by Burne-Jones in a letter to Lady Horner; J. A. Gere and John Sparrow (eds.) *Geoffrey Madan's Notebooks* (1981)

2 I'm not going to make the same mistake once.
on marriage

Warren Beatty 1937– : attributed; Bob Chieger *Was It Good For You Too?* (1983)

3 My only solution for the problem of habitual accidents . . . is to stay in bed all day. Even then, there is always the chance that you will fall out.

Robert Benchley 1889–1945: *Chips off the old Benchley* (1949) 'Safety Second'

4 George the Third
Ought never to have occurred.
One can only wonder
At so grotesque a blunder.

Edmund Clerihew Bentley 1875–1956: 'George the Third' (1929)

5 The younger Van Eyck
Was christened Jan, and not Mike,
The thought of this curious mistake
Often kept him awake.

Edmund Clerihew Bentley
1875-1956: 'Van Eyck' (1905)

6 My misdeeds are accidental happenings and merely the
result of having been in the wrong bar or bed at the wrong
time, say most days between midday and midnight.

Jeffrey Bernard 1932-97: in *The
Spectator* 18 July 1992

7 Calamities are of two kinds: misfortune to ourselves, and
good fortune to others.

Ambrose Bierce 1842-c.1914: *The
Cynic's Word Book* (1906)

8 Mr Hague may be good at telling jokes, but every time you
come to a critical question of judgement like this he gets it
wrong.
*on William Hague's endorsement of Jeffrey Archer as mayoral
candidate for London*

Tony Blair 1953- : in *Sunday Times*
28 November 1999; see **Mistakes** 16

9 Of all the horrid, hideous notes of woe,
Sadder than owl-songs or the midnight blast,
Is that portentous phrase, 'I told you so.'

Lord Byron 1788-1824: *Don Juan*
(1819-24)

Edith Evans repeatedly inserted the word 'very' into a line of Hay
Fever:
10 No, no, Edith. The line is, 'You can see as far as Marlow
on a clear day.' On a *very* clear day you can see Marlow
and Beaumont and Fletcher.

Noël Coward 1899-1973: Cole Lesley
The Life of Noël Coward (1976)

11 It was a moment of madness for which I have
subsequently paid a very, very heavy price.
*of the episode on Clapham Common leading to his resignation as
Welsh Secretary*

Ron Davies 1946- : interview with
BBC Wales and HTV, 30 October
1998

12 He has gone to the demnition bow-wows.

Charles Dickens 1812-70: *Nicholas
Nickleby* (1839)

13 If Gladstone fell into the Thames, that would be
misfortune; and if anybody pulled him out, that, I
suppose, would be a calamity.

Benjamin Disraeli 1804-81: Leon
Harris *The Fine Art of Political Wit*
(1965)

14 Something nasty in the woodshed.

Stella Gibbons 1902-89: *Cold
Comfort Farm* (1932)

15 I left the room with silent dignity, but caught my foot in
the mat.

George Grossmith 1847-1912 and
Weedon Grossmith 1854-1919: *The
Diary of a Nobody* (1894)

16 This is a candidate of probity and integrity—I am going to
back him to the full.
of Jeffrey Archer

William Hague 1961- : at the
Conservative party conference,
October 1999; see **Mistakes** 8

17 I was mistaken for a prostitute once in the last war. When
a GI asked me what I charged, I said, 'Well, dear, what do
your mother and sisters normally ask for?'

Thora Hird 1911- : in *Independent* 27
February 1999

18 Higgledy—Piggledy
Andrea Doria
Lines in the name of this
Glorious boat.
As I sit writing these
Non-navigational
Verses a—CRASH! BANG! BLURP!
GLUB . . . (end of quote).

John Hollander 1929- : 'Last
Words' (1966)

19 Well, I'm still here.

after erroneous reports of his death, marked by tributes paid to him in Congress

Bob Hope 1903- : in *Mail on Sunday* 7 June 1998 'Quotes of the Week'

20 When I make a mistake, it's a beaut.

Fiorello H. La Guardia 1882–1947: on his appointment of Herbert O'Brien as a judge; William Manners *Patience and Fortitude* (1976)

21 I've no sympathy with people to whom things happen. It may be that their luck was bad, but is that to count in their favour?

Cormac McCarthy 1933- : *All the Pretty Horses* (1993)

22 now and then
there is a person born
who is so unlucky
that he runs into accidents
which started to happen
to somebody else.

Don Marquis 1878–1937: *archys life of mehitabel* (1933) 'archy says'

a postcard of the Venus de Milo sent to his niece:
23 See what'll happen to you if you don't stop biting your finger-nails.

Will Rogers 1879–1935: Bennett Cerf *Shake Well Before Using* (1948)

24 *For* Pheasant *read* Peasant, throughout.

W. C. Sellar 1898–1951 and **R. J. Yeatman** 1898–1968: *1066 and All That* (1930); errata

25 Misery acquaints a man with strange bedfellows.

William Shakespeare 1564–1616: *The Tempest* (1611)

when the news that Sheridan's Drury Lane theatre was on fire reached the House of Commons, a motion was made to adjourn the debate on the campaign in Spain:
26 Whatever might be the extent of the individual calamity, I do not consider it of a nature worthy to interrupt the proceedings on so great a national question.

Richard Brinsley Sheridan 1751–1816: speech, House of Commons, 24 February 1809

27 Well, if I called the wrong number, why did you answer the phone?

James Thurber 1894–1961: cartoon caption in *New Yorker* 5 June 1937

Money See also **Debt, Poverty, Wealth**

1 Money is better than poverty, if only for financial reasons.

Woody Allen 1935- : *Without Feathers* (1976) 'Early Essays'

2 Money, it turned out, was exactly like sex, you thought of nothing else if you didn't have it and thought of other things if you did.

James Baldwin 1924–87: in *Esquire* May 1961 'Black Boy looks at the White Boy'

3 I'm tired of Love: I'm still more tired of Rhyme.
But Money gives me pleasure all the time.

Hilaire Belloc 1870–1953: 'Fatigued' (1923)

4 HOLDUP MAN: Quit stalling—I said your money or your life.
JACK BENNY: I'm thinking it over!

Jack Benny 1894–1974: one of Jack Benny's most successful gags; Irving Fein *Jack Benny* (1976)

5 'First you schange me schmall scheque?' 'No.'

Caryl Brahms 1901–82 and **S. J. Simon** 1904–48: *A Bullet in the Ballet* (1937)

6 I never loved a dear gazelle—
Nor anything that cost me much:

Lewis Carroll 1832–98: 'Tema con Variazioni'

High prices profit those who sell,
But why should I be fond of such?

7 Annual income twenty pounds, annual expenditure
nineteen nineteen six, result happiness. Annual income
twenty pounds, annual expenditure twenty pounds ought
and six, result misery.

Charles Dickens 1812–70: *David Copperfield* (1850)

8 When you don't have any money, the problem is food.
When you have money, it's sex. When you have both it's
health.

J. P. Donleavy 1926– : *The Ginger Man* (1955)

9 I like Chopin and Bizet, and the voice of Doris Day,
Gershwin songs and old forgotten carols.
But the music that excels is the sound of oil wells
As they slurp, slurp, slurp into the barrels.

My little home will be quaint as an old parasol,
Instead of fitted carpets I'll have money wall to wall.
I want an old-fashioned house
With an old-fashioned fence
And an old-fashioned millionaire.

Marve Fisher: 'An Old-Fashioned Girl' (1954)

10 Economy was always 'elegant', and money-spending
always 'vulgar' and ostentatious— a sort of sour-
grapeism, which made us very peaceful and satisfied.

Elizabeth Gaskell 1810–65: *Cranford* (1853)

11 Money, wife, is the true fuller's earth for reputations, there
is not a spot or a stain but what it can take out.

John Gay 1685–1732: *The Beggar's Opera* (1728)

12 The shares are a penny, and ever so many are taken by
Rothschild and Baring,
And just as a few are allotted to you, you awake with a
shudder despairing.

W. S. Gilbert 1836–1911: *Iolanthe* (1882)

13 Good news rarely comes in a brown envelope.

Henry D'Avigdor Goldsmid 1909–76: John Betjeman, letter to Tom Driberg, 21 July 1976

on being told that money doesn't buy happiness:
14 But it upgrades despair so beautifully.

Richard Greenberg: *Hurrah at Last* (1999)

15 Money is what you'd get on beautifully without if only
other people weren't so crazy about it.

Margaret Case Harriman: Laurence J. Peter (ed.) *Quotations for our Time* (1977)

16 A bank is a place that will lend you money if you can
prove that you don't need it.

Bob Hope 1903– : Alan Harrington *Life in the Crystal Palace* (1959)

17 Men are more often bribed by their loyalties and ambitions
than money.

Robert H. Jackson 1892–1954: dissenting opinion in *United States v. Wunderlich* 1951

to Joynson-Hicks, who had acquired his double-barrelled surname through marriage with an heiress:
18 On the spur of the moment I can think of no better
example of unearned increment than the hyphen in the
right honourable gentleman's name.

David Lloyd George 1863–1945: Leon Harris *The Fine Art of Political Wit* (1965)

19 I am in an age group where it is rude to discuss money,
and now it is all anyone cares about.

Jack Nicholson 1937– : in *Observer* 3 January 1999 'Sayings of the Week'

20 There's only one thing to do with loose change of course. Tighten it.

Flann O'Brien 1911–66: *The Best of Myles* (1968)

21 'My boy,' he says, 'always try to rub up against money, for if you rub up against money long enough, some of it may rub off on you.'

Damon Runyon 1884–1946: in *Cosmopolitan* August 1929, 'A Very Honourable Guy'

on being asked what Rosencrantz and Guildenstern are Dead *was about:*
22 It's about to make me very rich.

Tom Stoppard 1937– : attributed; in *Daily Telegraph* 27 February 1999

23 The elegant simplicity of the three per cents.

Lord Stowell 1745–1836: Lord Campbell *Lives of the Lord Chancellors* (1857)

24 Money won't buy happiness, but it will pay the salaries of a large research staff to study the problem.

Bill Vaughan: Laurence J. Peter (ed.) *Quotations for Our Time* (1977)

Morality See also **Virtue and Vice**

asking Robbie Ross to keep away from the scandal-touched Reggie Turner:
1 He is very weak and you, if I remember rightly, are wicked.

Max Beerbohm 1872–1956: letter, spring 1895

2 Morality's *not* practical. Morality's a gesture. A complicated gesture learned from books.

Robert Bolt 1924–95: *A Man for All Seasons* (1960)

3 I am all for morality now—and shall confine myself henceforward to the strictest adultery—which you will please recollect is all that that virtuous wife of mine has left me.

Lord Byron 1788–1824: letter 29 October 1819

4 I probably have a different sense of morality to most people.

Alan Clark 1928–99: in *The Times* 2 June 1994

5 To be absolutely honest, what I feel really bad about is that I don't feel worse. That's the ineffectual liberal's problem in a nutshell.

Michael Frayn 1933– : in *Observer* 8 August 1965

6 If people want a sense of purpose, they should get it from their archbishops. They should not hope to receive it from their politicians.

Harold Macmillan 1894–1986: in conversation 1963; Henry Fairlie *The Life of Politics* (1968)

7 Providing you have enough courage—or money—you can do without a reputation.
    said by Rhett Butler

Margaret Mitchell 1900–49: *Gone with the Wind* (1936)

8 I'm very mild, I'm very meek,
My will is strong, but my won't is weak;
So don't look at me that way!

Cole Porter 1891–1964: 'Don't Look at Me That Way' (*Paris*, 1928 musical)

9 People will do things from a sense of duty which they would never attempt as a pleasure.

Saki 1870–1916: *The Chronicles of Clovis* (1911)

10 There is such a thing as letting one's aesthetic sense override one's moral sense . . . I believe you would have condoned the South Sea Bubble and the persecution of the Albigenses if they had been carried out in effective colour schemes.

Saki 1870–1916: *The Toys of Peace* (1919)

11 Dost thou think, because thou art virtuous, there shall be no more cakes and ale?

William Shakespeare 1564–1616: *Twelfth Night* (1601)

12 When a stupid man is doing something he is ashamed of, he always declares that it is his duty.

George Bernard Shaw 1856–1950: *Caesar and Cleopatra* (1901)

13 PICKERING: Have you no morals, man?
DOOLITTLE: Can't afford them, Governor.

George Bernard Shaw 1856–1950: *Pygmalion* (1916)

14 BELINDA: Ay, but you know we must return good for evil.
LADY BRUTE: That may be a mistake in the translation.

John Vanbrugh 1664–1726: *The Provoked Wife* (1697)

15 Moral indignation is jealousy with a halo.

H. G. Wells 1866–1946: *The Wife of Sir Isaac Harman* (1914)

16 On an occasion of this kind it becomes more than a moral duty to speak one's mind. It becomes a pleasure.

Oscar Wilde 1854–1900: *The Importance of Being Earnest* (1895)

Murder

1 Lizzie Borden took an axe
And gave her mother forty whacks;
When she saw what she had done
She gave her father forty-one!

Anonymous: popular rhyme in circulation after the acquittal of Lizzie Borden, in June 1893, from the charge of murdering her father and stepmother at Fall River, Massachusetts on 4 August 1892

2 You can't chop your poppa up in Massachusetts,
Not even if it's planned as a surprise
No you can't chop your poppa up in Massachusetts
You know how neighbours love to criticize.

Michael Brown: 'Lizzie Borden' (1952)

3 The Stately Homes of England,
Tho' rather in the lurch,
Provide a lot of chances
For Psychical Research —
There's the ghost of a crazy younger son
Who murdered, in thirteen fifty-one,
An extremely rowdy Nun
Who resented it,
And people who come to call
Meet her in the hall.

Noël Coward 1899–1973: *The Stately Homes of England* (1938)

on being asked whether he thought that Dr John Bodkin Adams, acquitted of murdering an elderly female patient, had actually been guilty:
4 He must have had quite a lot of explaining to do to the recording angel.

Lord Hailsham 1907– : in an interview; John Mortimer *Character Parts* (1986)

5 Television has brought back murder into the home—where it belongs.

Alfred Hitchcock 1899–1980: in *Observer* 19 December 1965

6 It was not until several weeks after he had decided to murder his wife that Dr Bickleigh took any active steps in the matter. Murder is a serious business.

Francis Iles 1893–1970: *Malice Aforethought* (1931)

7 We'll murder them all amid laughter and merriment,
Except for a few we'll take home to experiment.
My pulse will be quickenin' with each drop of strychnine
    we feed to a pigeon.
(It just takes a smidgin!)
To poison a pigeon in the park.

Tom Lehrer 1928– : 'Poisoning Pigeons in the Park' (1953)

8 On the whole I am against mass murder: I rarely commit it myself, and often find myself quite out of sympathy with those who make a habit of it.

Bernard Levin 1928- : *In These Times* (1986)

9 You can always count on a murderer for a fancy prose style.

Vladimir Nabokov 1899–1977: *Lolita* (1955)

Julius Caesar of his assassins:
10 Infamy, infamy, they've all got it in for me!

Talbot Rothwell 1916–74: *Carry on, Cleo* (1964); according to Frank Muir's letter to the *Guardian*, 22 July 1995, the line had actually been written by him and Denis Norden for a radio sketch for 'Take It From Here', and was later used by Rothwell with their permission

11 I met Murder on the way—
He had a mask like Castlereagh.

Percy Bysshe Shelley 1792–1822: 'The Mask of Anarchy' (1819)

12 By the argument of counsel it was shown that at half-past ten in the morning on the day of the murder . . . [the defendant] became insane, and remained so for eleven and a half hours exactly.

Mark Twain 1835–1910: 'A New Crime' (1875)

13 When the peremptory challenges were all exhausted, a jury of twelve men were empaneled—a jury who swore that they had neither heard, read, talked about nor expressed an opinion concerning a murder which the very cattle in the corrals, the Indians in the sage-brush and the stones in the street were cognizant of!

Mark Twain 1835–1910: *Roughing It* (1872)

after another Jack the Ripper murder:
14 All these courts must be lit, and our detectives improved. They are not what they should be.

Queen Victoria 1819–1901: letter to Lord Salisbury, 10 November 1888

Music See also **Musicians, Songs and Singing**

1 I can't listen to too much Wagner, ya know? I start to get the urge to conquer Poland.

Woody Allen 1935- : *Manhattan Murder Mystery* (1998 film)

2 All music is folk music, I ain't never heard no horse sing a song.

Louis Armstrong 1901–71: in *New York Times* 7 July 1971

when asked what jazz is:
3 If you still have to ask . . . shame on you.

Louis Armstrong 1901–71: Max Jones et al. *Salute to Satchmo* (1970) (sometimes quoted 'Man, if you gotta ask you'll never know')

4 I love Wagner, but the music I prefer is that of a cat hung up by its tail outside a window and trying to stick to the panes of glass with its claws.

Charles Baudelaire 1821–67: Nat Shapiro (ed.) *An Encyclopedia of Quotations about Music* (1978)

5 What can you do with it? It's like a lot of yaks jumping about.
on the third movement of Beethoven's Seventh Symphony

Thomas Beecham 1879–1961: Harold Atkins and Archie Newman *Beecham Stories* (1978)

6 Why do we have to have all these third-rate foreign conductors around—when we have so many second-rate ones of our own?

Thomas Beecham 1879–1961: L. Ayre *Wit of Music* (1966)

7 The musical equivalent of the Towers of St Pancras Station.

Thomas Beecham 1879–1961: describing Elgar's 1st Symphony; Neville Cardus *Sir Thomas Beecham* (1961)

8 There are two golden rules for an orchestra: start together and finish together. The public doesn't give a damn what goes on in between.

Thomas Beecham 1879–1961: Harold Atkins and Archie Newman *Beecham Stories* (1978)

9 [The piano is] a parlour utensil for subduing the impenitent visitor. It is operated by depressing the keys of the machine and the spirits of the audience.

Ambrose Bierce 1842–c.1914: *The Enlarged Devil's Dictionary* (1967)

10 Extraordinary how potent cheap music is.

Noël Coward 1899–1973: *Private Lives* (1930); see **Music** 57

11 The tuba is certainly the most intestinal of instruments— the very lower bowel of music.

Peter de Vries 1910–93: *The Glory of the Hummingbird* (1974)

12 Dumb as a drum vith a hole in it, sir.

Charles Dickens 1812–70: *Pickwick Papers* (1837)

13 I don't like composers who think. It gets in the way of their plagiarism.

Howard Dietz 1896–1983: *Dancing in the Dark* (1974)

a trumpet player had been suggested with the endorsement 'he's a nice guy':
14 Nice guys are a dime a dozen! Get me a prick that can play!

Tommy Dorsey 1905–56: Bill Crow *Jazz Anecdotes* (1990)

15 I hate music, especially when it's played.

Jimmy Durante 1893–1980: Nat Shapiro (ed.) *An Encyclopedia of Quotations about Music* (1978)

16 Playing 'Bop' is like scrabble with all the vowels missing.

Duke Ellington 1899–1974: in *Look* 10 August 1954

17 'Tis wonderful how soon a piano gets into a log hut on the frontier.

Ralph Waldo Emerson 1803–82: 'Civilization' (1870)

18 Slap that bass—
Use it like a tonic.
Slap that bass
Keep your Philharmonic.
Zoom, zoom, zoom—
And the milk and honey'll flow!

Ira Gershwin 1896–1983: 'Slap that Bass' (1937)

19 The music-hall singer attends a series
Of masses and fugues and 'ops'
By Bach, interwoven
With Spohr and Beethoven,
At classical Monday Pops.

W. S. Gilbert 1836–1911: *The Mikado* (1885)

20 Then they began to sing
That extremely lovely thing,
'*Scherzando! ma non troppo ppp.*'

W. S. Gilbert 1836–1911: 'Story of Prince Agib' (1869)

21 What I love best about music is the women who listen to it.

Jules Goncourt 1830–70: Nat Shapiro (ed.) *An Encyclopedia of Quotations about Music* (1978)

22 I only know two tunes. One of them is 'Yankee Doodle' and the other isn't.

Ulysses S. Grant 1822–85: Nat Shapiro (ed.) *An Encyclopedia of Quotations about Music* (1978)

23 Music helps not the toothache.

George Herbert 1593–1633: *Outlandish Proverbs* (1640)

24 Classic music is th'kind that we keep thinkin'll turn into a tune.

Frank McKinney Hubbard 1868–1930: *Comments of Abe Martin and His Neighbors* (1923)

25 A pianoforte is a harp in a box.

Leigh Hunt 1784–1859: *The Seer* (1840)

On the performance of a celebrated violinist:
26 Difficult do you call it, Sir? I wish it were impossible.

Samuel Johnson 1709–84: William Seward *Supplement to the Anecdotes of Distinguished Persons* (1797)

27 If you play that score one more time before we open, people are going to think we're doing a revival.
   to George Gershwin

George S. Kaufman 1889–1961: Howard Teichmann *George S. Kaufman* (1973)

28 HAMMERSTEIN: Here is a story laid in China about an Italian told by an Irishman. What kind of music are you going to write?
   KERN: It'll be good Jewish music.
   in the 1930s, discussing with Oscar Hammerstein II a musical to be based on Donn Byrne's novel Messer Marco Polo

Jerome Kern 1885–1945: Gerald Bordman *Jerome Kern* (1980)

29 A carpenter's hammer, in a warm summer noon, will fret me into more than midsummer madness. But those unconnected, unset sounds are nothing to the measured malice of music.

Charles Lamb 1775–1834: *Elia* (1823)

30 A squeak's heard in the orchestra
   The leader draws across
   The intestines of the agile cat
   The tail of the noble hoss.

G. T. Lanigan 1845–86: *The Amateur Orlando* (1875)

31 Mine was the kind of piece in which nobody knew what was going on, including the composer, the conductor, and the critics. Consequently I got pretty good notices.

Oscar Levant 1906–72: *A Smattering of Ignorance* (1940)

32 If I play Tchaikovsky I play his melodies and skip his spiritual struggles . . . If there's any time left over I fill in with a lot of runs up and down the keyboard.

Liberace 1919–87: Stuart Hall and Paddy Whannel (eds.) *The Popular Arts* (1964)

33 I don't like my music, but what is my opinion against that of millions of others.

Frederick Loewe 1904–88: Nat Shapiro (ed.) *An Encyclopedia of Quotations about Music* (1978)

34 On seeing Niagara Falls, Mahler exclaimed: 'Fortissimo at last!'

Gustav Mahler 1860–1911: K. Blaukopf *Gustav Mahler* (1973)

35 If you're in jazz and more than ten people like you, you're labelled commercial.

Herbie Mann 1930– : Henry Pleasants *Serious Music and all that Jazz!* (1969)

36 If I had the power, I would insist on all oratorios being sung in the costume of the period—with a possible exception in the case of *The Creation*.

Ernest Newman 1868–1959: in *New York Post* 1924; Nat Shapiro (ed.) *An Encyclopedia of Quotations about Music* (1978)

37 I have been told that Wagner's music is better than it sounds.

Bill Nye 1850–96: Mark Twain *Autobiography* (1924)

38 What a terrible revenge by the culture of the Negroes on that of the whites!

Ignacy Jan Paderewski 1860–1941: of jazz; Nat Shapiro (ed.) *An Encyclopedia of Quotations about Music* (1978)

39 *Parsifal* is the kind of opera that starts at six o'clock. After it has been going three hours, you look at your watch and it says 6.20.

David Randolph 1914– : Nat Shapiro (ed.) *An Encyclopedia of Quotations about Music* (1978)

40 Of course we've all *dreamed* of reviving the *castrati*; but it's needed Hilda to take the first practical steps towards making them a reality . . . She's drawn up a list of well-known singers who she thinks would benefit . . . It's only a question of getting them to agree.

Henry Reed 1914–86: *Private Life of Hilda Tablet* (1954)

41 To the social-minded, a definition for Concert is: that which surrounds an intermission.

Ned Rorem 1923– : *The Final Diary* (1974)

42 It is a music one must hear several times. I am not going again.
of Tannhäuser

Gioacchino Rossini 1792–1868: L. de Hegermann-Lindencrone *In the Courts of Memory* (1912)

43 Wagner has lovely moments but awful quarters of an hour.

Gioacchino Rossini 1792–1868: to Emile Naumann, April 1867

44 Applause is a receipt, not a note of demand.

Artur Schnabel 1882–1951: in *Saturday Review of Literature* 29 September 1951

45 I know two kinds of audiences only—one coughing, and one not coughing.

Artur Schnabel 1882–1951: *My Life and Music* (1961)

46 You are there and I am here; but where is Beethoven?
to his conductor during a Beethoven rehearsal

Artur Schnabel 1882–1951: Nat Shapiro (ed.) *An Encyclopedia of Quotations about Music* (1978)

47 I have a reasonable good ear in music: let us have the tongs and the bones.

William Shakespeare 1564–1616: *A Midsummer Night's Dream* (1595–6)

48 Hell is full of musical amateurs: music is the brandy of the damned.

George Bernard Shaw 1856–1950: *Man and Superman* (1903)

49 I absolutely forbid such outrage. If *Pygmalion* is not good enough for your friends with its own verbal music . . . let them try Mozart's *Cosi Fan Tutti*, or at least Offenbach's *Grand Duchess*.

George Bernard Shaw 1856–1950: refusing to allow a musical based on *Pygmalion*; Caryl Brahms and Ned Sherrin *Song by Song* (1984)

50 If one will only take the precaution to go in long enough after it commences and to come out long before it is over you will not find it wearisome.

George Bernard Shaw 1856–1950: of Gounod's *La Rédemption*; in *The World* 22 February 1893

51 Nothing can be more disgusting than an oratorio. How absurd to see 500 people fiddling like madmen about Israelites in the Red Sea!

Sydney Smith 1771–1845: Hesketh Pearson *The Smith of Smiths* (1934)

52 Jazz will endure, just as long as people hear it through their feet instead of their brains.

John Philip Sousa 1854–1932: Nat Shapiro (ed.) *An Encyclopedia of Quotations about Music* (1978)

53 Satisfied great success.
reply to telegram from Billy Rose, suggesting that reorchestration by Robert Russell Bennett might make a ballet which was 'a great success' even more successful

Igor Stravinsky 1882–1971: in *Ned Sherrin in his Anecdotage* (1993)

54 I would like to thank Beethoven, Brahms, Wagner, Strauss, Rimsky-Korsakov.

Dmitri Tiomkin 1899–1979: Oscar acceptance speech for the score of *The High and the Mighty* in 1955

55 I assure you that the typewriting machine, when played with expression, is not more annoying than the piano when played by a sister or near relation.

Oscar Wilde 1854–1900: letter to Robert Ross from Reading Prison, 1 April 1897

56 Musical people are so absurdly unreasonable. They always want one to be perfectly dumb at the very moment when one is longing to be absolutely deaf.

Oscar Wilde 1854–1900: *An Ideal Husband* (1895)

57 He reminds us how cheap potent music can be.
   of the popular pianist Richard Clayderman

Richard Williams: Ned Sherrin *Cutting Edge* (1984); see **Music** 10

Musicians   See also **Music**

1 The music teacher came twice each week to bridge the awful gap between Dorothy and Chopin.

George Ade 1866–1944: attributed

2 There's no need for Peter Pears
To give himself airs.
He has them written
By Benjamin Britten.

Anonymous: a verse from *Punch*; in *Ned Sherrin in his Anecdotage* (1993)

3 I prefer to face the wrath of the police than the wrath of Sir John Barbirolli.
   a member of the Hallé orchestra on a speeding charge

Anonymous: Ned Sherrin *Cutting Edge* (1984)

   printed notice in an American dancing saloon:
4 Please do not shoot the pianist. He is doing his best.

Anonymous: Oscar Wilde *Impressions of America* 'Leadville' (c.1882–3)

5 A musicologist is a man who can read music but can't hear it.

Thomas Beecham 1879–1961: H. Proctor-Gregg *Beecham Remembered* (1976)

6 I am one of the three worst pianists in the world at the present time. The others are James Agate and somebody whose name I am not at liberty to mention—he is a very famous pianist.

Neville Cardus 1889–1975: *Autobiography* (1947)

7 Tchaikovsky thought of committing suicide for fear of being discovered as a homosexual, but today, if you are a composer and *not* homosexual, you might as well put a bullet through your head.

Sergei Diaghilev 1872–1929: Vernon Duke *Listen Here!* (1963)

8 QUESTION: Mr. Sullivan's music . . . reminds me so much of dear Baytch [Bach]. Do tell me: what is Baytch doing just now? Is he still composing?
   ANSWER: Just now, as a matter of fact, dear Baytch is by way of decomposing.

W. S. Gilbert 1836–1911: Hesketh Pearson *Gilbert and Sullivan* (1947)

9 There is no doubt that the first requirement for a composer is to be dead.

Arthur Honegger 1892–1955: *Je suis compositeur* (1951)

10 A review in the *Financial Times* said I was an extremely funky pub pianist. That was a good summing-up of what I am.

Elton John 1947– : in *Independent* 13 September 1997 'Quote Unquote'

11 Some cry up Haydn, some Mozart,
Just as the whim bites; for my part
I care not a farthing candle

Charles Lamb 1775–1834: 'Free Thoughts on Several Eminent Composers' (1830)

For either of them, or for Handel.

12 Leonard Bernstein has been disclosing musical secrets that have been known for over four hundred years.

Oscar Levant 1906–72: *Memoirs of an Amnesiac* (1965)

13 I'm told that Saint-Saëns has informed a delighted public that since the war began he has composed music for the stage, melodies, an elegy and a piece for the trombone. If he'd been making shell-cases instead it might have been all the better for music.

Maurice Ravel 1875–1937: letter to Jean Marnold, 7 October 1916

14 Ravel refuses the Legion of Honour, but all his music accepts it.

Erik Satie 1866–1925: Jean Cocteau *Le Discours d'Oxford* (1956)

asked how he could play so well when he was loaded:
15 I practise when I'm loaded.

Zoot Sims 1925–85: Bill Crow *Jazz Anecdotes* (1990)

16 'What do you think of Beethoven?'
'I love him, especially his poems.'

Ringo Starr 1940– : at a press conference during the Beatles' first American tour in 1964; Hunter Davies *The Beatles* (1985)

17 On matters of intonation and technicalities I am more than a martinet—I am a martinetissimo!

Leopold Stokowski 1882–1977: Nat Shapiro (ed.) *An Encyclopedia of Quotations about Music* (1978)

18 After I die, I shall return to earth as the doorkeeper of a bordello and I won't let one of you in.

Arturo Toscanini 1867–1957: to his orchestra during a difficult rehearsal; Nat Shapiro (ed.) *An Encyclopedia of Quotations about Music* (1978)

19 I wish I could write librettos for the rest of my life. It is the purest of human pleasures, a heavenly hermaphroditism of being both writer and musician. No wonder that selfish beast Wagner kept it all to himself.

Sylvia Townsend Warner 1893–1978: letter, 7 April 1949

Names

1 The reason Michael Jackson entitled his album *Bad* was because he couldn't spell *Indescribable*.

Anonymous: in 1987; Nigel Rees (ed.) *Cassell Dictionary of Humorous Quotations* (1999)

of Arianna Stassinopoulos:
2 So boring you fall asleep halfway through her name.

Alan Bennett 1934– : attributed; in *Observer* 18 September 1983

3 'You mustn't mention the Shah out loud.' . . . 'We had better call him Marjoribanks, if we want to remember who we mean.'

Robert Byron 1905–41: *The Road to Oxiana* (1937)

fashionable children's names of which Camden disapproved:
4 The new names, Free-gift, Reformation, Earth, Dust, Ashes . . . which have lately been given by some to their children.

William Camden 1551–1623: *Remains* (1605)

5 They *will* call me Mrs Pat. I can't stand it. The 'Pat' is the last straw that breaks the Campbell's back.

Mrs Patrick Campbell 1865–1940: attributed

of Alfred Bossom:
6 Who is this man whose name is neither one thing nor the other?

Winston Churchill 1874–1965: attributed

7 One theory is that I was named after the opera and the other that my mum was sitting in her boudoir wondering what to call me and glanced at her Carmen rollers. I prefer the Bizet theory.

Carmen Ejogo: in *Observer* 26 March 2000 'They said what . . . ?'

8 Every Tom, Dick and Harry is called Arthur.

Sam Goldwyn 1882–1974: to Arthur Hornblow, who was planning to name his son Arthur; Michael Freedland *The Goldwyn Touch* (1986)

9 *Yossarian*—the very sight of the name made him shudder. There were so many esses in it. It just had to be subversive.

Joseph Heller 1923–99: *Catch-22* (1961)

10 It was an odious, alien, distasteful name, that just did not inspire confidence. It was not at all like such clean, crisp, honest, American names as Cathcart, Peckem and Dreedle.

Joseph Heller 1923–99: *Catch-22* (1961)

11 The batsman's Holding, the bowler's Willey.

Brian Johnson: attributed; comment at a Test Match as Michael Holding faced Peter Willey

12 In the last Parliament, the House of Commons had more MPs called John than all the women MPs put together.

Tessa Jowell 1947– : in *Independent on Sunday* 14 March 1999 'Quotes'

13 If you should have a boy do not christen him John . . . 'Tis a bad name and goes against a man. If my name had been Edmund I should have been more fortunate.

John Keats 1795–1821: letter to his sister-in-law, 13 January 1820

14 One day I'll be famous! I'll be proper and prim; Go to St James so often I will call it St Jim!

Alan Jay Lerner 1918–86: 'Just You Wait' (*My Fair Lady*, 1956 musical)

pointing out that if she had kept her first husband's name she would still be 'Mrs Wisdom':
15 That would have been asking for trouble.

Doris Lessing 1919– : in *Times* 15 July 2000

16 Obadiah Bind-their-kings-in-chains-and-their-nobles-with-links-of-iron.

Lord Macaulay 1800–59: 'The Battle of Naseby' (1824), fictitious author's name

17 No, I'm breaking it in for a friend.

Groucho Marx 1895–1977: when asked if Groucho were his real name; attributed

on why she had named her canary 'Onan':
18 Because he spills his seed on the ground.

Dorothy Parker 1893–1967: John Keats *You Might as Well Live*

19 Why should people I have never met, who read me in bed and in the bathtub, think of me as 'Sam'.
  insisting that his first name be represented by the initial 'S.' on the title-pages of his books

Samuel ('Sam') Schoenbaum 1927–96: in *The Times* 25 April 1996; obituary

of Jeffrey Archer's title:
20 Lord Archer of Weston-Super-Mare—the only pier on which Danny La Rue has not performed.

Neil Shand: *Loose Ends* monologue, 1999

wondering why, since he was Irish, he was not O'Sheridan:
21 For in truth we owe everybody.

Richard Brinsley Sheridan 1751–1816: Walter Jerrold *Bon-Mots* (1893)

22 I remember your name perfectly; but I just can't think of
your face.

William Archibald Spooner
1844–1930: attributed; in *Penguin
Dictionary of Quotations* (1960)

23 MICHAEL WILDING: We have already been instructed to
refer to her at all times as Dame.
ELIZABETH TAYLOR: If I'm not being referred to as That
Broad.
*Elizabeth Taylor and her son, after the ceremony at which she
was appointed a DBE*

Elizabeth Taylor 1932– : in *Daily
Telegraph* 17 May 2000

24 Bingo Bolger-Baggins a bad name. Let Bingo = Frodo.
on the first draft of The Lord of the Rings

J. R. R. Tolkien 1892–1973: note,
c.1938; Humphrey Carpenter *J. R. R.
Tolkien* (1977)

25 We do have these extraordinary names . . . When you see
the sign 'African Primates Meeting' you expect someone to
produce bananas.
address at his retirement service, Cape Town, 23 June 1996

Desmond Tutu 1931– : in *Daily
Telegraph* 24 June 1996

*on being asked by William Carlos Williams how he had chosen the
name 'West':*

26 Horace Greeley said, 'Go West, young man. So I did.'

Nathanael West 1903–40: Jay
Martin *Nathanael West* (1970)

Nature and the Environment

1 The only place you can wake up in the morning and hear
the birds coughing in the trees.

Joe Frisco: of Hollywood; attributed

2 Every year, in the fulness o' summer, when the sukebind
hangs heavy from the wains . . . 'tes the same. And when
the spring comes her hour is upon her again. 'Tes the
hand of Nature and we women cannot escape it.

Stella Gibbons 1902–89: *Cold
Comfort Farm* (1932)

3 What do we chop, when we chop a tree?
A thousand things that you daily see.
A baby's crib, the poet's chair,
The soap box down in Union Square.
A pipe for Dad, a bat for brother,
An extra broom for dear old mother.

E. Y. Harburg 1898–1981: 'Song of
the Woodman' (1936)

4 Man he eat the barracuda,
Barracuda eat the bass
Bass he eat the little flounder,
'Cause the flounder lower class.
Little flounder eat the sardine
That's nature's plan.
Sardine eat the little worm,
Little worm eat man.

E. Y. Harburg 1898–1981: 'For Every
Fish' (1957)

5 I find it hard to accept, difficult to swallow, the new term
'ecology' which has come to us . . . It sounds a little too
much like being sick.

Stephen Leacock 1869–1944: *The
Boy I Left Behind Me* (1947)

6 I now promise that I will publicly eat an entire dolphin
without salt, when the last Green is stuffed with broccoli,
spinach, lettuce and dandelion-leaves, and boiled in a very
large bio-degradable iron cauldron, not that anyone would
notice a difference in the nonsense he would be spouting,
boiled or raw.

Bernard Levin 1928– : *If You Want
My Opinion* (1992)

on the possibility of golden plover being mistaken for grouse:

7 From a gastronomic point of view—that may be the wrong word—the golden plover are very good to eat but we must not think of our stomachs, but of conservation.

Lord Massereene and Ferrard 1914–93: speech on the Wildlife and Countryside Bill, House of Lords 2 February 1981

8 Worship of nature may be ancient, but seeing nature as cuddlesome, hug-a-bear and too cute for words is strictly a modern fashion.

P. J. O'Rourke 1947– : *Parliament of Whores* (1991)

9 [Richard Nixon is] the kind of politician who would cut down a redwood tree, and then mount the stump and make a speech on conservation.

Adlai Stevenson 1900–65: Fawn M. Brodie *Richard Nixon* (1983)

on the Falklands campaign, 1982:

10 It is exciting to have a real crisis on your hands, when you have spent half your political life dealing with humdrum issues like the environment.

Margaret Thatcher 1925– : speech to Scottish Conservative Party conference, 14 May 1982

11 BRICK: Well, they say nature hates a vacuum, Big Daddy.
BIG DADDY: That's what they say, but sometimes I think that a vacuum is a hell of a lot better than some of the stuff that nature replaces it with.

Tennessee Williams 1911–83: *Cat on a Hot Tin Roof* (1955)

Newspapers See also **Journalism**

1 HONG KONG POOH-POOHS NICHI NICHI'S DUM-DUMS.
reported headline in Australian newspaper, referring to reports that Hong Kong police denied a claim by the Japanese paper Nichi Nichi Shimbun *that they had used soft-nosed bullets against rioters*

Anonymous: attributed; in *Spectator* 19 December 1998

2 Sticks nix hick pix.

Anonymous: front-page headline on the lack of enthusiasm for farm dramas among rural populations; in *Variety* 17 July 1935

3 It's The Sun Wot Won It.
following the 1992 general election

Anonymous: headline in *Sun* 11 April 1992

4 NUT SCREWS WASHERS AND BOLTS.
reported headline in a Chinese newspaper above the story of an escapee from an asylum who broke into a laundry and raped several laundresses before escaping

Anonymous: Claud Cockburn *I, Claud* (1967)

5 If Kinnock wins today will the last person to leave Britain please turn out the lights.
on election day, showing Neil Kinnock's head inside a light bulb

Anonymous: headline in *Sun* 9 April 1992

6 If I rescued a child from drowning, the Press would no doubt headline the story 'Benn grabs child.'

Tony Benn 1925– : in *Observer* 2 March 1975

7 I read the newspapers avidly. It is my one form of continuous fiction.

Aneurin Bevan 1897–1960: in *The Times* 29 March 1960

8 More than one newspaper has been ruined by the brilliant writer in the editor's chair.

Lord Camrose 1879–1954: Leonard Russell et al. *The Pearl of Days: An Intimate Memoir of the Sunday Times* (1972)

9 If you are Editor [of *The Times*] you can never get away for an evening. It's worse than a herd of dairy cows.

Alan Clark 1928–99: diary 6 June 1984

with which Cockburn claimed to have won a competition at The
Times *for the dullest headline:*

10 Small earthquake in Chile. Not many dead.

Claud Cockburn 1904–81: *In Time of
Trouble* (1956)

11 It was mimeographed in dark brown ink on buff-coloured
foolscap. It was not merely noticeable, it was
unquestionably the nastiest-looking bit of work that ever
dropped on to a breakfast-table.

Claud Cockburn 1904–81: of his
periodical *The Week*; *In Time of
Trouble* (1956)

12 'I believe that nothing in the newspapers is ever true,' said
Madame Phoebus. 'And that is why they are so popular,'
added Euphrosyne, 'the taste of the age being decidedly for
fiction.'

Benjamin Disraeli 1804–81: *Lothair*
(1870)

13 Where it will all end, knows God!
   satirizing the style of Time *magazine*

Wolcott Gibbs 1902–58: in *New
Yorker* 28 November 1936

14 The witness replied that his leading articles [in *The
Observer*] were half-way between a cold bath and a
religious exercise, and that this was the place which they
occupied, very fitly, in the life of the nation.

A. P. Herbert 1890–1971: *Misleading
Cases* (1935)

15 Editor: a person employed by a newspaper, whose business
it is to separate the wheat from the chaff, and to see that
the chaff is printed.

Elbert Hubbard 1859–1915: *The
Roycroft Dictionary* (1914)

16 A newspaper which weighs as much as the *Oxford
Dictionary of Quotations* and a very large haddock.
   of the Sunday edition of the New York Times

Bernard Levin 1928– : *In These
Times* (1986)

17 The British Press is always looking for stuff to fill the space
between their cartoons.

Bernadette Devlin McAliskey
1947– : comment, 1970

18 You should always believe all you read in the newspapers,
as this makes them more interesting.

Rose Macaulay 1881–1958: *A Casual
Commentary* (1926)

19 People don't actually read newspapers. They get into them
every morning, like a hot bath.

Marshall McLuhan 1911–80: in 1965;
Jonathon Green (ed.) *A Dictionary of
Contemporary Quotations* (1982)

20 The art of newspaper paragraphing is to stroke a platitude
until it purrs like an epigram.

Don Marquis 1878–1937: E. Anthony
O Rare Don Marquis (1962)

21 When newspapers became solvent they lost a good deal of
their old venality, but at the same time they became
increasingly cautious, for capital is always timid.

H. L. Mencken 1880–1956: *Minority
Report* (1956)

22 Whenever I see a newspaper I think of the poor trees. As
trees they provide beauty, shade and shelter. But as paper
all they provide is rubbish.

Yehudi Menuhin 1916– : Jonathon
Green (ed.) *Contemporary Quotations*
(1982)

23 Exclusives aren't what they used to be. We tend to put
'exclusive' on everything just to annoy other papers. I
once put 'exclusive' on the weather by mistake.

Piers Morgan 1965– : in
Independent on Sunday 14 March 1999
'Quotes'

24 SIXTY HORSES WEDGED IN CHIMNEY
   The story to fit this sensational headline has not turned up
   yet.

J. B. Morton 1893–1975: Michael
Frayn (ed.) *The Best of Beachcomber*
(1963)

   asked why he had allowed Page 3 to develop:

25 I don't know. The editor did it when I was away.

Rupert Murdoch 1931– : in
Guardian 25 February 1994

on being telephoned by the Sunday Express *to ask what was his main wish for 1956:*

26 Not to be telephoned by the *Sunday Express* when I am busy.

Harold Nicolson 1886–1968: diary, 29 December 1955

27 If a newspaper prints a sex crime, it is smut: but when the *New York Times* prints it it is a sociological study.

Adolph S. Ochs 1858–1935: Laurence J. Peter (ed.) *Quotations for our Time* (1977)

28 No self-respecting fish would be wrapped in a Murdoch newspaper.

Mike Royko 1932– : before resigning from the Chicago *Sun-Times* when the paper was sold to Rupert Murdoch in 1984; Karl E. Meyer (ed.) *Pundits, Poets, and Wits* (1990)

of the Daily Mail*:*

29 By office boys for office boys.

Lord Salisbury 1830–1903: H. Hamilton Fyfe *Northcliffe, an Intimate Biography* (1930)

30 The newspapers! Sir, they are the most villainous— licentious—abominable—infernal—Not that I ever read them—No—I make it a rule never to look into a newspaper.

Richard Brinsley Sheridan 1751–1816: *The Critic* (1779)

31 Accuracy to a newspaper is what virtue is to a lady; but a newspaper can always print a retraction.

Adlai Stevenson 1900–65: *The Wit and Wisdom of Adlai Stevenson* (1965)

32 I'm with you on the free press. It's the newspapers I can't stand.

Tom Stoppard 1937– : *Night and Day* (1978)

33 Freedom of the press in Britain means freedom to print such of the proprietor's prejudices as the advertisers don't object to.

Hannen Swaffer 1879–1962: Tom Driberg *Swaff* (1974)

34 It is part of the social mission of every great newspaper to provide a refuge and a home for the largest possible number of salaried eccentrics.

Lord Thomson of Fleet 1894–1976: in *Observer* 22 November 1959 'Sayings of the Week'

35 There are laws to protect the freedom of the press's speech, but none that are worth anything to protect the people from the press.

Mark Twain 1835–1910: 'License of the Press' (1873)

36 None of the worst French novels from which careful parents try to protect their children can be as bad as what is daily brought and laid upon the breakfast-table of every educated family in England, and its effect must be most pernicious to the public morals of the country.
of the reporting of divorce cases in the press

Queen Victoria 1819–1901: letter to the Lord Chancellor, 26 December 1859

37 I don't do witty off the cuff remarks: it's like throwing £5 notes into the gutter.
speaking to Deborah Ross

Keith Waterhouse 1929– : in *Independent* 1 March 1999

38 *The Beast* stands for strong mutually antagonistic governments everywhere . . . Self-sufficiency at home, self-assertion abroad.

Evelyn Waugh 1903–66: *Scoop* (1938)

39 Newspapers, even, have degenerated. They may now be absolutely relied upon.

Oscar Wilde 1854–1900: *The Decay of Lying* (1891)

Old Age See also **Middle Age**, **Youth**

1 If you want to be adored by your peers and have standing ovations wherever you go—live to be over ninety.

George Abbott 1887–1995: in *The Times* 2 February 1995; obituary

2 Mr Salteena was an elderly man of 42.

Daisy Ashford 1881–1972: *The Young Visiters* (1919)

3 All I have to live on now is macaroni and memorial services.

Margot Asquith 1864–1945: Chips Channon diary 16 September 1943

4 To me old age is always fifteen years older than I am.

Bernard Baruch 1870–1965: in *Newsweek* 29 August 1955

5 Here I sit, alone and sixty,
Bald, and fat, and full of sin,
Cold the seat and loud the cistern,
As I read the Harpic tin.

Alan Bennett 1934– : 'Place Names of China'

6 In England, you see, age wipes the slate clean . . . If you live to be ninety in England and can still eat a boiled egg they think you deserve the Nobel Prize.

Alan Bennett 1934– : *An Englishman Abroad* (1989)

on reaching the age of 100:
7 If I'd known I was gonna live this long, I'd have taken better care of myself.

Eubie Blake 1883–1983: in *Observer* 13 February 1983 'Sayings of the Week'; also claimed by Adolph Zukor on reaching 100

8 'You are old, Father William,' the young man said,
'And your hair has become very white;
And yet you incessantly stand on your head—
Do you think, at your age, it is right?'

Lewis Carroll 1832–98: *Alice's Adventures in Wonderland* (1865)

9 I'll tell thee everything I can:
There's little to relate.
I saw an aged, aged man,
A-sitting on a gate.

Lewis Carroll 1832–98: *Through the Looking-Glass* (1872)

10 Old age is the outpatients' department of Purgatory.

Lord Hugh Cecil 1869–1956: John Betjeman, letter to Tom Driberg, 21 July 1976

in his old age Churchill overheard one of two new MPs whisper to the other, 'They say the old man's getting a bit past it':
11 And they say the old man's getting deaf as well.

Winston Churchill 1874–1965: K. Halle *The Irrepressible Churchill* (1985)

it was pointed out to the aged Winston Churchill that his fly-button was undone:
12 No matter. The dead bird does not leave the nest.

Winston Churchill 1874–1965: Rupert Hart-Davis letter to George Lyttelton, 5 January 1957

note left for traffic warden on illegally parked car:
13 Dearest Warden. Front tooth broken off; look like 81-year-old pirate, so at dentist 19a. Very old—very lame—no metras [sic].

Diana Cooper 1892–1986: Philip Ziegler *Diana Cooper* (1981)

14 How foolish to think that one can ever slam the door in the face of age. Much wiser to be polite and gracious and ask him to lunch in advance.

Noël Coward 1899–1973: diary, 3 June 1956

15 The late sixties is rather late to be orphaned.
on Clifton Webb's grief at his mother's death

Noël Coward 1899–1973: diary, 21 October 1960

16 To what do I attribute my longevity? Bad luck.

Quentin Crisp 1908–99: in *Spectator* 20 November 1999

17 Before I go to meet my Maker,
I want to use the salt left in my shaker.
I want to find out if it's true
The Blue Danube is really blue,
Before I kiss the world goodbye.

Howard Dietz 1896–1983: 'Before I Kiss the World Goodbye' (1963)

18 He who anticipates his century is generally persecuted when living, and is always pilfered when dead.

Benjamin Disraeli 1804–81: *Vivian Grey* (1826)

19 Being an old maid is like death by drowning, a really delightful sensation after you cease to struggle.

Edna Ferber 1887–1968: R. E. Drennan *Wit's End* (1973)

20 Methus'lah live nine hundred years,
Methus'lah live nine hundred years
But who calls dat livin'
When no gal'll give in
To no man what's nine hundred years?

Ira Gershwin 1896–1983: 'It Ain't Necessarily So' (1935)

21 I've got to take under my wing,
Tra la,
A most unattractive old thing,
Tra la,
With a caricature of a face.

W. S. Gilbert 1836–1911: *The Mikado* (1885)

22 At forty I lost my illusions,
At fifty I lost my hair,
At sixty my hope and teeth were gone,
And my feet were beyond repair.
At eighty life has clipped my claws,
I'm bent and bowed and cracked;
But I can't give up the ghost because
My follies are intact.

E. Y. Harburg 1898–1981: 'Gerontology or Springtime for Senility' (1965)

23 When our organs have been transplanted
And the new ones made happy to lodge in us,
Let us pray one wish be granted—
We retain our zones erogenous.

E. Y. Harburg 1898–1981: 'Seated One Day at the Organ' (1965)

24 W'en folks git ole en strucken wid de palsy, dey mus speck ter be laff'd at.

Joel Chandler Harris 1848–1908: *Nights with Uncle Remus* (1883)

25 Amidst the mortifying circumstances attendant upon growing old, it is something to have seen the *School for Scandal* in its glory.

Charles Lamb 1775–1834: *Elia* (1823)

26 H: We met at nine
G: We met at eight
H: I was on time
G: No, you were late
H: Ah yes! I remember it well.

Alan Jay Lerner 1918–86: 'I Remember It Well' (1957)

27 The fountain of youth is dull as paint.
Methuselah is my favourite saint.
I've never been so comfortable before.
Oh I'm so glad I'm not young any more.

Alan Jay Lerner 1918–86: 'I'm Glad I'm Not Young Any More' (1957)

28 The thing about getting old is the number of things you think that you can't say aloud because it would be too shocking.

Doris Lessing 1919– : in *Times* 15 July 2000

of an elderly guest:
29 Talk about over 70. She can do 8 times more than I can and reduces me to a pudding of exhaustion.

Nancy Mitford 1904–73: letter 15 October 1953

30 There's one more terrifying fact about old people: I'm going to be one soon.

P. J. O'Rourke 1947– : *Parliament of Whores* (1991)

31 I zeroed in and discovered I was easily the most decrepit. (Just funning, of course, show me a pretty woman and I immediately break into a lively hoedown, followed by Cheyne-Stokes breathing.)

S. J. Perelman 1904–79: letter, 27 January 1966

32 When men grow virtuous in their old age, they only make a sacrifice to God of the devil's leavings.

Alexander Pope 1688–1744: *Miscellanies* (1727) 'Thoughts on Various Subjects'

33 Growing old is like being increasingly penalized for a crime you haven't committed.

Anthony Powell 1905–2000: *Temporary Kings* (1973)

of Prince Philip on his sixty-fifth birthday:
34 A snappish OAP with a temper like an arthritic corgi.

Jean Rook 1931–91: in *Daily Express* 10 June 1986

35 As I grow older and older,
And totter towards the tomb,
I find that I care less and less
Who goes to bed with whom.

Dorothy L. Sayers 1893–1957: 'That's Why I Never Read Modern Novels'; Janet Hitchman *Such a Strange Lady* (1975)

36 A good old man, sir; he will be talking: as they say, 'when the age is in, the wit is out.'

William Shakespeare 1564–1616: *Much Ado About Nothing* (1598–9)

a final letter to a young correspondent, a year before his death:
37 Dear Elise,
Seek younger friends; I am extinct.

George Bernard Shaw 1856–1950: letter, 1949

38 The House of Lords is a perfect eventide home.

Baroness Stocks 1891–1975: *My Commonplace Book* (1970)

to a young diplomat who boasted of his ignorance of whist:
39 What a sad old age you are preparing for yourself.

Charles-Maurice de Talleyrand 1754–1838: J. Amédée Pichot *Souvenirs Intimes sur M. de Talleyrand* (1870)

40 One should never make one's début with a scandal. One should reserve that to give an interest to one's old age.

Oscar Wilde 1854–1900: *The Picture of Dorian Gray* (1891)

41 Though well stricken in years the old blister becomes on these occasions as young as he feels, which seems to be about twenty-two.

P. G. Wodehouse 1881–1975: *Uncle Dynamite* (1948)

Parents See also **Children, The Family**

1 The authoritarian, didactic, primitive Irish parent is world famous—as is his frequently neurotic, deceitful and anxious child.

Noel Browne 1915–97: in 1973, attributed

2 My parents and his mother ganged up and had pan-parent meetings.

Katy Hayes: *Forecourt* (1995)

3 Mom and Pop were just a couple of kids when they got married. He was eighteen, she was sixteen, and I was three.

Billie Holiday 1915-59: *Lady Sings the Blues* (1958) opening words

on hearing a report that his son Charles James Fox was to be married:
4 He will be obliged to go to bed at least one night of his life.

Lord Holland 1705-74: Christopher Hobhouse *Fox* (1934)

5 If I'm more of an influence to your son as a rapper than you are as a father . . . you got to look at yourself as a parent.

Ice Cube 1970- : to Mike Sager in *Rolling Stone* 4 October 1990

6 In case it is one of mine.
patting children in Chelsea on the head as he passed by

Augustus John 1878-1961: Michael Holroyd *Augustus John* (1975)

to Nina Hamnett:
7 We have become, Nina, the sort of people our parents warned us about.

Augustus John 1878-1961: attributed; Nigel Rees *Cassell Dictionary of Humorous Quotations* (1999)

8 Fathers don't curse, they disinherit. Mothers curse.

Irma Kurtz: *Malespeak* (1986)

explaining her mother's insistence on taking her own bidet with her when she travelled:
9 My poor, dear mother suffers from a bidet-fixe.

Karen Lancaster d. 1964: Osbert Lancaster *With an Eye to the Future* (1967)

10 They fuck you up, your mum and dad.
They may not mean to, but they do.
They fill you with the faults they had
And add some extra, just for you.

Philip Larkin 1922-85: 'This Be The Verse' (1974)

11 Parents should conduct their arguments in quiet, respectful tones, but in a foreign language. You'd be surprised what an inducement that is to the education of children.

Judith Martin 1938- : 'Advice from Miss Manners', column in *Washington Post* 1979-82

12 Because of their size, parents may be difficult to discipline properly.

P. J. O'Rourke 1947- : *Modern Manners* (1984)

13 A Jewish man with parents alive is a fifteen-year-old boy, and will remain a fifteen-year-old boy until *they die*!

Philip Roth 1933- : *Portnoy's Complaint* (1967)

14 I did not throw myself into the struggle for life: I threw my mother into it. I was not a staff to my father's old age: I hung on to his coat tails.

George Bernard Shaw 1856-1950: preface to *The Irrational Knot* (1905)

15 I wish either my father or my mother, or indeed both of them, as they were in duty both equally bound to it, had minded what they were about when they begot me.

Laurence Sterne 1713-68: *Tristram Shandy* (1759-67)

16 And her mother came too!

Dion Titheradge: title of song (1921)

17 The value to a child of poor role models is also underestimated. Parents have the idea that it is their duty to set a good example, never realizing that a bad one will do just as well, indeed better.

Jill Tweedie 1936-93: *Eating Children* (1993)

18 In our society . . . mothers go on getting blamed until they're eighty, but shouldn't take it personally.

Katharine Whitehorn 1926- : *Observations* (1970)

Parties See also **Society and Social Life**

1 I won't be going to any New Year's Eve parties because I think they're naff. The millennium is going to be the naffest of them all. No one over the age of 15 should bother going to parties.

Julie Burchill 1960– : in *Observer* 3 January 1999

2 I've been to a marvellous party,
We didn't start dinner till ten
And young Bobbie Carr
Did a stunt at the bar
With a lot of extraordinary men.

Noël Coward 1899–1973: 'I've been to a Marvellous Party' (1938)

3 You know I hate parties. My idea of hell is a very large party in a cold room, where everybody has to play hockey properly.

Stella Gibbons 1902–89: *Cold Comfort Farm* (1932)

4 Home is heaven and orgies are vile,
But you *need* an orgy, once in a while.

Ogden Nash 1902–71: 'Home, 99⁴⁴⁄₁₀₀% Sweet Home' (1935)

5 Unless your life is going well you don't dream of giving a party. Unless you can look in the mirror and see a benign and generous and healthy human being, you shrink from acts of hospitality.

Carol Shields 1935– : *Larry's Party* (1997)

6 Gee, what a terrific party. Later on we'll get some fluid and embalm each other.

Neil Simon 1927– : *The Gingerbread Lady* (1970)

7 I made a terrible social gaffe. I went to a Ken and Barbie party dressed as Klaus Barbie

Arthur Smith 1954– and **Chris England**: *An Evening with Gary Lineker* (1990)

8 An office party is not, as is sometimes supposed, the Managing Director's chance to kiss the tea-girl. It is the tea-girl's chance to kiss the Managing Director.

Katharine Whitehorn 1926– : *Roundabout* (1962) 'The Office Party'

9 Of course I don't want to go to a cocktail party . . . If I wanted to stand around with a load of people I don't know eating bits of cold toast I can get caught shoplifting and go to Holloway.

Victoria Wood 1953– : *Mens Sana in Thingummy Doodah* (1990)

Past and Present See also **The Future**

1 'The first ten million years were the worst,' said Marvin, 'and the second ten million years, they were the worst too. The third ten million I didn't enjoy at all. After that I went into a bit of a decline.'

Douglas Adams 1952– : *Restaurant at the End of the Universe* (1980)

2 Nostalgia isn't what it used to be.

Anonymous: graffito (taken as title of book by Simone Signoret, 1978)

3 It's not perfect, but to me on balance Right Now is a lot better than the Good Old Days.

Maeve Binchy 1940– : in *Irish Times* 15 November 1997

4 The rule is, jam to-morrow and jam yesterday—but never jam today.

Lewis Carroll 1832–98: *Through the Looking-Glass* (1872)

5 What a Royal Academy,
Too Alma-Tademy,
Practical, mystical,
Over-artistical,
Highly pictorial,

Noël Coward 1899–1973: 'What a Century' (1953)

Albert Memorial
Century this has been.

6 I don't look back in anger or even mild regret; it has all been most enjoyable.

Noël Coward 1899–1973: Sheridan Morley *The Quotable Noël Coward* (1999)

7 I do not know which makes a man more conservative—to know nothing but the present, or nothing but the past.

John Maynard Keynes 1883–1946: *The End of Laissez-Faire* (1926)

8 Industrial archaeology . . . believes that a thing that doesn't work any more is far more interesting than a thing that still works.

Miles Kington 1941– : *Nature Made Ridiculously Simple* (1983)

9 It was in the flood-tide of chivalry. Knighthood was in the pod.

Stephen Leacock 1869–1944: *Nonsense Novels* (1911) 'Guido the Gimlet of Ghent'

10 Stolen, perhaps, by Nicholas Udall, the Headmaster [of Eton] who stole the college plate, was homosexual, went to gaol, and on coming out was made Headmaster of Westminster. Those were the days!

George Lyttelton 1883–1962: letter to Rupert Hart-Davis, 17 September 1958

11 Victorians such as my grandmother always assumed, along with dreary old Isaac Watts who left us in 1748 and not one moment too soon, that Satan finds some mischief still for idle hands to do.

Arthur Marshall 1910–89: *Life's Rich Pageant* (1984)

12 Weren't the eighties grand? Cash grew on trees or, anyway, coca bushes. The rich roamed the land in vast herds hunted by proud, free tribes of investment brokers who lived a simple life in tune with money.

P. J. O'Rourke 1947– : introduction to the second edition of *The Bachelor Home Companion* (1993)

13 They spend their time mostly looking forward to the past.

John Osborne 1929– : *Look Back in Anger* (1956)

14 There's a million more important things going on in the world today. New countries are being born. They're getting ready to send men to the moon. I just can't get excited about making wax fruit.

Neil Simon 1927– : *Come Blow Your Horn* (1961)

15 It used to be a good hotel, but that proves nothing—I used to be a good boy.

Mark Twain 1835–1910: *The Innocents Abroad* (1869)

16 It is the spirit of the age to believe that any fact, no matter how suspect, is superior to any imaginative exercise, no matter how true.

Gore Vidal 1925– : in *Encounter* December 1967

17 We mustn't prejudge the past.

William Whitelaw 1918–99: in *Times* 2 July 1999; attributed

18 Hindsight is always twenty-twenty.

Billy Wilder 1906– : J. R. Columbo *Wit and Wisdom of the Moviemakers* (1979)

People and Personalities

1 In her early days she had that beatific expression characteristic of Victorian prettiness—like a sheep painted by Raphael.
  of Lillie Langtry

James Agate 1877–1947: diary, 10 April 1940

2 This was an actress who, for twenty years, had the world at her feet. She kicked it away, and the ball rolled out of her reach.
of Mrs Patrick Campbell

James Agate 1877–1947: diary, 12 April 1940

3 My name is George Nathaniel Curzon,
I am a most superior person.
My face is pink, my hair is sleek,
I dine at Blenheim once a week.
of Lord Curzon

Anonymous: *The Masque of Balliol* (c.1870), in W. G. Hiscock *The Balliol Rhymes* (1939, the last two lines are a later addition); see **People** 33

4 My God, there are two of them!
cry from the gallery of the Glasgow Empire as Mike Winters followed Bernie Winters on to the stage

Anonymous: unattributed

on Vita Sackville-West's appearance in a tableau vivant:
5 Dear old Vita, all aqua, no vita, was as heavy as frost.

Margot Asquith 1864–1945: Philip Ziegler *Diana Cooper* (1981)

6 He came to see me this morning—positively reeking of Horlicks.
of Adrian Boult

Thomas Beecham 1879–1961: Ned Sherrin *Cutting Edge* (1984)

7 Byron!—he would be all forgotten today if he had lived to be a florid old gentleman with iron-grey whiskers, writing very long, very able letters to *The Times* about the Repeal of the Corn Laws.

Max Beerbohm 1872–1956: *Zuleika Dobson* (1911)

8 He's always backing into the limelight.
of T. E. Lawrence

Lord Berners 1883–1950: oral tradition

9 The meringue-utan.
of Rosamond Lehmann

Maurice Bowra 1898–1971: in *Spectator* 17 July 1999; attributed

jumping from a second storey window:
10 I'm Superjew!

Lenny Bruce 1925–66: in *Observer* 21 August 1966

11 That's the trouble with Anthony—half mad baronet, half beautiful woman.
of Anthony Eden

R. A. Butler 1902–82: attributed

12 He is a person of very *epic* appearance—and has a fine head as far as the outside goes—and wants nothing but taste to make the inside equally attractive.
of Robert Southey

Lord Byron 1788–1824: letter, 30 September 1813

of the vegetarian George Bernard Shaw:
13 If you give him meat no woman in London will be safe.

Mrs Patrick Campbell 1865–1940: Frank Harris *Contemporary Portraits* (1919)

14 A magnificent sight presents itself: Barbara Cartland wearing an electric pink chiffon dress, with false eyelashes, as thick as those caterpillars that give you a rash if you handle them, was draped on the central staircase with her dress arranged like a caricature of the celebrated Cecil Beaton photograph of the Countess of Jersey.

Alan Clark 1928–99: diary, 12 May 1984

15 I do not wear a bleeper. I can't speak in soundbites. I refuse to repeat slogans. . . . I hate focus groups. I absolutely hate image consultants.

Kenneth Clarke 1940– : in *New Statesman* 12 February 1999

16 I had to pull him out, otherwise nobody would have believed I didn't push him in.
on rescuing David Frost from drowning

Peter Cook 1937–95: Nigel Rees (ed.) *A Year of Stings and Squelches* (1985)

17 Her shrill contralto could be heard urging friend and foe to go over the top. There is a quality to that gritty voice which . . . amounts to the infliction of pain.
of Margaret Thatcher

Julian Critchley 1930–2000: Kenneth Harris *Thatcher* (1988)

18 I view this able and energetic man with some detachment. He is loyal to his own career but only incidentally to anything or anyone else.
of Richard Crossman

Hugh Dalton 1887–1962: diary 17 September 1941

19 The laugh in mourning.
of Eamonn de Valera

Oliver St John Gogarty 1878–1957: Ulick O'Connor *Oliver St John Gogarty* (1964)

20 The good thing about them is that you can look at them with the sound turned down.
of the Spice Girls

George Harrison 1943– : in *Independent* 28 August 1997

21 Peter Mandelson is someone who can skulk in broad daylight.

Simon Hoggart 1946– : in *Guardian* 10 July 1998

22 A First Minister whose self-righteous stubbornness has not been equalled, save briefly by Neville Chamberlain, since Lord North.
of Margaret Thatcher

Roy Jenkins 1920– : in *Observer* 11 March 1990

23 I'd rather be Frank Capra than God. If there is a Frank Capra.

Garson Kanin 1912–99: in *Times* 16 March 1999; attributed

24 It was like watching someone organize her own immortality. Every phrase and gesture was studied. Now and again, when she said something a little out of the ordinary, she wrote it down herself in a notebook.
of Virginia Woolf

Harold Laski 1893–1950: letter to Oliver Wendell Holmes, 30 November 1930

25 Many people see Eva Peron as either a saint or the incarnation of Satan. That means I can definitely identify with her.

Madonna 1958– : in *Newsweek* 5 February 1996

26 There were three things that Chico was always on—a phone, a horse or a broad.

Groucho Marx 1895–1977: Ned Sherrin *Cutting Edge* (1984)

27 Nothing ever made me more doubtful of T. E. Lawrence's genuineness than that he so heartily trusted two persons whom I knew to be bogus.

W. Somerset Maugham 1874–1965: *A Writer's Notebook* (1949) written in 1941

Asked if she really had nothing on in the [calendar] *photograph:*
28 I had the radio on.

Marilyn Monroe 1926–62: in *Time* 11 August 1952

29 The triumph of sugar over diabetes.
of J. M. Barrie

George Jean Nathan 1882–1958: Robin May *The Wit of the Theatre* (1969)

30 [James Joyce] has the most lovely voice I know—liquid and soft with undercurrents of gurgle.

Harold Nicolson 1886–1968: letter to his wife Vita Sackville-West, 4 February 1934

31 Her interest in native things and people was not healthy when demented Black and Tans were at large and unused to making fine distinctions.
   of Lady Gregory

Flann O'Brien 1911–66: *Myles Away from Dublin* (1990)

32 A big cat detained briefly in a poodle parlour, sharpening her claws on the velvet.
   of Lady Thatcher in the House of Lords

Matthew Parris 1949– : *Look Behind You!* (1993)

33 My name is Mandy: Peter B.
I'm back in charge—don't mess with me.
My cheeks are drawn, my face is bony,
The line I take comes straight from Tony.

Matthew Parris 1949– : in *Times* 21 October 1999; see **People** 3

34 An elderly fallen angel travelling incognito.
   of André Gide

Peter Quennell 1905– : *The Sign of the Fish* (1960)

35 Poor George, he can't help it—he was born with a silver foot in his mouth.
   of George Bush

Ann Richards 1933– : keynote speech at the Democratic convention, in *Independent* 20 July 1988

36 Any man who hates dogs and babies can't be all bad.
   of W. C. Fields, and often attributed to him

Leo Rosten 1908– : speech at Masquers' Club dinner, 16 February 1939

37 Through it all, I have remained consistently and nauseatingly adorable. In fact, I have been known to cause diabetes.

Meg Ryan 1961– : at Women in Hollywood luncheon, 1999

38 He [Macaulay] is like a book in breeches.

Sydney Smith 1771–1845: Lady Holland *Memoir* (1855)

39 Daniel Webster struck me much like a steam-engine in trousers.

Sydney Smith 1771–1845: Lady Holland *Memoir* (1855)

40 That great Cham of literature, Samuel Johnson.

Tobias Smollett 1721–71: letter to John Wilkes, 16 March 1759

41 Her conception of God was certainly not orthodox. She felt towards Him as she might have felt towards a glorified sanitary engineer; and in some of her speculations she seems hardly to distinguish between the Deity and the Drains.
   of Florence Nightingale

Lytton Strachey 1880–1932: *Eminent Victorians* (1918)

42 Every Prime Minister needs a Willie.
   at the farewell dinner for William Whitelaw

Margaret Thatcher 1925– : in *Guardian* 7 August 1991

43 Rupert's idea of a better world is a world that's better for Rupert.
   of Rupert Murdoch

Ted Turner 1938– : in *Daily Telegraph* 6 November 1997

44 [Charles Laughton] walks top-heavily, like a salmon standing on its tail.

Kenneth Tynan 1927–80: *Profiles* (ed. Kathleen Tynan, 1989)

45 Forty years ago he was Slightly in *Peter Pan*, and you might say that he has been wholly in *Peter Pan* ever since.
   of Noël Coward

Kenneth Tynan 1927–80: *Curtains* (1961)

46 A triumph of the embalmer's art.
   of Ronald Reagan

Gore Vidal 1925– : in *Observer* 26 April 1981

47 Of course, I believe in the Devil. How otherwise would I account for the existence of Lord Beaverbrook?

Evelyn Waugh 1903–66: L. Gourlay *The Beaverbrook I Knew* (1984) *to a gentleman who had accosted him in the street saying, 'Mr Jones, I believe?':*

48 If you believe that, you'll believe anything.

Duke of Wellington 1769–1852: Elizabeth Longford *Pillar of State* (1972); George Jones RA (1786–1869), painter of military subjects, bore a striking resemblance to Wellington

49 The only Greek Tragedy I know.
of Spyros Skouras, Head of Fox Studios

Billy Wilder 1906– : attributed, perhaps apocryphal

50 She is so odd a blend of Little Nell and Lady Macbeth. It is not so much the familiar phenomenon of a hand of steel in a velvet glove as a lacy sleeve with a bottle of vitriol concealed in its folds.
of Dorothy Parker

Alexander Woollcott 1887–1943: *While Rome Burns* (1934)

Peoples See **Countries and Peoples**

Personalities See **People and Personalities**

Philosophy

intervening at a New York party between Mike Tyson and Naomi Campbell:

1 TYSON: Do you know who the f— I am? I'm the heavyweight champion of the world.
AYER: And I am the former Wykeham Professor of Logic. We are both pre-eminent in our field. I suggest we talk about this like rational men.

A. J. Ayer 1910–89: Ben Rogers *A. J. Ayer: a Life* (1999)

2 To take a gloomy view of life is not part of my philosophy; to laugh at the idiocies of my fellow creatures is. However, at this particular moment I cannot find so much to laugh at as I would like.

Noël Coward 1899–1973: diary 21 July 1963

3 I have tried too in my time to be a philosopher; but, I don't know how, cheerfulness was always breaking in.

Oliver Edwards 1711–91: James Boswell *Life of Samuel Johnson* (1934 ed.) 17 April 1778

4 The philosopher is like a mountaineer who has with difficulty climbed a mountain for the sake of the sunrise, and arriving at the top finds only fog . . . He must be an honest man if he doesn't tell you that the spectacle was stupendous.

W. Somerset Maugham 1874–1965: *A Writer's Notebook* (1949) written in 1896

5 Philosophy consists very largely of one philosopher arguing that all others are jackasses. He usually proves it, and I should add that he usually proves that he is one himself.

H. L. Mencken 1880–1956: *Minority Report* (1956)

6 Apart from the known and the unknown, what else is there?

Harold Pinter 1930– : *The Homecoming* (1965)

7 Sometimes I sits and thinks, and then again I just sits.

Punch 1841–1992: vol. 131 (1906)

on the speaker's choice of subject at university:
8 Almost everyone who didn't know what to do, did philosophy. Well, that's logical.

Tom Stoppard 1937– : *Albert's Bridge* (1969)

9 The safest general characterization of the European philosophical tradition is that it consists of a series of footnotes to Plato.

Alfred North Whitehead 1861–1947: *Process and Reality* (1929)

10 What is your aim in philosophy?—To show the fly the way out of the fly-bottle.

Ludwig Wittgenstein 1889–1951: *Philosophische Untersuchungen* (1953)

Places See also **America, Countries, England, Ireland, Scotland, Towns and Cities, Wales**

1 Stayed at the Randolph at Oxford. It is always good to return to places in which one has been thoroughly miserable. I hated Oxford—the rudest, meanest, sub-normallest hole I have ever struck.

James Agate 1877–1947: diary, 26 April 1942

2 He was glued to Soho, a fairly common but chronic attachment some of us formed. There is no known cure for it except the road to Golders Green.

Jeffrey Bernard 1932–97: in *The Spectator* 8 March 1986

3 For Cambridge people rarely smile,
Being urban, squat, and packed with guile.

Rupert Brooke 1887–1915: 'The Old Vicarage, Grantchester' (1915)

4 I had forgotten just how flat and empty it [middle America] is. Stand on two phone books almost anywhere in Iowa and you get a view.

Bill Bryson 1951– : *The Lost Continent* (1989)

of Herat:
5 Here at last is Asia without an inferiority complex.

Robert Byron 1905–41: *The Road to Oxiana* (1937)

6 BASIL: May I ask what you were hoping to see out of a Torquay bedroom window? Sydney Opera House, perhaps? The Hanging Gardens of Babylon? Herds of wildebeeste sweeping majestically . . .

John Cleese 1939– and **Connie Booth**: *Fawlty Towers* (1979) 'Communication Problems'

7 Very flat, Norfolk.

Noël Coward 1899–1973: *Private Lives* (1930)

8 In Manhattan, every flat surface is a potential stage and every inattentive waiter an unemployed, possibly unemployable, actor.

Quentin Crisp 1908–99: 'Love Lies Bleeding' (Channel 4 TV), 6 August 1991; Nigel Rees (ed.) *Cassell Dictionary of Humorous Quotations* (1999)

9 Kent, sir—everybody knows Kent—apples, cherries, hops, and women.

Charles Dickens 1812–70: *Pickwick Papers* (1837)

10 There's a famous seaside place called Blackpool,
That's noted for fresh air and fun,
And Mr and Mrs Ramsbottom
Went there with young Albert, their son.

Marriott Edgar 1880–1951: 'The Lion and Albert' (1932)

11 Mulberry Garden, now the only place of refreshment about the town for persons of the best quality to be exceedingly cheated at.

John Evelyn 1620–1706: diary 10 May 1654

12 They used to say that Cambridge was the first stopping place for the wind that swept down from the Urals: in the thirties that was as true of the politics as the weather.

Stephen Fry 1957– : *The Liar* (1991)

13 The Pacific Ocean was a body of water surrounded on all sides by elephantiasis and other dread diseases.

Joseph Heller 1923–99: *Catch-22* (1961)

14 I ascertained by looking down from Wenlock Edge that
Hughley Church could not have had much of a steeple.
But as I had already composed the poem and could not
invent another name that sounded so nice, I could only
deplore that the church at Hughley should follow the bad
example of the church at Brou, which persists in standing
on a plain after Matthew Arnold has said that it stands
among mountains.

A. E. Housman 1859–1936: letter to
Laurence Housman, 5 October 1896

15 The [Sydney] Opera House is a dud . . . It looks like a
portable typewriter full of oyster shells, and to the
contention that it echoes the sails of yachts on the harbour
I can only point out that the yachts on the harbour don't
waste any time echoing opera houses.

Clive James 1939– : *Flying Visits*
(1984)

16 Broadbosomed, bold, becalm'd, benign
Lies Balham foursquare on the Northern Line.
Matched by no marvel save in Eastern scene,
A rose-red city half as gold as green.

Frank Muir 1920–98 and **Denis
Norden** 1922– : 'Balham—Gateway
to the South' *Third Division* (BBC
Third Programme, 1948); Nigel Rees
(ed.) *Cassell Dictionary of Humorous
Quotations* (1999)

17 The lush pastrami beds of the West Forties knew him not.

S. J. Perelman 1904–79: 'The
Swirling Cape and the Low Bow'

18 Addresses are given to us to conceal our whereabouts.

Saki 1870–1916: *Reginald in Russia*
(1910)

19 Wensleydale lies between Tuesleydale and Thursleydale.

Arthur Smith 1954– : attributed

Poetry See also **Literature, Poets, Writers and
Writing**

1 There was a young man called MacNabbiter
Who had an organ of prodigious diameter.
But it was not the size
That gave girls the surprise,
'Twas his rhythm—Iambic Pentameter.

Anonymous: in *Ned Sherrin in his
Anecdotage* (1993)

2 There was a young man from Peru
Whose limericks stopped at line two.

Anonymous: Harry Mathews and
Alastair Brotchie (eds) *Oulipo
Compendium* (1998)

3 Poetry is the only art people haven't yet learnt to consume
like soup.

W. H. Auden 1907–73: in *New York
Times* 1960

4 I have but with some difficulty *not* added any more to this
snake of a poem [*The Giaour*]—which has been
lengthening its rattles every month.

Lord Byron 1788–1824: letter 26
August 1813

5 'I can repeat poetry as well as other folk if it comes to
that—' 'Oh, it needn't come to that!' Alice hastily said.

Lewis Carroll 1832–98: *Through the
Looking-Glass* (1872)

6 'By God,' quod he, 'for pleynly, at a word,
Thy drasty rymyng is nat worth a toord!'

Geoffrey Chaucer c.1343–1400: *The
Canterbury Tales* 'Sir Thopas'

7 Sometimes poetry is emotion recollected in a highly
emotional state.

Wendy Cope 1945– : 'An Argument
with Wordsworth' (1992)

*Laman Blanchard, a young poet, had submitted some verses
entitled 'Orient Pearls at Random Strung' to* Household Words:
8 Dear Blanchard, too much string—Yours. C.D.

Charles Dickens 1812–70: Frederick
Locker-Lampson *My Confidences*
(1896)

9 So poetry, which is in Oxford made
   An art, in London only is a trade.

John Dryden 1631–1700: 'Prologue
to the University of Oxon . . . at the
Acting of *The Silent Woman*' (1673)

10 Immature poets imitate; mature poets steal.

T. S. Eliot 1888–1965: *The Sacred
Wood* (1920) 'Philip Massinger'

11 I'd as soon write free verse as play tennis with the net
   down.

Robert Frost 1874–1963: Edward
Lathem *Interviews with Robert Frost*
(1966)

12 There are the women whose husbands I meet on
      aeroplanes
   Who close their briefcases and ask, 'What are *you* in?'
   I look in their eyes, I tell them I am in poetry . . . .

Donald Hall 1928– : 'To a
Waterfowl' (1971)

13 I did not begin to write poetry in earnest until the really
   emotional part of my life was over; and my poetry, so far
   as I could make out, sprang chiefly from physical
   conditions, such as a relaxed sore throat during my most
   prolific period.

A. E. Housman 1859–1936: letter, 5
February 1933

14 Mr Stone's hexameters are verses of no sort, but prose in
   ribands.

A. E. Housman 1859–1936: in
Classical Review 1899

of a poetry reading:
15 The audience swelled to six in the end and we all huddled
   in a corner.

P. J. Kavanagh 1931– : in *The
Spectator* 5 December 1992

16 The notion of expressing sentiments in short lines having
   similar sounds at their ends seems as remote as mangoes
   on the moon.

Philip Larkin 1922–85: letter to
Barbara Pym, 22 January 1975

17 Writing a book of poetry is like dropping a rose petal down
   the Grand Canyon and waiting for the echo.

Don Marquis 1878–1937: E. Anthony
O Rare Don Marquis (1962)

18 My favourite poem is the one that starts 'Thirty days hath
   September' because it actually tells you something.

Groucho Marx 1895–1977: Ned
Sherrin *Cutting Edge* (1984);
attributed

19 All that is not prose is verse; and all that is not verse is
   prose.

Molière 1622–73: *Le Bourgeois
Gentilhomme* (1671)

20 M. JOURDAIN: What? when I say: 'Nicole, bring me my
      slippers, and give me my night-cap,' is that prose?
   PHILOSOPHY TEACHER: Yes, Sir.
   M. JOURDAIN: Good heavens! For more than forty years I
      have been speaking prose without knowing it.

Molière 1622–73: *Le Bourgeois
Gentilhomme* (1671)

21 And he, whose fustian's so sublimely bad,
   It is not poetry, but prose run mad.

Alexander Pope 1688–1744: 'An
Epistle to Dr Arbuthnot' (1735)

22 Of all the literary scenes
   Saddest this sight to me:
   The graves of little magazines
   Who died to make verse free.

Keith Preston 1884–1927: 'The
Liberators'

23 I picture him as short and tan.
We'd meet, perhaps, in Hindustan.
I'd say, with admirable *élan*,
'Ah, Anantanarayanan—'.

John Updike 1932– : 'I Missed His Book, But I Read His Name' (1964)

24 All bad poetry springs from genuine feeling.

Oscar Wilde 1854–1900: 'The Critic as Artist' (1891)

25 Peotry is sissy stuff that rhymes. Weedy people sa la and fie and swoon when they see a bunch of daffodils.

Geoffrey Willans 1911–58 and **Ronald Searle** 1920– : *Down with Skool!* (1953)

Poets See also **Poetry**

1 The Edinburgh praises Jack Keats or Ketch or whatever his names are;—why his is the Onanism of poetry.

Lord Byron 1788–1824: letter to his publisher John Murray, 4 November 1820

2 I used to think all poets were Byronic —
Mad, bad and dangerous to know.
And then I met a few. Yes it's ironic —
I used to think all poets were Byronic.
They're mostly wicked as a ginless tonic
And wild as pension plans.

Wendy Cope 1945– : 'Triolet' (1986)

the young Stephen Spender had told Eliot of his wish to become a poet:
3 I can understand your wanting to write poems, but I don't quite know what you mean by 'being a poet' . . .

T. S. Eliot 1888–1965: Stephen Spender *World within World* (1951)

4 Osbert was wonderful, as you would expect, and Edith, of course, but then we had this rather lugubrious man in a suit, and he read a poem . . . I think it was called The Desert. And first the girls got the giggles and then I did and then even the King.
of an evening at Windsor during the war, arranged by Osbert Sitwell, at which T. S. Eliot read from 'The Waste Land' to the King and Queen and the Princesses

Queen Elizabeth, the Queen Mother 1900– : private conversation, reported in *Spectator* 30 June 1990

5 What is a modern poet's fate?
To write his thoughts upon a slate;
The critic spits on what is done,
Gives it a wipe—and all is gone.

Thomas Hood 1799–1845: 'A Joke', in Hallam Tennyson *Alfred Lord Tennyson* (1897); not found in Hood's *Complete Works*

a nineteenth-century headmaster of Eton:
6 I wish Shelley had been at Harrow.

James John Hornby 1826–1909: Henry S. Salt *Percy Bysshe Shelley* (1896)

7 In barrenness, at any rate, I hold a high place among English poets, excelling even Gray.

A. E. Housman 1859–1936: letter 28 February 1910

8 Dr Donne's verses are like the peace of God; they pass all understanding.

James I 1566–1625: remark recorded by Archdeacon Plume (1630–1704)

on the relative merits of two minor poets:
9 Sir, there is no settling the point of precedency between a louse and a flea.

Samuel Johnson 1709–84: James Boswell *Life of Samuel Johnson* (1791) 1783

10 We had the old crow over at Hull recently, looking like a Christmas present from Easter Island.

Philip Larkin 1922–85: letter, 1975

on being asked by Stephen Spender in the 1930s how best a poet could serve the Communist cause:

11 Go to Spain and get killed. The movement needs a Byron.

Harry Pollitt 1890–1960: Frank Johnson *Out of Order* (1982); attributed, perhaps apocryphal

12 While pensive poets painful vigils keep,
Sleepless themselves, to give their readers sleep.

Alexander Pope 1688–1744: *The Dunciad* (1742)

13 Sir, I admit your gen'ral rule
That every poet is a fool:
But you yourself may serve to show it,
That every fool is not a poet.

Alexander Pope 1688–1744: 'Epigram from the French' (1732)

14 For years a secret shame destroyed my peace—
I'd not read Eliot, Auden or MacNeice.
But then I had a thought that brought me hope—
Neither had Chaucer, Shakespeare, Milton, Pope.

Justin Richardson: 'Take Heart, Illiterates' (1966)

15 I made my then famous declaration (among 100 people) 'I am a Socialist, an Atheist and a Vegetarian' (ergo, a true Shelleyan), whereupon two ladies who had been palpitating with enthusiasm for Shelley under the impression that he was a devout Anglican, resigned on the spot.

George Bernard Shaw 1856–1950: letter 1 March 1908

16 Life's a curse, love's a blight, God's a blaggard, cherry blossom is quite nice.
on A. E. Housman

Tom Stoppard 1937– : *The Invention of Love* (1997)

17 I may as well tell you, here and now, that if you are going about the place thinking things pretty, you will never make a modern poet. Be poignant, man, be poignant!

P. G. Wodehouse 1881–1975: *The Small Bachelor* (1927)

Political Parties

1 CHILD: Mamma, are Tories born wicked, or do they grow wicked afterwards?
MOTHER: They are born wicked, and grow worse.

Anonymous: G. W. E. Russell *Collections and Recollections* (1898)

2 A liberal is a man who leaves the room before the fight begins.

Heywood Broun 1888–1939: R. E. Drennan *Wit's End* (1973)

3 Anyone in the Labour Party hierarchy who believes that New Labour is popular in Scotland should get out more.
after Labour was beaten into third place in the Ayr by-election for the Scottish Parliament

Ian Davidson 1950– : in *Scotsman* 18 March 2000

4 'A sound Conservative government,' said Taper, musingly. 'I understand: Tory men and Whig measures.'

Benjamin Disraeli 1804–81: *Coningsby* (1844)

5 The right hon. Gentleman caught the Whigs bathing, and walked away with their clothes.
on Sir Robert Peel's abandoning protection in favour of free trade, traditionally the policy of the [Whig] Opposition

Benjamin Disraeli 1804–81: speech, House of Commons 28 February 1845

6 I did not vote Labour because they've heard of Oasis and nobody is going to vote Tory because William Hague has got a baseball cap.

Ben Elton 1959– : in *Radio Times* 18 April 1998

7 I never dared be radical when young
For fear it would make me conservative when old.

Robert Frost 1874–1963: 'Precaution' (1936)

8 I often think it's comical
How Nature always does contrive
That every boy and every gal,
That's born into the world alive,
Is either a little Liberal,
Or else a little Conservative!

W. S. Gilbert 1836–1911: *Iolanthe* (1882)

9 Conservatives do not believe that the political struggle is the most important thing in life . . . The simplest of them prefer fox-hunting—the wisest religion.

Lord Hailsham 1907– : *The Case for Conservatism* (1947)

at a photocall when Lady Thatcher said to him 'You should be on my right':
10 That would be difficult.

Edward Heath 1916– : in *Times* 24 April 1999 'Quotes of the Week'

11 Testators would do well to provide some indication of the particular Liberal Party which they have in mind, such as a telephone number or a Christian name.

A. P. Herbert 1890–1971: *Misleading Cases* (1935)

12 The Tory Party only panics in a crisis.

Iain Macleod 1913–70: attributed

13 Labour is led by an upper-class public school man, the Tories by a self-made grammar school lass who worships her creator, though she is democratic enough to talk down to anyone.

Austin Mitchell 1934– : *Westminster Man* (1982)

14 The problem with New Labour is that they drink too much coffee, so they are always thinking up stupid ideas. Ordinary people have got a pint in hand and not a thought in their heads, and that's the way it should be.

Al Murray: in *Observer* 16 April 2000

15 I have only one firm belief about the American political system, and that is this: God is a Republican and Santa Claus is a Democrat.

P. J. O'Rourke 1947– : *Parliament of Whores* (1991)

on the contest for the Labour leadership, during a debate between himself, Tony Blair, and Margaret Beckett:
16 We're in danger of loving ourselves to death.

John Prescott 1938– : in *Observer* 19 June 1994 'Sayings of the Week'

17 Tory and Whig in turns shall be my host,
I taste no politics in boiled and roast.

Sydney Smith 1771–1845: letter to John Murray, November 1834

18 I like a lot of Republicans . . . Indeed, there are some I would trust with anything—anything, that is, except public office.

Adlai Stevenson 1900–65: in *New York Times* 15 August 1952

19 The Labour Party is going around stirring up apathy.

William Whitelaw 1918–99: recalled by Alan Watkins as a characteristic 'Willieism', in *Observer* 1 May 1983

20 The average footslogger in the New South Wales Right . . . generally speaking carries a dagger in one hand and a Bible in the other and doesn't put either to really elegant use.

Neville Wran 1926– : in 1973; Michael Gordon *A Question of Leadership* (1993)

Politicians See also **People and Personalities, Politics, Presidents, Prime Ministers**

1 In good King Charles's golden days,
When loyalty no harm meant;
A furious High-Churchman I was,

Anonymous: *British Musical Miscellany* (1734) 'The Vicar of Bray'

And so I gained preferment.
Unto my flock I daily preached,
Kings are by God appointed,
And damned are those who dare resist,
Or touch the Lord's Anointed.
And this is law, I will maintain,
Unto my dying day, Sir,
That whatsoever King shall reign,
I will be the Vicar of Bray, sir!

2 They [parliament] are a lot of hard-faced men who look as if they had done very well out of the war.

Stanley Baldwin 1867–1947: J. M. Keynes *Economic Consequences of the Peace* (1919)

3 Beaverbrook is so pleased to be in the Government that he is like the town tart who has finally married the Mayor!

Beverley Baxter 1891–1964: Chips Channon diary 12 June 1940

4 I am the very master of the multipurpose metaphor,
I put them into speeches which I always feel the better for.
The speed of my delivery is totally vehicular,
I'm burning with a passion about nothing in particular.
I'm well acquainted too with matters technological,
I'm able to explain myself in phrases tautological.
My language is poetical and full of hidden promises . . .
It's like the raging torrent of a thousand Dylan Thomases.

Alistair Beaton: 'I am the very Model . . . ', sung by Pooh-Bach (*Minister for everything else. Formerly Neil Kinnock*) in Ned Sherrin and Alistair Beaton *The Metropolitan Mikado* (1985)

5 Always threatening resignation, he never signed off.
of Lord Derby

Lord Beaverbrook 1879–1964: *Men and Power* (1956)

6 Sir! you have disappointed us!
We had intended you to be
The next Prime Minister but three:
The stocks were sold; the Press was squared;
The Middle Class was quite prepared.
But as it is! . . . My language fails!
Go out and govern New South Wales!

Hilaire Belloc 1870–1953: 'Lord Lundy' (1907)

7 I am not going to spend any time whatsoever in attacking the Foreign Secretary . . . If we complain about the tune, there is no reason to attack the monkey when the organ grinder is present.

Aneurin Bevan 1897–1960: during a debate on the Suez crisis, House of Commons 16 May 1957

8 The right kind of leader for the Labour Party . . . a desiccated calculating machine.
generally taken as referring to Hugh Gaitskell, although Bevan specifically denied it in an interview with Robin Day on 28 April 1959

Aneurin Bevan 1897–1960: Michael Foot *Aneurin Bevan* (1973) vol. 2

Attlee is said to have remarked that Herbert Morrison was his own worst enemy:
9 Not while I'm alive he ain't.

Ernest Bevin 1881–1951: Paul Johnson (ed.) *The Oxford Book of Political Anecdotes* (1986), introduction; also attributed to Bevin of Aneurin Bevan

of the popularity of Margaret Thatcher:
10 The further you got from Britain, the more admired you found she was.

James Callaghan 1912– : in *Spectator* 1 December 1990

11 Labour spin doctors aren't supposed to like Tory MPs. But Alan Clark was an exceptional man.

Alastair Campbell 1957- : in *Daily Mirror* 8 September 1999

12 QUESTION: What are the desirable qualifications for any young man who wishes to become a politician?
MR CHURCHILL: It is the ability to foretell what is going to happen tomorrow, next week, next month, and next year. And to have the ability afterwards to explain why it didn't happen.

Winston Churchill 1874–1965: B. Adler *Churchill Wit* (1965)

13 There but for the grace of God, goes God.
of Stafford Cripps

Winston Churchill 1874–1965: P. Brendon *Churchill* (1984)

14 a politician is an arse upon
which everyone has sat except a man.

e. e. cummings 1894–1962: *1 x 1* (1944)

15 My family was in politics while de Valera's was still bartering budgerigars in the back streets of Barcelona.

James Dillon 1902- : comment of the leader of Fine Gael, 1950s

16 It is not necessary that every time he rises he should give his famous imitation of a semi-house-trained polecat.
of Norman Tebbit

Michael Foot 1913- : speech in the House of Commons 2 March 1978

17 The Liberal Democrat leader [Charles Kennedy] has gone in a few short weeks from *Have I got News for You* to *I'm Sorry I Haven't a Clue*.

William Hague 1961- : in *Sunday Times* 21 November 1999

on being asked immediately after the Munich crisis if he were not worn out by the late nights:
18 No, not exactly. But it spoils one's eye for the high birds.

Lord Halifax 1881–1959: Paul Johnson (ed.) *The Oxford Book of Political Anecdotes* (1986)

19 Rum fellow, that Saddam [Hussein]. He's wearing an Eton Ramblers' tie.

Lord Home 1903- : while watching television; in *Ned Sherrin in his Anecdotage* (1993)

20 To represent Chamberlain as an injured man, and Balfour as the man who injured him, is like saying that Christ crucified Pontius Pilate.

A. E. Housman 1859–1936: letter 7 December 1922

21 The rich man's Roosevelt, the simple barefoot boy from Wall Street.
of Wendell Willkie, Republican presidential candidate in 1940

Harold Ickes 1874–1952: Leon Harris *The Fine Art of Political Wit* (1965)

22 He [Aneurin Bevan] enjoys prophesying the imminent fall of the capitalist system and is prepared to play a part, any part, in its burial, except that of mute.

Harold Macmillan 1894–1986: Michael Foot *Aneurin Bevan* (1962)

23 did you ever
notice that when
a politician
does get an idea
he usually
gets it all wrong.

Don Marquis 1878–1937: *archys life of mehitabel* (1933) 'archygrams'

24 He had the geniality of the politician who for years has gone out of his way to be cordial with everyone he meets.

W. Somerset Maugham 1874–1965: *A Writer's Notebook* (1949) written in 1938

25 If I saw Mr Haughey buried at midnight at a crossroads, with a stake driven through his heart—politically speaking—I should continue to wear a clove of garlic round my neck, just in case.

Conor Cruise O'Brien 1917- : in *Observer* 10 October 1982

26 DEMOSTHENES: The Athenians will kill thee, Phocion, should they go crazy.
PHOCION: But they will kill thee, should they come to their senses.

Phocion c.402–317 BC: Plutarch *Life of Phocion and Cato the Younger* (Loeb ed., 1919)

27 Gordon Brown is a bit like someone who takes great pride in how clean they leave the washing up, hoping we won't notice that they break and throw away all the really dirty plates and cups.

John Redwood 1951- : in *Observer* 7 May 2000 'They said what . . . ?'

28 He may be a son of a bitch, but he's our son of a bitch.
on President Somoza of Nicaragua, 1938

Franklin D. Roosevelt 1882–1945: Jonathon Green *The Book of Political Quotes* (1982)

29 I wouldn't vote for Ken Livingstone if he were running for Mayor of Toytown.

Arthur Scargill 1938- : in *Observer* 7 May 2000 'They said what . . . ?'

30 He didn't inhale, he didn't insert. He won't invade.
on Bill Clinton and Kosovo

Neil Shand: *Loose Ends* monologue, 1999

31 Austen [Chamberlain] always played the game, and he always lost it.

F. E. Smith 1872–1930: Lord Beaverbrook *Men and Power* (1956)

32 In his final desperate bid for a place in history, the Commander-in-Chief is in danger of finding he's got all the qualities of leadership except followers.
on Bill Clinton and Kosovo

Mark Steyn: in *Spectator* 17 April 1999

33 A politician is a man who understands government, and it takes a politician to run a government. A statesman is a politician who's been dead 10 or 15 years.

Harry S. Truman 1884–1972: in *New York World Telegram and Sun* 12 April 1958

34 The sad truth is that sunny, sensuous Edith was not up to the dossiers.
on Edith Cresson

George Walden 1939- : *Lucky George: Memoirs of an Anti-Politician* (1999)

35 A man whose ultimate priorities in life are books, trees and women cannot be all bad.
on François Mitterrand

George Walden 1939- : *Lucky George: Memoirs of an Anti-Politician* (1999)

of watching Harold Macmillan in operation:
36 Like watching a play by Harley Granville-Barker—you expected it to be passé Edwardian stuff and were agreeably surprised to get so much sense and entertainment from such a dated decor.

George Walden 1939- : *Lucky George* (1999)

37 There he sits, like a very old beast of the jungle or veldt, turning his great sad eyes now this way, now that, in an attempt to locate his enemies, and contemplating the while whether to take evasive action or mount a counter-attack.
of William Whitelaw at the Conservative Party Conference

Alan Watkins 1933- : in *Observer* 10 October 1982

38 I never saw so many shocking bad hats in my life.
on seeing the first Reformed Parliament

Duke of Wellington 1769–1852: W. Fraser *Words on Wellington* (1889)

39 If the country doesn't go to the dogs or the Radicals, we shall have you Prime Minister, some day.

Oscar Wilde 1854–1900: *An Ideal Husband* (1895)

Politics   See also **Democracy, Diplomacy, Government, Political Parties, Politicians, Presidents, Prime Ministers**

1 Being an MP is the sort of job all working-class parents want for their children—clean, indoors and no heavy lifting.

Diane Abbott 1953– : in *Observer* 30 January 1994 'Sayings of the Week'

2 When the political columnists say 'Every thinking man' they mean themselves, and when candidates appeal to 'Every intelligent voter' they mean everybody who is going to vote for them.

Franklin P. Adams 1881–1960: *Nods and Becks* (1944)

3 Practical politics consists in ignoring facts.

Henry Brooks Adams 1838–1918: *The Education of Henry Adams* (1907)

annotation to a ministerial brief, said to have been read out inadvertently in the House of Lords:
4 This is a rotten argument, but it should be good enough for their lordships on a hot summer afternoon.

Anonymous: Lord Home *The Way the Wind Blows* (1976)

5 Revolutions are not made with rosewater.

Anonymous: used by Disraeli in a speech at High Wycombe in 1847; Hesketh Pearson *Dizzy* (1951)

6 *Je suis Marxiste—tendance Groucho.*
I am a Marxist—of the Groucho tendency.

Anonymous: slogan found at Nanterre in Paris, 1968

7 [The War Office kept three sets of figures:] one to mislead the public, another to mislead the Cabinet, and the third to mislead itself.

Herbert Asquith 1852–1928: Alistair Horne *Price of Glory* (1962)

8 From politics, it was an easy step to silence.

Jane Austen 1775–1817: *Northanger Abbey* (1818)

9 There are three classes which need sanctuary more than others—birds, wild flowers, and Prime Ministers.

Stanley Baldwin 1867–1947: in *Observer* 24 May 1925

10 Vote for the man who promises least; he'll be the least disappointing.

Bernard Baruch 1870–1965: Meyer Berger *New York* (1960)

11 Damn it all, you can't have the crown of thorns *and* the thirty pieces of silver.
on his position in the Labour Party, c.1956

Aneurin Bevan 1897–1960: Michael Foot *Aneurin Bevan* (1973) vol. 2

12 There are two ways of getting into the Cabinet—you can crawl in or kick your way in.

Aneurin Bevan 1897–1960: attributed

13 A strife of interests masquerading as a contest of principles. The conduct of public affairs for private advantage.

Ambrose Bierce 1842–c.1914: *The Enlarged Devil's Dictionary* (1967)

14 A statesman who is enamoured of existing evils, as distinguished from the Liberal, who wishes to replace them with others.

Ambrose Bierce 1842–c.1914: definition of a Conservative; *The Cynic's Word Book* (1906)

15 My God! They've shot our fox!
on hearing of the resignation of Hugh Dalton, Chancellor of the Exchequer in the Labour Government, after a leakage of Budget secrets

Nigel Birch 1906–81: on 13 November 1947

16 Have you ever seen a candidate talking to a rich person on television?

Art Buchwald 1925– : Laurence J. Peter (ed.) *Quotations for our Time* (1977)

17 The US presidency is a Tudor monarchy plus telephones.

Anthony Burgess 1917–93: George Plimpton (ed.) *Writers at Work* 4th Series (1977)

18 In politics you must always keep running with the pack. The moment that you falter and they sense that you are injured, the rest will turn on you like wolves.

R. A. Butler 1902–82: Dennis Walters *Not Always with the Pack* (1989)

19 I have no consistency, except in politics; and *that* probably arises from my indifference on the subject altogether.

Lord Byron 1788–1824: letter, 16 January 1814

to Franklin Roosevelt on the likely duration of the Yalta conference with Stalin:

20 I do not see any other way of realizing our hopes about World Organization in five or six days. Even the Almighty took seven.

Winston Churchill 1874–1965: *The Second World War* (1954) vol. 6

21 Politics are almost as exciting as war and quite as dangerous. In war you can only be killed once, but in politics—many times.

Winston Churchill 1874–1965: attributed

22 There are no true friends in politics. We are all sharks circling, and waiting, for traces of blood to appear in the water.

Alan Clark 1928–99: diary, 30 November 1990

23 There's nothing so improves the mood of the Party as the imminent execution of a senior colleague.

Alan Clark 1928–99: diary 13 July 1990

24 Safe is spelled D-U-L-L. Politics has got to be a fun activity. *on being selected as parliamentary candidate for Kensington and Chelsea, 24 January 1997*

Alan Clark 1928–99: in *Daily Telegraph* 25 January 1997

25 M is for Marx
And Movement of Masses
And Massing of Arses.
And Clashing of Classes.

Cyril Connolly 1903–74: 'Where Engels Fears to Tread'

26 The only safe pleasure for a parliamentarian is a bag of boiled sweets.

Julian Critchley 1930–2000: in *Listener* 10 June 1982

27 The duty of an Opposition [is] very simple . . . to oppose everything, and propose nothing.

Lord Derby 1799–1869: quoting 'Mr Tierney, a great Whig authority'; House of Lords 4 June 1841

28 'It's always best on these occasions to do what the mob do.' 'But suppose there are two mobs?' suggested Mr Snodgrass. 'Shout with the largest,' replied Mr Pickwick.

Charles Dickens 1812–70: *Pickwick Papers* (1837)

29 'I am all for a religious cry,' said Taper. 'It means nothing, and, if successful, does not interfere with business when we are in.'

Benjamin Disraeli 1804–81: *Coningsby* (1844)

30 Men destined to the highest places should beware of badinage . . . An insular country subject to fogs, and with a powerful middle class, requires grave statesmen.

Benjamin Disraeli 1804–81: *Endymion* (1880)

31 Politics has everything you could want to throw into a novel, from the sordid to the sublime and the plain silly. You take reality and then water it down, just to make it credible.

Michael Dobbs 1948– : in *Observer* 7 May 2000 'They said what . . . ?'

32 Think of it! A second Chamber selected by the Whips. A seraglio of eunuchs.

Michael Foot 1913– : speech in the House of Commons 3 February 1969

33 The prospect of a lot
Of dull MPs in close proximity,
All thinking for themselves is what
No man can face with equanimity.

W. S. Gilbert 1836–1911: *Iolanthe* (1882)

34 When in that House MPs divide,
If they've a brain and cerebellum too,
They have to leave that brain outside,
And vote just as their leaders tell 'em to.

W. S. Gilbert 1836–1911: *Iolanthe* (1882)

35 Once the toothpaste is out of the tube, it is awfully hard to get it back in.

H. R. Haldeman 1929–93: to John Dean; *Hearings Before the Select Committee on Presidential Campaign Activities of US Senate: Watergate and Related Activities* (1973)

36 Fat filibusterers begat
Income tax adjusterers begat
'Twas Natchaler and Natchaler to Begat
And sometimes a bachelor, he begat . . .

E. Y. Harburg 1898–1981: 'The Begat' (1947)

37 DEALER: How about Dave Zimmerman?
BEN: Davie's too bright.
2: What about Walt Gustafson?
BEN: Walt died last night.
3:How about Frank Monohan?
4: What about George Gale?
BEN: Frank ain't a citizen
And George is in jail.
5: We could run Al Wallenstein.
BEN: He's only twenty three.
DEALER: How about Ed Peterson?
2: You idiot, that's me!
ALL: Politics and Poker . . .

Sheldon Harnick 1924– : 'Politics and Poker' (1959)

38 I cannot and will not cut my conscience to fit this year's fashions.

Lillian Hellman 1905–84: letter to John S. Wood, 19 May 1952, in *US Congress Committee Hearing on Un-American Activities* (1952)

39 A little rebellion now and then is a good thing.

Thomas Jefferson 1743–1826: letter to James Madison, 30 January 1787

40 BOSWELL: So, Sir, you laugh at schemes of political improvement.
JOHNSON: Why, Sir, most schemes of political improvement are very laughable things.

Samuel Johnson 1709–84: James Boswell *Life of Samuel Johnson* (1791) 26 October 1769

41 Gratitude is not a normal feature of political life.

Lord Kilmuir 1900–67: *Political Adventure* (1964)

42 Since when was fastidiousness a quality useful for political advancement?

Bernard Levin 1928– : *If You Want My Opinion* (1992)

43 If voting changed anything they'd abolish it.

Ken Livingstone 1945– : in *Independent* 12 April 1996

44 If you want to succeed in politics, you must keep your conscience well under control.

David Lloyd George 1863–1945: Lord Riddell diary 23 April 1919

45 As usual the Liberals offer a mixture of sound and original ideas. Unfortunately none of the sound ideas is original and none of the original ideas is sound.

Harold Macmillan 1894–1986: speech to London Conservatives, 7 March 1961

on privatization:

46 First of all the Georgian silver goes, and then all that nice furniture that used to be in the saloon. Then the Canalettos go.

Harold Macmillan 1894–1986: speech to the Tory Reform Group, 8 November 1985

statement at London airport on leaving for a Commonwealth tour, 7 January 1958, following the resignation of the Chancellor of the Exchequer and others:

47 I thought the best thing to do was to settle up these little local difficulties, and then turn to the wider vision of the Commonwealth.

Harold Macmillan 1894–1986: in *The Times* 8 January 1958

48 It has always seemed to me more artistic, when the curtain falls on the last performance, to accept the inevitable *E finita la commedia.* It is tempting, perhaps, but unrewarding to hang about the greenroom after final retirement from the stage.

Harold Macmillan 1894–1986: *At the End of the Day* (1973)

49 There are three bodies no sensible man directly challenges: the Roman Catholic Church, the Brigade of Guards and the National Union of Mineworkers.

Harold Macmillan 1894–1986: in *Observer* 22 February 1981

50 I have never found in a long experience of politics that criticism is ever inhibited by ignorance.

Harold Macmillan 1894–1986: Leon Harris *The Fine Art of Politcal Wit* (1965)

51 As socialists we want a socialist world not because we have the conceit that men would thereby be more happy . . . but because we feel the moral imperative in life itself to raise the human condition even if this should ultimately mean no more than that man's suffering has been lifted to a higher level.

Norman Mailer 1923– : 'David Riesman Reconsidered' (1954)

52 Welcome to Britain's New Political Order. No passion . . . No Right. No Left. Just multi-hued blancmange.

Austin Mitchell 1934– : in *Observer* 11 April 1999 'Sayings of the Week'

53 I thought you were the original professor of rotational medicine.
  to Bernard Ingham, who was appearing before the Commons public administration select committee

Rhodri Morgan 1939– : in *Mail on Sunday* 7 June 1998 'Quotes of the Week'

54 I'm not going to rearrange the furniture on the deck of the Titanic.
  having lost five of the last six primaries as President Ford's campaign manager

Rogers Morton 1914–79: in *Washington Post* 16 May 1976

55 Politics is the diversion of trivial men who, when they succeed at it, become important in the eyes of more trivial men.

George Jean Nathan 1882–1958: attributed

Nigel Nicolson, who in 1956 abstained from voting with the Government on the Suez Crisis and subsequently lost his seat, reflecting on the Maastricht vote:

56 One final tip to rebels: always have a second profession in reserve.

Nigel Nicolson 1917– : in *The Spectator* 7 November 1992

57 I will be sad if I either look up or down after my death and don't see my son fast asleep on the same benches on which I have slept.

Lord Onslow 1938– : in *Times* 31 October 1998 'Quotes of the Week'

58 Politics are, like God's infinite mercy, a last resort.

P. J. O'Rourke 1947– : *Parliament of Whores* (1991)

59 Men enter local politics solely as a result of being unhappily married.

C. Northcote Parkinson 1909–93: *Parkinson's Law* (1958)

60 Being an MP feeds your vanity and starves your self-respect.

Matthew Parris 1949– : in *The Times* 9 February 1994

61 Why waste it on some vanilla-flavoured pixie. Bring on the fruitcakes, we want a fruitcake for an unlosable seat. They enliven the Commons.
the day before the Kensington and Chelsea association chose Alan Clark as their parliamentary candidate

Matthew Parris 1949– : in *Mail on Sunday* 26 January 1997

62 Politics is supposed to be the second oldest profession. I have come to realize that it bears a very close resemblance to the first.

Ronald Reagan 1911– : at a conference in Los Angeles, 2 March 1977

63 The more you read and observe about this Politics thing, you got to admit that each party is worse than the other.

Will Rogers 1879–1935: *The Illiterate Digest* (1924)

64 It's not cricket to picket.

Harold Rome 1908– : song-title (1937)

65 Sing us a song
Of social significance.
All other tunes are taboo
It must be packed with social fact
Or we won't love you!

Harold Rome 1908– : 'Sing a Song of Social Significance' (1937)

66 He knows nothing; and he thinks he knows everything. That points clearly to a political career.

George Bernard Shaw 1856–1950: *Major Barbara* (1907)

67 Anarchism is a game at which the police can beat you.

George Bernard Shaw 1856–1950: *Misalliance* (1914)

68 Nature has no cure for this sort of madness [Bolshevism], though I have known a legacy from a rich relative work wonders.

F. E. Smith 1872–1930: *Law, Life and Letters* (1927)

69 Minorities . . . are almost always in the right.

Sydney Smith 1771–1845: H. Pearson *The Smith of Smiths* (1934)

on the quality of debate in the House of Lords:
70 It is, I think, good evidence of life after death.

Donald Soper 1903–98: in *Listener* 17 August 1978

71 An independent is a guy who wants to take the politics out of politics.

Adlai Stevenson 1900–65: Bill Adler *The Stevenson Wit* (1966)

72 I will make a bargain with the Republicans. If they will stop telling lies about Democrats, we will stop telling the truth about them.

Adlai Stevenson 1900–65: speech during 1952 Presidential campaign; Leon Harris *The Fine Art of Political Wit* (1965)

73 'Ominous' is not quite the right word for a situation where one of the most consistently unpopular politicians in American history [Richard Nixon] suddenly skyrockets to folk hero status while his closest advisers are being caught

Hunter S. Thompson 1939– : *Fear and Loathing: On the Campaign Trail* (1973)

almost daily in nazi-style gigs that would have
embarrassed Martin Bormann.

on why he did not become a politician:

74 I could not stand the strain of having to be right all the
time.

Peter Ustinov 1921– : in *Saga Magazine* August 1999

75 If you want to rise in politics in the United States there is
one subject you must stay away from, and that is politics.

Gore Vidal 1925– : in *Observer* 28 June 1987 'Sayings of the Week'

76 The amazing thing is not that we don't have Gladstones or
Disraelis as ministers for social security; it is that anyone
agrees to do the job.

George Walden 1939– : *Lucky George* (1999)

77 The public say they are getting cynical about politicians;
they should hear how politicians talk about them.

George Walden 1939– : *Lucky George* (1999)

Poverty See also **Debt**, **Money**

1 She was poor but she was honest
Victim of a rich man's game.
First he loved her, then he left her,
And she lost her maiden name . . .

It's the same the whole world over,
It's the poor wot gets the blame,
It's the rich wot gets the gravy.
Ain't it all a bleedin' shame?

Anonymous: 'She was Poor but she was Honest'; sung by British soldiers in the First World War

2 Anyone who has ever struggled with poverty knows how
extremely expensive it is to be poor.

James Baldwin 1924–87: *Nobody Knows My Name* (1961) 'Fifth Avenue, Uptown: a letter from Harlem'

3 Come away; poverty's catching.

Aphra Behn 1640–89: *The Rover* (1681)

4 Do you think Oxfam ever return anything? Oxfam
graciously acknowledges the receipt of your gift but feel
they must return this pair of your old knickers as they
would only aggravate the situation.

Alan Bennett 1934– : *Getting On* (1972)

5 He [Bill Bryson's father] was a child of the Depression and
where capital outlays were involved he always wore the
haunted look of a fugitive who had just heard
bloodhounds in the distance.

Bill Bryson 1951– : *The Lost Continent* (1989)

6 The murmuring poor, who will not fast in peace.

George Crabbe 1754–1832: 'The Newspaper' (1785)

7 There is a wealth of poverty in Northern Ireland which
must be overcome.

Lord Enniskillen 1918–89: speech in the House of Lords, 3 December 1968

8 Gee, I'd like to see you looking swell, Baby,
Diamond bracelets Woolworth doesn't sell, Baby,
Till that lucky day, you know darned well, Baby
I can't give you anything but love.

Dorothy Fields 1905–74: 'I Can't Give You Anything But Love' (1928)

9 What throws a monkey wrench in
A fella's good intention?
That nasty old invention—
Necessity!

E. Y. Harburg 1898–1981: 'Necessity' (1947)

10 It's no disgrace t'be poor, but it might as well be.

Frank McKinney Hubbard 1868–1930: *Short Furrows* (1911)

11 There seems to be much more in the New Testament in praise of poverty than we like to acknowledge.

Benjamin Jowett 1817–93: Kenneth Rose *Superior Person* (1969)

12 Everyone was poor and proud. My parents didn't know anything to be proud of, so they just carried on.

Patrick Kavanagh 1904–67: *The Green Fool* (1938)

13 Up and down the City Road,
In and out the Eagle,
That's the way the money goes—
Pop goes the weasel!

W. R. Mandale: 'Pop Goes the Weasel' (1853); also attributed to Charles Twiggs

14 If only Bapu [Gandhi] knew the cost of setting him up in poverty!

Sarojini Naidu 1879–1949: A. Campbell-Johnson *Mission with Mountbatten* (1951)

15 Look at me. Worked myself up from nothing to a state of extreme poverty.

S. J. Perelman 1904–79, **Will B. Johnstone**, and **Arthur Sheekman**: *Monkey Business* (1931 film)

16 LABRAX: One letter more than a medical man, that's what I am.
GRIPUS: Then you're a mendicant?
LABRAX: You've hit the point.

Plautus c.250–184 BC: *Rudens*

17 How can I ever start
To tell what's in my heart
At the sight of a dime
Of a shiny new dime.

Harold Rome 1908– : 'The Face on the Dime' (1946)

18 The greatest of evils and the worst of crimes is poverty . . . our first duty—a duty to which every other consideration should be sacrificed—is not to be poor.

George Bernard Shaw 1856–1950: *Major Barbara* (1907) preface

19 You may tempt the upper classes
With your villainous demi-tasses,
But: Heaven will protect a working-girl!

Edgar Smith 1857–1938: 'Heaven Will Protect the Working-Girl' (1909)

20 Poverty is no disgrace to a man, but it is confoundedly inconvenient.

Sydney Smith 1771–1845: J. Potter Briscoe *Sydney Smith: His Wit and Wisdom* (1900)

21 I am pent up in frowzy lodgings, where there is not room enough to swing a cat.

Tobias Smollett 1721–71: *Humphry Clinker* (1771)

22 He was a gentleman who was generally spoken of as having nothing a-year, paid quarterly.

R. S. Surtees 1805–64: *Mr Sponge's Sporting Tour* (1853)

23 How to live well on nothing a year.

William Makepeace Thackeray 1811–63: *Vanity Fair* (1847–8)

24 As for the virtuous poor, one can pity them, of course, but one cannot possibly admire them.

Oscar Wilde 1854–1900: *Sebastian Melmoth* (1891)

25 Like dear St Francis of Assisi I am wedded to Poverty: but in my case the marriage is not a success.

Oscar Wilde 1854–1900: letter June 1899

Power

1 Whatever happens we have got
The Maxim Gun, and they have not.

Hilaire Belloc 1870–1953: *The Modern Traveller* (1898)

2 Anybody that wants the presidency so much that he'll spend two years organizing and campaigning for it is not to be trusted with the office.

David Broder 1929– : in *Washington Post* 18 July 1973

3 She cannot see an institution without hitting it with her handbag.
of Margaret Thatcher

Julian Critchley 1930–2000: in *The Times* 21 June 1982

4 So long as men worship the Caesars and Napoleons, Caesars and Napoleons will duly arise and make them miserable.

Aldous Huxley 1894–1963: *Ends and Means* (1937)

5 I don't want loyalty. I want *loyalty*. I want him to kiss my ass in Macy's window at high noon and tell me it smells like roses. I want his pecker in my pocket.

Lyndon Baines Johnson 1908–73: David Halberstam *The Best and the Brightest* (1972)

6 Better to have him inside the tent pissing out, than outside pissing in.
of J. Edgar Hoover

Lyndon Baines Johnson 1908–73: David Halberstam *The Best and the Brightest* (1972)

7 Eight years of playing second fiddle is not doing me any good.
to Bob Hawke in 1988

Paul Keating 1944– : Michael Gordon *A Question of Leadership* (1993)

8 I'll make him an offer he can't refuse.

Mario Puzo 1920–99: *The Godfather* (1969)

9 Seven months ago I could give a single command and 541,000 people would immediately obey it. Today I can't get a plumber to come to my house.

H. Norman Schwarzkopf III 1934– : in *Newsweek* 11 November 1991; see **Presidents** 17

10 The Pope! How many divisions has *he* got?
on being asked to encourage Catholicism in Russia by way of conciliating the Pope

Joseph Stalin 1879–1953: on 13 May 1935

11 If you were handed power on a plate you'd be left fighting over the plate.

Tom Stoppard 1937– : *Squaring the Circle* (1984)

12 He seemed much greater than a private citizen while he still was a private citizen, and by everyone's consent capable of reigning if only he had not reigned.
of the Emperor Galba

Tacitus AD 56–after 117: *Histories*

13 Children and zip fasteners do not respond to force . . .
Except occasionally.

Katharine Whitehorn 1926– : *Observations* (1970)

Praise and Flattery

1 If you are flattering a woman, it pays to be a little more subtle. You don't have to bother with men, they believe any compliment automatically.

Alan Ayckbourn 1939– : *Round and Round the Garden* (1975)

2 We authors, Ma'am.
to Queen Victoria after the publication of Leaves from the Journal of our Life in the Highlands *in 1868*

Benjamin Disraeli 1804–81: Elizabeth Longford *Victoria R.I.* (1964); attributed

3 Your Majesty is the head of the literary profession.
to Queen Victoria after the publication of Leaves from the Journal of our Life in the Highlands *in 1868*

Benjamin Disraeli 1804–81: Hesketh Pearson *Dizzy* (1951); attributed

4 Please don't be too effusive.
adjuration to the Prime Minister, at their weekly meeting on the speech he was to make to celebrate her golden wedding; see
Prime Ministers 6

Elizabeth II 1926– : in *Daily Telegraph* 21 November 1997

5 I live for your agglomerated lucubrations.
   to H. G. Wells

Henry James 1843–1916: letter, 18 November 1902

6 Consider with yourself what your flattery is worth before you bestow it so freely.
   to Hannah More

Samuel Johnson 1709–84: James Boswell *Life of Johnson* (1791)

7 You're the top! You're the Coliseum,
You're the top! You're the Louvre Museum,
You're a melody
From a symphony by Strauss,
You're a Bendel bonnet,
A Shakespeare sonnet,
You're Mickey Mouse!

Cole Porter 1891–1964: 'You're the Top' (1934)

8 I used your soap two years ago; since then I have used no other.

Punch 1841–1992: vol. 86 (1884)

9 What really flatters a man is that you think him worth flattering.

George Bernard Shaw 1856–1950: *John Bull's Other Island* (1907)

10 Among the smaller duties of life, I hardly know one more important than that of not praising where praise is not due.

Sydney Smith 1771–1845: Saba Holland *Memoir* (1855)

11 I suppose flattery hurts no one, that is, if he doesn't inhale.

Adlai Stevenson 1900–65: television broadcast, 30 March 1952

Prejudice and Tolerance

1 Being a star has made it possible for me to get insulted in places where the average Negro could never *hope* to go and get insulted.

Sammy Davis Jnr. 1925–90: *Yes I Can* (1965)

2 I always suspected she had Scotch blood in her veins, anything else I could have looked over in her from a regard to the family.

Maria Edgeworth 1767–1849: *Castle Rackrent* (1800)

3 CONGRESSMAN STARNES: You are quoting from this Marlowe. Is he a Communist?
HALLIE FLANAGAN: I am very sorry. I was quoting from Christopher Marlowe.

Hallie Flanagan 1890–1969: in hearing on the Federal Theatre Project by the House Un-American Activities Committee, 6 December 1938

4 CONGRESSMAN STARNES: I believe Mr Euripides was guilty of teaching class consciousness also, wasn't he?
HALLIE FLANAGAN: I believe that was alleged against all the Greek dramatists.

Hallie Flanagan 1890–1969: in hearing on the Federal Theatre Project by the House Un-American Activities Committee, 6 December 1938

5 Wouldn't it be a hell of a thing if all this was burnt cork and you people were being tolerant for nothing?

Dick Gregory 1932– : *Nigger* (1965)

6 You gotta say this for the white race—its self-confidence knows no bounds. Who else could go to a small island in the South Pacific where there's no poverty, no crime, no unemployment, no war and no worry—and call it a 'primitive society'?

Dick Gregory 1932– : *From the Back of the Bus* (1962)

7 Without the aid of prejudice and custom, I should not be able to find my way across the room.

William Hazlitt 1778–1830: 'On Prejudice' (1830)

8 'It's powerful,' he said.
'What?'
'That one drop of Negro blood—because just *one* drop of black blood makes a man coloured. *One* drop—you are a Negro!'

Langston Hughes 1902–67: *Simple Takes a Wife* (1953)

9 If there were any of Australia's original inhabitants living in Melbourne they were kept well out of the way of nice people; unless, of course, they could sing.

Barry Humphries 1934– : *More Please* (1992)

10 When they call you articulate, that's another way of saying 'He talks good for a black guy'.

Ice-T 1958– : in *Independent* 30 December 1995 'Interviews of the Year'

refused admittance to a smart Californian beach club:
11 Since my daughter is only half-Jewish, could she go in the water up to her knees?

Groucho Marx 1895–1977: in *Observer* 21 August 1977

12 Tolerance is only another name for indifference.

W. Somerset Maugham 1874–1965: *A Writer's Notebook* (1949) written in 1896

13 The South African police would leave no stone unturned to see that nothing disturbed the even terror of their lives.

Tom Sharpe 1928– : *Indecent Exposure* (1973)

14 You must always look for the *Ulsterior motive*.
of C. S. Lewis as an Ulsterman

J. R. R. Tolkien 1892–1973: A. N. Wilson *Life of C. S. Lewis* (1986)

15 I have a distinct impression that the anthropologists' version of that famous quote from Alexander Pope's essay runs: 'The proper study of mankind is *black* man, or if not actually black, at least poor and a long way off.'

Jill Tweedie 1936–93: *It's Only Me* (1980)

Present see Past and Present

Presidents See also **Politicians**, **Politics**

1 Richard Nixon impeached himself. He gave us Gerald Ford as his revenge.

Bella Abzug 1920– : in *Rolling Stone*; Linda Botts *Loose Talk* (1980)

2 I worship the quicksand he walks in.
of Richard Nixon (later also applied to Jimmy Carter)

Art Buchwald 1925– : Jonathon Green (ed.) *The Book of Political Quotes* (1982)

3 God Almighty was satisfied with Ten Commandments. Mr Wilson requires Fourteen Points.

Georges Clemenceau 1841–1929: during the Peace Conference negotiations in 1919; Leon Harris *The Fine Art of Political Wit* (1965)

4 A hard dog to keep on the porch.
on her husband, Bill Clinton

Hillary Rodham Clinton 1947– : in *Guardian* 2 August 1999

5 Mr Speaker, the Honourable Gentleman has conceived three times and brought forth nothing.
when Lincoln, making his first speech in the Illinois legislature, had three times begun 'Mr Speaker, I conceive'

Stephen A. Douglas 1813–61: Leon Harris *The Fine Art of Political Wit* (1965)

6 Reagan was probably the first modern president to treat the post as a part-time job, one way of helping to fill the otherwise blank days of retirement.

Simon Hoggart 1946– : *America* (1990)

7 Higgledy-Piggledy
Benjamin Harrison
Twenty-third President,

John Hollander 1929– : 'Historical Reflections' (1966)

Was, and, as such,
Served between Clevelands, and
Save for this trivial
Idiosyncrasy
Didn't do much.

8 Ronald Reagan, the President who never told bad news to the American people.

Garrison Keillor 1942– : *We Are Still Married* (1989), introduction

9 The pay is good and I can walk to work.

John F. Kennedy 1917–63: attributed; James B. Simpson (ed.) *Simpson's Contemporary Quotations* (1988)

10 Many a time have I stood on one side of the counter and sold whiskey to Mr Douglas, but the difference between us now is this. I have left my side of the counter, but Mr Douglas still sticks to his as tenaciously as ever.
  during a debate with Stephen A. Douglas in 1858

Abraham Lincoln 1809–65: Leon Harris *The Fine Art of Political Wit* (1965)

11 If there had been any formidable body of cannibals in the country he would have promised to provide them with free missionaries fattened at the taxpayer's expense.
  of Harry Truman's success in the 1948 presidential campaign

H. L. Mencken 1880–1956: in *Baltimore Sun* 7 November 1948

12 The battle for the mind of Ronald Reagan was like the trench warfare of World War I. Never have so many fought so hard for such barren terrain.

Peggy Noonan 1950– : *What I Saw at the Revolution* (1990)

13 McKinley has no more backbone than a chocolate éclair!

Theodore Roosevelt 1858–1919: Harry Thurston Peck *Twenty Years of the Republic* (1906)

14 If I talk over people's heads, Ike must talk under their feet.

Adlai Stevenson 1900–65: during the Presidential campaign of 1952; Bill Adler *The Stevenson Wit* (1966)

  of Eisenhower's presidential campaign in 1956:
15 The General has dedicated himself so many times he must feel like the cornerstone of a public building.

Adlai Stevenson 1900–65: Leon Harris *The Fine Art of Political Wit* (1965)

16 We elected a President, not a Pope.
  to journalists at the White House, 5 February 1998

Barbra Streisand 1942– : reported by James Naughtie, BBC Radio 4, Today programme, 6 February 1998

17 He'll sit right here and he'll say do this, do that! And nothing will happen. Poor Ike—it won't be a bit like the Army.

Harry S. Truman 1884–1972: *Harry S. Truman* (1973); see **Power** 9

Pride and Humility

1 His opinion of himself, having once risen, remained at 'set fair'.

Arnold Bennett 1867–1931: *The Card* (1911)

  on stepping from his bath in the presence of a startled President Roosevelt:
2 The Prime Minister has nothing to hide from the President of the United States.

Winston Churchill 1874–1965: as recalled by Roosevelt's son in *Churchill* (BBC television series presented by Martin Gilbert, 1992)

3 Every day when he looked into the glass, and gave the last touch to his consummate toilette, he offered his grateful thanks to Providence that his family was not unworthy of him.

Benjamin Disraeli 1804–81: *Lothair* (1870)

4 In 1969 I published a small book on Humility. It was a pioneering work which has not, to my knowledge, been superseded.

Lord Longford 1905– : in *The Tablet* 22 January 1994

5 Modest? My word, no . . . He was an all-the-lights-on man.

Henry Reed 1914–86: *A Very Great Man Indeed* (1953 radio play) in *Hilda Tablet and Others*

6 But be not afraid of greatness: some men are born great, some achieve greatness, and some have greatness thrust upon them.

William Shakespeare 1564–1616: *Twelfth Night* (1601)

7 I have often wished I had time to cultivate modesty . . . But I am too busy thinking about myself.

Edith Sitwell 1887–1964: in *Observer* 30 April 1950

8 We have the highest authority for believing that the meek shall inherit the earth; though I have never found any particular corroboration of this aphorism in the records of Somerset House.

F. E. Smith 1872–1930: *Contemporary Personalities* (1924) 'Marquess Curzon'

9 I am the Dean of Christ Church, Sir:
There's my wife; look well at her.
She's the Broad and I'm the High;
We are the University.

Cecil Spring-Rice 1859–1918: *The Masque of Balliol* (composed by and current among members of Balliol College, Oxford, in the 1870s); the first couplet was unofficially altered to: 'I am the Dean, and this is Mrs Liddell; / She the first, and I the second fiddle.'

10 Of all my verse, like not a single line;
But like my title, for it is not mine.
That title from a better man I stole;
Ah, how much better, had I stol'n the whole!

Robert Louis Stevenson 1850–94: *Underwoods* (1887) foreword

11 When I pass my name in such large letters I blush, but at the same time instinctively raise my hat.

Herbert Beerbohm Tree 1852–1917: Hesketh Pearson *Beerbohm Tree* (1956)

12 Do you imagine I am going to pronounce the name of my beautiful theatre in a hired cab?
refusing to give directions to His Majesty's theatre to a cab-driver

Herbert Beerbohm Tree 1852–1917: Neville Cardus *Sir Thomas Beecham* (1961)

13 The cross of the Legion of Honour has been conferred upon me. However, few escape that distinction.

Mark Twain 1835–1910: *A Tramp Abroad* (1880)

14 Charity, dear Miss Prism, charity! None of us are perfect. I myself am peculiarly susceptible to draughts.

Oscar Wilde 1854–1900: *The Importance of Being Earnest* (1895)

on being asked to name the best living author writing in English:
15 No one working in the English language now comes close to my exuberance, my passion, my fidelity to words.

Jeanette Winterson 1959– : in *Sunday Times* 13 March 1994

Prime Ministers See also **Politicians, Politics**

1 It is fitting that we should have buried the Unknown Prime Minister [Bonar Law] by the side of the Unknown Soldier.

Herbert Asquith 1852–1928: Robert Blake *The Unknown Prime Minister* (1955)

2 He [Lloyd George] can't see a belt without hitting below it.

Margot Asquith 1864–1945: in *Listener* 11 June 1953 'Margot Oxford' by Lady Violet Bonham Carter

3 Few thought he was even a starter
There were many who thought themselves smarter
But he ended PM
CH and OM
An earl and a knight of the garter.

Clement Attlee 1883–1967: describing himself; letter to Tom Attlee, 8 April 1956

4 [Lloyd George] did not seem to care which way he travelled providing he was in the driver's seat.

Lord Beaverbrook 1879–1964: *The Decline and Fall of Lloyd George* (1963)

5 Listening to a speech by Chamberlain is like paying a visit to Woolworth's: everything in its place and nothing above sixpence.

Aneurin Bevan 1897–1960: Michael Foot *Aneurin Bevan* (1962) vol.1

6 I am from the Disraeli school of Prime Ministers in their relations with the Monarch.
at the Queen's golden wedding celebration; see **Praise** 4

Tony Blair 1953– : speech, 20 November 1997

7 If he ever went to school without any boots it was because he was too big for them.
referring to Harold Wilson in a speech at the Conservative Party Conference

Ivor Bulmer-Thomas 1905–93: in *Manchester Guardian* 13 October 1949

on the younger Pitt's maiden speech:
8 Not merely a chip of the old 'block', but the old block itself.

Edmund Burke 1729–97: N. W. Wraxall *Historical Memoirs of My Own Time* (1904 ed.)

9 Pitt is to Addington
As London is to Paddington.

George Canning 1770–1827: 'The Oracle' (*c.*1803)

10 For the purposes of recreation he [Gladstone] has selected the felling of trees, and we may usefully remark that his amusements, like his politics, are essentially destructive . . . The forest laments in order that Mr Gladstone may perspire.

Lord Randolph Churchill 1849–94: speech on Financial Reform, delivered in Blackpool, 24 January 1884

11 I remember, when I was a child, being taken to the celebrated Barnum's circus, which contained an exhibition of freaks and monstrosities, but the exhibit on the programme which I most desired to see was the one described as 'The Boneless Wonder'. My parents judged that that spectacle would be too revolting and demoralizing for my youthful eyes, and I have waited 50 years to see the boneless wonder sitting on the Treasury Bench.
of Ramsay Macdonald

Winston Churchill 1874–1965: speech in the House of Commons 28 January 1931

12 In the depths of that dusty soul is nothing but abject surrender.
of Neville Chamberlain

Winston Churchill 1874–1965: Leon Harris *The Fine Art of Political Wit* (1965)

13 At the best only ginger-beer and not champagne, and now an old painted pantaloon, very deaf, very blind, and with false teeth which would fall out of his mouth when speaking if he did not hesitate and halt so in his talk.
of Palmerston in 1855

Benjamin Disraeli 1804–81: Algernon Cecil *Queen Victoria and her Prime Ministers* (1953)

14 Palmerston is now seventy. If he could prove evidence of his potency in his electoral address he'd sweep the country.

to the suggestion that capital could be made from one of Palmerston's affairs

Benjamin Disraeli 1804–81: Hesketh Pearson *Dizzy* (1951); attributed, probably apocryphal

Disraeli was asked on what, offering himself for Marylebone, he intended to stand:
15 On my head.

Benjamin Disraeli 1804–81: *Lord Beaconsfield's Correspondence with his Sister 1832–1852* (1886)

16 I've known every Prime Minister to a greater or lesser extent since Balfour, and most of them have died unhappy.

Lord Hailsham 1907– : attributed

17 INTERVIEWER: What three skills should every great Prime Minister have? Did you have them?
HEATH: Patience, stamina and good luck. Two out of three isn't bad!

Edward Heath 1916– : in *Independent* 25 November 1998

on being asked what place Arthur Balfour would have in history:
18 He will be just like the scent on a pocket handkerchief.

David Lloyd George 1863–1945: Thomas Jones diary, 9 June 1922

19 [Churchill] would make a drum out of the skin of his mother in order to sound his own praises.

David Lloyd George 1863–1945: Paul Johnson (ed.) *The Oxford Book of Political Anecdotes* (1986)

20 He might make an adequate Lord Mayor of Birmingham in a lean year.
of Neville Chamberlain

David Lloyd George 1863–1945: Leon Harris *The Fine Art of Political Wit* (1965)

21 Well, it was the best I could do, seated as I was between Jesus Christ and Napoleon Bonaparte.
on the outcome of the Peace Conference negotiations in 1919 between himself, Woodrow Wilson, and Georges Clemenceau

David Lloyd George 1863–1945: Leon Harris *The Fine Art of Political Wit* (1965)

after forming the National Government, 25 August 1931:
22 Tomorrow every Duchess in London will be wanting to kiss me!

Ramsay MacDonald 1866–1937: Viscount Snowden *An Autobiography* (1934)

23 I think sometimes the Prime Minister should be intimidating. There's not much point being a weak, floppy thing in the chair, is there?

Margaret Thatcher 1925– : on 'The Thatcher Years' (BBC 1), 21 October 1993

Prizes See **Awards and Prizes**

Progress See also **Science, Technology**

1 Everywhere one looks, decadence. I saw a bishop with a moustache the other day.

Alan Bennett 1934– : *Forty Years On* (1969)

2 Is this what we were promised when we emerged from the Dark Ages? Is this Civilization? I'm only thankful Kenneth Clark isn't here to see it.

Alan Bennett 1934– : *Habeas Corpus* (1973)

3 All progress is based upon a universal innate desire on the part of every organism to live beyond its income.

Samuel Butler 1835–1902: *Notebooks* (1912)

4 Now, *here*, you see, it takes all the running *you* can do, to keep in the same place. If you want to get somewhere else, you must run at least twice as fast as that!

Lewis Carroll 1832–98: *Through the Looking-Glass* (1872)

5 To you, Baldrick, the Renaissance was just something that happened to other people, wasn't it?

Richard Curtis 1956- and **Ben Elton** 1959- : *Blackadder II* (1987) television series

6 Mechanics, not microbes, are the menace to civilization.

Norman Douglas 1868–1952: introduction to *The Norman Douglas Limerick Book* (1967)

7 Think what we would have missed if we had never . . . used a mobile phone or surfed the Net—or, to be honest, listened to other people talking about surfing the Net.
reflecting on developments in the past 50 years

Elizabeth II 1926- : in *Daily Telegraph* 21 November 1997

8 The civilized man has built a coach, but has lost the use of his feet.

Ralph Waldo Emerson 1803–82: 'Self-Reliance' (1841)

on being asked what he thought of modern civilization:
9 That would be a good idea.
while visiting England in 1930

Mahatma Gandhi 1869–1948: E. F. Schumacher *Good Work* (1979)

10 They all laughed at Christopher Columbus
When he said the world was round
They all laughed when Edison recorded sound
They all laughed at Wilbur and his brother
When they said that man could fly;
They told Marconi
Wireless was a phony—
It's the same old cry!

Ira Gershwin 1896–1983: 'They All Laughed' (1937)

11 Don't get smart alecksy,
With the galaxy
Leave the atom alone.

E. Y. Harburg 1898–1981: 'Leave the Atom Alone' (1957)

12 Push de button!
Up de elevator!
Push de button!
Out de orange juice!
Push de button!
From refrigerator
Come banana short-cake and frozen goose!

E. Y. Harburg 1898–1981: 'Push de Button' (1957)

13 You can't say civilization don't advance, however, for in every war they kill you in a new way.

Will Rogers 1879–1935: in *New York Times* 23 December 1929

14 The cry was for vacant freedom and indeterminate progress: *Vorwärts! Avanti! Onwards! Full speed ahead!*, without asking whether directly before you was not a bottomless pit.

George Santayana 1863–1952: *My Host the World* (1953)

15 You started something which you can't stop. You want a self-limiting revolution but it's like trying to limit influenza.

Tom Stoppard 1937- : *Squaring the Circle* (1984)

16 A swell house with . . . all the modern inconveniences.

Mark Twain 1835–1910: *Life on the Mississippi* (1883)

Publishing

1 If I had been someone not very clever, I would have done an easier job like publishing. That's the easiest job I can think of.

A. J. Ayer 1910–89: attributed

2 Times have changed since a certain author was executed for murdering his publisher. They say that when the author was on the scaffold he said goodbye to the minister and to the reporters, and then he saw some publishers sitting in the front row below, and to them he did not say goodbye. He said instead, 'I'll see you later.'

J. M. Barrie 1860–1937: speech at Aldine Club, New York, 5 November 1896

3 In a profession where simple accountancy is preferable to a degree in English, illiteracy is not considered to be a great drawback.

Dominic Behan 1928– : *The Public World of Parable Jones* (1989)

4 The ever-increasing dullness and oddity of Oxford books is an old favourite among humorists, who are always trying to think up new and hilariously tedious 'The Oxford Book of . . . ' titles.

Craig Brown 1957– : *Craig Brown's Greatest Hits* (1993)

5 I have seen enough of my publishers to know that they have no ideas of their own about literature save what they can clutch at as believing it to be a straight tip from a business point of view.

Samuel Butler 1835–1902: *Notebooks* (1912)

6 The poem will please if it is lively—if it is stupid it will fail—but I will have none of your damned cutting and slashing.

Lord Byron 1788–1824: letter to his publisher John Murray, 6 April 1819

at a literary dinner during the Napoleonic Wars, Thomas Campbell proposed a toast to Napoleon:
7 Gentlemen, you must not mistake me. I admit that the French Emperor is a tyrant. I admit he is a monster. I admit that he is the sworn foe of our nation, and, if you will, of the whole human race. But, gentlemen, we must be just to our great enemy. We must not forget that he once shot a bookseller.

Thomas Campbell 1777–1844: G. O. Trevelyan *The Life of Lord Macaulay* (1876)

8 Now Barabbas was a publisher.

Thomas Campbell 1777–1844: attributed, in Samuel Smiles *A Publisher and his Friends: Memoir and Correspondence of the late John Murray* (also attributed, wrongly, to Byron); see **Publishing** 12

9 Aren't we due a royalty statement?
to his literary agent

Charles, Prince of Wales 1948– : Giles Gordon *Aren't We Due a Royalty Statement?* (1993)

10 An author who shouts 'You mean bastard' at a publisher is not going to be popular. However, I do have the satisfaction of having been rude to some of the most famous publishers in London.

Michael Green 1927– : *The Boy Who Shot Down an Airship* (1988)

on being sent the manuscript of Travels with my Aunt, *Greene's American publishers had cabled, 'Terrific book, but we'll need to change the title':*
11 No need to change title. Easier to change publishers.

Graham Greene 1904–91: telegram to his American publishers in 1968; Giles Gordon *Aren't We Due a Royalty Statement?* (1993)

12 I always thought Barabbas was a much misunderstood man . . .
a publisher's view

Peter Grose: letter, 25 May 1983; see **Publishing** 8

13 One envies a publisher because of course he can help himself cheaply to anything he produces. To listen to these two Macmillans one might imagine that their publishing business was almost run at a loss and that the authors got away with the swag! Being an author in a very mild way I hold a contrary view.

Cuthbert Morley Headlam 1876–1964: diary, 10 April 1932

14 A new firm of publishers has written to me proposing to publish 'the successor' of *A Shropshire Lad*. But as they don't also offer to write it, I have had to put them off.

A. E. Housman 1859–1936: letter to Laurence Housman, 5 October 1896

15 You cannot or at least you should not try to argue with authors. Too many are like children whose tears can suddenly be changed to smiles if they are handled in the right way.
    a publisher's view

Michael Joseph 1897–1958: *The Adventure of Publishing* (1949)

16 The relationship of an agent to a publisher is that of a knife to a throat.
    an American agent's view

Marvin Josephson: Ned Sherrin *Cutting Edge* (1984)

17 A publisher who writes is like a cow in a milk bar.

Arthur Koestler 1905–83: Jonathon Green (ed.) *A Dictionary of Contemporary Quotations* (1982)

18 The publishers contend that you only advertise a book to any extent *after* it's beginning to sell, which is certainly Alice-in-Wonderland thinking.

S. J. Perelman 1904–79: letter 22 November 1956

19 There is some kind of notion abroad that because a book is humorous the publisher has to be funnier and madder than hell in marketing it.

S. J. Perelman 1904–79: letter to Bennett Cerf, 23 July 1937

20 I suppose publishers are untrustworthy. They certainly always look it.

Oscar Wilde 1854–1900: letter February 1898

21 All a publisher has to do is write cheques at intervals, while a lot of deserving and industrious chappies rally round and do the real work.

P. G. Wodehouse 1881–1975: *My Man Jeeves* (1919)

22 Being published by the Oxford University Press is rather like being married to a duchess: the honour is almost greater than the pleasure.

G. M. Young 1882–1959: Rupert Hart-Davis letter to George Lyttelton, 29 April 1956

Punishment See **Crime and Punishment**

Quotations

1 To-day I am a lamppost against which no anthologist lifts his leg.

James Agate 1877–1947: diary, 21 August 1941

2 Ah, yes! I wrote the 'Purple Cow'—
I'm sorry, now, I wrote it!
But I can tell you anyhow,
I'll kill you if you quote it!

Gelett Burgess 1866–1951: *The Burgess Nonsense Book* (1914) 'Confessional'

3 For quotable good things, for pregnant aphorisms, for touchstones of ready application, the opinions of the English judges are a mine of instruction and a treasury of joy.

Benjamin N. Cardozo 1870–1938: *Law and Literature* (1931)

4 It would be nice if sometimes the kind things I say were considered worthy of quotation. It isn't difficult, you know, to be witty or amusing when one has something to say that is destructive, but damned hard to be clever and quotable when you are singing someone's praises.

Noël Coward 1899–1973: William Marchant *The Pleasure of His Company* (1981)

5 I know heaps of quotations, so I can always make quite a fair show of knowledge.

O. Douglas 1877–1948: *The Setons* (1917)

6 Next to the originator of a good sentence is the first quoter of it.

Ralph Waldo Emerson 1803–82: *Letters and Social Aims* (1876)

advice for House of Commons quotations:
7 No Greek; as much Latin as you like: never French in any circumstance: no English poet unless he has completed his century.

Charles James Fox 1749–1806: J. A. Gere and John Sparrow (eds.) *Geoffrey Madan's Notebooks* (1981)

8 A cannibal, but one with better table manners.
of the editor of the Oxford Dictionary of Twentieth Century Quotations

Bevis Hillier 1940– : in *Spectator* 19 December 1998

9 But I have long thought that if you knew a column of advertisements by heart, you could achieve unexpected felicities with them. You can get a happy quotation anywhere if you have the eye.

Oliver Wendell Holmes Jr. 1841–1935: letter to Harold Laski, 31 May 1923

10 You must not treat my immortal works as quarries to be used at will by the various hacks whom you may employ to compile anthologies.

A. E. Housman 1859–1936: letter to his publisher Grant Richards, 29 June 1907

11 He wrapped himself in quotations—as a beggar would enfold himself in the purple of emperors.

Rudyard Kipling 1865–1936: *Many Inventions* (1893)

12 There is no reason why a book of quotations should be dull; it has its uses in idleness as well as in study.

H. L. Mencken 1880–1956: introduction to *H. L. Mencken's Dictionary of Quotations* (1942)

13 My favourite quotation is eight pounds ten for a second-hand suit.

Spike Milligan 1918– : on *Quote . . . Unquote* (BBC Radio) 1 January 1979; Nigel Rees (ed.) *Cassell Dictionary of Humorous Quotations* (1999)

14 He liked those literary cooks
Who skim the cream of others' books;
And ruin half an author's graces
By plucking bon-mots from their places.

Hannah More 1745–1833: *Florio* (1786)

15 I . . . try much to my fury to find quotations in my own books for Doubleday Doran's *Dictionary of Quotations*. It doesn't work. I am not given to apophthegms. My gift is to explain things at length and convey atmosphere.

Harold Nicolson 1886–1968: diary, 7 November 1948

16 His works contain nothing worth quoting; and a book that furnishes no quotations is, *me judice*, no book—it's a plaything.

Thomas Love Peacock 1785–1866: *Crotchet Castle* (1831)

17 Misquotation is, in fact, the pride and privilege of the learned. A widely-read man never quotes accurately, for the rather obvious reason that he has read too widely.

Hesketh Pearson 1887–1964: *Common Misquotations* (1934) introduction

18 I was both horrified and immeasurably flattered by your confession that you had in the past quoted from my work: horrified because unbeknownst to yourself, you ran the risk of verbal infection (the kind of words I use are liable to

S. J. Perelman 1904–79: letter to Betsy Drake, 1951

become imbedded and fester, like the steel wool
housewives use).

19 An anthology is like all the plums and orange peel picked
out of a cake.

Walter Raleigh 1861–1922: letter to
Mrs Robert Bridges, 15 January 1915

20 I always have a quotation for everything—it saves original
thinking.

Dorothy L. Sayers 1893–1957: *Have
His Carcase* (1932)

21 It seems pointless to be quoted if one isn't going to be
quotable . . . It's better to be quotable than honest.

Tom Stoppard 1937– : in *Guardian*
21 March 1973

22 What a good thing Adam had. When he said a good thing
he knew nobody had said it before.

Mark Twain 1835–1910: *Notebooks*
(1935)

23 Anthologies are mischievous things. Some years ago there
was a rage for chemically predigested food, which was
only suppressed when doctors pointed out that since
human beings had been given teeth and digestive organs
they had to be used or they degenerated very rapidly.
Anthologies are predigested food for the brain.

Rebecca West 1892–1983: in *The
Clarion* 27 December 1912

Reading

1 The world may be full of fourth-rate writers but it's also
full of fourth-rate readers.

Stan Barstow 1928– : in *Daily Mail*
15 August 1989

on hearing that Watership Down *was a novel about rabbits
written by a civil servant:*
2 I would rather read a novel about civil servants written by
a rabbit.

Craig Brown 1957– : attributed;
probably apocryphal

3 The ideal reader of my novels is a lapsed Catholic and a
failed musician, short-sighted, colour-blind, auditorily
biased, who has read the books that I have read. He
should also be about my age.

Anthony Burgess 1917–93: George
Plimpton (ed.) *Writers at Work* 4th
Series (1977)

4 You couldn't even read the Gettysburg Address.
So who cares anyway where Gettysburg lived?

Betty Comden 1919– and **Adolph
Green** 1915– : *Singin' in the Rain*
(1952)

5 Arrival of Book of the Month choice, and am disappointed.
History of a place I am not interested in, by an author I do
not like.

E. M. Delafield 1890–1943: *The Diary
of a Provincial Lady* (1930)

to an author who had presented him with an unwelcome book:
6 Many thanks. I shall lose no time in reading it.

Benjamin Disraeli 1804–81: Wilfrid
Meynell *The Man Disraeli* (1903)

on the difficulties of reading the novels of Sir Walter Scott:
7 He shouldn't have written in such small print.

O. Douglas 1877–1948: *The Setons*
(1917)

8 I read part of it all the way through.

Sam Goldwyn 1882–1974: N. Zierold
Hollywood Tycoons (1969)

*to Melvyn Bragg, when no one in the studio audience claimed to
have read his novels:*
9 You're going to have to slow down. We can't keep up
with you!

Barry Humphries 1934– : *An
Audience With Dame Edna Everage*
(TV show, early 1980s); Nigel Rees
(ed.) *Cassell Dictionary of Humorous
Quotations* (1999)

10 Henry Kissinger may be a great writer, but anyone who finishes his book is definitely a great reader.

Walter Isaacson: in *The Week* 20 March 1999 'Wit and Wisdom'

11 [ELPHINSTON:] What, have you not read it through? [JOHNSON:] No, Sir, do *you* read books *through*?

Samuel Johnson 1709–84: James Boswell *Life of Samuel Johnson* (1791) 19 April 1773

12 [*The Compleat Angler*] is acknowledged to be one of the world's books. Only the trouble is that the world doesn't read its books, it borrows a detective story instead.

Stephen Leacock 1869–1944: *The Boy I Left Behind Me* (1947)

13 We shouldn't trust writers, but we should read them.

Ian McEwan 1948– : in BBC2 'Late Show' 7 February 1990

14 Don't read much but love books about homos.
   to Gore Vidal, on her taste in reading

Ethel Merman 1909–84: Fred Kaplan *Gore Vidal* (1999)

15 Reading isn't an occupation we encourage among police officers. We try to keep the paper work down to a minimum.

Joe Orton 1933–67: *Loot* (1967)

16 What really knocks me out is a book that, when you're all done reading it, you wish the author that wrote it was a terrific friend of yours and you could call him up on the phone whenever you felt like it.

J. D. Salinger 1919– : *Catcher in the Rye* (1951)

17 People say that life is the thing, but I prefer reading.

Logan Pearsall Smith 1865–1946: *Afterthoughts* (1931) 'Myself'

18 '*Classic.*' A book which people praise and don't read.

Mark Twain 1835–1910: *Following the Equator* (1897)

Religion See also **The Clergy, God**

1 We have in England a particular bashfulness in every thing that regards religion.

Joseph Addison 1672–1719: *The Spectator* 15 August 1712

2 As Sir Roger is landlord to the whole congregation, he keeps them in very good order, and will suffer nobody to sleep in it [the church] besides himself; for if by chance he has been surprised into a short nap at sermon, upon recovering out of it, he stands up, and looks about him; and if he sees anybody else nodding, either wakes them himself, or sends his servant to them.

Joseph Addison 1672–1719: *The Spectator* 9 July 1711

a rhyming marriage license, said to have been composed for an al fresco ceremony outside Lichfield:
3 Under an oak in stormy weather
I joined this rogue and whore together;
And none but he who rules the thunder
Can put this rogue and whore asunder.

Anonymous: has been attributed to Swift, but of doubtful authenticity; C. H. Wilson *Swiftiana* (1804)

4 Bernard always had a few prayers in the hall and some whiskey afterwards as he was rarther pious but Mr Salteena was not very addicted to prayers so he marched up to bed.

Daisy Ashford 1881–1972: *The Young Visiters* (1919)

5 Gentlemen, I am a Catholic . . . If you reject me on account of my religion, I shall thank God that He has spared me the indignity of being your representative.

Hilaire Belloc 1870–1953: speech to voters of South Salford, 1906

6 FOSTER: I'm still a bit hazy about the Trinity, sir.
SCHOOLMASTER: Three in one, one in three, perfectly
 straightforward. Any doubts about that see your maths
 master.

Alan Bennett 1934– : *Forty Years On*
(1969)

7 The attitude that regards entanglement with religion as
something akin to entanglement with an infectious disease
must be confronted broadly and directly.

William J. Bennett 1943– : in *New
York Times* 8 August 1985

of Dr Arnold when St Paul was by someone put above St John:
8 He burst into tears and begged that the subject might
never again be mentioned in his presence.

A. C. Benson 1862–1925: George
Lyttelton letter to Rupert Hart-Davis,
20 August 1958

9 Broad of Church and 'broad of Mind',
Broad before and broad behind,
A keen ecclesiologist,
A rather dirty Wykehamist.

John Betjeman 1906–84: 'The
Wykehamist' (1931)

10 The Church's Restoration
In eighteen-eighty-three
Has left for contemplation
Not what there used to be.

John Betjeman 1906–84: 'Hymn'
(1931)

11 Thanks to God, I am still an atheist.

Luis Buñuel 1900–83: *Le Monde* 16
December 1959

12 An atheist is a man who has no invisible means of
support.

John Buchan 1875–1940: H. E.
Fosdick *On Being a Real Person* (1943)

13 Christians have burnt each other, quite persuaded
That all the Apostles would have done as they did.

Lord Byron 1788–1824: *Don Juan*
(1819–24)

14 I am always most religious upon a sunshiny day.

Lord Byron 1788–1824: 'Detached
Thoughts' 15 October 1821

15 The two dangers which beset the Church of England are
good music and bad preaching.

Lord Hugh Cecil 1869–1956: K. Rose
The Later Cecils (1975)

16 Lord Hugh Cecil preaching (Miss Goodford present) and
saying that eternal torment was almost certain: but a very
few might hope for merciful annihilation.

Lord Hugh Cecil 1869–1956: sermon
at Eton, 25 November 1944; J. A.
Gere and John Sparrow (eds.)
Geoffrey Madan's Notebooks (1981)

17 Is man an ape or an angel? Now I am on the side of the
angels.

Benjamin Disraeli 1804–81: speech
at Oxford, 25 November 1864

18 A Protestant, if he wants aid or advice on any matter, can
only go to his solicitor.

Benjamin Disraeli 1804–81: *Lothair*
(1870)

19 Said Waldershare, 'Sensible men are all of the same
religion.' 'And pray what is that?' . . . 'Sensible men never
tell.'

Benjamin Disraeli 1804–81:
Endymion (1880)

20 A lady, if undressed at Church, looks silly,
One cannot be devout in dishabilly.

George Farquhar 1678–1707: *The
Stage Coach* (1704)

21 'I know of no joy,' she airily began, 'greater than a cool
white dress after the sweetness of confession.'

Ronald Firbank 1886–1926:
Valmouth (1919)

*Lady Carina Fitzalan-Howard was asked if her future husband
David Frost were religious:*
22 Yes, he thinks he's God Almighty.

Carina Frost 1952– : in *Sunday Times*
28 July 1985

23   What after all
Is a halo? It's only one more thing to keep clean.

Christopher Fry 1907– : *The Lady's not for Burning* (1949)

24 A Consumer's Guide to Religion—The Best Buy—Church
of England. It's a jolly friendly faith. If you are one, there's
no onus to make everyone else join. In fact no one need
ever know.

Robert Gillespie and **Charles Lewson**: *That Was The Week That Was* BBC television 1962

25 If Evan gave *all* his reasons for joining the Church he'd be
excommunicated.
of an acquaintance who had become a convert to Catholicism

Oliver St John Gogarty 1878–1957: Ulick O'Connor *Oliver St John Gogarty* (1964)

*at Oxford, to an angry crowd who thought she was Charles II's
French Catholic mistress the Duchess of Portsmouth:*
26 Pray, good people, be civil. I am the Protestant whore.

Nell Gwyn 1650–87: B. Bevan *Nell Gwyn* (1969)

27 No matter how I probe and prod
I cannot quite believe in God.
But oh! I hope to God that he
Unswervingly believes in me.

E. Y. Harburg 1898–1981: 'The Agnostic' (1965)

28 For a halo up in heaven
I have never been too keen.
Who needs another gadget
That a fellow has to clean?

E. Y. Harburg 1898–1981: 'The Man who has Everything' (1965)

29 When Messiah comes,
He will say to us
'I apologise that I took so long,
But I had a little trouble finding you.
Over here a few and over there a few—
You were hard to reunite,
But everything is going to be all right.
Up in heaven there
How I wrang my hands
When they exiled you from the Promised Land.
In Babylon you went like castaways
On the first of many, many moving days.
What a day and what a blow,
How terrible I felt you'll never know!'

Sheldon Harnick 1924– : 'When Messiah Comes' (1964)

30 Much as Field-Marshal Goering sought to confer Aryan
status on the Jewish tenor Richard Tauber, so my mother
spared Pat Bagott [her gardener] her usual strictures
against Catholicism. Without knowing it, the spotless and
particular Bagotts were granted a unique amnesty; in my
mother's eyes at least they were honorary Protestants.

Barry Humphries 1934– : *More Please* (1992)

31 The Revised Prayer Book: a sort of attempt to suppress
burglary by legalizing petty larceny.

Dean Inge 1860–1954: J. A. Gere and John Sparrow (eds.) *Geoffrey Madan's Notebooks* (1981)

32 All moanday, tearsday, wailsday, thumpsday, frightday,
shatterday till the fear of the Law.

James Joyce 1882–1941: *Finnegans Wake* (1939)

33 When suave politeness, tempering bigot zeal,
Corrected *I believe* to *One does feel*.

Ronald Knox 1888–1957: 'Absolute and Abitofhell' (1913)

34 In the course of one of his most rousing sermons,
fortunately at Evensong, he announced that it had
recently been revealed to him in a dream that there were

Osbert Lancaster 1908–80: *All Done From Memory* (1953)

no women in heaven, the female part of mankind having finally been judged incapable of salvation. While those of his hearers who were acquainted with the Canon's wife could quite appreciate the obvious satisfaction with which the Vicar promulgated this new dogma, few among a congregation that was largely female could be expected to share it.

35 'Oh, a cheque, I think,' said the rector; 'one can do so much more with it, after all.' 'Precisely,' said his father; he was well aware of many things that can be done with a cheque that cannot possibly be done with a font.

Stephen Leacock 1869–1944: *Arcadian Adventures with the Idle Rich* (1914)

36 Food was a very big factor in Christianity. What would the miracle of the loaves and fishes have been without it? And the Last Supper—how effective would that have been?

Fran Lebowitz 1946– : *Metropolitan Life* (1978)

37 Redemption does, on the whole, play a rather important part in the Christian religion, and . . . the Founder of it was particularly taken with the idea.

Bernard Levin 1928– : *If You Want My Opinion* (1992)

38 That the Almighty would send down His wisdom on the Queen's Ministers, who sorely need it.
prayer delivered in Crathie church, to Queen Victoria's amusement

Dr Macgregor: Arthur Ponsonby *Henry Ponsonby* (1942)

Mahaffy had been asked 'Are you saved?' by 'a zealot who cornered him in a railway carriage':

39 To tell you the truth, my good fellow, I am; but it was such a narrow squeak it does not bear talking about.

John Pentland Mahaffy 1839–1919: Oliver St John Gogarty *It Isn't This Time of Year at All* (1954)

40 The spirituality of man is most apparent when he is eating a hearty dinner.

W. Somerset Maugham 1874–1965: *A Writer's Notebook* (1949) written in 1897

41 Things have come to a pretty pass when religion is allowed to invade the sphere of private life.

Lord Melbourne 1779–1848: on hearing an evangelical sermon; G. W. E. Russell *Collections and Recollections* (1898)

42 Puritanism. The haunting fear that someone, somewhere, may be happy.

H. L. Mencken 1880–1956: *Chrestomathy* (1949)

43 It is now quite lawful for a Catholic woman to avoid pregnancy by a resort to mathematics, though she is still forbidden to resort to physics and chemistry.

H. L. Mencken 1880–1956: *Notebooks* (1956) 'Minority Report'

44 I went to Duff [Cooper]'s service—C of E at its most uncompromising. Our Bishop is so low church that he thinks singing hymns is idolatry so we sat while one was *played*.

Nancy Mitford 1904–73: letter, 8 January 1954

45 The orgasm has replaced the Cross as the focus of longing and the image of fulfilment.

Malcolm Muggeridge 1903–90: *Tread Softly* (1966)

46 King David and King Solomon
Led merry, merry lives,
With many, many lady friends,
And many, many wives;
But when old age crept over them—
With many, many qualms!—

James Ball Naylor 1860–1945: 'King David and King Solomon' (1935)

King Solomon wrote the Proverbs
And King David wrote the Psalms.

47 God is a man, so it must be all rot.
just before her marriage to Robert Graves in 1917

Nancy Nicholson d. 1977: R. Graves *Goodbye to All That* (1929)

48 You are not an agnostic . . . You are just a fat slob who is too lazy to go to Mass.

Conor Cruise O'Brien 1917- : attributed

49 There's no reason to bring religion into it. I think we ought to have as great a regard for religion as we can, so as to keep it out of as many things as possible.

Sean O'Casey 1880–1964: *The Plough and the Stars* (1926)

50 Good manners can replace religious beliefs. In the Anglican Church they already have. Etiquette (and quiet, well-cut clothes) are devoutly worshipped by Anglicans.

P. J. O'Rourke 1947- : *Modern Manners* (1984)

51 He was an embittered atheist (the sort of atheist who does not so much disbelieve in God as personally dislike Him), and took a sort of pleasure in thinking that human affairs would never improve.

George Orwell 1903-50: *Down and Out in Paris and London* (1933)

52 No praying, it spoils business.

Thomas Otway 1652-85: *Venice Preserved* (1682)

53 God and the doctor we alike adore
But only when in danger, not before;
The danger o'er, both are alike requited,
God is forgotten, and the Doctor slighted.

John Owen c.1563-1622: *Epigrams*

54 I've been a sinner, I've been a scamp,
But now I'm willin' to trim my lamp,
So blow, Gabriel, blow!

Cole Porter 1891-1964: 'Blow, Gabriel, Blow' (1934)

55 How can you expect to convert England if you use a cope like that?

Augustus Welby Pugin 1812-52: to an unidentified Catholic priest; Bernard Ward *The Sequel to Catholic Emancipation* (1915)

56 Prove to me that you're no fool
Walk across my swimming pool.

Tim Rice 1944- : 'Herod's Song' (1970)

57 I always claim the mission workers came out too early to catch any sinners on this part of Broadway. At such an hour the sinners are still in bed resting up from their sinning of the night before, so they will be in good shape for more sinning a little later on.

Damon Runyon 1884-1946: in *Collier's* 28 January 1933, 'The Idyll of Miss Sarah Brown'

58 I was told that the Chinese said they would bury me by the Western Lake and build a shrine to my memory. I have some slight regret that this did not happen as I might have become a god, which would have been very *chic* for an atheist.

Bertrand Russell 1872-1970: *Autobiography* (1968)

59 People may say what they like about the decay of Christianity; the religious system that produced green Chartreuse can never really die.

Saki 1870-1916: *Reginald* (1904)

60 Every reformation must have its victims. You can't expect the fatted calf to share the enthusiasm of the angels over the prodigal's return.

Saki 1870-1916: *Reginald* (1904)

61 The conversion of England was thus effected by the landing of St Augustine in Thanet and other places, which resulted in the country being overrun by a Wave of Saints. Among these were St Ive, St Pancra, the great St Bernard (originator of the clerical collar), St Bee, St Ebb, St Neot (who invented whisky), St Kit and St Kin, and the Venomous Bead (author of *The Rosary*).

W. C. Sellar 1898–1951 and **R. J. Yeatman** 1898–1968: *1066 and All That* (1930)

62 There is only one religion, though there are a hundred versions of it.

George Bernard Shaw 1856–1950: preface to *Plays Pleasant and Unpleasant* (1898) vol. 2

63 Christianity never got any grip of the world until it virtually reduced its claims on the ordinary citizen's attention to a couple of hours every seventh day, and let him alone on week-days.

George Bernard Shaw 1856–1950: preface to *Getting Married* (1911)

64 How can what an Englishman believes be heresy? It is a contradiction in terms.

George Bernard Shaw 1856–1950: *Saint Joan* (1924)

65 I have not the smallest influence over Lord Byron, in this particular, and if I had, I certainly should employ it to eradicate from his great mind the delusions of Christianity, which, in spite of his reason, seem perpetually to recur.

Percy Bysshe Shelley 1792–1822: letter 11 April 1822

66 Baptists are only funny underwater.

Neil Simon 1927– : *Laughter on the 23rd Floor* (1994)

67 Deserves to be preached to death by wild curates.

Sydney Smith 1771–1845: Lady Holland *Memoir* (1855)

68 His followers threw a Rosary and a Bible at me, which I felt was at least an ecumenical gesture, and there was a near riot.
  of Ian Paisley

Donald Soper 1903–98: speech in the House of Lords, 3 December 1968

69 I was going to be a nun, but they wouldn't have me because I didn't believe . . . not about him being the son of God, for instance, that's the part that put paid to my ambition, that's where we didn't see eye to eye.

Tom Stoppard 1937– : *If You're Glad I'll Be Frank* (1973)

70 Protestant women may take the pill. Roman Catholic women must keep taking The Tablet.

Irene Thomas 1919–2001: in *Guardian* 28 December 1990

71 Dr Gwynne himself, though a religious man, was also a thoroughly practical man of the world, and he regarded with no favourable eye the tenets of anyone who looked on the two things as incompatible.

Anthony Trollope 1815–82: *Barchester Towers* (1857)

72 Why did the Catholics invent the confessional? What is that but a phone box?

Peter Ustinov 1921– : *Monsieur René* (1999)

73 Religions are manipulated by those who govern society and not the other way around. This is a brand-new thought to Americans, whether once or twice or never bathed in the Blood of the Lamb.

Gore Vidal 1925– : *Pink Triangle and Yellow Star* (1982)

74 THE ARCHDEACON: Her deafness is a great privation to her. She can't even hear my sermons now.

Oscar Wilde 1854–1900: *A Woman of No Importance* (1893)

75 'God knows how you Protestants can be expected to have any sense of direction,' she said. 'It's different with us, I haven't been to mass for years, I've got every mortal sin

Angus Wilson 1913–91: *The Wrong Set* (1949)

on my conscience, but I know when I'm doing wrong. I'm still a Catholic, it's there, nothing can take it away from me.' 'Of course, duckie,' said Jeremy . . . 'once a Catholic always a Catholic.'

Royalty

1 She is only 5ft 4in, and to make someone that height look regal is difficult. Fortunately she holds herself very well.
   of Queen Elizabeth II

Hardy Amies 1909– : interview in *Sunday Telegraph* 9 February 1997

2 When I appear in public people expect me to neigh, grind my teeth, paw the ground and swish my tail—none of which is easy.

Anne, Princess Royal 1950– : in *Observer* 22 May 1977

notice affixed to the gates of St James's Palace during one of George II's absences in Hanover:
3 Lost or strayed out of this house a man who has left a wife and six children on the parish . . . [A reward of four shillings and sixpence is offered] Nobody judging him to deserve a crown.

Anonymous: Duke of Windsor 'My Hanoverian Ancestors' (unpublished reminiscences); Elizabeth Longford (ed.) *The Oxford Book of Royal Anecdotes* (1989)

4 King's Moll Reno'd in Wolsey's Home Town.

Anonymous: US newspaper headline on Wallis Simpson's divorce proceedings in Ipswich

it was said that during a cruise Caroline of Brunswick would sleep in a tent on deck with her majordomo, and take a bath in her cabin either with him or in his presence:
5 The Grand Master of St Caroline has found promotion's path;
He is made both Knight Companion and Commander of the Bath.

Anonymous: Roger Fulford *The Trial of Queen Caroline* (1967)

Caroline of Brunswick, estranged wife of George IV, while attending the debate in the House of Lords on the Bills of Pains and Penalties whereby George IV was attempting to divorce her, habitually fell asleep:
6 Her conduct at present no censure affords,
She sins not with courtiers but sleeps with the Lords.

Anonymous: Roger Fulford *The Trial of Queen Caroline* (1967)

7 Most Gracious Queen, we thee implore
To go away and sin no more,
But if that effort be too great,
To go away at any rate.

Anonymous: epigram on Queen Caroline, quoted in a letter from Francis Burton to Lord Colchester, 15 November 1820

8 As Jordan's high and mighty squire
Her playhouse profits deigns to skim,
Some folks audaciously enquire:
If *he* keeps *her*, or *she* keeps *him*?
   of the Duke of Clarence (later William IV) and his mistress, the actress Mrs Jordan

Anonymous: Philip Ziegler *King William IV* (1971)

9 Lousy but loyal.

Anonymous: London East End slogan at George V's Jubilee, 1935

10 How different, how very different from the home life of our own dear Queen!

Anonymous: comment overheard at a performance of Cleopatra by Sarah Bernhardt (probably apocryphal)

11 Which King did you say?

Anonymous: BBC receptionist to King Haakon of Norway; in *Ned Sherrin in his Anecdotage* (1993)

12 One of Edward's Mistresses was Jane Shore, who has had a play written about her, but it is a tragedy and therefore not worth reading.

Jane Austen 1775–1817: *The History of England* (written 1791)

13 Fate wrote her a most tremendous tragedy, and she played it in tights.

Max Beerbohm 1872–1956: of Caroline of Brunswick, wife of George IV; *The Yellow Book* (1894)

14 Spirits of well-shot woodcock, partridge, snipe
Flutter and bear him up the Norfolk sky.

John Betjeman 1906–84: 'Death of King George V' (1937)

William IV, on his way to dissolve Parliament, with uproar growing in both Houses over the Reform Bill and a cannon heralding his approach, asked his Lord Chancellor what the noise could be:
15 If you please, Your Majesty, it is the Lords debating.

Lord Brougham 1778–1868: *Works of Henry Lord Brougham* (1872)

16 'Where shall I begin, please your Majesty?' he asked.
'Begin at the beginning,' the King said, gravely, 'and go on till you come to the end: then stop.'

Lewis Carroll 1832–98: *Alice's Adventures in Wonderland* (1865)

17 I shall be an autocrat: that's my trade. And the good Lord will forgive me: that's his.

Catherine the Great 1729–96: attributed

18 We saw Queen Mary looking like the Jungfrau, white and sparkling in the sun.

Chips Channon 1897–1958: diary, 22 June 1937

19 He had been, he said, an unconscionable time dying; but he hoped that they would excuse it.

Charles II 1630–85: Lord Macaulay *History of England* (1849)

20 I've tried him drunk and I've tried him sober but there's nothing in him.

Charles II 1630–85: of his niece Anne's husband George of Denmark; Gila Curtis *The Life and Times of Queen Anne* (1972)

21 This is very true: for my words are my own, and my actions are my ministers'.

Charles II 1630–85: reply to 'The King's Epitaph'; *Thomas Hearne: Remarks and Collections* (1885–1921) 17 November 1706; see **Royalty** 60

22 Ma'am or Sir,
Sir or Ma'am
Makes every royal personage as happy as a clam.

Noël Coward 1899–1973: 'Sir or Ma'am' (1962)

on being asked the identity of the small man sharing an open carriage with the large Queen Salote of Tonga in the British Coronation procession:
23 Her lunch.

Noël Coward 1899–1973: attributed, but denied by Coward as offensive to Queen Salote; Dick Richards *The Wit and Wisdom of Noël Coward* (1968)

24 Everyone likes flattery; and when you come to Royalty you should lay it on with a trowel.

Benjamin Disraeli 1804–81: G. W. E. Russell *Collections and Recollections* (1898)

25 I never deny; I never contradict; I sometimes forget.

Benjamin Disraeli 1804–81: of his dealings as Prime Minister with Queen Victoria; Elizabeth Longford *Victoria R. I.* (1964)

26 I had three concubines, who in three diverse properties diversely excelled. One, the merriest; another the wiliest; the third, the holiest harlot in my realm, as one whom no man could get out of the church lightly to any place but it were to his bed.

Edward IV 1442–83: Thomas More *The History of Richard III*, composed about 1513

to the Archbishop of Canterbury after the service of celebration at St Paul's for Queen Victoria's Diamond Jubilee in 1897:
27 I have no objection whatsoever to the notion of the Eternal Father, but every objection to the concept of an eternal mother.

Edward VII 1841–1910: attributed, perhaps apocryphal

on being asked if Queen Victoria would be happy in heaven:
28 She will have to walk behind the angels—and she won't like that.

Edward VII 1841–1910: attributed, perhaps apocryphal

on being asked, just after George VI's accession, if she had seen Chips Channon's new gold dinner service in his Belgravia home:
29 Oh no, we're not nearly grand enough to be asked there.

Queen Elizabeth, the Queen Mother 1900– : attributed, perhaps apocryphal

30 I think everybody really will concede that on this, of all days, I should begin my speech with the words 'My husband and I'.

Elizabeth II 1926– : speech at Guildhall, London, on her 25th wedding anniversary

31 His Weariness the Prince entered the room in all his tinted orders.

Ronald Firbank 1886–1926: *The Flower Beneath the Foot* (1923)

32 I hate all Boets and Bainters.

George I 1660–1727: John Campbell *Lives of the Chief Justices* (1849) 'Lord Mansfield'

when Queen Caroline, on her deathbed, urged him to marry again:
33 No, I shall have mistresses.
  the Queen replied, 'Oh, my God! That won't make any difference'

George II 1683–1760: John Hervey *Memoirs of the Reign of George II* (1848)

the Duke of Clarence had told his father that he made his mistress Mrs Jordan an allowance of £1000 per year:
34 A thousand, a thousand; too much; too much! Five hundred quite enough! Quite enough!

George III 1738–1820: Brian Fothergill *Dorothy Jordan* (1965)

on first seeing Caroline of Brunswick, his future wife:
35 Harris, I am not well; pray get me a glass of brandy.

George IV 1762–1830: Earl of Malmesbury *Diaries and Correspondence* (1844), 5 April 1795

in conversation with Anthony Eden, 23 December 1935, following Samuel Hoare's resignation as Foreign Secretary:
36 I said to your predecessor: 'You know what they're all saying, no more coals to Newcastle, no more Hoares to Paris.' The fellow didn't even laugh.

George V 1865–1936: Earl of Avon *Facing the Dictators* (1962)

on H. G. Wells's comment on 'an alien and uninspiring court':
37 I may be uninspiring, but I'll be damned if I'm an alien!

George V 1865–1936: Sarah Bradford *George VI* (1989); attributed *to Brigadier Hinde, who had replied to the question, 'Have we met before?' with 'I don't think so':*

38 You should bl-bloody well know.

George VI 1895–1952: Lord Carver *Out of Step* (1989)

39 Ah'm sorry your Queen has to pay taxes. She's not a wealthy woman.

John Paul Getty 1892–1976: in *Ned Sherrin in his Anecdotage* (1993); attributed

of the Emperor Gordian:

40 Twenty-two acknowledged concubines, and a library of sixty-two thousand volumes, attested the variety of his inclinations, and from the productions which he left behind him, it appears that the former as well as the latter were designed for use rather than ostentation. [Footnote] By each of his concubines the younger Gordian left three or four children. His literary productions were by no means contemptible.

Edward Gibbon 1737–94: *The Decline and Fall of the Roman Empire* (1776–88)

41 Another damned, thick, square book! Always scribble, scribble, scribble! Eh! Mr Gibbon?

Duke of Gloucester 1743–1805: Henry Best *Personal and Literary Memorials* (1829); also attributed to the Duke of Cumberland and King George III

42 I left England when I was four because I found out I could never be King.

Bob Hope 1903– : from the Bob Hope Joke Files stored in two vaults of his Toluca Lake estate office; William Robert Faith *Bob Hope* (1983)

Housman had been asked to choose a selection of his poems for the library of Queen Mary's doll's house:

43 I selected the 12 shortest and least likely to fatigue the attention of dolls or members of the illustrious House of Hanover.

A. E. Housman 1859–1936: letter 4 May 1923

notice on a playbill sent to her former lover, the Duke of Clarence, refusing repayment of her allowance:

44 Positively no money refunded after the curtain has risen.

Mrs Jordan 1762–1816: Duke of Windsor 'My Hanoverian Ancestors' (unpublished reminiscences); Elizabeth Longford (ed.) *The Oxford Book of Royal Anecdotes* (1989)

45 Not a fatter fish than he
Flounders round the polar sea.
See his blubber—at his gills
What a world of drink he swills . . .
By his bulk and by his size
By his oily qualities
This (or else my eyesight fails)
This should be the Prince of Wales.

Charles Lamb 1775–1834: anonymously written in 1812; Elizabeth Longford (ed.) *Oxford Book of Royal Anecdotes* (1989)

46 What do the simple folk do?
. . . I have been informed
By those who know them well,
They find relief in quite a clever way.
When they're sorely pressed
They whistle for a spell:
And whistling seems to brighten up their day.

Alan Jay Lerner 1918–86: 'What Do the Simple Folk Do?' (1960)

And that's what simple folk do;
So they say.

*England had declared war on France two weeks after the accession
of Queen Anne:*
47 It means I'm growing old when ladies declare war on me.

Louis XIV 1638–1715: Gila Curtis *The Life and Times of Queen Anne* (1972)

48 My children are not royal, they just happen to have the Queen as their aunt.

Princess Margaret 1930– : Elizabeth Longford (ed.) *The Oxford Book of Royal Anecdotes* (1989)

on being told that one of the Royal paintings was a Mercier, not by Nollekens:
49 We prefer the picture to remain as by Nollekens.

Queen Mary 1867–1953: Michael Hill (ed.) 'Right Royal Remarks' (unpublished compilation); in *Ned Sherrin in his Anecdotage* (1993)

50 Superior to her waiting nymphs,
As lobster to attendant shrimps.
of Queen Caroline of Ansbach when dressed in pink

Lady Mary Wortley Montagu 1689–1762: 'Epistle to Lord Hervey on the King's Birthday'

51 It will be fun being 'In search of George'—but it will be hell writing the thing. I quite see that the Royal Family feel their myth is a piece of gossamer and must not be blown upon. So George VI will cut out all the jokes about George V.
on his biography of George V

Harold Nicolson 1886–1968: diary, 9 September 1948

Harold Nicolson had failed to recognize immediately that the 'dear little woman in black' to whom he was talking was the Duchess of York:
52 I steered my conversation onwards in the same course as before but with different sails: the dear old jib of comradeship was lowered and very slowly the spinnaker of 'Yes Ma'am' was hoisted in its place.

Harold Nicolson 1886–1968: diary, 20 February 1936

53 It used to occur to me when I lived in London . . . that it can't be easy being a queen. The poor old dear has had one *annus horribilis* after another. The kids are splitting up, the palace is falling down, the mother is on the gin. It is all like a particularly atrocious episode of *Eastenders*.

Joseph O'Connor 1963– : *The Secret World of the Irish Male* (1995)

54 She has become a parrot.
on the perceived readiness of the Queen to repeat the views of her Prime Minister

Ian Paisley 1926– : in *Daily Telegraph* 27 May 1998

55 She's head of a dysfunctional family—if she lived on a council estate in Sheffield, she'd probably be in council care.
on the Queen

Michael Parkinson 1935– : in *Mail on Sunday* 17 January 1999 'Quotes of the Week'

after the death in childbirth of the Prince Regent's daughter Charlotte, four of the Regent's brothers married in an attempt to provide an heir to the throne:
56 Yoics! the Royal sport's begun!
I'faith but it is glorious fun,
For hot and hard each Royal pair
Are at it hunting for an heir.

Peter Pindar 1738–1819: Elizabeth Longford (ed.) *The Oxford Book of Royal Anecdotes* (1989)

57 Here thou, great Anna! whom three realms obey,
Dost sometimes counsel take—and sometimes tea.

Alexander Pope 1688–1744: *The Rape of the Lock* (1714)

58 The Right Divine of Kings to govern wrong.

Alexander Pope 1688–1744: *The Dunciad* (1742)

59 I am his Highness' dog at Kew;
Pray, tell me sir, whose dog are you?

Alexander Pope 1688–1744: 'Epigram Engraved on the Collar of a Dog which I gave to his Royal Highness' (1738)

60 Here lies a great and mighty king
Whose promise none relies on;
He never said a foolish thing,
Nor ever did a wise one.

Lord Rochester 1647–80: 'The King's Epitaph' (an alternative first line reads: 'Here lies our sovereign lord the King')

at the funeral of Edward VII the Kaiser asked Roosevelt to call on him the next day 'at two o'clock sharp—for I can give you only 45 minutes':
61 I will be there at two, but unfortunately I have just 20 minutes to give you.

Theodore Roosevelt 1858–1919: attributed, perhaps apocryphal

62 The *éminence cerise*, the bolster behind the throne.
of Queen Elizabeth the Queen Mother

Will Self 1961– : in *Independent on Sunday* 8 August 1999

questionnaire for would-be Kings in the Wars of the Roses:
63 Are you Edmund Mortimer? If not, have you got him?

W. C. Sellar 1898–1951 and **R. J. Yeatman** 1898–1968: *1066 and All That* (1930)

64 The cruel Queen died and a post-mortem examination revealed the word 'CALLOUS' engraved on her heart.

W. C. Sellar 1898–1951 and **R. J. Yeatman** 1898–1968: of Mary Tudor; *1066 and All That* (1930)

65 Charles II was always very merry and was therefore not so much a king as a Monarch.

W. C. Sellar 1898–1951 and **R. J. Yeatman** 1898–1968: *1066 and All That* (1930)

when preaching before Charles II and his court:
66 My lord, you snore so loud you will wake the king.

Dr South 1634–1716: to Lord Lauderdale; Arthur Bryant *King Charles II* (rev. ed. 1964)

to Harold Nicolson on the Abdication crisis:
67 And now 'ere we 'ave this obstinate little man with 'is Mrs Simpson. Hit won't do, 'arold, I tell you that straight.

J. H. Thomas 1874–1949: Harold Nicolson letter, 26 February 1936

of the British people:
68 They 'ate 'aving no family life at Court.

J. H. Thomas 1874–1949: Harold Nicolson letter, 26 February 1936

69 Sire, your majesty seems to have won the race.
after the Battle of the Boyne to James II, who had complained that Lady Tyrconnel's countrymen had run away

Lady Tyrconnel d. 1731: Elizabeth Longford (ed.) *The Oxford Book of Royal Anecdotes* (1989)

70 He speaks to Me as if I was a public meeting.
of Gladstone

Queen Victoria 1819–1901: G. W. E. Russell *Collections and Recollections* (1898)

71 Lord Granville has not the courage of his opinions and therefore is of not the slightest use to the Queen.

Queen Victoria 1819–1901: letter to Sir Henry Ponsonby, 21 May 1882

When forced by a mob to cheer George IV's wife Caroline of Brunswick:

72 God Save the Queen, and may all your wives be like her!

Duke of Wellington 1769–1852: Elizabeth Longford *Wellington: Pillar of State* (1972); also attributed to Lord Anglesey and others

having been wakened with the news of his accession, William IV returned to bed:

73 To enjoy the novelty of sleeping with a queen.

William IV 1765–1837: Duke of Windsor 'My Hanoverian Ancestors' (unpublished reminiscences); Elizabeth Longford (ed.) *The Oxford Book of Royal Anecdotes* (1989)

Satisfaction and Discontent See also
Happiness and Unhappiness, Hope and Despair

comment made to Cecil Beaton by a lady-in-waiting to the exiled Queen Geraldine of Albania:

1 Of course, we'll go back there one day. Meanwhile, we have to make a new life for ourselves at the Ritz.

Anonymous: Cecil Beaton diary 1940

Mr Bennet dissuading his daughter Mary from continuing to sing:

2 You have delighted us long enough.

Jane Austen 1775–1817: *Pride and Prejudice* (1813)

asked if he had any regrets:

3 Yes, I haven't had enough sex.

John Betjeman 1906–84: on *Time With Betjeman* (BBC TV), February 1983; Nigel Rees (ed.) *Cassell Dictionary of Humorous Quotations* (1999)

4 There was a jolly miller once,
Lived on the river Dee;
He worked and sang from morn till night;
No lark more blithe than he . . .
And this the burthen of his song,
For ever used to be,
I care for nobody, not I,
If no one cares for me.

Isaac Bickerstaffe 1733–c.1808: *Love in a Village* (1762)

5 Does he paint? He would fain write a poem.
Does he write? He would fain paint a picture.

Robert Browning 1812–89: 'One Word More' (1855)

6 I ask very little. Some fragments of Pamphilides, a Choctaw blood-mask, the prose of Scaliger the Elder, a painting by Fuseli, an occasional visit to the all-in wrestling, or to my meretrix; a cook who can produce a passable 'poulet à la Khmer', a Pong vase. Simple tastes, you will agree, and it is my simple habit to indulge them.

Cyril Connolly 1903–74: *The Condemned Playground* 'Told in Gath', a parody of Aldous Huxley

7 If, of all words of tongue and pen,
The saddest are, 'It might have been,'
More sad are these we daily see:
'It is, but hadn't ought to be!'

Bret Harte 1836–1902: 'Mrs Judge Jenkins' (1867)

8 I can tolerate without discomfort being waited on hand and foot.

Osbert Lancaster 1908–80: *All Done From Memory* (1953)

9 I test my bath before I sit,
And I'm always moved to wonderment
That what chills the finger not a bit
Is so frigid upon the fundament.

Ogden Nash 1902–71: 'Samson Agonistes' (1942)

10 My life was simply hellish
I didn't stand a chance
I thought that I would relish
A tomb like General Grant's
But now I feel so swellish
So Elsa Maxwellish
That I'm giving a dance.

Cole Porter 1891–1964: 'I'm Throwing a Ball Tonight' (1940)

11 'I must be going,' said Mrs Eggelby, in a tone which had been thoroughly sterilised of even perfunctory regret.

Saki 1870–1916: *Beasts and Super-Beasts* (1914)

12 His strongest tastes were negative. He abhorred plastics, Picasso, sunbathing and jazz—everything in fact that had happened in his own lifetime.

Evelyn Waugh 1903-66: *The Ordeal of Gilbert Pinfold* (1957)

13 It's better to be looked over than overlooked.

Mae West 1892–1980: *Belle of the Nineties* (1934 film)

14 Ice formed on the butler's upper slopes.

P. G. Wodehouse 1881–1975: *Pigs Have Wings* (1952)

15 He spoke with a certain what-is-it in his voice, and I could see that, if not actually disgruntled, he was far from being gruntled.

P. G. Wodehouse 1881–1975: *The Code of the Woosters* (1938)

Science See also **Progress, Technology**

1 All I know about the becquerel is that, like the Italian lira, you need an awful lot to amount to very much.

Arnold Allen 1924– : in *Financial Times* 19 September 1986

2 Multiplication is vexation,
Division is as bad;
The Rule of Three doth puzzle me,
And Practice drives me mad.

Anonymous: in *Lean's Collectanea* (1904), possibly 16th-century

3 When I find myself in the company of scientists, I feel like a shabby curate who has strayed by mistake into a drawing room full of dukes.

W. H. Auden 1907-73: *The Dyer's Hand* (1963)

4 The Microbe is so very small
You cannot make him out at all.
But many sanguine people hope
To see him through a microscope.

Hilaire Belloc 1870–1953: 'The Microbe' (1897)

5 Sir Humphrey Davy
Abominated gravy.
He lived in the odium
Of having discovered Sodium.

Edmund Clerihew Bentley 1875–1956: 'Sir Humphrey Davy' (1905)

6 Basic research is what I am doing when I don't know what I am doing.

Werner von Braun 1912-77: R. L. Weber *A Random Walk in Science* (1973)

7 Let's be frank, the Italians' technological contribution to humankind stopped with the pizza oven.

Bill Bryson 1951– : *Neither Here Nor There* (1991)

8 There was a young lady named Bright,
Whose speed was far faster than light;
She set out one day
In a relative way
And returned on the previous night.

Arthur Buller 1874–1944: 'Relativity' (1923)

9 If they are worthy of the name, they are indeed about God's path and about his bed and spying out all his ways.
of scientists

Samuel Butler 1835–1902: *Notebooks* (1912)

10 The Scylla's cave which men of science are preparing for themselves to be able to pounce out upon us from it, and into which we cannot penetrate.

Samuel Butler 1835–1902: of scientific terminology; *Notebooks* (1912)

to an elderly scientist who had bored her by talking interminably about the social organization of ants, which have 'their own police force and their own army':
11 No navy, I suppose?'

Mrs Patrick Campbell 1865–1940: James Agate diary, 11 February 1944

12 If an elderly but distinguished scientist says that something is possible he is almost certainly right, but if he says that it is impossible he is very probably wrong.

Arthur C. Clarke 1917– : in *New Yorker* 9 August 1969

13 I have no more faith in men of science being infallible than I have in men of God being infallible, principally on account of them being men.

Noël Coward 1899–1973: diary, 1 July 1946

14 Equations are more important to me, because politics is for the present, but an equation is something for eternity.

Albert Einstein 1879–1955: Stephen Hawking *A Brief History of Time* (1988)

15 If I could remember the names of all these particles I'd be a botanist.

Enrico Fermi 1901–54: R. L. Weber *More Random Walks in Science* (1973)

16 Someone told me that each equation I included in the book would halve the sales.

Stephen Hawking 1942– : *A Brief History of Time* (1988)

17 Why is it that the scholar is the only man of science of whom it is ever demanded that he should display taste and feeling?

A. E. Housman 1859–1936: 'Cambridge Inaugural Lecture' (1911)

18 The way botanists divide up flowers reminds me of the way Africa was divided into countries by politicians.

Miles Kington 1941– : *Nature Made Ridiculously Simple* (1983)

19 I read with infinite pleasure Eddington's *Nature of the Physical World* which for 24 hours almost persuaded me that I had caught a glimpse of what the new physics was really about. It wasn't, of course, true; but the sensation, while it lasted, was charming.

Harold Laski 1893–1950: letter to Oliver Wendell Holmes, 30 November 1928

20 It was Einstein who made the real trouble. He announced in 1905 that there was no such thing as absolute rest. After that there never was.

Stephen Leacock 1869–1944: *The Boy I Left Behind Me* (1947)

21 When Rutherford was done with the atom all the solidity was pretty well knocked out of it.

Stephen Leacock 1869–1944: *The Boy I Left Behind Me* (1947)

22 Scientists are rarely to be counted among the fun people. Awkward at parties, shy with strangers, deficient in irony—they have had no choice but to turn their attention to the close study of everyday objects.

Fran Lebowitz 1946– : *Metropolitan Life* (1978)

23 My theory [is] that modern science was largely conceived of as an answer to the servant problem and that it is generally practised by those who lack a flair for conversation.

Fran Lebowitz 1946– : *Metropolitan Life* (1978)

24 It is a good morning exercise for a research scientist to discard a pet hypothesis every day before breakfast.

Konrad Lorenz 1903–89: *On Aggression* (1966)

25 The scientist who yields anything to theology, however slight, is yielding to ignorance and false pretences, and as certainly as if he granted that a horse-hair put into a bottle of water will turn into a snake.

H. L. Mencken 1880–1956: *Minority Report* (1956)

26 To mistrust science and deny the validity of the scientific method is to resign your job as a human. You'd better go look for work as a plant or wild animal.

P. J. O'Rourke 1947– : *Parliament of Whores* (1991)

27 Realistically, the argument saying that you won't find a good scientist without industry connections is almost certainly right.

Doug Parr: in *Independent* 12 June 1999

28 Aristotle maintained that women have fewer teeth than men; although he was twice married, it never occurred to him to verify this statement by examining his wives' mouths.

Bertrand Russell 1872–1970: *Impact of Science on Society* (1952)

29 Science becomes dangerous only when it imagines that it has reached its goal.

George Bernard Shaw 1856–1950: preface to *The Doctor's Dilemma* (1911)

30 He had been eight years upon a project for extracting sun-beams out of cucumbers, which were to be put into vials hermetically sealed, and let out to warm the air in raw inclement summers.

Jonathan Swift 1667–1745: *Gulliver's Travels* (1726)

31 Her own mother lived the latter years of her life in the horrible suspicion that electricity was dripping invisibly all over the house.

James Thurber 1894–1961: *My Life and Hard Times* (1933)

32 There is something fascinating about science. One gets such wholesale returns of conjecture out of such a trifling investment of fact.

Mark Twain 1835–1910: *Life on the Mississippi* (1883)

33 It was absolutely marvellous working for Pauli. You could ask him anything. There was no worry that he would think a particular question was stupid, since he thought *all* questions were stupid.

Victor Weisskopf 1908– : in *American Journal of Physics* 1977

Scotland and the Scots See also **Countries and Peoples**, **Places**

1 There are few more impressive sights in the world than a Scotsman on the make.

J. M. Barrie 1860–1937: *What Every Woman Knows* (performed 1908)

2 A young Scotsman of your ability let loose upon the world with £300, what could he not do? It's almost appalling to think of; especially if he went among the English.

J. M. Barrie 1860–1937: *What Every Woman Knows* (1918)

3 I had occasion, not for the first time, to thank heaven for that state of mind which cartographers seek to define as Scotland.

Claud Cockburn 1904–81: *Crossing the Line* (1958)

4 They christened their game golf because they were
Scottish and revelled in meaningless Celtic noises in the
back of the throat.

Stephen Fry 1957– : *Paperweight*
(1992)

5 Norway, too, has noble wild prospects; and Lapland is
remarkable for prodigious noble wild prospects. But, Sir,
let me tell you, the noblest prospect which a Scotchman
ever sees, is the high road that leads him to England!

Samuel Johnson 1709–84: James
Boswell *Life of Samuel Johnson* (1791)
6 July 1763

6 *Oats*. A grain, which in England is generally given to
horses, but in Scotland supports the people.

Samuel Johnson 1709–84: *A
Dictionary of the English Language*
(1755)

7 Can the United States ever become genuinely civilized?
Certainly it is possible. Even Scotland has made enormous
progress since the Eighteenth Century, when, according to
Macaulay, most of it was on the cultural level of Albania.

H. L. Mencken 1880–1956: *Minority
Report* (1956)

8 No McTavish
Was ever lavish.

Ogden Nash 1902–71: 'Genealogical
Reflection' (1931)

9 Scotland has too many ninety-minute patriots whose
nationalist outpourings are expressed only at major
sporting events.

Jim Sillars 1937– : television
interview following the 1992 general
election; in *The Herald* 24 April 1992

10 That knuckle-end of England—that land of Calvin, oat-
cakes, and sulphur.

Sydney Smith 1771–1845: Lady
Holland *Memoir* (1855)

11 It requires a surgical operation to get a joke well into a
Scotch understanding. Their only idea of wit . . . is
laughing immoderately at stated intervals.

Sydney Smith 1771–1845: Lady
Holland *Memoir* (1855)

12 It is never difficult to distinguish between a Scotsman with
a grievance and a ray of sunshine.

P. G. Wodehouse 1881–1975:
Blandings Castle and Elsewhere (1935)

Secrecy

1 A Company for carrying on an undertaking of Great
Advantage, but no one to know what it is.

Anonymous: Company Prospectus
at the time of the South Sea Bubble
(1711)

2 I came to the conclusion that a man who could give such
pleasure with his pen couldn't be much of a secret agent. I
may well be wrong.
*view of the IRA army council's head of civilian intelligence on
John Betjeman's role as a press attaché in wartime Dublin*

Diarmuid Brennan: report, c.1941;
in *Guardian* 22 April 2000

3 Is that man crazy? He thinks there's a bug behind all the
pictures.
*as Director of the CIA, having visited Harold Wilson during
Wilson's last premiership*

George Bush 1924– : Peter
Hennessy *The Prime Minister: the
Office and its Holders since 1945*
(2000)

4 The best leaks always take place in the urinal.

John Cole 1927– : in *Independent* 3
June 1996

5 The spy who came in for a cardie.
*on 85-year-old Melita Nelson, exposed in 1999 as having spied
for Russia in the Cold War*

Mike Coleman 1946– : on *Loose
Ends* (BBC Radio 4) 18 September
1999

6 Secrets with girls, like loaded guns with boys,
Are never valued till they make a noise.

George Crabbe 1754–1832: *Tales of
the Hall* (1819) 'The Maid's Story'

7 We never knows wot's hidden in each other's hearts; and
if we had glass winders there, we'd need keep the shutters
up, some on us, I do assure you!

Charles Dickens 1812–70: *Martin Chuzzlewit* (1844)

8 If a man cannot keep a measly affair secret, what is he
doing in charge of the Intelligence Service?
on the break-up of the marriage of Foreign Secretary Robin Cook

Frederick Forsyth 1938– : in *Guardian* 14 January 1998

9 Anonymous, unseen—
You're dealing with the all-time king or queen
Of undercover loves.
The author of this valentine wore gloves.

Sophie Hannah 1971– : 'Poem for a Valentine Card' (1995)

10 Truth is suppressed, not to protect the country from
enemy agents but to protect the Government of the day
against the people.

Roy Hattersley 1932– : in *Independent* 18 February 1995

11 That's another of those irregular verbs, isn't it? I give
confidential briefings; you leak; he has been charged
under Section 2a of the Official Secrets Act.

Jonathan Lynn 1943– and **Antony Jay** 1930– : *Yes Prime Minister* (1987) vol. 2 'Man Overboard'

12 BLAIR: Everybody knows their safe house. Red Square we
call it.
HOGBIN: We call it Dunkremlin.

Tom Stoppard 1937– : *The Dog It Was That Died* (1983)

Self-Knowledge and Self-Deception See
also **Character**

1 Lady Kill-Chairman, who is one of the greatest gossips in
the kingdom, and knows everybody but herself.

Anonymous: in *The Female Tatler* December 1709

2 I do not stare at myself in the mirror. For one thing I can't
see myself properly without my glasses and because I can't
bear looking at myself in glasses because I look so terrible
in them, I never look at myself at all.

Alan Ayckbourn 1939– : *Table Manners* (1975)

3 A person of low taste, more interested in himself than in
me.

Ambrose Bierce 1842–c.1914: definition of an egotist; *Cynic's Word Book* (1906)

4 Our polite recognition of another's resemblance to
ourselves.

Ambrose Bierce 1842–c.1914: definition of admiration; *Cynic's Word Book* (1906)

5 It exactly resembles a superannuated Jesuit . . . though my
mind misgives me that it is hideously like. If it is—I can
not be long for this world—for it overlooks seventy.

Lord Byron 1788–1824: of a bust of himself by Bartolini; letter 23 September 1822

6 The Crown Prince Umberto is charm itself, but has no
great intelligence. He reminds me of myself.

Chips Channon 1897–1958: diary (undated entry); introduction to *Chips: the Diaries of Sir Henry Channon* (1993)

7 Long experience has taught me that to be criticized is not
always to be wrong.

Anthony Eden 1897–1977: speech at Lord Mayor's Guildhall banquet during the Suez crisis; in *Daily Herald* 10 November 1956

to a footman who had accidentally spilt cream over him:
8 My good man, I'm not a strawberry!

Edward VII 1841–1910: William Lanceley *From Hall-Boy to House-Steward* (1925)

9 I tell you,
Miss, I knows an undesirable character
When I see one; I've been one myself for years.

Christopher Fry 1907– : *Venus Observed* (1950)

10 All my shows are great. Some of them are bad. But they are all great.

Lew Grade 1906–98: in *Observer* 14 September 1975

11 This piece of writing had all the characteristics of my later work, namely that it was plagiarized, not very funny and in slightly bad taste.

Michael Green 1927– : *The Boy Who Shot Down an Airship* (1988)

12 The photograph is not quite true to my own notion of my gentleness and sweetness of nature, but neither perhaps is my external appearance.

A. E. Housman 1859–1936: letter, 12 June 1922

Housman was a pall-bearer at Thomas Hardy's funeral:
13 A journalist present in the abbey says that my person proved as polished as my verse, after which I desire to be for ever invisible.

A. E. Housman 1859–1936: letter, 24 January 1928

14 Without exactly *telling* them that I felt like a man swimming towards a raft in a sea of circling fins, I constructed a cry for help masterfully disguised as a manifesto.

Clive James 1939– : *The Dreaming Swimmer* (1992)

15 For self-revelation, whether it be a Tudor villa on the by-pass or a bomb-proof chalet at Berchtesgaden, there's no place like home.

Osbert Lancaster 1908–80: *Homes Sweet Homes* (1939)

16 I am not the type who wants to go back to the land; I am the type who wants to go back to the hotel.

Fran Lebowitz 1946– : *Social Studies* (1981)

17 Underneath this flabby exterior is an enormous lack of character.

Oscar Levant 1906–72: *Memoirs of an Amnesiac* (1965)

18 I believe that Sir Isaiah Berlin is the only man in Britain who talks more rapidly than I do, and even that is a close-run thing.

Bernard Levin 1928– : *In These Times* (1986)

19 If it were an innocent, passive gullibility it would be excusable; but all too clearly, alas, it is an active willingness to be deceived.

Peter Medawar 1915–87: review of Teilhard de Chardin *The Phenomenon of Man* (1961)

20 [I am] a doormat in a world of boots.

Jean Rhys c.1890–1979: in *Guardian* 6 December 1990

21 You're so vain
You probably think this song is about you.

Carly Simon 1945– : 'You're So Vain' (1972 song)

22 I can put two and two together, you know. Do not think you are dealing with a man who has lost his grapes.

Tom Stoppard 1937– : *Another Moon Called Earth* (1983)

23 Satire is a sort of glass, wherein beholders do generally discover everybody's face but their own.

Jonathan Swift 1667–1745: *The Battle of the Books* (1704) preface

24 'He has a profound contempt for human nature.'
'Of course, he is much given to introspection.'
of Fouché

Charles-Maurice de Talleyrand 1754–1838: Leon Harris *The Fine Art of Political Wit* (1965)

25 I am extraordinarily patient, provided I get my own way in the end.

Margaret Thatcher 1925– : in *Observer* 4 April 1989

26 As a lady of a certain age, I am willing to let the photographers and their zoom lenses stay, but only if they use their Joan Collins lens on me for close-ups.
on the decision to ban photographers from the debating chamber of the Scottish Parliament

Kay Ullrich 1943– : in *Scotsman* 18 March 2000

27 Pavarotti is not vain, but conscious of being unique.

Peter Ustinov 1921– : in *Independent on Sunday* 12 September 1993

28 I'm the girl who lost her reputation and never missed it.

Mae West 1892–1980: P. F. Boller and R. L. Davis *Hollywood Anecdotes* (1988)

29 I don't at all like knowing what people say of me behind my back. It makes me far too conceited.

Oscar Wilde 1854–1900: *An Ideal Husband* (1895)

Sex See also **Love, Marriage**

1 Don't knock masturbation. It's sex with someone I love.

Woody Allen 1935– : *Annie Hall* (1977 film, with Marshall Brickman)

2 A fast word about oral contraception. I asked a girl to go to bed with me and she said 'no'.

Woody Allen 1935– : at a night-club in Washington, April 1965

3 On bisexuality: It immediately doubles your chances for a date on Saturday night.

Woody Allen 1935– : in *New York Times* 1 December 1975

4 That [sex] was the most fun I ever had without laughing.

Woody Allen 1935– : *Annie Hall* (1977 film, with Marshall Brickman)

a former girlfriend's description of being made love to by Nicholas Soames:
5 Like having a large wardrobe fall on top of you with the key still in the lock.

Anonymous: Gyles Brandreth *Breaking the Code* (1999)

6 You should make a point of trying every experience once, excepting incest and folk-dancing.

Anonymous: Arnold Bax *Farewell My Youth* (1943), quoting 'a sympathetic Scot'

7 Would you like to sin
With Elinor Glyn
On a tigerskin?
Or would you prefer
To err
With her
On some other fur?

Anonymous: verse alluding to Elinor Glyn's romantic novel *Three Weeks* (1907); A. Glyn *Elinor Glyn* (1955)

8 You're the burning heat of a bridal suite in use.
You're the breasts of Venus,
You're King Kong's penis,
You're self abuse.
You're an arch
In the Rome collection
You're the starch
In a groom's erection.

Anonymous: parody version of Cole Porter's 'You're the Top' (1934), possibly by Porter

9 'My mother made me a homosexual.'
'If I send her the wool will she make me one?'

Anonymous: New York graffito of the 1970s

10 Let us honour if we can
   The vertical man
   Though we value none
   But the horizontal one.

W. H. Auden 1907–73: 'To Christopher Isherwood' (1930)

11 Give me chastity and continency—but not yet!

St Augustine of Hippo AD 354–430: *Confessions* (AD 397–8)

12 Norman doesn't bother with secret signals. It was just wham, thump and there we both were on the rug.

Alan Ayckbourn 1939– : *Table Manners* (1975)

13 My mother used to say, Delia, if S-E-X ever rears its ugly head, close your eyes before you see the rest of it.

Alan Ayckbourn 1939– : *Bedroom Farce* (1978)

14 I'll come and make love to you at five o'clock. If I'm late start without me.

Tallulah Bankhead 1903–68: Ted Morgan *Somerset Maugham* (1980)

15 I've no feeling in this arm and I can hardly see. Which knocks out at least three erogenous zones for a kick-off.

Alan Bennett 1934– : *Enjoy* (1980)

16 In the Garden City Café with its murals on the wall
   Before a talk on 'Sex and Civics' I meditated on the Fall.

John Betjeman 1906–84: 'Huxley Hall' (1954)

at the age of ninety-seven, Blake was asked at what age the sex drive goes:
17 You'll have to ask somebody older than me.

Eubie Blake 1883–1983: in *Ned Sherrin in his Anecdotage* (1993)

on being told he should not marry anyone as plain as his fiancée:
18 My dear fellow, buggers can't be choosers.

Maurice Bowra 1898–1971: Hugh Lloyd-Jones *Maurice Bowra: a Celebration* (1974)

19 Genitals are a great distraction to scholarship.

Malcolm Bradbury 1932–2000: *Cuts* (1987)

20 If homosexuality were the normal way, God would have made Adam and Bruce.

Anita Bryant 1940– : in *New York Times* 5 June 1977

21 He said it was artificial respiration, but now I find I am to have his child.

Anthony Burgess 1917–93: *Inside Mr Enderby* (1963)

22 It was the afternoon of my eighty-first birthday, and I was in bed with my catamite when Ali announced that the archbishop had come to see me.

Anthony Burgess 1917–93: *Earthly Powers* (1980); opening sentence

23 What men call gallantry, and gods adultery,
   Is much more common where the climate's sultry.

Lord Byron 1788–1824: *Don Juan* (1819–24)

24 A little still she strove, and much repented,
   And whispering 'I will ne'er consent'—consented.

Lord Byron 1788–1824: *Don Juan* (1819–24)

on homosexuality:
25 It doesn't matter what you do in the bedroom as long as you don't do it in the street and frighten the horses.

Mrs Patrick Campbell 1865–1940: Daphne Fielding *The Duchess of Jermyn Street* (1964)

26 Do not adultery commit;
   Advantage rarely comes of it.

Arthur Hugh Clough 1819–61: 'The Latest Decalogue' (1862)

27 The House of Commons en bloc do it,
   Civil Servants by the clock do it.

Noël Coward 1899–1973: 'Let's Do It' (with acknowledgements to Cole Porter) (1940s)

28 I became one of the stately homos of England.

Quentin Crisp 1908–99: *The Naked Civil Servant* (1968)

29 For flavour, Instant Sex will never supersede the stuff you had to peel and cook.

Quentin Crisp 1908–99: in *Sunday Telegraph* 28 September 1999

in 1951 the homosexual Labour politician Tom Driberg married a widow; he later complained:

30 She broke her marriage vows; she tried to sleep with me.

Tom Driberg 1905–76: in *Ned Sherrin in his Anecdotage* (1993)

31 Seduction is often difficult to distinguish from rape. In seduction, the rapist bothers to buy a bottle of wine.

Andrea Dworkin 1946– : *Letters from a War Zone* (1988)

32 He in a few minutes ravished this fair creature, or at least would have ravished her, if she had not, by a timely compliance, prevented him.

Henry Fielding 1707–54: *Jonathan Wild* (1743)

33 My dad told me, 'Anything worth having is worth waiting for.' I waited until I was fifteen.

Zsa Zsa Gabor 1919– : attributed; Bob Chieger *Was It Good For You?* (1983)

34 Sex was a competitive event in those days and the only thing you could take as a certainty was that everyone else was lying, just as you were.

Bob Geldof 1954– : *Is That It?* (1986)

35 Only the Lion and the Cock;
As Galen says, withstand Love's shock.
So, dearest, do not think me rude
If I yield now to lassitude,
But sympathize with me. I know
You would not have me roar or crow.

Oliver St John Gogarty 1878–1957: 'After Galen' (1957)

36 'Ye'es, ye'es,' he finally observed with a certain dry relish, 'ye'es, I think I see some adulterers down there.'
in the Press Gallery of the House of Commons during the Profumo scandal

Maurice Green 1906–87: recorded by Colin Welch; Ned Sherrin *Cutting Edge* (1984)

37 Masturbation is the thinking man's television.

Christopher Hampton 1946– : *The Philanthropist* (1970)

38 The trouble with a virgin is
She's always on the verge.
A virgin is the worst
Her method is reversed
She'll lead a horse to water
And then let him die of thirst.

E. Y. Harburg 1898–1981: 'Never Trust a Virgin' (1961)

39 I regret to say that we of the FBI are powerless to act in cases of oral-genital intimacy, unless it has in some way obstructed interstate commerce.

J. Edgar Hoover 1895–1972: Irving Wallace et al. *Intimate Sex Lives of Famous People* (1981)

40 The sexophones wailed like melodious cats under the moon.

Aldous Huxley 1894–1963: *Brave New World* (1932)

41 I can't get no satisfaction
I can't get no girl reaction.

Mick Jagger 1943– and **Keith Richard** 1943– : '(I Can't Get No) Satisfaction' (1965)

42 There is no unhappier creature on earth than a fetishist who yearns to embrace a woman's shoe and has to embrace the whole woman.

Karl Kraus 1874–1936: *Aphorisms and More Aphorisms* (1909)

43 Sexual intercourse began
In nineteen sixty-three
(Which was rather late for me)—

Philip Larkin 1922–85: 'Annus Mirabilis' (1974)

Between the end of the *Chatterley* ban
And the Beatles' first L.P.

44 Surely the sex business isn't worth all this damned fuss?
I've met only a handful of people who cared a biscuit for it.
on reading Lady Chatterley's Lover

T. E. Lawrence 1888–1935:
Christopher Hassall *Edward Marsh*
(1959)

45 He was into animal husbandry—until they caught him at
it.

Tom Lehrer 1928– : in *An Evening
Wasted with Tom Lehrer* (record
album, 1953); Nigel Rees (ed.) *Cassell
Dictionary of Humorous Quotations*
(1999)

on lesbianism:
46 I can understand two men. There is something to get hold
of. But how do two insides make love?

Lydia Lopokova 1892–1981: A. J. P.
Taylor letter 5 November 1973

47 BARNARDINE: Thou hast committed—
BARABAS: Fornication? But that was in another country:
and besides, the wench is dead.

Christopher Marlowe 1564–93: *The
Jew of Malta* (c.1592)

48 Many years ago I chased a woman for almost two years,
only to discover that her tastes were exactly like mine: we
both were crazy about girls.

Groucho Marx 1895–1977: letter 28
March 1955

49 I've been around so long, I knew Doris Day before she was
a virgin.

Groucho Marx 1895–1977: Max Wilk
The Wit and Wisdom of Hollywood
(1972)

50 I always thought music was more important than sex—
then I thought if I don't hear a concert for a year-and-
a-half it doesn't bother me.

Jackie Mason 1931– : in *Guardian* 17
February 1989

51 Continental people have sex life; the English have hot-
water bottles.

George Mikes 1912– : *How to be an
Alien* (1946)

on British attitudes to homosexuality:
52 Half the public wants it officially recognized and the other
half wants burning alive quartering etc. etc. to be restored
as the normal penalty.

Nancy Mitford 1904–73: letter, 21
November 1953

53 An orgy looks particularly alluring seen through the mists
of righteous indignation.

Malcolm Muggeridge 1903–90: *The
Most of Malcolm Muggeridge* (1966)
'Dolce Vita in a Cold Climate'

54 Not tonight, Josephine.

Napoleon I 1769–1821: attributed,
but probably apocryphal; R. H.
Horne *The History of Napoleon* (1841)
describes the circumstances in which
the affront might have occurred

55 I toiled on a farm tilling soybeans,
In a struggle to chasten my brain,
But the girl beans got in with the boy beans,
And I never struggled again.

Ogden Nash 1902–71: in *One Touch
of Venus* (1943 musical film)

56 She was as happy as the dey was long.
*of the relationship between Caroline of Brunswick, estranged
wife of George IV, and the dey (or governor) of Algiers*

Lord Norbury 1745–1831: attributed;
Nigel Rees *Cassell Dictionary of
Humorous Quotations* (1998)

57 GARY: She put me right on a few technical details, yes.
DERMOT: She said it was like sleeping with a badly-
informed labrador.

Simon Nye 1958– : *Men Behaving
Badly* (ITV, series 1, 1992) 'Intruders'

58 You were born with your legs apart. They'll send you to the grave in a Y-shaped coffin.

Joe Orton 1933–67: *What the Butler Saw* (1969)

59 MIKE: There's no word in the Irish language for what you were doing.
WILSON: In Lapland they have no word for snow.

Joe Orton 1933–67: *The Ruffian on the Stair* (rev. ed. 1967)

60 His second question was, 'How queer are you?' If I myself had small talent to amuse, I could at least make an effort to please. 'Oh, about twenty per cent.' 'Really! Are you? I'm ninety-five.'

John Osborne 1929– : recollection of a conversation with Noël Coward in 1966; *Almost a Gentleman* (1991)

61 Thank God we're normal,
Yes, this is our finest shower!

John Osborne 1929– : *The Entertainer* (1957)

on her abortion:
62 It serves me right for putting all my eggs in one bastard.

Dorothy Parker 1893–1967: John Keats *You Might as well Live* (1970)

63 Nobody in their right minds would call me a nymphomaniac. I only sleep with good-looking men.

Fiona Pitt-Kethley 1954– : in *Listener* 17 November 1988

64 On a sofa upholstered in panther skin
Mona did researches in original sin.

William Plomer 1903–73: 'Mews Flat Mona' (1960)

65 Birds do it, bees do it,
Even educated fleas do it.
Let's do it, let's fall in love.

Cole Porter 1891–1964: 'Let's Do It' (1954; words added to the 1928 original)

66 Mister Harris, Plutocrat,
Wants to give my cheek a pat.
If a Harris pat
Means a Paris hat,
Bébé!

Cole Porter 1891–1964: 'Always True to You in my Fashion' (*Kiss Me Kate* 1949 musical)

67 No, no; for my virginity,
When I lose that, says Rose, I'll die:
Behind the elms last night, cried Dick,
Rose, were you not extremely sick?

Matthew Prior 1664–1721: 'A True Maid' (1718)

68 Your idea of fidelity is not having more than one man in bed at the same time.

Frederic Raphael 1931– : *Darling* (1965)

69 Sex is something I really don't understand too hot. You never know *where* the hell you are. I keep making up these sex rules for myself, and then I break them right away.

J. D. Salinger 1919– : *The Catcher in the Rye* (1951)

70 Is it not strange that desire should so many years outlive performance?

William Shakespeare 1564–1616: *Henry IV, Part 2* (1597)

of Marina, a beautiful virgin
71 She would serve after a long voyage at sea.

William Shakespeare 1564–1616: *Pericles* (1606–8)

72 How long do you want to wait until you start enjoying life? When you're sixty-five you get social security, not girls.

Neil Simon 1927– : *Come Blow Your Horn* (1961)

73 Where is she at the moment? Alone with probably the most attractive man she's ever met. Don't tell me *that* doesn't beat hell out of hair curlers and the *Late Late Show*.

Neil Simon 1927– : *Barefoot in the Park* (1964)

74 Fancy meeting someone and forgetting you've slept with them. It's not good, is it?

Arthur Smith 1954– : *The Live Bed Show* (1995)

75 How can a bishop marry? How can he flirt? The most he can say is, 'I will see you in the vestry after service.'

Sydney Smith 1771–1845: Lady Holland *Memoir* (1855)

76 BONES: A consummate artist, sir. I felt it deeply when she retired.
GEORGE: Unfortunately she retired from consummation about the same time as she retired from artistry.

Tom Stoppard 1937– : *Jumpers* (rev. ed. 1986)

77 It's an odd thing but travel broadens the mind in a way that the proverbialist didn't quite intend. It's only at airports and railway stations that one finds in oneself a curiosity about er—er—erotica, um, girlie magazines.

Tom Stoppard 1937– : *Professional Foul* (1978)

78 [CHAIRMAN OF MILITARY TRIBUNAL:] What would you do if you saw a German soldier trying to violate your sister? [STRACHEY:] I would try to get between them.

Lytton Strachey 1880–1932: in Robert Graves *Good-bye to All That* (1929); otherwise rendered as, 'I should interpose my body'

79 Masturbation: the primary sexual activity of mankind. In the nineteenth century, it was a disease; in the twentieth, it's a cure.

Thomas Szasz 1920– : *The Second Sin* (1973)

80 Gomer Owen who kissed her once by the pig-sty when she wasn't looking and never kissed her again although she was looking all the time.

Dylan Thomas 1914–53: *Under Milk Wood* (1954)

81 Chasing the naughty couples down the grassgreen gooseberried double bed of the wood.

Dylan Thomas 1914–53: *Under Milk Wood* (1954)

82 She kissed her way into society. I don't like her. But don't misunderstand me: my dislike is purely platonic.
of an actress whose reputation as a lover was higher than her reputation as an artist

Herbert Beerbohm Tree 1852–1917: Hesketh Pearson *Beerbohm Tree* (1956)

83 Enjoy your supper, Mr Percy, the port is on the chim-a-ney piece, and it's *still* adultery!
on finding her husband Herbert Beerbohm Tree dining à deux with the young and handsome actor Esmé Percy

Lady Tree 1863–1937: attributed, perhaps apocryphal

84 Enter the strumpet voluntary.

Kenneth Tynan 1927–80: of a guest at an Oxford party; attributed

85 I'm all for bringing back the birch, but only between consenting adults.

Gore Vidal 1925– : in *Sunday Times Magazine* 16 September 1973

86 All this fuss about sleeping together. For physical pleasure I'd sooner go to my dentist any day.

Evelyn Waugh 1903–66: *Vile Bodies* (1930)

87 In my day, I would only have sex with a man if I found him extremely attractive. These days, girls seem to choose them in much the same way as they might choose to suck on a boiled sweet.

Mary Wesley 1912– : in *Independent* 18 October 1997 'Quote Unquote'

88 Why don't you come up sometime, and see me?
usually quoted as, 'Why don't you come up and see me sometime?'

Mae West 1892–1980: in *She Done Him Wrong* (1933 film)

89 It's not the men in my life that counts—it's the life in my men.

Mae West 1892–1980: in *I'm No Angel* (1933 film)

90 'But what *is* the love life of newts, if you boil it right down? Didn't you tell me once that they just waggled their tails at one another in the mating season?' 'Quite correct.'

P. G. Wodehouse 1881–1975: *The Code of the Woosters* (1938)

I shrugged my shoulders.
'Well, all right, if they like it. But it's not my idea of
molten passion.'

Sickness See also **Health**, **Medicine**

1 About five o'clock I am convinced, as of old, that I am
suffering from a combination of D.T.'s and G.P.I. Think of
making my will, but make some tea instead.

James Agate 1877–1947: diary, 1
June 1943

*Christopher Isherwood, apologising for his bad cold, had said that
he should probably have cancelled his dinner invitation to Axelrod
and Frederic Raphael:*
2 My dear Christopher, any cold of yours is a cold of mine.

George Axelrod 1922– : quoted by
Frederic Raphael in *Times Literary
Supplement* 4 February 2000

3 He was a very fine doctor. Very little he couldn't put right
when he set his mind to it. Rita's knee got the better of
him, though.

Alan Ayckbourn 1939– : *Sisterly
Feelings* (1981)

4 What's happened to the galloping consumption you had
last Thursday? Slowed down to a trot I suppose.

Alan Bennett 1934– : *Habeas Corpus*
(1973)

5 DENNIS: It's called Brett's Palsy.
He shows her a medical book.
MRS WICKSTEED: Tiredness, irritability, spots, yes. And
generally confined to the Caucasus. If this germ is
confined to the Caucasus what's it doing in Hove?

Alan Bennett 1934– : *Habeas Corpus*
(1973)

6 I'm not unwell. I'm fucking dying.

Jeffrey Bernard 1932–97: in
conversation with Dominic Lawson;
in *The Spectator* 19 February 1994

7 A cough so robust that I tapped into two new seams of
phlegm.

Bill Bryson 1951– : *Neither Here Nor
There* (1991)

8 What fun—dear little Sidney
Produced a spectacular stone in his kidney,
He's had eleven
So God's in His heaven
And that is the end of the news.

Noël Coward 1899–1973: 'That is
the End of the News' (1945)

9 The nurse sleeps sweetly, hired to watch the sick,
Whom, snoring, she disturbs.

William Cowper 1731–1800: *The
Task* (1785)

10 This cough I've got is hacking,
The pain in my head is wracking,
I hardly need to mention my flu.
The Board of Health has seen me
They want to quarantine me,
I might as well be miserable with you.

Howard Dietz 1896–1983:
'Miserable with You' (1931)

11 I wish I had the voice of Homer
To sing of rectal carcinoma,
Which kills a lot more chaps, in fact,
Than were bumped off when Troy was sacked.

J. B. S. Haldane 1892–1964:
'Cancer's a Funny Thing'; Ronald
Clark *J. B. S.* (1968)

12 My final word, before I'm done,
Is 'Cancer can be rather fun'.
Thanks to the nurses and Nye Bevan

J. B. S. Haldane 1892–1964:
'Cancer's a Funny Thing'; Ronald
Clark *J. B. S.* (1968)

The NHS is quite like heaven
Provided one confronts the tumour
With a sufficient sense of humour.

13 You can feed her all day with the vitamin A and the
    Bromo fizz,
But the medicine never gets anywhere near where the
    trouble is,
If she's getting a kind of a name for herself, and the name
    ain't his—
A person . . . can develop a cough.

Frank Loesser 1910–69: 'Adelaide's
Lament', reprise (1950)

14 In other words just from waiting around
For that plain little band of gold
A person . . . can develop a cold.
You can spray her wherever you figure the streptococci
    lurk.
You can give her a shot for whatever she's got but it just
    won't work.
If she's tired of getting the fish-eye from the hotel clerk,
A person . . . can develop a cold.

Frank Loesser 1910–69: 'Adelaide's
Lament' (1950)

15 Besides death, constipation is the big fear in hospitals.

Robert McCrum 1953– : *My Year Off*
(1998)

*on hearing of the illness of Traill, who in 1904 had beaten him for
the Provostship of Trinity Dublin:*
16 Nothing trivial, I hope.

John Pentland Mahaffy 1839–1919:
Ulick O'Connor *Oliver St John Gogarty*
(1964)

17 When they catch some sickness—which they rarely
do—usually they do not have to send for a doctor. They
know the cure . . . horrified though the doctor might be if
he heard what it was.
    of the older inhabitants of the Irish Gaeltacht

Flann O'Brien 1911–66: *Myles Away
from Dublin* (1990)

18 To talk of diseases is a sort of *Arabian Nights*
entertainment.

William Osler 1849–1919: Oliver
Sacks *The Man Who Mistook his Wife
for a Hat* (1985)

19 London is in the grip of a smog attack that makes
anything we've ever seen look trifling; it's a wonder to me
that everyone here isn't hospitalized with some kind of
pulmonary illness, because breathing is like burying your
head in a smokestack.

S. J. Perelman 1904–79: letter 13
December 1953

20 Hypochondria is the one disease I haven't got.

David Renwick 1951– and **Andrew
Marshall**: *The Burkiss Way* (BBC
Radio, 1978); Nigel Rees *Cassell
Dictionary of Humorous Quotations*
(1999)

21 In rural cottage life not to have rheumatism is as glaring
an omission as not to have been presented at Court would
be in more ambitious circumstances.

Saki 1870–1916: *The Toys of Peace*
(1919)

22 When men die of disease they are said to die from natural
causes. When they recover (and they mostly do) the doctor
gets the credit of curing them.

George Bernard Shaw 1856–1950:
preface to *The Doctor's Dilemma*
(1911)

23 My aunt died of influenza: so they said. But it's my belief they done the old woman in.

George Bernard Shaw 1856–1950: *Pygmalion* (1916)

24 BUDDY: . . . Do you feel any better?
MOTHER: How do I know? I feel too sick to tell.

Neil Simon 1927– : *Come Blow Your Horn* (1961)

Singing see **Songs and Singing**

Sleep and Dreams

1 There is a school of thought that believes that sleep is for the night. You seem to be out to disprove them.

Alan Ayckbourn 1939– : *Woman in Mind* (1986)

2 'It would make anyone go to sleep, that bedstead would, whether they wanted to or not.' 'I should think,' said Sam . . . 'poppies was nothing to it.'

Charles Dickens 1812–70: *Pickwick Papers* (1837)

3 Try thinking of love, or something.
Amor vincit insomnia.

Christopher Fry 1907– : *A Sleep of Prisoners* (1951)

4 Sleep is when all the unsorted stuff comes flying out as from a dustbin upset in a high wind.

William Golding 1911–93: *Pincher Martin* (1956)

5 I want something that will keep me awake thinking it was the food I ate and not the show I saw.
after a disastrous preview

George S. Kaufman 1889–1961: Howard Teichmann *George S. Kaufman* (1973)

6 I love sleep because it is both pleasant and safe to use.

Fran Lebowitz 1946– : *Metropolitan Life* (1978)

7 And so to bed.

Samuel Pepys 1633–1703: diary 20 April 1660

8 Men who are unhappy, like men who sleep badly, are always proud of the fact.

Bertrand Russell 1872–1970: *The Conquest of Happiness* (1930)

9 I have had a dream, past the wit of man to say what dream it was.

William Shakespeare 1564–1616: *A Midsummer Night's Dream* (1595–6)

10 Many's the long night I've dreamed of cheese—toasted, mostly.

Robert Louis Stevenson 1850–94: *Treasure Island* (1883)

11 There ain't no way to find out why a snorer can't hear himself snore.

Mark Twain 1835–1910: *Tom Sawyer Abroad* (1894)

12 I haven't been to sleep for over a year. That's why I go to bed early. One needs more rest if one doesn't sleep.

Evelyn Waugh 1903–66: *Decline and Fall* (1928)

Smoking

1 I have to smoke more [cigarettes] than most people— because the ones I smoke are very small and full of holes.

Beryl Bainbridge 1933– : in *Daily Telegraph* 28 February 1998

2 It has been said that cigarettes are the only product that, if used according to the manufacturer's instructions, have a very high chance of killing you.

Michael Buerk 1946– : in *Sunday Times* 11 July 1999

3 The pipe with solemn interposing puff,
Makes half a sentence at a time enough;
The dozing sages drop the drowsy strain,
Then pause, and puff—and speak, and pause again.

William Cowper 1731–1800: 'Conversation' (1782)

4 A custom loathsome to the eye, hateful to the nose, harmful to the brain, dangerous to the lungs, and in the black, stinking fume thereof, nearest resembling the horrible Stygian smoke of the pit that is bottomless.

James I 1566–1625: *A Counterblast to Tobacco* (1604)

5 This very night I am going to leave off tobacco! Surely there must be some other world in which this unconquerable purpose shall be realized.

Charles Lamb 1775–1834: letter to Thomas Manning, 26 December 1815

6 I smoked my first cigarette and kissed my first woman on the same day. I have never had time for tobacco since.

Arturo Toscanini 1867–1957: in *Observer* 30 June 1946

Snobbery See also **Class**

1 I am not quite a gentleman but you would hardly notice it but can't be helped anyhow.

Daisy Ashford 1881–1972: *The Young Visiters* (1919)

2 Sir Walter Elliot, of Kellynch-hall, in Somersetshire, was a man who, for his own amusement, never took up any book but the Baronetage; there he found occupation for an idle hour, and consolation in a distressed one.

Jane Austen 1775–1817: *Persuasion* (1818)

3 Vulgarity has its uses. Vulgarity often cuts ice which refinement scrapes at vainly.

Max Beerbohm 1872–1956: letter, 21 May 1921

4 Sapper, Buchan, Dornford Yates, practitioners in that school of Snobbery with Violence that runs like a thread of good-class tweed through twentieth-century literature.

Alan Bennett 1934– : *Forty Years On* (1969)

5 From Poland to polo in one generation.

Arthur Caesar d. 1953: of Darryl Zanuck; Max Wilk *The Wit and Wisdom of Hollywood* (1972)

6 Just because I have made a point of never losing my accent it doesn't mean I am an eel-and-pie yob.

Michael Caine 1933– : in *Times* 15 April 2000 'Quotes of the Week'

7 Yeats is becoming so aristocratic, he's evicting imaginary tenants.

Oliver St John Gogarty 1878–1957: Ulick O'Connor *Oliver St John Gogarty* (1964)

8 Why cannot you go down to Bristol and see some of the third and fourth class people there, and they'll do just as well?
to *Charles Dickens, who had told her of his proposed trip to America*

Lady Holland 1770–1845: U. Pope-Hennessy *Charles Dickens* (1947)

9 The trouble with Michael is that he had to buy all his furniture.

Michael Jopling 1930– : of Michael Heseltine; Alan Clark diary 17 June 1987

as an undergraduate Curzon requested permission to be allowed to attend a ball in London in honour of the Empress Augusta of Germany:
10 I don't think much of Empresses. Good morning.

Benjamin Jowett 1817–93: Kenneth Rose *Superior Person* (1969)

11 These are the same old fogies who doffed their lids and tugged the forelock to the British establishment.

Paul Keating 1944– : of Australian Conservative supporters of Great Britain, House of Representatives, 27 February 1992

12 People like a bit of humbug. If a reader of this book heard that the King had appointed him Keeper of the Swans, he'd be all over town with it in a minute.

Stephen Leacock 1869–1944: *The Boy I Left Behind Me* (1947)

the Duchess of Devonshire had called on Queen Mary to apologize
for her son's marrying the dancer Adele Astaire:

13 Don't worry. I have a niece called Smith.

Queen Mary 1867–1953: in *Times* 1 June 1994; obituary of Lady May Abel Smith

14 Aunt Bess, a built-in snob and prig,
Considered all gnomes infra dig;
Not things one readily forgives
On lawns of true Conservatives.

Alan Melville 1910–83: *Gnomes and Gardens* (1983)

on being told that Clare Boothe Luce was always kind to her
inferiors:

15 And where does she find them?

Dorothy Parker 1893–1967: Marion Meade *What Fresh Hell is This?* (1988)

16 Whenever he met a great man he grovelled before him,
and my-lorded him as only a free-born Briton can do.

William Makepeace Thackeray 1811–63: *Vanity Fair* (1847–8)

17 There is much to be said for the *nouveau riche* and the
Reagans intend to say it all.

Gore Vidal 1925– : attributed

Society and Social Life See also **Parties**

1 CECIL BEATON: What on earth can I become?
FRIEND: I shouldn't bother too much. Just become a friend
of the Sitwells and see what happens.

Anonymous: at the outset of Cecil Beaton's career; Laurence Whistler *The Laughter and the Urn* (1985)

2 Though you would often in the fifteenth century have
heard the snobbish Roman say, in a would-be off-hand
tone, 'I am dining with the Borgias tonight,' no Roman
ever was able to say, 'I dined last night with the Borgias.'

Max Beerbohm 1872–1956: *And Even Now* (1920)

3 Phone for the fish-knives, Norman
As Cook is a little unnerved;
You kiddies have crumpled the serviettes
And I must have things daintily served.

John Betjeman 1906–84: 'How to get on in Society' (1954)

4 Gaily into Ruislip Gardens
Runs the red electric train,
With a thousand Ta's and Pardon's
Daintily alights Elaine;
Hurries down the concrete station
With a frown of concentration,
Out into the outskirt's edges
Where a few surviving hedges
Keep alive our lost Elysium—rural Middlesex again.

John Betjeman 1906–84: 'Middlesex' (1954)

5 I'm a man more dined against than dining.

Maurice Bowra 1898–1971: John Betjeman *Summoned by Bells* (1960)

6 NINOTCHKA: Why should you carry other people's bags?
PORTER: Well, that's my business, Madame.
NINOTCHKA: That's no business. That's social injustice.
PORTER: That depends on the tip.

Charles Brackett 1892–1969 and **Billy Wilder** 1906– : *Ninotchka* (1939 film, with Walter Reisch)

7 The bar was like a funeral parlour with a beverage service.

Bill Bryson 1951– : *Neither Here Nor There* (1991)

8 Children of the Ritz,
Mentally congealed
Lilies of the Field

Noël Coward 1899–1973: 'Children of the Ritz' (1932)

We say just how we want our quails done,
And then we go and have our nails done.

9 In London, at the Café de Paris, I sang to café society; in Las Vegas, at the Desert Inn, I sang to Nescafé society.

Noël Coward 1899–1973: Sheridan Morley *The Quotable Noël Coward* (1999)

10 I notice she likes lights and commotion, which goes to show she has social instincts.

Ronald Firbank 1886–1926: *Valmouth* (1919)

11 The very pink of perfection.

Oliver Goldsmith 1730–74: *She Stoops to Conquer* (1773)

12 To hear Alice [Keppel] talk about her escape from France, one would think she had swum the Channel, with her maid between her teeth.

Mrs Ronnie Greville d. 1942: Chips Channon diary 19 August 1940

13 I'm Burlington Bertie
I rise at ten thirty and saunter along like a toff,
I walk down the Strand with my gloves on my hand,
Then I walk down again with them off.

W. F. Hargreaves 1846–1919: 'Burlington Bertie from Bow' (1915)

14 I do wish we could chat longer, but I'm having an old friend for dinner.

Thomas Harris 1940– and **Ted Tally** 1952– : *The Silence of the Lambs* (1991 film)

15 Already at four years of age I had begun to apprehend that refinement was very often an extenuating virtue; one that excused and eclipsed almost every other unappetizing trait.

Barry Humphries 1934– : *More Please* (1992)

16 Hail him like Etonians, without a single word,
Absolutely silent and indefinitely bored.

Ronald Knox 1888–1957: 'Magister Reformator' (1906)

17 PLEASE ACCEPT MY RESIGNATION. I DON'T WANT TO BELONG TO ANY CLUB THAT WILL ACCEPT ME AS A MEMBER.

Groucho Marx 1895–1977: telegram; *Groucho and Me* (1959)

18 You can be in the Horseguards and still be common, dear.

Terence Rattigan 1911–77: *Separate Tables* (1954) 'Table Number Seven'

on showing guests their rooms at Belvoir Castle, at a country-house weekend at the turn of the century:
19 If you are frightened in the night, Lord Kitchener, dear Lady Salisbury is just next door.

Duchess of Rutland d. 1937: Philip Ziegler *Diana Cooper* (1981)

20 All decent people live beyond their incomes nowadays, and those who aren't respectable live beyond other peoples'.

Saki 1870–1916: *Chronicles of Clovis* (1911)

21 MENDOZA: I am a brigand: I live by robbing the rich.
TANNER: I am a gentleman: I live by robbing the poor.

George Bernard Shaw 1856–1950: *Man and Superman* (1903)

22 MRS CANDOUR: I'll swear her colour is natural—I have seen it come and go—
LADY TEAZLE: I dare swear you have, ma'am; it goes of a night and comes again in the morning.

Richard Brinsley Sheridan 1751–1816: *The School for Scandal* (1777)

23 I must say I take off my hat to you, coming home with Rembrandt place mats for your mother. It's those little touches that lift adultery out of the moral arena and make it a matter of style.

Tom Stoppard 1937– : *The Real Thing* (1988 rev. ed.)

24 GERALD: I suppose society is wonderfully delightful!
LORD ILLINGWORTH: To be in it is merely a bore. But to be out of it simply a tragedy.

Oscar Wilde 1854–1900: *A Woman of No Importance* (1893)

25 Never speak disrespectfully of Society, Algernon. Only people who can't get into it do that.

Oscar Wilde 1854–1900: *The Importance of Being Earnest* (1895)

26 Yes, dear Frank [Harris], we believe you: you have dined in every house in London, *once*.

Oscar Wilde 1854–1900: William Rothenstein *Men and Memories* (1931)

27 Radical Chic . . . is only radical in Style; in its heart it is part of Society and its tradition—Politics, like Rock, Pop, and Camp, has its uses.

Tom Wolfe 1931– : in *New York* 8 June 1970

Songs and Singing

1 A town-and-country soprano of the kind often used for augmenting grief at a funeral.

George Ade 1866–1944: Nat Shapiro (ed.) *An Encyclopedia of Quotations about Music* (1978)

2 It is a pity that the composer did not leave directions as to how flat he really did want it sung.

Anonymous: review in *West Wilts Herald* 1893; Ned Sherrin *Cutting Edge* (1984)

3 In saloons and drab hallways
You are what I'll grab, always
Our love will be as grand
As Paul Whiteman's band
And will weigh as much as Paul weighs.
See how I dispense
Rhymes which are immense;
But do they make sense?
Not
Always.

Anonymous: a 1930s parody of Irving Berlin's 'Always' in Lorenz Hart's rhyming style; Ned Sherrin *Cutting Edge* (1984)

4 I do not mind what language an opera is sung in so long as it is a language I don't understand.

Edward Appleton 1892–1965: in *Observer* 28 August 1955

5 A gender bender I
A creature of illusion,
Of genital confusion,
A gorgeous butterfly.
My list of hits is long
Through every passion ranging,
To every fashion changing,
I tune my latent song.

Alistair Beaton and **Ned Sherrin** 1931– : a parody of Gilbert and Sullivan's 'A Wandering Minstrel I' in *The Metropolitan Mikado* (1985)

6 Today if something is not worth saying, people sing it.

Pierre-Augustin Caron de Beaumarchais 1732–99: *Le Barbier de Séville* (1775)

7 'Mr Nash, I can't hear you. Sing up!'
'How do you expect me to sing my best in this position, Sir Thomas?'
'In that position, my dear fellow, I have given some of my best performances.'

Thomas Beecham 1879–1961: to a tenor in rehearsals for *La Bohème* while lying on Mimi's bed; Ned Sherrin *Cutting Edge* (1984)

8 I was just wondering, is this the place where I'm supposed to be drowned by the waves or by the orchestra?
the tenor in The Wreckers *explaining to Sir Thomas Beecham why he had stopped*

John Coates 1865–1941: ; C. Reid *Sir Thomas Beecham* (1961)

9 The opera ain't over 'til the fat lady sings.

Dan Cook: in *Washington Post* 3 June 1978

10 Nonsense. Has he not moved the Queen of Portugal to tears?

when Noël was denied a place in the Chapel Royal School choir because his voice was unsuitable

Violet Coward: Caryl Brahms and Ned Sherrin *Song by Song* (1984)

11 People are wrong when they say that the opera isn't what it used to be. It is what it used to be—that's what's wrong with it.

Noël Coward 1899–1973: *Design for Living* (1933)

12 In writing songs I've learned as much from Cézanne as I have from Woody Guthrie.

Bob Dylan 1941– : Clinton Heylin *Dylan: Behind the Shades* (1991)

13 Maybe the most that you can expect from a relationship that goes bad is to come out of it with a few good songs.

Marianne Faithfull 1946– : *Faithfull* (1994)

14 LEW FIELDS: Ladies don't write lyrics.
DOROTHY FIELDS: I'm no lady, I'm your daughter.
to her father

Dorothy Fields 1905–74: Caryl Brahms and Ned Sherrin *Song by Song* (1984)

15 Opera is when a guy gets stabbed in the back and, instead of bleeding, he sings.

Ed Gardner 1901–63: *Duffy's Tavern* (US radio programme, 1940s)

16 Opera in English is, in the main, just about as sensible as baseball in Italian.

H. L. Mencken 1880–1956: Laurence J. Peter (ed.) *Quotations for our Time* (1977)

refusing to accept further changes to lyrics:
17 Call me Miss Birdseye. This show is frozen!

Ethel Merman 1909–84: in *Times* 13 July 1985

18 Clichés make the best songs. I put down every one I can find.

Bob Merrill 1921–98: in *New York Times* 19 February 1998

19 'Who wrote that song?'
'Rodgers and Hammerstein. If you can imagine it taking *two* men to write one song.'
of 'Some Enchanted Evening' (1949)

Cole Porter 1891–1964: G. Eells *The Life that Late He Led* (1967)

20 I lift up my finger and I say 'tweet tweet'.

Leslie Sarony 1897–1985: title of song (1929)

21 Tenors are usually short, stout men (except when they are Wagnerian tenors, in which case they are large, stout men) made up predominantly of lungs, rope-sized vocal chords, large frontal sinuses, thick necks, thick heads, tantrums and *amour propre* . . . It is certain that they are a race apart, a race that tends to operate reflexively rather than with due process of thought.

Harold Schonberg 1915– : in *Show* December 1961

22 All the grittiness of *The Fantastics*.

Stephen Sondheim 1930– : of one of his own lyrics; in conversation

23 The first act of the three occupied two hours. I enjoyed that in spite of the singing.

Mark Twain 1835–1910: *What is Man?* (1906)

24 By the Great Wobbly top note of Jeanette Macdonald!

Dick Vosburgh: *A Saint She Ain't* (1999)

Speeches and Speechmaking

1 I do not object to people looking at their watches when I am speaking. But I strongly object when they start shaking them to make certain they are still going.

Lord Birkett 1883–1962: in *Observer* 30 October 1960

2 ALEXANDER SMYTH: You, sir, speak for the present
generation, but I speak for posterity.
HENRY CLAY: Yes, and you seem resolved to speak until the
arrival of *your* audience.

Henry Clay 1777–1852: in the US
Senate; Robert V. Remini *Henry Clay*
(1991)

opening a Red Cross bazaar at Oxford:
3 Desperately accustomed as I am to public speaking.

Noël Coward 1899–1973: Dick
Richards *The Wit of Noël Coward*
(1968)

4 Hubert Humphrey talks so fast that listening him is like
trying to read *Playboy* magazine with your wife turning
the pages.

Barry Goldwater 1909–98:
attributed; Ned Sherrin *Cutting Edge*
(1984)

5 Lisp: to call a spade a thpade.

Oliver Herford 1863–1935:
attributed; Evan Esar and Nicolas
Bentley (eds.) *The Treasury of
Humorous Quotations* (1951)

6 I may not know much, but I know chicken shit from a
chicken salad.

Lyndon Baines Johnson 1908–73:
on a speech by Richard Nixon; Merle
Miller *Lyndon* (1980)

7 Did you ever think that making a speech on economics is a
lot like pissing down your leg? It seems hot to you, but it
never does to anyone else.
to J. K. Galbraith

Lyndon Baines Johnson 1908–73: J.
K. Galbraith *A Life in Our Times* (1981)

*on Winston Churchill at a dinner at the London School of
Economics:*
8 He searched always to end a sentence with a climax. He
looked for antithesis like a monkey looking for fleas.

Harold Laski 1893–1950: letter to
Oliver Wendell Holmes, 7 May 1927

9 The most popular speaker is the one who sits down before
he stands up.

John Pentland Mahaffy 1839–1919:
W. B. Stanford and R. B. McDowell
Mahaffy (1971)

*with reference to William Jennings Bryan's speech at the
Democratic National Convention in 1896:*
10 Democracy seldom had a ruder shock than when a
phrase—you shall not crucify mankind upon a cross of
gold—nearly put an ignorant and conceited fool in the
White House.

W. Somerset Maugham 1874–1965:
A Writer's Notebook (1949) written in
1941

11 I am hopeless at making an amusing speech, since my
jokes never seem to the British public to be jokes at all. The
only thing I am at all good at is making funeral orations.

Harold Nicolson 1886–1968: diary 12
October 1954

12 The . . . reason why MPs now speak for so long is that
padding takes longer than substance . . . having nothing
to say, they have no way of knowing when they have said
it.

Matthew Parris 1949– : in *Times* 4
March 1999

13 When someone asks a question about sex in Hyde Park
you double the crowd and halve the argument.

Donald Soper 1903–98: attributed,
in *The Times* 23 December 1998

14 I fear I cannot make an amusing speech. I have just been
reading a book which says that 'all geniuses are devoid of
humour'.

Stephen Spender 1909– : speech in
a debate at the Cambridge Union,
January 1938

15 Nixon's farm policy is vague, but he is going a long way
towards slowing the corn surplus by his speeches.

Adlai Stevenson 1900–65: Bill Adler
The Stevenson Wit (1966)

16 Someone must fill the gap between platitudes and bayonets.

Adlai Stevenson 1900–65: Leon Harris *The Fine Art of Political Wit* (1965)

17 Reading a speech with his usual sense of discovery.
of ex-President Eisenhower at the Republican convention of 1964

Gore Vidal 1925– : in *New York Review of Books* 29 September 1983

Sports and Games See also **Baseball**, **Boxing**, **Cricket**, **Football**, **Golf**, **Tennis**

1 DORCAS: I thought runners were all sportsmen and totally honest.
LEN: Not this lot. They're all as bent as hell.

Alan Ayckbourn 1939– : *Sisterly Feelings* (1981)

on being asked why he did not hunt:
2 I do not see why I should break my neck because a dog chooses to run after a nasty smell.

Arthur James Balfour 1848–1930: Ian Malcolm *Lord Balfour: A Memory* (1930)

3 Playing snooker gives you firm hands and helps to build up character. It is the ideal recreation for dedicated nuns.
view of the Pope's emissary, attending a sponsored snooker championship at Tyburn convent

Luigi Barbarito 1922– : in *Daily Telegraph* 15 November 1989

4 If you think squash is a competitive activity, try flower arrangement.

Alan Bennett 1934– : *Talking Heads* (1988)

5 Oh wasn't it naughty of Smudges?
Oh, Mummy, I'm sick with disgust.
She threw me in front of the Judges
And my silly old collarbone's bust.

John Betjeman 1906–84: 'Hunter Trials' (1954)

6 A man described as a 'sportsman' is generally a bookmaker who takes actresses to night clubs.

Jimmy Cannon 1910–73: in *New York Post c.*1951–54 'Nobody Asked Me, But . . .'

7 The trouble with referees is that they just don't care which side wins.
a US basketball player's view

Tom Canterbury: in *Guardian* 24 December 1980 'Sports Quotes of the Year'

8 His blade struck the water a full second before any other: the lad had started well. Nor did he flag as the race wore on . . . as the boats began to near the winning-post, his oar was dipping into the water nearly *twice* as often as any other.
often quoted as, 'All rowed fast, but none so fast as stroke'

Desmond Coke 1879–1931: *Sandford of Merton* (1903)

9 He just can't believe what isn't happening to him.

David Coleman: in *Guardian* 24 December 1980 'Sports Quotes of the Year'

10 That's the fastest time ever run—but it's not as fast as the world record.

David Coleman: Barry Fantoni (ed.) *Private Eye's Colemanballs 3* (1986)

11 Makes me want to yell from St Paul's steeple
The people I'd like to shoot are the shooting people.

Howard Dietz 1896–1983: 'By Myself' (1937)

12 The thing about sport, any sport, is that swearing is very much part of it.

Jimmy Greaves 1940– : in *Observer* 1 January 1989 'Sayings of the Year'

13 Vladimir, Vladimir, Vladimir Kuts
Nature's attempt at an engine in boots.
on the Russian runner Vladimir Kuts in 1956

A. P. Herbert 1890–1971: Ned Sherrin *Cutting Edge* (1984)

14 The only athletic sport I ever mastered was backgammon.

Douglas Jerrold 1803–57: Walter Jerrold *Douglas Jerrold* (1914)

15 It is very strange, and very melancholy, that the paucity of human pleasures should persuade us ever to call hunting one of them.

Samuel Johnson 1709–84: Hester Lynch Piozzi *Anecdotes of . . . Johnson* (1786)

16 I remain of the opinion that there is no game from bridge to cricket that is not improved by a little light conversation; a view which . . . is shared only by a small and unjustly despised minority.

Osbert Lancaster 1908–80: *All Done From Memory* (1953)

17 It is to be observed that 'angling' is the name given to fishing by people who can't fish.

Stephen Leacock 1869–1944: attributed

18 Rodeoing is about the only sport you can't fix. You'd have to talk to the bulls and the horses, and they wouldn't understand you.

Bill Linderman 1922–61: in 1961; Jonathon Green and Don Atyeo (eds.) *The Book of Sports Quotes* (1979)

19 If you shout hooray for the Pennsylvania Dutchmen
Every team that they play will be carried away with a
    crutch when
They're out on the field if they're wearing the shield of the
    Dutchmen.

Hugh Martin and **Ralph Blane**: 'Buckle Down Winsocki' (1941)

20 I hate all sports as rabidly as a person who likes sports hates common sense.

H. L. Mencken 1880–1956: Laurence J. Peter (ed.) *Quotations for our Time* (1977)

21 Sport, as I have discovered, fosters international hostility and leads the audience, no doubt from boredom, to assault and do grievous bodily harm while watching it.

John Mortimer 1923– : *Clinging to the Wreckage* (1982)

22 There's been a colour clash: both teams are wearing white.

John Motson: in 'Colemanballs' column in *Private Eye*; Ned Sherrin *Cutting Edge* (1984)

23 All winter long I am one for whom the bell is tolling
I can arouse no interest in basketball, indoor fly casting or
    bowling.
The sports pages are strictly no soap
And until the cry of 'Play Ball', I mope!

Ogden Nash 1902–71: in *Sports Illustrated* 1957

24 The sport of ski-ing consists of wearing three thousand dollars' worth of clothes and equipment and driving two hundred miles in the snow in order to stand around at a bar and get drunk.

P. J. O'Rourke 1947– : *Modern Manners* (1984)

25 Most of their discourse was about hunting, in a dialect I understand very little.

Samuel Pepys 1633–1703: diary, 22 November 1663

Goering's excuse for being late was a shooting party:
26 Animals, I hope.

Eric Phipps 1875–1945: Ned Sherrin *Cutting Edge* (1984); attributed

27 SHE: Are you fond of riding, dear?
Kindly tell me, if so.
HE: Yes, I'm fond of riding, dear,
But in the morning, no.

Cole Porter 1891–1964: 'But in the Morning, No' (1939)

28 A handicapper being a character who can dope out from the form what horses ought to win the races, and as long as his figures turn out all right, a handicapper is spoken of

Damon Runyon 1884–1946: *Take it Easy* (1938); 'All Horse Players Die Broke'

most respectfully by one and all, although of course when
he begins missing out for any length of time as
handicappers are bound to do, he is no longer spoken of
respectfully, or even as a handicapper. He is spoken of as a
bum.

29 You do not keep accounts and tell everybody that you
think you are all square at the end of the year. You lie and
you know it.

S. J. Simon 1904–48: *Why You Lose at Bridge* (1945)

30 I can't see who's in the lead but it's either Oxford or
Cambridge.

John Snagge 1904– : C. Dodd *Oxford and Cambridge Boat Race* (1983)

31 It ar'n't that I loves the fox less, but that I loves the 'ound
more.

R. S. Surtees 1805–64: *Handley Cross* (1843)

32 'Unting is all that's worth living for—all time is lost wot is
not spent in 'unting—it is like the hair we breathe—if we
have it not we die—it's the sport of kings, the image of
war without its guilt, and only five-and-twenty per cent of
its danger.

R. S. Surtees 1805–64: *Handley Cross* (1843)

33 I am here to propose a toast to the sports writers. It's up to
you whether you stand or not.

Freddie Trueman 1931– : Michael Parkinson *Sporting Lives* (1993)

34 I have observed in women of her type a tendency to regard
all athletics as inferior forms of foxhunting.

Evelyn Waugh 1903–66: *Decline and Fall* (1928)

35 I used to think the only use for it [sport] was to give small
boys something else to kick besides me.

Katharine Whitehorn 1926– : *Observations* (1970)

36 The English country gentleman galloping after a fox—the
unspeakable in full pursuit of the uneatable.

Oscar Wilde 1854–1900: *A Woman of No Importance* (1893); see **The Law** 42

37 The fascination of shooting as a sport depends almost
wholly on whether you are at the right or wrong end of a
gun.

P. G. Wodehouse 1881–1975: attributed

38 Jogging is for people who aren't intelligent enough to
watch television.

Victoria Wood 1953– : *Mens Sana in Thingummy Doodah* (1990)

Success and Failure

*during a rehearsal at the Royal Court, Beckett encouraged an actor
who had lamented, 'I'm failing':*
1 Go on failing. Go on. Only next time, try to fail better.

Samuel Beckett 1906–89: Tony Richardson *Long Distance Runner* (1993)

2 Success is the one unpardonable sin against our fellows.

Ambrose Bierce 1842–c.1914: *The Enlarged Devil's Dictionary* (1967)

3 Where did we go right?
of an unexpected success

Mel Brooks 1926– : *The Producers* (1967 film), spoken by Zero Mostel

4 There are three things you can't do in life. You can't beat
the phone company, you can't make a waiter see you
until he's ready to see you, and you can't go home again.

Bill Bryson 1951– : *The Lost Continent* (1989)

5 In the end we are all sacked and it's always awful. It is as
inevitable as death following life. If you are elevated there
comes a day when you are demoted. Even Prime Ministers.

Alan Clark 1928–99: diary 21 June 1983

6 I am that twentieth-century failure, a happy undersexed celibate.

Denise Coffey: Ned Sherrin *Cutting Edge* (1984)

7 Whom the gods wish to destroy they first call promising.

Cyril Connolly 1903–74: *Enemies of Promise* (1938)

8 Success took me to her bosom like a maternal boa constrictor.

Noël Coward 1899–1973: Sheridan Morley *A Talent to Amuse* (1969)

9 If at first you don't succeed, failure may be your style.

Quentin Crisp 1908–99: in *Sunday Telegraph* 28 September 1999

10 The trouble with fulfilling your ambitions is you think you will be transformed into some sort of archangel and you're not. You still have to wash your socks.

Louis de Bernières 1954– : in *Independent* 14 February 1999

11 I think that's just another word for a washed-up has-been.
on being an 'icon'

Bob Dylan 1941– : in *Mail on Sunday* 18 January 1998 'Quotes of the Week'

12 I don't think we have failed, we have just found another way that doesn't work.
on the ending of an attempted round-the-world balloon flight

Andy Ellson: comment, Hamamatsu, Japan, 7 March 1999

13 If at first you don't succeed, try, try again. Then quit. No use being a damn fool about it.

W. C. Fields 1880–1946: attributed

of David Steel, Leader of the Liberal Party:
14 He's passed from rising hope to elder statesman without any intervening period whatsoever.

Michael Foot 1913– : in the House of Commons, 28 March 1979

15 My son, the world is your lobster.

Leon Griffiths 1928–92: *Minder* (TV series); Nigel Rees (ed.) *Cassell Dictionary of Humorous Quotations* (1999)

16 Well, we knocked the bastard off!
on conquering Mount Everest, 1953

Edmund Hillary 1919– : *Nothing Venture, Nothing Win* (1975)

17 Come forth, Lazarus! And he came fifth and lost the job.

James Joyce 1882–1941: *Ulysses* (1922)

18 We would prefer to see the House run by a philistine with the requisite financial acumen than by the succession of opera and ballet lovers who have brought a great and valuable institution to its knees.

Gerald Kaufman 1930– : report of the Commons' Culture, Media and Sport select committee on Covent Garden, 3 December 1997

19 It is sobering to consider that when Mozart was my age he had already been dead for a year.

Tom Lehrer 1928– : N. Shapiro (ed.) *An Encyclopedia of Quotations about Music* (1978)

20 Success. I don't believe it has any effect on me. For one thing I always expected it.

W. Somerset Maugham 1874–1965: *A Writer's Notebook* (1949) written in 1908

21 How to succeed in business without really trying.

Shepherd Mead 1914– : title of book (1952)

22 The theory seems to be that as long as a man is a failure he is one of God's children, but that as soon as he succeeds he is taken over by the Devil.

H. L. Mencken 1880–1956: *Minority Report* (1956)

23 Be nice to people on your way up because you'll meet 'em on your way down.

Wilson Mizner 1876–1933: Alva Johnston *The Legendary Mizners* (1953)

24 The world is divided into people who do things and people who get the credit. Try, if you can, to belong to the first class. There's far less competition.

Dwight Morrow 1873–1931: letter to his son; Harold Nicolson *Dwight Morrow* (1935)

25 David Frost has risen without trace.

Kitty Muggeridge 1903–94: said c.1965 to Malcolm Muggeridge

as the disastrous 1958 electoral results for the Canadian Liberal Party were announced, Lester Pearson's wife had comforted herself with the hope of 'an honourable if unflattering' exit from politics for her husband:

26 We've lost everything, we've even won our own constituency!

Maryon Pearson: Lester Pearson *Memoirs* (1975) vol. 3

a choice of explanations for Dan Quayle's success at various critical points in his career:

27 His family knew people/calls were made/luck would have it.

Joe Queenan: *Imperial Caddy* (1992)

28 Failure is human, after all, and you grow up by making mistakes. I've made a ton of them, but as long as I keep on failing better, I don't mind.

Joely Richardson 1958– : in *Observer* 14 May 2000 'They said what . . . ?'

29 She regretted that Fate had not seen its way to reserve for her some of the ampler successes for which she felt herself well qualified.

Saki 1870–1916: *The Toys of Peace* (1919)

30 I never climbed any ladder: I have achieved eminence by sheer gravitation.

George Bernard Shaw 1856–1950: preface to *The Irrational Knot* (1905)

31 Lord Rosebery had ambition of an unusual kind. His lifelong dream was that, without effort or preparation, he should be offered the post of Prime Minister, and that he should then gracefully refuse. He nearly attained this ambition.

A. J. P. Taylor 1906–90: in *Observer* 17 February 1963

32 People who reach the top of the tree are only those who haven't got the qualifications to detain them at the bottom.

Peter Ustinov 1921– : interview with David Frost in 1969

33 Whenever a friend succeeds, a little something in me dies.

Gore Vidal 1925– : in *Sunday Times Magazine* 16 September 1973

34 He turned being a Big Loser into a perfect triumph by managing to lose the presidency in a way bigger and more original than anyone else had ever lost it before.
   of Richard Nixon

Gore Vidal 1925– : in *Esquire* December 1983

35 Anybody seen in a bus over the age of 30 has been a failure in life.

Loelia, Duchess of Westminster 1902–93: in *The Times* 4 November 1993; habitual remark

36 Moderation is a fatal thing, Lady Hunstanton. Nothing succeeds like excess.

Oscar Wilde 1854–1900: *A Woman of No Importance* (1893)

37 Success is a science; if you have the conditions, you get the result.

Oscar Wilde 1854–1900: letter ?March–April 1883

to the actor Victor Spinetti:

38 Ah, Victor, still struggling to keep your head below water.

Emlyn Williams 1905–87: attributed; Ned Sherrin *Cutting Edge* (1984)

Taxes

1 Tax collectors who'll never know the invigorating joys of treading water in the deep end without a life belt.

Jeffrey Bernard 1932–97: in *The Spectator* 3 March 1984

2 It was as true . . . as taxes is. And nothing's truer than them.

Charles Dickens 1812–70: *David Copperfield* (1850)

3 To be consistent the potato, introduced by Raleigh, would be extradited and smoking taxed as a foreign game.
   on the introduction to the Irish Senate in 1932 of the Emergency Imposition of Duties Bill

Oliver St John Gogarty 1878–1957: Ulick O'Connor *Oliver St John Gogarty* (1964)

4 The collection of a lunatic and inequitable tax, however few the victims, must tend to breed an un-English dislike of taxation in general.

A. P. Herbert 1890–1971: *Misleading Cases* (1935)

5 *Excise.* A hateful tax levied upon commodities.

Samuel Johnson 1709–84: *A Dictionary of the English Language* (1755)

6 Logic and taxation are not always the best of friends.

James C. McReynolds 1862–1946: concurring in *Sonneborn Bros. v. Cureton* 1923

7 I'm up to my neck in the real world, every day. Just you try doing your VAT return with a head full of goblins

Terry Pratchett 1948– : in *Sunday Times* 27 February 2000 'Talking Heads'

8 Income Tax has made more Liars out of the American people than Golf.

Will Rogers 1879–1935: *The Illiterate Digest* (1924) 'Helping the Girls with their Income Taxes'

9 The average homebred Englishman . . . will shut his eyes to the most villainous abuses if the remedy threatens to add another penny in the pound to the rates and taxes which he has to be half cheated, half coerced into paying.

George Bernard Shaw 1856–1950: preface to *Plays Unpleasant* (1898)

10 What is the difference between a taxidermist and a tax collector? The taxidermist takes only your skin.

Mark Twain 1835–1910: *Notebook* 30 December 1902

11 I sincerely hope that increased taxation, necessary to meet the expenses of the war, will not fall upon the working classes; but I fear they will be most affected by the extra sixpence on beer.

Queen Victoria 1819–1901: letter to Lord Salisbury, 21 October 1899

Technology See also **Progress, Science**

1 When man wanted to make a machine that would walk he created the wheel, which does not resemble a leg.

Guillaume Apollinaire 1880–1918: *Les Mamelles de Tirésias* (1918)

2 Inanimate objects are classified scientifically into three major categories—those that don't work, those that break down, and those that get lost.

Russell Baker 1925– : in *New York Times* 18 June 1968

3 Electric typewriters keep going 'mmmmmmm—what are you waiting for?'

Anthony Burgess 1917–93: Clare Boylan (ed.) *The Agony and the Ego* (1993)

4 The first rule of intelligent tinkering is to save all the parts.

Paul Ralph Ehrlich 1932- : in *Saturday Review* 5 June 1971

5 Why sir, there is every possibility that you will soon be able to tax it!
to Gladstone, when asked about the usefulness of electricity

Michael Faraday 1791–1867: W. E. H. Lecky *Democracy and Liberty* (1899 ed.)

6 For a successful technology, reality must take precedence over public relations, for nature cannot be fooled.

Richard Phillips Feynman 1918–88: Appendix to the *Rogers Commission Report on the Space Shuttle Challenger Accident* 6 June 1986

7 Technology . . . the knack of so arranging the world that we need not experience it.

Max Frisch 1911–91: *Homo Faber* (1957)

8 The itemised phone bill ranks up there with suspender belts, Sky Sports Channels and Loaded magazine as inventions women could do without.

Maeve Haran 1932- : in *Mail on Sunday* 25 April 1999

9 The thing with high-tech is that you always end up using scissors.

David Hockney 1937- : in *Observer* 10 July 1994 'Sayings of the Week'

10 Take up car maintenance and find the class is full of other thirty-something women like me, looking for a fella.

Marian Keyes: 'Late Opening at the Last Chance Saloon' (1997)

11 How very bold of you to buy an electric typewriter; the only time I tried one I was scared to death, as it seemed to be running away with me. I felt as if I had been put at the controls of Concorde after five minutes' tuition.

Philip Larkin 1922–85: letter to Anthony Powell, 7 August 1985

12 Dr Strabismus (Whom God Preserve) of Utrecht has patented a new invention. It is an illuminated trouser-clip for bicyclists who are using main roads at night.

J. B. Morton 1893–1975: *Morton's Folly* (1933)

13 Father had a secret of making inanimate objects appear to possess malevolent life of their own, and sometimes it was hard to believe that his tools and materials were not really in a conspiracy against him.

Frank O'Connor 1903–66: *An Only Child* (1961)

14 The photographer is like the cod which produces a million eggs in order that one may reach maturity.

George Bernard Shaw 1856–1950: introduction to the catalogue for Alvin Langdon Coburn's exhibition at the Royal Photographic Society, 1906

15 I was right about the skate-board, I was right about *nouvelle cuisine*, and I'll be proved right about the digital watch. Digitals have got no class, you see. They're science and technology.

Tom Stoppard 1937- : *The Real Thing* (1988 rev. ed.)

16 He put this engine [a watch] to our ears, which made an incessant noise like that of a water-mill; and we conjecture it is either some unknown animal, or the god that he worships; but we are more inclined to the latter opinion.

Jonathan Swift 1667–1745: *Gulliver's Travels* (1726)

17 Molesworth 2 . . . is inventing the wheel as he feel in science nothing should be accepted he is uterly wet.

Geoffrey Willans 1911–58 and **Ronald Searle** 1920- : *Down with Skool!* (1953)

18 JACKIE: (*very slowly*) Take Tube A and apply to Bracket D.
VICTORIA: Reading it slower does not make it any easier to do.

Victoria Wood 1953- : *Mens Sana in Thingummy Doodah* (1990)

Telegrams

1 Along the electric wire the message came:
He is not better—he is much the same.

Anonymous: parodic poem on the illness of the Prince of Wales, later King Edward VII, in F. H. Gribble *Romance of the Cambridge Colleges* (1913); sometimes attributed to Alfred Austin (1835–1913), Poet Laureate

as a young Times *correspondent in America, Claud Cockburn received a telegram authorizing him to report a murder in Al Capone's Chicago:*

2 BY ALL MEANS COCKBURN CHICAGOWARDS. WELCOME STORIES EX-CHICAGO NOT UNDULY EMPHASISING CRIME.

Anonymous: Claud Cockburn *In Time of Trouble* (1956)

telegraph message on arriving in Venice:

3 STREETS FLOODED. PLEASE ADVISE.

Robert Benchley 1889–1945: R. E. Drennan *Wit's End* (1973)

4 HOW DARE YOU BECOME PRIME MINISTER WHEN I'M AWAY GREAT LOVE CONSTANT THOUGHT VIOLET.
to her father, H. H. Asquith, 7 April 1908

Violet Bonham Carter 1887–1969: Mark Bonham Carter and Mark Pottle (eds.) *Lantern Slides* (1996)

to Irving Thalberg on the birth of his son:

5 CONGRATULATIONS ON YOUR LATEST PRODUCTION. AM SURE IT WILL LOOK BETTER AFTER IT'S BEEN CUT.

Eddie Cantor 1892–1964: Max Wilk *The Wit and Wisdom of Hollywood* (1972)

from G. K. Chesterton to his wife:

6 AM IN MARKET HARBOROUGH. WHERE OUGHT I TO BE?

G. K. Chesterton 1874–1936: *Autobiography* (1936)

7 Dear Mrs A.,
Hooray, hooray,
At last you are deflowered.
On this as every other day
I love you—Noel Coward.

Noël Coward 1899–1973: telegram to Gertrude Lawrence, 5 July 1940 (the day after her wedding)

8 HAVE MOVED HOTEL EXCELSIOR COUGHING MYSELF INTO A FIRENZE.

Noël Coward 1899–1973: telegram from Florence; Angus McGill and Kenneth Thomson *Live Wires* (1982)

9 LEGITIMATE AT LAST WONT MOTHER BE PLEASED.
on Gertrude Lawrence's first straight role

Noël Coward 1899–1973: Sheridan Morley *A Talent to Amuse* (1969)

sent to his partner Jack Wilson in New York in 1938 as the threat of war increased:

10 GRAVE POSSIBILITY WAR WITHIN FEW WEEKS OR DAYS MORE IF THIS HAPPENS POSTPONEMENT REVUE INEVITABLE AND ANNIHILATION ALL OF US PROBABLE.

Noël Coward 1899–1973: Sheridan Morley *A Talent to Amuse* (1969)

despite the threat of war, arrangements for the revue Set to Music *went ahead:*

11 SUGGEST YOU ENGAGE EIGHT REALLY BEAUTIFUL SHOWGIRLS MORE OR LESS SAME HEIGHT NO REAL TALENT REQUIRED.

Noël Coward 1899–1973: telegram to Jack Wilson; Sheridan Morley *A Talent to Amuse* (1969)

in 1916 Norman Douglas had slipped bail on a charge of an indecent offence with a young man. He returned twenty-five years later, sending this telegram to a friend:

12 FEEL LIKE A BOY AGAIN.

Norman Douglas 1868–1952: Angus McGill and Kenneth Thomson *Live Wires* (1982)

sent by a cricket-playing coroner, W. G. Grace's elder brother, to postpone an inquest:

13 PUT CORPSE ON ICE TILL CLOSE OF PLAY.

E. M. Grace d. 1911: A. A. Thomson *The Great Cricketer* (1957); perhaps apocryphal

response to a telegraphic enquiry, HOW OLD CARY GRANT?:

14 OLD CARY GRANT FINE. HOW YOU?

Cary Grant 1904–86: R. Schickel *Cary Grant* (1983)

15 LAST SUPPER AND ORIGINAL CAST COULDN'T DRAW IN THIS HOUSE.
    telegram to his father during a bad week with a stock company

George S. Kaufman 1889–1961: Angus McGill and Kenneth Thomson *Live Wires* (1982)

Carl Laemmle Jr. had sent a telegram to his father, PLEASE WIRE MORE MONEY AM TALKING TO FRENCH COUNT RE MOVIE:

16 NO MONEY TILL YOU LEARN TO SPELL.

Carl Laemmle 1867–1939: Angus McGill and Kenneth Thomson *Live Wires* (1982)

an estate agent in Bermuda told her that the house she was considering came with a maid, a secretary, and a chauffeur:

17 AIRMAIL PHOTOGRAPH OF CHAUFFEUR.

Beatrice Lillie 1894–1989: Angus McGill and Kenneth Thomson *Live Wires* (1982)

telegram to Mrs Sherwood on the arrival of her baby:

18 GOOD WORK, MARY. WE ALL KNEW YOU HAD IT IN YOU.

Dorothy Parker 1893–1967: Alexander Woollcott *While Rome Burns* (1934)

to a couple who had married after living together:

19 WHAT'S NEW?

Dorothy Parker 1893–1967: S. T. Brownlow (ed.) *The Sayings of Dorothy Parker* (1992)

cables were soon arriving . . . 'Require earliest name life story photograph American nurse upblown Adowa.' We replied:

20 NURSE UNUPBLOWN.

Evelyn Waugh 1903–66: *Waugh in Abyssinia* (1936)

21 FEAR I MAY NOT BE ABLE TO REACH YOU IN TIME FOR THE CEREMONY. DON'T WAIT.
    telegram of apology for missing Oscar Wilde's wedding

James McNeill Whistler 1834–1903: E. J. and R. Pennell *The Life of James McNeill Whistler* (1908)

his wife had requested him, when in Paris, to buy and send her a bidet:

22 UNABLE OBTAIN BIDET. SUGGEST HANDSTAND IN SHOWER.

Billy Wilder 1906– : Leslie Halliwell *Filmgoer's Book of Quotes* (1973)

23 At this point in the proceedings there was another ring at the front door. Jeeves shimmered out and came back with a telegram.

P. G. Wodehouse 1881–1975: *Carry On, Jeeves!* (1925)

24 I HAVE BEEN LOOKING AROUND FOR AN APPROPRIATE WOODEN GIFT AND AM PLEASED HEREBY TO PRESENT YOU WITH ELSIE FERGUSON'S PERFORMANCE IN HER NEW PLAY.

Alexander Woollcott 1887–1943: congratulatory telegram for George S. Kaufman's fifth wedding anniversary; Howard Teichmann *George S. Kaufman* (1973)

Television See also **Broadcasting**

1 TV—a clever contraction derived from the words Terrible Vaudeville . . . we call it a medium because nothing's well done.

Goodman Ace 1899–1982: letter to Groucho Marx, *c.*1953

2 The new series of Kavanagh QC is so true-to-life that I fell fast asleep during the last ten minutes of counsel's speech to the jury.
a judge's view

Barrington Black 1932– : in *Mail on Sunday* 14 March 1999

3 The best that can be said for Norwegian television is that it gives you the sensation of a coma without the worry and inconvenience.

Bill Bryson 1951– : *Neither Here Nor There* (1991)

4 Television is more interesting than people. If it were not, we should have people standing in the corners of our rooms.

Alan Coren 1938– : attributed; in *The Penguin Dictionary of Twentieth-Century Quotations* (1993)

5 Television is for appearing on, not looking at.

Noël Coward 1899–1973: Dick Richards *The Wit of Noël Coward* (1968)

6 We exercise the ultimate sanction of switching off only in an extreme case, like a heroin addict rejecting the needle in the face of death.
on television as an agent of cultural destruction

Richard Eyre 1943– : attributed, 1995

7 There was never sex in Ireland before television.

Oliver J. Flanagan 1920–87: *c.*1965, attributed

8 Let's face it, there are no plain women on television.

Anna Ford 1943– : in *Observer* 23 September 1979

9 I don't watch television, I think it destroys the art of talking about oneself.

Stephen Fry 1957– : *Paperweight* (1992)

10 Being taken no notice of in 10 million homes.
of appearing on television

David Hare 1947– : *Amy's View* (1997)

11 It's television, you see. If you are not on the thing every week, the public think you are either dead or deported.

Frankie Howerd 1922–92: attributed

12 Television is simultaneously blamed, often by the same people, for worsening the world and for being powerless to change it.

Clive James 1939– : *Glued to the Box* (1981); introduction

13 We are surfing food.
on cable television

Kelvin Mackenzie 1946– : in *Trouble at the Top* (BBC2) 12 February 1997, a documentary on the launch of Live TV, originally run by Janet Street-Porter

14 *Television?* The word is half Greek, half Latin. No good can come of it.

C. P. Scott 1846–1932: view of the editor of the *Manchester Guardian*; Asa Briggs *The BBC: the First Fifty Years* (1985)

15 I didn't create Alf Garnett. Society did. I just grassed on him.

Johnny Speight 1921– : in *Mail on Sunday* 27 December 1998 'Quotes of the Year'

16 My show is the stupidest show on TV. If you are watching it, get a life.

Jerry Springer 1944– : in *Independent on Sunday* 7 March 1999

17 It is stupidvision—where most of the presenters look like they have to pretend to be stupid because they think their audience is . . . It patronises. It talks to the vacuum cleaner and the washing machine without much contact with the human brain.

of daytime television

Polly Toynbee 1946– : in *Daily Telegraph* 7 May 1996

18 It always makes me laugh when people ask why anyone would want to do a sitcom in America. If it runs five years, you never have to work again.

Twiggy 1949– : in *Independent* 4 October 1997 'Quote Unquote'

19 Never miss a chance to have sex or appear on television.

Gore Vidal 1925– : attributed; Bob Chieger *Was It Good For You Too?* (1983)

of television:
20 It used to be that we in films were the lowest form of art. Now we have something to look down on.

Billy Wilder 1906– : A. Madsen *Billy Wilder* (1968)

21 You know daytime television? You know what it's supposed to be for? It's to keep unemployed people happy. It's supposed to stop them running to the social security demanding mad luxuries like cookers and windows.

Victoria Wood 1953– : *Mens Sana in Thingummy Doodah* (1990)

Tennis

1 In other sports, the lateral euphemism is still in its infancy (at Wimbledon, for example, they have only just realized that 'perfectionist' can be used to represent 'extremely bad-tempered'). In soccer, the form of the encoded adjective is well developed. 'Tenacious', for example, always means 'small'.

Julian Barnes 1946– : in *Observer* 4 July 1982

2 Miss J. Hunter Dunn, Miss J. Hunter Dunn,
Furnish'd and burnish'd by Aldershot sun,
What strenuous singles we played after tea,
We in the tournament—you against me.
Love-thirty, love-forty, oh! weakness of joy,
The speed of a swallow, the grace of a boy,
With carefullest carelessness, gaily you won,
I am weak from your loveliness, Joan Hunter Dunn.

John Betjeman 1906–84: 'A Subaltern's Love-Song' (1945)

3 No one is more sensitive about his game than a weekend tennis player.

Jimmy Cannon 1910–73: in *New York Post* c.1955 'Nobody Asked Me, But . . .'

4 I call tennis the McDonald's of sport—you go in, they make a quick buck out of you, and you're out.

Pat Cash 1965– : in *Independent on Sunday* 4 July 1999

5 New Yorkers love it when you spill your guts out there. Spill your guts at Wimbledon and they make you stop and clean it up.

Jimmy Connors 1952– : at Flushing Meadow; in *Guardian* 24 December 1984 'Sports Quotes of the Year'

6 Like a Volvo, Borg is rugged, has good after-sales service, and is very dull.

Clive James 1939– : in *Observer* 29 June 1980

7 You cannot be serious!

John McEnroe 1959– : said to tennis umpire at Wimbledon, early 1980s

8 All gong and no dinner . . . we just wish Anna would finally win something aside from hearts.
   of the Russian tennis star Anna Kournikova at Wimbledon 2000

Tim Sheridan: 'The Word from Wimbledon' (online report) 10 July 2000

The Theatre See also **Actors and Acting**

1 Welcome to the Theatre,
   To the magic, to the fun!
   Where painted trees and flowers grow,
   And laughter rings fortissimo,
   And treachery's sweetly done.

Lee Adams: 'Welcome to the Theatre' (1970)

2 Shaw's plays are the price we pay for Shaw's prefaces.

James Agate 1877–1947: diary 10 March 1933

3 STUDENT: Did Hamlet actually have an affair with Ophelia?
   ACTOR-MANAGER: In our company, always.

Anonymous: Cedric Hardwicke *A Victorian in Orbit* (1961)

4 There is less in this than meets the eye.

Tallulah Bankhead 1903–68: of a revival of Maeterlinck's play 'Aglavaine and Selysette'; Alexander Woollcott *Shouts and Murmurs* (1922)

5 This [*Oh, Calcutta!*] is the kind of show to give pornography a dirty name.

Clive Barnes 1927– : in *New York Times* 18 June 1969

6 God, send me some good actors. Cheap

Lilian Baylis 1874–1937: Sybil Thorndike *Lilian Baylis* (1938)

7 Enter Michael Angelo. Andrea del Sarto appears for a moment at a window. Pippa passes.

Max Beerbohm 1872–1956: *Seven Men* (1919)

   on being asked 'What was the message of your play' after a performance of The Hostage:
8 Message? Message? What the hell do you think I am, a bloody postman?

Brendan Behan 1923–64: Dominic Behan *My Brother Brendan* (1965)

9 And remember, this is the School play. You are not here to enjoy yourselves.

Alan Bennett 1934– : *Forty Years On* (1969)

10 A play wot I wrote.

Eddie Braben: spoken by Ernie Wise; Gary Morecambe and Martin Stirling *Behind the Sunshine* (1994)

   on hearing the Cockney playwright Henry Arthur Jones reading his play Michael and his Lost Angel (*1896*):
11 But it's so *long*, Mr. Jones—even *without* the *h*'s.

Mrs Patrick Campbell 1865–1940: Margot Peters *Mrs Pat* (1984)

   of Lionel Bart's musical Blitz:
12 Just as long as the real thing and twice as noisy.

Noël Coward 1899–1973: Sheridan Morley *The Quotable Noël Coward* (1999)

13 Stop being gallant
   And don't be such a bore,
   Pack up your talent,

Noël Coward 1899–1973: 'Why Must the Show Go On?' (1955)

There's always plenty more
And if you lose hope
Take dope
And lock yourself in the John,
Why must the show go on?

14 It's about as long as *Parsifal*, and not as funny.

Noël Coward 1899–1973: on *Camelot*; Dick Richards *The Wit of Noël Coward* (1968)

15 Shut up, Arnold, or I'll direct this play the way you wrote it!

John Dexter: to the playwright Arnold Wesker; in *Ned Sherrin in his Anecdotage* (1993)

16 The plot can be hot—simply teeming with sex,
A gay divorcee who is after her ex.
It could be Oedipus Rex,
Where a chap kills his father
And causes a lot of bother.
The clerk
Who is thrown out of work
By the boss
Who is thrown for a loss
By the skirt
Who is doing him dirt.
The world is a stage
The stage is a world of entertainment.

Howard Dietz 1896–1983: 'That's Entertainment' (1953)

17 Theatre is often regarded in Britain as the cricket of the performing arts, meaning archaic, quaint, thinly attended, and not done as well as it used to be.

Richard Eyre 1943– : in *Observer* 26 March 'They said what . . . ?'

18 Ridiculous farces worthy of Canadian savages.
  of Shakespeare's plays

Frederick the Great 1712–86: Giles MacDonogh *Frederick the Great* (1999)

19 Prologues precede the piece—in mournful verse;
As undertakers—walk before the hearse.

David Garrick 1717–79: prologue to Arthur Murphy's *The Apprentice* (1756)

20 Applause, applause!
Vociferous applause
From orchestra to gallery
Could mean a raise in salary.
Give out, give in!—
Be noisy, make a din!
(The manager, he audits our plaudits.)

Ira Gershwin 1896–1983: 'Applause, Applause' (1953)

a Broadway producer after a play about Napoleon had failed:
21 Never, never, will I do another play where a guy writes with a feather.

Max Gordon: attributed by Arthur Miller; in *Ned Sherrin's Theatrical Anecdotes* (1991)

22 I have knocked everything but the knees of the chorus girls, and nature has anticipated me there.

Percy Hammond: Ned Sherrin *Cutting Edge* (1984)

23 If any play has been produced only twice in three hundred years, there must be some good reason for it.

Rupert Hart-Davis 1907–99: letter to George Lyttelton, 7 July 1957

24 The difficulty about a theatre job is that it interferes with party-going.

Barry Humphries 1934– : *More Please* (1992)

25 I'll come no more behind your scenes, David; for the silk stockings and white bosoms of your actresses excite my amorous propensities.

Samuel Johnson 1709-84: James Boswell *Life of Samuel Johnson* (1791) 1750; John Wilkes recalls the remark [to Garrick] in the form: 'the silk stockings and white bosoms of your actresses do make my genitals to quiver'

26 For so many people, going to the theatre is just a little bit of a nuisance. When going out to have a good old laugh gets worthy, the writing is on the wall.

Griff Rhys Jones 1953- : in *Daily Telegraph* 22 January 1994

27 Mixed notices—they were good and rotten.
after sharing a flop, The Channel Road *(1929), with Alexander Woollcott*

George S. Kaufman 1889-1961: Howard Teichmann *George S. Kaufman* (1973)

28 I understand your play is full of single entendre.
to Howard Dietz on Beat the Devil

George S. Kaufman 1889-1961: attributed; Ned Sherrin *Cutting Edge* (1984)

29 I thought I heard one of the original lines of the show.
of the Marx Brothers' ad-libbing

George S. Kaufman 1889-1961: Howard Teichmann *George S. Kaufman* (1973)

30 There was laughter in the back of the theatre, leading to the belief that someone was telling jokes back there.

George S. Kaufman 1889-1961: Howard Teichmann *George S. Kaufman* (1973)

31 Well, Marc, there's only one thing we can do. We've got to call the audience in tomorrow morning for a ten o'clock rehearsal.
to convince Marc Connelly that a line would not work

George S. Kaufman 1889-1961: Howard Teichmann *George S. Kaufman* (1973)

32 Satire is what closes Saturday night.

George S. Kaufman 1889-1961: Scott Meredith *George S. Kaufman and his Friends* (1974)

33 Murder was one thing Hamlet sure did enjoy.
He was, how shall I say, quite a mischievious boy;
And the moral of this story was very, very plain;
You'd better get a mussle if you've got a great Dane!

Frank Loesser 1910-69: 'Hamlet' (1949)

34 I didn't like the play, but then I saw it under adverse conditions—the curtain was up.

Groucho Marx 1895-1977: ad-lib, attributed in an interview by Marx to George S. Kaufman; Peter Hay *Broadway Anecdotes* (1989)

35 This play is rather your line of country I should have thought, all about incest and the early days of aviation.

Joe Orton 1933-67 and **Kenneth Halliwell**: *The Boy Hairdresser* (1960)

36 Don't clap too hard—it's a very old building.

John Osborne 1929- : *The Entertainer* (1957)

37 In fact, now that you've got me right down to it, the only thing I didn't like about *The Barretts of Wimpole Street* was the play.

Dorothy Parker 1893-1967: review in *New Yorker* 21 February 1931

38 *House Beautiful* is play lousy.

Dorothy Parker 1893-1967: review in *New Yorker* 1933

39 'Ah,' I said to myself, for I love a responsive audience, 'so it's one of those plays.'

Dorothy Parker 1893-1967: review of A. A. Milne's *Give Me Yesterday* in *New Yorker* 14 March 1931

40 There still remains, to mortify a wit,
The many-headed monster of the pit.

Alexander Pope 1688–1744:
Imitations of Horace (1737)

41 Another pain where the ulcers grow,
Another op'nin' of another show.

Cole Porter 1891–1964: 'Another
Op'nin', Another Show' (1948)

42 We open in Venice,
We next play Verona,
Then on to Cremona.
Lotsa laughs in Cremona.

Cole Porter 1891–1964: 'We Open in
Venice' (1948)

43 Brush up your Shakespeare,
Start quoting him now.
Brush up your Shakespeare
And the women you will wow . . .

If she says your behaviour is heinous
Kick her right in the 'Coriolanus'.
Brush up your Shakespeare
And they'll all kowtow.

Cole Porter 1891–1964: 'Brush Up
your Shakespeare' (1948)

44 It is better to have written a damned play, than no play at
all—it snatches a man from obscurity.

Frederic Reynolds 1764–1841: *The
Dramatist* (1789)

45 You've got to perform in a role hundreds of times. In
keeping it fresh one can become a large, madly humming,
demented refrigerator.

Ralph Richardson 1902–83: in *Time*
21 August 1978

46 A buzz of recognition came from the front rows of the pit,
together with a craning of necks on the part of those in
less favoured seats. It heralded the arrival of Sherard Blaw,
the dramatist who had discovered himself, and who had
given so ungrudgingly of his discovery to the world.

Saki 1870–1916: *The Unbearable
Bassington* (1912)

47 The most lamentable comedy, and most cruel death of
Pyramus and Thisby.

William Shakespeare 1564–1616: *A
Midsummer Night's Dream* (1595–6)

48 *Exit, pursued by a bear.*

William Shakespeare 1564–1616:
stage direction in *The Winter's Tale*
(1610–11)

49 You don't expect me to know what to say about a play
when I don't know who the author is, do you?

George Bernard Shaw 1856–1950:
Fanny's First Play (1914)

50 My intention is to do to the play what Hamlet himself
longed to do to his mother.

Arthur Smith 1954– : *Arthur Smith's
Hamlet*

51 Something appealing,
Something appalling,
Something for everyone:
A comedy tonight!

Stephen Sondheim 1930– :
'Comedy Tonight' (1962)

52 It's pure theatrical Viagra.
on The Blue Room, *starring Nicole Kidman*

Charles Spencer 1955– : in *Daily
Telegraph* 24 September 1999

53 I can do you blood and love without the rhetoric, and I
can do you blood and rhetoric without the love, and I can
do you all three concurrent or consecutive, but I can't do
you love and rhetoric without the blood. Blood is
compulsory—they're all blood, you see.

Tom Stoppard 1937– : *Rosencrantz
and Guildenstern are Dead* (1967)

54 To sum up: your father, whom you love, dies, you are his heir, you come back to find that hardly was the corpse cold before his young brother popped onto his throne and into his sheets, thereby offending both legal and natural practice. Now why exactly are you behaving in this extraordinary manner?

Tom Stoppard 1937– : *Rosencrantz and Guildenstern Are Dead* (1967)

55 *Moby Dick* nearly became the tragedy of a man who could not make up his nose.
on Welles's production of Moby Dick *in 1955, when his false nose fell off on the first night, alluding to the publicity for Olivier's* Hamlet *as 'the tragedy of a man who could not make up his mind'*

Kenneth Tynan 1927–80: *A View of the English Stage* (1975)

56 I've never much enjoyed going to plays . . . The unreality of painted people standing on a platform saying things they've said to each other for months is more than I can overlook.

John Updike 1932– : George Plimpton (ed.) *Writers at Work* 4th Series (1977)

57 When you think about it, what other playwrights are there besides O'Neill, Tennessee and me?

Mae West 1892–1980: G. Eells and S. Musgrove *Mae West* (1989)

58 The play was a great success, but the audience was a total failure.

Oscar Wilde 1854–1900: after the first performance of *Lady Windermere's Fan*; Peter Hay *Theatrical Anecdotes* (1987)

on Irving's revival of Macbeth *at the Lyceum, with Ellen Terry as Lady Macbeth:*
59 Judging from the banquet, Lady Macbeth seems an economical housekeeper and evidently patronises local industries for her husband's clothes and the servants' liveries, but she takes care to do all her shopping in Byzantium.

Oscar Wilde 1854–1900: Rupert Hart-Davis (ed.) *The Letters of Oscar Wilde* (1962)

on the Company of Four's poorly attended revival of his play Spring 1600 *in 1945:*
60 The Lyric housed the Company of Four and the Audience of Two.

Emlyn Williams 1905–87: James Harding *Emlyn Williams* (1987)

the impresario Binkie Beaumont had been greatly impressed by The Wind of Heaven *(1945):*
61 BEAUMONT: I've read your new play, Emlyn, and I like it twice as much as your last.
WILLIAMS: Does that mean you're going to pay me twice my usual royalties?

Emlyn Williams 1905–87: James Harding *Emlyn Williams* (1987)

Time

on receiving an invitation for 9 a.m.:
1 Oh, are there two nine o'clocks in the day?

Tallulah Bankhead 1903–68: attributed, perhaps apocryphal

to an effusive greeting 'I haven't seen you for 41 years':
2 I thought I told you to wait in the car.

Tallulah Bankhead 1903–68: attributed; Nigel Rees *Cassell Dictionary of Humorous Quotations* (1999)

3 VLADIMIR: That passed the time.
ESTRAGON: It would have passed in any case.
VLADIMIR: Yes, but not so rapidly.

Samuel Beckett 1906–89: *Waiting for Godot* (1955)

4 I am a sundial, and I make a botch
Of what is done much better by a watch.

Hilaire Belloc 1870–1953: 'On a Sundial' (1938)

arriving at Dublin Castle for the handover by British forces on 16 January 1922, and being told that he was seven minutes late:
5 We've been waiting 700 years, you can have the seven minutes.

Michael Collins 1880–1922: Tim Pat Coogan *Michael Collins* (1990); attributed, perhaps apocryphal

6 Life is too short to stuff a mushroom.

Shirley Conran 1932– : *Superwoman* (1975)

7 There was a pause—just long enough for an angel to pass, flying slowly.

Ronald Firbank 1886–1926: *Vainglory* (1915)

8 I'll be with you in the squeezing of a lemon.

Oliver Goldsmith 1730–74: *She Stoops to Conquer* (1773)

9 We have passed a lot of water since then.

Sam Goldwyn 1882–1974: E. Goodman *The Fifty-Year Decline of Hollywood* (1961); attributed, possibly apocryphal

10 The ability of dandelions to tell the time is somewhat exaggerated, owing to the fact that there is always one seed that refuses to be blown off; the time usually turns out to be 37 o'clock.

Miles Kington 1941– : *Nature Made Ridiculously Simple* (1983)

11 'Twenty three and a quarter minutes past,' Uncle Matthew was saying furiously, 'in precisely six and three-quarter minutes the damned fella will be late.'

Nancy Mitford 1904–73: *Love in a Cold Climate* (1949)

12 Time spent on any item of the agenda will be in inverse proportion to the sum involved.

C. Northcote Parkinson 1909–93: *Parkinson's Law* (1958)

13 Eternity's a terrible thought. I mean, where's it all going to end?

Tom Stoppard 1937– : *Rosencrantz and Guildenstern are Dead* (1967)

to a man in the street, carrying a grandfather clock:
14 My poor fellow, why not carry a watch?

Herbert Beerbohm Tree 1852–1917: Hesketh Pearson *Beerbohm Tree* (1956)

Titles

1 Your official signature 'Archibald the Arctic' is the most romantic signature in the world and just one point ahead of 'William of Argyll and the Isles'.
to first Bishop of the Arctic, 1937

John Buchan 1875–1940: Archibald Lang Fleming *Archibald the Arctic* (1957)

2 Hit me with your Rhythm Stick.

Ian Dury 1942–2000: (song title, 1978)

leading title on the autumn list of 'a new publishing house that would be sure to fail':
3 Canada, Our Good Neighbour to the North.

Robert Gottlieb: in *Ned Sherrin in his Anecdotage* (1993)

4 Rum, Bum and Concertina.

George Melly 1926– : title of autobiography (1977)

Tolerance See **Prejudice and Tolerance**

Towns and Cities

1 God made the harbour, and that's all right, but Satan made Sydney.

Anonymous: unnamed Sydney citizen; Mark Twain *More Tramps Abroad* (1897)

2 Toronto the Good.
  ironic nickname used by 'hilarious drunks'

Anonymous: Robert Thomas Allen *When Toronto was for Kids* (1961)

3 One has no great hopes from Birmingham. I always say there is something direful in the sound.

Jane Austen 1775–1817: *Emma* (1816)

4 So literary a little town is Oxford that its undergraduates see a newspaper nearly as seldom as the Venetians see a horse.

Max Beerbohm 1872–1956: letter, May 1894

5 New York makes one think of the collapse of civilization, about Sodom and Gomorrah, the end of the world. The end wouldn't come as a surprise here. Many people already bank on it.

Saul Bellow 1915– : *Mr Sammler's Planet* (1970)

6 Come, friendly bombs, and fall on Slough!
  It isn't fit for humans now.

John Betjeman 1906–84: 'Slough' (1937)

7 And this is good old Boston,
  The home of the bean and the cod,
  Where the Lowells talk to the Cabots
  And the Cabots talk only to God.

John Collins Bossidy 1860–1928: verse spoken at Holy Cross College alumni dinner in Boston, Massachusetts, 1910

8 Wakefield is a bit like Wollongong except there aren't any beaches.
  Australian rugby league player on the delights of his adopted Yorkshire home

Josh Bostock: in *Daily Telegraph* 28 December 1998

9 A big hard-boiled city with no more personality than a paper cup.

Raymond Chandler 1888–1959: *The Little Sister* (1949)

10 People don't talk in Paris; they just look lovely . . . and eat.

Chips Channon 1897–1958: diary 22 May 1951

11 New York, New York,—a helluva town,
  The Bronx is up but the Battery's down,
  And people ride in a hole in the ground:
  New York, New York,—It's a helluva town.

Betty Comden 1919– and **Adolph Green** 1915– : 'New York, New York' (1945)

12 For some guys
  The dream is Paris,
  But I found a shrine
  Where Hollywood Boulevard crosses Vine.

Ervin Drake: 'My Hometown' (1964)

13 Nearly all th' most foolish people in th' counthry an' manny iv th' wisest goes to Noo York. Th' wise people ar-re there because th' foolish wint first. That's th' way th' wise men make a livin'.

Finley Peter Dunne 1867–1936: *Mr. Dooley's Opinions* (1902)

14 Last week, I went to Philadelphia, but it was closed.

W. C. Fields 1880–1946: Richard J. Anobile *Godfrey Daniels* (1975); attributed

15 The people of Berlin are doing very exciting things with their city at the moment. Basically they had this idea of just knocking it through.

Stephen Fry 1957– and **Hugh Laurie:** *A Bit More Fry and Laurie* (1991)

16 Cities are above
The quarrels that were hapless.
Look who's making love:
St Paul and Minneap'lis!

Ira Gershwin 1896–1983: 'Love is Sweeping the Country' (1931)

17 I met him in Boston
In the native quarter.
He was from Harvard
Just across the border.

Sheldon Harnick 1924– : 'The Boston Beguine' (1952)

18 Broadway's turning into Coney,
Champagne Charlie's drinking gin.
Old New York is new and phoney—
Give it back to the Indians.

Lorenz Hart 1895–1943: 'Give it back to the Indians' (1940)

19 I still felt like an exile in Sydney. I was stranded among
people who could not even muster the glottal energy to
pronounce the 'd' in the name of their own city.

Barry Humphries 1934– : *More Please* (1992)

20 Try Manchester after midnight and you'll think you've
walked into the Book of Revelations.

Howard Jacobson: *The Mighty Waltzer* (1999)

21 When a man is tired of London, he is tired of life; for there
is in London all that life can afford.

Samuel Johnson 1709–84: James Boswell *Life of Samuel Johnson* (1791) 20 September 1777

22 Fleet-street has a very animated appearance; but I think
the full tide of human existence is at Charing-Cross.

Samuel Johnson 1709–84: James Boswell *Life of Samuel Johnson* (1791) 2 April 1775

23 [Sydney] was all London without being London. Without
any of the lovely old glamour that invests London. This
London of the Southern hemisphere was all, as it were,
made in five minutes, a substitute for the real thing. Just a
substitute—as margarine is a substitute for butter.

D. H. Lawrence 1885–1930: *Kangaroo* (1923)

24 You're from Big D,
My, oh yes, I mean Big D, little a, double l-a-s
And that spells Dallas, my darlin' darlin' Dallas,
Don't it give you pleasure to confess
That you're from Big D?
My, oh yes!

Frank Loesser 1910–69: 'Big D' (1956)

Ogden Nash had had his car broken into in Boston:
25 I'd expect to be robbed in Chicago
But not in the land of the cod,
So I hope that the Cabots and Lowells
Will mention the matter to God.

Ogden Nash 1902–71: David Frost and Michael Shea *The Mid-Atlantic Companion* (1986)

26 Saigon is like all the other great modern cities of the world.
It's the mess left over from people getting rich.

P. J. O'Rourke 1947– : *Give War a Chance* 1992)

27 Last Sunday afternoon
I took a trip to Hackensack
But after I gave Hackensack the once-over
I took the next train back.
I happen to like New York.

Cole Porter 1891–1964: 'I Happen to Like New York' (1931)

28 City of perspiring dreams.

Frederic Raphael 1931– : of Cambridge; *The Glittering Prizes* (1976)

29 He took offence at my description of Edinburgh as the Reykjavik of the South.

Tom Stoppard 1937– : *Jumpers* (1972)

30 Toronto is a kind of New York operated by the Swiss.

Peter Ustinov 1921– : in *Globe & Mail* 1 August 1987; attributed

Transport

of Annie's parking:
1 That's OK, we can walk to the kerb from here.

Woody Allen 1935– : *Annie Hall* (1977 film)

2 Railways and the Church have their critics, but both are the best ways of getting a man to his ultimate destination.

Revd W. Awdry 1911–97: in *Daily Telegraph* 22 March 1997; obituary

3 The freeway is . . . the place where they [Angelenos] spend the two calmest and most rewarding hours of their daily lives.

Reynar Banham 1922–88: *Los Angeles: the Architecture of Four Ecologies* (1971)

4 He [Benchley] came out of a night club one evening and, tapping a uniformed figure on the shoulder, said, 'Get me a cab.' The uniformed figure turned around furiously and informed him that he was not a doorman but a rear admiral. 'O.K.,' said Benchley, 'Get me a battleship.'

Robert Benchley 1889–1945: in *New Yorker* 5 January 1946

5 Boston's freeway system . . . was clearly designed by a person who had spent his childhood crashing toy trains.

Bill Bryson 1951– : *The Lost Continent* (1989)

6 Q: If Mrs Thatcher were run over by a bus . . . ?
LORD CARRINGTON: It wouldn't dare.

Lord Carrington 1919– : during the Falklands War; Russell Lewis *Margaret Thatcher* (1984)

7 Many people were quite upset that there was a large uncontrollable pig on board, especially those in the first class cabin.
a US Airways spokesman, after a pig travelling in first class as a 'therapeutic companion pet' had rampaged through the aisles

David Castleveter: in *Daily Telegraph* 30 October 2000

8 The only way of catching a train I ever discovered is to miss the train before.

G. K. Chesterton 1874–1936: attributed; Evan Esar and Nicolas Bentley (eds.) *Treasury of Humorous Quotations* (1951)

9 That monarch of the road,
Observer of the Highway Code,
That big six-wheeler
Scarlet-painted
London Transport
Diesel-engined
Ninety-seven horse power
Omnibus!

Michael Flanders 1922–75 and **Donald Swann** 1923–94: 'A Transport of Delight' (c.1956)

10 Sir, Saturday morning, although recurring at regular and well-foreseen intervals, always seems to take this railway by surprise.

W. S. Gilbert 1836–1911: letter to the station-master at Baker Street, on the Metropolitan line; John Julius Norwich *Christmas Crackers* (1980)

11 For you dream you are crossing the Channel, and tossing about in a steamer from Harwich—
Which is something between a large bathing machine and a very small second class carriage.

W. S. Gilbert 1836–1911: *Iolanthe* (1882)

12 What is this that roareth thus?
  Can it be a Motor Bus?
  Yes, the smell and hideous hum
  Indicat Motorem Bum! . . .
  How shall wretches live like us
  Cincti Bis Motoribus?
  Domine, defende nos
  Contra hos Motores Bos!

A. D. Godley 1856–1925: letter to C. R. L. Fletcher, 10 January 1914

13 Aunt Jane observed, the second time
  She tumbled off a bus,
  'The step is short from the Sublime
  To the Ridiculous.'

Harry Graham 1874–1936: 'Equanimity' (1899)

14 'Glorious, stirring sight!' murmured Toad, never offering to move. 'The poetry of motion! The *real* way to travel! The *only* way to travel! Here today—in next week tomorrow! Villages skipped, towns and cities jumped— always somebody else's horizon! O bliss! O poop-poop! O my! O my!'

Kenneth Grahame 1859–1932: *The Wind in the Willows* (1908)

15 A Deputy Prime Minister whose idea of a park and ride scheme is to park one Jaguar and drive away in another.
  of John Prescott's transport policy

William Hague 1961– : in House of Commons, 17 November 1999

of Bishop Patrick's fatal error in crossing the street:
16 The light of God was with him,
  But the traffic light was not.

E. Y. Harburg 1898–1981: 'Lead Kindly Light' (1965)

17 There once was an old man who said, 'Damn!
  It is borne in upon me I am
  An engine that moves
  In determinate grooves,
  I'm not even a bus, I'm a tram.'

Maurice Evan Hare 1886–1967: 'Limerick' (1905)

18 The defendant is clearly one who insufficiently appreciates the value of the motor car to the human race. But we must not allow our natural detestation for such an individual to cloud our judgment.

A. P. Herbert 1890–1971: *Misleading Cases* (1935)

19 Home James, and don't spare the horses.

Fred Hillebrand 1893– : title of song (1934)

20 My inclination to go by Air Express is confirmed by the crash they had yesterday, which will make them careful in the immediate future.

A. E. Housman 1859–1936: letter 17 August 1920

21 The automobile changed our dress, manners, social customs, vacation habits, the shape of our cities, consumer purchasing patterns, common tastes and positions in intercourse.

John Keats 1920– : *The Insolent Chariots* (1958)

22 For sheer pleasure few methods of progression, one comes gradually to realise, can compare with the perambulator. The motion is agreeable, the range of vision extensive and one has always before one's eyes the rewarding spectacle of a grown-up maintaining prolonged physical exertion.

Osbert Lancaster 1908–80: *All Done From Memory* (1953)

23 FATHER STACK: While you were out, I got the keys to your car. And drove it into a big wall. And if you don't like it, tough. I've had my fun, and that's all that matters.

Graham Linehan and **Arthur Mathews**: 'New Jack City' (1996), episode from *Father Ted* (Channel 4 TV, 1994–8)

24 'Take my camel, dear,' said my aunt Dot, as she climbed down from this animal on her return from High Mass.

Rose Macaulay 1881–1958: *The Towers of Trebizond* (1956)

on a car called by Macmillan 'Mrs Thatcher':
25 This car makes a noise if you don't fasten your seat belt, and a light starts flashing if you don't close the door. It's a *very bossy* car.

Harold Macmillan 1894–1986: Ludovic Kennedy *On My Way to the Club* (1989)

on the Channel Tunnel:
26 I have always been pro-tunnel, although I should have preferred a bridge. The people of Kent have been anti-tunnel, but I hope they will soon grow out of that.

Lord Massereene and Ferrard 1914–93: speech in the House of Lords, 26 March 1990

seeing the Morris Minor prototype in 1945:
27 It looks like a poached egg—we can't make that.

Lord Nuffield 1877–1963: attributed

28 People who spend most of their natural lives riding iron bicycles over the rocky roadsteads of this parish get their personalities mixed up with the personalities of their bicycles as a result of the interchanging of the atoms of each of them and you would be surprised at the number of people in these parts who nearly are half people and half bicycles.

Flann O'Brien 1911–66: *The Third Policeman* (1967)

29 Why is it no one ever sent me yet
One perfect limousine, do you suppose?
Ah no, it's always just my luck to get
One perfect rose.

Dorothy Parker 1893–1967: 'One Perfect Rose' (1937)

30 The wife does not like her hair blown about.
  explaining why he had driven from his hotel to the conference centre at the Labour Party Conference

John Prescott 1938– : in *Daily Telegraph* 1 October 1999; see **Appearance** 12

31 Back in the house, I felt someone had put planks in my legs and turned my buttocks into wooden boxes.
  his first experience of riding

V. S. Pritchett 1900–97: *Midnight Oil* (1971)

32 Sure, the next train has gone ten minutes ago.

Punch 1841–1992: vol. 60 (1871)

33 What is better than presence of mind in a railway accident? Absence of body.

Punch 1841–1992: vol. 16 (1849)

34 Denis Norden thought that Johann Strauss's car would have been registered as—123 123.

Steve Race 1921– : in *The Bibliophile* September 2000; attributed

35 Take most people, they're crazy about cars. They worry if they get a little scratch on them, and they're always talking about how many miles they get to a gallon . . . I don't even like *old* cars. I mean they don't even interest me. I'd rather have a goddam horse. A horse is at least *human*, for God's sake.

J. D. Salinger 1919– : *The Catcher in the Rye* (1951)

36 Walk! Not bloody likely. I am going in a taxi.

George Bernard Shaw 1856–1950: *Pygmalion* (1916)

37 I wonder if there are enough traffic cones for every student to have one in their bedroom.

Arthur Smith 1954– and **Chris England**: *An Evening with Gary Lineker* (1990)

38 BOATMAN: I 'ad that Christopher Marlowe in the back of my boat.

Tom Stoppard 1937– : *Shakespeare in Love* (1999 film, screenplay by Tom Stoppard and Mark Norman)

Travel and Exploration

1 In America there are two classes of travel—first class, and with children.

Robert Benchley 1889–1945: *Pluck and Luck* (1925)

2 I encountered Mr. Hackman, an Englishman, who has been walking the length and breadth of Europe for several years. I enquired of him what were his chief observations. He replied gruffly, 'I never look up', and went on his way.

N. Brooke: in 1796; Duncan Minshull *The Vintage Book of Walking* (2000)

3 What an odd thing tourism is. You fly off to a strange land, eagerly abandoning all the comforts of home, and then expend vast quantities of time and money in a largely futile attempt to recapture the comforts that you wouldn't have lost if you hadn't left home in the first place.

Bill Bryson 1951– : *Neither Here Nor There* (1991)

4 But the principal failing occurred in the sailing,
And the Bellman, perplexed and distressed,
Said he *had* hoped, at least, when the wind blew due East,
That the ship would *not* travel due West!

Lewis Carroll 1832–98: *The Hunting of the Snark* (1876) 'Fit the Second: The Bellman's Speech'

5 They say travel broadens the mind; but you must have the mind.

G. K. Chesterton 1874–1936: 'The Shadow of the Shark' (1921)

6 Why do the wrong people travel, travel, travel,
When the right people stay back home?
What compulsion compels them
And who the hell tells them
To drag their cans to Zanzibar
Instead of staying quietly in Omaha?

Noël Coward 1899–1973: 'Why do the Wrong People Travel?' (1961)

on his arrival in Turkey:
7 I am of course known here as English Delight.

Noël Coward 1899–1973: Sheridan Morley *The Quotable Noël Coward* (1999)

8 A person can be stranded and get by, even though she will be imperilled; two people with a German shepherd and no money are in a mess.

Andrea Dworkin 1946– : *Letters from a War Zone* (1988)

9 At my age travel broadens the behind.

Stephen Fry 1957– : *The Liar* (1991)

10 Abroad is bloody.

George VI 1895–1952: W. H. Auden *A Certain World* (1970)

11 So think twice my friends, before you doubt Columbus,
Just imagine what happens to Posterity without
    Columbus.
No New York, and no skyscrapers,
No funnies in the papers,
No automat nickels,
No Heinz and his pickles,
No land of the Brave and the Free.

Ira Gershwin 1896–1983: 'The Nina, the Pinta, the Santa Maria' (1945)

12 And bound on that journey you find your attorney (who
    started that morning from Devon);
He's a bit undersized, and you don't feel surprised when he
    tells you he's only eleven.

W. S. Gilbert 1836–1911: *Iolanthe* (1882)

13 In your shirt and your socks (the black silk with gold clocks), crossing Salisbury Plain on a bicycle.

W. S. Gilbert 1836–1911: *Iolanthe* (1882)

14 On arrival in that loathsome land of frog-eatg. Toads, Pederasts and Dancing Masters, I went ashore with only Roderick as my companion. Grunge had got on the wrong boat at Dover and was now on his way to Sweden.

Michael Green 1927– : in *Daily Telegraph* 21 August 1993 'Squire Haggard's Journal'

on the difficulties of the Passport Regulations:
15 Drake himself, confronted with the same discouragements, might well have degenerated into a stay-at-home.

A. P. Herbert 1890–1971: *Misleading Cases* (1935)

on the Giant's Causeway:
16 Worth seeing, yes; but not worth going to see.

Samuel Johnson 1709–84: James Boswell *Life of Samuel Johnson* (1791) 12 October 1779

17 What good is speed if the brain has oozed out on the way?

Karl Kraus 1874–1936: 'The Discovery of the North Pole'

18 Thanks to the interstate highway system, it is now possible to travel from coast to coast without seeing anything.

Charles Kuralt 1934–97: *On the Road* (1980)

filling in an embarkation form on a channel crossing:
19 HAROLD NICOLSON: What age are you going to put, Osbert?
OSBERT SITWELL: What sex are you going to put, Harold?

Harold Nicolson 1886–1968: attributed, perhaps apocryphal

of someone suffering from sea-sickness:
20 His condition was not enhanced by the titters of passers-by, chiefly women who should in justice be far sicker than he.

Flann O'Brien 1911–66: *The Best of Myles* (1968)

21 Everybody in fifteenth-century Spain was wrong about where China was and as a result, Columbus discovered Caribbean vacations.

P. J. O'Rourke 1947– : *Parliament of Whores* (1991)

22 The whistle shrilled and in a moment I was chugging out of Grand Central's dreaming spires followed only by the anguished cries of relatives who would now have to go to work. I had chugged only a few feet when I realized that I had left without the train, so I had to run back and wait for it to start.

S. J. Perelman 1904–79: *The Most of S. J. Perelman* (1959) 'Strictly from Hunger'

23 If only I could get down to Sidcup! I've been waiting for the weather to break. He's got my papers, this man I left them with, it's got it all down there, I could prove everything.

Harold Pinter 1930– : *The Caretaker* (1960)

24 In these days of rapid and convenient travel . . . to come from Leighton Buzzard does not necessarily denote any great strength of character. It might only mean mere restlessness.

Saki 1870–1916: *The Chronicles of Clovis* (1911)

25 If it's Tuesday, this must be Belgium.

David Shaw: film title (1969)

26 In Turkey it was always 1952, in Malaysia 1937; Afghanistan was 1910 and Bolivia 1949. It is twenty years ago in the Soviet Union, ten in Norway, five in France. It is always last year in Australia and next week in Japan.

Paul Theroux 1941– : *The Kingdom by the Sea* (1983)

asked why he had come to America:
27 In pursuit of my life-long quest for naked women in wet mackintoshes.

Dylan Thomas 1914–53: Constantine Fitzgibbon *Dylan Thomas* (1965); attributed

28 It is not worthwhile to go around the world to count the cats in Zanzibar.

Henry David Thoreau 1817-62: *Walden* (1854) 'Conclusion'

29 Done the elephants, done the poverty.
after a cricket tour of India

Phil Tufnell 1961- : attributed; in *Times Literary Supplement* 28 July 2000

of the Prince of Wales's trip to India:
30 Bertie's progresses lose a little interest and are very wearing—as there is such a constant repetition of elephants—trappings—jewels—illuminations and fireworks.

Queen Victoria 1819-1901: letter to the Crown Princess of Prussia, 2 February 1876

31 Commuter—one who spends his life
In riding to and from his wife;
A man who shaves and takes a train,
And then rides back to shave again.

E. B. White 1899-1985: 'The Commuter' (1982)

Trust and Treachery

1 Outside Shakespeare the word treason to me means nothing. Only, you pissed in our soup and we drank it.

Alan Bennett 1934- : *An Englishman Abroad* (1989)

2 To have betrayed two leaders—to have wrecked two historic parties—reveals a depth of infamy never previously reached, compared with which the Thugs of India are faithful friends and Judas Iscariot is entitled to a crown of glory.
of Joseph Chamberlain

John Burns 1858-1943: Leon Harris *The Fine Art of Political Wit* (1965)

3 The only recorded instance in history of a rat swimming *towards* a sinking ship.

Winston Churchill 1874-1965: of a former Conservative who proposed to stand as a Liberal; Leon Harris *The Fine Art of Political Wit* (1965)

4 You're . . . turning into a kind of serial monogamist.

Richard Curtis 1956- : *Four Weddings and a Funeral* (1994 film)

5 Frankly speaking it is difficult to trust the Chinese. Once bitten by a snake you feel suspicious even when you see a piece of rope.

Dalai Lama 1935- : attributed, 1981

discussing a friend with Robert Lajeunesse:
6 LAJEUNESSE: He deserves to be betrayed.
FEYDEAU: And even so, his wife has to help him.

Georges Feydeau 1862-1921: Caryl Brahms and Ned Sherrin *Ooh! La-La!* (1973)

7 When I was at Cambridge it was, naturally enough I felt, my ambition to be approached in some way by an elderly homosexual don and asked to spy for or against my country.

Stephen Fry 1957- : *Paperweight* (1992)

8 It is rather like sending your opening batsmen to the crease only for them to find the moment that the first balls are bowled that their bats have been broken before the game by the team captain.

Geoffrey Howe 1926- : resignation speech as Deputy Prime Minister, House of Commons 13 November 1990

9 *Pension.* Pay given to a state hireling for treason to his country.

Samuel Johnson 1709-84: *A Dictionary of the English Language* (1755)

10 He that hath a Gospel
Whereby Heaven is won
(Carpenter, or Cameleer,
Or Maya's dreaming son),
Many swords shall pierce Him,
Mingling blood with gall;
But His Own Disciple
Shall wound Him worst of all!

Rudyard Kipling 1865–1936: *Limits and Renewals* (1932)

11 Never trust a man who combs his hair straight from his left armpit.
of the careful distribution of hair on General MacArthur's balding head

Alice Roosevelt Longworth 1884–1980: Michael Teague *Mrs L* (1981)

12 Defectors are like grapes. The first pressings from them are the best. The third and fourth lack body.

Maurice Oldfield 1915–81: Chapman Pincher in *Mail on Sunday* 19 September 1982; attributed

13 Never take a reference from a clergyman. They always want to give someone a second chance.

Lady Selborne 1858–1950: K. Rose *The Later Cecils* (1975)

14 [Treason], Sire, is a question of dates.

Charles-Maurice de Talleyrand 1754–1838: Duff Cooper *Talleyrand* (1932)

15 He trusted neither of them as far as he could spit, and he was a poor spitter, lacking both distance and control.

P. G. Wodehouse 1881–1975: *Money in the Bank* (1946)

Truth See also **Lies**

1 The pursuit of truth is chimerical . . . What we should pursue is the most convenient arrangement of our ideas.

Samuel Butler 1835–1902: *Notebooks* (1912)

2 'Tis strange—but true; for truth is always strange; Stranger than fiction.

Lord Byron 1788–1824: *Don Juan* (1819–24)

3 The 'Sunday Express' today published a most extraordinary paragraph to the effect that I am really 41 instead of 39, and hinted that I had faked my age in the reference books. The awful thing is that it is true.

Chips Channon 1897–1958: diary, 19 June 1938

4 He occasionally stumbled over the truth, but hastily picked himself up and hurried on as if nothing had happened.
of Stanley Baldwin

Winston Churchill 1874–1965: J. L. Lane (ed.) *The Sayings of Winston Churchill* (1992)

5 Our old friend . . . economical with the *actualité*.

Alan Clark 1928–99: under cross-examination at the Old Bailey during the Matrix Churchill case; in *Independent* 10 November 1992

6 Something unpleasant is coming when men are anxious to tell the truth.

Benjamin Disraeli 1804–81: *The Young Duke* (1831)

7 It is always the best policy to speak the truth—unless, of course, you are an exceptionally good liar.

Jerome K. Jerome 1859–1927: in *The Idler* February 1892

8 Never tell a story because it is true: tell it because it is a good story.

John Pentland Mahaffy 1839–1919: W. B. Stanford and R. B. McDowell *Mahaffy* (1971)

9 Blurting out the complete truth is considered adorable in the young, right smack up to the moment that the child says, 'Mommy, is this the fat lady you can't stand?'

Judith Martin 1938– : *Miss Manners' Guide to Rearing Perfect Children* (1985)

10 I never give them [the public] hell. I just tell the truth, and they think it is hell.

Harry S. Truman 1884–1972: in *Look* 3 April 1956

11 'The Adventures of Tom Sawyer' . . . was made by Mr Mark Twain, and he told the truth, mainly. There was things which he stretched, but mainly he told the truth.

Mark Twain 1835–1910: *The Adventures of Huckleberry Finn* (1884)

12 I don't always admit to being an MP. If I'm in a bar with people I don't know, to say you're a Labour MP isn't always a good move. I have said I'm a solicitor.

Claire Ward 1972– : in *Independent on Sunday* 14 March 1999 'Quotes'

13 The truth is rarely pure, and never simple.

Oscar Wilde 1854–1900: *The Importance of Being Earnest* (1895)

Unhappiness See **Happiness and Unhappiness**

The Universe

1 Had I been present at the Creation, I would have given some useful hints for the better ordering of the universe.

Alfonso, King of Castile 1221–84: on studying the Ptolemaic system (attributed)

2 'I quite realized,' said Columbus,
'That the Earth was not a rhombus,
But I *am* a little annoyed
To find it an oblate spheroid.'

Edmund Clerihew Bentley 1875–1956: 'Columbus' (1929)

3 This is the first convention of the Space Age—when a candidate can promise the moon and mean it.

David Brinkley: Laurence J. Peter (ed.) *Quotations for our Time* (1977)

on hearing that Margaret Fuller 'accepted the universe':
4 Gad! she'd better!

Thomas Carlyle 1795–1881: William James *Varieties of Religious Experience* (1902)

5 Twinkle, twinkle, little bat!
How I wonder what you're at!
Up above the world you fly!
Like a teatray in the sky.

Lewis Carroll 1832–98: *Alice's Adventures in Wonderland* (1865)

6 The world has treated me very well, but then I haven't treated it so badly either.

Noël Coward 1899–1973: Sheridan Morley *The Quotable Noël Coward* (1999)

7   Listen: there's a hell
Of a good universe next door; let's go.

e. e. cummings 1894–1962: *1 x 1* (1944)

8 The world is disgracefully managed, one hardly knows to whom to complain.

Ronald Firbank 1886–1926: *Vainglory* (1915)

9 Now, my own suspicion is that the universe is not only queerer than we suppose, but queerer than we *can* suppose.

J. B. S. Haldane 1892–1964: *Possible Worlds* (1927)

10 If this planet is a sample,
Or a preview if you will,
Or a model demonstration
Of the great designer's stall,
I say without hesitation,
'Thank you, no reincarnation.'

E. Y. Harburg 1898–1981: 'Letter to my Gaza' (1976)

11 To make the longest story terse,
Be it blessing, be it curse

E. Y. Harburg 1898–1981: 'The Odds on Favourite' (1976)

The Lord designed the Universe
With built in obsolescence . . .

12 The only lyric writer on the Broadway treadmill to get comic with the cosmic.

John Lahr 1941– : of E. Y. Harburg; Ned Sherrin *Cutting Edge* (1984)

13 The whole thing was so amazingly simple . . . Once started, the nebulous world condensed into suns, the suns threw off planets, the planets cooled, life resulted and presently became conscious, conscious life got higher up and higher up till you had apes, then Bishop Wilberforce, and then Professor Huxley.

Stephen Leacock 1869–1944: *The Boy I Left Behind Me* (1947)

14 The Greeks said God was always doing geometry, modern physicists say he's playing roulette, everything depends on the observer, the universe is a totality of observations, it's a work of art created by us.

Iris Murdoch 1919–99: *The Good Apprentice* (1985)

15 Space is almost infinite. As a matter of fact, we think it is infinite.

Dan Quayle 1947– : in *Daily Telegraph* 8 March 1989

Virtue and Vice See also **Morality**

1 I'm as pure as the driven slush.

Tallulah Bankhead 1903–68: in *Saturday Evening Post* 12 April 1947

2 All things are capable of excess. Absence of morbid moisture is a Whig virtue. But morbid dryness is a Whig vice.

Max Beerbohm 1872–1956: letter July 1928

3 A dead sinner revised and edited.

Ambrose Bierce 1842–c.1914: definition of a saint; *The Devil's Dictionary* (1911)

4 The rain, it raineth on the just
And also on the unjust fella:
But chiefly on the just, because
The unjust steals the just's umbrella.

Lord Bowen 1835–94: Walter Sichel *Sands of Time* (1923)

5 An original something, fair maid, you would win me
To write—but how shall I begin?
For I fear I have nothing original in me—
Excepting Original Sin.

Thomas Campbell 1777–1844: 'To a Young Lady, Who Asked Me to Write Something Original for Her Album' (1843)

6 In former days, everyone found the assumption of innocence so easy; today we find fatally easy the assumption of guilt.

Amanda Cross 1926– : *Poetic Justice* (1970)

7 Lydia was tired of being good. She felt it didn't altogether suit her. It made her feel a little dowdy, as though she had taken up residence in the suburbs of morality.

Alice Thomas Ellis 1932– : *Unexplained Laughter* (1985)

8 The louder he talked of his honour, the faster we counted our spoons.

Ralph Waldo Emerson 1803–82: *The Conduct of Life* (1860)

9 I do not look with favour on the collecting of first editions and autographs, but it is a vice which is sometimes found in otherwise virtuous persons.

A. E. Housman 1859–1936: letter, 28 March 1933

10 But if he does really think that there is no distinction between virtue and vice, why, Sir, when he leaves our houses, let us count our spoons.

Samuel Johnson 1709–84: James Boswell *Life of Samuel Johnson* (1791) 14 July 1763

11 He that but looketh on a plate of ham and eggs to lust after it, hath already committed breakfast with it in his heart.

C. S. Lewis 1898–1963: letter, 10 March 1954

12 honesty is a good
thing but
it is not profitable to
its possessor
unless it is
kept under control.

Don Marquis 1878–1937: *archys life of mehitabel* (1933) 'archygrams'

13 Goodness never means simply acceding to everyone else's idea of what you ought to be doing (for them). Adult virtue includes being able to decide what you can do, in terms of the importance you assign a task and the cost to you of performing it.

Judith Martin 1938– : *Miss Manners' Guide to Rearing Perfect Children* (1985)

on being discovered by his wife with a chorus girl:
14 I wasn't kissing her, I was just whispering in her mouth.

Chico Marx 1891–1961: Groucho Marx and Richard J. Anobile *Marx Brothers Scrapbook* (1973)

15 If only the good were a little less heavy-footed!

W. Somerset Maugham 1874–1965: *A Writer's Notebook* (1949) written in 1896

16 Beaverbrook, as it seemed to me, was a perfect example of the validity of the Faust myth; he really did believe he had sold his soul to the Devil, and was terrified of having to settle the account.

Malcolm Muggeridge 1903–90: *The Infernal Grove* (1975)

17 Temptations came to him, in middle age, tentatively and without insistence, like a neglected butcher-boy who asks for a Christmas box in February for no more hopeful reason than that he didn't get one in December.

Saki 1870–1916: *The Chronicles of Clovis* (1911)

18 Decency is Indecency's conspiracy of silence.

George Bernard Shaw 1856–1950: *Man and Superman* (1903) 'Maxims: Decency'

19 Self-denial is not a virtue: it is only the effect of prudence on rascality.

George Bernard Shaw 1856–1950: *Man and Superman* (1903)

20 There is nothing in this world constant, but inconstancy.

Jonathan Swift 1667–1745: *A Critical Essay upon the Faculties of the Mind* (1709)

21 I think I could be a good woman if I had five thousand a year.

William Makepeace Thackeray 1811–63: *Vanity Fair* (1847–8)

22 Barring that natural expression of villainy which we all have, the man looked honest enough.

Mark Twain 1835–1910: *A Curious Dream* (1872) 'A Mysterious Visit'

23 When I'm good, I'm very, very good, but when I'm bad, I'm better.

Mae West 1892–1980: in *I'm No Angel* (1933 film)

24 I've been things and seen places.

Mae West 1892–1980: in *I'm No Angel* (1933 film)

25 I used to be Snow White . . . but I drifted.

Mae West 1892–1980: Joseph Weintraub *Peel Me a Grape* (1975)

26 Between two evils, I always pick the one I never tried before.

Mae West 1892–1980: in *Klondike Annie* (1936 film)

27 To err is human—but it feels divine.

Mae West 1893–1980: attributed; Fred Metcalf (ed.) *Penguin Dictionary of Modern Humorous Quotations* (1987)

28 Like a monkey scratching for the wrong fleas, every age assiduously seeks out in itself those vices which it does not in fact have, while ignoring the large, red, beady-eyed crawlers who scuttle around unimpeded.

Katharine Whitehorn 1926– : *Observations* (1970)

29 I can resist everything except temptation.

Oscar Wilde 1854–1900: *Lady Windermere's Fan* (1892)

30 A little sincerity is a dangerous thing, and a great deal of it is absolutely fatal.

Oscar Wilde 1854–1900: 'The Critic as Artist' (1891)

Wales and the Welsh See also **Countries and Peoples**, **Places**

a Board Member objecting to Richard Burton's candidature for leading a Welsh National Theatre Company, after hearing of Burton's international triumphs:

1 Yes, but what has he done for Wales?

Anonymous: in *Ned Sherrin's Theatrical Anecdotes* (1992)

2 It profits a man nothing to give his soul for the whole world . . . But for Wales—!

Robert Bolt 1924–95: *A Man for All Seasons* (1960)

3 Now I perceive the devil understands Welsh.

William Shakespeare 1564–1616: *Henry IV, Part 1* (1597)

4 Not for Cadwallader and all his goats.

William Shakespeare 1564–1616: *Henry V* (1599)

5 The land of my fathers. My fathers can have it.

Dylan Thomas 1914–53: *Adam* December 1953

6 There are still parts of Wales where the only concession to gaiety is a striped shroud.

Gwyn Thomas 1913– : in *Punch* 18 June 1958

7 'I often think,' he continued, 'that we can trace almost all the disasters of English history to the influence of Wales!'

Evelyn Waugh 1903–66: *Decline and Fall* (1928)

8 The Welsh remain the only race whom you can vilify without being called a racist.

A. N. Wilson 1950– : in *Sunday Times* 23 April 2000 'Talking Heads'

War See also **The Armed Forces**

of the retreat from Dunkirk, May 1940:

1 The noise, my dear! And the people!

Anonymous: Anthony Rhodes *Sword of Bone* (1942)

2 Kitchener is a great poster.

Margot Asquith 1864–1945: *More Memories* (1933)

3 After each war there is a little less democracy to save.

Brooks Atkinson 1894–1984: *Once Around the Sun* (1951) 7 January

4 Well, if you knows of a better 'ole, go to it.

Bruce Bairnsfather 1888–1959: *Fragments from France* (1915)

5 I have never understood this liking for war. It panders to instincts already catered for within the scope of any respectable domestic establishment.

Alan Bennett 1934– : *Forty Years On* (1969)

on becoming aware of the Nazi threat:
6 I shall put warmonger on my passport.

Robert Byron 1905–41: *The Road to Oxiana* (1980 ed.); introduction

of Viscount Montgomery:
7 In defeat unbeatable: in victory unbearable.

Winston Churchill 1874–1965: Edward Marsh *Ambrosia and Small Beer* (1964)

to Peter Quennell, who had been complaining that he had to do fire-watching:
8 Can't you get out of it on the ground that you have a child and three wives to support?

Cyril Connolly 1903–74: Harold Nicolson *Diaries* (1980 ed.)

9 Though Waterloo was won upon the playing fields of Eton, The next war will be photographed, and lost, by Cecil Beaton.

Noël Coward 1899–1973: 'Bright Young People' (1931)

10 The nine o'clock news announced the discovery of the German blacklist. Among the people to be dealt with when England was invaded were Winston, Vic Oliver, Sybil Thorndyke, Rebecca West and me. What a cast!

Noël Coward 1899–1973: diary, 13 September 1945

when Park Lane was bombed:
11 I was under the table with the telephone and Shakespeare.

Emerald Cunard 1872–1948: Chips Channon diary, 20 March 1945

12 I gave my life for freedom—This I know: For those who bade me fight had told me so.

William Norman Ewer 1885–1976: 'Five Souls' (1917)

13 There never was a good war, or a bad peace.

Benjamin Franklin 1706–90: letter to Josiah Quincy, 11 September 1783

14 Fortunately, just when things were blackest, the war broke out.

Joseph Heller 1923–99: *Catch-22* (1961)

15 I'd like to see the government get out of war altogether and leave the whole field to private industry.

Joseph Heller 1923–99: *Catch-22* (1961)

16 The last European war (commonly called Great, as all wars are called by those concerned in them).

A. P. Herbert 1890–1971: *Misleading Cases* (1935)

17 All the same, sir, I would put some of the colonies in your wife's name.
   the Chief Rabbi to George VI, summer 1940

Joseph Herman Hertz 1872–1946: Chips Channon diary, 3 June 1943

18 TRENTINO (Louis Calhern): I am willing to do anything to prevent this war.
   FIREFLY (Groucho Marx): It's too late. I've already paid a month's rent on the battlefield.

Bert Kalmar 1884–1947 et al.: *Duck Soup* (1933 film)

19 I think from now on they're shooting without a script.

George S. Kaufman 1889–1961: comment on German strategy when the Germans invaded Russia; Howard Teichmann *George S. Kaufman* (1973)

20 Gentlemen, you can't fight in here. This is the war room.

Stanley Kubrick 1928–99, **Terry Southern**, and **Peter George**: *Dr Strangelove* (1963 film)

21 The first step in having any successful war is getting people to fight it.

Fran Lebowitz 1946– : *Social Studies* (1981)

22 If we'd had as many soldiers as that, we'd have won the war!
    on seeing the number of Confederate troops in Gone with the Wind *at the 1939 premiere*

Margaret Mitchell 1900–49: W. G. Harris *Gable and Lombard* (1976)

23 Like many men of my generation, I had an opportunity to give war a chance, and I promptly chickened out.

P. J. O'Rourke 1947– : *Give War a Chance* (1992)

24 The quickest way of ending a war is to lose it.

George Orwell 1903–50: in *Polemic* May 1946 'Second Thoughts on James Burnham'

25 Little girl . . . Sometime they'll give a war and nobody will come.

Carl Sandburg 1878–1967: *The People, Yes* (1936); 'Suppose They Gave a War and Nobody Came?' was the title of a 1970 film

26 'Our armies swore terribly in Flanders,' cried my uncle Toby,—'but nothing to this.'

Laurence Sterne 1713–68: *Tristram Shandy* (1759–67)

27 War is capitalism with the gloves off and many who go to war know it but they go to war because they don't want to be a hero.

Tom Stoppard 1937– : *Travesties* (1975)

28 The First World War had begun—imposed on the statesmen of Europe by railway timetables. It was an unexpected climax to the railway age.

A. J. P. Taylor 1906–90: *The First World War* (1963)

Evelyn Waugh, returning from Crete in 1941, was asked his impression of his first battle:
29 Like German opera, too long and too loud.

Evelyn Waugh 1903–66: Christopher Sykes *Evelyn Waugh* (1975)

30 As Lord Chesterfield said of the generals of his day, 'I only hope that when the enemy reads the list of their names, he trembles as I do.'

Duke of Wellington 1769–1852: letter, 29 August 1810, usually quoted 'I don't know what effect these men will have upon the enemy, but, by God, they frighten me'

31 Good-bye-ee! — Good-bye-ee!
Wipe the tear, baby dear, from your eye-ee.
Tho' it's hard to part, I know,
I'll be tickled to death to go.
Don't cry-ee — don't sigh-ee!
There's a silver lining in the sky-ee!
Bonsoir, old thing! cheerio! chin-chin!
Nahpoo! Toodle-oo! Good-bye-ee!

R. P. Weston 1878–1936 and **Bert Lee** 1880–1936: 'Good-bye-ee!' (c.1915)

32 The day war broke out.

Robb Wilton 1881–1957: customary preamble to radio monologues in the role of a Home Guard, from c.1940

of Sir Charles Napier's conquest of Sindh:
33 *Peccavi*—I have Sindh.
    reworking Latin peccavi *I have sinned*

Catherine Winkworth 1827–78: in *Punch* 18 May 1844, supposedly sent by Napier to Lord Ellenborough

34 'Anything in the papers, Jeeves?' 'Some slight friction threatening in the Balkans, sir.'

P. G. Wodehouse 1881–1975: *The Inimitable Jeeves* (1923)

Wealth See also **Money, Poverty**

1 'Whatever happened to the good old-fashioned City gent?'
'He's helping police with their enquiries.'

Anonymous: graffito in City of London lavatory, 1980s.

2 It was a sumpshous spot all done up in gold with plenty of looking glasses.

Daisy Ashford 1881–1972: *The Young Visiters* (1919)

3 If you would know what the Lord God thinks of money, you have only to look at those to whom he gives it.

Maurice Baring 1874–1945: Malcolm Cowley (ed.) *Writers at Work* (1958) 1st series

4 I can walk. It's just that I'm so rich I don't need to.

Alan Bennett 1934– : *Forty Years On* (1969)

5 People say I wasted my money. I say 90 per cent went on women, fast cars and booze. The rest I wasted.

George Best 1946– : in *Daily Telegraph* 29 December 1990

6 Mrs Budge Bulkeley, worth £32,000,000, has arrived here [Isfahan] accompanied by some lesser millionairesses. They are in great misery because the caviare is running out.
   on fellow travellers in Persia

Robert Byron 1905–41: *The Road to Oxiana* (1937)

7 When I hear a rich man described as a colourful character I figure he's a bum with money.

Jimmy Cannon 1910–73: in *New York Post* c.1955 'Nobody Asked Me, But . . .'

8 No wonder they fall for air hostesses and marry them, though only too often to ruin them by turning them into patrons of the arts.
   on American millionaires

Alexander Chancellor 1940– : *Some Times in America* (1999)

9 It is very difficult to spend less than £200 a morning when one goes out shopping.

Chips Channon 1897–1958: diary, 27 September 1934

10 I've got £700,000 in my Abbey National Crazy-High-Interest account. But what's the use?

Alan Clark 1928–99: diary, 24 December 1987

11 The Rich aren't like us—they pay less taxes.

Peter de Vries 1910–93: in *Washington Post* 30 July 1989

12 £40,000 a year [is] a moderate income—such a one as a man might jog on with.

Lord Durham 1792–1840: Herbert Maxwell *The Creevey Papers* (1903); letter from Mr Creevey to Miss Elizabeth Ord, 13 September 1821

13 I used to walk in the shade,
With those blues on parade,
But I'm not afraid.
This Rover crossed over.
If I never have a cent
I'll be rich as Rockefeller,
Gold dust on my feet,
On the sunny side of the street.

Dorothy Fields 1905–74: 'On the Sunny Side of the Street' (1930)

14 A rich man is nothing but a poor man with money.

W. C. Fields 1880–1946: attributed

15 To trust people is a luxury in which only the wealthy can indulge; the poor cannot afford it.

E. M. Forster 1879–1970: *Howards End* (1910)

16 The meek shall inherit the earth, but not the mineral rights.

John Paul Getty 1892–1976: Robert Lenzner *The Great Getty*; attributed

17 Poor Harold, he can live on his income all right, but he no longer can live on the income from his income.
of Harold Vanderbilt

George S. Kaufman 1889–1961: Howard Teichmann *George S. Kaufman* (1973)

18 I have never seen any rich people. Very often I have thought that I had found them. But it turned out that it was not so. They were not rich at all. They were quite poor. They were hard up. They were pushed for money. They didn't know where to turn for ten thousand dollars.

Stephen Leacock 1869–1944: *Further Foolishness* (1917) 'Are the Rich Happy?'

19 Wealth and power are much more likely to be the result of breeding than they are of reading.

Fran Lebowitz 1946– : on self-help books; *Social Studies* (1981)

20 When I want a peerage, I shall buy it like an honest man.

Lord Northcliffe 1865–1922: Tom Driberg *Swaff* (1974)

21 Chapman insisted, however, that the poet should come along . . . holding that millionaires were necessarily personable folk whose friendship could be very beautiful.

Flann O'Brien 1911–66: *The Best of Myles* (1968)

22 There is no stronger craving in the world than that of the rich for titles, except perhaps that of the titled for riches.

Hesketh Pearson 1887–1964: *The Pilgrim Daughters* (1961)

23 Where would the Rockefellers be today if sainted old John D. had gone on selling short-weight kerosene (paraffin to you) to widows and orphans instead of wisely deciding to mulct the whole country?

S. J. Perelman 1904–79: letter 25 October 1976

24 I've a shooting box in Scotland,
I've a chateau in Touraine,
I've a silly little chalet
In the Interlaken Valley,
I've a hacienda in Spain,
I've a private fjord in Norway,
I've a villa close to Rome,
And in travelling
It's really quite a comfort to know
That you're never far from home!

Cole Porter 1891–1964: 'I've a Shooting Box in Scotland' (1916)

25 HE: Who wants to be a millionaire?
SHE: I don't.
HE: Have flashy flunkeys ev'rywhere?
SHE: I don't . . .
HE: Who wants a marble swimming pool too?
SHE: I don't.
HE: And I don't,
BOTH: 'Cause all I want is you.

Cole Porter 1891–1964: 'Who Wants to be a Millionaire?' (1956)

26 A kiss on the hand may be quite continental,
But diamonds are a girl's best friend . . .

Men grow cold as girls grow old
And we all lose our charms in the end.
But square cut or pear shape,
These rocks won't lose their shape,
Diamonds are a girl's best friend.

Leo Robin 1900–84: 'Diamonds are a Girl's Best Friend' (1949)

27 I am a Millionaire. That is my religion.

George Bernard Shaw 1856–1950: *Major Barbara* (1907)

28 It is the wretchedness of being rich that you have to live with rich people.

Logan Pearsall Smith 1865–1946: *Afterthoughts* (1931)

29 To suppose, as we all suppose, that we could be rich and not behave as the rich behave, is like supposing that we could drink all day and keep absolutely sober.

Logan Pearsall Smith 1865–1946: *Afterthoughts* (1931)

30 It was very prettily said, that we may learn the little value of fortune by the persons on whom heaven is pleased to bestow it.

Richard Steele 1672–1729: *The Tatler* 27 July 1710

31 I've been poor and I've been rich—rich is better.

Sophie Tucker 1884–1966: attributed

32 I sometimes wished he would realize that he was poor instead of being that most nerve-racking of phenomena, a rich man without money.

Peter Ustinov 1921– : *Dear Me* (1977)

The Weather

1 When the foal and broodmare hinny,
And in every cut-down spinney
Ladysmocks grow mauve and mauver,
Then the winter days are over.
   Sometimes misquoted as, 'Spring is here, winter is over; the cuckoo-flower gets mauver and mauver'

Alfred Austin 1835–1913: *Fortunatus the Pessimist* (1892)

2 If this was Australia, this would be mid-winter. Think of that. Thick snow on the coolibah trees, koala bears rushing about in gum boots.

Alan Ayckbourn 1939– : *Table Manners* (1975)

on being asked why he never sunbathed in California instead of sitting under a sun-lamp:
3 And get hit by a meteor?

Robert Benchley 1889–1945: R. E. Drennan *Wit's End* (1973)

4 Wet spring had merged imperceptibly into bleak autumn. For months the sky had remained a depthless grey. Sometimes it rained, but mostly it was just dull . . . It was like living inside Tupperware.

Bill Bryson 1951– : *The Lost Continent* (1989)

5 The English winter—ending in July,
To recommence in August.

Lord Byron 1788–1824: *Don Juan* (1819–24)

6 Summer has set in with its usual severity.

Samuel Taylor Coleridge 1772–1834: letter to Vincent Novello, 9 May 1826

7 We sat on the front [at Deal] and watched the hardy English children and a few adults advancing, mauve with cold, into the cheerless waves.

Noël Coward 1899–1973: diary, 1 July 1946

8 It ain't a fit night out for man or beast.

W. C. Fields 1880–1946: adopted by Fields but claimed by him not to be original; letter 8 February 1944

9 A woman rang to say she heard there was a hurricane on the way. Well don't worry, there isn't.
   weather forecast on the night before serious gales in southern England

Michael Fish 1944– : BBC TV, 15 October 1987

10 Some are weather-wise, some are otherwise.

Benjamin Franklin 1706–90: *Poor Richard's Almanac* (1735) February

11 I said, 'It is most extraordinary weather for this time of year.' He replied, 'Ah, it isn't this time of year at all.'

Oliver St John Gogarty 1878–1957: *It Isn't This Time of Year At All* (1954)

12 April in Fairbanks
There's nothing more appealing
You feel your blood congealing
In April in Fairbanks.

Murray Grand: 'April in Fairbanks' (1952)

13 When two Englishmen meet, their first talk is of the weather.

Samuel Johnson 1709–84: *The Idler* 24 June 1758

14 The most serious charge which can be brought against New England is not Puritanism but February.

Joseph Wood Krutch 1893–1970: *The Twelve Seasons* (1949) 'February'

15 The Gulf Stream, as it nears the shores of the British Isles and feels the propinquity of Ireland, rises into the air, turns into soup, and comes down on London . . . London people are a little sensitive on the point and flatter their atmosphere by calling it a fog; but it is not: it is soup.

Stephen Leacock 1869–1944: *My Discovery of England* (1922) 'Impressions of London'

16 It was a wild and stormy night on the West Coast of Scotland. This, however, is immaterial to the present story, as the scene is not laid in the West of Scotland. For the matter of that the weather was just as bad on the East Coast of Ireland.

Stephen Leacock 1869–1944: *Nonsense Novels* (1911) 'Gertrude the Governess'

17 By and large the world considers weather to be something, if not all, of a romantic—given to dashing about hither and yon raining and snowing and cooling and heating with a capriciousness astonishing if not downright ridiculous in one so mature.

Fran Lebowitz 1946– : *Metropolitan Life* (1978)

18 SHE: I really can't stay
HE: But baby it's cold outside.

Frank Loesser 1910–69: 'Baby, It's Cold Outside' (1949)

19 The rain drove us into the church—our refuge, our strength, our only dry place . . . Limerick gained a reputation for piety, but we knew it was only the rain.

Frank McCourt 1930– : *Angela's Ashes* (1996)

20 It was such a lovely day I thought it was a pity to get up.

W. Somerset Maugham 1874–1965: *Our Betters* (1923)

21 Winter is icummen in,
Lhude sing Goddamm,
Raineth drop and staineth slop,
And how the wind doth ramm!
Sing: Goddamm.

Ezra Pound 1885–1972: 'Ancient Music' (1917)

22 'Anyhow,' Mme de Cambremer went on, 'I have a horror of sunsets, they're so romantic, so operatic.'

Marcel Proust 1871–1922: *Sodome et Gomorrhe* (Cities of the Plain, 1922)

23 Come December, people always say, 'Isn't it cold?' Well, of course it's cold. It's the middle of winter. You don't wander around at midnight saying, 'Isn't it dark?'

Arthur Smith 1954– : *Arthur Smith's Hamlet*

24 Thank heavens, the sun has gone in, and I don't have to go out and enjoy it.

Logan Pearsall Smith 1865–1946: *Afterthoughts* (1931)

25 Let no man boast himself that he has got through the perils of winter till at least the seventh of May.

Anthony Trollope 1815–82: *Doctor Thorne* (1858)

26 The way to ensure summer in England is to have it framed and glazed in a comfortable room.

Horace Walpole 1717–97: letter to Revd William Cole, 28 May 1774

27 It was the wrong kind of snow.

Terry Worrall: explaining disruption on British Rail; in *The Independent* 16 February 1991

Wit and Wordplay See also **Humour**

1 An ill-favoured thing, but Minoan
supposedly a comment by the archaeologist Sir Arthur Evans on finding a fragment of Cretan pottery

Anonymous: in 'Quote . . . Unquote' Newsletter, April 1995

2 Wild horses on their bended knees would not get me out there.

Alan Bennett 1934– : *Forty Years On* (1969)

3 There's an element of mockery here I don't like. I don't mind your tongue being in your cheek, but I suspect your heart is there with it.

Alan Bennett 1934– : *Forty Years On* (1969)

4 'That's the reason they're called lessons,' the Gryphon remarked: 'because they lessen from day to day.'

Lewis Carroll 1832–98: *Alice's Adventures in Wonderland* (1865)

5 'Curiouser and curiouser!' cried Alice.

Lewis Carroll 1832–98: *Alice's Adventures in Wonderland* (1865)

6 A wit should be no more sincere than a woman constant; one argues a decay of parts, as t'other of beauty.

William Congreve 1670–1729: *The Way of the World* (1700)

7 His wit invites you by his looks to come, But when you knock it never is at home.

William Cowper 1731–1800: 'Conversation' (1782)

8 Staircase wit.

Denis Diderot 1713–84: the witty riposte one thinks of only when one has left the drawing-room and is already on the way downstairs, in *Paradoxe sur le Comédien* (written 1773–8, published 1830)

9 O lovely O most charming pug
Thy graceful air and heavenly mug . . .
His noses cast is of the roman
He is a very pretty weoman
I could not get a rhyme for roman
And was oblidged to call it weoman.

Marjory Fleming 1803–11: 'Sonnet'

10 You've got to take the bull between your teeth.

Sam Goldwyn 1882–1974: N. Zierold *Hollywood Tycoons* (1969)

11 I can answer you in two words, im-possible.

Sam Goldwyn 1882–1974: Alva Johnston *The Great Goldwyn* (1937); apocryphal

12 Those who cannot miss an opportunity of saying a good thing . . . are not to be trusted with the management of any great question.

William Hazlitt 1778–1830: *Characteristics* (1823)

13 Dentist fills wrong cavity.
report of a dentist convicted of interfering with a patient

on being told that the publisher of Bentley's Miscellany *had thought of calling it* The Wits' Miscellany:

Ben Hecht 1894–1964: attributed

14 You need not have gone to the other extremity.

Douglas Jerrold 1803–57: Charles Cowden Clarke *Recollections of Writers* (1878)

15 It's hard not to write satire.

Juvenal AD c.60–c.130: *Satires*

Ira Gershwin had noticed two aged men entering the theatre:

16 GERSHWIN: That must be Gilbert and Sullivan coming to fix the show.

KAUFMAN: Why don't you put jokes like that into your lyrics?

George S. Kaufman 1889–1961: Howard Teichmann *George S. Kaufman* (1973)

17 '*Succès d'estime*' translates as 'a success that ran out of steam'.

George S. Kaufman 1889–1961: Philip Furia *Ira Gershwin* (1996)

18 The greatest thing since they reinvented unsliced bread.

William Keegan 1938– : in *Observer* 13 December 1987

19 [*Shogun* ended with] almost everybody except Richard Chamberlain being killed in the city of Osaka. *Moral—* Never give Osaka an even break.

Herbert Kretzmer: review of the miniseries *Shogun*; Ned Sherrin *Cutting Edge* (1984)

20 Many of us can still remember the social nuisance of the inveterate punster. This man followed conversation as a shark follows a ship.

Stephen Leacock 1869–1944: *The Boy I Left Behind Me* (1947)

21 Epigram: a wisecrack that played Carnegie Hall.

Oscar Levant 1906–72: in *Coronet* September 1958

on being asked how to make an epigram by a young man in the flying corps:

22 You merely loop the loop on a commonplace and come down between the lines.

W. Somerset Maugham 1874–1965: *A Writer's Notebook* (1949) written in 1933

23 Satire is a lesson, parody is a game.

Vladimir Nabokov 1899–1977: *Strong Opinions* (1974)

24 The dusk was performing its customary intransitive operation of 'gathering'.

Flann O'Brien 1911–66: *The Best of Myles* (1968)

to the British actor Herbert Marshall who annoyed her by repeated references to his busy 'shedule':

25 I think you're full of skit.

Dorothy Parker 1893–1967: Marion Meade *What Fresh Hell Is This?* (1988)

26 The pellet with the poison's in the vessel with the pestle. The chalice from the palace has the brew that is true.

Norman Panama 1914– and **Melvin Frank** 1913–88: *The Court Jester* (1955 film); spoken by Danny Kaye)

27 You beat your pate, and fancy wit will come: Knock as you please, there's nobody at home.

Alexander Pope 1688–1744: 'Epigram: You beat your pate' (1732)

28 I see a voice: now will I to the chink, To spy an I can hear my Thisby's face.

William Shakespeare 1564–1616: *A Midsummer Night's Dream* (1595–6)

29 Most forcible Feeble.

William Shakespeare 1564–1616: *Henry IV, Part 2* (1597)

30 Comparisons are odorous.

William Shakespeare 1564–1616: *Much Ado About Nothing* (1598–9)

31 An aspersion upon my parts of speech!

Richard Brinsley Sheridan 1751–1816: *The Rivals* (1775)

32 He is the very pineapple of politeness!

Richard Brinsley Sheridan 1751–1816: *The Rivals* (1775)

33 If I reprehend any thing in this world, it is the use of my oracular tongue, and a nice derangement of epitaphs!

Richard Brinsley Sheridan 1751–1816: *The Rivals* (1775)

34 No caparisons, Miss, if you please!—Caparisons don't become a young woman.

Richard Brinsley Sheridan
1751–1816: *The Rivals* (1775)

35 She's as headstrong as an allegory on the banks of the Nile.

Richard Brinsley Sheridan
1751–1816: *The Rivals* (1775)

36 'I can't see the Speaker,
Pray, Hal, do you?'
'Not see the Speaker, Bill?
Why I see *two*.'

Richard Brinsley Sheridan
1751–1816: recalling an epigram commemorating the drunkenness of Pitt and Henry Dundas in the House of Commons; Walter Jerrold *Bon-Mots* (1893)

37 LADY SNEERWELL: There's no possibility of being witty without a little ill-nature; the malice of a good thing is the barb that makes it stick.

Richard Brinsley Sheridan
1751–1816: *The School for Scandal* (1777)

38 A man might sit down as systematically, and successfully, to the study of wit as he might to the study of mathematics . . . By giving up only six hours a day to being witty, he should come on prodigiously before midsummer.

Sydney Smith 1771–1845: *Sketches of Moral Philosophy* (1849)

on seeing Mrs Grote in a huge rose-coloured turban:
39 Now I know the meaning of the word 'grotesque'.

Sydney Smith 1771–1845: Peter Virgin *Sydney Smith* (1994)

40 You will find as you grow older that the weight of rages will press harder and harder upon the employer.

William Archibald Spooner
1844–1930: William Hayter *Spooner* (1977)

41 To our queer old dean.

William Archibald Spooner
1844–1930: a toast; *Oxford University What's What* (1948); attributed, perhaps apocryphal

42 You have tasted your worm, you have hissed my mystery lectures, and you must leave by the first town drain.

William Archibald Spooner
1844–1930: to an undergraduate; *Oxford University What's What* (1948); attributed, perhaps apocryphal

43 My parents bought a lavatory from a travelling circus, under the fond delusion that a Chipperfield commode was a desirable thing to have about the house.
at a British Antique Dealers' Association dinner in the 1970s

Tom Stoppard 1937– : attributed; in *Spectator* 19 December 1998

44 Do you think Diaghilev was the kind of person about whom you could say, 'Hail, Fellatio, well met?'

Peter Ustinov 1921– : John Drummond *Tainted by Experience* (2000); attributed

45 I'm aghast! If there ever was one.

Dick Vosburgh: *A Saint She Ain't* (1999)

46 I'm on the horns of a Dalai Lama.

Dick Vosburgh: *A Saint She Ain't* (1999)

the American lexicographer Noah Webster was said to have been found by his wife embracing a chambermaid:
47 MRS WEBSTER: Noah, I'm surprised.
NOAH WEBSTER: No, my dear. You are amazed. It is we who are surprised.

Noah Webster 1758–1843: apocryphal; William Safire in *New York Times* 15 October 1973

48 'Sesquippledan,' he would say. 'Sesquippledan verboojuice.'

H. G. Wells 1866–1946: *The History of Mr Polly* (1909)

49 OSCAR WILDE: How I wish I had said that.
WHISTLER: You will, Oscar, you will.

James McNeill Whistler 1834–1903:
in R. Ellman *Oscar Wilde* (1987)

50 Oscar . . . picks from our platters the plums for the
puddings he peddles in the provinces.

James McNeill Whistler 1834–1903:
in *World* November 1886

51 I summed up all systems in a phrase, and all existence in
an epigram.

Oscar Wilde 1854–1900: letter, from
Reading Prison, to Lord Alfred
Douglas, January–March 1897

Women and Woman's Role See also **Men and Women**

1 The only options open for girls then were of course
mother, secretary or teacher . . . Now, I must say how
lucky we are, as women, to live in an age where 'Dental
Hygienist' has been added to the list.

Roseanne Arnold 1953– : *Roseanne*
(1990)

2 The trouble with women in an orchestra is that if they are
attractive it will upset my players and if they're not it will
upset me.

Thomas Beecham 1879–1961:
Harold Atkins and Archie Newman
Beecham Stories (1978)

3 Zuleika, on a desert island, would have spent most of her
time in looking for a man's footprint.

Max Beerbohm 1872–1956: *Zuleika
Dobson* (1911)

4 The suffragettes were triumphant. Woman's place was in
the gaol.

Caryl Brahms 1901–82 and **S. J.
Simon** 1904–48: *No Nightingales*
(1944)

5 I will vote for it [female suffrage] when women have left off
making a noise in the reading-room of the British
Museum.

Samuel Butler 1835–1902: *Notebooks*
(1912)

6 I heard a man say that brigands demand your money *or*
your life, whereas women require both.

Samuel Butler 1835–1902: *Further
Extracts from Notebooks* (1934)

7 It was a blonde. A blonde to make a bishop kick a hole in a
stained glass window.

Raymond Chandler 1888–1959:
Farewell, My Lovely (1940)

8 I let go of her wrists, closed the door with my elbow and
slid past her. It was like the first time. 'You ought to carry
insurance on those,' I said.

Raymond Chandler 1888–1959: *The
Little Sister* (1949)

9 Ful weel she soong the service dyvyne,
Entuned in hir nose ful semely;
And Frenssh she spak ful faire and fetisly,
After the scole of Stratford atte Bowe,
For Frenssh of Parys was to hire unknowe.

Geoffrey Chaucer c.1343–1400: of
the Prioress; *The Canterbury Tales*
'The General Prologue'

10 When a woman isn't beautiful, people always say, 'You
have lovely eyes, you have lovely hair.'

Anton Chekhov 1860–1904: *Uncle
Vanya* (1897)

11 A woman can become a man's friend only in the following
stages—first an acquaintance, next a mistress, and only
then a friend.

Anton Chekhov 1860–1904: *Uncle
Vanya* (1897)

12 Why do you rush through the fields in trains,
Guessing so much and so much.
Why do you flash through the flowery meads,
Fat-head poet that nobody reads;
And why do you know such a frightful lot
About people in gloves and such?

G. K. Chesterton 1874–1936: 'The
Fat White Woman Speaks' (1933); an
answer to Frances Cornford

13 As the Prime Minister developed her case she, as it were, auto-fed her own indignation. It was a prototypical example of an argument with a woman—no rational sequence, associative, lateral thinking, jumping the rails the whole time.

Alan Clark 1928–99: diary, 14 June 1988

14 O'erjoy'd was he to find
That, though on pleasure she was bent,
She had a frugal mind.

William Cowper 1731–1800: 'John Gilpin' (1785)

15 I'd have opened a knitting shop in Carlisle and been a part of life.
on his regret at not being born female

Quentin Crisp 1908–99: in *Spectator* 20 November 1999

16 A good uniform must work its way with the women, sooner or later.

Charles Dickens 1812–70: *Pickwick Papers* (1837)

17 She's the sort of woman . . . one would almost feel disposed to bury for nothing: and do it neatly, too!

Charles Dickens 1812–70: *Martin Chuzzlewit* (1844)

18 It used to be almost the first question (just after 'Can you type?') in the standard female job interview: 'Are you now, or have you ever, contemplated marriage, motherhood, or the violent overthrow of the US government?'

Barbara Ehrenreich 1941– : *The Worst Years of our Lives* (1991)

19 Plain women he regarded as he did the other severe facts of life, to be faced with philosophy and investigated by science.

George Eliot 1819–80: *Middlemarch* (1871–2)

20 When lovely woman stoops to folly and
Paces about her room again, alone,
She smoothes her hair with automatic hand,
And puts a record on the gramophone.

T. S. Eliot 1888–1965: *The Waste Land* (1922)

21 No woman can be a beauty without a fortune.

George Farquhar 1678–1707: *The Beaux' Stratagem* (1707)

22 'O! help me, heaven,' she prayed, 'to be decorative and to do right!'

Ronald Firbank 1886–1926: *The Flower Beneath the Foot* (1923)

23 The more underdeveloped the country, the more overdeveloped the women.

J. K. Galbraith 1908– : in *Time* 17 October 1969

24 I must have women. There is nothing unbends the mind like them.

John Gay 1685–1732: *The Beggar's Opera* (1728)

25 She may very well pass for forty-three
In the dusk with a light behind her!

W. S. Gilbert 1836–1911: *Trial by Jury* (1875)

26 I'm called Little Buttercup—dear Little Buttercup, Though I could never tell why.

W. S. Gilbert 1836–1911: *HMS Pinafore* (1878)

27 To everybody's prejudice I know a thing or two;
I can tell a woman's age in half a minute—and I do!

W. S. Gilbert 1836–1911: *Princess Ida* (1884)

28 When lovely woman stoops to folly
And finds too late that men betray,
What charm can soothe her melancholy,
What art can wash her guilt away?

Oliver Goldsmith 1730–74: *The Vicar of Wakefield* (1766)

29 I didn't fight to get women out from behind the vacuum cleaner to get them onto the board of Hoover.

Germaine Greer 1939– : in *Guardian* 27 October 1986

30 She who must be obeyed.

Rider Haggard 1856–1925: *She* (1887)

31 Other girls are coy and hard to catch,
But other girls ain't havin' any fun.
Ev'ry time I lose a wrestlin' match
I have a funny feelin' that I won.

Oscar Hammerstein II 1895–1960: 'I Cain't Say No' (1943)

32 When she's narrow, she's narrow as an arrow
And she's broad, where a broad, should be broad.

Oscar Hammerstein II 1895–1960: 'Honey Bun' (1949)

33 I'm just a fool when lights are low,
I cain't be prissy and quaint.
I ain't the type thet c'n faint,
How c'n I be whut I ain't,
I cain't say no!

Oscar Hammerstein II 1895–1960: 'I Cain't Say No' (1943)

34 When Grandma was a lassie
That tyrant known as man
Thought a woman's place
Was just the space
Around a fryin' pan.

It was good enough for Grandma
But it ain't good enough for us!

E. Y. Harburg 1898–1981: 'It was Good Enough for Grandma' (1944)

35 Starlet is the name for any woman under thirty not actively employed in a brothel.

Ben Hecht 1894–1964: E. Goodman *The Fifty-Year Decline and Fall of Hollywood* (1961)

36 Other people's babies—
That's my life!
Mother to dozens,
And nobody's wife.
    of a nanny

A. P. Herbert 1890–1971: 'Other People's Babies' (1930)

37 A woman's preaching is like a dog's walking on his hinder legs. It is not done well; but you are surprised to find it done at all.

Samuel Johnson 1709–84: James Boswell *Life of Samuel Johnson* (1791) 31 July 1763

38 Remember, you're fighting for this woman's honour . . . which is probably more than she ever did.

Bert Kalmar 1884–1947 et al.: *Duck Soup* (1933 film); spoken by Groucho Marx

39 When you get to a man in the case,
They're like as a row of pins—
For the Colonel's Lady an' Judy O'Grady
Are sisters under their skins!

Rudyard Kipling 1865–1936: 'The Ladies' (1896)

40 I can stretch a greenback dollar from here to Kingdom Come.
I can play the numbers, pay my bills, an' still end up with some
I got a twenty dollar piece says
There ain't nothin' I can't do.
I can make a dress out of a feed bag an' I can make a man out of you.
'Cause I'm a woman
W-O-M-A-N
I'll say it again.

Jerry Leiber 1933– : 'I'm a Woman' (1962)

41 Thank heaven for little girls!
For little girls get bigger every day.

Alan Jay Lerner 1918–86: 'Thank Heaven for Little Girls' (1958)

42 Women do not find it difficult nowadays to behave like men, but they often find it extremely difficult to behave like gentlemen.

Compton Mackenzie 1883–1972: *Literature in My Time* (1933)

43 Miss Manners cannot think of a more succinct definition of a lady than 'someone who wants to punch another person in the nose, but doesn't.'

Judith Martin 1938– : *Miss Manners' Guide to Rearing Perfect Children* (1985)

44 When women kiss it always reminds one of prize-fighters shaking hands.

H. L. Mencken 1880–1956: *Chrestomathy* (1949)

45 'Always be civil to the girls, you never know who they may marry' is an aphorism which has saved many an English spinster from being treated like an Indian widow.

Nancy Mitford 1904–73: *Love in a Cold Climate* (1949)

46 I have never had any great esteem for the generality of the fair sex, and my only consolation for being of that gender has been the assurance it gave me of never being married to anyone amongst them.

Lady Mary Wortley Montagu 1689–1762: letter to Mrs Calthorpe, 7 December 1723

47 Be plain in dress and sober in your diet;
In short my deary, kiss me, and be quiet.

Lady Mary Wortley Montagu 1689–1762: 'A Summary of Lord Lyttelton's Advice'

48 My only books
Were woman's looks,
And folly's all they've taught me.

Thomas Moore 1779–1852: *Irish Melodies* (1807) 'The time I've lost in wooing'

49 The sight of a woman at my public school was almost as rare as a Cockney accent in class; and if we spotted one it was, as often as not, a fierce and elderly matron.

John Mortimer 1923– : *Clinging to the Wreckage* (1982)

50 The thinking man's crumpet.
of Joan Bakewell

Frank Muir 1920–98: attributed

51 There was a young belle of old Natchez
Whose garments were always in patchez.
When comment arose
On the state of her clothes,
She drawled, When Ah itchez, Ah scratchez.

Ogden Nash 1902–71: 'Requiem' (1938)

52 Feminism is the result of a few ignorant and literal-minded women letting the cat out of the bag about which is the superior sex.

P. J. O'Rourke 1947– : *Modern Manners* (1984)

53 I'd the upbringing a nun would envy . . . Until I was fifteen I was more familiar with Africa than my own body.

Joe Orton 1933–67: *Entertaining Mr Sloane* (1964)

54 She's like the old line about justice—not only must be done, but must be seen to be done.

John Osborne 1929– : *Time Present* (1968)

55 That woman speaks eighteen languages, and can't say No in any of them.

Dorothy Parker 1893–1967: Alexander Woollcott *While Rome Burns* (1934)

56 And there was that wholesale libel on a Yale prom. If all the girls attending it were laid end to end, Mrs Parker said, she wouldn't be at all surprised.

Dorothy Parker 1893–1967: Alexander Woollcott *While Rome Burns* (1934)

57 You can lead a horticulture, but you can't make her think.

Dorothy Parker 1893–1967: John Keats *You Might as well Live* (1970)

58 A busted, disgusted cocotte am I,
Undesired on my tired little bottom, I,
While those fat femmes du monde

Cole Porter 1891–1964: 'The Cocotte' (1933)

With the men whom once I owned
Splash around like hell-bound hippopotami.

59 It's not 'cause I wouldn't,
It's not 'cause I shouldn't,
And, Lord knows, it's not 'cause I couldn't,
It's simply because I'm the laziest gal in town.

Cole Porter 1891–1964: 'The Laziest Girl in Town' (1927)

60 I do see her in tough joints more than somewhat.

Damon Runyon 1884–1946: in *Collier's* 22 May 1930 'Social Error'

61 O! when she's angry she is keen and shrewd.
She was a vixen when she went to school:
And though she be but little, she is fierce.

William Shakespeare 1564–1616: *A Midsummer Night's Dream* (1595-6)

62 The lady doth protest too much, methinks.

William Shakespeare 1564–1616: *Hamlet* (1601)

63 The fickleness of the women I love is only equalled by the infernal constancy of the women who love me.

George Bernard Shaw 1856–1950: *The Philanderer* (1898)

64 Here's to the ladies who lunch—
Everybody laugh—
Lounging in their caftans and planning a brunch
On their own behalf . . .
Off to the gym
Then to a fitting
Claiming they're fat,
And looking grim
'Cause they've been sitting
Choosing a hat—
Does anyone still wear a hat?
I'll drink to that . . .

. . . Another long exhausting day,
Another thousand dollars
A Matinée, a Pinter play,
Perhaps a piece of Mahler's—
I'll drink to that.
And one for Mahler . . .

. . . A toast to that invincible bunch
The dinosaurs surviving the crunch
Let's hear it for the ladies who lunch.

Stephen Sondheim 1930– : 'The Ladies who Lunch' (1970)

65 A woman seldom writes her mind but in her postscript.

Richard Steele 1672–1729: *The Spectator* 31 May 1711

66 A woman without a man is like a fish without a bicycle.

Gloria Steinem 1934– : attributed

67 We are becoming the men we wanted to marry.

Gloria Steinem 1934– : in *Ms* July/August 1982

68 There are worse occupations in this world than feeling a woman's pulse.

Laurence Sterne 1713–68: *A Sentimental Journey* (1768)

69 I had never seen a naked woman, and the way things were going I was never likely to. My family owned land.

Tom Stoppard 1937– : *Artist Descending a Staircase* (1973)

70 It's the last thing one would have expected of a woman who runs a donkey sanctuary—concubine to an opium addict.

Tom Stoppard 1937– : *The Dog It Was That Died* (1983)

71 Women never look so well as when one comes in wet and dirty from hunting.

R. S. Surtees 1805–64: *Mr Sponge's Sporting Tour* (1853)

72 I blame the women's movement for 10 years in a boiler suit.

Jill Tweedie 1936–93: attributed

73 Surely that shove I feel between my shoulder blades isn't liberation?

Jill Tweedie 1936–93: *Letters From a Fainthearted Feminist* (1982)

74 When once a woman has given you her heart, you can never get rid of the rest of her body.

John Vanbrugh 1664–1726: *The Relapse* (1696)

75 The Queen is most anxious to enlist every one who can speak or write to join in checking this mad, wicked folly of 'Woman's Rights', with all its attendant horrors, on which her poor feeble sex is bent, forgetting every sense of womanly feeling and propriety.

Queen Victoria 1819–1901: letter to Theodore Martin, 29 May 1870

76 The world is full of care, much like unto a bubble;
Woman and care, and care and women, and women and care and trouble.

Nathaniel Ward 1578–1652: epigram, attributed by Ward to a lady at the Court of the Queen of Bohemia; *The Simple Cobbler of Aggawam in America* (1647)

77 I will not stand for being called a woman in my own house.

Evelyn Waugh 1903–66: *Scoop* (1938)

78 I myself have never been able to find out precisely what feminism is: I only know that people call me a feminist whenever I express sentiments that differentiate me from a doormat or a prostitute.

Rebecca West 1892–1983: in 1913; *The Young Rebecca* (1982)

79 Glitter and be gay,
That's the part I play.
Here I am, unhappy chance.
Forced to bend my soul
To a sordid role,
Victimized by bitter, bitter circumstance.

Richard Wilbur 1921– : 'Glitter and be Gay' (1956)

80 One should never trust a woman who tells one her real age. A woman who would tell one that, would tell one anything.

Oscar Wilde 1854–1900: *A Woman of No Importance* (1893)

81 Many a woman has a past, but I am told that she has at least a dozen, and that they all fit.

Oscar Wilde 1854–1900: *Lady Windermere's Fan* (1892)

82 Could you not get Mrs Marshall to send down one of her typewriting girls—women are the most reliable, as they have no memory for the important.

Oscar Wilde 1854–1900: letter to Robert Ross from Reading Prison, 1 April 1897

Wordplay See **Wit and Wordplay**

Words See also **Language**

1 HONEY: I wonder if you could show me where the . . . I want to . . . put some powder on my nose.
GEORGE: Martha, won't you show her where we keep the . . . euphemism?

Edward Albee 1928– : *Who's Afraid of Virginia Woolf* (1964)

as a young serviceman Dennis Potter was summoned for help with spelling by an elderly Major:

2 How you do spell 'accelerator'? I've been all through the blasted 'Ex's' in this bloody dictionary.

Anonymous: related by Dennis Potter during the launch of his television show *Lipstick on Your Collar*; in *Ned Sherrin in his Anecdotage* (1993)

3 Serendipity means searching for a needle in a haystack and instead finding a farmer's daughter.

Anonymous: in 'Quote . . . Unquote' Newsletter, July 1995, as quoted by Sir Herman Bondi

4 You see it's like a portmanteau—there are two meanings packed up into one word.

Lewis Carroll 1832–98: *Through the Looking-Glass* (1872)

5 'There's glory for you!' 'I don't know what you mean by "glory",' Alice said. 'I meant, "there's a nice knock-down argument for you!" ' 'But "glory" doesn't mean "a nice knock-down argument",' Alice objected. 'When *I* use a word,' Humpty Dumpty said in a rather scornful tone, 'it means just what I choose it to mean—neither more nor less.'

Lewis Carroll 1832–98: *Through the Looking-Glass* (1872)

6 It depends on what the meaning of 'is' is.
videotaped evidence to the grand jury; tapes broadcast 21 September 1998

Bill Clinton 1946– : in *Guardian* 22 September 1998

7 'Do you spell it with a "V" or a "W"?' inquired the judge. 'That depends upon the taste and fancy of the speller, my Lord,' replied Sam [Weller].

Charles Dickens 1812–70: *Pickwick Papers* (1837)

8 Two such wonderful phrases—'I understand perfectly' and 'That is a lie'—a précis of life, aren't they?

Brian Friel 1929– : *The Communication Cord* (1983)

9 Excluding two-letter prepositions and 'an', I imagine *me* is the most used two-letter word in Songdom. 'I' (leaving out indefinite article 'a') is doubtless the most used one-letter word (and everywhere else, for that matter). 'You' (if definite article 'the' bows out) is the most frequent three-letter word. 'Love' probably gets the four-letter nod (referring strictly to songs that can be heard in the home). In the five-letter stakes I would wager that 'heart' and 'dream' photo-finish in a dead heat. As for words of more than five letters, you're on your own.

Ira Gershwin 1896–1983: *Lyrics on Several Occasions: A Brief Concordance* (1977)

10 Some word that teems with hidden meaning—like Basingstoke.

W. S. Gilbert 1836–1911: *Ruddigore* (1887)

11 It's exactly where a thought is lacking
That, just in time, a word shows up instead.

Goethe 1749–1832: *Faust* (1808) pt 1

12 Words are chameleons, which reflect the colour of their environment.

Learned Hand 1872–1961: in *Commissioner v. National Carbide Corp.* (1948)

13 Together they go places . . . Words make you think a thought. Music makes you feel a feeling. A song makes you feel a thought . . . The greatest romance in the life of a lyricist is when the right word meets the right note; often however, a Park Avenue phrase elopes with a Bleeker Street chord resulting in a shotgun wedding and a quickie divorce.

E. Y. Harburg 1898–1981: lecture given at the New York YMCA in 1970

14 Is there, can there be, such a word as *purposive?* There is: it was invented by a surgeon in 1855; and instead of being kept on the top shelf of an anatomical museum it is exhibited in both these volumes.

A. E. Housman 1859–1936: in *Cambridge Review* 1917

15 I understand your new play is full of single entendre.

George S. Kaufman 1889–1961: to Howard Dietz on *Between the Devil*; Howard Teichmann *George S. Kaufman* (1973)

16 I can't do splat . . . It doesn't translate.
the British Consul when asked to translate a description of the effect of a dum-dum bullet on the human skull

John le Carré 1931– : *Single & Single* (1999)

17 In my youth there were words you couldn't say in front of a girl; now you can't say 'girl'.

Tom Lehrer 1928– : in *Sunday Telegraph* 10 March 1996 'Spirits of the Age'

18 I know
That's she's sweeter 'n sugar—
But oh!
You can't rhyme 'sugar'!

Frank Loesser 1910–69: 'I'm Ridin' for a Fall' in *Thank Your Lucky Stars* (1943 musical film)

19 They say the definition of ambivalence is watching your mother-in-law drive over a cliff in your new Cadillac.

David Mamet 1947– : in *Guardian* 19 February 2000

20 I often think how much easier life would have been for me and how much time I should have saved if I had known the alphabet. I can never tell where I and J stand without saying G, H to myself first.

W. Somerset Maugham 1874–1965: *A Writer's Notebook* (1949) written in 1941

21 He respects Owl, because you can't help respecting anybody who can spell TUESDAY, even if he doesn't spell it right; but spelling isn't everything. There are days when spelling Tuesday simply doesn't count.

A. A. Milne 1882–1956: *The House at Pooh Corner* (1928)

22 The present age shrinks from precision and 'understands' only soft woolly words which really have no particular meaning, like 'cultural heritage' or 'the exigent dictates of modern traffic needs'.

Flann O'Brien 1911–66: *The Hair of the Dogma* (1977)

23 My stomach turned over twice at the thought of you sitting in a hot little office in South Beverly Hills scratching adjectives. Or verbs. They are the least responsive, most ornery little critters in the world to work with, and I needn't tell you how exasperating, befuddling, and dismaying a full day of struggling with them can be.

S. J. Perelman 1904–79: letter to Betsy Drake, 12 May 1952

24 Words are like leaves; and where they most abound, Much fruit of sense beneath is rarely found.

Alexander Pope 1688–1744: *An Essay on Criticism* (1711)

25 Make me a beautiful word for doing things tomorrow; for that surely is a great and blessed invention.

George Bernard Shaw 1856–1950: *Back to Methuselah* (1921)

26 I asked my teacher what an oxymoron was and he said, 'I don't know what an "oxy" is, bastard.

Arthur Smith 1954– and **Chris England**: *An Evening with Gary Lineker* (1990)

prescription when J. H. Thomas complained of 'an 'ell of an 'eadache':
27 A couple of aspirates.

F. E. Smith 1872–1930: in *Ned Sherrin in his Anecdotage* (1993)

28 Man does not live by words alone, despite the fact that he sometimes has to eat them.

Adlai Stevenson 1900–65: *The Wit and Wisdom of Adlai Stevenson* (1965)

29 By hard, honest labour I've dug all the large words out of my vocabulary . . . I never write metropolis for seven cents because I can get the same money for city. I never write policeman, because I can get the same money for *Cop*.

Mark Twain 1835–1910: *Mark Twain's Speeches* (1923)

30 It is a pity that Chawcer, who had geneyus, was so unedicated. He's the wuss speller I know of.

Artemus Ward 1834–67: *Artemus Ward in London* (1867)

31 In modern life nothing produces such an effect as a good platitude. It makes the whole world kin.

Oscar Wilde 1854–1900: *An Ideal Husband* (1895)

Work and Leisure

1 I will undoubtedly have to seek what is happily known as gainful employment, which I am glad to say does not describe holding public office.

Dean Acheson 1893–1971: in *Time* 22 December 1952

2 A professional is a man who can do his job when he doesn't feel like it. An amateur is a man who can't do his job when he does feel like it.

James Agate 1877–1947: diary, 19 July 1945

3 If I am doing nothing, I like to be doing nothing to some purpose. That is what leisure means.

Alan Bennett 1934– : *A Question of Attribution* (1989)

4 I realized I could have written two songs and made myself some money in that time.

Irving Berlin 1888–1989: after taking two days of piano lessons; Caryl Brahms and Ned Sherrin *Song by Song* (1984)

5 I suspect guys who say, 'I just send out for a sandwich for lunch,' as lazy men trying to impress me.

Jimmy Cannon 1910–73: in *New York Post* c.1955 'Nobody Asked Me, But . . .'

when criticized for continually arriving late for work:
6 But think how early I go.

Lord Castlerosse 1891–1943: while working in the City in 1919 for his uncle Lord Revelstoke; Leonard Mosley *Castlerosse* (1956); remark also claimed by Howard Dietz at MGM

7 Mr Chamberlain loves the working man, he loves to see him work.
of Joseph Chamberlain in 1903

Winston Churchill 1874–1965: K. Halle *The Irrepressible Churchill* (1985)

8 I do nothing, granted. But I see the hours pass—which is better than trying to fill them.

E. M. Cioran 1911– : in *Guardian* 11 May 1993

9 Work is always so much more fun than fun.

Noël Coward 1899–1973: Sheridan Morley *The Quotable Noël Coward* (1999)

10 I never work. Work does age you so.

Quentin Crisp 1908–99: in *Observer* 10 January 1999 'Sayings of the Week'

11 People who are lonely are those who do not know what to do with the time when they are alone.

Quentin Crisp 1908–99: in *Sunday Telegraph* 28 September 1999

12 My life is one demd horrid grind!

Charles Dickens 1812–70: *Nicholas Nickleby* (1839)

13 Anythin' for a quiet life, as the man said wen he took the sitivation at the lighthouse.

Charles Dickens 1812–70: *Pickwick Papers* (1837)

14 I was proud to work with the great Gershwin, and I would have done it for nothing, which I did.

Howard Dietz 1896–1983: *Dancing in the Dark* (1974)

15 I have long been of the opinion that if work were such a splendid thing the rich would have kept more of it for themselves.

Bruce Grocott 1940– : in *Observer* 22 May 1988 'Sayings of the Week'

16 Never work for a liberal employer, dear boy, they'll sack you on Christmas Eve.
  learned at his father's knee

Philip Hope-Wallace 1911–79: in *Spectator* 7 August 1999; attributed

17 It is impossible to enjoy idling thoroughly unless one has plenty of work to do.

Jerome K. Jerome 1859–1927: *Idle Thoughts of an Idle Fellow* (1886) 'On Being Idle'

18 Astronomers, like burglars and jazz musicians, operate best at night.

Miles Kington 1941– : *Welcome to Kington* (1989)

19 Being a specialist is one thing, getting a job is another.

Stephen Leacock 1869–1944: *The Boy I Left Behind Me* (1947)

20 A secretary is not a toy.

Frank Loesser 1910–69: song title (1961)

21 I can think of few nobler callings for elderly persons with leisure than to provide unindexed books with indexes.

E. V. Lucas 1868–1938: *365 Days and One More* (1926)

22 Employers have a very bad time these days, what with the Protection of Employment Act and various other acts. You may give your employees intructions but you cannot ensure that they are carried out.

Lord Massereene and Ferrard 1914–93: speech on the Wildlife and Countryside Bill, House of Lords 3 February 1981

23 Why do men delight in work? Fundamentally, I suppose, because there is a sense of relief and pleasure in getting something done—a kind of satisfaction not unlike that which a hen enjoys on laying an egg.

H. L. Mencken 1880–1956: *Minority Report* (1956)

24 Work expands so as to fill the time available for its completion.

C. Northcote Parkinson 1909–93: *Parkinson's Law* (1958)

25 It's true hard work never killed anybody, but I figure why take the chance?

Ronald Reagan 1911– : interview; in *Guardian* 31 March 1987

26 Most memorable . . . was the discovery (made by all the rich men in England at once) that women and children could work twenty-five hours a day in factories without many of them dying or becoming excessively deformed. This was known as the Industrial Revelation.

W. C. Sellar 1898–1951 and **R. J. Yeatman** 1898–1968: *1066 and All That* (1930)

27 I understand. You work very hard two days a week and you need a five-day weekend. That's normal.

Neil Simon 1927– : *Come Blow Your Horn* (1961)

28 It's dogged as does it. It ain't thinking about it.

Anthony Trollope 1815–82: *The Last Chronicle of Barset* (1867)

29 How to be an effective secretary is to develop the kind of lonely self-abnegating sacrificial instincts usually possessed only by the early saints on their way to martyrdom.

Jill Tweedie 1936–93: *It's Only Me* (1980)

30 Work is the curse of the drinking classes.

Oscar Wilde 1854–1900: Hesketh Pearson *Life of Oscar Wilde* (1946)

Writers See also **Books, Literature, Poetry, Poets, Reading, Writing**

1 I do think . . . the mighty stir made about scribbling and scribes, by themselves and others—a sign of effeminacy, degeneracy, and weakness. Who would write, who had any thing better to do?

Lord Byron 1788–1824: diary, 24 November 1813

2 In general I do not draw well with literary men—not that I dislike them but—I never know what to say to them after I have praised their last publication.

Lord Byron 1788–1824: 'Detached Thoughts' 15 October 1821

his Intourist guide had protested that Shakespeare's plays could never have been written by a grocer from Stratford-upon-Avon:
3 They are exactly the sort of plays I would expect a grocer to write.

Robert Byron 1905–41: *The Road to Oxiana* (1980 ed.); introduction

4 I met Aldous Huxley slinking out of a bank, as if he was afraid to be seen emerging from a capitalist institution, from where he had doubtless withdrawn large sums.

Chips Channon 1897–1958: diary 16 December 1935

5 The compulsion to make rhymes was born in me. For those sated readers of my work who wish ardently that I would stop, the future looks dark indeed.

Noël Coward 1899–1973: foreword to the *The Lyrics of Noel Coward* (1965)

6 HANNEN SWAFFER: I have always said that you act much better than you write.
NOËL COWARD: How odd, I'm always saying the same about you.

Noël Coward 1899–1973: Sheridan Morley *A Talent to Amuse* (1969)

7 There are three reasons for becoming a writer. The first is that you need the money; the second, that you have something to say that you think the world should know; and the third is that you can't think what to do with the long winter evenings.

Quentin Crisp 1908–99: *The Naked Civil Servant* (1968)

8 Most people are vain, so I try to ensure that any author who comes to stay will find at least one of their books in their room.

Duke of Devonshire 1920– : in *The Spectator* 22 January 1994

9 I love being a writer. What I can't stand is the paperwork.

Peter de Vries 1910–93: Laurence J. Peter (ed.) *Quotations for our Time* (1977)

10 An author who speaks about his own books is almost as bad as a mother who talks about her own children.

Benjamin Disraeli 1804–81: at a banquet given in Glasgow on his installation as Lord Rector, 19 November 1873

11 The nicest old lady I ever met.
of Henry James

William Faulkner 1897–1962: Edward Stone *The Battle and the Books* (1964)

12 A New Jersey Nero who mistakes his pinafore for a toga.
of Alexander Woollcott

Edna Ferber 1887–1968: R. E. Drennan *Wit's End* (1973)

13 It is splendid to be a great writer, to put men into the frying pan of your words and make them pop like chestnuts.

Gustave Flaubert 1821–80: letter to Louise Colet, 3 November 1851

14 I learned to read and write with unusual speed, a facility the book-buying public would regret forty years later.

Michael Green 1927– : *The Boy Who Shot Down an Airship* (1988)

15 The defendant, Mr. Haddock, is, among other things, an author, which fact should alone dispose you in the plaintiff's favour.

A. P. Herbert 1890–1971: *Misleading Cases* (1935)

16 He can't write fiction and he can't write non-fiction, so he's invented a bogus category in between.
    on Jeffrey Archer's 'novelography', based on Rupert Murdoch and Robert Maxwell

Ian Hislop 1960– : in *Observer* 14 April 1996

17 The book of my enemy has been remaindered
And I rejoice . . .
What avail him now his awards and prizes,
The praise expended upon his meticulous technique,
His individual new voice?

Clive James 1939– : 'The Book of My Enemy has been Remaindered' (1986)

a young admirer had asked if he might kiss the hand that wrote Ulysses:
18 No, it did lots of other things too.

James Joyce 1882–1941: Richard Ellmann *James Joyce* (1959)

19 Tell them the author giveth and the author taketh away.
    to a playwright afraid to tell the cast of cuts he had made

George S. Kaufman 1889–1961: Howard Teichmann *George S. Kaufman* (1973)

objecting to having been appointed a Companion of Honour without his consent:
20 How would you like it if you woke up and found yourself Archbishop of Canterbury?

Rudyard Kipling 1865–1936: letter to Bonar Law, 1917; Charles Carrington *Rudyard Kipling* (1978)

21 Mr. Ruskin, whose distinction it was to express in prose of incomparable grandeur thought of an unparalleled confusion.

Osbert Lancaster 1908–80: *Pillar to Post* (1938)

22 To read Swift is like being locked up on a desert island with Napoleon in the capacity of secretary. There is no prospect of relief.

Harold Laski 1893–1950: letter to Oliver Wendell Holmes, 12 January 1919

23 We writers all act and react on one another; and when I see a good thing in another man's book I react on it at once.

Stephen Leacock 1869–1944: *My Discovery of England* (1922) 'Impressions of London'

24 The writer is to the real world what Esperanto is to the language world—funny, maybe, but not *that* funny.

Fran Lebowitz 1946– : *Metropolitan Life* (1978)

25 E. M. Forster never gets any further than warming the teapot. He's a rare fine hand at that. Feel this teapot. Is it not beautifully warm? Yes, but there ain't going to be no tea.

Katherine Mansfield 1888–1923: diary, May 1917

26 The humour of Dostoievsky is the humour of a bar-loafer who ties a kettle to a dog's tail.

W. Somerset Maugham 1874–1965: *A Writer's Notebook* (1949) written in 1917

27 There is no need for the writer to eat a whole sheep to be able to tell you what mutton tastes like. It is enough if he eats a cutlet. But he should do that.

W. Somerset Maugham 1874–1965: *A Writer's Notebook* (1949) written in 1941

28 Poor Henry [James], he's spending eternity wandering round and round a stately park and the fence is just too high for him to peep over and they're having tea just too far away for him to hear what the countess is saying.

W. Somerset Maugham 1874–1965: *Cakes and Ale* (1930)

29 Dear Willie, you may well be right in thinking you write like Shakespeare. Certainly I have noticed during these last few months an adulation of your name in the more vulgar portions of the popular press. And one word of brotherly advice. *Do Not Attempt the Sonnets.*

Viscount Maugham d. 1958: letter to his brother Somerset Maugham, in *Ned Sherrin in his Anecdotage* (1993)

30 What obsesses a writer starting out on a lifetime's work is the panic-stricken search for a voice of his own.

John Mortimer 1923– : *Clinging to the Wreckage* (1982)

31 I am the kind of writer that people think other people are reading.

V. S. Naipaul 1932– : in *Radio Times* 14 March 1979

32 THE EDITOR: We can't have much more of this, space must also be found for my stuff.
MYSELF: All right, never hesitate to say so. I can turn off the tap at will.

Flann O'Brien 1911–66: *The Best of Myles* (1968)

33 [David Merrick] liked writers in the way that a snake likes live rabbits.

John Osborne 1929– : *Almost a Gentleman* (1991)

34 He's a writer for the ages—for the ages of four to eight.

Dorothy Parker 1893–1967: R. E. Drennan *Wit's End* (1973)

35 Authors are judged by strange capricious rules
The great ones are thought mad, the small ones fools.

Alexander Pope 1688–1744: prologue to *Three Hours after Marriage* (1717)

36 No, on the whole I think all writers should be in prison.

Ralph Richardson 1902–83: on being asked to appear in a charity programme in support of imprisoned writers; in *Ned Sherrin in his Anecdotage* (1993)

37 A confessional passage has probably never been written that didn't stink a little bit of the writer's pride in having given up his pride.

J. D. Salinger 1919– : *Catcher in the Rye* (1951)

38 Virginia Woolf, I enjoyed talking to her, but thought *nothing* of her writing. I considered her 'a beautiful little knitter'.

Edith Sitwell 1887–1964: letter to Geoffrey Singleton, 11 July 1955

39 The shelf life of the modern hardback writer is somewhere between the milk and the yoghurt.

Calvin Trillin 1935– : in *Sunday Times* 9 June 1991; attributed

40 He never leaves off . . . and he always has two packages of manuscript in his desk, besides the one he's working on, and the one that's being published.
on her husband Anthony Trollope

Rose Trollope 1820–1917: Julian Hawthorne *Shapes that Pass: Memories of Old Days* (1928)

41 What other culture could have produced someone like Hemingway and *not* seen the joke?

Gore Vidal 1925– : *Pink Triangle and Yellow Star* (1982)

42 To see him [Stephen Spender] fumbling with our rich and delicate language is to experience all the horror of seeing a Sèvres vase in the hands of a chimpanzee.

Evelyn Waugh 1903–66: in *The Tablet* 5 May 1951

43 Let Shakespeare do it his way, I'll do it mine. We'll see who comes out better.

Mae West 1892–1980: G. Eells and S. Musgrove *Mae West* (1989)

44 Mr. [Henry] James writes fiction as if it were a painful duty.

Oscar Wilde 1854–1900: 'The Decay of Lying' (1891)

45 Meredith! Who can define him? His style is chaos illuminated by flashes of lightning. As a writer he has mastered everything except language: as a novelist he can

Oscar Wilde 1854–1900: 'The Decay of Lying' (1891)

do everything except tell a story. As an artist he is
everything, except articulate.

46 I know no person so perfectly disagreeable and even
dangerous as an author.

William IV 1765–1837: Philip Ziegler
King William IV (1971)

47 Every author really wants to have letters printed in the
papers. Unable to make the grade, he drops down a rung
of the ladder and writes novels.

P. G. Wodehouse 1881–1975: *Louder
and Funnier* (1932)

A. A. Milne had written a hostile letter to the Daily Telegraph *on
the report of Wodehouse's broadcasting from Germany:*

48 My personal animosity against a writer never affects my
opinion of what he writes. Nobody could be more anxious
than myself, for instance, that Alan Alexander Milne
should trip over a loose bootlace and break his bloody
neck, yet I re-read his early stuff at regular intervals with
all the old enjoyment.

P. G. Wodehouse 1881–1975: letter
27 November 1945

Writing See also **Books, Literature, Poetry, Poets, Reading, Writers**

1 If you can't annoy somebody with what you write, I think
there's little point in writing.

Kingsley Amis 1922–95: in *Radio
Times* 1 May 1971

2 The biggest obstacle to professional writing is the necessity
for changing a typewriter ribbon.

Robert Benchley 1889–1945: *Chips
off the old Benchley* (1949)

3 The only thing that goes missing in Nature is a pencil.

Robert Benchley 1889–1945:
attributed, perhaps apocryphal

4 In the mind, as in the body, there is the necessity of
getting rid of waste, and a man of active literary habits
will write for the fire as well as for the press.

Jerome Cardan 1501–76: William
Osler *Aequanimites* (1904); epigraph

5 Writing, I explained, was mainly an attempt to out-argue
one's past; to present events in such a light that battles
lost in life were either won on paper or held to a draw.

Jules Feiffer 1929– : *Ackroyd* (1977)

6 No plagiarist can excuse the wrong by showing how much
of his work he did not pirate.

Learned Hand 1872–1961: *Sheldon v.
Metro-Goldwyn Pictures Corp.* 1936

7 I had my fill of this dreamy abstract thing called business
and I decided to face reality by writing lyrics . . . the
capitalists saved me in 1929 . . . I was left with a pencil
and finally had to write for a living.

E. Y. Harburg 1898–1981: lecture
given at the New York YMCA in 1970

explaining why he wrote opinions while standing:

8 Nothing conduces to brevity like a caving in of the knees.

Oliver Wendell Holmes Jr.
1841–1935: Catherine Drinker Bowen
Yankee from Olympus (1944);
attributed

9 Whence came the intrusive comma on p. 4? It did not fall
from the sky.

A. E. Housman 1859–1936: letter to
the Richards Press, 3 July 1930

10 Written English is now inert and inorganic: not stem and
leaf and flower, not even trim and well-joined masonry,
but a daub of untempered mortar.

A. E. Housman 1859–1936: in
Cambridge Review 1917

11 Let alone re-write, he doesn't even re-read.

Clive James 1939– : *The Dreaming
Swimmer* (1992)

12 Read over your compositions, and where ever you meet with a passage which you think is particularly fine, strike it out.

Samuel Johnson 1709–84: quoting a college tutor; James Boswell *Life of Samuel Johnson* (1791) 30 April 1773

13 No man but a blockhead ever wrote, except for money.

Samuel Johnson 1709–84: James Boswell *Life of Samuel Johnson* (1791) 5 April 1776

14 If you want to get rich from writing, write the sort of thing that's read by persons who move their lips when reading.

Don Marquis 1878–1937: attributed; Peter Kemp (ed.) *Oxford Dictionary of Literary Quotations* (1997)

15 The art of writing, like the art of love, runs all the way from a kind of routine hard to distinguish from piling bricks to a kind of frenzy closely related to delirium tremens.

H. L. Mencken 1880–1956: *Minority Report* (1956)

16 If you steal from one author, it's plagiarism; if you steal from many, it's research.

Wilson Mizner 1876–1933: Alva Johnston *The Legendary Mizners* (1953)

17   I'm glad you'll write,
You'll furnish paper when I shite.

Lady Mary Wortley Montagu 1689–1762: 'Reasons that Induced Dr S— to write a Poem called the Lady's Dressing Room'

18 It is our national joy to mistake for the first-rate, the fecund rate.

Dorothy Parker 1893–1967: review of Sinclair Lewis *Dodsworth*; in *New Yorker* 16 March 1929

19 As to the Adjective: when in doubt, strike it out.

Mark Twain 1835–1910: *Pudd'nhead Wilson* (1894)

20 Anyone could write a novel given six weeks, pen, paper, and no telephone or wife.

Evelyn Waugh 1903–66: Chips Channon diary 16 December 1934

Youth See also **Children, Middle Age, Old Age**

1 It is better to waste one's youth than to do nothing with it at all.

Georges Courteline 1858–1929: *La Philosophie de Georges Courteline* (1948)

2 I am just an ingénue
And shall be till I'm eighty-two.

Noël Coward 1899–1973: 'Little Women' (1928)

3 She's shy—of the Violet persuasion, but that's not a bad thing in a young girl.

Ronald Firbank 1886–1926: *The Flower Beneath the Foot* (1923)

4 Remember that as a teenager you are at the last stage in your life when you will be happy to hear that the phone is for you.

Fran Lebowitz 1946– : *Social Studies* (1981)

5 Youth is wasted on the young. I'm 52 now and I just can't stay up all night like I did.

Camille Paglia 1947– : interview in *Sunday Times* 6 June 1999

6 It's all that the young can do for the old, to shock them and keep them up to date.

George Bernard Shaw 1856–1950: *Fanny's First Play* (1914) 'Induction'

7 What music is more enchanting than the voices of young people, when you can't hear what they say?

Logan Pearsall Smith 1865–1946: *Afterthoughts* (1931)

8 Give me a girl at an impressionable age, and she is mine for life.

Muriel Spark 1918– : *The Prime of Miss Jean Brodie* (1961)

9 One's prime is elusive. You little girls, when you grow up, must be on the alert to recognize your prime at whatever time of your life it may occur.

Muriel Spark 1918– : *The Prime of Miss Jean Brodie* (1961)

10 Being young is not having any money; being young is not minding not having any money.

Katharine Whitehorn 1926– : *Observations* (1970)

11 I have been in a youth hostel. I know what they're like. You are put in a kitchen with seventeen venture scouts with behavioural difficulties and made to wash swedes.

Victoria Wood 1953– : *Mens Sana in Thingummy Doodah* (1990)

Author Index

Bagehot, Walter (1826–77)
  Economics 1
Bailey, David (1938–)
  Fashion 3
  Football 3
  Men and Women 1
Bailey, F. Lee (1933–)
  Law 1
Bailey, Richard W. (1939–)
  Dictionaries 1
Bainbridge, Beryl (1933–)
  Marriage 10
  Men 1
  Smoking 1
Bairnsfather, Bruce
  (1888–1959)
  War 4
Baker, Russell (1925–)
  Advertising 2
  Alcohol 6
  Languages 3
  Literature 2
  Technology 2
Bakewell, Joan (1933–)
  Food 5
Baldwin, James (1924–87)
  Money 2
  Poverty 2
Baldwin, Stanley (1867–1947)
  Politicians 2
  Politics 9
Balfour, Arthur James
  (1848–1930)
  Biography 1
  Sports 2
Balzac, Honoré de
  (1799–1850)
  Marriage 11
Banham, Reynar (1922–88)
  Transport 3
Bankhead, Tallulah (1903–68)
  Behaviour 1
  Description 3
  Education 2
  Film Stars 2
  Life 3, 4
  Sex 14
  Theatre 4
  Time 1, 2
  Virtue 1
Banks-Smith, Nancy
  Actors 1
  Books 2
Barbarito, Luigi (1922–)
  Sports 3

Barber, Eric Arthur
  (1888–1965)
  Education 3
Baring, Maurice (1874–1945)
  Wealth 3
Barker, Ronnie (1929–)
  Humour 3
Barnes, Clive (1927–)
  Theatre 5
Barnes, Julian (1946–)
  Men 2
  Tennis 1
Barnes, Peter (1931–)
  God 8
Barrie, J. M. (1860–1937)
  Acting 3
  Class 2
  Publishing 2
  Scotland 1, 2
Barry, Dave (1948–)
  Journalism 1
Barrymore, Ethel (1879–1959)
  Actors 2
Barrymore, John (1882–1942)
  Actors 3
Barstow, Stan (1928–)
  Reading 1
Bart, Lionel (1930–)
  Marriage 12
Baruch, Bernard (1870–1965)
  Old Age 4
  Politics 10
Baudelaire, Charles (1821–67)
  Music 4
Baxter, Beverley (1891–1964)
  Politicians 3
Baylis, Lilian (1874–1937)
  Theatre 6
Beaton, Alistair
  Politicians 4
Beaton, Alistair and **Sherrin,
Ned** (1931–)
  Songs 5
Beaton, Cecil (1904–80)
  Appearance 2
  Languages 4
Beatty, Warren (1937–)
  Mistakes 2
**Beaumarchais, Pierre-
Augustin Caron de**
  (1732–99)
  Songs 6
Beaverbrook, Lord
  (1879–1964)
  Certainty 2

  Countries 1
  Heaven 1
  Politicians 5
  Prime Ministers 4
Beckett, Samuel (1906–89)
  Body 3
  Censorship 2
  Certainty 3
  Death 8
  God 9
  Success 1
  Time 3
Beebe, Lucius (1902–)
  Food 6
Beecham, Thomas
  (1879–1961)
  Art 3
  Dance 1
  England 3
  Insults 7
  Medicine 4
  Music 5, 6, 7, 8
  People 6
  Songs 7
  Women 2
Beecher, Henry Ward
  (1813–87)
  Law 2
Beerbohm, Max (1872–1956)
  America 3
  Appearance 3
  Art 4
  Class 3
  Cricket 5
  Critics 5, 6
  Education 4
  History 1
  Intelligence 2
  Literature 3, 4
  Love 3
  Men 3
  Morality 1
  People 7
  Royalty 13
  Snobbery 3
  Society 2
  Theatre 7
  Towns 4
  Virtue 2
  Women 3
Beethoven, Ludwig van
  (1770–1827)
  Cookery 3
Behan, Brendan (1923–64)
  Alcohol 7

Brickman, Marshall (1941–)
see Allen, Woody and
Brickman, Marshall

Bridges, Edward (1892–1969)
Civil Servants 3

Brien, Alan (1925–)
Acting 6

Brillat-Savarin, Anthelme
(1755–1826)
Cookery 6

Brindley, Brian
Letters 2

Brinkley, David
Universe 3

Britchky, Seymour
Food 10, 11

Britten, Philip (1957–)
Cookery 7

Broder, David (1929–)
Power 2

Brooke, N.
Travel 2

Brooke, Rupert (1887–1915)
History 3
Places 3

Brookner, Anita (1938–)
Literature 8

Brooks, Mel (1926–)
Comedy 20
Success 3

Brooks, Mel (1926–) see
Bergman, Andrew and
Brooks, Mel

Brougham, Lord (1778–1868)
Royalty 15

Broun, Heywood (1888–1939)
Censorship 4
Future 3
Love 6
Political Parties 2

Brown, Craig (1957–)
Food 12
Humour 6
Hypocrisy 1
Publishing 4
Reading 2

Brown, John (1810–82)
Dictionaries 2

Brown, John Mason
(1900–69)
Actors 4

Brown, Michael
Murder 2

Brown, Thomas (1663–1704)
Friends 4

Browne, Cecil (1932–)
God 13

Browne, Coral (1913–91)
Actors 5, 6
Critics 9

Browne, Noel (1915–97)
Parents 1

Browning, Robert (1812–89)
Bible 1
Gardens 5
Satisfaction 5

Bruce, Lenny (1925–66)
Drugs 2
Family 6
People 10

Bruno, Frank
Boxing 3

Bryant, Anita (1940–)
Sex 20

Bryson, Bill (1951–)
Animals 9
Appearance 5
Baseball 4
Business 2
Children 5
Countries 5
Education 10
Fame 7
Fashion 5
Food 13
Human Race 1
Humour 7
Places 4
Poverty 5
Science 7
Sickness 7
Society 7
Success 4
Television 3
Transport 5
Travel 3
Weather 4

Buchan, John (1875–1940)
Humour 8
Religion 12
Titles 1

Buchwald, Art (1925–)
Advertising 3
Politics 16
Presidents 2

Buerk, Michael (1946–)
Smoking 2

Buller, Arthur (1874–1944)
Science 8

Bulmer-Thomas, Ivor
(1905–93)
Prime Ministers 7

Buñuel, Luis (1900–83)
Religion 11

Burchill, Julie (1960–)
Indexes 2
Insults 8
Men and Women 4
Parties 1

Burgess, Anthony (1917–93)
Politics 17
Reading 3
Sex 21, 22
Technology 3

Burgess, Gelett (1866–1951)
Quotations 2

Burke, Edmund (1729–97)
Prime Ministers 8

Burke, Johnny (1908–64)
Dictionaries 3

Burney, Fanny (1752–1840)
Literature 9

Burns, George (1896–1996)
Comedy 12

Burns, John (1858–1943)
Trust 2

Burt, Benjamin Hapgood
(1880–1950)
Alcohol 12

Busby, Matt (1909–94)
Football 4

Bush, George (1924–)
Bores 4
Food 14
Secrecy 3

Butler, R. A. (1902–82)
People 11
Politics 18

Butler, Samuel (1835–1902)
Birds 3
Bores 5
Children 6
Food 15
God 14
Marriage 23
Progress 3
Publishing 5
Science 9, 10
Truth 1
Women 5, 6

Carroll, Lewis *(cont.)*:
Poetry 5
Progress 4
Royalty 16
Travel 4
Universe 5
Wit 4, 5
Words 4, 5
Carter, Jimmy (1924–)
Argument 3
Cartland, Barbara
(1901–2000)
Colours 1
Countries 7
Health 2
Middle Age 5
Casey, Warren see Jacobs, Jim
and Casey, Warren
Cash, Pat (1965–)
Tennis 4
Casson, Anne
Actors 11
Castlerosse, Lord (1891–1943)
Golf 2
Work 6
Castleveter, David
Transport 7
Catherine the Great
(1729–96)
Royalty 17
Causley, Charles (1917–)
Children 10
Cecil, Lord Hugh (1869–1956)
Old Age 10
Religion 15, 16
Chancellor, Alexander
(1940–)
Wealth 8
Chandler, Raymond
(1888–1959)
Bible 3
Language 4
Literature 14
Towns 9
Women 7, 8
Chanel, Coco (1883–1971)
Fashion 6
Channon, Chips (1897–1958)
Aristocracy 2
Autobiography 5
Conversation 6
Countries 8, 9
Diaries 3

Diplomacy 4
Libraries 4
Royalty 18
Self-Knowledge 6
Towns 10
Truth 3
Wealth 9
Writers 4
Chapman, Graham (1941–89),
John Cleese (1939–), et al.
Comedy 29
Charles II (1630–85)
Royalty 19, 20, 21
Charles, Prince of Wales
(1948–)
Architecture 6
Conversation 7
Publishing 9
Chaucer, Geoffrey
(c.1343–1400)
Marriage 32
Poetry 6
Women 9
Chekhov, Anton (1860–1904)
Happiness 5
Women 10, 11
Cher (1946–)
Body 8
Chesterfield, Lord
(1694–1773)
Books 5
Chesterton, G. K. (1874–1936)
Alcohol 13
Argument 4
Art 5
Crime 5
Food 19
Government 3, 4
History 4
Hypocrisy 3
Journalism 8
Telegrams 6
Transport 8
Travel 5
Women 12
Chiles, Lawton (1930–)
Journalism 9
Choate, Rufus (1799–1859)
Judges 4
Christie, Agatha (1890–1976)
Marriage 33
Churchill, Charles (1731–64)
Humour 10

Churchill, Lord Randolph
(1849–94)
Economics 3
Prime Ministers 10
Churchill, Randolph (1911–68)
Friends 6
God 16
Churchill, Winston
(1874–1965)
Alcohol 14
Animals 11
Armed Forces 3
Colours 2
Description 8
Examinations 1
Fashion 7
Food 20
Insults 10, 11, 12
Language 5
Names 6
Old Age 11, 12
Politicians 12, 13
Politics 20, 21
Pride 2
Prime Ministers 11, 12
Trust 3
Truth 4
War 7
Work 7
Cioran, E.M. (1911–)
Work 8
Clark, Alan (1928–99)
Civil Servants 4
Epitaphs 8
Government 5
Morality 4
Newspapers 9
People 14
Politics 22, 23, 24
Success 5
Truth 5
Wealth 10
Women 13
Clark, Jane
Class 5
Clarke, Arthur C. (1917–)
Certainty 7
Science 12
Clarke, Kenneth (1940–)
Medicine 7
People 15
Clarkson, Jeremy (1960–)
Countries 10

Cornford, Francis M. (*cont.*):
Lies 5
Costello, Lou (1906–59) see
Abbott, Bud and Costello,
Lou
Courteline, Georges
(1858–1929)
Youth 1
Coward, Noël (1899–1973)
Acting 8, 9, 10
Actors 12, 13
America 10
Appearance 8
Architecture 7
Aristocracy 3
Armed Forces 5, 6
Behaviour 9, 10
Body 10
Broadcasting 1
Children 11
Class 8
Clergy 5
Countries 14, 15, 16
Crime 7, 8
Dance 5
Death 15, 16, 17
Description 11
Diaries 4
England 8
Fame 9, 10
Family 8
Film Stars 4
Food 21
God 18
Holidays 5
Home 9, 10
Hope 3
Letters 5, 6
Love 9
Marriage 44, 45, 46
Men 5
Men and Women 6
Mistakes 10
Murder 3
Music 10
Old Age 14, 15
Parties 2
Past 5, 6
Philosophy 2
Places 7
Quotations 4
Royalty 22, 23
Science 13
Sex 27
Sickness 8

Society 8, 9
Songs 11
Speeches 3
Success 8
Telegrams 7, 8, 9, 10, 11
Television 5
Theatre 12, 13, 14
Travel 6, 7
Universe 6
War 9, 10
Weather 7
Work 9
Writers 5, 6
Youth 2
Coward, Violet
Songs 10
Cowper, William (1731–1800)
Armed Forces 7
Clergy 6, 7
Country 1, 2
Crime 9
Family 9
Foolishness 6
Home 11
Journalism 11
Sickness 9
Smoking 3
Wit 7
Women 14
Crabbe, George (1754–1832)
Poverty 6
Secrecy 6
Craigie, W. A. (1867–1967)
Dictionaries 6
Crèvecoeur, St John de
(1735–1813)
Food 22
Crisp, Quentin (1908–99)
Appearance 9
Autobiography 8
Character 4
Home 12
Human Race 3
Life 8, 9
Old Age 16
Places 8
Sex 28, 29
Success 9
Women 15
Work 10, 11
Writers 7
Critchley, Julian (1930–2000)
People 17
Politics 26
Power 3

Crompton, Richmal
(1890–1969)
Children 12
Crooks, Garth (1958–)
Football 5
Cross, Amanda (1926–)
Virtue 6
Cross, Eric (1905–80)
Critics 11
cummings, e. e. (1894–1962)
Epitaphs 27
Politicians 14
Universe 7
Cunard, Emerald (1872–1948)
War 11
Curran, John Philpot
(1750–1817)
Description 12
Curry, John (1949–94)
Fashion 8
Curtis, Richard (1956–)
Appearance 10
Marriage 47, 48
Trust 4
Curtis, Richard (1956–) and
Elton, Ben (1959–)
Comedy 22
Progress 5
Curtis, Tony (1925–)
Film Stars 5
Curtiz, Michael (1888–1962)
Cinema 5
Curzon, Lord (1859–1925)
Class 9, 10
Colours 3
Death 18

Dalai Lama (1935–)
Trust 5
Dalton, Hugh (1887–1962)
People 18
Daninos, Pierre
Behaviour 11
England 9
Darling, Lord (1849–1936)
Crime 10
Darlington, W. A.
(1890–1979)
Actors 14
Darrow, Clarence (1857–1938)
America 11
Certainty 9
God 19
Davidson, Ian (1950–)
Political Parties 3

Disraeli, Benjamin (*cont.*):
Religion 17, 18, 19
Royalty 24, 25
Truth 6
Writers 10
Disraeli, Mary Anne (d. 1872)
Body 14
Dobbs, Michael (1948–)
Comedy 43
Politics 31
Docherty, Tommy (1928–)
Football 6
Dodd, Ken (1931–)
Humour 13
Donleavy, J. P. (1926–)
Death 21
Human Race 4
Money 8
Donne, John (1572–1631)
Family 14
Dorsey, Tommy (1905–56)
Music 14
Douglas, Norman (1868–1952)
Class 11
Friends 7
Government 8
Progress 6
Telegrams 12
Douglas, O. (1877–1948)
Letters 8
Quotations 5
Reading 7
Douglas, Stephen A. (1813–61)
Presidents 5
Douglas, William O.
(1898–1980)
Censorship 6
Government 9
Douglas-Home, Caroline
(1937–)
Class 12
Doyle, Arthur Conan
(1859–1930)
Crime 12, 13
Mind 4
Drake, Ervin
Towns 12
Driberg, Tom (1905–76)
Country 3
Sex 30
Drummond, John (1934–)
Bureaucracy 6
Dryden, John (1631–1700)
England 11
Marriage 53

Poetry 9
Dunne, Finley Peter
(1867–1936)
Alcohol 23
Libraries 5
Towns 13
Dunsany, Lord (1878–1957)
Aristocracy 4
Durante, Jimmy (1893–1980)
Music 15
Durham, Lord (1792–1840)
Wealth 12
Dury, Ian (1942–2000)
Titles 2
Dworkin, Andrea (1946–)
Sex 31
Travel 8
Dylan, Bob (1941–)
Songs 12
Success 11

Eban, Abba (1915–)
History 5
Ebb, Fred
Life 12
Edelman, Maurice (1911–75)
Censorship 7
Eden, Anthony (1897–1977)
Self-Knowledge 7
Edgar, Marriott (1880–1951)
Places 10
Edgeworth, Maria
(1767–1849)
Prejudice 2
Edison, Thomas Alva
(1847–1931)
Intelligence 5
Edward IV (1442–83)
Royalty 26
Edward VII (1841–1910)
Fashion 11, 12
Royalty 27, 28
Self-Knowledge 8
Edward VIII (1894–1972)
America 12
Edwards, Oliver (1711–91)
Philosophy 3
Edwards, Sherman
America 13
Ehrenreich, Barbara (1941–)
Health 4
Women 18
Ehrlich, Paul Ralph (1932–)
Technology 4

Einstein, Albert (1879–1955)
Future 5
Life 13
Science 14
Ejogo, Carmen
Names 7
Eliot, George (1819–80)
Humour 14
Women 19
Eliot, T. S. (1888–1965)
Poetry 10
Poets 3
Women 20
Elizabeth I (1533–1603)
Body 15
Clergy 8
Elizabeth II (1926–)
Football 7
Praise 4
Progress 7
Royalty 30
**Elizabeth, Queen, the Queen
Mother** (1900–)
Alcohol 24
Animals 12
Countries 22
Poets 4
Royalty 29
Ellington, Duke (1899–1974)
Music 16
Ellis, Alice Thomas (1932–)
Behaviour 12
Character 6
God 20
Virtue 7
Ellson, Andy
Success 12
Elton, Ben (1959–)
Fashion 13
Political Parties 6
Elton, Ben (1959–) see Curtis,
Richard and Elton, Ben
Elyot, Thomas (1499–1546)
Football 8
Emerson, Ralph Waldo
(1803–82)
Children 15
Music 17
Progress 8
Quotations 6
Virtue 8
Empson, William (1906–84)
Dictionaries 7
Enfield, Harry (1961–)
Comedy 24

Certainty 12
Critics 16
Sex 37
Hand, Learned (1872–1961)
  Words 12
  Writing 6
Hannah, Sophie (1971–)
  Secrecy 9
Haran, Maeve (1932–)
  Technology 8
Harburg, E. Y. (1898–1981)
  America 17
  Animals 16
  Body 20
  Class 20
  Debt 4
  Economics 7
  Family 19
  Food 33
  Foolishness 10, 11
  Future 6
  God 23
  Government 14
  Intelligence 6
  Love 22, 23
  Men and Women 14
  Nature 3, 4
  Old Age 22, 23
  Politics 36
  Poverty 9
  Progress 11, 12
  Religion 27, 28
  Sex 38
  Transport 16
  Universe 10, 11
  Women 34
  Words 13
  Writing 7
Harding, Gilbert (1907–60)
  America 18
Hare, David (1947–)
  Anger 5
  Television 10
Hare, Maurice Evan
(1886–1967)
  Transport 17
Hare, Robertson (1891–1979)
  Comedy 31
Hargreaves, W. F. (1846–1919)
  Acting 14
  Society 13
Harman, Lord Justice
(1894–1970)
  Business 5

Harnick, Sheldon (1924–)
  Politics 37
  Religion 29
  Towns 17
Harriman, Margaret Case
  Money 15
Harris, Joel Chandler
(1848–1908)
  Alcohol 33
  Animals 17, 18
  Old Age 24
Harris, Thomas (1940–) and
Tally, Ted (1952–)
  Food 34
  Society 14
Harrison, George (1943–)
  Cinema 24
  People 20
Hart, Lorenz (1895–1943)
  Behaviour 16
  Class 21
  Country 7
  Description 16
  Hotels 3
  Insults 18
  Intelligence 7
  Love 24, 25
  Marriage 69
  Men and Women 15, 16
  Towns 18
Hart, Moss (1904–61)
  Cinema 25
Hart-Davis, Rupert (1907–99)
  Bores 7
  Family 20
  Handwriting 2
  Theatre 23
Harte, Bret (1836–1902)
  Satisfaction 7
Hattersley, Roy (1932–)
  Dogs 1
  Secrecy 10
Hawking, Stephen (1942–)
  Science 16
Hawthorne, Nathaniel
(1804–64)
  Death 28
Hay, Ian (1876–1952)
  Handwriting 3
  Humour 20
Hayes, Katy
  Parents 2
Hazlitt, William (1778–1830)
  Country 8
  Letters 9

Prejudice 7
Wit 12
Headlam, Cuthbert Morley
(1876–1964)
  Publishing 13
Healey, Denis (1917–)
  Insults 19
Heath, Edward (1916–)
  Friends 8
  Marriage 70
  Political Parties 10
  Prime Ministers 17
Hecht, Ben (1894–1964)
  Wit 13
  Women 35
Hedren, Tippi (1935–)
  Body 21
Heine, Heinrich (1797–1856)
  God 24
Heller, Joseph (1923–99)
  Armed Forces 13
  Character 7
  Clergy 13
  Critics 17
  Humour 21
  Insults 20
  Literature 21
  Medicine 16
  Mind 5
  Names 9, 10
  Places 13
  War 14, 15
Hellman, Lillian (1905–84)
  Politics 38
Helpmann, Robert (1909–86)
  Dance 10
Henahan, Donal
  Autobiography 11
Hendrix, Jimi (1942–70)
  Death 57
Henley, Arthur W. D.
  Middle Age 6
Henry, O. (1862–1910)
  Crime 20
Herbert, A. P. (1890–1971)
  Argument 10
  Aristocracy 11
  Art 12
  Betting 8
  Censorship 9
  Country 9
  Education 19
  Golf 6
  Government 15, 16

Hughes Jr., Howard (1905–76)
Film Stars 8
Hull, Josephine (1886–1957)
Acting 15
Humphries, Barry (1934–)
Alcohol 34
Armed Forces 16
Art 14
Bores 8
Comedy 16
Countries 31
Education 20
Fashion 17
Food 35
Gardens 7
Prejudice 9
Reading 9
Religion 30
Society 15
Theatre 24
Towns 19
Hunt, Leigh (1784–1859)
Conversation 12
Music 25
Hurley, Jack
Boxing 7
Death 32
Huxley, Aldous (1894–1963)
Advertising 6
Argument 11
Bureaucracy 9
Countries 32
Men and Women 18
Power 4
Sex 40
Hyland, Richard (1949–)
Law 15

Ibsen, Henrik (1828–1906)
Fashion 18
Ice Cube (1970–)
Parents 5
Ice-T (1958–)
Prejudice 10
Ickes, Harold (1874–1952)
Politicians 21
Idi Amin (1925–)
Marriage 4
Iles, Francis (1893–1970)
Murder 6
Inge, Charles (1868–1957)
Future 7
Inge, Dean (1860–1954)
Religion 31

Ingham, Bernard (1932–)
Government 18
Ingrams, Richard (1937–)
Appearance 14
Ingrams, Richard (1937–)
and **Wells, John** (1936–)
Gardens 8
Ionesco, Eugène (1912–94)
Civil Servants 5
Future 8
Isaacson, Walter
Reading 10
Issigonis, Alec (1906–88)
Bureaucracy 10
Ivins, Molly (1944–)
Generation Gap 5

Jackson, Donald L.
Acting 16
Jackson, Robert H.
(1892–1954)
Books 7
Judges 11, 12
Money 17
Jacobs, Jim and **Casey, Warren**
Education 21
Jacobs, Joe (1896–1940)
Baseball 7
Boxing 8
Jacobson, Howard
Towns 20
Jagger, Mick (1943–) and
Richard, Keith (1943–)
Sex 41
James I (1566–1625)
Poets 8
Smoking 4
James, Clive (1939–)
Anger 6
Broadcasting 4
Business 6
Clergy 14
Description 17
England 17
Food 36
Language 12
Places 15
Self-Knowledge 14
Television 12
Tennis 6
Writers 17
Writing 11
James, Henry (1843–1916)
Actors 24

America 19
Biography 7
Foolishness 13
Literature 22
Praise 5
James, P. D. (1920–)
Architecture 9
James, William (1842–1910)
Marriage 76
Jarrell, Randall (1914–65)
America 20
Ideas 5
Jay, Antony (1930–) see Lynn,
Jonathan and Jay, Antony
Jefferson, Thomas (1743–1826)
Censorship 10
Government 19
Politics 39
Jellinek, Roger (1938–)
Autobiography 12
Jenkins, Roy (1920–)
People 22
Jerome, Jerome K.
(1859–1927)
Alcohol 35
Death 33
Home 16
Humour 22
Truth 7
Work 17
Jerrold, Douglas (1803–57)
Countries 33, 34
Love 26
Sports 14
Wit 14
John, Augustus (1878–1961)
Parents 6, 7
John, Elton (1947–)
Musicians 10
Johnson, Brian
Names 11
Johnson, Lyndon Baines
(1908–73)
Insults 23
Power 5, 6
Speeches 6, 7
Johnson, Nunnally
(1897–1977)
Film Stars 9
Johnson, Philander Chase
(1866–1939)
Future 9
Johnson, Samuel (1709–84)
Alcohol 36
Armed Forces 17

McWilliam, Candia (1955-)
Children 25
Madan, Falconer (1851–1935)
Libraries 9
Madonna (1958-)
People 25
Mahaffy, John Pentland
(1839–1919)
Autobiography 16
Religion 39
Sickness 16
Speeches 9
Truth 8
Maher, Mary
Conversation 18
Mahler, Gustav (1860–1911)
Music 34
Mahy, Margaret (1937-)
Countries 41
Mailer, Norman (1923-)
Politics 51
Major, John (1943-)
Foolishness 19
Malahide, Patrick (1945-)
Actors 26
Mamet, David (1947-)
Cinema 30
Words 19
Mancroft, Lord (1914-)
Cricket 11
Mandale, W. R.
Poverty 13
Mankiewicz, Herman J.
(1897–1953)
Films 8
Food 46
Insults 29
Mankiewicz, Joseph L.
(1909-)
Films 9
Mann, Herbie (1930-)
Music 35
Mansfield, Katherine
(1888–1923)
Writers 25
Margaret, Princess (1930-)
Royalty 48
Margolyes, Miriam (1941-)
Life 17
Marks, Johnny (1909–85)
Animals 26
Marlowe, Christopher
(1564–93)
Sex 47

Marquis, Don (1878–1937)
Alcohol 41
Hope 5, 6
Mistakes 22
Newspapers 20
Poetry 17
Politicians 23
Virtue 12
Writing 14
Marriott, Anthony (1931-)
and **Foot, Alistair**
Comedy 30
Marryat, Frederick
(1792–1848)
Children 24
Marshall, Andrew see
Renwick, David and Marshall,
Andrew
Marshall, Arthur (1910–89)
Autobiography 17
Death 41
Dictionaries 10
Family 27
God 31
Life 18
Past 11
Martin, Dean (1917-)
Alcohol 42
Martin, Dick (1923-) see
Rowan, Dan and Martin, Dick
Martin, Hugh and **Blane,**
Ralph
Sports 19
Martin, Judith (1938-)
Argument 14
Behaviour 23
Hypocrisy 6
Love 32
Parents 11
Truth 9
Virtue 13
Women 43
Marx, Chico (1891–1961)
Virtue 14
Marx, Groucho (1895–1977)
Clergy 21
Death 42
Food 47
Humour 25
Insults 30
Literature 25
Medicine 22

Men and Women 28
Names 17
People 26
Poetry 18
Prejudice 11
Sex 48, 49
Society 17
Theatre 34
Mary, Queen (1867–1953)
Country 11
Royalty 49
Snobbery 13
Mason, Jackie (1931-)
England 21
Food 48
Sex 50
Mathews, Arthur see
Linehan, Graham and
Mathews, Arthur
Matthau, Carol
Marriage 84
Mature, Victor (1915-)
Actors 27
Maugham, Viscount (d. 1958)
Writers 29
Maugham, W. Somerset
(1874–1965)
Acting 17
Advertising 9
Books 13
Censorship 17
Certainty 17
Class 23
Conversation 19, 20
Crime 24
Fame 13
Family 28
Food 49, 50
God 32
Happiness 7, 8
Human Race 7
Language 13
Law 21
Literature 26
Love 33
Men 11
People 27
Philosophy 4
Politicians 24
Prejudice 12
Religion 40
Speeches 10

Plautus (c.250–184 BC)
Poverty 16
Plomer, William (1903–73)
Art 21
Conversation 22
Description 28
Sex 64
Pollitt, Harry (1890–1960)
Poets 11
Pope, Alexander (1688–1744)
Children 28
Cookery 16
Critics 27
Death 54, 55, 56
England 25
Hope 8
Insults 35, 36, 37
Marriage 100
Old Age 32
Poetry 21
Poets 12, 13
Royalty 57, 58, 59
Theatre 40
Wit 27
Words 24
Writers 35
Porter, Cole (1891–1964)
Alcohol 51
Art 22
Behaviour 26, 27
Birds 7
Countries 46, 47
Country 16
Dance 15
Food 61, 62
Golf 9
Hope 9
Love 37, 38
Marriage 101, 102, 103
Medicine 28
Men and Women 36, 37, 38, 39
Middle Age 10
Morality 8
Praise 7
Religion 54
Satisfaction 10
Sex 65, 66
Songs 19
Sports 27
Theatre 41, 42, 43
Towns 27
Wealth 24, 25
Women 58, 59

Porter, Peter (1929–)
Countries 48
Potter, Beatrix (1866–1943)
Animals 38
Food 63
Potter, Gillie (1887–1975)
England 26
Potter, Stephen (1900–69)
Alcohol 52
Conversation 23
Critics 28
Education 35
Pound, Ezra (1885–1972)
Weather 21
Powell, Anthony (1905–2000)
Character 9
Children 29
Food 64
Old Age 33
Powell, Enoch (1912–98)
Diaries 6
Pratchett, Terry (1948–)
Libraries 11
Taxes 7
Prescott, John (1938–)
Class 25
Political Parties 16
Transport 30
Preston, Keith (1884–1927)
Poetry 22
Price, Anthony (1928–)
Heaven 4
Priestland, Gerald (1927–91)
Fame 15
Priestley, J. B. (1894–1984)
Biography 9
Conversation 24
England 27
Football 17
God 39
Journalism 17
Prior, Matthew (1664–1721)
Medicine 29
Sex 67
Pritchett, V. S. (1900–97)
Fashion 30
Transport 31
Proust, Marcel (1871–1922)
Behaviour 28
Weather 22
Pugin, Augustus Welby (1812–52)
Religion 55
Punch (1841–1992)
Animals 39

Children 30
Economics 12
Food 65, 66, 67
Insults 38
Literature 31
Marriage 104, 105, 106
Philosophy 7
Praise 8
Transport 32, 33
Puttnam, Roger
Business 11
Puzo, Mario (1920–99)
Power 8
Pym, Barbara (1913–80)
Love 39

Quayle, Dan (1947–)
Foolishness 23
Universe 15
Queenan, Joe
Success 27
Quennell, Peter (1905–)
People 34

Race, Steve (1921–)
Transport 34
Raleigh, Walter (1861–1922)
Examinations 4
Human Race 9
Quotations 19
Randolph, David (1914–)
Music 39
Raphael, Frederic (1931–)
Sex 68
Towns 28
Ratner, Gerald (1949–)
Business 12
Rattigan, Terence (1911–77)
Languages 19
Society 18
Ravel, Maurice (1875–1937)
Musicians 13
Ray, John (1627–1705)
Food 68
Ray, Ted (1906–77)
Comedy 8, 17
Reading, Peter (1946–)
Art 23
Reagan, Ronald (1911–)
Character 10
Politics 62
Work 25
Redwood, John (1951–)
Politicians 27

Sterne, Laurence (*cont.*):
Women 68
Stevas, Norman St John
(1929–)
Judges 17
Stevenson, Adlai (1900–65)
America 26
Law 35
Nature 9
Newspapers 31
Political Parties 18
Politics 71, 72
Praise 11
Presidents 14, 15
Speeches 15, 16
Words 28
Stevenson, Robert Louis
(1850–94)
Insults 47
Marriage 120
Pride 10
Sleep 10
Steyn, Mark
Description 30
Politicians 32
Sting (1951–)
Fame 18
Stocks, Baroness (1891–1975)
Old Age 38
Stockwood, Mervyn
(1913–95)
Food 81
Medicine 34
Stokowski, Leopold
(1882–1977)
Musicians 17
Stoller, Mike (1933–) see
Leiber, Jerry and Stoller, Mike
Stone, Oliver (1946–) see
Weiser, Stanley and Stone,
Oliver
Stoppard, Tom (1937–)
Actors 34
Alcohol 61
Architecture 16
Argument 22
Art 26
Autobiography 23
Baseball 12
Biography 11
Broadcasting 7
Bureaucracy 15
Character 15
Children 34
Conversation 27

Countries 58
Country 19
Death 65
Democracy 15
Football 24
Friends 20
Future 14
God 41
Government 39, 40
Human Race 11
Intelligence 15
Journalism 19, 20
Language 15, 16
Life 22
Literature 35
Middle Age 13
Money 22
Newspapers 32
Philosophy 8
Poets 16
Power 11
Progress 15
Quotations 21
Religion 69
Secrecy 12
Self-Knowledge 22
Sex 76, 77
Society 23
Technology 15
Theatre 53, 54
Time 13
Towns 29
Transport 38
War 27
Wit 43
Women 69, 70
Stowe, Harriet Beecher
(1811–96)
Children 35
Family 40
Stowell, Lord (1745–1836)
Money 23
Strachan, Gordon
Football 25
Strachey, Lytton (1880–1932)
Biography 12
Last Words 8
People 41
Sex 78
Stravinsky, Igor (1882–1971)
Music 53
Straw, Jack (1946–)
Drugs 8
Streisand, Barbra (1942–)
Presidents 16

Strong, Roy (1935–)
Art 27
Suckling, John (1609–42)
Love 43, 44
Surtees, R. S. (1805–64)
Alcohol 62
Appearance 26
Behaviour 30
Class 31
Family 41
Food 82
Foolishness 28
Happiness 15
Poverty 22
Sports 31, 32
Women 71
Swaffer, Hannen (1879–1962)
Newspapers 33
Swann, Donald (1923–94) see
Flanders, Michael and
Swann, Donald
Swift, Jonathan (1667–1745)
Conversation 28
Critics 35
Epitaphs 21, 22
Fashion 35
Foolishness 29
Home 24
Science 30
Self-Knowledge 23
Technology 16
Virtue 20
**Swinburne, Algernon
Charles** (1837–1909)
Epitaphs 23
Sykes, Eric and **Bygraves,
Max** (1922–)
Comedy 10, 25
Szasz, Thomas (1920–)
Sex 79

Tacitus (AD 56–after 117)
Power 12
**Talleyrand, Charles-Maurice
de** (1754–1838)
Life 23
Old Age 39
Self-Knowledge 24
Trust 14
Tally, Ted (1952–) see Harris,
Thomas and Tally, Ted
Tarkington, Booth
(1869–1946)
Alcohol 63

Keyword Index

admiral not a doorman but a rear a.   TRANSPORT 4

admirals A. extolled for standing   ARMED FORCES 7

admire cannot possibly a. them   POVERTY 24

admired more a. she was   POLITICIANS 10

admirer enthusiastic a. of mine   LITERATURE 24

admit a. to being an MP   TRUTH 12

    Whenever you're wrong, a. it   MARRIAGE 91

adorable a. pancreas   APPEARANCE 16

    nauseatingly a.   PEOPLE 37

adore a. those sort of people   BEHAVIOUR 31

    need to a. me   FAME 16

adored I was a. once too   LOVE 40

adornment from the a. of his person   INSULTS 48

ads watched the a.   EPITAPHS 18

adult A. virtue includes being   VIRTUE 13

    with the a. world   CHILDREN 37

adulterers I see some a. down there   SEX 36

adulterous would be a.   ARCHITECTURE 2

adultery a. out of the moral arena   SOCIETY 23

    common as a.   AUTOBIOGRAPHY 10

    Do not a. commit   SEX 26

    gallantry, and gods a.   SEX 23

    henceforward to the strictest a.   MORALITY 3

    it's still a.   SEX 83

adults how I regarded a.   GENERATION GAP 6

    only between consenting a.   SEX 85

advanced a. state of nudity   BODY 27

advancement useful for political a.   POLITICS 42

advantage A. rarely comes of it   SEX 26

    take a mean a.   BEHAVIOUR 39

    undertaking of Great A.   SECRECY 1

adversary mine a. had written   BOOKS 4

advertise eat what I a.   ALCOHOL 19

    only a. a book   PUBLISHING 18

advertisement one effective a.   ADVERTISING 6

    same as that of a.   ADVERTISING 9

advertisements column of a. by heart   QUOTATIONS 9

    real estate a.   AUTOBIOGRAPHY 11

advertisers a. don't object to   NEWSPAPERS 33

advertising A. is the most   ADVERTISING 4

    A. is the rattling   ADVERTISING 13

    A. may be described   ADVERTISING 8

    calls it a.   ADVERTISING 7

advise STREETS FLOODED. PLEASE A.   TELEGRAMS 3

advises It's my old girl that a.   MARRIAGE 49

advocate art of the a.   ARGUMENT 16

aesthete perfect a.   ART 20

aesthetic letting one's a. sense override   MORALITY 10

affair a. between Margot Asquith   INSULTS 34

    a. with Ophelia   THEATRE 3

    keep a measly a. secret   SECRECY 8

afford Can't a. them, Governor   MORALITY 13

afraid a. to die   DEATH 1

Africa more familiar with A.   WOMEN 53

    way A. was divided   SCIENCE 18

African A. Primates Meeting   NAMES 25

Afro A.-Asian studies   COUNTRIES 28

after A. you, Claude   COMEDY 1

afternoon make love in the a.   COUNTRIES 7

against always vote a.   DEMOCRACY 6

    life is 6 to 5 a.   BETTING 13

    most people vote a.   DEMOCRACY 1

agapanthus Beware of the a.   COUNTRY 12

age A. before Beauty   INSULTS 33

    a. is not estimable   CHARACTER 3

    can tell a woman's a.   WOMEN 27

    every a. assiduously seeks   VIRTUE 28

    faked my age   TRUTH 3

    in an a. group   MONEY 19

    lie about his a.   HUMOUR 21

    Mozart was my a.   SUCCESS 19

    reached the a. to write   AUTOBIOGRAPHY 24

    slam the door in the face of a.   OLD AGE 14

    talk turns to a.   MIDDLE AGE 4

    Thirty-five is a very attractive a.   MIDDLE AGE 15

    What a. are you going to put   TRAVEL 19

    when the a. is in   OLD AGE 36

    when you've the a.   ACTING 19

    woman who tells her real a.   WOMEN 80

    Work does a. you so   WORK 10

aged I saw an a., aged man   OLD AGE 9

agenda a. will be in inverse proportion   TIME 12

    breakfast-time a.   CONVERSATION 2

agent a. to a publisher   PUBLISHING 16

    much of a secret a.   SECRECY 2

agents and west by a.   CINEMA 7

ages He's a writer for the a.   WRITERS 34

agglomerated your a. lucubrations   PRAISE 5

aghast I'm a.   WIT 45

AGM address the A.   BUSINESS 16

agnostic I have been an a.   GOD 11

    You are not an a.   RELIGION 48

agnosticism that a. means   CERTAINTY 9

agnostics fans and a.   BASEBALL 4

agony a. is abated   BEHAVIOUR 22

    it was a., Ivy   COMEDY 8

agreeable idea of an a. person   ARGUMENT 5

agreement public a. among doctors   MEDICINE 31

    Too much a.   CONVERSATION 8

agrees person who a. with me   ARGUMENT 5

ahead a. in this world   LAW 3

ain't a. a fit night out for man   WEATHER 8

air apple-scented a. freshener   DESCRIPTION 25

    fall for a. hostesses   WEALTH 8

airplanes feel about a.   FOOD 39

airport observing a. layouts HEAVEN 4
airs give himself a. MUSICIANS 2
Albanian A. . . . a language that sounded
LANGUAGES 4
Albert A. must have married ACTING 10
take a message to A. LAST WORDS 2
Went there with young A. PLACES 10
albino a. curate FRIENDS 23
alcohol A. . . . enables Parliament ALCOHOL 55
a. was a food ALCOHOL 69
Mere a. doesn't thrill me at all LOVE 38
pleasant effects of a. ALCOHOL 34
taken more out of a. ALCOHOL 14
ale no more cakes and a. MORALITY 11
Alec Dull A. versus CHOICE 5
Alf didn't creat A. Garnett TELEVISION 15
algebra no such thing as a. EDUCATION 26
Alice may call me A. INSULTS 28
Pass the sick bag, A. COMEDY 33
alien I'll be damned if I'm an a. ROYALTY 37
alike do everything a. FAMILY 13
alive Botticelli were a. today ART 29
if I am a. DEATH 29
lucky if he gets out of it a. LIFE 10
no longer a. DEATH 12
not dead but a. GOD 4
Not while I'm a. he ain't POLITICIANS 9
To keep my love a. MARRIAGE 69
all a. go together COUNTRIES 37
A. my shows are great SELF-KNOWLEDGE 10
allegory headstrong as an a. WIT 35
allergies provide the a. GOD 23
all-round a.-round man ART 4
almighty ear of the A. GOD 30
Even the A. took seven POLITICS 20
relieves the A. ENGLAND 2
thinks he's God A. RELIGION 22
alone A. with probably the most SEX 73
sleeps a. at last EPITAPHS 6
that he is a. ENGLAND 16
alphabet if I had known the a. WORDS 20
altar high a. on the move DESCRIPTION 6
alternative a. were immortality DEATH 65
always Not A. SONGS 3
amateur a. is a man who can't WORK 2
amateurs Hell is full of musical a. MUSIC 48
supporting a. BUREAUCRACY 6
that afflicts a. ART 5
amazed You are a. WIT 47
ambassador a. is an honest man DIPLOMACY 18
Russian a. DIPLOMACY 4
ambassadors A. cropped up GOVERNMENT 10
amber a. foam FOOD 28
ambiguity is its a. HUMOUR 17
ambition a. of an unusual kind SUCCESS 31

ambitions their loyalties and a. MONEY 17
ambitious less a. project GOD 4
ambivalence definition of a. WORDS 19
amendment Fourteenth A. GOVERNMENT 9
America A. is a model AMERICA 5
A. is a vast conspiracy AMERICA 27
A. was thus HISTORY 9
arts in A. ART 3
come back to A. AMERICA 19
do a sitcom in A. TELEVISION 18
England and A. COUNTRIES 55
I like A. AMERICA 10
like to be in A. AMERICA 24
most about A. AMERICA 12
what makes A. AMERICA 25
youth of A. AMERICA 30
American A. *diplomacy* DIPLOMACY 6
A. girls turn AMERICA 16
A. joke HUMOUR 40
A. names as Cathcart NAMES 10
A. president GOVERNMENT 43
bad news to the A. people PRESIDENTS 8
Every A. woman AMERICA 1
living the A. dream GENERATION GAP 8
nod from an A. AMERICA 6
pay for my A. Express ADVERTISING 14
play A. music COUNTRIES 12
Americans All A. FILM STARS 14
always liked A. AMERICA 8
A. have a perfect right AMERICA 3
bad A. are slobs COUNTRIES 52
bad A. die AMERICA 29
Canadians are A. COUNTRIES 41
is concerned, the A. AMERICA 4
Never criticize A. AMERICA 21
To A., English manners AMERICA 20
amoebae a. getting married MARRIAGE 83
amor A. vincit insomnia SLEEP 3
amount awful lot to a. to much SCIENCE 1
amused a. by its presumption ALCOHOL 65
One is not a. at that FOOTBALL 7
Anantanarayanan Ah, A. POETRY 23
anarchism A. is a game POLITICS 67
anatomist bad a. LAST WORDS 9
anatomy before he has studied a. MARRIAGE 11
learned all my a. EDUCATION 12
portions of the human a. DANCE 10
ancestor I am an a. ARISTOCRACY 13
ancestors pricey a. GENERATION GAP 7
ancestry trace my a. back ARISTOCRACY 6
angel a. to pass, flying slowly TIME 7
a. travelling incognito PEOPLE 34
Is man an ape or an a. RELIGION 17
to the recording a. MURDER 4
wrote like an a. EPITAPHS 13

angels walk behind the a.   ROYALTY 28
anger A. makes dull men witty   ANGER 2
  don't look back in a.   PAST 6
Anglicans devoutly worshipped by A.
       RELIGION 50
angling 'a.' is the name given to fishing
       SPORTS 17
Anglish A. is what we don' know   LANGUAGES 9
Anglo-Irishman He was an A.   IRELAND 1
angry a. with my friend   ANGER 3
  when she's a. she is keen   WOMEN 61
  when very a.   ANGER 10
  when you get a.   ANGER 5
animal a. husbandry   SEX 45
  a. lover   HUMAN RACE 11
  Man is the Only A.   HUMAN RACE 13
  what a. would you like to be   BORES 20
animals All a. are equal   DEMOCRACY 13
  A., I hope   SPORTS 26
  distinguishes man from a.   MEDICINE 26
  Men are a.   MEN 9
  of Music Among A.   CRITICS 31
  woollier a.   ART 18
animosity a. against a writer   WRITERS 48
  sisterly a.   FAMILY 41
annihilation A. ALL OF US PROBABLE
       TELEGRAMS 10
  hope for merciful a.   RELIGION 16
annoy A. 'im   GOD 6
  a. somebody with what you write   WRITING 1
annoyance a. of a good example   CHARACTER 17
annuals a. are the ones   GARDENS 17
annus horribilis one *a.* after another
       ROYALTY 53
anomalies a. exist   GOVERNMENT 46
anorak chancellor is an a.   BORES 1
another A. bride, another June   LOVE 27
  that was in a. country   SEX 47
answer a. letters back   CENSORSHIP 25
  a. the phone   MISTAKES 27
  believe that men were the a.   MEN 2
  love is the a.   LOVE 45
  thought of the a.   CINEMA 27
answering a. you in French   COUNTRIES 36
answers figure out the funny a.   HUMOUR 25
antagonistic a. governments   NEWSPAPERS 38
antediluvian a. families   CLASS 6
anthologies A. are predigested food
       QUOTATIONS 23
  employ to compile a.   QUOTATIONS 10
anthologist no a. lifts his leg   QUOTATIONS 1
anthology a. is like all the plums   QUOTATIONS 19
anthrax a. bacillus   HUMAN RACE 8
anthropology familiar facts of a.   MARRIAGE 57
anticipates He who a. his century   OLD AGE 18

anticlimax kind of a.   FILMS 14
ants social organization of a.   SCIENCE 11
anxious a. to tell the truth   TRUTH 6
anybody a.'s weddings   MARRIAGE 56
  no one's a.   CLASS 18
anything A. goes   BEHAVIOUR 27
  give you a. but love   POVERTY 8
apart You mean a. from my own   MARRIAGE 60
apathy stirring up a.   POLITICAL PARTIES 19
ape Is man an a. or an angel   RELIGION 17
apes higher up till you had a.   UNIVERSE 13
aphorisms for pregnant a.   QUOTATIONS 3
apologize never to a.   BEHAVIOUR 39
apologizes a. to the truck   ENGLAND 21
apology a. for the Devil   GOD 14
  God's a. for relations   FRIENDS 10
apostles A. would have done as they did
       RELIGION 13
apothegms I am not given to a.   QUOTATIONS 15
appearance my external a.   SELF-KNOWLEDGE 12
  person of very *epic* a.   PEOPLE 12
appearing Television is for a. on   TELEVISION 5
appendix Like an a.   CENSORSHIP 7
appendixes errors that lead to burst a.
       MEDICINE 23
appetite a. for lunch   DEATH 41
  gratify the a.   GOSSIP 9
  satisfying a voracious a.   LOVE 15
applause A., applause   THEATRE 20
  A. is a receipt   MUSIC 44
apple greedy boy takes a. pie   CRITICS 21
apples a., cherries, hops, and women   PLACES 9
  a. short of a picnic   FOOLISHNESS 19
  begin to think of a.   CRICKET 9
  what a. smell like   DESCRIPTION 25
applications filling out prize a.   JOURNALISM 1
appointment making an a.   GOVERNMENT 30
approved I a. of it   DEATH 69
April A. in Fairbanks   WEATHER 12
aprons dress up in leather a.   MEN AND WOMEN 4
aqua all a., no vita   PEOPLE 5
Arabian A. *Nights* entertainment   SICKNESS 18
Arabs A. are only Jews   COUNTRIES 21
  A. of means   ANIMALS 22
archaeologist marry an a.   MARRIAGE 33
archaeology Industrial a.   PAST 8
archangel A. Gabriel   DEMOCRACY 2
  some sort of a.   SUCCESS 10
archbishop a. had come to see me   SEX 22
  found yourself A. of Canterbury   WRITERS 20
archbishops get it from their a.   MORALITY 6
archdeacon (by way of turbot) an a.
       THE CLERGY 23
archfiend terrible fault for an a.   ACTORS 24

atheist A. and a Vegetarian POETS 15
a. is a man RELIGION 12
He was an embittered a. RELIGION 51
I am still an a. RELIGION 11
remain a sound a. CERTAINTY 15
very *chic* for an a. RELIGION 58
atheistical 'Tis a damned a. age, wife
MARRIAGE 125
atheists realise that they are a. THE CLERGY 14
athletic only a. sport I ever mastered SPORTS 14
athletics all a. as inferior forms SPORTS 34
Atlantic cheaper to lower the A. FILMS 7
atmosphere at length and convey a.
QUOTATIONS 15
atom Leave the a. alone PROGRESS 11
Rutherford was done with the a. SCIENCE 21
atoms interchanging of the a. TRANSPORT 28
attachment a. à la Plato ART 9
attack a. from Mars ARMED FORCES 23
a. the monkey POLITICIANS 7
dared a. my Chesterton LITERATURE 5
attendance a. at the House of Commons
MARRIAGE 52
attendant lobster to a. shrimps ROYALTY 50
attention compelled one's a. FASHION 33
give their entire a. to it MARRIAGE 14
paid constant a. CHILDREN 11
withdrew my a. CONVERSATION 13
Attlee [A. is] a modest man INSULTS 10
attorney gentleman was an *a.* LAW 16
office boy to an A.'s firm LAW 10
rich a.'s Elderly ugly daughter LOVE 21
attractive grows increasingly a. MARRIAGE 33
if they are a. WOMEN 2
if they are in the least a. MARRIAGE 30
you are not a. APPEARANCE 17
audience arrival of *your* a. SPEECHES 2
A. of Two THEATRE 60
a. swelled to six POETRY 15
a. was a total failure THEATRE 58
call the a. in tomorrow THEATRE 31
ignores her a. ACTORS 35
I love a responsive a. THEATRE 39
looks at the a. MEDICINE 34
audiences English-speaking a. LANGUAGES 24
I know two kinds of a. MUSIC 45
August To recommence in A. WEATHER 5
aunt A. in Yucatan ANIMALS 7
A. is calling to Aunt FAMILY 55
Charley's a. FAMILY 46
have the Queen as their a. ROYALTY 48
aunts bad a. FAMILY 53
cousins and his a. FAMILY 18
Austen A. doesn't sell high-tech BUSINESS 11

Australia A., *Inter alia* COUNTRIES 48
A., this would be mid-winter WEATHER 2
A. is a huge rest home COUNTRIES 29
A.'s original inhabitants PREJUDICE 9
A.'s very own way BETTING 7
last year in A. TRAVEL 26
Australian A. humour COUNTRIES 31
authentic a. self into a letter LETTERS 11
author among other things, an a. WRITERS 15
a. giveth WRITERS 19
a. of this valentine SECRECY 9
a. that wrote it was READING 16
a. was entitled CRITICS 2
a. was executed PUBLISHING 2
a. who comes to stay WRITERS 8
a. who speaks about WRITERS 10
dangerous as an a. WRITERS 46
don't know who the a. is THEATRE 49
Every a. really wants WRITERS 47
friends of the a. ADVERTISING 3
authority Distrust of a. GOVERNMENT 8
authors A. are judged WRITERS 35
a. got away with the swag PUBLISHING 13
towards noble a. ARISTOCRACY 15
try not to argue with a. PUBLISHING 15
We a., Ma'am PRAISE 2
autobiographer a. is the most
AUTOBIOGRAPHY 11
autobiographies in later life to a.
AUTOBIOGRAPHY 20
reader of a. AUTOBIOGRAPHY 17
autobiography A. comes out AUTOBIOGRAPHY 1
a. is an obituary AUTOBIOGRAPHY 8
a. is a sin AUTOBIOGRAPHY 14
A. is now as common AUTOBIOGRAPHY 10
a. is the most AUTOBIOGRAPHY 23
a. should give AUTOBIOGRAPHY 6
Every a. AUTOBIOGRAPHY 19
you've read his a. INSULTS 32
autocrat I shall be an a. ROYALTY 17
autographs first editions and a. VIRTUE 9
Autolycus named me A. CHARACTER 11
automatic with a. hand WOMEN 20
automobile a. changed our dress TRANSPORT 21
available time I've been a. AWARDS 2
average too good for the a. man CLASS 21
aversion begin with a little a. MARRIAGE 114
closely bordering on a. INSULTS 47
aviation early days of a. THEATRE 35
Avon down the A. in a gondola INTELLIGENCE 13
awake a. thinking it was the food SLEEP 5
you'll a. FOOD 16
away WHEN I'M A. TELEGRAMS 4
axe Lizzie Borden took an a. MURDER 1
axes no a. are being ground CENSORSHIP 4

bedroom French widow in every b.　　HOTELS 4
　have one in their b.　　TRANSPORT 37
　take care of the b. bit　　MARRIAGE 68
　what you do in the b.　　SEX 25
beds lush pastrami b.　　PLACES 17
bedstead that b. would　　SLEEP 2
bee hero is a b.　　ANIMALS 15
Beecham's Pills B. are just the thing　　MEDICINE 4
beef b.-faced boys　　CHILDREN 14
　love British b.　　FOOD 5
　Roast B., Medium　　FOOD 27
been I've b. things　　VIRTUE 24
beer B. and Britannia　　ENGLAND 33
　b. teetotaller　　ALCOHOL 56
　b. to cry into　　ALCOHOL 41
　desire small b.　　ALCOHOL 53
　extra sixpence on b.　　TAXES 11
beers other b. cannot reach　　ALCOHOL 39
Beethoven Anything but B.　　FILMS 12
　What do you think of B.　　MUSICIANS 16
　where is B.　　MUSIC 46
　would like to thank B.　　MUSIC 54
begat Fat filibusterers b.　　POLITICS 36
begin B. at the beginning　　ROYALTY 16
　should b. at home　　CENSORSHIP 16
beginning b., a middle　　CINEMA 12
　b., a muddle　　LITERATURE 23
begot were about when they b. me　　PARENTS 15
behave b. like gentlemen　　WOMEN 42
behaving b. in this extraordinary manner
　　THEATRE 54
behaviour b. everywhere　　COUNTRIES 53
　mitigate b.　　GOLF 6
behind it will be b. me　　LETTERS 14
　no bosom and no b.　　ENGLAND 32
　no more b. your scenes　　THEATRE 25
　travel broadens the b.　　TRAVEL 9
　walk b. the angels　　ROYALTY 28
beige just my colour: it's *b.*　　COLOURS 5
Belgium must be B.　　TRAVEL 25
Belgrave beat in B. Square　　ARISTOCRACY 7
believe b. all you read in the newspapers
　　NEWSPAPERS 18
　b. almost anything provided　　INTELLIGENCE 15
　b. I am between both　　ARGUMENT 17
　can't b. what isn't happening　　SPORTS 9
　Corrected I *b.*　　RELIGION 33
　don't b. in God　　GOD 19
　don't b. in it　　CERTAINTY 5
　I cannot quite b. in God　　RELIGION 27
　I don't *b.* it　　COMEDY 32
　If you b. that　　PEOPLE 48
believed b. of any man　　ALCOHOL 63
　I should not be b.　　MARRIAGE 125
believers b. in Clough　　EPITAPHS 23

bell sexton tolled the b.　　DEATH 30
bellman B., perplexed and distressed　　TRAVEL 4
belly-tension b. between a man and a woman
　　MARRIAGE 65
belong B. TO ANY CLUB　　SOCIETY 17
beloved B. friends　　HANDWRITING 7
below b.-stairs class　　CLASS 5
　belt without hitting b. it　　PRIME MINISTERS 2
belt b. without hitting below it　　PRIME MINISTERS 2
belted b. you and flayed you　　ARMED FORCES 19
bench he fancied he was on the b.　　JUDGES 14
benches asleep on the same b.　　POLITICS 57
beneath married b. him　　ACTING 10
Benn B. grabs child　　NEWSPAPERS 6
Benois B. . . . . If 'e come　　DANCE 3
bent all as b. as hell　　SPORTS 1
bereaved would be b.　　HUMOUR 41
Berlin people of B.　　TOWNS 15
Berlitz glibness of the B.-school　　LANGUAGES 11
Bernstein B. has been disclosing　　MUSICIANS 12
berth lying in the upper b.　　MARRIAGE 22
best b. of us being unfit　　DEATH 28
　in the b. of things　　HAPPINESS 14
　Reagan for his b. friend　　FILM STARS 15
bestest b. of friends　　FRIENDS 28
best-seller b. is the gilded tomb　　BOOKS 18
betrayed He deserves to be b.　　TRUST 6
　To have b. two leaders　　TRUST 2
better b. in France　　COUNTRIES 57
　b. man than I am　　ARMED FORCES 19
　b. than we thought　　FOOTBALL 18
　b. to be looked over　　SATISFACTION 13
　Discretion is not the b.　　BIOGRAPHY 12
　don't know b.　　CHILDREN 32
　expected b. manners　　BEHAVIOUR 9
　Gad! she'd b.　　UNIVERSE 4
　He is not b.　　TELEGRAMS 1
　if they had been any b.　　LITERATURE 14
　keep on failing b.　　SUCCESS 28
　rich is b.　　WEALTH 31
　things I'd been b. without　　LOVE 36
　Wagner's music is b.　　MUSIC 37
　when I'm bad, I'm better　　VIRTUE 23
　who had any thing b.　　WRITERS 1
　world that's b. for Rupert　　PEOPLE 43
better-class b. people get it apparently
　　MEDICINE 6
betting keeps horse from b.　　BETTING 5
between believe I am b. both　　ARGUMENT 17
　I would try to get b. them　　SEX 78
　something b. us　　BODY 19
Beulah B., peel me a grape　　FOOD 86
Bevan [Aneurin B.] enjoys prophesying
　　POLITICIANS 22
beverage parlour with a b. service　　SOCIETY 7

beware B. of men bearing flowers
　　　　　　　　　　　　　　MEN AND WOMEN 47
　B. of the agapanthus　　　　　　COUNTRY 12
bewildered Bewitched, bothered and b.
　　　　　　　　　　　　　　MEN AND WOMEN 15
bewitched B., bothered and bewildered
　　　　　　　　　　　　　　MEN AND WOMEN 15
bible B. in the other　　POLITICAL PARTIES 20
bicycle cannot even use a b.　COMPUTERS 3
　fish without a b.　　　　　　　WOMEN 66
　king rides a b.　　　　　　　COUNTRIES 4
　Salisbury Plain on a b.　　　　TRAVEL 13
　so is a b. repair kit　　　　　MARRIAGE 41
bicycles half people and half b.　TRANSPORT 28
bicyclists trouser-clip for b.　TECHNOLOGY 12
bidet b.-fixe　　　　　　　PARENTS 9
　keep it in the b.　　　　　　　CLASS 25
　UNABLE OBTAIN B.　　　　TELEGRAMS 22
biennials b. are the ones　　GARDENS 17
big b. game hunting　　　　BIOGRAPHY 5
　born with b. bones　　　　　　BODY 5
　Hey! b. spender　　MEN AND WOMEN 11
　I am b.　　　　　　　　FILM STARS 3
　too b. for them　　　PRIME MINISTERS 7
bigamy b., Sir, is a crime　　MARRIAGE 88
　B. is having one husband　　MARRIAGE 7
　maximum punishment for b.　MARRIAGE 108
bigger b. they are　　　　　BOXING 5
　little girls get b.　　　　　WOMEN 41
bike Mind my b.　　　　　COMEDY 28
bikers one-word nickname for b.　MEDICINE 12
bill very large b.　　　　　DEBT 7
billboard b. lovely as a tree　ADVERTISING 11
bills I have the b. to prove it　MEN AND WOMEN 21
　two things about b.　　　　　DEBT 5
Billy poke poor B.　　　　　DEATH 27
bind B.-their-kings-in-chains　NAMES 16
bingo Let B. = Frodo　　　　NAMES 24
biographers love of b.　　　BIOGRAPHY 8
biographical b. friend　　　BIOGRAPHY 16
biographies reading b.　　　BIOGRAPHY 14
biography better part of b.　BIOGRAPHY 12
　B., like big game hunting　　BIOGRAPHY 5
　B. is about chaps　　　　　BIOGRAPHY 3
　B. should be written　　　　BIOGRAPHY 1
　writes the b.　　　　　　BIOGRAPHY 17
birch bringing back the b.　　SEX 85
bird dead b.　　　　　　　FASHION 7
　　　　　　　　　　　　　　OLD AGE 12
Birdie lady whose name is B.　LETTERS 10
birds b., wild flowers, and Prime Ministers
　　　　　　　　　　　　　　POLITICS 9
　b. coughing in the trees　　　NATURE 1
　b. were trying to communicate　DRUGS 1

　merciful to the b.　　　ARISTOCRACY 1
　one's eye for the high b.　　POLITICIANS 18
Birkenhead B. is very clever　INSULTS 2
Birmingham no great hopes from B.　TOWNS 3
birth b. of each child　　　CHILDREN 25
birth control she had not thought of b.
　　　　　　　　　　　　　　INSULTS 46
birthday my eighty-first b.　　SEX 22
biscuit people who cared a b.　SEX 44
bisexuality On b.: It immediately doubles
　　　　　　　　　　　　　　SEX 3
bishop b. kick a hole　　　WOMEN 7
　b. with a moustache　　　　PROGRESS 1
　How can a b. marry　　　　SEX 75
bishopric *merit* for a b.　　THE CLERGY 26
bishops B. treat everyone　THE CLERGY 12
　Don't like b.　　　　　THE CLERGY 3
　many of its b.　　　　　THE CLERGY 14
bison water b.　　　　　　ANIMALS 25
bite hope he will *b.*　　ARMED FORCES 9
biting b. my knuckles　　　FILMS 9
　b. the hand　　　　　　CINEMA 20
　don't stop b.　　　　　MISTAKES 23
bitten b. in half by a shark　CHOICE 13
　Once b. by a snake　　　　TRUST 5
Bizet I prefer the B. theory　NAMES 7
black blacker than b.　　　COLOURS 7
　b. was　　　　　　　　FAMILY 26
　one drop of b. blood　　　PREJUDICE 8
　so long as it's b.　　　　COLOURS 4
　study of mankind is *b.*　　PREJUDICE 15
　talks good for a b. guy　　PREJUDICE 10
　unexpectedly turned b.　　ACTING 1
　Why do you wear b.　　　HAPPINESS 5
　will be b. holes　　　　　FAME 5
Black and Tans B. were at large　PEOPLE 31
blacker b. than black　　　COLOURS 7
blackest just when things were b.　WAR 14
blacklist discovery of the German b.　WAR 10
Blackpool famous seaside place called B.
　　　　　　　　　　　　　　PLACES 10
blade bloody, blameful b.　　ANGER 8
　His b. struck the water　　SPORTS 8
blaggard God's a b.　　　　POETS 16
blame It's the poor wot gets the b.　POVERTY 1
　manager gets the b.　　　FOOTBALL 11
　pass the b.　　　　BUREAUCRACY 15
blamed mothers go on getting b.　PARENTS 18
blameless led b. lives　　　LAW 3
blamelessness B. runs riot　BIOGRAPHY 15
blancmange multi-hued b.　POLITICS 52
blazer make them wear a b.　MEN AND WOMEN 1
bleeding instead of b., he sings　SONGS 15
bleeper I do not wear a b.　　PEOPLE 15

blind b. composer — FILMS 12
  deaf man to a b. woman — MARRIAGE 34
  dust on a Venetian b. — CRITICS 9
  Shakespeare Sonnets to the b. — ACTORS 11
blitz b. of a boy — CHILDREN 10
block old b. itself — PRIME MINISTERS 8
blockhead No man but a b. — WRITING 13
blonde b. to make a bishop kick — WOMEN 7
blood B., as all men know — COUNTRIES 32
  b. and thirsty — FILMS 6
  B. pressure — HANDWRITING 7
  b. to appear in the water — POLITICS 22
  Fats Waller's b. — ALCOHOL 16
  I can do you b. and love — THEATRE 53
  one drop of Negro b. — PREJUDICE 8
  Scotch b. in her veins — PREJUDICE 2
  show-business with b. — BOXING 2
bloody Abroad is b. — TRAVEL 10
  b., blameful blade — ANGER 8
  Walk! Not b. likely — TRANSPORT 36
  wipe a b. nose — ARGUMENT 7
bloom destined to b. late — APPEARANCE 20
blooming b. well dead — DEATH 62
blotched great b. moon — APPEARANCE 28
blow otherwise you b. up — LIFE 17
  So b., Gabriel, blow — RELIGION 54
blown her hair b. about — TRANSPORT 30
bludgeoning b. of the people — DEMOCRACY 17
blue Blue Danube is really b. — OLD AGE 17
  brilliant b. garment — COLOURS 6
  invented b. jeans — FASHION 32
  pale b. eyes — ACTORS 26
  there isn't much b. — LITERATURE 33
Bluebird B. complex — ARCHITECTURE 10
blues future of the b. — FILMS 10
blunder wonder At so grotesque a b. — MISTAKES 4
blurbs B. that appear on the back — ADVERTISING 3
blurting B. out the complete truth — TRUTH 9
blush b. into the cheek — ENGLAND 10
  let other people b. — FOOLISHNESS 2
  such large letters I b. — PRIDE 11
blushes B.. Or needs to — HUMAN RACE 13
blushing I always take b. — BEHAVIOUR 7
boa constrictor like a maternal b. — SUCCESS 8
board b. of gods — GOD 34
  wasn't any B. — GOVERNMENT 15
boasting B. about modesty — ENGLAND 1
boat back of my b. — TRANSPORT 38
  wrong b. at Dover — TRAVEL 14
boats sink my b. — MARRIAGE 3
bodega home is the b. — ALCOHOL 44
Bodley losing a book from B. — LIBRARIES 9
body approaching the age when your b.
— MIDDLE AGE 3
  borrow his b. — BODY 25

get rid of the rest of her b. — WOMEN 74
I should interpose my b. — SEX 78
looking for a b. — CINEMA 26
my b. and your brains — MEN AND WOMEN 43
places on one's b. — APPEARANCE 17
use of my b. — BODY 3
with Africa than my own b. — WOMEN 53
boets I hate all B. and Bainters — ROYALTY 32
Bognor Bugger B. — LAST WORDS 3
bogus b. for some time — HEALTH 7
  persons whom I knew to be b. — PEOPLE 27
Bohemian B. and artistic quarter — ART 38
boil vulgar b. — COOKERY 16
boiled bag of b. sweets — POLITICS 26
  cold b. veal — FRIENDS 11
  no politics in b. and roast — POLITICAL PARTIES 17
  suck on a b. sweet — SEX 87
boiler 10 years in a b. suit — WOMEN 72
boiling b. oil — CRIME 19
Bolshevism B. triumphs — FOOLISHNESS 16
  this sort of madness [B.] — POLITICS 68
bolster b. behind the throne — ROYALTY 62
bomb atomic b. — FOOLISHNESS 20
bombazine B. would have shown — DEATH 23
bombs Come, friendly b. — TOWNS 6
bond handle a b. offering — LAW 4
boneless see the b. wonder — PRIME MINISTERS 11
bones tongs and the b. — MUSIC 47
bonhomie natural *b.* — ECONOMICS 2
bon-mots plucking b. from their places
— QUOTATIONS 14
bonnet b. in Germany — COUNTRIES 53
bonus that's a b. — BODY 39
book Another damned, thick, square b.
— ROYALTY 41
Arrival of B. of the Month — READING 5
because a b. is humorous — PUBLISHING 19
b.-buying public would regret — WRITERS 14
b. flying a bullet — CRIME 3
b. in breeches — PEOPLE 38
B. of Life begins — BIBLE 7
b. of my enemy — WRITERS 17
b. publication — BOOKS 11
b. which people praise — READING 18
b. would have been finished — FAMILY 54
enjoy your b. — AUTOBIOGRAPHY 3
finishes his b. — READING 10
get a lawyer—not a b. — LAW 18
had written a b. — BOOKS 4
knocks me out is a b. — READING 16
knows this out of the b. — EDUCATION 14
large b. is depicted — FASHION 27
losing a b. from Bodley — LIBRARIES 9
moment I picked up your b. — LITERATURE 25
no b.—it's a plaything — QUOTATIONS 16

book (*cont.*):

only advertise a b.	PUBLISHING 18
only ever read one b. in my life	LITERATURE 27
rather read a b.	DANCE 5
read the b.	CRITICS 22
read the b. of Job	BIBLE 8
sent a new b.	INDEXES 2
What is the use of a b.	LITERATURE 13
with a good b.	HOLIDAYS 10
without mentioning a single b.	LITERATURE 32
written a b.	BOOKS 8

bookmaker b. who takes actresses — SPORTS 6

bookmaking tax on b. — BETTING 14

books any good b. lately — COMEDY 14

b., trees and women	POLITICIANS 35
b. about homos	READING 14
b. about living men	BIOGRAPHY 6
B. are well written	BOOKS 25
B. from Boots'	ENGLAND 6
b. were read	DEATH 11
cream of other's b.	QUOTATIONS 14
do *you* read b. *through*	READING 11
had a lot of b.	BOOKS 15
If my b. had been any worse	LITERATURE 14
I hate b.	BOOKS 17
learned from b.	MORALITY 2
My only b.	WOMEN 48
oddity of Oxford b.	PUBLISHING 4
one of their b. in their room	WRITERS 8
provided with no b.	BOOKS 7
regular supply of b.	LIFE 26
respected b.	LIBRARIES 11
showed me his b.	LIBRARIES 7
so charming as b.	BOOKS 19
unindexed b. with indexes	WORK 21
world doesn't read its b.	READING 12
wrote a few b.	MARRIAGE 40

bookseller he once shot a b. — PUBLISHING 7

If Kafka had been a b. — BOOKS 1

bootboy b. at Claridges — BOOKS 27

bootlace trip over a loose b. — WRITERS 48

boots doormat in a world of b. — SELF-KNOWLEDGE 20

engine in b.	SPORTS 13
look at his b.	CLASS 28
school without any b.	PRIME MINISTERS 7
top of his b.	ARMED FORCES 22
when I take my b. off	BODY 12

booze fool with b. — ALCOHOL 25

bop 'B.' is like scrabble — MUSIC 16

bordello doorkeeper of a b. — MUSICIANS 18

bore b. is a man — BORES 15

b. is simply a nonentiy	BORES 11
b. you to sleep	BORES 7
God is a b.	GOD 33

is an old b.	BORES 17
merely a b.	SOCIETY 24
not only a b.	BORES 13
not to b. yourself	BORES 12
Thou shalt not b.	CINEMA 51

bored b. with good wine — ALCOHOL 22

I'd get b.	CRICKET 8
indefinitely b.	SOCIETY 16
man is b.	MEN AND WOMEN 35

boredom b. occasioned — BORES 10

b. threshold — BORES 18

bores destiny of b. — BORES 8

Borg B. is rugged — TENNIS 6

Borgias I dined last night with the B. — SOCIETY 2

boring b. kind of guy — BORES 4

b. you fall asleep	NAMES 2
Somebody's b. me	BORES 16

born b. an Englishman — ENGLAND 4

b. in a manger	CHILDREN 1
b. with your legs apart	SEX 58
man is b. in a stable	IRELAND 13
Never was b.	FAMILY 40
person b. who is so unlucky	MISTAKES 22
refusing to be b.	FUTURE 1
some men are b. great	PRIDE 6
That's b. into the world alive	POLITICAL PARTIES 8

borrow b. his body — BODY 25

b. the money	HAPPINESS 17
b. the words	DICTIONARIES 10
well enough to b. from	FRIENDS 3

borrowers to catch out b. — BOOKS 14

borrows b. a detective story — READING 12

Borstal it may have been B. — EDUCATION 7

bosom no b. and no behind — ENGLAND 32

bossy It's a *very* b. car — TRANSPORT 25

Boston B., the home of the bean — TOWNS 7

B. social zones	CLASS 15
I met him in B.	TOWNS 17

botanist I'd be a b. — SCIENCE 15

botanists way b. divide up flowers — SCIENCE 18

botch I make a b. — TIME 4

both friends in b. places — HEAVEN 6

bother B. it — LANGUAGE 10

no time to b. — LETTERS 1

bothered Bewitched, b. and bewildered — MEN AND WOMEN 15

Botticelli B.'s a *cheese* — FOOD 65

B. were alive today	ART 29
If B. were alive	FASHION 36

bottle b. just going to sit — HOME 22

b. of hay	FOOD 73
b. on the chimley-piece	ALCOHOL 21
catsup b.	FOOD 2
little for the b.	LOVE 11

bottles English have hot-water b. — SEX 51

bottom baby, I'm the b. — MEN AND WOMEN 39
reach the b. first — CHILDREN 16
Undesired on my tired little b. — WOMEN 58
Boule Little sticks of B. — ART 16
bounded b. on the north — CINEMA 7
bouquet b. is better — ALCOHOL 52
Bourbon Wheaties with B. — ALCOHOL 19
Bovril does her hair with B. — FRIENDS 5
made into B. when she dies — INSULTS 3
bow b., ye tradesmen — CLASS 17
bowel lower b. of music — MUSIC 11
bowl not to see you b. — CRICKET 4
bowler b.'s Willey — NAMES 11
bow-wows gone to the demnition b. — MISTAKES 12
box pianoforte is a harp in a b. — MUSIC 25
boxes buttocks into wooden b. — TRANSPORT 31
boxing B. is show-business — BOXING 2
boy any b. ever had — CINEMA 46
b. as he really is — CHILDREN 19
Can befall a b. — FAMILY 28
FEEL LIKE A B. AGAIN — TELEGRAMS 12
fifteen-year-old b. — PARENTS 13
I used to be a good b. — PAST 15
mad about the b. — FILM STARS 4
no longer a b. — CHARACTER 3
quite a little b. — CONVERSATION 4
to your little b. — CHILDREN 9
boyfriend having no b. — MEN AND WOMEN 10
boys b. something else to kick — SPORTS 35
B. were so simple — EDUCATION 8
By office boys for office b. — NEWSPAPERS 29
Faded b., jaded boys — MEN 5
Hello b. — BODY 4
liked little b. too little — EDUCATION 46
loaded guns with b. — SECRECY 6
two sorts of b. — CHILDREN 14
brain b. and his expression — HUMOUR 7
b. has oozed out — TRAVEL 17
b.? It's my second favourite — BODY 1
b. like Swiss cheese — FILM STARS 18
certain to b. — ART 38
definition of the b. — MIND 3
If I only had a b. — INTELLIGENCE 6
leave that b. outside — POLITICS 34
Very Little B. — ANIMALS 30
with b. surgeons — JOURNALISM 5
brains b. are in the right place — DESCRIPTION 2
b. of a Minerva — ACTORS 2
feet instead of their b. — MUSIC 52
his b. go to his head — INSULTS 2
husbands having b. — MARRIAGE 136
intelligence and no b. — CHARACTER 7
my body and your b. — MEN AND WOMEN 43

brandy music is the b. of the damned — MUSIC 48
must drink b. — ALCOHOL 36
pray get me a glass of b. — ROYALTY 35
braw b. bricht moonlicht nicht' — ALCOHOL 43
Bray I will be the Vicar of B., sir — POLITICIANS 1
Brazil aunt from B. — FAMILY 46
bread piece of b. and butter — FOOD 44
reinvented unsliced b. — WIT 18
She was cutting b. and butter — MEN AND WOMEN 49
break day will b. — FOOD 16
give Osaka an even b. — WIT 19
one-year b. — HOLIDAYS 3
sucker an even b. — BETTING 4
those that b. down — TECHNOLOGY 2
breakages B., Limited — BUSINESS 15
breakfast b. three times — FOOD 50
brilliant at b. — BORES 21
hath already committed b. — VIRTUE 11
spoil your b. — CRITICS 3
touch my b. — FOOD 89
breakfast-time b. agenda — CONVERSATION 2
period in matrimony is b. — MARRIAGE 71
breaking b. it in for a friend — NAMES 17
b. my heart — HAPPINESS 3
breast boiling bloody b. — ANGER 8
breasts Big b. — BODY 34
b. like granite — FILM STARS 18
You're the b. of Venus — SEX 8
breath use your b. — ALCOHOL 29
breathe like the hair we b. — SPORTS 32
breathing b. is like burying your head — SICKNESS 19
followed by Cheyne-Stokes b. — OLD AGE 31
stopped b. — DEATH 47
bred B. en bawn — ANIMALS 18
breeches book in b. — PEOPLE 38
in my riding b. — FASHION 30
breeding b. our own team — FOOTBALL 25
or of ill b. — BEHAVIOUR 7
result of b. — WEALTH 19
brevity Nothing conduces to b. — WRITING 8
bribe b. or twist — JOURNALISM 26
Marriage is a b. — MARRIAGE 135
bribed b. by their loyalties — MONEY 17
bribes b. he had taken — CRIME 1
bricht braw b. moonlicht nicht' — ALCOHOL 43
brick b. in his pocket — HOME 24
threw it a b. at a time — ACTING 14
bricks pile of b. — ARCHITECTURE 17
bride Including the b. and groom — MARRIAGE 95
It feels so fine to be a b. — MARRIAGE 102
bridegroom close as a b. — GARDENS 4

bridge Beautiful Railway B.   DEATH 40
 b. to the future   FUTURE 10
 I should have preferred a b.   TRANSPORT 26
brief B., to the point   MARRIAGE 46
briefing off-the-record b.   GOD 28
brier in a b.-patch   ANIMALS 18
brigade B. of Guards   POLITICS 49
brigand I am a b.   SOCIETY 21
brigands b. demand your money   WOMEN 6
bright quit looking on the b. side
                                          GOVERNMENT 33
brilliant b. at breakfast   BORES 21
 b. on paper   FOOTBALL 22
 b.—to the top   ARMED FORCES 22
 b. writer in the editor's chair   NEWSPAPERS 8
 less b. pen   HISTORY 1
bring b. it to you, free   DEATH 3
 do b. him   BEHAVIOUR 31
Britain B. was no part of Europe   COUNTRIES 1
 care about B.   ENGLAND 17
 further you got from B.   POLITICIANS 10
Britannia Beer and B.   ENGLAND 33
British B. are not given   ENGLAND 39
 B. government   FAME 2
 B. history   ECONOMICS 10
 rules of B. conduct   BEHAVIOUR 11
 we're B.   COMEDY 30
Briton only a free-born B. can   SNOBBERY 16
Britons brave b.   ENGLAND 25
 B. were only natives   ENGLAND 28
 we B. alone   ENGLAND 42
Brits bad B. are snobs   COUNTRIES 52
Britten written By Benjamin B.   MUSICIANS 2
broad b., where a broad should be   WOMEN 32
 B. of Church   RELIGION 9
 phone, a horse or a b.   PEOPLE 26
 referred to as That Kw.   NAMES 23
 She's the B. and I'm the High   PRIDE 9
broadens travel b. the behind   TRAVEL 9
 travel b. the mind   TRAVEL 5
Broadstairs Good old B.   HOLIDAYS 8
Broadway B.'s turning into Coney   TOWNS 18
 sinners on this part of B.   RELIGION 57
broccoli eat any more b.   FOOD 14
 It's b.   FOOD 87
broken baying for b. glass   ENGLAND 41
 b. my bloody leg   CRICKET 1
 Sound of B. Glass   CLASS 4
 their bats have been b.   TRUST 8
bronchial my b. tubes were entrancing
                                          MEDICINE 28
brooch Cartier b.   MEN AND WOMEN 62
broom extra b. for dear old mother   NATURE 3

brothel actively employed in a b.   WOMEN 35
 celibate b.   ALCOHOL 66
 male b. in Norway   BIOGRAPHY 4
brother B., can you spare   AMERICA 17
 had a younger b.   ACTING 3
 let my b. take over   BOXING 1
brow b. lifts are getting scary   MEDICINE 21
Brown Gordon B. is a bit like someone
                                          POLITICIANS 27
brown in a b. envelope   MONEY 13
 mimeographed in dark b. ink   NEWSPAPERS 11
 never wear b.   COLOURS 3
Browning B.'s translation   CRITICS 39
browning Meredith's a prose B.   LITERATURE 39
browns sorry for the poor b.   COLOURS 2
browsing b. and sluicing   FOOD 91
Bruce made Adam and B.   SEX 20
brush B. up your Shakespeare   THEATRE 43
brutal something positively b.   MEN 18
brute Feed the b.   MARRIAGE 104
bubble like unto a b.   WOMEN 76
bucket from any old b.   LOVE 46
 inside a swill b.   ADVERTISING 13
 kicked the b.   DEATH 4
budgerigars bartering b.   POLITICIANS 15
budget Balancing the b.   ECONOMICS 6
buff on b.-coloured foolscap   NEWSPAPERS 11
bug As a b.   EPITAPHS 12
 thinks there's a b.   SECRECY 3
bugger B. Bognor   LAST WORDS 3
 not to b. badgers   ANIMALS 2
buggers b. can't be choosers   SEX 18
 little b. hop   DANCE 1
build b. shopping malls   HUMAN RACE 1
building it's a very old b.   THEATRE 36
 something like a public b.   MARRIAGE 131
built b. it to last   BODY 32
 b. on large lines   BODY 38
bulimia yuppie version of b.   HEALTH 4
bull Beware of the b.   COUNTRY 12
 bullslinging, and b.—   INSULTS 15
 Cock and a B.   CONVERSATION 26
 take the b. between your teeth   WIT 10
bulldozers in front of the b.   GARDENS 16
bullet book flying a b.   CRIME 3
bullfighting b., bullslinging   INSULTS 15
bulls endearing b.   ANIMALS 27
bum every b. gets one   AWARDS 5
 he's a b. with money   WEALTH 7
 Indicat Motorem B.   TRANSPORT 12
 Rum, B. and Concertina   TITLES 4
 spoken of as a b.   SPORTS 28
 you can say b.   HUMOUR 43
bun like a damp b.   DESCRIPTION 4
bunk more or less b.   HISTORY 6

calves susceptible to c.　　　MEN AND WOMEN 18
Calvin C., oat-cakes, and sulphur　　SCOTLAND 10
Cambridge C. people rarely smile　　PLACES 3
　C. was the first stopping place　　PLACES 12
　it's either Oxford or C.　　SPORTS 30
　When I was at C.　　TRUST 7
camel c. is a horse designed　　BUREAUCRACY 10
　come on a c.　　COUNTRIES 47
　Take my c., dear　　TRANSPORT 24
camelopardalis c. or giraffe　　ANIMALS 14
camels none but she-c.　　ANIMALS 22
campaigning two years organizing and c.
　　　POWER 2
Campbell breaks the C.'s back　　NAMES 5
can C. I do you now　　COMEDY 2
　He who c., does　　EDUCATION 39
　horse c. do　　BETTING 10
　I c. do that　　AMERICA 22
　think you c.　　FUTURE 7
Canada all over C.　　COUNTRIES 49
　C., Our Good Neighbour　　TITLES 3
　C. is a country　　COUNTRIES 3
　Drink C. Dry　　ALCOHOL 7
　see C. as a country　　COUNTRIES 17
Canadian C. savages　　THEATRE 18
　little time left to be C.　　COUNTRIES 45
Canadians C. are Americans　　COUNTRIES 41
Canaletto stare at C.　　ART 31
Canalettos Then the C. go　　POLITICS 46
canaries C., caged　　BIRDS 7
can-can you can c. too　　DANCE 15
cancer C. can be rather fun　　SICKNESS 12
candidate c. can promise the moon　　UNIVERSE 3
　c. of probity　　MISTAKES 16
　c. talking to a rich person　　POLITICS 16
candidates when c. appeal　　POLITICS 2
candle I care not a farthing c.　　MUSICIANS 11
candy C. is dandy　　ALCOHOL 45
cannabis import c.　　CRIME 23
canned c. food came in　　FOOD 41
cannibal c., but one　　QUOTATIONS 8
　Said the c.　　FOOD 33
cannibalism C. went right out　　FOOD 41
cannibals formidable body of c.　　PRESIDENTS 11
cannon c.-ball took off his legs　　ARMED FORCES 14
cant c. of criticism　　HYPOCRISY 9
Canterbury vacancy at C.　　THE CLERGY 4
canting this c. world　　HYPOCRISY 9
cap Housman's c.　　DESCRIPTION 4
capable c. of reigning　　POWER 12
caparisons No c., Miss　　WIT 34
cape Risorgimento c.　　APPEARANCE 8
capital c. is always timid　　NEWSPAPERS 21
　where c. outlays were involved　　POVERTY 5

capitalism c. with the gloves off　　WAR 27
　definition of c.　　AMERICA 16
capitalist emerging from a c. institution
　　　WRITERS 4
Capra rather be Frank C.　　PEOPLE 23
captain by the team c.　　TRUST 8
　nobody like the C.　　JOURNALISM 21
car It's a *very bossy* c.　　TRANSPORT 25
　keys to your c.　　TRANSPORT 23
　motor c. to the human race　　TRANSPORT 18
　Strauss's c.　　TRANSPORT 34
　Take up c. maintenance　　TECHNOLOGY 10
　took the c.　　APPEARANCE 12
　wait in the c.　　TIME 2
carbuncle monstrous c.　　ARCHITECTURE 6
carcases c., which are to rise　　BODY 6
carcinoma sing of rectal c.　　SICKNESS 11
card c. to play for Honours　　LITERATURE 7
　insulting Christmas c.　　CHRISTMAS 7
cardie spy who came in for a c.　　SECRECY 5
care I c. for nobody　　SATISFACTION 4
　I c. less and less　　OLD AGE 35
　Take c. of him　　MARRIAGE 115
　taken better c. of myself　　OLD AGE 7
　women and c. and trouble　　WOMEN 76
career c. must be slipping　　AWARDS 2
　Good c. move　　DEATH 70
　loyal to his own c.　　PEOPLE 18
careful cannot be too c.　　FRIENDS 27
　c. in the immediate future　　TRANSPORT 20
　C. now　　CENSORSHIP 14
carelessness looks like c.　　FAMILY 51
Caribbean Columbus discovered C. vacations
　　　TRAVEL 21
caricature With a c. of a face　　OLD AGE 21
Carlyle good of God to let C.　　MARRIAGE 23
Carmen glanced at her C. rollers　　NAMES 7
carnation We all wear a green c.　　MEN 5
Carnegie wisecrack that played C. Hall　　WIT 21
Carnera C. hadn't stunted　　BODY 38
car park We sat in the c.　　MEN AND WOMEN 3
carrier c. who carried his can　　EPITAPHS 7
carrots naked, raw c.　　FOOD 42
cars crazy about c.　　TRANSPORT 35
Cartier C. brooch　　MEN AND WOMEN 62
Cartland C. wearing an electric pink　　PEOPLE 14
cartographers c. seek to define　　SCOTLAND 3
cartoons space between their c.　　NEWSPAPERS 17
Cary OLD C. GRANT FINE　　TELEGRAMS 14
Casanova would like to be, a C.　　MEN 11
case civil servant a good c.　　CIVIL SERVANTS 4
　In c. it is one of mine　　PARENTS 6
cash C. grew on trees　　PAST 12
　she needs good c.　　MIDDLE AGE 14
cassowary If I were a c.　　BIRDS 8

change c. from talking — CONVERSATION 7
  c. my plan — FASHION 10
  First you c. me schmall scheque — MONEY 5
  one thing to do with loose c. — MONEY 20
changed If voting c. anything — POLITICS 43
changes c. it more often — MEN AND WOMEN 17
  I make c. — FOOTBALL 19
changing c. a typewriter ribbon — WRITING 2
  not c. one's mind — CERTAINTY 17
channel she had swum the C. — SOCIETY 12
  you are crossing the C. — TRANSPORT 11
chaos emotional c. — HUMOUR 39
  His style is c. — WRITERS 45
  primordial c. — BODY 35
chaplain c. around Headquarters — THE CLERGY 13
chaps Biography is about C. — BIOGRAPHY 3
chapters no Previous C. — BOOKS 10
character about a fellow's c. — CHARACTER 10
  any great strength of c. — TRAVEL 24
  c. dead — GOSSIP 12
  c. is to be abused — FAMILY 43
  enormous lack of c. — SELF-KNOWLEDGE 17
  I knows an undesirable c. — SELF-KNOWLEDGE 9
  leave my c. behind — GOSSIP 11
characters too many c. — CINEMA 34
charge in c. of the Intelligence — SECRECY 8
charged asked me what I c. — MISTAKES 17
  c. straight through — ART 31
  he has been c. — SECRECY 11
Charing Cross human existence is at C. — TOWNS 22
charity C., dear Miss Prism — PRIDE 14
Charles C. II was always very merry — ROYALTY 65
  In good King C.'s golden days — POLITICIANS 1
  used by C. the First — HOME 9
Charlotte Werther had a love for C. — MEN AND WOMEN 49
charm By my c. — BEHAVIOUR 10
  know what c. is — BEHAVIOUR 4
  Prince Umberto is c. itself — SELF-KNOWLEDGE 6
charmer Were t'other dear c. away — LOVE 17
charming c. face — ANIMALS 3
  Farming is so c. — COUNTRY 16
Chartreuse C. can never really die — RELIGION 59
chasing always c. Rimbauds — LITERATURE 29
  nobody's c. me — MEN AND WOMEN 38
chaste c. whore — HUMOUR 28
chastity c. and continency — SEX 11
chat kills a c. — CONVERSATION 8
chateau I've a c. in Touraine — WEALTH 24
Chatterley end of the C. ban — SEX 43
Chaucer C., who had geneyus — WORDS 30
cheap good actors—c. — THEATRE 6
  handy and c. — FAMILY 1
  how c. potent music — MUSIC 57

how potent c. music is — MUSIC 10
  in c. shoes — FASHION 1
cheaper c. to lower the Atlantic — FILMS 7
cheapish C., reddish — ALCOHOL 61
cheat lucrative to c. — CRIME 6
  trying to c. you — MIDDLE AGE 7
cheated to be exceedingly c. at — PLACES 11
cheek blush into the c. — ENGLAND 10
  C. to Cheek — DANCE 11
  tongue being in your c. — WIT 3
cheekbones high c. — ACTORS 1
cheerful being so c. — COMEDY 23
cheerfulness c. was always breaking in — PHILOSOPHY 3
cheerio c. my deario — HOPE 5
cheese Botticelli's a c. — FOOD 65
  C. it is a peevish elf — FOOD 68
  chinks with c. — FOOD 82
  dreamed of c. — SLEEP 10
  soft c. will kill you — FOOD 48
  varieties of c. — COUNTRIES 18
  very new c. — FOOD 76
cheesed humanity soon had me c. off — LITERATURE 6
cheetah like a c. — HUMOUR 11
chef c. and a cook — COOKERY 10
chemotherapy sessions of c. — MEDICINE 30
cheque be done with a c. — RELIGION 35
  c.-book journalism — JOURNALISM 18
  mail that c. to the Judge — JUDGES 6
  schange me schmall c. — MONEY 5
  written a bad c. — DEBT 6
cheques publisher has to do is write c. — PUBLISHING 21
cherries c., hops, and women — PLACES 9
cherry c. blossom is quite nice — POETS 16
cherub c.'s face, a reptile all — INSULTS 36
chest c. to slip down — FOOD 90
Chesterton dared attack my C. — LITERATURE 5
chestnuts pop like c. — WRITERS 13
chew fart and c. gum — INSULTS 23
chianti bottles of C. — COUNTRIES 51
  nice c. — FOOD 34
chic Radical C. — SOCIETY 27
  very c. for an atheist — RELIGION 58
Chicago I'd expect to be robbed in C. — TOWNS 25
Chicagowards COCKBURN C. — TELEGRAMS 2
chicken c. and gravy — FOOD 53
  c. whose head has been — ARISTOCRACY 16
  frozen c. — COOKERY 5
  I know c. shit — SPEECHES 6
chickened I promptly c. out — WAR 23
child Any c. with sense — CHILDREN 37
  Ask your c. — CHILDREN 20
  Benn grabs c. — NEWSPAPERS 6

church (*cont.*):
pray that the c. — MARRIAGE 128
Railways and the C. — TRANSPORT 2
Churchill never was a C. — ARISTOCRACY 9
Randolph C. went into hospital — MEDICINE 36
churchman British c. — THE CLERGY 2
Modern C. — THE CLERGY 25
churchyards gloomy c. — DESCRIPTION 32
chutzpah C. is that quality — FAMILY 35
cigarette c. into the lake — COUNTRIES 25
c. is the perfect type — HAPPINESS 18
I smoked my first c. — SMOKING 6
Put that bloody c. out — LAST WORDS 6
cigarettes c. are the only product — SMOKING 2
more c. than most — SMOKING 1
Cinderella If I made C. — CINEMA 26
cinemas screens at c. — CINEMA 9
circumcision breast-feeding, c. — CHILDREN 27
circumference c. to rival — BODY 37
circumlocution C. Office — BUREAUCRACY 5
circumstance bitter, bitter c. — WOMEN 79
circumstantial c. evidence is very strong
— LAW 36
circus celebrated Barnum's c. — PRIME MINISTERS 11
cistern loud the c. — OLD AGE 5
cities shape of our c. — TRANSPORT 21
city big hard-boiled c. — TOWNS 9
good old-fashioned C. gent — WEALTH 1
I can get the same money for c. — WORDS 29
stay in the c. — COUNTRY 15
civil Always be c. to the girls — WOMEN 45
c. To everyone — CIVIL SERVANTS 8
Pray good people, be c. — RELIGION 26
civilisation collapse of c. — TOWNS 5
civilities groundless c. — BEHAVIOUR 15
civilization can't say c. don't advance
— PROGRESS 13
Is this C. — PROGRESS 2
menace to c. — PROGRESS 6
thought of modern c. — PROGRESS 9
veneer of c. — HOME 1
civilizations build c. — HUMAN RACE 1
civilized become genuinely c. — SCOTLAND 7
c. man has built a coach — PROGRESS 8
civil servant c. doesn't make jokes
— CIVIL SERVANTS 5
Give a c. a good case — CIVIL SERVANTS 4
Here lies a c. — CIVIL SERVANTS 8
civil servants c. are human beings
— CIVIL SERVANTS 6
C. by the clock — SEX 27
novel about c. — READING 2
persecuting c. — CIVIL SERVANTS 2
civil service c. has finished — CIVIL SERVANTS 7
claiming each c. to be — ARGUMENT 23

clam personage as happy as a c. — ROYALTY 22
clap Don't c. too hard — THEATRE 36
claret C. is the liquor for boys — ALCOHOL 36
Clark C. isn't here to see it — PROGRESS 2
class c. distinctions — CLASS 23
c.-ridden society — CLASS 22
Digitals have got no c. — TECHNOLOGY 15
fourth c. people — SNOBBERY 8
Infants' Bible C. — EDUCATION 51
merciless c. distinction — APPEARANCE 19
teaching c. consciousness — PREJUDICE 4
classes better c. — CLASS 19
Clashing of C. — POLITICS 25
three c. which need sanctuary — POLITICS 9
two great c. — CLASS 3
classic 'C.' A book — READING 18
c. is a synonym for narcotic — LITERATURE 2
C. music is th'kind — MUSIC 24
classics great homicidal c. — LITERATURE 35
classroom in every c. — COMPUTERS 4
walks in the c. — EDUCATION 27
clatter c. of Sir James Barrie's cans
— LITERATURE 20
Claude After you, C. — COMEDY 1
Claus ain't no Sanity C. — CHRISTMAS 8
claws panes of glass with its c. — MUSIC 4
clean c., verb active — EDUCATION 14
how c. they leave the washing up
— POLITICIANS 27
one more thing to keep c. — RELIGION 23
cleaner c. than a man's — MEN AND WOMEN 17
cleanliness c. everywhere — COUNTRIES 25
Cleopatra C.—and sank — ACTORS 4
clergy rising generation of c. — THE CLERGY 18
clergyman beneficed c. — THE CLERGY 25
take a reference from a c. — TRUST 13
clergymen men, women, and c. — THE CLERGY 22
clever c. men at Oxford — EDUCATION 17
provided he is c. enough — INTELLIGENCE 15
cleverness C. is a quality — INTELLIGENCE 10
cliché c. and an indiscretion — DIPLOMACY 9
clichés C. make the best songs — SONGS 18
have some new c. — CINEMA 19
wreck it with c. — CIVIL SERVANTS 4
climax end a sentence with a c. — SPEECHES 8
works its way up to a c. — CINEMA 22
clipboards people with c. — FUTURE 12
Clive like about C. — DEATH 12
close c. your eyes — SEX 13
ON ICE TILL C. OF PLAY — TELEGRAMS 13
closed Philadelphia, but it was c. — TOWNS 14
with a c. door — CINEMA 50
closes Satire is what c. Saturday — THEATRE 32

close-ups Collins lens on me for c.

comedy (*cont.*):
most lamentable c.   THEATRE 47
rules for great c.   HUMOUR 36
comes c. again in the morning   SOCIETY 22
comfort not ecstasy but it was c.   MARRIAGE 50
comfortable c. estate of widowhood
    MARRIAGE 61
comfortably lived c. so long together
    MARRIAGE 62
comforts attempt to recapture the c.   TRAVEL 3
comic c. with the cosmic   UNIVERSE 12
comma Whence came the intrusive c.
    WRITING 9
command give a single c.   POWER 9
commander C. of the Bath   ROYALTY 5
commandments first nine c.   CINEMA 51
Five C.   FILMS 3
only ten c.   BIBLE 2
satisfied with Ten C.   PRESIDENTS 3
ten c.   HANDWRITING 8
commences long enough after it c.   MUSIC 50
commendably speaking c. of anybody
    CONVERSATION 1
comment C. is free   JOURNALISM 19
couldn't possibly c.   COMEDY 43
commentators learned c.   CRITICS 35
commerce obstructed interstate c.   SEX 39
commercial you're labelled c.   MUSIC 35
commercialism [C.] is doing well   BUSINESS 21
commit refusing to c. oneself   BEHAVIOUR 20
committed c. breakfast with it   VIRTUE 11
committee c. discussions   BUREAUCRACY 12
c.'s idea   DESCRIPTION 25
horse designed by a c.   BUREAUCRACY 10
written by a c.   BIBLE 6
commode Chipperfield c.   WIT 43
common c. murderer   COOKERY 19
c. where the climate's sultry   SEX 23
Horseguards and still be c.   SOCIETY 18
members of the c. throng   ARISTOCRACY 8
commonplace loop on a c.   WIT 22
commons C. must bray   ARISTOCRACY 11
common sense defiance of c.   ARCHITECTURE 9
importance of things which c.   LITERATURE 26
likes sports hates c.   SPORTS 20
never ascribe c.   GOD 32
Nothing but c.   LAW 27
commotion she likes lights and c.   SOCIETY 10
communicate trying to c. with me   DRUGS 1
communist C. Party   ACTING 16
Is he a C.   PREJUDICE 3
commuter C.—one who spends his life
    TRAVEL 31

company C. for carrying on   SECRECY 1
c. he chooses   ALCOHOL 12
C. of Four   THEATRE 60
play it the c. way   BUSINESS 9
Running a c.   BUSINESS 13
steal out of your c.   CRIME 28
comparisons C. are odorous   WIT 30
compassion c. in the very name   THE CLERGY 24
compensate c. people for the damage
    LITERATURE 38
competition home c.   HUMOUR 4
competitive Sex was a c. event   SEX 34
squash is a c. activity   SPORTS 4
complain hardly knows to whom to c.
    UNIVERSE 8
complexion convictions and her c.   COLOURS 6
compliance by a timely c.   SEX 32
compos non c. penis   CRITICS 23
composed c. for the retreat   ARMED FORCES 20
composer blind c.   FILMS 12
c. and *not* homosexual   MUSICIANS 7
c. did not leave directions   SONGS 2
c. is to be dead   MUSICIANS 9
composers I don't like c. who think   MUSIC 13
composing Is he still c.   MUSICIANS 8
compromise c. with being swallowed
    CHOICE 13
compulsion What c. compels them   TRAVEL 6
compulsory Blood is c.   THEATRE 53
computer c. in every   COMPUTERS 4
modern c.   COMPUTERS 2
never was in my c.   HAPPINESS 16
requires a c.   COMPUTERS 1
conceal c. our whereabouts   PLACES 18
conceited It makes me far too c.
    SELF-KNOWLEDGE 29
conceived c. three times   PRESIDENTS 5
concentrates c. his mind   DEATH 34
concert definition for C.   MUSIC 41
concertina Rum, Bum and C.   TITLES 4
concerts c. you enjoy together   MARRIAGE 118
concession only c. to gaiety   WALES 6
conclaves in stately c.   GOVERNMENT 4
Concorde put at the controls of C.
    TECHNOLOGY 11
concubine c. to an opium addict   WOMEN 70
concubines I had three c.   ROYALTY 26
Twenty-two acknowledged c.   ROYALTY 40
concussed born c.   CLASS 19
concussion Acquired c.   CLASS 19
condemned c. veal   ACTORS 5
conditions if you have the c.   SUCCESS 37
conducting c. an orchestra   DIPLOMACY 15
conductor affair with a c.   MEN AND WOMEN 51
conductors foreign c.   MUSIC 6

cones enough traffic c. — TRANSPORT 37
confession after the sweetness of c. — RELIGION 21
confessional c. passage has probably — WRITERS 37
   invent the c. — RELIGION 72
confidential I give c. briefings — SECRECY 11
conflict C. and Art — FOOTBALL 17
confused but a bit c. — BODY 29
   more c. than it found it — LAW 31
confusion of an unparalleled c. — WRITERS 21
congealing You feel your blood c. — WEATHER 12
congeals When love c. — LOVE 25
congratulation matter for c. — IDEAS 6
congregation landlord to the whole c. — RELIGION 2
conjecture wholesale returns of c. — SCIENCE 32
conked c. out on November 15th — EPITAPHS 14
connections scientist without industry c. — SCIENCE 27
conquer urge to c. Poland — MUSIC 1
conscience cut my c. — POLITICS 38
   live with a good c. — HYPOCRISY 8
   your c. well under control — POLITICS 44
conscious c. life got higher up — UNIVERSE 13
consent I will ne'er c. — SEX 24
consenting only between c. adults — SEX 85
conservation make a speech on c. — NATURE 9
   our stomachs, but of c. — NATURE 7
conservative c. when old — POLITICAL PARTIES 7
   nothing if not c. — FOOD 15
   Or else a little C. — POLITICAL PARTIES 8
   sound C. government — POLITICAL PARTIES 4
   which makes a man more c. — PAST 7
conservatives C. do not believe — POLITICAL PARTIES 9
   On lawns of true C. — SNOBBERY 14
consistency I have no c. — POLITICS 19
consolation c. in a distressed one — SNOBBERY 2
   that's one c. — CRIME 11
conspiracy c. theory — GOVERNMENT 18
   c. to make you happy — AMERICA 27
   Indecency's c. of silence — VIRTUE 18
   really in a c. against him — TECHNOLOGY 13
constable C. had taken — ART 31
constabulary c. duty's to be done — HAPPINESS 6
constancy c. of the women who love me — WOMEN 63
constant nothing in this world c. — VIRTUE 20
   Such a c. lover — LOVE 43
   than a woman c. — WIT 6
constipation c. is the big fear — SICKNESS 15
constituency won our own c. — SUCCESS 26
constitution holy resignation and an iron c. — MEDICINE 25
   left out of the C. — GOD 43

consume can c. locally — COUNTRIES 50
   c. like soup — POETRY 3
consumer c. isn't a moron — ADVERTISING 12
consumerism first rule of c. — BUSINESS 2
consummation retired from c. — SEX 76
consumption galloping c. you had — SICKNESS 4
contemplation Has left for c. — RELIGION 10
contempt c. for human nature — SELF-KNOWLEDGE 24
   Familiarity breeds c. — FAMILY 49
contest end a c. quicker — ALCOHOL 58
continency chastity and c. — SEX 11
continental C. people have sex life — SEX 51
   may be quite c. — WEALTH 26
contraception word about oral c. — SEX 2
contract c. is so one-sided — LAW 9
   not yet signed her c. — ACTORS 30
   verbal c. — CINEMA 21
contractions cheap c. — ADVERTISING 2
   uterine c. — HEALTH 7
contradict I never c. — ROYALTY 25
contradiction c. in terms — RELIGION 64
contralto Her shrill c. — PEOPLE 17
contraption TV —a clever c. — TELEVISION 1
contribution valuable c. — DEATH 47
control conscience well under c. — POLITICS 44
   kept rigidly under c. — CENSORSHIP 3
   unless it is kept under c. — VIRTUE 12
conversation art of c. — CONVERSATION 9
   elegant c. — CONVERSATION 3
   flagging c. — CONVERSATION 12
   followed c. as a shark — WIT 20
   go on with the c. — CONVERSATION 32
   improved by a little light c. — SPORTS 16
   I steered my c. onwards — ROYALTY 52
   lack a flair for c. — SCIENCE 23
   lady's c. — COUNTRY 13
   make his c. — CONVERSATION 25
   ordinary c. — CONVERSATION 15
   pause in c. — MARRIAGE 47
conversational c. overachiever — CONVERSATION 17
conversations without pictures or c. — LITERATURE 13
convert expect to c. England — RELIGION 55
convictions c. for drunken driving — ALCOHOL 10
   man of no c. — CERTAINTY 12
convincing less c. than one — ARGUMENT 11
cook chef and a c. — COOKERY 10
   c. in the kitchen — MARRIAGE 68
   C. is a little unnerved — SOCIETY 3
   C. my own lunch — COOKERY 1
   uncommon c. — COOKERY 19
cooked c. a few meals — MARRIAGE 40

cousins sisters and his c.   FAMILY 18
Coutts banks with C.   CLASS 16
cover arrived to c. it   JOURNALISM 20
cow c. is of the bovine ilk   ANIMALS 35
   Don't have a c., man   COMEDY 5
   it was an open c.   LAW 13
   like a c. in a milk bar   PUBLISHING 17
   pet is a c.   ANIMALS 9
cows worse than a herd of dairy c.   NEWSPAPERS 9
coy c. desperation   ARCHITECTURE 16
   Other girls are c.   WOMEN 31
crab grimly playful c.   CRICKET 13
cradle hand that rocked the c.   DEATH 4
crap Copperfield kind of c.   AUTOBIOGRAPHY 22
   floating c. game   BETTING 11
crash c.! BANG! BLURP   MISTAKES 18
   c. is coming   ALCOHOL 48
   c. they had yesterday   TRANSPORT 20
crashing c. toy trains   TRANSPORT 5
craving no stronger c.   WEALTH 22
crawl c. in or kick your way in   POLITICS 12
crazy football c.   FOOTBALL 13
   Is that man c.   SECRECY 3
   should they go c.   POLITICIANS 26
creation exception in the case of *The C.*   MUSIC 36
   Had I been present at the C.   UNIVERSE 1
creator C. made Italy   COUNTRIES 59
creatures animated c.   HUMAN RACE 8
credit greatly to his c.   ENGLAND 13
   I never seek to take the c.   LITERATURE 30
   people who get the c.   SUCCESS 24
   very much to his c.   EXAMINATIONS 1
creditors c. press you for debts   DEBT 9
creep Almost any c.'ll   GOVERNMENT 14
crème c. de la crème   EDUCATION 43
Crete people of C.   COUNTRIES 50
crew haircut will be c.   FAMILY 17
cricket c. of the performing arts   THEATRE 17
   It's not c. to picket   POLITICS 64
   looked upon c.   CRICKET 15
   not in support of c.   CRICKET 5
   to dare in c.   CRICKET 12
cricketer modern professional c.   CRICKET 7
crime c. you haven't committed   OLD AGE 33
   newspaper prints a sex c.   NEWSPAPERS 27
   UNDULY EMPHASISING C.   TELEGRAMS 2
   We like c.   CRIME 8
crimes respect of those c.   CRIME 30
   worst of c. is poverty   POVERTY 18
criminal c. investigation   CRIME 26
   ends I think c.   GOVERNMENT 22
crinolines top hats and C.   BUSINESS 11
cripple cannot meet a c.   CONVERSATION 3

crisis cannot be a c.   DIPLOMACY 8
   only panics in a c.   POLITICAL PARTIES 12
   real c. on your hands   NATURE 10
critic c. is a man   CRITICS 38
   c. spits on what is done   POETS 5
   in honour of a c.   CRITICS 33
   is a dramatic c.   CRITICS 25
   Times c. said   CRITICS 2
critical c. period in matrimony   MARRIAGE 71
criticism cant of c.   HYPOCRISY 9
   C. is a study   CRITICS 20
   c. is ever inhibited by ignorance   POLITICS 50
   C. is not only   CRITICS 32
criticize Never c. Americans   AMERICA 21
criticized c. is not always to be wrong   SELF-KNOWLEDGE 7
critics all good dramatic c.   CRITICS 11
   C. are like eunuchs   CRITICS 7
   C. search for ages   CRITICS 40
   know who the c. are   CRITICS 12
   lot of c.   CRITICS 24
   murderers or c.   ART 14
   of Music Among C.   CRITICS 31
crochet c. week in Rhyl   HOLIDAYS 13
crook told him he was a c.   CRIME 24
crooning c. like a bilious pigeon   LANGUAGES 20
cross adjective 'c.'   ANGER 11
   having a c. word   ARGUMENT 10
   orgasm has replaced the C.   RELIGION 45
   un-nailed from the c.   ACTORS 12
cross-dressing about c.   FASHION 28
crossed Was the cow c.   LAW 13
crossing double c. of a pair of heels   LOVE 25
crossroads faces a c.   CHOICE 1
crow arse of a c.   FOOTBALL 2
   had the old c. over   POETS 10
crown c. of thorns *and* the thirty   POLITICS 11
   deserve a c.   ROYALTY 3
crucifixion after the C.   FILMS 14
cruel Such c. glasses   INSULTS 22
cruelty supposed act of c.   LOVE 32
crumpet thinking man's c.   WOMEN 50
Crusades book about the C.   BOOKS 3
crushed c. life is what I lead   MARRIAGE 93
crutch kick in the c.   ANGER 4
   Reality is a c.   DRUGS 9
cry babe with a c.   DEATH 25
   c. into your beer   ALCOHOL 41
cryptogram charm of a c.   AUTOBIOGRAPHY 19
crystal C. Palace was   ARCHITECTURE 10
cuckoo c. clock   COUNTRIES 61
   sudden c.   COUNTRIES 62
cucumber c. should be well sliced   COOKERY 12
   when c. is added   FOOD 44

cucumbers extracting sun-beams out of c. SCIENCE 30
cuddlesome seeing nature as c. NATURE 8
cuddly c. in a frightening DOGS 1
kissable, c., and smelling good MEN AND WOMEN 9
culture c. could have produced WRITERS 41
pursue C. in bands ART 32
cultured real or c. FAME 13
cumbersome ridiculously c. INSULTS 16
cunning I have a c. plan COMEDY 22
cup c. of tea in the morning DRUGS 4
curable Love's a disease. But c. LOVE 31
curate albino c. FRIENDS 23
bland country c. APPEARANCE 2
I feel like a shabby c. SCIENCE 3
like a Protestant c. DANCE 12
pale young c. THE CLERGY 10
remember the average c. THE CLERGY 9
very name of a C. THE CLERGY 24
curates preached to death by wild c. RELIGION 67
cure in the twentieth, it's a c. SEX 79
no C. for this Disease MEDICINE 5
They know the c. SICKNESS 17
you have a c. MEDICINE 35
cured C. yesterday of my disease MEDICINE 29
cures No herb ever c. anything MEDICINE 20
curiosity lost all c. AUTOBIOGRAPHY 24
Love, c., freckles, and doubt LOVE 36
curious like c. clothes FASHION 30
curiouser C. and curiouser WIT 5
curse c. of the drinking classes WORK 30
Fathers don't c. PARENTS 8
journalistic c. of Eve JOURNALISM 24
curtail desire to c. CENSORSHIP 12
curtain after the c. has risen ROYALTY 44
c. was up THEATRE 34
her c. calls ACTORS 12
remove the c. rings FASHION 17
curtains C. in orange nylon HOME 1
c. looked like duvets HOTELS 2
sew rings on the new c. INSULTS 9
curtsey C. while you're thinking BEHAVIOUR 6
Curzon second Lady C. DEATH 18
cushions c. had cushions HOTELS 2
custard bathed us like warm c. DESCRIPTION 5
custom aid of prejudice and c. PREJUDICE 7
cut BETTER AFTER IT'S BEEN C. TELEGRAMS 5
c. my conscience to fit POLITICS 38
right of final c. CINEMA 51
cuter When I was c. MIDDLE AGE 10
cutlet enough if he eats a c. WRITERS 27
cutting damned c. and slashing PUBLISHING 6
cuttings press c. to prove it ACTORS 27
cymbal like an ill-tuned c. JUDGES 16

cynic What is a c. CHARACTER 19
cynical c. about politicians POLITICS 77
cynics composed of c. GOVERNMENT 29

d I mean Big D. TOWNS 24
I never use a big, big D. LANGUAGE 10
dad your mum and d. PARENTS 10
dada art belongs to D. ART 22
mama of d. LITERATURE 17
daddy D. sat up very late ALCOHOL 9
English teacher D.-o EDUCATION 27
dagger d. in one hand POLITICAL PARTIES 20
daintily must have things d. served SOCIETY 3
Dalai horns of a D. Lama WIT 46
Dallas that spells D. TOWNS 24
damage compensate people for the d. LITERATURE 38
dame refer to her at all times as D. NAMES 23
dameship recipient of a D. HAPPINESS 16
dammed saved by being d. COUNTRIES 30
damn no general idea is worth a d. IDEAS 4
old man who said 'D.' TRANSPORT 17
damnation didn't mind d. FUTURE 11
damnations Twenty-nine distinct d. BIBLE 1
damned lies, d. lies and statistics LIES 6
Life is just one d. thing LIFE 15
music is the brandy of the d. MUSIC 48
public be d. BUSINESS 20
those d. dots ECONOMICS 3
written a d. play THEATRE 44
damp like a d. mackintosh DESCRIPTION 11
damped d. by ceaseless CHARACTER 2
dance I'm giving a d. SATISFACTION 10
join the d. DANCE 4
no d. on Sunday DANCE 17
dances Also d. FILM STARS 1
dancing mature women, d. DANCE 7
dandelion parsnip or d. ALCOHOL 5
dandelions ability of d. to tell the time TIME 10
dandy Candy is d. ALCOHOL 45
Dane if you've got a great D. THEATRE 33
play a D. ACTING 5
danger be in less d. FAMILY 29
But only when in d. RELIGION 53
dangerous d. as an author WRITERS 46
D. Dan McGrew MEN AND WOMEN 41
d. when active CENSORSHIP 7
Science becomes d. SCIENCE 29
Daniel lionized was D. HUMAN RACE 12
Daniels den of D. FRIENDS 25
dank d. rock pools FOOD 45
dare It wouldn't d. TRANSPORT 6
dark those d. glasses FILM STARS 10
darken Never d. my Dior FASHION 22
darling oh, he's a d. man MEN 12

date keep them up to date — YOUTH 6
dated d. decor — POLITICIANS 36
dates broken d. — LOVE 24
  question of d. — TRUST 14
daughter Don't put your d. — ACTING 8
  Elderly ugly d. — LOVE 21
  I'm your d. — SONGS 14
daughter-in-law her own d. — FAMILY 21
daughters D. are best — FAMILY 5
David D. wrote the Psalms — RELIGION 46
Davy D. Abominated gravy — SCIENCE 5
day Another d. gone — HUMOUR 29
  as his 'd. mayor' — CHOICE 7
  d. away from Tallulah — DESCRIPTION 13
  d. war broke out — WAR 32
  D. will break — FOOD 16
  During the d. — MARRIAGE 116
  I knew Doris D. — SEX 49
  when people write every other d. — LETTERS 8
daylight skulk in broad d. — PEOPLE 21
days five or six d. — POLITICS 20
daytime You know d. television — TELEVISION 21
dead all our best men are d. — LITERATURE 31
  blooming well d. — DEATH 62
  character d. — GOSSIP 12
  composer is to be d. — MUSICIANS 9
  d., and buried at last — DEATH 39
  d., or my watch has stopped — DEATH 42
  d. bird — FASHION 7
  d. bird — OLD AGE 12
  d. for a year — SUCCESS 19
  d. for the next two months — LETTERS 15
  d. or deported — TELEVISION 11
  d. sinner revised — VIRTUE 3
  For being d. — DEATH 12
  hopes of dropping d. — DEATH 31
  if I am d. — DEATH 29
  Lord Jones D. — JOURNALISM 8
  Mayfair of the d. — DEATH 59
  must be d. — DEATH 7
  Not many d. — NEWSPAPERS 10
  Once you're d. — DEATH 57
  rot the d. talk — DEATH 6
  seen d. with — DEATH 72
  think that Ned Sherrin is d. — BROADCASTING 3
  was alive and is d. — EPITAPHS 4
  wealthy and d. — DEATH 66
  wench is d. — SEX 47
deaded told you I'd be d. — DEATH 43
deadlock Holy d. — MARRIAGE 72
deadly d. in the long run — EDUCATION 44
deaf d. man to a blind woman — MARRIAGE 34
  longing to be absolutely d. — MUSIC 56
  old man's getting d. as well — OLD AGE 11
deafness Her d. is a great privation — RELIGION 74

dean I am the D. of Christ Church — PRIDE 9
  To our queer old d. — WIT 41
dear D. 338171 — LETTERS 6
dearth d. of bad pictures — CINEMA 15
death between wife and d. — DEATH 49
  d., sex and jewels — ART 27
  d., which happened — DEATH 30
  D. and marriage are raging — MARRIAGE 75
  d. and taxes — DEATH 22
  D. and taxes and childbirth — DEATH 44
  D. has got something — DEATH 3
  D. is always a great pity — DEATH 65
  D. is the most convenient — DEATH 38
  d. is unreliable — DEATH 8
  d. of a political economist — ECONOMICS 1
  improved by d. — DEATH 61
  in the face of d. — TELEVISION 6
  loving ourselves to d. — POLITICAL PARTIES 16
  makes d. a long-felt want — INSULTS 49
  my d. duties — DEATH 67
  no drinking after d. — ALCOHOL 29
  old maid is like d. by drowning — OLD AGE 19
  preached to d. — RELIGION 67
  put the worst to d. — DEATH 28
  quality of d. — COUNTRIES 10
  Reports of my d. — DEATH 68
  terror to d. — BIOGRAPHY 16
  thought of d. — DEATH 63
debating d. competition — MARRIAGE 82
  It is the Lords d. — ROYALTY 15
debauchery Drink and d. — GOLF 2
debt National D. — DEBT 8
debts get caught up on your d. — CINEMA 37
  If I hadn't my d. — DEBT 10
  press you for d. — DEBT 9
début never make one's d. with a scandal — OLD AGE 40
decadence Everywhere one looks, d. — PROGRESS 1
decay one argues a d. of parts — WIT 6
deceived willingness to be d. — SELF-KNOWLEDGE 19
deceiving nearly d. your friends — LIES 5
decency D. is Indecency's conspiracy — VIRTUE 18
  d. is sort of secret — CHARACTER 15
decent d. people live beyond — SOCIETY 20
decipherable was d. — HANDWRITING 6
deciphering only hope of d. — HANDWRITING 2
decisions d. he is allowed to take — BUREAUCRACY 13
declare nothing to d. except my genius — INTELLIGENCE 17
decline d. two drinks — LANGUAGES 23
  I went into a bit of a d. — PAST 1
decompose d. in a barrel — DEATH 21
decomposing Baytch is d. — MUSICIANS 8

decorative be d. and to do right WOMEN 22
decoyed see these poor fools d. MARRIAGE 97
decrepit I was easily the most d. OLD AGE 31
dedicated d. follower FASHION 9
d. himself so many times PRESIDENTS 15
deduct teach him to d. EDUCATION 25
deep d. peace of the double-bed MARRIAGE 29
treading water in the d. end TAXES 1
deeper shown a d. sense DEATH 23
defeat d. *a law of God* FOOLISHNESS 31
In d. unbeatable WAR 7
defectors D. are like grapes TRUST 12
defendant d., Mr Haddock WRITERS 15
d. became insane MURDER 12
defining d. what is unknown DICTIONARIES 12
definite d. maybe CERTAINTY 11
deflowered At last you are d. TELEGRAMS 7
defoliant aerosol d. GARDENS 8
degenerated Newspapers, even, have d.
NEWSPAPERS 39
degree I know I've got a d. INTELLIGENCE 20
deity between the D. and the Drains PEOPLE 41
delayed d. till I am indifferent INSULTS 24
deliberately d. tries to hurt MEN 1
delight English D. TRAVEL 7
delighted You have d. us long enough
SATISFACTION 2
delightful It's d., it's delicious MARRIAGE 102
delinquents Three juvenile d. CRIME 8
delusion Love is the d. LOVE 34
delusions d. of Christianity RELIGION 65
demand not a note of d. MUSIC 44
some less delightful d. MARRIAGE 22
demented d. refrigerator THEATRE 45
d. typewriter ACTORS 14
de Mille Cecil B. d. CINEMA 2
demi-tasses With your villainous d.
POVERTY 19
democracy D. is the name DEMOCRACY 7
D. is the recurrent DEMOCRACY 16
D. is the theory DEMOCRACY 10
D. means DEMOCRACY 3
D. means GOVERNMENT 3
D. means simply DEMOCRACY 17
D. seldom had a ruder shock SPEECHES 10
less d. to save WAR 3
not the voting that's d. DEMOCRACY 15
say about d. DEMOCRACY 4
triumph for d. DEMOCRACY 9
Under d. DEMOCRACY 11
democrat Santa Claus is a D.
POLITICAL PARTIES 15
democrats stop telling lies about D. POLITICS 72
demonstrator obligation of the d. ARGUMENT 14
dental 'D. Hygienist' has been added WOMEN 1

dentist consulting a d. regularly MEDICINE 27
D. fills WIT 13
I'd sooner go to my d. SEX 86
talk like a d. BEHAVIOUR 37
dentists on a level with d. ECONOMICS 8
dentures find her d. FOOD 13
denunciation d. of the young GENERATION GAP 10
deny d. nothing CERTAINTY 6
I never d. ROYALTY 25
denying not d. anything CERTAINTY 19
deoch-an-doris Just a wee d. ALCOHOL 43
department outpatient's d. OLD AGE 10
deported dead or d. TELEVISION 11
they would be d. CHRISTMAS 5
deposit d. in my name GOD 2
depressing d. the keys of the machine MUSIC 9
depression child of the D. POVERTY 5
d. when you lose BUSINESS 18
got him on tablets for d. MEDICINE 6
source of d. APPEARANCE 23
depths Down in the d. HOPE 9
derangement nice d. of epitaphs WIT 33
description Damn d. DESCRIPTION 7
desert d. island with Napoleon WRITERS 22
Zuleika on a d. island WOMEN 3
deserve d. a crown ROYALTY 3
d. to get it DEMOCRACY 10
desiccated d. calculating machine POLITICIANS 8
design there is a d. BORES 14
designer d. jeans FASHION 31
designs His d. were strictly honourable
MARRIAGE 55
desire d. should so many years SEX 70
get your heart's d. HAPPINESS 13
horizontal d. DANCE 16
provokes the d. ALCOHOL 54
desk manuscript in his d. WRITERS 40
subservience to the d. BUREAUCRACY 7
desks Stick close to your d. ARMED FORCES 10
despair form of d. HOPE 1
leads to d. CHOICE 1
sign of d. FASHION 40
upgrades d. MONEY 14
desperately D. accustomed SPEECHES 3
desperation coy d. ARCHITECTURE 16
despised I always d. Mr Tattle MARRIAGE 37
destination getting man to his ultimate d.
TRANSPORT 2
destined d. to bloom late APPEARANCE 20
destiny d. of bores BORES 8
destroy Whom the gods wish to d. SUCCESS 7
destruction Total d. GOD 30
detective borrows a d. story READING 12
detectives our d. improved MURDER 14
detest d. him more FRIENDS 11

dip quick d. in bed — HEALTH 11
diplomacy D.—lying in state — DIPLOMACY 7
diplomat D. these days — DIPLOMACY 17
distinction of a d. — DIPLOMACY 14
diplomats D. tell lies — GOVERNMENT 24
direct d. this play the way you — THEATRE 15
direful something d. in the sound — TOWNS 3
dirt d. doesn't get any worse — HOME 12
not a d. gardener — GARDENS 1
dirty At D. Dick's — ALCOHOL 4
d. minds — CENSORSHIP 23
d. or not — BEHAVIOUR 2
give pornography a d. name — THEATRE 5
in a d. glass — FOOD 56
wet and d. from hunting — APPEARANCE 26
disagreeable no person so perfectly d.
— WRITERS 46
disappointed been d. as often as I have
— MEN AND WOMEN 9
d. in human nature — HUMAN RACE 4
never be d. — HOPE 8
Sir! you have d. us — POLITICIANS 6
disappointment are a bitter d. — CHILDREN 38
bitter d. — FOOTBALL 10
ceaseless d. — CHARACTER 2
disasters d. of English history — WALES 7
disbelief ferocious d. — DESCRIPTION 22
disciple His Own D. Shall wound him — TRUST 10
disciples has his d. — BIOGRAPHY 17
discipline D. must be maintained — MARRIAGE 49
parents may be difficult to d. — PARENTS 12
discomfort tolerate without d. — SATISFACTION 8
discourage d. our better emotions — CHILDREN 33
discouragements with the same d. — TRAVEL 15
discovered dramatist who had d. himself
— THEATRE 46
discovery d. of a new dish — COOKERY 6
his usual sense of d. — SPEECHES 17
Medicinal d. — MEDICINE 3
discreet more dull than a d. diary — DIARIES 3
discretion D. is not the better — BIOGRAPHY 12
discuss stay and d. them — GOVERNMENT 44
discussing d. on the same level — DIPLOMACY 3
d. sex — CHILDREN 21
disdain my dear Lady D. — INSULTS 40
disease Cured yesterday of my d. — MEDICINE 29
d. I haven't got — SICKNESS 20
d. that afflicts — ART 5
entanglement with an infectious d. — RELIGION 7
if they cannot ascertain a d. — MEDICINE 19
Life is a sexually transmitted d. — LIFE 2
Love's a d. But curable — LOVE 31
nineteenth century, it was a d. — SEX 79
no Cure for this D. — MEDICINE 5
When men die of d. — SICKNESS 22

diseases d. are innumerable — COOKERY 20
lists of fatal d. — MEDICINE 16
scientific treatment for all d. — MEDICINE 32
To talk of d. — SICKNESS 18
disgrace It's no d. t'be poor — POVERTY 10
tinge of d. — GOSSIP 10
disgruntled if not actually d. — SATISFACTION 15
disgusting it is always d. — DESCRIPTION 7
more d. than an oratorio — MUSIC 51
dish discovery of a new d. — COOKERY 6
dishabilly One cannot be devout in d.
— RELIGION 20
disinherit Fathers don't curse, they d.
— PARENTS 8
disinherited d. by the out of pocket — MIND 2
disinheriting d. countenance — CHARACTER 12
disinterred sometimes be d. by chance — LAW 26
dislike my d. is purely platonic — SEX 82
with that d. — FRIENDS 19
Disney Walt D. Corporation — FAME 2
Disneyland Americans with no D. — COUNTRIES 41
dispoged when I am so d. — ALCOHOL 21
Disraeli D. school of Prime Ministers
— PRIME MINISTERS 6
Disraelis Gladstones or D. — POLITICS 76
disrespectfully d. of Society — SOCIETY 25
dissected d. at the least one woman
— MARRIAGE 11
dissed royally d. — AWARDS 1
distinction d. between virtue and vice
— VIRTUE 10
few escape that d. — PRIDE 13
man of d. — MEN AND WOMEN 11
merciless class d. — APPEARANCE 19
distinctions class d. — CLASS 23
unused to making fine d. — PEOPLE 31
distraction Genitals are a great d. — SEX 19
diver Don't forget the d. — COMEDY 4
divine it feels d. — VIRTUE 27
Right D. of Kings — ROYALTY 58
division D. is as bad — SCIENCE 2
divisions How many d. has *he* got — POWER 10
divorce D. never — MARRIAGE 73
when I d. I keep the house — MARRIAGE 58
divorced If Gloria hadn't divorced me — FAMILY 21
my fault that we got d. — MARRIAGE 2
divorcee gay d. — THEATRE 16
do by the clock d. it — SEX 27
Can I d. you now — COMEDY 2
d. just what you like — BEHAVIOUR 29
d. to his mother — THEATRE 50
d. what I say — GOVERNMENT 41
he'll say d. this, do that — PRESIDENTS 17

down D. in the depths — HOPE 9
 meet 'em on your way d. — SUCCESS 23
downcast feel a little d. — DEATH 39
dozens Mother to d. — WOMEN 36
drag being a d. queen — FASHION 14
 d. queen's like — APPEARANCE 11
 D. them down — LIFE 9
dragon father was a d. — FAMILY 34
drain leave by the first town d. — WIT 42
drains Better D. — GARDENS 6
 between the Deity and the D. — PEOPLE 41
 unblock your d. — HOME 14
drake D. himself, confronted — TRAVEL 15
dramatic all good d. critics — CRITICS 11
 is a d. critic — CRITICS 25
dramatist d. who had discovered himself
      THEATRE 46
drank at dinner and supper, I d. — ALCOHOL 50
draughts peculiarly susceptible to d. — PRIDE 14
draw COULDN'T D. IN THIS HOUSE — TELEGRAMS 15
 d. right to the finish — DEATH 32
 right arm to d. — ART 2
drawback considered to be a great d.
      PUBLISHING 3
drawbacks everything has its d. — DEATH 33
dream d. you are crossing the Channel
      TRANSPORT 11
 living the American d. — GENERATION GAP 8
 say what d. it was — SLEEP 9
 They d. in courtship — MARRIAGE 100
dreamed d. of cheese — SLEEP 10
dreams City of perspiring d. — TOWNS 28
dredger sharp end of a d. — ARGUMENT 22
dress All women d. like their mothers
      MEN AND WOMEN 2
 automobile changed our d. — TRANSPORT 21
 cool, white d. — RELIGION 21
 like to d. egos — FASHION 37
 plain in d. — WOMEN 47
dressed d. with pepper — COOKERY 12
drier Or come up d. — FOOLISHNESS 17
drifted Snow White . . . but I d. — VIRTUE 25
drink buy a d. from both — HEALTH 10
 don't d. liquor — ALCOHOL 38
 D., sir, is a great provoker — ALCOHOL 54
 D. and debauchery — GOLF 2
 d. and women — EDUCATION 41
 D. Canada Dry — ALCOHOL 7
 D.! Drink — COMEDY 6
 d. it himself — FOOD 89
 d. one another's healths — ALCOHOL 35
 d. too much coffee — POLITICAL PARTIES 14
 gave up d. — FOOD 1
 has taken to d. — ALCOHOL 63
 in favour iv d. — ALCOHOL 23

meat, d. and cigarettes — HEALTH 9
One more d. — ALCOHOL 49
we could d. all day — WEALTH 29
What a world of d. he swills — ROYALTY 45
woman drove me to d. — ALCOHOL 28
your husband I would d. it — INSULTS 6
drinking curse of the d. classes — WORK 30
 no d. after death — ALCOHOL 29
drinks d. as much as you do — ALCOHOL 64
dripping electricity was d. invisibly — SCIENCE 31
drive can't d. the car — CRITICS 38
 d. away in another — TRANSPORT 15
 d. has gone to pieces — GOLF 1
driven pure as the d. slush — VIRTUE 1
driver in the d.'s seat — PRIME MINISTERS 4
drop don't d. players — FOOTBALL 19
 one d. of Negro blood — PREJUDICE 8
drove d. it into a big wall — TRANSPORT 23
 woman d. me to drink — ALCOHOL 28
drowned d. by the waves — SONGS 8
drowning death by d. — OLD AGE 19
drudge harmless d. — DICTIONARIES 8
drug depends what miracle d. — MEDICINE 2
 d. is neither — DRUGS 10
drugs can't cope with d. — DRUGS 9
 D. have taught — DRUGS 6
 D. is like getting up — DRUGS 4
 quality of his d. — DRUGS 5
drum d. out of the skin — PRIME MINISTERS 19
 Dumb as a d. — MUSIC 12
drunk d. for about a week — LIBRARIES 6
 I've tried him d. — ROYALTY 20
 not get d. at Lord's — CRICKET 7
 not so think as you d. — ALCOHOL 60
 stand around at a bar and get d. — SPORTS 24
 Winston, you're d. — INSULTS 12
 You're not d. — ALCOHOL 42
drunken convictions for d. driving — ALCOHOL 10
 d. porter — GOVERNMENT 31
dry Drink Canada D. — ALCOHOL 7
 d. she ain't — FILM STARS 12
 into a d. Martini — ALCOHOL 2
 Those d. Martinis — ALCOHOL 1
dryness morbid d. is a Whig vice — VIRTUE 2
Dubliners real D. lead — IRELAND 10
duchess every D. in London — PRIME MINISTERS 22
 married to a d. — PUBLISHING 22
duchesses four bereaved D. — ARISTOCRACY 2
duke avoided either d. — BIRDS 5
 D. of Fife — BEHAVIOUR 3
 enough who knows a d. — THE CLERGY 6
 palace of the D. of Ferrara — ARISTOCRACY 19
dukes drawing room full of d. — SCIENCE 3
 d. were three a penny — GOVERNMENT 10

dull always d. — ENGLAND 43
 Anger makes d. men witty — ANGER 2
 d. in a new way — BORES 9
 d. in himself — BORES 6
 land of the d. — AMERICA 28
 more d. than a discreet diary — DIARIES 3
 mostly it was just d. — WEATHER 4
 Only d. people — BORES 21
 paper appears d. — BORES 14
 quotations should be d. — QUOTATIONS 12
 service, and is very d. — TENNIS 6
 so d. that I can scarcely — BOOKS 3
 that he be d. — GOVERNMENT 1
dullness cardinal sin is d. — CINEMA 4
 cause of d. — BORES 6
 D. is so much stronger — BORES 5
dumb D. as a drum — MUSIC 12
 d. at the very moment when — MUSIC 56
 Our D. Friends — ALCOHOL 48
 so d. he can't fart — INSULTS 23
dum-dums NICHI NICHI'S D. — NEWSPAPERS 1
dumping eternal d. ground — FAME 6
dunce d. with wits — INSULTS 37
 How much a d. — FOOLISHNESS 6
Dunkremlin We call it D. — SECRECY 12
Dunlopillo preferred D. — ACTORS 37
Dunn Miss Joan Hunter D. — MEN AND WOMEN 3
dusk d. was performing — WIT 24
 d. with a light behind — WOMEN 25
dust d. on a Venetian blind — CRITICS 9
 Excuse My D. — EPITAPHS 19
dustbin d. upset in a high wind — SLEEP 4
Dutchmen wearing the shield of the D.
 — SPORTS 19
duties my death d. — DEATH 67
 neglect of his d. — INSULTS 48
 smaller d. of life — PRAISE 10
duty as if it were a painful d. — WRITERS 44
 declares that it is his d. — MORALITY 12
 do things from a sense of d. — MORALITY 9
 D. is what one expects — BEHAVIOUR 38
 d. of an Opposition — POLITICS 27
 d. to speak one's mind — MORALITY 16
 one d. we owe — HISTORY 17
duvets curtains looked like d. — HOTELS 2
dwarfs dozen red-bearded d. — JUDGES 13
dying Here I am, d. — DEATH 54
 If this is d. — LAST WORDS 8
 I'm fucking d. — SICKNESS 6
 stay d. here all night — ACTING 26
 through not d. — DEATH 2
 unconscionable time d. — ROYALTY 19
 without many of them d. — WORK 26
dynamite Several tons of d. — FILMS 2

dysfunctional head of a d. family — ROYALTY 55
ear cut his e. off — ART 19
 out of your wife's e. — ANIMALS 32
earl fourteenth e. is concerned — ARISTOCRACY 12
early came out too e. — RELIGION 57
 E. Grey omelettes — COOKERY 2
 E. to rise — DEATH 66
 think how e. I go — WORK 6
earn do least to e. it — HAPPINESS 2
earrings e. probably won't last — BUSINESS 12
ears E. like bombs — CHILDREN 10
 has long e. — APPEARANCE 4
 That man's e. — FILM STARS 8
earth E. is here so kind — COUNTRIES 34
 E. was not a rhombus — UNIVERSE 2
 heavy on him, E. — EPITAPHS 10
 meek shall inherit the e. — PRIDE 8
 — WEALTH 16
earthquake Small e. in Chile — NEWSPAPERS 10
 starts with an e. — CINEMA 22
easier e. job like publishing — PUBLISHING 1
Eastenders atrocious episode of E. — ROYALTY 53
Easter from E. Island. — POETS 10
eat E. my shorts — COMEDY 7
 E. the cast — COOKERY 13
 e. what I advertise — ALCOHOL 19
 I'll e. this planet — BOXING 6
 kill and e. them — ANIMALS 9
 look lovely and e. — TOWNS 10
 Man he e. the barracuda — NATURE 4
 publicly e. an entire dolphin — NATURE 6
 see what I e. — CONVERSATION 5
 sometimes has to e. them — WORDS 28
eating subject of e. — CONVERSATION 12
eats gentleman never e. — CLASS 1
eccentricity E., to be socially — BEHAVIOUR 19
eccentrics number of salaried e. — NEWSPAPERS 34
ecclesiologist keen e. — RELIGION 9
echo waiting for the e. — POETRY 17
echoes e. the sails of the yachts — PLACES 15
éclair backbone than a chocolate é.
 — PRESIDENTS 13
ecology new term 'e.' — NATURE 5
economical e. with the *actualité* — TRUTH 5
economics knew more about e. — EXAMINATIONS 3
 speech on e. — SPEECHES 7
economist death of a political e. — ECONOMICS 1
economists e. could manage — ECONOMICS 8
economy E. is going without — CHOICE 10
 E. was always 'elegant' — MONEY 10
 Political E. — DEBT 8
 Political E. — ECONOMICS 9
 Principles of Political E. — ECONOMICS 2
ecstasy not e. but it was comfort — MARRIAGE 50

ecumenical e. gesture	RELIGION 68
edible e. and the readable	FOOD 81
Edinburgh description of E.	TOWNS 29
Edith E. was not up to the dossiers	POLITICIANS 34
editions collecting of first editions	VIRTUE 9
e. and title-pages	BOOKS 5
editor brilliant writer in the e.'s chair	
	NEWSPAPERS 8
E.: a person employed	NEWSPAPERS 15
e. did it while I was away	NEWSPAPERS 25
If you are E. [of *The Times*]	NEWSPAPERS 9
editorial e. chair	MIND 6
editors e., and people with tapeworms	
	LANGUAGE 17
lazy e.	CRITICS 18
educate e. him first	EDUCATION 36
educated Cabinet ministers are e.	LITERATURE 7
education branch of e.	EDUCATION 35
e., taste	BEHAVIOUR 24
e. and catastrophe	HISTORY 16
E. in those elementary	EDUCATION 19
e. is what is left	EDUCATION 5
e. of men	EDUCATION 48
E. with socialists	EDUCATION 6
liberal e.	EDUCATION 2
poor e. I have received	EDUCATION 9
Soap and e.	EDUCATION 44
what I call e.	EDUCATION 42
educator overpaid as an e.	EDUCATION 33
Edwardian E. stuff	POLITICIANS 36
Edwardians E., on the contrary	HOLIDAYS 12
eel e.-and-pie yob	SNOBBERY 6
pick an e. out	HUMOUR 16
Eeyore E., the old grey Donkey	ANIMALS 29
effect believe it has any e. on me	SUCCESS 20
get the full e.	APPEARANCE 11
effort if that e. be too great	ROYALTY 7
effusive don't be too e.	PRAISE 4
egg demnition e.	FOOD 23
e.'s way of making	BIRDS 3
It looks like a poached e.	TRANSPORT 27
learned roast, an e.	COOKERY 16
like eating an e. without salt	
	MEN AND WOMEN 20
never see an e.	FOOD 22
still eat a boiled e.	OLD AGE 6
you've got a bad e.	FOOD 66
egghead E. weds hourglass	MARRIAGE 5
eggs all my e. in one bastard	SEX 62
e. are FANTASTIC	COOKERY 14
e. in one basket	BUSINESS 19
hardboiled e.	CHARACTER 21
Lays her e.	ANIMALS 28
ways to dress e.	COUNTRIES 44
egos like to dress e.	FASHION 37

Egypt Remember you're in E.	ACTING 28
eiderdown flurry of e.	BIRDS 4
eight We met at e.	OLD AGE 26
eighth I'm Henery the E., I am	MARRIAGE 90
eighty At e. life has clipped my claws	
	OLD AGE 22
eighty-two And shall be till I'm e.	YOUTH 2
Einstein E. who made the real trouble	
	SCIENCE 20
either How happy I could be with e.	LOVE 17
élan with admirable é.	POETRY 23
elbow e. has a fascination	BODY 18
elder to e. statesman	SUCCESS 14
elderly e. fellow	GOD 37
Judges commonly are e. men	JUDGES 9
Mr Salteena was an e. man of 42	OLD AGE 2
writing for an e. lady	JOURNALISM 14
eldest not the e. son	FAMILY 15
elected e. a President, not a Pope	PRESIDENTS 16
elections E. are won	DEMOCRACY 1
electric biggest e. train set	CINEMA 46
e. typewriters keep going	TECHNOLOGY 3
mend the E. Light	DEATH 10
electricity e. was dripping invisibly	SCIENCE 31
usefulness of e.	TECHNOLOGY 5
elegant Economy was always 'e.'	MONEY 10
e. simplicity	MONEY 23
elementary E., my dear Watson	CRIME 13
elephant e. seal	ANIMALS 37
life an e.'s	BODY 7
saw an E.	ANIMALS 10
They couldn't hit an e.	LAST WORDS 7
elephantiasis e. and other dread diseases	
	PLACES 13
elephants constant repetition of e.	TRAVEL 30
done the e.	TRAVEL 29
eleven e. at night	ALCOHOL 55
elf Cheese it is a peevish e.	FOOD 68
Elginbrodde Martin E.	EPITAPHS 16
Eliot I'd not read E.	POETS 14
élitist well-known é.	ARISTOCRACY 10
Elizabeth wickedness of E.	HISTORY 15
elms Behind the e. last night	SEX 67
elopement e. would be preferable	MARRIAGE 1
else does it to somebody e.	GOVERNMENT 32
happening to Somebody E.	HUMOUR 34
elsewhere something that happens e.	LIFE 5
elusive One's prime is e.	YOUTH 9
emasculated has not been e.	AUTOBIOGRAPHY 18
embalm e. each other	PARTIES 6
embalmer triumph of the e.'s art	PEOPLE 46
embarrass begins to e. other people	
	MIDDLE AGE 3

embarrassing e. pause   MARRIAGE 47
embarrassment Think of the e.   FAME 7
emblem e. of mortality   DEATH 20
embody e. the Law   LAW 11
embrace e. your Lordship's principles

    INSULTS 53
eminence e. by sheer gravitation   SUCCESS 30
éminence cerise *é. cerise*   ROYALTY 62
emotion poetry is an e.   POETRY 7
emotions gamut of the e.   ACTORS 31
emperor snuff-box from an E.   AMERICA 6
employees give your e. instructions   WORK 22
employer press harder upon the e.   WIT 40
employment known as gainful e.   WORK 1
empresses I don't think much of E.

    SNOBBERY 10
emptiness posed e.   FILM STARS 13
empty Bring on the e. horses   CINEMA 5
emulate most wanted to e.   ALCOHOL 6
encoded e. adjective is well developed   TENNIS 1
encouragement sympathy and e.   FAMILY 54
encyclopedia *Children's E.*   EDUCATION 12
end at his wit's e.   FOOLISHNESS 4
go on till you come to the e.   ROYALTY 16
ignorance that it can ever e.   LOVE 14
noise at one e.   CHILDREN 18
Where it will all e., knows God   NEWSPAPERS 13
where's it all going to e.   TIME 13
endangered even as an e. species   LAW 15
they were an e. species   LOVE 10
endearing e. bulls   ANIMALS 27
ending quickest way of e. a war   WAR 24
ends e. I think criminal   GOVERNMENT 22
see how it e.   EXAMINATIONS 7
similar sounds at their e.   POETRY 16
enemies choice of his e.   FRIENDS 27
conciliates e.   FRIENDS 1
forgiving one's e.   FRIENDS 26
hundred e.   HUMOUR 38
no time for making new e.   LAST WORDS 10
wish their e. dead   FRIENDS 13
enemy acute e.   BIOGRAPHY 1
better class of e.   FRIENDS 12
book of my e.   WRITERS 17
e. of good art   MARRIAGE 42
hasn't an e.   FRIENDS 24
men will have upon the e.   WAR 30
Morrison was his own worst e.   POLITICIANS 9
sleeps with the e.   MARRIAGE 6
your e. and your friend   FRIENDS 22
energy muster the glottal e.   TOWNS 19
engaged now I'm e.   MEN AND WOMEN 3
engagement e. should come   MARRIAGE 130
sort of eternal e.   MARRIAGE 9

engine e. [a watch] to our ears   TECHNOLOGY 16
e. in boots   SPORTS 13
e. of pollution   DOGS 7
e. that moves   TRANSPORT 17
England amusements in E.   ENGLAND 34
dowdiness in E.   ENGLAND 29
E. and America   COUNTRIES 55
expect to convert E.   RELIGION 55
France and E.   COUNTRIES 33
Good evening, E.   ENGLAND 26
he bored for E.   BORES 13
I left E. when I was four   ROYALTY 42
in E. a particular bashfulness   RELIGION 1
road that leads him to E.   SCOTLAND 5
stately homos of E.   SEX 28
summer in E.   WEATHER 26
taken for granted in E.   COUNTRY 19
English E., not being a spiritual   CRICKET 11
E. approach to ideas   IDEAS 9
E. are busy   ENGLAND 23
E. can be explained   ENGLAND 9
E. completely disappears   LANGUAGES 14
E. Delight   TRAVEL 7
E. have hot-water bottles   SEX 51
E. how to talk   CONVERSATION 31
E. manners   AMERICA 20
E. servants   COUNTRIES 6
E. up with which I will not put   LANGUAGE 5
if he went among the E.   SCOTLAND 2
it's in E.   CENSORSHIP 5
Larkin was so E.   ENGLAND 17
No one working in the E. language   PRIDE 15
Not to be E.   ENGLAND 18
of the E. language   LANGUAGES 16
old E. belief   ENGLAND 19
Opera in E.   SONGS 16
our E. nation   ENGLAND 11
speaking to you in E.   ENGLAND 26
strong E. accent   FASHION 34
think of the E. for a thing   LANGUAGES 7
understand E.   LANGUAGES 2
We E.   ENGLAND 5
Why can't the E. teach   LANGUAGES 14
Written E. is now inert   WRITING 10
Englishman average E.   ENGLAND 16
born an E.   ENGLAND 4
E., even if he is alone   ENGLAND 22
E. believes be heresy   RELIGION 64
E. considers   ENGLAND 2
E. does not travel   ENGLAND 36
E.'s house   ENGLAND 15
E. thinks   ENGLAND 30
genial E.   ENGLAND 38
He is an E.   ENGLAND 13
in the E.   ENGLAND 10

Englishman (*cont.*):

never find an E.	ENGLAND 40
remains an E.	COUNTRIES 26
to be an E.	ENGLAND 24
typical E.	ENGLAND 43
upstanding E.	ENGLAND 45

Englishmen E. never will be ENGLAND 31

honorary E.	COUNTRIES 35
Mad dogs and E.	ENGLAND 8
When two E. meet	WEATHER 13

Englishwoman E. is so refined ENGLAND 32

enjoy e. your book AUTOBIOGRAPHY 3

except how to e. it	LITERATURE 21
have to go out and e. it	WEATHER 24
not here to e. yourselves	THEATRE 9

enjoyment e. you've taken out THE CLERGY 21

their own e. FOOD 49

enjoyments for its e. HAPPINESS 15

enlightenment spread e. EDUCATION 31

enough Five hundred quite e. ROYALTY 34

entanglement e. with religion RELIGION 7

entendre full of single e. WORDS 15

single e. THEATRE 28

entertain e. an idea IDEAS 5

entertained e. by some of your grosser

LETTERS 17

entertainment *Arabian Nights* e. SICKNESS 18

stage is a world of e. THEATRE 16

enthusiasm uncontrolled e. BORES 10

envelope in a brown e. MONEY 13

environment humdrum issues like the e.

NATURE 10

envy thing I e. you for GENERATION GAP 1

epic person of very *e.* appearance PEOPLE 12

epicure e. would say FOOD 77

epiglottis My e. filled him with glee MEDICINE 28

epigram all existence in an e. WIT 51

E.: a wisecrack that played	WIT 21
Impelled to try an e.	LITERATURE 30
until it purrs like an e.	NEWSPAPERS 20

epitaph No e. EPITAPHS 24

epitaphs nice derangement of e. WIT 33

Epstein never forgive Mr E. ART 1

equal all shall e. be CLASS 16

more e. than others DEMOCRACY 13

equality e. in the servants' hall CLASS 2

true sexual e. MEN AND WOMEN 29

equanimity No man can face with e.

POLITICS 33

equation each e. I included SCIENCE 16

e. is something for eternity SCIENCE 14

equator rival the E. BODY 37

equipment only item of essential e.

MARRIAGE 92

equity E. does not demand LAW 3

erections Friends who give you e.

MEN AND WOMEN 60

erogenous e. zones for a kick-off SEX 15

We retain our zones e. OLD AGE 23

erotic you're an erratic e. MEN AND WOMEN 14

err e. is human COMPUTERS 1

e. is human VIRTUE 27

errands run on little e. GOVERNMENT 11

erratic For I'm a neurotic e. MEN AND WOMEN 14

erroneous e. opinion HUMAN RACE 7

error confessions of e. BEHAVIOUR 40

errors factual e. BIOGRAPHY 11

escape few e. that distinction PRIDE 13

Eskimo proud to be an E. ARCHITECTURE 13

Esperanto E. is to the language world

WRITERS 24

essential e. ingredient MARRIAGE 99

only item of e. equipment MARRIAGE 92

esses so many e. in it NAMES 9

establishment forelock to the British e.

SNOBBERY 11

estate dealing with e. workers CLASS 12

eternal concept of an e. mother ROYALTY 27

eternity equation is something for e. SCIENCE 14

E.'s a terrible thought	TIME 13
some conception of e.	CRICKET 11

ethics yob e. FOOTBALL 24

etiquette E., sacred subject BEHAVIOUR 23

E. (and quiet, well-cut clothes)	RELIGION 50
It isn't e.	BEHAVIOUR 5

Eton boys of E. must not CENSORSHIP 9

hoidays from E.	EDUCATION 40
wearing an E. Ramblers' tie	POLITICIANS 19

Etonians Hail him like E. SOCIETY 16

Ettie E. is an ox INSULTS 3

eunuch e. and a snigger THE CLERGY 9

eunuchs Critics are like e. CRITICS 7

seraglio of e. POLITICS 32

euphemism keep the . . . e. WORDS 1

lateral e. TENNIS 1

Euripides Mr E. was guilty PREJUDICE 4

Europe Britain was no part of E. COUNTRIES 1

In E., when a rich woman	MEN AND WOMEN 51
length and breadth of E.	TRAVEL 2

European every E. language except one

LANGUAGES 12

evacuated e. children CHRISTMAS 2

evasive take e. action POLITICIANS 37

even e. terror of their lives PREJUDICE 13

evening never get away for the e. NEWSPAPERS 9

evenings do with the long winter e. WRITERS 7

exciting e. HOLIDAYS 10

eventide perfect e. home OLD AGE 38

ever Well, did you e. MARRIAGE 101

fatal deal of it is absolutely f.   VIRTUE 30
I am a f. man   MEN AND WOMEN 48
fate f. became a cert   BIRDS 5
F. cannot harm me   FOOD 77
F. had not seen its way   SUCCESS 29
f. worse than marriage   MARRIAGE 9
F. wrote her a most tremendous   ROYALTY 13
I have a bone to pick with f.   MIDDLE AGE 8
father as a rapper than you are as a f.
                    PARENTS 5
bed fell on my f.   FAMILY 47
called F. by everyone   THE CLERGY 1
either my f. or my mother   PARENTS 15
f. had an accident   ANIMALS 38
f.'s an actor   BEHAVIOUR 14
f. was a dragon   FAMILY 34
f. was so ignorant   GENERATION GAP 12
gave her f. forty-one   MURDER 1
leave my f. alone   INSULTS 27
poor f. used to say   ART 12
whistle your f.   FAMILY 3
wise f.   FAMILY 37
You are old, F. William   OLD AGE 8
your f. whom you love, dies   THEATRE 54
fathers F. don't curse   PARENTS 8
My f. can have it   WALES 5
fathom f. the inscrutable   ARGUMENT 18
fatigue f. the attention of dolls   ROYALTY 43
fattening immoral, or f.   HAPPINESS 19
fault anybody's f.   EDUCATION 32
no f. or flaw   LAW 11
Faust validity of the F. myth   VIRTUE 16
fava with some f. beans   FOOD 34
favour count in their f.   MISTAKES 21
in f. iv dhrink   ALCOHOL 23
favourite second f. organ   BODY 1
fax fox from a f.-machine   COUNTRY 4
faxed proposal which my secretary f.   LOVE 16
FBI F. and the CIA   BIOGRAPHY 2
F. are powerless   SEX 39
fear constipation is the big f.   SICKNESS 15
f. of the Law   RELIGION 32
feast Marriage is a f.   MARRIAGE 35
feather writes with a f.   THEATRE 21
feather-footed F. through the plashy fen
                    LANGUAGE 18
feathers three white f.   CLASS 8
February not Puritanism but F.   WEATHER 14
fecund first-rate, the f. rate   WRITING 18
fee small f. in America   AMERICA 24
feeble Most forcible F.   WIT 29
feed F. the brute   MARRIAGE 104
starlings could f. off him   DESCRIPTION 17

feel f. a thought   WORDS 13
F. LIKE A BOY AGAIN   TELEGRAMS 12
how the Taj Mahal must f.   MARRIAGE 13
I don't f. worse   MORALITY 5
One does f.   RELIGION 33
tragedy to those that f.   HUMAN RACE 15
feeling display taste and f.   SCIENCE 17
springs from genuine f.   POETRY 24
fees as they took their F.   MEDICINE 5
My f. are sufficient punishment   LAW 1
Whatever f. we earn   LAW 19
feet difficult f.   BODY 7
don't have to look at his f.   INSULTS 39
hear it through their f.   MUSIC 52
lost the use of his f.   PROGRESS 8
talking about f.   CONVERSATION 3
talk under their f.   PRESIDENTS 14
felicity more f.   GENERATION GAP 11
fell F. half so flat   CRITICS 4
f. in love with a rich   LOVE 21
not love thee, Dr F.   FRIENDS 4
fellatio Hail, F.   WIT 44
fellow women like me, looking for a f.
                    TECHNOLOGY 10
female f. equivalent   BODY 8
f. llama   DESCRIPTION 8
God has become f.   GOD 44
standard f. job interview   WOMEN 18
females eighty mile o' f.   MEN AND WOMEN 7
feminism F. is the result   WOMEN 52
feminist anti-f. books to review   JOURNALISM 24
early f.   GOVERNMENT 45
people call me a f.   WOMEN 78
fen through the plashy f.   LANGUAGE 18
fence colours to the f.   CERTAINTY 10
f. is just too high for him   WRITERS 28
fermented drink f. liquids   ALCOHOL 68
ferocious f. disbelief   DESCRIPTION 22
ferret enthusiasm of a f.   FOOD 71
fertile to be so f.   ANIMALS 34
fetish as a savage approaches his f.   JUDGES 4
fetishist f. who years   SEX 42
fetlocks f. blowing   ANIMALS 24
fettle I'm in fine f.   HEALTH 9
few f. who know her   CRITICS 41
fickleness f. of the women I love   WOMEN 63
fiction all forms of f.   AUTOBIOGRAPHY 23
being decidedly for f.   NEWSPAPERS 12
best thing in f.   ENGLAND 44
f. as if it were a painful duty   WRITERS 44
He can't write f.   WRITERS 16
one form of continuous f.   NEWSPAPERS 7
Stranger than f.   TRUTH 2
what f. means   BOOKS 26
work of f.   AUTOBIOGRAPHY 19

fiddle I the second f.   PRIDE 9
    playing second f.   POWER 7
fidelity f. is not having more than one   SEX 68
field loaf with a f. in it   FOOD 88
fielder bad f.   BASEBALL 8
fields lies W. C. F.   EPITAPHS 11
fife practised on a f.   ANIMALS 10
fifteen always f. years older than I am
     OLD AGE 4
    until I was f.   SEX 33
fifth came f. and lost the job   SUCCESS 17
fifty At f. I lost my hair   OLD AGE 22
    f.-fifty proposition   CRIME 24
    f. million Frenchmen   FOOD 62
    until he's f.   ALCOHOL 25
fight before the f. begins   POLITICAL PARTIES 2
    Can't f. in here   WAR 20
    f. for freedom   FASHION 18
    getting people to f. it   WAR 21
    If I don't f.   BOXING 6
    those who bade me f.   WAR 12
    will f.   ARMED FORCES 4
fighter f. in the business world   BOXING 7
fighting f. for this woman's honour   WOMEN 38
    stop f. for it   FOOTBALL 1
figment like it to say 'f.'   EPITAPHS 24
figs Mashed f.   FOOD 13
figure f. is unbelievable   MARRIAGE 40
    losing her f. or her face   MIDDLE AGE 5
figurehead you're just a f.   ARGUMENT 22
file f. your waste-paper basket   LIBRARIES 2
    must be a f. somewhere   GOD 30
files splash your f.   BIOGRAPHY 2
filibusters Fat f. begat   POLITICS 36
filing mental capacities of a f. cabinet   LAW 4
fill better than trying to f. them   WORK 8
    f. hup the chinks   FOOD 82
    stuff to f. the space   NEWSPAPERS 17
fills f. wrong cavity   WIT 13
film and that is f.   CINEMA 43
    deal with the f. lab   FILM STARS 11
    psychological f.   FILMS 1
filmmaking no rules in f.   CINEMA 4
films f. were the lowest form   TELEVISION 20
financial seek f. succour   BETTING 1
Finchley Lord F. tried   DEATH 10
find f. a friend   FRIENDS 7
    f. God by tomorrow   GOD 26
    f. it in the index   INDEXES 1
    f. out what everyone is doing   LAW 12
    f. out why a snorer   SLEEP 11
    where does she f. them   SNOBBERY 15
finding I had a little trouble f. you   RELIGION 29

fine f., strike it out   WRITING 12
    f. romance with no kisses   MEN AND WOMEN 12
    OLD CARY GRANT F.   TELEGRAMS 14
finer for the f. folk   CLASS 21
finest this is our f. shower   SEX 61
finger I lift up my f.   SONGS 20
    looking at your f.   FAME 18
    what chills the f. not a bit   SATISFACTION 9
fingernails biting your f.   MISTAKES 23
    finished the f.   FILMS 9
    see his f.   INSULTS 39
finish draw right to the f.   DEATH 32
    start together and f. together   MUSIC 8
finished f. in half the time   FAMILY 54
    Then he's f.   MARRIAGE 59
fire had to do f.-watching   WAR 8
    shouted 'F.'   LIES 4
    supplied the f. themselves   MARRIAGE 18
    write for the f.   WRITING 4
fired just got f. for it   APPEARANCE 15
Firenze COUGHING MYSELF INTO A F.   TELEGRAMS 8
fires having inner f.   CHARACTER 2
fireside by his own f.   HOME 21
firing faced the f. squad   CHARACTER 16
first f. class, and with children   TRAVEL 1
    f. class cabin   TRANSPORT 7
    f. ten million years   PAST 1
    to mistake for the f.-rate   WRITING 18
fish came up with the f.   FOOD 46
    f. are having their revenge   ANIMALS 12
    f. without a bicycle   WOMEN 66
    He eats a lot of f.   INTELLIGENCE 18
    no self-respecting f.   NEWSPAPERS 28
    Not a fatter f. than he   ROYALTY 45
    surrounded by f.   BUREAUCRACY 4
    throw her a f.   ACTORS 36
fishing 'angling' is the name given to f.
     SPORTS 17
    basis from which to go f.   MARRIAGE 79
fish-knives Phone for the f., Norman   SOCIETY 3
    sling out the f.   BEHAVIOUR 12
fishy f. about the French   COUNTRIES 16
fit It isn't f. for humans now   TOWNS 6
five count to f.   ANGER 5
    f.-day weekend   WORK 27
    I have wedded f.   MARRIAGE 32
fiver No woman is worth more than a f.
     LOVE 33
fix coming to f. the show   WIT 16
    only sport you can't f.   SPORTS 18
flag High as a f.   AMERICA 15
flair You have f.   HAPPINESS 2
flamingo very large f.   DEBT 7
flap I can't f.   ACTORS 8
flappers London wants f.   ACTORS 8

flared copiously f. FASHION 5
flashes f. of silence CONVERSATION 25
flat Fell half so f. CRITICS 4
   how f. he really did want it SONGS 2
   just how f. and empty PLACES 4
   Very f., Norfolk PLACES 7
flats can't walk in f. FASHION 14
flattered f. by the censorship CENSORSHIP 19
flattering If you are f. a woman PRAISE 1
   you think him worth f. PRAISE 9
flattery Everyone likes f. ROYALTY 24
   f. hurts no one PRAISE 11
   objects of f. GOSSIP 8
   what your f. is worth PRAISE 6
flaunt f. it COMEDY 20
flavour spearmint lose its f. FOOD 70
flaw f. in any argument ARGUMENT 16
   no fault or f. LAW 11
flea between a louse and a f. POETS 9
fleas Even educated f. do it SEX 65
   reasonable amount o' f. DOGS 9
   scratching for the wrong f. VIRTUE 28
fleet F.'s lit up ALCOHOL 70
Fleet-street F. has a very animated appearance
  TOWNS 22
flesh delicate white human f. LOVE 15
   have more f. BODY 31
   makes man and wife one f. MARRIAGE 38
flood f. could not wash away CLASS 6
flooded STREETS F. PLEASE ADVISE TELEGRAMS 3
floor lie on the f. ALCOHOL 42
   table near the f. FOOD 47
floozie f. in the jacuzzi ARCHITECTURE 1
flopping f. yourself down FAMILY 10
floppy weak, f. thing in the chair
  PRIME MINISTERS 23
flower damned f.-pots GARDENS 5
   try f. arrangement SPORTS 4
flowers Beware of men bearing f.
  MEN AND WOMEN 47
   heard about f. FASHION 25
   smelling f. HEALTH 6
   way botanists divide up f. SCIENCE 18
   wild f., and Prime Ministers POLITICS 9
fluid get some f. and embalm each other
  PARTIES 6
flutter F. and bear him up ROYALTY 14
fly f. which had been trained HANDWRITING 1
   made the f. ANIMALS 33
   show the f. the way out PHILOSOPHY 10
   with an open f. CINEMA 50
foal f. and broodmare WEATHER 1
foam amber f. FOOD 28
foe angry with my f. ANGER 3
   find a f. FRIENDS 16

fogs insular country subject to f. POLITICS 30
foible omniscience is his f. INSULTS 45
Folies-Bergère goes to the F. MEDICINE 34
folk All music is f. music MUSIC 2
   incest and f.-dancing SEX 6
folks W'en f. git ole OLD AGE 24
follies author's f. AUTOBIOGRAPHY 6
   f. which a man regrets most MEN 13
   My f. are intact OLD AGE 22
follow F. the van HOME 6
follower f. of fashion FASHION 9
followers except f. POLITICIANS 32
follows lie f. BEHAVIOUR 28
folly f. of 'Woman's Rights' WOMEN 75
   f.'s all they've taught me WOMEN 48
   woman stoops to f. WOMEN 20
   woman stoops to f. WOMEN 28
Fondas Henry F. lay on the evening
  DESCRIPTION 11
font be done with a f. RELIGION 35
   portable, second-hand f. THE CLERGY 16
food aftertaste of foreign f. ALCOHOL 15
   alcohol was a f. ALCOHOL 69
   f. a tragedy FOOD 64
   f. enough for a week BIRDS 6
   f. I ate and not the show SLEEP 5
   f. is more dangerous FOOD 48
   f. was a very big factor RELIGION 36
   predigested f. for the brain QUOTATIONS 23
   problem is f. MONEY 8
   We are surfing f. TELEVISION 13
fool conceited f. in the White House SPEECHES 10
   every f. is not a poet POETS 13
   f. and his money BETTING 7
   f. and his wife COUNTRY 15
   f.'s paradise FOOLISHNESS 15
   f. with booze ALCOHOL 25
   I'm just a f. WOMEN 33
   let a kiss f. you FOOLISHNESS 10
   Prove to me that you're no f. RELIGION 56
   that does not marry a f. MARRIAGE 138
   without being a f. FOOLISHNESS 28
foolish He never said a f. thing ROYALTY 60
   most f. people TOWNS 13
   saying a f. thing FOOLISHNESS 27
foolproof f. items FOOLISHNESS 5
fools all the f. in town FOOLISHNESS 30
   f. of gardeners GARDENS 9
   house for f. and mad EPITAPHS 21
   leaves 'em still two f. MARRIAGE 38
   see these poor f. decoyed MARRIAGE 97
   the small ones f. WRITERS 35
   tolerate f. FOOLISHNESS 1
foolscap on buff-coloured f. NEWSPAPERS 11

freckles Love, curiosity, f., and doubt — LOVE 36
Fred Here lies F. — EPITAPHS 4
free bring it to you, f. — DEATH 3
  favours f. speech — CENSORSHIP 4
  f. in America — AMERICA 24
  F. speech is not — CENSORSHIP 6
  I'd as soon write f. verse — POETRY 11
  in favour of f. expression — CENSORSHIP 3
  This is a f. country — BEHAVIOUR 32
  where the press is f. — CENSORSHIP 10
freedom achieve fuller f. — CENSORSHIP 20
  fight for f. — FASHION 18
  F. of the press — CENSORSHIP 13
  F. of the press in Britain — NEWSPAPERS 33
  I gave my life for f. — WAR 12
  undue f. — CENSORSHIP 12
  vacant f. — PROGRESS 14
freemasonry have a kind of bitter f. — LOVE 3
freeway Boston's f. system — TRANSPORT 5
  f. is . . . the place — TRANSPORT 3
French answering you in F. — COUNTRIES 36
  fishy about the F. — COUNTRIES 16
  F. are awful — COUNTRIES 58
  F. are masters — DIPLOMACY 11
  F. of Parys — WOMEN 9
  F. Revolution — FAMILY 52
  F. went in — COUNTRIES 40
  F. widow in every bedroom — HOTELS 4
  gave the F. the third way — CHOICE 8
  hate the F. — COUNTRIES 27
  how it's improved her F. — LANGUAGES 13
  much more in F. — CENSORSHIP 5
  not too F. French bean — ART 9
  reading a F. novel — CRITICS 28
  serve the F. — FOOD 8
  Speak in F. — LANGUAGES 7
  speaking F. fluently — LANGUAGES 8
  worst F. novels — NEWSPAPERS 36
Frenchmen fifty million F. — FOOD 62
frenzy f. closely related to delirium — WRITING 15
fresh noted for f. air and fun — PLACES 10
Freud investigations of Herr F. — ART 17
  trouble with F. — HUMOUR 13
Freudian F. nightmare — FAMILY 32
friction f. threatening — WAR 34
fridge in the f. — AWARDS 4
fried in which their fat was f. — MARRIAGE 18
friend angry with my f. — ANGER 3
  become a man's f. — WOMEN 11
  breaking it in for a f. — NAMES 17
  Diamonds are a girl's best f. — WEALTH 26
  find a f. — FRIENDS 7
  f. is not standing — DEMOCRACY 18
  f. of the Sitwells — SOCIETY 1
  goodnatured f. — FRIENDS 17

  having an old f. for dinner — SOCIETY 14
  my f. Evelyn Waugh — FRIENDS 6
  Reagan for his best f. — FILM STARS 15
  terrific f. of yours — READING 16
  Whenever a f. succeeds — SUCCESS 33
  your enemey and your f. — FRIENDS 22
friends at all her f. — GOSSIP 7
  bestest of f. — FRIENDS 28
  couldn't buy f. — FRIENDS 12
  deserting one's f. — FRIENDS 1
  documents and trusted f. — FRIENDS 18
  f. are true — FUTURE 2
  f. except two — CHRISTMAS 6
  f. he loved — EPITAPHS 25
  f. in both places — HEAVEN 6
  f. of the author — ADVERTISING 3
  F. who give you erections — MEN AND WOMEN 60
  f. who took exercise — HEALTH 8
  lay down his f. — FRIENDS 21
  make f. fall out — MARRIAGE 109
  make new f. — FRIENDS 2
  nearly deceiving your f. — LIES 5
  none of his f. — FRIENDS 24
  not always the best of f. — TAXES 6
  no true f. in politics — POLITICS 22
  only two f. — FRIENDS 20
  Seek younger f. — OLD AGE 37
  two real f. — LIFE 26
friendship f. could be very beautiful — WEALTH 21
  sort of f. — MARRIAGE 120
frighten by God, they f. me — WAR 30
  f. the horses — SEX 25
frightened If you are f. in the night — SOCIETY 19
frightening f. sort of way — DOGS 1
frivolity how precious is f. — LITERATURE 18
frivolous Memoirs of the f. — AUTOBIOGRAPHY 5
frivolously ability to make love f. — LOVE 6
frock history of that f. — FASHION 17
frocks f. are built — FASHION 34
Frodo Let Bingo = F. — NAMES 24
front f.-page news — DOGS 5
frown Say that she f. — MEN AND WOMEN 42
frozen show is f. — SONGS 17
frugal She had a f. mind — WOMEN 14
fruit delicate exotic f. — FOOLISHNESS 33
  Old Trafford f. machine — FOOTBALL 6
fruitcakes Bring on the f. — POLITICS 61
frustration sexual f. — FRIENDS 14
frying f. pan of your words — WRITERS 13
fuck couldn't write 'f.' — CRITICS 9
  They f. you up, your mum and dad — PARENTS 10
fugues Of masses and f. — MUSIC 19
fule As any f. kno — FOOLISHNESS 34
fulfilment image of f. — RELIGION 45
full f. tide of human existence — TOWNS 22

fuller's earth Money, wife, is the true f. | MONEY 11
fume black, stinking f. thereof | SMOKING 4
fun Cancer can be rather fun | SICKNESS 12
counted among the f. people | SCIENCE 22
damps the f. | HOME 10
got to be a f. activity | POLITICS 24
I've had my fun | TRANSPORT 23
more f. than fun | WORK 9
most f. I ever had | SEX 4
most f. you can have | ADVERTISING 4
no concept of f. | COUNTRIES 5
no reference to f. | GOVERNMENT 16
Other girls ain't havin' any f. | WOMEN 31
stop people having f. | DRUGS 8
fundament frigid on the f. | SATISFACTION 9
funeral bar was like a f. parlour | SOCIETY 7
making f. orations | SPEECHES 11
next day there's a f. | MEDICINE 33
nothing like a morning f. | DEATH 41
refused to attend his f. | DEATH 69
upon him for the f. | DEATH 33
funky f. pub pianist | MUSICIANS 10
funny but not *that* f. | WRITERS 24
don't think that's f. | HUMOUR 32
Everything is f. | HUMOUR 34
F.-peculiar | HUMOUR 20
It's a f. old world | LIFE 10
Life is the f. thing | LIFE 8
not very f. | SELF-KNOWLEDGE 11
saw anything so f. | ACTORS 20
fur bred for food or f. | MEN 9
F. is a subject | FASHION 29
Three kinds of f. | CLASS 13
furniture all that nice f. | POLITICS 46
buy all his f. | SNOBBERY 9
cumbersome f. | HOME 25
mere church f. | THE CLERGY 7
No f. so charming | BOOKS 19
rearrange the f. | POLITICS 54
twice as much f. | HOME 23
further f. they have to fall | BOXING 5
f. you got from Britain | POLITICIANS 10
fury beastly f. | FOOTBALL 8
fustian whose f.'s so sublimely bad | POETRY 21
future about the f. | AUTOBIOGRAPHY 24
bridge to the f. | FUTURE 10
f. looks dark indeed | WRITERS 5
f. refusing | FUTURE 1
never think of the f. | FUTURE 5

Gabor G. marrying Freddie Ayer | MARRIAGE 87
Gabriel Archangel G. | DEMOCRACY 2
So blow, G., blow | RELIGION 54
Gaelic restore the old G. | IRELAND 6

gaffe terrible social g. | PARTIES 7
gaiety g. is a striped shroud | WALES 6
gaily G. into Ruislip Gardens | SOCIETY 4
gainful happily known as g. employment | WORK 1
gaining Something may be g. | BASEBALL 10
Galatians text in G. | BIBLE 1
galaxy smart alecksy, With the g. | PROGRESS 11
gallant Stop being g. | THEATRE 13
gallantry What men call g. | SEX 23
galleon Stately as a g. | DANCE 8
galloping g. consumption you had | SICKNESS 4
gallows upon the g. or of the pox | INSULTS 53
galoshes vest and g. | CHARACTER 14
gamble Life is a g. | LIFE 22
gamblers g. are as happy | BETTING 2
game always played the g. | POLITICIANS 31
Anarchism is a g. | POLITICS 67
g. at which only one | EDUCATION 30
g. which takes less | BASEBALL 12
get a g. now | FOOTBALL 16
latest popular g. | FAMILY 20
no g. from bridge to cricket | SPORTS 16
only a g. | BASEBALL 13
parody is a g. | WIT 23
Take me out to the ball g. | BASEBALL 9
wouldn't be the g. it is | FOOTBALL 5
gamut g. of the emotions | ACTORS 31
Gandhi [G.] knew the cost | POVERTY 14
ganged my parents and his mother g. up | PARENTS 2
gap g. between Dorothy and Chopin | MUSICIANS 1
g. between platitudes | SPEECHES 16
garbage week of the g. strike | APPEARANCE 25
garbled Rather g. | MARRIAGE 44
Garbo unwelcoming Greta G. | MEN AND WOMEN 28
garden G. City Café | SEX 16
g. is a loathsome thing | GARDENS 14
led up the g. path | DIPLOMACY 1
man and a woman in a g. | BIBLE 7
gardener not a dirt g. | GARDENS 1
gardeners fools of g. | GARDENS 9
grim g. | GARDENS 13
gardens Irish g. | GARDENS 11
garlic clove of g. round my neck | POLITICIANS 25
gas G. smells awful | DEATH 53
Had silicon been a g. | EXAMINATIONS 6
read the g.-meter | EDUCATION 31
gate A-sitting on a g. | OLD AGE 9
gathering intransitive operation of g. | WIT 24
gauze shoot her through g. | FILM STARS 2
gay g. or not | FOOTBALL 14
Glitter and be g. | WOMEN 79
gazelle love a dear g. | MONEY 6
geisha Get yourself a G. | COUNTRIES 20

got If not, have you g. him | ROYALTY 63
If you've g. it | COMEDY 20
gourmet g. can tell | FOOD 6
gout give them the g. | FRIENDS 13
govern Go out and g. New South Wales | POLITICIANS 6
g. a country | COUNTRIES 18
those who g. society | RELIGION 73
government art of g. | GOVERNMENT 37
Every g. | DEMOCRACY 12
get good g. | GOVERNMENT 27
given to g. | FAMILY 11
G. and public opinion | ENGLAND 31
g. by discussion | DEMOCRACY 3
g. get out of war | WAR 15
G. I despise | GOVERNMENT 22
g. of laws | GOVERNMENT 21
hands of the general g. | GOVERNMENT 19
man who understands g. | POLITICIANS 33
no g. in history | JOURNALISM 16
no law or g. | GOVERNMENT 2
Overthrow the G. | AMERICA 18
prefer that the g. | GOVERNMENT 32
they want Irish g. | IRELAND 5
governor *Stewart* for g. | FILM STARS 15
goyim g. Annoy 'im | GOD 6
GP more suspicious of our G.s | MEDICINE 7
grabs Benn g. child | NEWSPAPERS 6
grace does it with a better g. | FOOLISHNESS 25
g. is sometimes better | MARRIAGE 35
There but for the g. of God | POLITICIANS 13
graceful g. exit | BEHAVIOUR 17
Gracie goodnight, G. | COMEDY 12
grades into four g. | EDUCATION 45
graffiti No g. | COUNTRIES 25
grammar don't want to talk g. | CLASS 27
self-made g. school lass | POLITICAL PARTIES 13
talking bad g. | LAST WORDS 1
grammatical seven g. errors | EPITAPHS 27
grand Ain't it g. | DEATH 62
doing a g. job | COMEDY 35
g. enough to be asked there | ROYALTY 29
Grand Canyon rose petal down the G. | POETRY 17
grandchild fourteenth g. | CHILDREN 39
granddaughter seventh g. | CHILDREN 39
grandeur prose of incomparable g. | WRITERS 21
grandiose taste for the g. | ARCHITECTURE 11
grandma It was good enough for G. | WOMEN 34
grandmother g. took a bath | BEHAVIOUR 2
We have become a g. | FAMILY 44
granite breasts like g. | FILM STARS 18
grape how to jump on a g. | COUNTRIES 12
peel me a g. | FOOD 86

grapes Defectors are like g. | TRUST 12
man who has lost his g. | SELF-KNOWLEDGE 22
grass shit on g. | FOOTBALL 22
grassed I just g. on him | TELEVISION 15
grassroots Springing from the g. | DESCRIPTION 20
gratitude G. is not a normal feature | POLITICS 41
gratuitous is the most g. | AUTOBIOGRAPHY 23
grave g. in a Y-shaped coffin | SEX 58
g. yawns for him | BORES 17
kind of healthy g. | COUNTRY 18
on the way to the g. | LIFE 8
graves g. of little magazines | POETRY 22
have no g. as yet | GOVERNMENT 4
look at the g. | BUSINESS 14
gravitate constantly tending to g. | LAW 2
gravitation eminence by sheer g. | SUCCESS 30
gravy chicken and g. | FOOD 53
It's the rich wot gets the g. | POVERTY 1
great All my shows are g. | SELF-KNOWLEDGE 10
commonly called G. | WAR 16
feeling that he is g. | JUDGES 4
g. being a priest | THE CLERGY 17
some men are born g. | PRIDE 6
think him *g.* | BORES 9
Whenever he met a g. man | SNOBBERY 16
greater G. love | FRIENDS 9
| FRIENDS 21
greatly g. to his credit | ENGLAND 13
greatness g. thrust upon them | PRIDE 6
greed G. is right | ECONOMICS 13
swallow with g. | COUNTRIES 13
Greek half G., half Latin | TELEVISION 14
No G.; as much Latin | QUOTATIONS 7
only G. Tragedy I know | PEOPLE 49
original G. | CRITICS 39
green dyeing their hair g. | GENERATION GAP 5
just as g. | GARDENS 4
greenery mountain g. | COUNTRY 7
greenery-yallery g., Grosvenor Gallery | MEN 8
greenfly dosing the g. | GARDENS 8
greenroom hang about the g. | POLITICS 48
grew when I g. up | GENERATION GAP 13
grey seemed a g. crew | GENERATION GAP 6
six g. suits | FOOD 10
sky had remained a depthless g. | WEATHER 4
grief used for augmenting g. | SONGS 1
grievance Scotsman with a g. | SCOTLAND 12
grieve will g. a month | EPITAPHS 22
grind My life is one demd horrid g. | WORK 12
grittiness g. of the Fantastics | SONGS 22
gritty that g. voice | PEOPLE 17
grocer expect a g. to write | WRITERS 3
photograph of the G. | DIPLOMACY 15
groom Including the bride and g. | MARRIAGE 95
grooves In determinate g. | TRANSPORT 17

grosser your g. reminiscences	LETTERS 17
Grosvenor violence in G. Square	EDUCATION 49
Grosvenor Gallery greenery-yallery, G.	MEN 8
grotesque meaning of the word g.	WIT 39
Groucho Marxist—of the G. tendency	POLITICS 6
ground worship the g. you walk on	
	MARRIAGE 134
grounds walks round the g.	GARDENS 12
grouse g. do it	BIRDS 7
grovelled g. before him	SNOBBERY 16
grow never g. out of it	ARMED FORCES 29
growed s'pect I g.	CHILDREN 35
growing hard price to pay for g. up	
	MIDDLE AGE 13
grown-up rewarding spectacle of a g.	
	TRANSPORT 22
grown-ups G. never understand	
	GENERATION GAP 3
When g. pretend	MIDDLE AGE 7
grunt guttural g.	BEHAVIOUR 20
gruntled he was far from being g.	
	SATISFACTION 15
guaranteed g. only to those	CENSORSHIP 13
guardian reading *The G.*	FOOTBALL 14
guess In disease Medical Men g.	MEDICINE 19
Let me g.	DEATH 60
guessing g. so much and so much	WOMEN 12
guests hosts and g.	CLASS 3
guile squat, and packed with g.	PLACES 3
guilt easy the assumption of g.	VIRTUE 6
sign of g.	BEHAVIOUR 7
guilty g. never escape unscathed	LAW 1
guineas two hundred g.	ART 34
Guinness G., sarcasm and late nights	
	IRELAND 10
gulf G. Stream, as it nears	WEATHER 15
gum chew g. at the same time	INSULTS 23
gun Is that a g. in your pocket	
	MEN AND WOMEN 54
we have got The Maxim G.	POWER 1
wrong end of a g.	SPORTS 37
Gunga G. Din	ARMED FORCES 19
guns G. aren't lawful	DEATH 53
loaded g. with boys	SECRECY 6
gurgles undercurrents of g.	PEOPLE 30
Guthrie as I have from Woody G.	SONGS 12
guts Spill your g. at Wimbledon	TENNIS 5
gutter into the g.	NEWSPAPERS 37
guy g.'s only doing it	MEN AND WOMEN 26
h even *without* the h.'s	THEATRE 11
ha funny h.-ha	HUMOUR 20
habit-forming Cocaine h.	LIFE 4
habits Inhibit their h.	ANIMALS 16
hack some government h.	GOVERNMENT 21

Hackensack I took a trip to H.	TOWNS 27
had been h. by all	CHARACTER 18
WE ALL KNEW YOU H. IT IN YOU	TELEGRAMS 18
haddock *Quotations* and a very large h.	
	NEWSPAPERS 16
sausage and h.	COOKERY 22
Hague H. has got a baseball cap	
	POLITICAL PARTIES 6
hail H., Fellatio	WIT 44
H. him like Etonians	SOCIETY 16
hair At fifty I lost my h.	OLD AGE 22
beat hell out of h. curlers	SEX 73
did to their h.	APPEARANCE 12
does her h. with Bovril	FRIENDS 5
h. of the horse	HYPOCRISY 7
h. straight from his left armpit	TRUST 11
have their h. done	APPEARANCE 27
her h. blown about	TRANSPORT 30
let his h. grow	LAW 22
like the h. we breathe	SPORTS 32
pin up my h. with prose	LETTERS 4
Presbyterian h.	BODY 23
rich mouse h.	APPEARANCE 9
smoothes her hair	WOMEN 20
You have lovely h.	WOMEN 10
your h. has become very white	OLD AGE 8
haircut h. will be crew	FAMILY 17
really awful h.	FASHION 4
hairpieces reliable as his h.	AUTOBIOGRAPHY 20
hairs h. weakly curled	APPEARANCE 3
half h. mad baronet	PEOPLE 11
halo For a h. up in heaven	RELIGION 28
jealousy with a h.	MORALITY 15
What after all Is a h.	RELIGION 23
ham don't take a h. sandwich	MARRIAGE 122
when there's h.	MEDICINE 10
Hamlet Briers played H.	ACTORS 14
Did H. actually	THEATRE 3
H. himself longed	THEATRE 50
H. in invisible	ACTORS 10
H. sure did enjoy	THEATRE 33
I'm doing H.	ACTING 27
hand h. that lays	CINEMA 20
H. that rocked the cradle	DEATH 4
kiss on the h.	WEALTH 26
'Tes the h. of Nature	NATURE 2
with automatic h.	WOMEN 20
handbag bred in a h.	FAMILY 52
hitting it with her h.	POWER 3
Handel For either of them, or for H.	
	MUSICIANS 11
handicap terrible a h.	ENGLAND 18
What is your h.	GOLF 2
What's your h.	GOLF 3

handicapper h. is spoken of most respectfully

SPORTS 28

handkerchief like a damp h.   FOOD 44

scent on a pocket h.   PRIME MINISTERS 18

handle doesn't h. very well   HUMAN RACE 14

hands has the most beautiful h.   ART 11

Holding h. at midnight   LOVE 18

ice on your h.   FASHION 8

into the wrong h.   CENSORSHIP 8

prize-fighters shaking h.   WOMEN 44

handstand H. IN SHOWER   TELEGRAMS 22

handwriting exquisite h.   HANDWRITING 1

in his h.   HANDWRITING 3

your own h.   HANDWRITING 9

handy h. and cheap   FAMILY 1

hang they h. a man first   LAW 24

hanged burnt or h.   HUMOUR 22

h. in a fortnight   DEATH 34

hanging H. is too good   CRIME 16

h. prevents a bad marriage   MARRIAGE 111

one of them is my h.   ARISTOCRACY 4

happen accidents which started to h.

MISTAKES 22

foretell what is going to h.   POLITICIANS 12

to whom things h.   MISTAKES 21

happened after they have h.   FUTURE 8

what h. to him   ARMED FORCES 5

happening believe what isn't h.   SPORTS 9

happens there when it h.   DEATH 1

happily h. a woman may be married

MARRIAGE 85

happiness h. is assured   FUTURE 2

Last Chance Gulch for h.   CHILDREN 34

lifetime of h.   HAPPINESS 12

man in pursuit of h.   MARRIAGE 25

Money won't buy h.   MONEY 24

result h.   MONEY 7

sacrifice one's own h.   HAPPINESS 7

happy conspiracy to make you h.   AMERICA 27

h. as most people   BETTING 2

h. as the dey   SEX 56

h. families   FAMILY 48

h. New Year   INSULTS 50

haven't been so h.   BOOKS 23

How h. I could be with either   LOVE 17

keep unemployed people h.   TELEVISION 21

man can be h. with any woman

MEN AND WOMEN 58

not a h. one   HAPPINESS 6

someone, somewhere, may be h.   RELIGION 42

very h. life   FAMILY 8

will never be h.   COUNTRY 9

harbour God made the h.   TOWNS 1

hard h. dog to keep   PRESIDENTS 4

h.-faced men   POLITICIANS 2

h. man is good to find   MEN 17

very h. guy   BETTING 12

hardback modern h. writer   WRITERS 39

hard-boiled big h. city   TOWNS 9

h. eggs   CHARACTER 21

harem eunuchs in a h.   CRITICS 7

hark H.! the herald angels sing   MEDICINE 4

harlot holiest h. in my realm   ROYALTY 26

prerogative of the h.   JOURNALISM 13

harmless h. drudge   DICTIONARIES 8

harp pianoforte is a h. in a box   MUSIC 25

Harpic As I read the H. tin   OLD AGE 5

Harrow H. man, I expect   EDUCATION 50

I wish Shelley had been at H.   POETS 6

Harry Any Tom, Dick or H.   MARRIAGE 103

Uncle H.'s not a missionary   THE CLERGY 5

Harvard He was from H.   TOWNS 17

harvest laughs with a h.   COUNTRIES 34

harvesting h. and crop spraying   BODY 16

Harwich steamer from H.   TRANSPORT 11

has-been word for washed-up h.   SUCCESS 11

haste repent in h.   MARRIAGE 39

hat brim of her floppy h.   MEN AND WOMEN 28

exactly the right h.   FASHION 39

means a Paris h.   SEX 66

hate h. for queers   EPITAPHS 9

h. the French   COUNTRIES 27

If h. killed men   GARDENS 5

I h. all Boets and Bainters   ROYALTY 32

I h. men   MEN AND WOMEN 37

I h. music   MUSIC 15

players who h. your guts   BASEBALL 11

hated I h. it   ARMED FORCES 16

hates hateful h.   LOVE 24

h. dogs and babies   PEOPLE 36

h. them for it   HOPE 10

man who h. his mother   MARRIAGE 15

hating h., my boy   FRIENDS 15

hatred h. of domestic work   HOME 26

Oxford's instinctive h.   EDUCATION 35

hats h. were nearly all   FASHION 25

so many shocking bad h.   POLITICIANS 38

Haughey H. buried at midnight   POLITICIANS 25

haunt certain to h. her   FAMILY 7

have already h. it   GOVERNMENT 46

having have what she's h.   CHOICE 3

h. an old friend for dinner   SOCIETY 14

hawkish consider myself h.   ARMED FORCES 24

hay bottle of h.   FOOD 73

eating h.   FOOD 18

what h. looks like   COUNTRY 11

Haydn Some cry up H.   MUSICIANS 11

Hays H. is my shepherd — CINEMA 11
he H. would, wouldn't he — LIES 9
head for your good h. — BODY 15
　h. below water — SUCCESS 38
　h. in the sand — INTELLIGENCE 4
　h. of a dysfunctional family — ROYALTY 55
　his brains go to his h. — INSULTS 2
　incessantly stand on your h. — OLD AGE 8
　On my h. — PRIME MINISTERS 15
　popular h. girl — ACTING 30
　rears its ugly h. — SEX 13
　should have his h. examined — MEDICINE 14
　wrong man's h. off — CRIME 11
headache with a dismal h. — LANGUAGE 9
headline h. has not turned up — NEWSPAPERS 24
headmaster made H. of Westminster — PAST 10
headquarters chaplain around H.
　 — THE CLERGY 13
　got his h. — ARMED FORCES 21
heads lay their h. together — INSULTS 44
headstrong h. as an allegory — WIT 35
health interests of my h. — ALCOHOL 34
healths drink one another's h. — ALCOHOL 35
healthy h. and wealthy — DEATH 66
hear can't h. it — MUSICIANS 5
　can't h. what they say — YOUTH 7
　h. it through their feet — MUSIC 52
　h. my Thisby's face — WIT 28
　music one must h. several times — MUSIC 42
heard h. one of the original lines — THEATRE 29
　neither h., read, talked — MURDER 13
hearse walk before the h. — THEATRE 19
heart breaking my h. — HAPPINESS 3
　'CALLOUS' engraved on her h. — ROYALTY 64
　fart Of every h. — LOVE 44
　Fourteen h. attacks — DEATH 35
　get your h.'s desire — HAPPINESS 13
　h. belongs to Daddy — GOLF 9
　h. is on the left — MEDICINE 24
　h. of stone — CRITICS 44
　Irishman's h. is nothing — IRELAND 12
　occasional h. attack — HEALTH 1
　sake of my h. — HEALTH 5
　ways of mending a broken h. — LOVE 39
　What they call 'h.' — BODY 22
　woman has given you her h. — WOMEN 74
　your h. is there with it — WIT 3
hearts H. just as pure — ARISTOCRACY 7
　hidden in each other's h. — SECRECY 7
　hidden each other's h. — CHARACTER 5
　jining of h. and house-keeping — LOVE 13
heaven between H. and Hell — HEAVEN 7
　Germans went to h. — COUNTRIES 54
　h. is pleased to bestow it — WEALTH 30
　H. will protect a working-girl — POVERTY 19

　H. would be too dull — EPITAPHS 20
　it's the Hebrew in H. — LANGUAGES 10
　journey to h. — HEAVEN 1
　leave to h. — CHOICE 11
　leaving mercy to h. — CRIME 15
　like going to h. — ECONOMICS 6
　my idea of h. — HEAVEN 5
　NHS is quite like h. — SICKNESS 12
　no women in h. — RELIGION 34
　to h. might have gone — EPITAPHS 26
heavier seven stones h. — HEALTH 5
heavy less h.-footed — VIRTUE 15
heavyweight anything but a h. — BOXING 11
Hebrew I hear it's the H. in Heaven
　 — LANGUAGES 10
Hebrews H. 13.8 — CRITICS 8
hedgehog h. all in primroses — FASHION 24
heels double crossing of a pair of h. — LOVE 25
　shoes with high h. — FASHION 20
height down to my h. — BOXING 4
　MORE OR LESS THE SAME H. — TELEGRAMS 11
Heineken H. refreshes the parts — ALCOHOL 39
heir at it hunting for an h. — ROYALTY 56
hell between Heaven and H. — HEAVEN 7
　h. is a very large party — PARTIES 3
　H. is full of musical amateurs — MUSIC 48
　H. would not be Hell — EPITAPHS 20
　I say the h. with it — FOOD 87
　my idea of h. — FOOTBALL 3
　probably re-designed H. — HEAVEN 4
　they think it is h. — TRUTH 10
　want to go to H. — HEAVEN 3
　would be h. on earth — HAPPINESS 12
hellhound h. is always a hellhound
　 — CHARACTER 22
hellish My life was simply h. — SATISFACTION 10
hello H. boys — BODY 4
　H. possums — COMEDY 16
helluva New York,—a h. town — TOWNS 11
help his wife has to h. him — TRUST 6
　I constructed a cry for h. — SELF-KNOWLEDGE 14
　I will h. them there — HEAVEN 3
　'O! h. me, heaven,' she prayed — WOMEN 22
　sick enough to call for h. — MEDICINE 23
　very present h. — LIES 1
　you can't h. it — INSULTS 43
helped can't be h. — CRIME 11
helping h. police with their enquiries — WEALTH 1
Hemingway H. and *not* seen the joke
　 — WRITERS 41
hen gentle useful h. — FOOD 22
　h. is only an egg's way — BIRDS 3
　h. you ran over the other day — MARRIAGE 93
Henery I'm H. the Eighth, I am — MARRIAGE 90

hen-pecked have they not h. you all

INTELLIGENCE 3

hens h. who've earned privileges   BIRDS 2

herald Hark! the h. angels sing   MEDICINE 4

herb No h. ever cures anything   MEDICINE 20

herbaceous h. border   LIES 7

herbs intolerance to h.   ALCOHOL 68

herds H. of wildebeeste   PLACES 6

here H. at last is Asia   PLACES 5

I'm still h.   MISTAKES 19

want you to be h. and sexy   MARRIAGE 116

heresy Englishman believes be h.   RELIGION 64

hermaphroditism heavenly h.   MUSICIANS 19

hero aspires to be a h.   ALCOHOL 36

h. is a bee   ANIMALS 15

h. is the author   BOOKS 24

I may be the H. of a novel yet   LITERATURE 24

they don't want to be a h.   WAR 27

Herod character of H.   CHILDREN 7

hour of H.   CHILDREN 17

heroes h. were good   BOOKS 13

heroine when a h. goes mad   MIND 8

heron H. flies   BIRDS 1

h.'s eggs   FOOD 28

herring these pickle h.   FOOD 74

Herveys men, women, and H.   ARISTOCRACY 17

Herzog thought Moses H.   MIND 1

hesitate h. and halt so in his talk

PRIME MINISTERS 13

heterodox It would have been less h.   LETTERS 2

heterodoxy another man's h.   BEHAVIOUR 33

hick Sticks nix h. pix   NEWSPAPERS 2

hidden h. in each other's hearts   SECRECY 7

h. in each other's hearts   CHARACTER 5

teems with h. meaning   WORDS 10

hide Minister has nothing to h.   PRIDE 2

hideous horrid, h. notes of woe   MISTAKES 9

high her h. days and low days   MEDICINE 2

h. altar on the move   DESCRIPTION 6

h. cheekbones   ACTORS 1

h. road that leads   SCOTLAND 5

h.-water mark   FAMILY 47

I'm getting h.   ALCOHOL 16

She's the Broad and I'm the H.   PRIDE 9

walk along H. Holborn   HOPE 7

highballs Three h. and I think   ALCOHOL 48

highbrow What is a h.   INTELLIGENCE 16

higher capable of h. things   LITERATURE 18

high-tech h. is that you always end up

TECHNOLOGY 9

highway Thanks to the interstate h.   TRAVEL 18

himself more interested in h.   SELF-KNOWLEDGE 3

hindquarters h. ought to be   ARMED FORCES 21

hindsight h. attachment   HOME 3

H. is always twenty-twenty   PAST 18

hinges more h. in it   GOLF 1

hippopotami like hell-bound h.   WOMEN 58

hippopotamus shoot the H.   ANIMALS 5

hips Mae West's h.   ACTORS 16

tight about the h.   DESCRIPTION 35

when your h. stick   MEN AND WOMEN 30

hired h. the money   DEBT 2

hireling Pay given to a state h.   TRUST 9

historians H. repeat one another   HISTORY 3

history disasters of English h.   WALES 7

H. came to a stop   HISTORY 9

h. comes equipped   HISTORY 14

H. gets thicker   HISTORY 12

H. is more or less   HISTORY 6

H. is not what you thought   HISTORY 8

H. repeats itself   HISTORY 3

H. started badly   HISTORY 18

H. teaches us   HISTORY 5

make more h.   COUNTRIES 50

owe to h.   HISTORY 17

People who make h.   HISTORY 4

place in h.   POLITICIANS 32

takes a great deal of h.   LITERATURE 22

telescope h.   CRITICS 2

What will h. say   HISTORY 10

hit h. 'em in the body   BOXING 4

H. me with   TITLES 2

they'll all h. you   EDUCATION 28

think and h.   BASEBALL 2

Hitler kissing H.   FILM STARS 5

hitter poor h.   BASEBALL 8

ho What h.   CONVERSATION 32

hoarder h. of two things   FRIENDS 18

Hoare H.-Laval pact   DIPLOMACY 10

Hoares No more H. to Paris   ROYALTY 36

hockey play h. properly   PARTIES 3

hoedown break into a lively h.   OLD AGE 31

Hoffa H.'s most valuable   DEATH 47

hog disadvantage of being a h.   ANIMALS 32

hogamus H., higamous   MARRIAGE 76

hokum Of all the h.   CLASS 23

holding batsman's H.   NAMES 11

without h. on   ALCOHOL 42

holds she h. herself very well   ROYALTY 1

hole h. in a stained glass window   WOMEN 7

knows of a better h.   WAR 4

only a h.   BASEBALL 13

sub-normallest h. I ever struck   PLACES 1

holes small and full of h.   SMOKING 1

holiday Welcome to H. Inn   HOTELS 1

What kind of h.   HOLIDAYS 4

when on a h.   HOLIDAYS 6

holidays during the h.   EDUCATION 40

earlier h.   HOLIDAYS 9

holiness like your h.   FRIENDS 6

Holland H. . . . lies so low — COUNTRIES 30
Holloway caught shoplifting and go to H.
  — PARTIES 9
Hollywood H. Boulevard — TOWNS 12
  H. is a place — CINEMA 1
  H. is bounded — CINEMA 7
  H. money — CINEMA 38
  Hooray for H. — CINEMA 31
  invited to H. — LITERATURE 14
  Lunch H.-style — FOOD 40
  only 'ism' in H. — CINEMA 36
  tinsel of H. — CINEMA 28
holy devil and the H. See — CENSORSHIP 18
  dropped the word 'H.' — BIBLE 9
  H. deadlock — MARRIAGE 72
homage h. which they pay — HYPOCRISY 2
home all the comforts of h. — TRAVEL 3
  Boston, the h. of the bean — TOWNS 7
  geriatric h. — HAPPINESS 1
  good of a h. — HOME 15
  H., James — TRANSPORT 19
  H. is heaven — PARTIES 4
  h. keeps you from — FAMILY 31
  h. life as we understand it — HOME 20
  h. life of our own dear Queen — ROYALTY 10
  h. of the literal — AMERICA 28
  it never is at h. — WIT 7
  murder into the h. — MURDER 5
  no place like h. — SELF-KNOWLEDGE 15
  refuge from h. life — HOTELS 5
  should begin at h. — CENSORSHIP 16
  there's nobody at h. — WIT 27
  you can't go h. again — SUCCESS 4
  you're never far from h. — WEALTH 24
Homer H. sometimes sleeps — LITERATURE 11
  more than H. knew — CRITICS 35
  voice of H. — SICKNESS 11
homes Stately H. — ARISTOCRACY 3
  Stately H. of England — MURDER 3
homework dog ate my h. — DIPLOMACY 11
homicidal great h. classics — LITERATURE 35
homos books about h. — READING 14
  stately h. of England — SEX 28
homosexual composer and *not* h. — MUSICIANS 7
  My mother made me a h. — SEX 9
homosexuality If h. were the normal way
  — SEX 20
honest better to be quotable than h.
  — QUOTATIONS 21
  buy it like an h. man — WEALTH 20
  man looked h. enough — VIRTUE 22
  Men are so h. — MEN AND WOMEN 22
honesty h. is a good thing — VIRTUE 12
honey month of h. — MARRIAGE 19

honeymooning unusual emotion for a h.
  husband — MARRIAGE 22
Hong Kong H. POOH-POOHS — NEWSPAPERS 1
honorary h. Protestants — RELIGION 30
honour fighting for this woman's h. — WOMEN 38
  h. is almost greater — PUBLISHING 22
  in h. of a critic — CRITICS 33
  Let us h. if we can — SEX 10
  loss of h. was a wrench — LANGUAGES 13
  louder he h. of his h. — VIRTUE 8
honourable His designs were strictly h.
  — MARRIAGE 55
honoured deeply h. — BODY 29
honours good card to play for H. — LITERATURE 7
hooray H. for Hollywood — CINEMA 31
Hoover onto the board of H. — WOMEN 29
hop little buggers h. — DANCE 1
hope from rising h. — SUCCESS 14
  h. that keeps up a wife's spirits — MARRIAGE 61
  triumph of h. over experience — MARRIAGE 77
hopeless To inspire h. passion
  — MEN AND WOMEN 48
hopes no great h. from Birmingham — TOWNS 3
hops cherries, h., and women — PLACES 9
horizontal But the h. one — SEX 10
  h. desire — DANCE 16
Horlick reeking of H. — PEOPLE 6
horns h. of a Dalai Lama — WIT 46
horrible awe-inspiringly h. — CHILDREN 36
horror bristling with h. — HOLIDAYS 9
  h. and struck — FILMS 6
  I have a h. of sunsets — WEATHER 22
horse about the h. — ANIMALS 41
  does not make him a h. — IRELAND 13
  got a h. right here — BETTING 10
  hair of the h. — HYPOCRISY 7
  heard no h. sing a song — MUSIC 2
  h. designed by a committee — BUREAUCRACY 10
  h. is at least *human* — TRANSPORT 4
  h. is to the Arab — ANIMALS 20
  H. sense is a good judgement — BETTING 5
  like a h. and carriage — MARRIAGE 27
  phone, a h. or a broad — PEOPLE 26
  tail of the noble h. — MUSIC 30
  to the h. dentist — ANIMALS 24
  where's the bloody h. — LITERATURE 12
horseback Jews upon h. — COUNTRIES 21
  On h. after we — FAMILY 9
Horseguards You can be in the H. — SOCIETY 18
horses Bring on the empty h. — CINEMA 5
  don't spare the h. — TRANSPORT 19
  frighten the h. — SEX 25
  given to h. — SCOTLAND 6
  sixty h. wedged in a chimney — NEWSPAPERS 24

horses (cont.):

They eat h.	FOOD 62
Wild h. on their bended knees	WIT 2

horseshoe h. hanging over — CERTAINTY 5
horticulture lead a h. — WOMEN 57
Hoskin loo-vely, Mrs H. — COMEDY 17
hospital doctor whispers in the h. — MEDICINE 33

is his h.	ENGLAND 15
patient in any h. in Ireland	MEDICINE 25

hospitality h. I have enjoyed — AUTOBIOGRAPHY 16

shrink from acts of h.	PARTIES 5

hospitals big fear in h. — SICKNESS 15
host have been under the h. — ALCOHOL 49
hostages taking of h. — BROADCASTING 5
hostesses fall for air h. — WEALTH 8
hostility based on h. — HUMOUR 35

fosters international h.	SPORTS 21

hosts h. and guests — CLASS 3
hot It's Rome, it's h. — CINEMA 3

red h., mate	CENSORSHIP 8

hot dog h. and vintage wine — FOOD 40
hotel back to the h. — SELF-KNOWLEDGE 16

from h. to hotel	JOURNALISM 20
great advantage of a h.	HOTELS 5
It used to be a good h.	PAST 15

hound I loves the h. more — SPORTS 31

nothin' but a h. dog	LOVE 29

hour h. of Herod — CHILDREN 17
hourglass Egghead weds h. — MARRIAGE 5
hours But I see the h. pass — WORK 8

it has been going three h.	MUSIC 39
most rewarding h.	TRANSPORT 3

house called a woman in my own h. — WOMEN 77

COULDN'T DRAW IN THIS H.	TELEGRAMS 15
Englishman's h.	ENGLAND 15
every h. in London	SOCIETY 26
H. at Pooh Corner	CRITICS 26
H. Beautiful is play lousy	THEATRE 38
H. of Peers	GOVERNMENT 12
in the way in the h.	FAMILY 16
I want a h.	HOME 16
leaving her present h.	CLASS 26
see the H. run by a philistine	SUCCESS 18
sell his h.	HOME 24
Spinks will come to your h.	BOXING 10
swell h.	PROGRESS 16
when I divorce I keep the h.	MARRIAGE 58

householder housekeeper think she's a h.

MARRIAGE 135

housekeeper h. think she's a householder

MARRIAGE 135

seems an economical h.	THEATRE 59

housekeeping He taught me h. — MARRIAGE 58
house-keepings jining of hearts and h.

LOVE 13

House of Commons advice for H. quotations

QUOTATIONS 7

attendance at the H.	MARRIAGE 52
H. en bloc do it	SEX 27
H. is trying	GOVERNMENT 47
libraries of the H.	LIBRARIES 4
untrue in the H.	LIES 12

House of Lords H. is a perfect eventide home

OLD AGE 38

houses books in their h. — BOOKS 15
housework law of H. — HOME 8

no need to do any h.	HOME 12

hove what's it doing in H. — SICKNESS 5
how H. can they tell — DEATH 52

say why and h.	AUTOBIOGRAPHY 25

hucksters h.' shops — DICTIONARIES 11
hugged h. by Diana Rigg — MEDICINE 30
human bona fide h. being — HUMAN RACE 10

civil servants are h. beings	CIVIL SERVANTS 6
contempt for h. nature	SELF-KNOWLEDGE 24
disappointed in h. nature	HUMAN RACE 4
err is h.	COMPUTERS 1
err is h.	VIRTUE 27
falure is h.	SUCCESS 28
full tide of h. existence	TOWNS 22
horse is at least h.	TRANSPORT 35
h. race doesn't handle	HUMAN RACE 14
h. race would never	FOOLISHNESS 3
loved the H. Race	HUMAN RACE 9
motor car to the h. race	TRANSPORT 18
people are only h.	HUMAN RACE 2
resign your job as a h.	SCIENCE 26

humanity unremitting h. — LITERATURE 6
humans It isn't fit for h. now — TOWNS 6
Humber look at H. Bridge — AWARDS 4
humble so very h. — HYPOCRISY 4
humbug People like a bit of h. — SNOBBERY 12

Yes we have. H.	LANGUAGES 18

humdrum h. issues — NATURE 10
humiliation shame and h. — FAME 14
humility small book on H. — PRIDE 4
hummy that word 'h.' — CRITICS 26
humorists great h. — HUMOUR 23
humorous because a book is h. — PUBLISHING 19

h. resignation	HAPPINESS 8

humour Australian h. — COUNTRIES 31

deliberate h.	DICTIONARIES 6
flummoxed by h.	COUNTRIES 5
geniuses are devoid of h.	SPEECHES 14
have a sense of h.	APPEARANCE 5
h. from women	HUMOUR 9
H. is, but its nature	HUMOUR 31
h. is based	HUMOUR 35
h. of a bar-loafer	WRITERS 26
H. studies	HUMOUR 42

industry scientist without i. connections

SCIENCE 27

whole field to private i. WAR 15

inebriated i. with the exuberance INSULTS 14

ineffectual Remote and i. Don LITERATURE 5

inexperienced young and i. HOME 16

infallible i. rule CLASS 31

men of science being i. SCIENCE 13

infamy I., infamy MURDER 10

infant i. phenomenon ACTORS 15

infantry posted to the i. CRIME 16

infants I.' Bible Class EDUCATION 51

infection risk of verbal i. QUOTATIONS 18

inferiority Asia without an i. complex PLACES 5

inferiors kind to her i. SNOBBERY 15

infinite Space is almost i. UNIVERSE 15

infinitive when I split an i. LANGUAGE 4

infinitives i. neatly down the middle

LANGUAGE 19

inflation soaring i. LANGUAGES 16

influence i. over Lord Byron RELIGION 65

not susceptible to i. CHARACTER 20

influenza My aunt died of i. SICKNESS 23

inform not to i. the reader BUREAUCRACY 1

information i. and wit CONVERSATION 15

i. leavened BOOKS 9

Minister of I. GOVERNMENT 6

informed badly-i. labrador SEX 57

far better i. JUDGES 15

infra dig Considered all gnomes i. SNOBBERY 14

ingénue I am just an i. YOUTH 2

inhale didn't i. POLITICIANS 30

I didn't i. DRUGS 3

if he doesn't i. PRAISE 11

iniquity den of i. HOTELS 3

injured Chamberlain as an i. man POLITICIANS 20

injustice I. is relatively easy to bear LAW 23

That's social i. SOCIETY 6

ink mimeographed in dark brown i.

NEWSPAPERS 11

innocence assumption of i. so easy VIRTUE 6

innocent I am i. JUDGES 3

inorganic English is now inert and i. WRITING 10

Inquisition expects the Spanish I. COMEDY 29

insane defendant became i. MURDER 12

insanity any i. in her family MIND 7

insect some hapless i. ANIMALS 21

insensibility stark i. EDUCATION 22

insert didn't i. POLITICIANS 30

inside i. the tent pissing out POWER 6

insides how do two i. make love SEX 46

insomnia Amor vincit i. SLEEP 3

inspiration Genius is one percent i.

INTELLIGENCE 5

instalment last i. missing AUTOBIOGRAPHY 8

instant I. Sex SEX 29

instinct i. for being unhappy HAPPINESS 11

instincts It panders to i. WAR 5

institution I'm not ready for an i. yet

MARRIAGE 129

see an i. without hitting it POWER 3

institutions Laws and i. LAW 2

instructions give your employees i. WORK 22

I have no i. DIPLOMACY 3

impossible i. ARMED FORCES 12

manufacturer's i. SMOKING 2

insufferable made me i. EDUCATION 4

insular i. country subject to fogs POLITICS 30

insult not i. his wife publicly MARRIAGE 123

insulted never *hope* to go and get i. PREJUDICE 1

insulting i. Christmas card CHRISTMAS 7

insuppressible i. island IRELAND 4

insurance life-i. agents DEATH 37

ought to carry i. on those WOMEN 8

integral very good at i. ARMED FORCES 11

intellect his i. is improperly exposed MIND 9

intellectual lords of ladies i. INTELLIGENCE 3

more i. THE CLERGY 18

word 'I.' INTELLIGENCE 1

intellectuals spend my life with i.

INTELLIGENCE 20

intelligence i. and no brains CHARACTER 7

i. of the great masses INTELLIGENCE 12

no great i. SELF-KNOWLEDGE 6

Intelligence Service in charge of the I.

SECRECY 8

intelligent Every i. voter POLITICS 2

first rule of i. tinkering TECHNOLOGY 4

must be i. ACTING 18

only a very i. person IDEAS 8

only look i. COUNTRIES 23

intentions Good i. LANGUAGE 20

interest Crazy-High-I. account WEALTH 10

give an i. to one's old age OLD AGE 40

interested i. in art CINEMA 42

in which he has been greatly i. LETTERS 1

interesting in an i. condition APPEARANCE 6

i., but tough BOOKS 22

something more i. than women INTELLIGENCE 16

this makes them more i. NEWSPAPERS 18

Very i. COMEDY 39

interests i. masquerading as a contest

POLITICS 13

interfere does not i. with business POLITICS 29

interior i. decorators ART 14

intermission surrounds an i. MUSIC 41

international fosters i. hostility SPORTS 21

Internet posted on the I. COMPUTERS 4

thanks to the I. COMPUTERS 5

interpose in quarrels i.   ARGUMENT 7
interpreter i. is the hardest   LANGUAGES 21
interstate Thanks to the i. highway   TRAVEL 18
interview *marvellous* i.   BEHAVIOUR 1
  standard female job i.   WOMEN 18
intestinal most i. of instruments   MUSIC 11
intimacy oral-genital i.   SEX 39
intimate i. spectacle   CINEMA 14
intimidating Prime Minister should be i.
   PRIME MINISTERS 23
intoxication mild i.   ALCOHOL 3
intransitive customary i. operation   WIT 24
introduced been i. to   BEHAVIOUR 5
introduction buy back my i.   BEHAVIOUR 25
introspection much given to i.
   SELF-KNOWLEDGE 24
introspective said Shakespeare. 'I.'   ACTING 5
intrusion call it i.   EDUCATION 42
intrusive Whence came the i. comma
   WRITING 9
intuition explanation of i.   ADVERTISING 9
invade won't i.   POLITICIANS 30
invented i. blue jeans   FASHION 32
  speech to finish being i.   LANGUAGE 6
inventing Molesworth 2 . . . is i. the wheel
   TECHNOLOGY 17
invention i. of a mouse   FAME 11
  Marriage is a wonderful i.   MARRIAGE 41
  pure i.   LITERATURE 10
  That nasty old i.   POVERTY 9
inventions i. women could do without
   TECHNOLOGY 8
inverse i. proportion to the sum   TIME 12
investigations i. of Herr Freud   ART 17
investment it's a good i.   LOVE 4
  tribes of i. brokers   PAST 12
  trifling i. of fact   SCIENCE 32
invisible no i. means of support   RELIGION 12
invitations *her* i.   HANDWRITING 2
Iowa people from I.   CINEMA 1
IQ I. of 170   INTELLIGENCE 14
  I. of a moron   ART 30
Ireland East Coast of I.   WEATHER 16
  I. is a small   IRELAND 4
  never sex in I.   TELEVISION 7
  now handling I.   GOVERNMENT 45
  patient in any hospital in I.   MEDICINE 25
Irish answer to the I. Question   IRELAND 11
  I'm I.   IRELAND 7
  I. gardens   GARDENS 11
  I. have wit   HUMOUR 19
  I. how to listen   CONVERSATION 31
  I. people all over   HUMOUR 30
  I. politics   IRELAND 9
  part played by the I. Navy   ARMED FORCES 2

primitive I. parent   PARENTS 1
someone to be I. at   IRELAND 2
symbol of I. art   ART 15
they want I. government   IRELAND 5
Irishman I.'s heart is nothing   IRELAND 12
  lying in an I.   LIES 7
iron i. ladies   BIOGRAPHY 13
ironic skipped the i.   COUNTRIES 31
irrelevant word 'i.'   EDUCATION 13
irritate can't afford to i.   FRIENDS 20
is meaning of 'i.'   WORDS 6
island i. is made mainly   BUREAUCRACY 4
ism only 'i.' in Hollywood   CINEMA 36
Isosceles ran into I.   IDEAS 1
Israel O I.   FAMILY 33
Israelite I. leaders   GOD 28
Italian baseball in I.   SONGS 16
  old I. stereotype   COMEDY 13
Italians I.' technological contribution   SCIENCE 7
Italy Creator made I.   COUNTRIES 59
itemised i. phone bill ranks up there
   TECHNOLOGY 8
iterated i. before   CONVERSATION 29
ivy it was agony, I.   COMEDY 8

jackasses all others are j.   PHILOSOPHY 5
jacket *short* j. is always   FASHION 11
jacuzzi floozie in the j.   ARCHITECTURE 1
jaguar park one J.   TRANSPORT 15
jail being in a j.   ARMED FORCES 17
  j. birds sing   CRIME 22
jam j. tomorrow   PAST 4
jamais j. triste   HOPE 6
James death of Jesse J.   ART 37
  Home, J.   TRANSPORT 19
  J. I, James II   LITERATURE 19
  J. writes fiction   WRITERS 44
  Poor Henry J.   WRITERS 28
Jane you J.   FILMS 13
janitor j. to the looney-bin   MEDICINE 37
Japanese get away with in J.   CENSORSHIP 5
  J. maple   GARDENS 7
jazz burglars and j. musicians   WORK 18
  in j. and more than ten   MUSIC 35
  J. will endure   MUSIC 52
jealousy j. with a halo   MORALITY 15
jeans designer j.   FASHION 31
  invented blue j.   FASHION 32
Jeeves J. is a wonder   INTELLIGENCE 18
  J. shimmered out   TELEGRAMS 23
Jefferson when J. ate alone   INTELLIGENCE 8
jelly Meaty j.   MEDICINE 10
  shivers like a j.   DANCE 14
jellybeans way of eating j.   CHARACTER 10
je-ne-sais-quoi *J.* young man   MEN 7

Jesuit J. practitioners   ARGUMENT 15
    resembles a superannuated J.   SELF-KNOWLEDGE 5
Jesuits telling jokes to J.   HUMOUR 24
Jesus J. Christ and Napoleon   PRIME MINISTERS 21
    J. was a normal   MEDICINE 17
Jew I'm Super-j.   PEOPLE 10
    not really a J.   COUNTRIES 42
    one-eyed J.   GOLF 3
jewels sex and j.   ART 27
Jewish I'm not J.   COUNTRIES 23
    It'll be good J. music   MUSIC 28
    J. man with parents alive   PARENTS 13
    only half-J.   PREJUDICE 11
Jews choose The J.   GOD 21
    J. upon horseback   COUNTRIES 21
    place was run by J.   EPITAPHS 26
    spurn the J.   GOD 13
Jim call it St J.   NAMES 14
job any j. men willingly vacate
    MEN AND WOMEN 50
    came fifth and lost the j.   SUCCESS 17
    difficulty about a theatre j.   THEATRE 24
    doing a grand j.   COMEDY 35
    easier j. like publishing   PUBLISHING 1
    getting a j. is another   WORK 19
    husband is a whole-time j.   MARRIAGE 14
    j. when he doesn't feel like it   WORK 2
    loses his j.   BUSINESS 18
    MP is the sort of j.   POLITICS 1
    offering them your j.   GOVERNMENT 17
    read the book of J.   BIBLE 8
    resign your j. as a human   SCIENCE 26
    standard female j. interview   WOMEN 18
jogging J. is for people   SPORTS 38
John do not christen him J.   NAMES 13
    more MPs called J.   NAMES 12
Johnson Cham of literature, Samuel J.
    PEOPLE 40
    no arguing with J.   ARGUMENT 8
joinery j. with a chainsaw   DIPLOMACY 6
joining j. of hearts and house-keepings   LOVE 13
joint minute you walked in the j.
    MEN AND WOMEN 11
    Remove the j.   BEHAVIOUR 5
joints I do see her in tough j.   WOMEN 60
joke American j.   HUMOUR 40
    Hemingway and *not* seen the j.   WRITERS 41
    idea of a good j.   HUMOUR 21
    j. as a serious thing   HUMOUR 30
    j.'s a very serious thing   HUMOUR 10
    j. well into a Scotch   SCOTLAND 11
    j. with a double meaning   HUMOUR 3
    tell an Iowan a j.   HUMOUR 7

jokes all the j. about George V   ROYALTY 51
    and no j.   HUMOUR 29
    apocryphal j.   DEATH 15
    doesn't make j.   CIVIL SERVANTS 5
    every ten j.   HUMOUR 38
    good at telling j.   MISTAKES 8
    J. are fast running out   HUMOUR 6
    j. never seem to the British   SPEECHES 11
    little j. on thee   GOD 22
    one of his own j.   HUMOUR 4
    someone was telling j.   THEATRE 30
    taste in j.   HUMOUR 14
    telling j. to Jesuits   HUMOUR 24
    things which are not j.   ARISTOCRACY 4
jolly Awfully j. of you   LAST WORDS 4
Jones Lord J. Dead   JOURNALISM 8
Joneses keep up with the J.   LIFE 9
Josephine Not tonight, J.   SEX 54
journal keep a full j.   DIARIES 7
    page of my J.   DIARIES 2
    regret, dear j.   DIARIES 4
journalism cheque-book j.   JOURNALISM 18
    first law of j.   JOURNALISM 10
    J. is unreadable   JOURNALISM 25
    J. largely consists   JOURNALISM 8
journalist British j.   JOURNALISM 26
    than a j.   JOURNALISM 17
journalists lies to j.   GOVERNMENT 24
Jovelike his J. side   FAMILY 25
    J. wrath   ANGER 11
Joyce [J.] has the most lovely voice   PEOPLE 30
Judas J. who writes   BIOGRAPHY 17
judge best j. of a run   CRICKET 17
    God is my j.   JUDGES 3
    j. goes to the lawyer   CINEMA 10
    j. had slept through his play   JUDGES 14
    know who the j. is   JUDGES 5
    mail that cheque to the J.   JUDGES 6
    talking J. is like   JUDGES 16
    they j. them   CHILDREN 41
judgement not give his j. rashly   ARGUMENT 1
    question of j.   MISTAKES 8
judges j. are a mine of instruction   QUOTATIONS 3
    J. commonly are elderly men   JUDGES 9
    She threw me in front of the j.   SPORTS 5
judging never had the Latin for the j.   JUDGES 7
Judy O'Grady Colonel's Lady an' J.   WOMEN 39
jug loose fum de j.   ALCOHOL 33
juice j. of two quarts   ALCOHOL 18
Julian I'm J.   COMEDY 15
Julius here comes J.   CINEMA 3
July fourth of J.   AMERICA 15
June J. is bustin' out   COUNTRY 6
Jungfrau looking like the J.   ROYALTY 18

up to her k. | PREJUDICE 11
valuable institution to its k. | SUCCESS 18
Wild horses on their bended k. | WIT 2
knew WE ALL K. YOU HAD IT IN YOU | TELEGRAMS 18
knife k. to a throat | PUBLISHING 16
using a k. | BEHAVIOUR 3
knighted I didn't know he'd been k. | INSULTS 7
knighthood K. was in the pod | PAST 9
knitter beautiful little k. | WRITERS 38
knitting opened a k. shop | WOMEN 15
knock K. as you please | WIT 27
k. it never is at home | WIT 7
nice k.-down argument | WORDS 5
knocked k. everything but the knees

THEATRE 22
we k. the bastard off | SUCCESS 16
knocking just k. it through | TOWNS 15
knocks k. you down with the butt | ARGUMENT 8
knot there's no k. for me | LOVE 19
know do not wish to k. | EXAMINATIONS 4
don't k. what I am doing | SCIENCE 6
How do you k. | GOD 8
I Don't K. | COMEDY 40
merely k. more | CHILDREN 32
not pretend to k. | CERTAINTY 9
things we k. nothing about | BOOKS 17
You k. | BOXING 3
You lie and you k. it | SPORTS 29
You should bl-bloody well k. | ROYALTY 38
knowledge k. of a lifetime | ART 34
quite a fair show of k. | QUOTATIONS 5
known apart from the k. and the unknown

PHILOSOPHY 6
k., and do not want it | INSULTS 24
very well k. | CRITICS 41
knows He k. nothing | POLITICS 66
if you k. of a better 'ole | WAR 4
man who k. more | CENSORSHIP 21
knuckle k.-end of England | SCOTLAND 10
knuckles biting my k. | FILMS 9
koala k. bears rushing about | WEATHER 2
Krakatoa K. number | ANGER 6
Kruschev married Mrs K. | HISTORY 13

labels l. served up | FOOD 93
laboratory used to be a l. | DRUGS 7
labour Barking L. Party | MARRIAGE 87
I did not vote L. | POLITICAL PARTIES 6
L. is led by an upper class | POLITICAL PARTIES 13
L. Party is going round stirring

POLITICAL PARTIES 19
L. spin doctors | POLITICIANS 11
L.-voting Scotland | DIPLOMACY 16
leader for the L. Party | POLITICIANS 8

New L. is popular in Scotland

POLITICAL PARTIES 3
problem with New L. | POLITICAL PARTIES 14
two days' l. | ART 34
labrador badly-informed l. | SEX 57
ladder I never climbed any l. | SUCCESS 30
ladies Here's to the l. who lunch | WOMEN 64
L., just a little more | ACTING 29
l. and their dogs | GARDENS 16
l. apparently rolled along | MEN AND WOMEN 18
lords of l. intellectual | INTELLIGENCE 3
than leading l. | ACTORS 28
when l. declare war on me | ROYALTY 47
lads We are l. | MEN 6
lady definition of a l. | WOMEN 43
I'm no l. | SONGS 14
l. doth protest too much | WOMEN 62
l. is a tramp | BEHAVIOUR 16
l.'s conversation | COUNTRY 13
l. that's known as Lou | MEN AND WOMEN 41
nicest old l. | WRITERS 11
talk like a l. | CLASS 27
tattooed l. | BODY 20
writing for an elderly l. | JOURNALISM 14
young l. named Bright | SCIENCE 8
ladysmocks L. grow | WEATHER 1
lagoon goona goona l. | LOVE 28
laid l. end to end | WOMEN 56
lake meal on a l. | FOOD 51
lama horns of a Dalai L. | WIT 46
lame Very old—very l.—no metras | OLD AGE 13
laments forest l. | PRIME MINISTERS 10
lamp smell too strong of the l. | LITERATURE 34
turn it into a l. | HOME 22
lamppost asking a l. | CRITICS 16
To-day I am a l. | QUOTATIONS 1
land back to the l. | SELF-KNOWLEDGE 16
l. of my fathers | WALES 5
l. of the dull | AMERICA 28
My family owned l. | WOMEN 69
landlord L. says | DEBT 4
Sir Roger is l. | RELIGION 2
Landseer L. whose only merit | ART 18
langlish Spanglish is l. we know | LANGUAGES 9
language divided by a common l. | COUNTRIES 55
every European l. except one | LANGUAGES 12
in a foreign l. | PARENTS 11
l. an opera is sung in | SONGS 4
l. being the aniseed | CONVERSATION 27
l. of Shakespeare | LANGUAGES 20
L. was not powerful enough | ACTORS 15
mastered everything except l. | WRITERS 45
our rich and delicate l. | WRITERS 42

leaks l. always take place — SECRECY 4
leap milk's l. — FOOD 26
leaping l.-before-you-look — LANGUAGES 8
leaps It moves in mighty l. — MEDICINE 3
learn don't want to l. — EDUCATION 37
learned all you have ever l. — EDUCATION 5
 going to a l. conference — LOVE 39
 l. as much from Cézanne — SONGS 12
 l. in seven years — GENERATION GAP 12
 Quote L. — JUDGES 11
lease Imagine signing a l. together — MARRIAGE 64
least man who promises l. — POLITICS 10
leather dress up in chamois l. — HAPPINESS 10
 in their l. shoes — FASHION 29
leave just who would have to l. — LAW 33
 l. off tobacco — SMOKING 5
 L. out the cherry — ALCOHOL 51
leaves man who l. the room — POLITICAL PARTIES 2
 Words are like l. — WORDS 24
lecture tire of a l. — EDUCATION 24
lecturer extension l. — ACTORS 10
leeks cabbages and l. — CENSORSHIP 15
left I had l. without the train — TRAVEL 22
leftovers nothing but l. — COOKERY 21
leg anthologist lifts his l. — QUOTATIONS 1
 broken my bloody l. — CRICKET 1
 leave my second l. — ARMED FORCES 15
 which does not resemble a l. — TECHNOLOGY 1
legacy l. from a rich relative — POLITICS 68
legal l. writing is one of those — LAW 15
 some l. experience — FAMILY 23
legality taint of l. — LAW 17
legalizing l. petty larceny — RELIGION 31
legend l. in his own lunchtime — FAME 8
legibility dawn of l. — HANDWRITING 3
legible is to be l. — ARGUMENT 14
legion L. of Honour has been conferred
 — PRIDE 13
 Ravel refuses the L. of Honour — MUSICIANS 14
legitimate AT LAST — TELEGRAMS 9
legs born with your l. apart — SEX 58
 chop off her l. and read the rings — MARRIAGE 84
 l. round his neck — ANGER 1
 not for your bad l. — BODY 15
 planks in my l. — TRANSPORT 31
 recuvver the use of his l. — LETTERS 7
 see my l. — BODY 12
 took off his l. — ARMED FORCES 14
 two l. bad — ANIMALS 36
 uglier a man's l. are — GOLF 12
 walking on his hinder l. — WOMEN 37
Leighton Buzzard to come from L. — TRAVEL 24
leisure At l. married — MARRIAGE 39
 elderly persons with l. — WORK 21
 That is what l. means — WORK 3

lemon in the squeezing of a l. — TIME 8
lemonade I'll take a l. — FOOD 56
lend not well enough to l. to — FRIENDS 3
length exactly the same l. — AUTOBIOGRAPHY 9
lens use their Joan Collins l. — SELF-KNOWLEDGE 26
lent In L. she ate onion soup — FOOD 1
Léonie Weep not for little L. — LANGUAGES 13
leopard There was a l. — ANIMALS 19
lepers Shakepeare to the l. — ACTORS 11
lesbian l. mud-wrestling — DESCRIPTION 30
 politest l. — BEHAVIOUR 1
less can't take l. — FOOD 17
 l. in this than meets the eye — THEATRE 4
lessen l. from day to day — WIT 4
lesser l. of two weevils — CHOICE 15
lesson l. to all us men — MARRIAGE 4
 satire is a l. — WIT 23
lessons reason they're called l. — WIT 4
let L. my people go — CRITICS 30
lets I l. 'em — MEDICINE 11
letter authentic self into a l. — LETTERS 11
 cautious l.-writer — LETTERS 3
 [l.] longer than usual — LETTERS 12
 plaintive l. — BIOGRAPHY 11
 put the l. in the letter-o-box — LETTERS 2
 replied to your l. — LETTERS 13
letters able l. to *The Times* — PEOPLE 7
 Any further l. — DEBT 3
 l. get in the wrong places — LANGUAGE 14
 l. printed in the papers — WRITERS 47
 like women's l. — LETTERS 9
 man of l. — FOOLISHNESS 27
 my name in such large l. — PRIDE 11
 reading l. — CENSORSHIP 25
lettuce crop of l. — FOOD 4
 too much l. — FOOD 63
level discussing on the same l. — DIPLOMACY 3
leveller great l. — INDEXES 4
lexicographer L. A writer — DICTIONARIES 8
lexicographers these l. — DICTIONARIES 2
lexicon Two men wrote a l. — DICTIONARIES 13
liaisons L.! What's happened — ARISTOCRACY 19
liar answered 'Little L.' — LIES 4
 exceptionally good l. — TRUTH 7
 ignorant, uncultivated l. — LAW 37
 talent of a l. — LITERATURE 10
liars Income Tax has made more L. — TAXES 8
libel Beaverbrook for l. — LIES 13
liberal ineffectual l.'s problem — MORALITY 5
 Is either a little L. — POLITICAL PARTIES 8
 L., who wishes to replace them — POLITICS 14
 L. Democrat leader — POLITICIANS 17

liberal (*cont.*):
l. education   EDUCATION 2
l. employer   WORK 16
l. is a man who leaves the room
    POLITICAL PARTIES 2
particular L. Party   POLITICAL PARTIES 11
liberals L. have invented   EDUCATION 32
L. offer a mixture   POLITICS 45
liberation shoulder blades isn't l.   WOMEN 73
liberty consistent with the l.   MARRIAGE 54
safeguards of l.   HISTORY 7
libraries l. of the House of Commons   LIBRARIES 4
library Another corpse in the l.   LIBRARIES 10
go to the l.   APPEARANCE 27
l. must be full of them   IDEAS 2
l. of sixty-two thousand volumes   ROYALTY 40
Majesty's l. in every county   LIBRARIES 3
sit in a l.   LIBRARIES 6
thing to have in a l. is a shelf   LIBRARIES 5
you have a public l.   LIBRARIES 2
librettos l. for the rest of my life   MUSICIANS 19
licence temporary l.   DRUGS 10
lid Don't slam the l.   MEDICINE 38
Liddell right part wrote L.   DICTIONARIES 13
lie Here l. I   EPITAPHS 16
l. diagonally in his bed again   MARRIAGE 119
l. follows   BEHAVIOUR 28
L. heavy on him   EPITAPHS 10
l. is an abomination   LIES 1
l. less convincingly   JOURNALISM 15
sent to l. abroad   DIPLOMACY 18
You l. and you know it   SPORTS 29
lies Diplomats tell l.   GOVERNMENT 24
enough white l.   LIES 2
John Adams l. here   EPITAPHS 7
l., damned lies and statistics   LIES 6
l. he has been telling   CONVERSATION 10
Matilda told such Dreadful L.   LIES 3
spring of endless l.   JOURNALISM 11
stop telling l. about Democrats   POLITICS 72
tell l. as usual   HISTORY 10
told some l. about me   LIES 13
life been a part of l.   WOMEN 15
Book of L. begins   BIBLE 7
crushed l. is what I lead   MARRIAGE 93
evidence of l. after death   POLITICS 70
get a l.   TELEVISION 16
goes through l.   CHARACTER 6
I gave my l. for freedom   WAR 12
in mourning for my l.   HAPPINESS 5
isn't l. a terrible thing   LIFE 24
it's the l. in my men   SEX 89
let a woman in your l.   MEN AND WOMEN 23
L. as we know it   CRICKET 3
l. for ourselves at the Ritz   SATISFACTION 1

l. had been ruined by literature   LITERATURE 8
L. imitates Art   ART 36
l.-insurance agents   DEATH 37
L. in the movies   CINEMA 30
l. is 6 to 5 against   BETTING 13
L. is a Cabaret   LIFE 12
L. is a gamble at terrible odds   LIFE 22
l. is a glorious cycle of song   LOVE 35
L. is a sexually transmitted   LIFE 2
l. is a shit sandwich   LIFE 20
l. is generally something   LIFE 5
L. is just one damned thing   LIFE 15
L. is something to do   LIFE 16
L. is the funny thing   LIFE 8
l. is the thing   READING 17
L. is too short   TIME 6
l.-saving certificate   INTELLIGENCE 20
l.'s rich pageant   LIFE 18
l.'s story   AUTOBIOGRAPHY 2
l. was coming to consist   LIFE 1
l. will perhaps seem   DIARIES 7
L. would be very pleasant   HAPPINESS 15
made for l.   DEATH 57
malevolent l. of their own   TECHNOLOGY 13
matter of l. and death   FOOTBALL 20
My l. was simply hellish   SATISFACTION 10
never lived his l. at all   LIFE 6
new terror to l.   INSULTS 49
no quality of l.   COUNTRIES 10
Not too much of l.   LIFE 19
on a l.-support machine   APPEARANCE 7
planets cooled, l. resulted   UNIVERSE 13
précis of l.   WORDS 8
read the l.   BIOGRAPHY 9
sech is l.   LIFE 11
some problems with my l.   LIFE 21
stretch your l. out   MEDICINE 22
third of my l.   MIDDLE AGE 2
tired of l.   TOWNS 21
University of L.   EDUCATION 9
What a queer thing L. is   LIFE 25
write *A L.*   AUTOBIOGRAPHY 13
your money *or* your l.   WOMEN 6
life belt deep end without a l.   TAXES 1
lifelong l. romance   LOVE 48
lifetime knowledge of a l.   ART 34
l. of happiness   HAPPINESS 12
lift can't even l. them   GOVERNMENT 34
light dusk with a l. behind   WOMEN 25
l. at the end of the tunnel   BETTING 3
l. of God was with him   TRANSPORT 16
speed was faster than l.   SCIENCE 8
travel l.   BODY 17
lighthouse sitivation at the l.   WORK 13

lightning illuminated by flashes of l.   WRITERS 45
  not struck by l.   MARRIAGE 128
lights all-the-l.-on man   PRIDE 5
  fool when l. are low   WOMEN 33
  she likes l. and commotion   SOCIETY 10
  switch off the l.   NEWSPAPERS 5
like I didn't l. the play   THEATRE 34
  I l. America   AMERICA 10
  l. cures like   BORES 19
  l. it twice as much   THEATRE 61
  made me l. him less   MARRIAGE 37
  man you don't l.   ALCOHOL 64
  of his friends l. him   FRIENDS 24
  only thing I didn't l.   THEATRE 37
liked always l. Americans   AMERICA 8
likely A mighty l. speech   MARRIAGE 63
  Walk! Not bloody l.   TRANSPORT 36
liking understood this l. for war   WAR 5
Lillabullero bars of L.   ARGUMENT 21
limbo l. which divides   ALCOHOL 3
limbs Yours are the l.   APPEARANCE 21
limelight backing into the l.   PEOPLE 8
Limerick L. gained a reputation   WEATHER 19
limericks l. stopped   POETRY 2
limes two gin-and-l.   FOOD 60
limousine One perfect l.   TRANSPORT 29
Lincoln I could be another L.   INTELLIGENCE 6
line along the l.   BUREAUCRACY 15
  l. I take   PEOPLE 33
  stopped at l. two   POETRY 2
lines come down between the l.   WIT 22
  knew these l. backwards   ACTING 9
  l. having similar sounds   POETRY 16
  original lines of the l.   THEATRE 29
lingering Something l.   CRIME 19
linguistic L. analysis   LANGUAGE 16
linoleum shoot me through l.   FILM STARS 2
lion achieve a l. by hearsay   DESCRIPTION 19
  l. and the calf   ANIMALS 1
  l. in a den   FRIENDS 25
lionized spoilt by being l.   HUMAN RACE 12
lip Stiff upper l.   ENGLAND 12
lips Lombard's l.   ACTORS 16
  move their l.   WRITING 14
  put my l. to it   ALCOHOL 21
lipstick too much l.   MEN AND WOMEN 30
liquor bumper of good l.   ALCOHOL 58
  don't drink l.   ALCOHOL 38
  drank our l. straight   ALCOHOL 4
  l. Is quicker   ALCOHOL 45
  L. talks mighty loud   ALCOHOL 33
  Lord above made l.   ALCOHOL 37
lira like the Italian l.   SCIENCE 1
lisp L.: call a spade   SPEECHES 5
lisped l. in numbers   CHILDREN 28

list I've got a little l.   CRIME 18
listen people don't l.   CONVERSATION 30
  women who l. to it   MUSIC 21
  you wish him to l.   BORES 3
listener was a good l.   CONVERSATION 24
listening ain't l.   ACTORS 21
lit courts must be l.   MURDER 14
  Fleet's l. up   ALCOHOL 70
literal home of the l.   AMERICA 28
  ignorant and l.-minded   WOMEN 52
literary draw well with l. men   WRITERS 2
  head of the l. profession   PRAISE 3
  l. censorship   CENSORSHIP 20
  l. gift is a mere accident   LITERATURE 4
  l. man—*with* a wooden leg   LITERATURE 15
  l. offspring   CHILDREN 6
  Of all the l. scenes   POETRY 22
  So l. a town is Oxford   TOWNS 4
  those l. cooks   QUOTATIONS 14
literate If, with the l., I am impelled
  LITERATURE 30
literature failed in l.   CRITICS 12
  great Cham of l.   PEOPLE 40
  He knew everything about l.   LITERATURE 21
  history to produce a little l.   LITERATURE 22
  ideas of their own about l.   PUBLISHING 5
  life had been ruined by l.   LITERATURE 8
  l. is not read   JOURNALISM 25
  L.'s always a good card to play   LITERATURE 7
  locks of l.   CRITICS 36
litigant l. drawn to the United States   LAW 5
littered come down and l.   ARCHITECTURE 15
little I ask very l.   SATISFACTION 6
  l. local difficulties   POLITICS 47
  Thank heaven for l. girls   WOMEN 41
  though she be but l.   WOMEN 61
  very l. one   CHILDREN 24
live All I have to l. on now is macaroni
  OLD AGE 3
  gonna l. this long   OLD AGE 7
  l. to be over ninety   OLD AGE 1
  l. well on nothing a year   POVERTY 23
  never to l.   AMERICA 19
  you have to l. with rich people   WEALTH 28
  You might as well l.   DEATH 53
lived never l. his life at all   LIFE 6
  where Gettysburg l.   READING 4
liver ate his l.   FOOD 34
  l. is on the right   MEDICINE 24
  l.-wing of a fowl   AWARDS 6
living books about l. men   BIOGRAPHY 6
  But who calls dat l.   OLD AGE 20
  Dogs who earn their l.   DOGS 2
  had to write for a l.   WRITING 7
  I *love* l.   LIFE 21

living (*cont.*):

Lady Disdain, are you yet l.   INSULTS 40

l. for one's diary   DIARIES 1

Livingstone I wouldn't vote for Ken L.

    POLITICIANS 29

Lizzie Borden L. took an axe   MURDER 1

llama female l.   DESCRIPTION 8

Lloyd George L. did not seem to care

    PRIME MINISTERS 4

loaded I practise when I'm l.   MUSICIANS 15

loafing organized l.   CRICKET 15

loathsome l. thing   GARDENS 14

lobster l. to attendant shrimps   ROYALTY 50

small l.   FOOD 59

world is your l.   SUCCESS 15

local little l. difficulties   POLITICS 47

lock key still in the l.   SEX 5

locks louse in the l.   CRITICS 36

lodging count l. houses   EDUCATION 3

lodgings pent up in a frowzy l.   POVERTY 21

log hut piano gets into a l.   MUSIC 17

logic L. and taxation   TAXES 6

[L.] is neither   ARGUMENT 12

Professor of L.   PHILOSOPHY 1

logical l. positivists   LOVE 2

Well, that's l.   PHILOSOPHY 8

London comes down on L.   WEATHER 15

in L. only is a trade   POETRY 9

L. at night   CRIME 7

L. of the Southern Hemisphere   TOWNS 23

L. Transport Diesel-engined   TRANSPORT 9

tired of L.   TOWNS 21

wear brown in L.   COLOURS 3

lonely People who are l.   WORK 11

troubled with her l. life   MARRIAGE 98

long as the dey was l.   SEX 56

But it's so *l.*   THEATRE 11

gonna live this l.   OLD AGE 7

It often lasts too l.   LIFE 19

Like German opera, too l.   WAR 29

l., long time   BROADCASTING 1

l. as the real thing   THEATRE 12

longevity attribute my l.   OLD AGE 16

longing focus of l.   RELIGION 45

longitude l. with no platitude   LANGUAGE 7

look don't l. back in anger   PAST 6

I never l. up   TRAVEL 2

l. another   BODY 21

l. at me that way   MORALITY 8

l. at them with the sound turned   PEOPLE 20

l. like the second week   APPEARANCE 25

looked better to be l. over   SATISFACTION 13

looking she was l. all the time   SEX 80

looking-glass cracked l.   ART 15

looks One of those l.   MARRIAGE 43

she needs good l.   MIDDLE AGE 14

looney-bin janitor to the l.   MEDICINE 37

loop l. on a commonplace   WIT 22

loose one thing to do with l. change   MONEY 20

lord liaison with the L.   THE CLERGY 13

L. above made liquor   ALCOHOL 37

L. designed the Universe   UNIVERSE 11

L. says   DEBT 4

representation of Our L.   ART 1

to a point, L. Copper   JOURNALISM 22

lords it is the L. debating   ROYALTY 15

only a wit among L.   INSULTS 25

sleeps with the L.   ROYALTY 6

to be said for the L.   ARISTOCRACY 11

lordships good enough for their l.   POLITICS 4

lose l. no time   READING 6

l. one parent   FAMILY 51

l. one's mind   FOOLISHNESS 23

l. them   FRIENDS 2

l. the presidency   SUCCESS 34

way of ending a war is to l.   WAR 24

loss sense of her l.   DEATH 23

lost he always l. it   POLITICIANS 31

l. for words   CRITICS 42

l. her reputation   SELF-KNOWLEDGE 28

those that get l.   TECHNOLOGY 2

We've l. everything   SUCCESS 26

lottery l.-ticket   HEAVEN 2

National L.   FOOD 5

Lou lady that's known as L.   MEN AND WOMEN 41

loud too long and too l.   WAR 29

louder l. he talked of his honour   VIRTUE 8

loudspeaker listening to a l.   ADVERTISING 5

louse between a l. and a flea   POETS 9

l. in the locks   CRITICS 36

lousy L. but loyal   ROYALTY 9

lovable extremely l.   CHILDREN 11

love ability to make l. frivolously   LOVE 6

as long as he does not l. her   MEN AND WOMEN 58

beginning of a l. affair   CINEMA 30

capable of l.   LOVE 2

do not l. thee   FRIENDS 4

fall in l. with yourself   LOVE 30

give you anything but l.   POVERTY 8

Greater l.   FRIENDS 9

Greater l.   FRIENDS 21

He was all for l.   LOVE 11

I can do you blood and l.   THEATRE 53

If this be not l.   LOVE 8

I l. the girl I'm near   LOVE 23

I'm tired of L.   MONEY 3

I wish I were in l. again   LOVE 24

let's fall in l.   SEX 65

Look who's making l.   TOWNS 16

lying (*cont.*):

One of you is l.	LIES 8
truth and l.	LIES 11

Lyme old man of L. · MARRIAGE 88

lyrics Ladies don't write l. · SONGS 14

ma'am M. or Sir · ROYALTY 22

spinnaker of 'Yes M.' · ROYALTY 52

macaroni m. and memorial services · OLD AGE 3

MacArthur General Douglas M. · GOD 38

Macaulay M. is like a book in breeches · PEOPLE 38

Macbeth don't care for Lady M. · ACTING 23

hit in *M.* · ACTING 13

Little Nell and Lady M. · PEOPLE 50

McDonald M.'s of sport · TENNIS 4

McGregor Mr M.'s garden · ANIMALS 38

machine desiccated calculating m. · POLITICIANS 8

I have tested your m. · INSULTS 49

ingenious m. · BODY 13

make a m. that would walk · TECHNOLOGY 1

mackintosh bit of black m. · FOOD 85

burnt his m. · THE CLERGY 5

like a damp m. · DESCRIPTION 11

mackintoshes wet m. · TRAVEL 27

McTavish No M. Was ever lavish · SCOTLAND 8

mad half of the nation is m. · ENGLAND 35

How m. I am, sad I am · LOVE 5

M., is he? · ARMED FORCES 9

m. about the boy · FILM STARS 4

M. dogs · ENGLAND 8

m. till you have your mistresses · MEN 16

The great ones are thought m. · WRITERS 35

when a heroine goes m. · MIND 8

made m. for life · DEATH 57

madness If this be not love, it is m. · LOVE 8

moment of m. · MISTAKES 11

sort of m. [Bolshevism] · POLITICS 68

Mafia it's the M. · CRIME 29

magazine falsehoods for a m. · JOURNALISM 4

magazines girlie m. · SEX 77

graves of little m. · POETRY 22

magic m. in a pint bottle · MARRIAGE 50

m. of first love · LOVE 14

magnificent more than m. · FILMS 5

maid her m. between her teeth · SOCIETY 12

lugger and the m. is mine · MARRIAGE 78

m. in the living room · MARRIAGE 68

old m. is like death by drowning · OLD AGE 19

Mailer M. is, as usual · CRITICS 42

maintenance Take up car m. · TECHNOLOGY 10

majesty M.'s library in every county · LIBRARIES 3

Major M. Major it had been all three · INSULTS 20

Major-General modern M. · ARMED FORCES 11

Majoribanks call him M. · NAMES 3

majority admit to be the m. · DEMOCRACY 14

big enough m. · FOOLISHNESS 30

m. is always the best · DEMOCRACY 5

majors college m. · EDUCATION 32

make movie I want to m. · CINEMA 44

People who m. history · HISTORY 4

Scotsman on the m. · SCOTLAND 1

to m. it up · MIND 10

You cannot m. him out at all · SCIENCE 4

male as my m. organ · AUTOBIOGRAPHY 9

middle-aged m. · GOD 37

males coarser m. · ANIMALS 22

malice m. of a good thing · WIT 37

measured m. of music · MUSIC 29

malignant part of Randolph that was not m. · MEDICINE 36

Mall kicked down the m. · DESCRIPTION 26

malls build shopping m. · HUMAN RACE 1

Malvern Perrier or M. water · CHOICE 2

mama m. of dada · LITERATURE 17

Mammon God and M. · GOD 40

man Clothes by a m. · FASHION 6

fit night out for m. or beast · WEATHER 8

get M. to shut up · GOD 3

God is a m. · RELIGION 47

hard m. is good to find · MEN 17

let him pass for a m. · MEN 14

make a m. by standing a sheep · MEN 3

makes m. and wife one flesh · MARRIAGE 38

m. bites a dog · JOURNALISM 2

m. can be happy with any woman · MEN AND WOMEN 58

M. does not live by words · WORDS 28

M. he eat the barracuda · NATURE 4

m. in love is incomplete · MARRIAGE 59

m.-in-the-street · INTELLIGENCE 1

M. is one of the toughest · HUMAN RACE 8

m. is *so* in the way · FAMILY 16

M. is the Only Animal · HUMAN RACE 13

m. more dined against than dining · SOCIETY 5

m. to a worm · FOOD 7

married at all . . . I'm a m. · MARRIAGE 133

single m. in possession · MARRIAGE 8

woman be more like a m. · MEN AND WOMEN 22

woman without a m. · WOMEN 66

Women who love the same m. · LOVE 3

managed world is disgracefully m. · UNIVERSE 8

manager m. gets the blame · FOOTBALL 11

winning one as a m. · FOOTBALL 15

Managing Director M.'s chance to kiss the tea-girl · PARTIES 8

Manchester M. after midnight · TOWNS 20

Mandelson M. is someone who can skulk · PEOPLE 21

Mandy My name is M.: Peter B · PEOPLE 33

marry (*cont.*):

  some m. them   MEN AND WOMEN 1

  that does not m. a fool   MARRIAGE 138

Mars attack from M.   ARMED FORCES 23

Martha had enough of M.   THE CLERGY 20

martinet I am more than a m.   MUSICIANS 17

martinetissimo I am a m.   MUSICIANS 17

Martini into a dry M.   ALCOHOL 2

Martinis Those dry M.   ALCOHOL 1

martyrdom saints on their way to m.   WORK 29

Marx M is for M.   POLITICS 25

Marxist M.—of the Groucho tendency

                           POLITICS 6

Mary time for some M.   THE CLERGY 20

marzipan made out of pink m.   APPEARANCE 2

Masefield To M. something more   LITERATURE 3

mask m. like Castlereagh   MURDER 11

mass I am against m. murder   MURDER 8

  too lazy to go to M.   RELIGION 48

Massachusetts chop your poppa up in M.

                           MURDER 2

massage went to a m. parlour   COMPUTERS 6

masses Movement of M.   POLITICS 25

  Of m. and fugues   MUSIC 19

master m. of the multipurpose metaphor

                       POLITICIANS 4

  One m. will hit you   EDUCATION 28

masters like the old m.   CINEMA 47

  m. came and went   EDUCATION 46

mastodons like m.   FAMILY 55

masturbation Don't knock m.   SEX 1

  M. is the thinking man's   SEX 37

  M.: the primary sexual activity   SEX 79

maternal like a m. boa constrictor SUCCESS 8

mathematics resort to m.   RELIGION 43

maths see your m. master   RELIGION 6

Matilda M. told such Dreadful Lies   LIES 3

Matisse hanging a M. together   MARRIAGE 64

matrimony critical period in m. MARRIAGE 71

  m. at its lowest   MARRIAGE 120

  m. consistent with the liberty MARRIAGE 54

  more of love than m.   MARRIAGE 67

  safest in m. to begin   MARRIAGE 114

matron fierce and elderly m.   WOMEN 49

mature m. poets steal   POETRY 10

maturing my mind is m. late   MIDDLE AGE 8

maturity M. is a hard price to pay

                      MIDDLE AGE 13

mausoleum built like a brick m. INSULTS 41

mauver mauve and m.   WEATHER 1

maxim we have got The M. Gun   POWER 1

maximum m. of temptation   MARRIAGE 113

may at least the seventh of M.   WEATHER 25

maybe definite m.   CERTAINTY 11

Mayfair M. of the dead   DEATH 59

mayonnaise on m.   FOOD 8

mayor as his 'night m.'   CHOICE 7

  married the M.   POLITICIANS 3

  m. gave no other   BEHAVIOUR 20

  M. of Birmingham in a lean year

                    PRIME MINISTERS 20

  running for M. of Toytown   POLITICIANS 29

MCC M. ends   ENGLAND 27

me interested in himself than in m.

                  SELF-KNOWLEDGE 3

  m. is the most used two-letter word   WORDS 9

  M. Tarzan   FILMS 13

meal building a m.   FOOD 51

  m. was never found   COOKERY 21

  of a good m.   FOOD 49

mealy M. boys   CHILDREN 14

mean only m. one thing   HUMOUR 3

  say what you m.   CONVERSATION 5

meaning m. of 'is'   WORDS 6

  really have no particular m.   WORDS 22

  teems with hidden m.   WORDS 10

meanings two m. packed up into one word

                      WORDS 4

means die beyond my m.   DEATH 73

  live within our m.   HAPPINESS 17

  m. just what I choose   WORDS 5

meant say what we m.   LANGUAGE 16

measles Love's like the m.   LOVE 26

measured m. malice of music   MUSIC 29

meat If you give him m.   PEOPLE 13

  sends us good m.   COOKERY 9

  very old m.   FOOD 76

mechanics M. not microbes   PROGRESS 6

mechanism m. that prides itself CIVIL SERVANTS 1

media m.. It sounds like   BROADCASTING 7

medical advance of m. thought ALCOHOL 69

medicinal M. discovery   MEDICINE 3

medicinally m. salutary   CRITICS 32

medicine desire to take m.   MEDICINE 26

  home studying m.   MEDICINE 18

  m. by a completely new method MEDICINE 24

  m. never gets anywhere near SICKNESS 13

  No patent m.   GOVERNMENT 9

  professor of rotational m.   POLITICS 53

mediocre it's m.   FILMS 5

  m. judges   JUDGES 10

mediocrities M. Think   COUNTRIES 48

mediocrity m. thrust upon them INSULTS 20

Mediterranean from the M. COUNTRIES 51

medium m. because nothing's well done

                   TELEVISION 1

  Roast Beef, M.   FOOD 27

medley m. of extemporanea   LOVE 35

Mee give a child to Arthur M. EDUCATION 12

meek m. shall inherit the earth — PRIDE 8
m. shall inherit the earth — WEALTH 16
meekness Ever heard of m. stopping — THE CLERGY 3
meeting hearing, or m. — HOME 4
meetings pan-parent m. — PARENTS 2
melodies I play his melodies — MUSIC 32
member ACCEPT ME AS A M. — SOCIETY 17
members m. of the common throng — ARISTOCRACY 8
memoirs Like all good m. — AUTOBIOGRAPHY 18
M. of the frivolous — AUTOBIOGRAPHY 5
write no m. — AUTOBIOGRAPHY 16
write one's m. — AUTOBIOGRAPHY 21
memoranda read these m. — GOVERNMENT 34
memorandum m. is written — BUREAUCRACY 1
memorial macaroni and m. services — OLD AGE 3
memory no m. for the important — WOMEN 82
men all our best m. are dead — LITERATURE 31
believe that m. were the answer — MEN 2
education of m. — EDUCATION 48
gets to know of m. — DOGS 8
If m. could get pregnant — MEN AND WOMEN 19
I hate m. — MEN AND WOMEN 37
I swear by m. — MEDICINE 8
It's not the m. in my life — SEX 89
manners out of m. — MEN AND WOMEN 8
m., women, and Herveys — ARISTOCRACY 17
m. cannot help not loving you — MEN 1
m. had to have babies — CHILDREN 13
m. have got love well weighed up — LOVE 1
M. seldom make passes — MEN AND WOMEN 34
m. we wanted to marry — WOMEN 67
on account of them being m. — SCIENCE 13
Some m. are born mediocre — INSULTS 20
too late that m. betray — WOMEN 28
You m. are unaccountable things — MEN 16
mendicant you're a mendicant — POVERTY 16
mending ways of m. a broken heart — LOVE 39
mental It's not m. — MEDICINE 6
Those who were bad were m. — THE CLERGY 19
mention Don't m. the war — COUNTRIES 11
resolved not to m. — CONVERSATION 6
mentioned might never again be m. — RELIGION 8
menu waiters discussing the m. — FOOD 11
merciful hope for m. annihilation — RELIGION 16
mercury littered under M. — CHARACTER 11
mercy leaving m. to heaven — CRIME 15
like God's infinite m. — POLITICS 58
m. o' my soul — EPITAPHS 16
Meredith M., we're in — COMEDY 27
M.'s a prose Browning — LITERATURE 39
meretricious m. and a happy — INSULTS 50
merger trying to pull off a m. — HEAVEN 7

meringue like a big m. — APPEARANCE 10
m.-utan — PEOPLE 9
merit m. for a bishopric — THE CLERGY 26
merriment m. of parsons — THE CLERGY 15
merry M. Christmas — CHRISTMAS 6
mésalliance it was an absolute m. — MARRIAGE 87
mess m. left over from other people — TOWNS 26
why I'm a m. — FAMILY 39
message if there is a m. — JOURNALISM 16
M.? What the hell do you think I am — THEATRE 8
take a m. to Albert — LAST WORDS 2
messages M. should be delivered — CINEMA 17
messenger as the m. — ACTING 13
Messiah When M. comes — RELIGION 29
met Have we m. before — ROYALTY 38
how he first m. her — MEN AND WOMEN 49
they still m. — BODY 33
metaphor master of the multipurpose m. — POLITICIANS 4
metaphysical m. fox — CONVERSATION 27
meteor And get hit by a m. — WEATHER 3
meter read the gas-m. — EDUCATION 31
Methuselah M. is my favourite saint — OLD AGE 27
M. live nine hundred years — OLD AGE 20
metras Very old—very lame—no m. — OLD AGE 13
metric m. system — DRUGS 6
metropolis I never write m. — WORDS 29
mezzanine down into the m. floor — FOOD 90
mice jobs minding m. at crossroads — INSULTS 31
slept with m. — FAME 10
Michelangelo designs by M. — COUNTRIES 59
Mickey Mouse make the M. brand — CINEMA 8
You're M. — PRAISE 7
microbe M. is so very small — SCIENCE 4
microbes Mechanics not m. — PROGRESS 6
microscope m. at a drop of pond water — MARRIAGE 83
middle m. of the road — LIFE 14
middle age dead centre of m. — MIDDLE AGE 1
Temptations came to him, in m. — VIRTUE 17
middle-aged m. reformers — MIDDLE AGE 12
middle class flagrantly m. — CLASS 33
M. was quite prepared — POLITICIANS 6
with a powerful m. — POLITICS 30
middle classes lower m. — CLASS 17
midnight Holding hands at m. — LOVE 18
Manchester after m. — TOWNS 20
mid-winter Australia, this would be m. — WEATHER 2
might It m. have been — SATISFACTION 7
migrate they don't m. — FAMILY 5

mild drawed m. ALCOHOL 20
I'm very m. MORALITY 8
prefer m. hale ALCOHOL 62
military m. man approaches ARMED FORCES 27
unfit for m. service ARMED FORCES 13
milk between the m. and the yoghurt
WRITERS 39
find a trout in the m. LAW 36
Gin was mother's m. ALCOHOL 57
m. of human kindness LITERATURE 20
m.'s leap FOOD 26
other m. ANIMALS 35
mill John Stuart M. ECONOMICS 2
millennium m. is going to be PARTIES 1
million first ten m. years PAST 1
millionaire m. has just as good DEMOCRACY 9
M. That is my religion WEALTH 27
old-fashioned m. MONEY 9
Who wants to be a m. WEALTH 25
millionaires m. were necessarily personable
WEALTH 21
millionairesses some lesser m. WEALTH 6
millions opinion against that of m. MUSIC 33
miminy m., piminy MEN 7
mind characteristic of a m. at bay LETTERS 13
don't m. if I do COMEDY 19
duty to speak one's m. MORALITY 16
full of the sound of m. MIND 2
have any women got a right m. MARRIAGE 17
If I am out of my m. MIND 1
m. and spirit GOVERNMENT 42
M. my bike COMEDY 28
m. of Ronald Reagan PRESIDENTS 12
my m. is maturing late MIDDLE AGE 8
nothing unbends the m. WOMEN 24
not to have a m. FOOLISHNESS 23
prodigious quantity of m. MIND 10
travel broadens the m. TRAVEL 5
until reeled the m. LANGUAGE 8
woman's m. MEN AND WOMEN 17
minding not m. not having any money
YOUTH 10
minds dirty m. CENSORSHIP 23
mindset m. changed considerably CRIME 26
mine In case it is one of m. PARENTS 6
she is m. for life YOUTH 8
minefield if you're fat, is a m. LIFE 17
miner I became a m. instead JUDGES 7
mineral not the m. rights WEALTH 16
mineworkers National Union of M. POLITICS 49
minister inadequate ex-m. AUTOBIOGRAPHY 26
ministers how much my M. talk
GOVERNMENT 41
M. of State GOVERNMENT 11

my actions are my m. ROYALTY 21
wisdom on the Queen's m. RELIGION 38
Minneapolis St Paul and M. TOWNS 16
Minoan but M. WIT 1
minorities M. . . . are almost always POLITICS 69
mints After-Eight thin m. FOOD 36
minute m. you walked in the joint
MEN AND WOMEN 11
minutes I have just 20 m. to give you
ROYALTY 61
M. of the last meal CONVERSATION 2
ninety m. BROADCASTING 1
six and three-quarter m. TIME 11
You can have the seven m. TIME 5
mirror in the rear view m. BUSINESS 13
stare at myself in the m. SELF-KNOWLEDGE 2
miscarry apt to m. HUMOUR 1
miscast He's m. ACTORS 39
mischief m. still for idle hands PAST 11
miserable arise and make them m. POWER 4
I might as well be m. with you SICKNESS 10
two people m. instead of four MARRIAGE 23
misery find a little m. HAPPINESS 14
M. acquaints a man MISTAKES 25
m. of a man in pursuit MARRIAGE 25
result m. MONEY 7
misfortune m. to ourselves MISTAKES 7
that would be a m. MISTAKES 13
misfortunes Few m. FAMILY 28
mislead one to m. the public POLITICS 7
misquotation M. is, in fact, the pride
QUOTATIONS 17
misquotations gleeful m. DEATH 15
miss don't m. being smacked BOXING 9
m. the train before TRANSPORT 8
Never m. a chance TELEVISION 19
missed never m. it SELF-KNOWLEDGE 28
who never would be m. CRIME 18
missing m. in Nature is a pencil WRITING 3
mission social m. of every great newspaper
NEWSPAPERS 34
missionaries m. fattened PRESIDENTS 11
missionary eat a m. BIRDS 8
m. position of cooking COOKERY 17
m.'s shank FOOD 33
Uncle Harry's not a m. THE CLERGY 5
missus The M., my Lord MARRIAGE 106
mistake m. in the translation MORALITY 14
same m. once MISTAKES 2
Shome m. COMEDY 36
thought of this curious m. MISTAKES 5
usually a m. HUMAN RACE 3
When I make a m., it's a beaut MISTAKES 20
mistakes learned from the m. HISTORY 11
make all the same m. LIFE 3

movies Life in the m. — CINEMA 30
  m. are the only court — CINEMA 10
  M. should have — CINEMA 12
  not to write for the m. — BIBLE 3
moving first of many, many m. days — RELIGION 29
  often m. in opposite directions — MARRIAGE 117
  On m. house — HOME 3
Mozart M. was my age — SUCCESS 19
  Some cry up Haydn, some M. — MUSICIANS 11
MP admit to being an M. — TRUTH 12
  Being an M. feeds your vanity — POLITICS 60
  M. is the sort of job — POLITICS 1
MPs dull M. in close proximity — POLITICS 33
  more M. called John — NAMES 12
  When in that House M. divide — POLITICS 34
much Didn't do m. — PRESIDENTS 7
  guessing so much and so m. — WOMEN 12
  seem m. for them to be — HUMAN RACE 2
muddle beginning, a m. — LITERATURE 23
muddy m. horsepond — MARRIAGE 96
muffin well-buttered m. — FOOD 59
muffs huge m. of horror — FASHION 25
mug heavenly m. — WIT 9
mulct m. the whole country — WEALTH 23
multi-hued m. blancmange — POLITICS 52
multiplication M. is vexation — SCIENCE 2
multipurpose master of the m. metaphor — POLITICIANS 4
mum 'M.'s the word' — ADVERTISING 5
  They fuck you up, your m. and dad — PARENTS 10
mummy make one's m. just as nice — ART 33
murals with its m. on the wall — SEX 16
murder brought back m. into the home — MURDER 5
  I am against mass m. — MURDER 8
  if m. had been allowed — DEATH 45
  I met M. on the way — MURDER 11
  m. a tiger — ANIMALS 42
  M. is a serious business — MURDER 6
  m. often — MARRIAGE 73
  M. was one thing — THEATRE 33
murdered m. reputations — GOSSIP 2
murderer common m. — COOKERY 19
  m. for a fancy prose style — MURDER 9
murderers mass m. — ART 14
murdering executed for m. his publisher — PUBLISHING 2
Murdoch wrapped in a M. newspaper — NEWSPAPERS 28
museum shelf of an anatomical m. — WORDS 14
mushroom too short to stuff a m. — TIME 6
music all his m. accepts it — MUSICIANS 14
  All m. is folk music — MUSIC 2
  all the better for m. — MUSICIANS 13

Appreciation of M. — CRITICS 31
But the m. that excels — MONEY 9
Classic m. is th'kind — MUSIC 24
good m. and bad preaching — RELIGION 15
how potent cheap m. is — MUSIC 10
I don't like my m. — MUSIC 33
I hate m. — MUSIC 15
It'll be good Jewish m. — MUSIC 28
love best about m. — MUSIC 21
may not like m. — ENGLAND 3
measured malice of m. — MUSIC 29
m. and football — LITERATURE 37
m. had finished — DANCE 10
M. helps not the toothache — MUSIC 23
m. is the brandy of the damned — MUSIC 48
M. makes you feel a feeling — WORDS 13
m. of our own opinions — LAW 35
m. one must hear several times — MUSIC 42
m. was more important than sex — SEX 50
play American m. — COUNTRIES 12
plays good m. — CONVERSATION 30
potent m. can be — MUSIC 57
reasonable good ear in m. — MUSIC 47
What m. is more enchanting — YOUTH 7
with its own verbal m. — MUSIC 49
musical disclosing m. secrets — MUSICIANS 12
  M. people are so absurdly — MUSIC 56
  not unduly m. — MARRIAGE 46
music-hall m. singer attends a series — MUSIC 19
musician both writer and m. — MUSICIANS 19
musicologist m. is a man who — MUSICIANS 5
mustard Pass the m. — HUMOUR 18
mute except that of m. — POLITICIANS 22
mutton make them into m.-pies — COOKERY 8
  what m. tastes like — WRITERS 27
mutual m. knowledge — FRIENDS 23
my-lorded m. him — SNOBBERY 16
myopia all we got was Dev's m. — IRELAND 3
myself He reminds me of m. — SELF-KNOWLEDGE 6
mystery hissed my m. lectures — WIT 42
  wrap it up in m. — MEDICINE 35
myth m. is a piece of gossamer — ROYALTY 51

naff I think they're n. — PARTIES 1
nailing n. his colours — CERTAINTY 10
nails have our n. done — SOCIETY 8
  relatively clean finger n. — LAW 27
naive n. domestic Burgundy — ALCOHOL 65
naïve both a little n. — FOOLISHNESS 11
naked I had never seen a n. woman — WOMEN 69
  n. women — TRAVEL 27
name alien, distasteful n. — NAMES 10
  colonies in your wife's n. — WAR 17
  halfway through her n. — NAMES 2
  has got a bad n. — ARGUMENT 15

name (*cont.*):

I don't wish to sign my n.	LETTERS 16
If my n. had been Edmund	NAMES 13
if my n. occurs	AUTOBIOGRAPHY 1
I write my n.	BOOKS 14
my n. in such large letters	PRIDE 11
n. is neither one thing	NAMES 6
n. is not in the obits	DEATH 17
n. *not* suggest	COUNTRIES 2
n. that sounded so nice	PLACES 14
n. we give the people	DEMOCRACY 7
remember your n.	NAMES 22
Under an assumed n.	BETTING 9

named n. a country — FILMS 4

names American n. as Cathcart — NAMES 10
n. of all these particles — SCIENCE 15
new n. — NAMES 4

Napoleon Jesus Christ and N. — PRIME MINISTERS 21
N. in the capacity of secretary — WRITERS 22
N.'s armies — ARMED FORCES 25

Napoleons worship the Caesars and N.
— POWER 4

narcotic classic is a synonym for n. — LITERATURE 2

narrow notions should be so n. — THE CLERGY 8

nasty n., expensive — MEDICINE 35
n. as himself — HOPE 10
Something n. in the woodshed — MISTAKES 14
when we turn n. — CHARACTER 8

Natchez young belle of old N. — WOMEN 51

nation let alone a n. — HUMOUR 8
Our N. stands for — ENGLAND 6
top n. — HISTORY 9

national N. Debt — DEBT 8

nations n. behave wisely — HISTORY 5
Other n. use force — ENGLAND 42

native interest in n. things — PEOPLE 31

natural her colour is n. — SOCIETY 22
I do it more n. — FOOLISHNESS 25
On the stage he was n. — ACTORS 23
twice as n. — LIFE 7

nature missing in N. is a pencil — WRITING 3
n. has anticipated me — THEATRE 22
N. has no cure — POLITICS 68
N. is creeping up — ART 35
N.'s way of telling you — DEATH 5
phenomenon of n. — FILM STARS 9
position in n. — HUMAN RACE 7
seeing n. as cuddlesome — NATURE 8
stuff that n. replaces it with — NATURE 11
'Tes the hand of N. — NATURE 2

natures terribly weak n. — CHARACTER 20

naughty Oh wasn't it n. of Smudges — SPORTS 5

Navaho than Basque or N. — LANGUAGES 3

naval n. tradition — ARMED FORCES 3

navy joined the N. — ARMED FORCES 1
n. blue of India — COLOURS 8
No n., I suppose — SCIENCE 11
of the Queen's N. — ARMED FORCES 10
part played by the Irish N. — ARMED FORCES 2
Ruler of the Queen's N. — LAW 10

near When I'm not n. the girl I love — LOVE 23

necessarily It ain't n. so — BIBLE 5

necessity nasty old invention—N. — POVERTY 9
n. invented — HOME 11

neck break his bloody n. — WRITERS 48
legs round his n. — ANGER 1
why I should break my n. — SPORTS 2

need whenever we n. them — DEMOCRACY 7

needle addict rejecting the n. — TELEVISION 6
n. in a haystack — WORDS 3

neglect die of n. — IDEAS 9
n. of his duties — INSULTS 48
perfectly understandable n. — MEN AND WOMEN 25

Negro N. could never *hope* — PREJUDICE 1
one drop of N. blood — PREJUDICE 8

Negroes culture of the N. — MUSIC 38

neigh people expect me to n. — ROYALTY 2

neighbour Our Good N. — TITLES 3

neighbourhood if you only lived in a better n.
— MARRIAGE 134

neighbours n. do wrong — CRIME 21
N. you annoy together — MARRIAGE 118

neither N. am I — BOOKS 6

Nell death of Little N. — CRITICS 44
Little N. and Lady Macbeth — PEOPLE 50

nephews erring n. — FAMILY 56

Nero New Jersey N. — WRITERS 12

nerve after the n. has been extracted
— MARRIAGE 107
always called a n. specialist — MEDICINE 37

nervous disease, they call it n. — MEDICINE 19
n. to kill himself — CHARACTER 13

Nescafé N. society — SOCIETY 9

nest does not leave the n. — FASHION 7
does not leave the n. — OLD AGE 12

net surfed the N. — PROGRESS 7
tennis with the n. down — POETRY 11
too old to rush up to the n. — MIDDLE AGE 1

neurosis n. is a secret — MIND 11

neurotic For I'm a n. erratic — MEN AND WOMEN 14

never I n. use a big, big D — LANGUAGE 10
n. can tell — CERTAINTY 21
N. give a sucker — BETTING 4

new all the n. boys — GOVERNMENT 17
happy N. Year — INSULTS 50
have some n. clichés — CINEMA 19
kill you in a n. way — PROGRESS 13
make n. friends — FRIENDS 2
making n. enemies — LAST WORDS 10

non is a n.-starter · COMPUTERS 3
  n. compos penis · CRITICS 23
none If Nun, write *N*. · FAMILY 36
nonentity n. who resents · BORES 11
nonexistent obsolescent and the n. · COMPUTERS 2
non-fiction he can't write n. · WRITERS 16
Norfolk bear him up the N. sky · ROYALTY 14
  Very flat, N. · PLACES 7
normal Thank God we're n. · SEX 61
north Good Neighbour to the N. · TITLES 3
Norway male brothel in N. · BIOGRAPHY 4
Norwegian N. language · LANGUAGES 1
  N. television · TELEVISION 3
Norwegians don't like the N. · COUNTRIES 60
nose Entuned in hir n. · WOMEN 9
  insinuated n. · EPITAPHS 25
  lifts his n. · FOOLISHNESS 29
  man who could not make up his n. · THEATRE 55
  not a n. at all · BODY 35
  punch another person in the n. · WOMEN 43
  wipe a bloody n. · ARGUMENT 7
nostalgia N. isn't what it used to be · PAST 2
not N. while I'm alive he ain't · POLITICIANS 9
note Wobbly top n. · SONGS 24
notebook wrote it down herself in a n. · PEOPLE 24
notes throwing £5 n. · NEWSPAPERS 37
nothing absolutely n. could be said · IRELAND 8
  doing absolutely n. · HOLIDAYS 3
  doing n. · ARMED FORCES 7
  doing n. to some purpose · WORK 3
  going to do n. · EPITAPHS 3
  I do n., granted · WORK 8
  live well on n. a year · POVERTY 23
  n. a-year, paid quarterly · POVERTY 22
  N. for nothink · ECONOMICS 12
  n. *like* it · FOOD 18
  n. on in the photograph · PEOPLE 28
  n. to say · SPEECHES 12
  of you with n. on · HOPE 7
  Worked myself up from n. · POVERTY 15
  would have done it for n. · WORK 14
notice hand-painted n. · DANCE 17
  taken no n. of · TELEVISION 10
notices I got pretty good n. · MUSIC 31
  Mixed n. · THEATRE 27
notions n. should be so narrow · THE CLERGY 8
nouveau riche much to be said for the n. · SNOBBERY 17
novel Anyone could write a n. · WRITING 20
  I may be the Hero of a n. yet · LITERATURE 24
  In ever first n. · BOOKS 24
  n. about civil servants · READING 2
  n. was self-administered · LITERATURE 28

reading a French n. · CRITICS 28
  want to throw into a n. · POLITICS 31
novelists easier for the old n. · BOOKS 13
novels ideal reader of my n. · READING 3
  lose two n. · CHILDREN 25
  worst French n. · NEWSPAPERS 36
novelties fall in love with n. · JUDGES 9
novelty n. of sleeping with a queen · ROYALTY 73
now If they could see me n. · CLASS 13
nudity advanced state of n. · BODY 27
  enjoy their own n. · DIARIES 5
nuisance really rather a n. · ARISTOCRACY 20
null N. an' Void · LAW 29
number called the wrong n. · MISTAKES 27
  n. for a dinner · FOOD 32
numbers lisped in n. · CHILDREN 28
nun extremely rowdy N. · MURDER 3
  If N., write *None* · FAMILY 36
  I was going to be a n. · RELIGION 69
nuns n. in a rugger scrum · ARCHITECTURE 12
  recreation for dedicated n. · SPORTS 3
nurse keep a-hold of N. · CHILDREN 3
  n. sleeps sweetly · SICKNESS 9
  N. UNUPBLOWN · TELEGRAMS 20
nut N. SCREWS WASHERS · NEWSPAPERS 4
nuts where the n. come from · FAMILY 46
nylon Curtains in orange n. · HOME 1
nymphomaniac call me a n. · SEX 63

oafish o. louts remember · CHRISTMAS 3
OAP snappish O. with a temper · OLD AGE 34
oasis they've heard of O. · POLITICAL PARTIES 6
oatcakes Calvin, o., and sulphur · SCOTLAND 10
oats feeds the horse enough o. · ECONOMICS 4
  O.. A grain, which in England · SCOTLAND 6
Obadiah O. Bind-their-kings · NAMES 16
OBE O. goes on for ever · AWARDS 7
obedient now totally o. · GARDENS 1
obey people would immediately o. · POWER 9
obeyed She who must be o. · WOMEN 30
obits name is not in the o. · DEATH 17
obituaries read the o. · DEATH 63
obituary autobiography is an o. · AUTOBIOGRAPHY 8
  just read o. · DEATH 50
  to the o. page · MIDDLE AGE 9
oblate o. spheroid · UNIVERSE 2
oblivion O. (noun) · FAME 6
obscurity snatches a man from o. · THEATRE 44
observation faculty for o. · BOOKS 15
observations universe is a totality of o. · UNIVERSE 14
observer keen o. of life · INTELLIGENCE 1
obsolescence With built in o. · UNIVERSE 11

opera echoing o. houses   PLACES 15
    language an o. is sung in   SONGS 4
    Like O. opera, too long   WAR 29
    o. ain't over   SONGS 9
    O. in English   SONGS 16
    o. isn't what it used to be   SONGS 11
    O. is when a guy gets stabbed   SONGS 15
    Parsifal is the kind of o.   MUSIC 39
operas French o. sung by Swedish artists
    LANGUAGES 24
operatic sunsets, they're so o.   WEATHER 22
operation o. to get a joke   SCOTLAND 11
Ophelia affair with O.   THEATRE 3
    she is not O.   INSULTS 9
opinion His o. of himself   PRIDE 1
    o. against that of millions   MUSIC 33
opinions courage of his o.   ROYALTY 71
    high quality of early o.   BOOKS 7
    music of our own o.   LAW 35
opium concubine to an o. addict   WOMEN 70
opportunity commit when he had the o.
    MEN 13
    manhood was an o.   MEN 10
    maximum of o.   MARRIAGE 113
    o. of saying a good thing   WIT 12
oppose o. everything   POLITICS 27
opposite o. of people   ACTORS 34
    o. of talking   CONVERSATION 16
opposites O., opposites   MARRIAGE 12
opposition duty of an O. is very simple
    POLITICS 27
    It's called o.   GOVERNMENT 25
options o. open for girls   WOMEN 1
oracular use of my o. tongue   WIT 33
oral word about o. contraception   SEX 2
oral-genital cases of o. intimacy   SEX 39
orange happen to be an o.   AMERICA 2
oranges flew at the o.   FOOD 71
orations making funeral o.   SPEECHES 11
oratorio more disgusting than an o.   MUSIC 51
oratorios o. being sung in the costume
    MUSIC 36
orchard Trees in the o.   COUNTRY 5
orchestra by the waves or by the o.   SONGS 8
    squeak's heard in the o.   MUSIC 30
    two golden rules for an o.   MUSIC 8
    women in an o.   WOMEN 2
order dictionary out of o.   DICTIONARIES 5
    not necessarily in that o.   CINEMA 12
    o. of importance   CHOICE 14
    O. TOILET PAPER   HOME 5
    They o., said I   COUNTRIES 57
ordering better o. of the universe   UNIVERSE 1
orders don't take o. from you   ARGUMENT 22
    gave them their o.   GOVERNMENT 44

organ as my male o.   AUTOBIOGRAPHY 9
    mellering to the o.   MEDICINE 10
    o. grinder is present   POLITICIANS 7
    o. of prodigious diameter   POETRY 1
    second favourite o.   BODY 1
organism o. to live beyond its income
    PROGRESS 3
organization o. of idolatry   GOVERNMENT 37
organize o. her own immortality   PEOPLE 24
organized o. loafing   CRICKET 15
organs inner o. of beasts   FOOD 37
    When our o. have been transplanted
    OLD AGE 23
orgasm o. has replaced the Cross   RELIGION 45
orgy But you *need* an o.   PARTIES 4
    o. looks particularly alluring   SEX 53
oriental Like an O. tart   ARCHITECTURE 7
original I have nothing o. in me   VIRTUE 5
    it saves o. thinking   QUOTATIONS 20
    none of the o. ideas is sound   POLITICS 45
    one of the o. lines   THEATRE 29
    o. idea   IDEAS 2
originator o. of a good sentence   QUOTATIONS 6
orphan as an o.   FAMILY 35
orphaned rather late to be o.   OLD AGE 15
orthodoxy O. is my doxy   BEHAVIOUR 33
Osaka Never give O. an even break   WIT 19
Oscar We all assume that O. said it
    LITERATURE 30
ostentation use rather than o.   ROYALTY 40
ostrich behaved like an o.   INTELLIGENCE 4
Othello man of affairs like O.   ACTING 2
    O. had the naturalness   ACTING 1
other Every o. inch a gentleman   INSULTS 51
    for o. people to go on   FOOD 39
    happened to o. people   PROGRESS 5
    it did lots of o. things too   WRITERS 18
    think o. people are reading   WRITERS 31
    Were t'o. dear charmer away   LOVE 17
otherwise some are o.   WEATHER 10
Otis Miss O. regrets   BEHAVIOUR 26
ought It is, but hadn't o. to be   SATISFACTION 7
    WHERE O. I TO BE   TELEGRAMS 6
our o. son of a bitch   POLITICIANS 28
out include me o.   CINEMA 13
    say he is o. of touch   CLASS 12
    should get o. more   POLITICAL PARTIES 3
out-argue attempt to o. one's past   WRITING 5
outpatients o.' department   OLD AGE 10
outrageous o. young fellow   GENERATION GAP 4
outside baby, it's cold o.   WEATHER 18
    o. pissing in   POWER 6
ovaltine art to be like o.   ART 23
oven self-cleaning o.   HOME 27

perspiration ninety-nine percent p. INTELLIGENCE 5
perspire Gladstone may p. PRIME MINISTERS 10
perspiring City of p. dreams TOWNS 28
persuasion of the Violet p. YOUTH 3
Peru young man from P. POETRY 2
pessimist what a p. is HOPE 10
pet p. is a cow ANIMALS 9
petal p. down the Grand Canyon POETRY 17
Peter Pan wholly in P. ever since PEOPLE 45
pews p. and steeples HYPOCRISY 3
phagocytes stimulate the p. MEDICINE 32
phallus is the p. FUTURE 10
pharynx wild about my p. MEDICINE 28
pheasant *For* P. *read* Peasant MISTAKES 24
p., the pheasant FOOD 78
phenomenon infant p. ACTORS 15
p. of nature FILM STARS 9
Philadelphia I went to P. TOWNS 14
living in P. EPITAPHS 11
philanthropy It is p. BUSINESS 1
Philharmonic Keep your P. MUSIC 18
philistine see the House run by a p. SUCCESS 18
philosopher one p. arguing PHILOSOPHY 5
p. is like a mountaineer PHILOSOPHY 4
to be a p. PHILOSOPHY 3
philosophy did p. PHILOSOPHY 8
faced with p. WOMEN 19
What is your aim in p. PHILOSOPHY 10
phlegm two new seams of p. SICKNESS 7
phone answer the p. MISTAKES 27
couldn't take a p. call CONVERSATION 18
p., a horse or a broad PEOPLE 26
P. for the fish-knives, Norman SOCIETY 3
p. is for you YOUTH 4
p. whenever you felt like it READING 16
Stand on two p. books PLACES 4
What is that but a p. box RELIGION 72
You can't beat the p. company SUCCESS 4
phone bill itemised p. ranks up there TECHNOLOGY 8
photograph AIRMAIL P. OF CHAUFFEUR TELEGRAMS 17
p. is not quite true SELF-KNOWLEDGE 12
p. of the Grocer DIPLOMACY 15
photographed next war will be p. WAR 9
p. in bed FAME 9
photographer p. is like the cod TECHNOLOGY 14
photographers don't trust p. APPEARANCE 14
phrase all systems in a p. WIT 51
p. becomes current LANGUAGE 11
ruder shock than when a p. SPEECHES 10
phrases p. out of newspapers DICTIONARIES 4
physical chiefly from p. conditions POETRY 13
For p. pleasure SEX 86

physically p. desirable APPEARANCE 19
physician died last might of my p. MEDICINE 29
p. can bury ARCHITECTURE 18
physicians P. of the Utmost Fame MEDICINE 5
physics new p. was really about SCIENCE 19
pianist funky pub p. MUSICIANS 10
Please do not shoot the p. MUSICIANS 4
pianists one of the three worst p. MUSICIANS 6
piano p. gets into a log hut MUSIC 17
p. is a parlour utensil MUSIC 9
p. when played by a sister MUSIC 55
push a grand p. CHILDREN 23
pianoforte p. is a harp in a box MUSIC 25
Picasso P., sunbathing and jazz SATISFACTION 12
piccola bar on the P. Marina COUNTRIES 14
picket It's not cricket to p. POLITICS 64
pickle open p. jars MEN AND WOMEN 13
weaned on a p. DESCRIPTION 1
picnic apples short of a p. FOOLISHNESS 19
picture It was a cute p. FILMS 11
p. to remain as by Nollekens ROYALTY 49
set off in this p. FILMS 2
pictures behind all the p. SECRECY 3
dearth of bad p. CINEMA 15
know which p. are yours CINEMA 8
P. are for entertainment CINEMA 17
p. that got small FILM STARS 3
without p. or conversations LITERATURE 13
pie put into a p. ANIMALS 38
piece p. of cod FOOD 43
pier only seaside p. on which NAMES 20
piety reputation for p. WEATHER 19
pig p. got up and slowly walked ALCOHOL 12
p. is to the Irishman ANIMALS 20
p. on board TRANSPORT 7
shrewd, levelheaded p. INTELLIGENCE 19
silk stockings on a p. BOXING 7
When not, a p. CHILDREN 11
pigeon crooning like a bilious p. LANGUAGES 20
To poison a p. in the park MURDER 7
pigs fond of p. ANIMALS 11
Pilate Christ crucified Pontius P. POLITICIANS 20
since Pontius P. JUDGES 8
piles Awards are like p. AWARDS 5
pilfered always p. when dead OLD AGE 18
Pilgrim 'P.'s Progress' BOOKS 22
pill Protestant women may take the p. RELIGION 70
pillow like the feather p. INSULTS 17
pills don't believe in vitamin p. MEDICINE 8
piminy miminy, p. MEN 7
pimples scratching of p. BOOKS 27
pin p. up my hair with prose LETTERS 4
pinafore mistakes his p. for a toga WRITERS 12
pince-nez invisible p. ACTORS 10

pine as a Scots p. tree · LOVE 46
pineapple p. of politeness · WIT 32
pink all this wonderful p. · COLOURS 1
bright p. dress · BUSINESS 16
made out of p. marzipan · APPEARANCE 2
P. is the navy blue · COLOURS 8
p. plate of a face · APPEARANCE 4
very p. of perfection · SOCIETY 11
pint p. . . . why that's very nearly · MEDICINE 13
pious he was rarther p. · RELIGION 4
pipe p. with solemn interposing puff · SMOKING 3
three-p. problem · CRIME 12
Pippa P. passes · THEATRE 7
pirate like 81-year-old p. · OLD AGE 13
pissed you p. in our soup · TRUST 1
pissing inside the tent p. out · POWER 6
like p. down your leg · SPEECHES 7
pistol Is that a p. in your pocket · MEN AND WOMEN 54
p. misses fire · ARGUMENT 8
pit many-headed monster of the p. · THEATRE 40
pitchfork thrown on her with a p. · FASHION 35
pith p. is in the postscript · LETTERS 9
Pitt P. is to Addington · PRIME MINISTERS 9
Pittsburgh guy I knew in P. · MEN AND WOMEN 28
pity it was a p. to get up · WEATHER 20
pix Sticks nix hick p. · NEWSPAPERS 2
pixie vanilla-flavoured p. · POLITICS 61
pizza stopped with the p. oven · SCIENCE 7
place good p. to have them · BEHAVIOUR 36
know your p. · CLASS 22
our only dry p. · WEATHER 19
to keep in the same p. · PROGRESS 4
place mats coming home with Rembrandt p. · SOCIETY 23
places been things and seen p. · VIRTUE 24
friends in both p. · HEAVEN 6
plagiarised namely that it was p. · SELF-KNOWLEDGE 11
plagiarism gets in the way of their p. · MUSIC 13
is p. · CINEMA 36
steal from one author, it's p. · WRITING 16
plagiarist No p. can excuse the wrong · WRITING 6
plain I was very p. · APPEARANCE 9
need of the p. · BEHAVIOUR 34
no plain p. on television · TELEVISION 8
'p.' cooking · COOKERY 15
p. in dress · WOMEN 47
P. women he regarded · WOMEN 19
plan change my p. · FASHION 10
I have a cunning p. · COMEDY 22
planet If this p. is a sample · UNIVERSE 10
planks p. in my legs · TRANSPORT 31
plants talking to p. · CONVERSATION 7

plashy through the p. fen · LANGUAGE 18
plastic with a p. spoon · DESCRIPTION 31
plastics He abhorred p. · SATISFACTION 12
plate pink p. of a face · APPEARANCE 4
power on a p. · POWER 11
platinum bullets made of p. · ANIMALS 5
platitude effect as a good p. · WORDS 31
longitude with no p. · LANGUAGE 7
stroke a p. until it purrs · NEWSPAPERS 20
platitudes p. and bayonets · SPEECHES 16
sea of p. · CONVERSATION 20
Plato attachment à la P. · ART 9
foootnotes to P. · PHILOSOPHY 9
platonic my dislike is purely p. · SEX 82
plausibility dreadful p. · GOVERNMENT 26
play bad as the p. was · ACTORS 32
House Beautiful is p. lousy · THEATRE 38
I didn't like the p. · THEATRE 34
know what to say about a p. · THEATRE 49
not the way I p. it · BETTING 6
p. Ercles rarely · ACTING 25
p. has been produced only twice · THEATRE 23
p. is full · THEATRE 28
p. is full of single entendre · WORDS 15
p. it · GOLF 7
p. was a great success · THEATRE 58
p. was consumed in wholesome · LITERATURE 28
p. wot I wrote · THEATRE 10
prick that can p. · MUSIC 14
read your p. · CRITICS 37
(the professor) can p. · EDUCATION 30
this is the School p. · THEATRE 9
this p. the way you wrote it · THEATRE 15
Wimpole Street was the p. · THEATRE 37
witty prologue to a very dull p. · MARRIAGE 36
written a damned p. · THEATRE 44
y is p. · LIFE 13
playboy read *P.* magazine · SPEECHES 4
played always p. the game · POLITICIANS 31
especially when it's p. · MUSIC 15
p. the King · ACTORS 17
players don't drop p. · FOOTBALL 19
for 22 p. · FOOTBALL 1
p. who hate your guts · BASEBALL 11
playground laid to adventure p. · GARDENS 3
three times round the p. · ACTING 13
playhouse Paper Mill P. · DESCRIPTION 27
playing P. around · CHARACTER 14
p. in the other room · CHARACTER 4
p. like Tarzan · GOLF 10
p. second fiddle · POWER 7
terribly hard at p. · EDUCATION 29
where it's p. · FILMS 8

power (*cont.*):
  responsibility without p.   GOVERNMENT 40
  Wealth and p. are much more   WEALTH 19
powers all the state p.   GOVERNMENT 19
pox upon the gallows or of the p.   INSULTS 53
practical failed his p.   EXAMINATIONS 2
  most p. plan   FUTURE 7
  p. man of the world   RELIGION 71
practice had plenty of p.   CONVERSATION 24
practise I p. when I'm loaded   MUSICIANS 15
  p. this without me   ACTING 26
prairie like the p. flowers   AMERICA 7
praise people p. and don't read   READING 18
  p. is not due   PRAISE 10
  took the p.   CRITICS 21
praised p. their last publication   WRITERS 2
praises sound his own p.   PRIME MINISTERS 19
pram p. in the hall   MARRIAGE 42
prattle pleasantly they p.   CONVERSATION 19
prawn cheaper than a p. sandwich   BUSINESS 12
  swallowed the last p.   FOOD 35
pray p. for the country   GOVERNMENT 13
  p. that the church   MARRIAGE 128
prayer Revised P. Book   RELIGION 31
prayers not very addicted to p.   RELIGION 4
praying No p., it spoils business   RELIGION 52
preached p. to death   RELIGION 67
preaching gone about p.   HUMOUR 22
  good music and bad p.   RELIGION 15
  woman's p. is like a dog   WOMEN 37
precedency p. between a louse and a flea
     POETS 9
précis p. of life   WORDS 8
precision present age shrinks from p.   WORDS 22
predict only p. things   FUTURE 8
predigested p. food for the brain   QUOTATIONS 23
prefaces price we pay for his p.   THEATRE 2
pregnancy p. by a resort to mathematics
     RELIGION 43
pregnant If men could get p.   MEN AND WOMEN 19
prejudge mustn't p.   PAST 17
prejudice aid of p. and custom   PREJUDICE 7
  confirm existing p.   JOURNALISM 10
  personal p.   BOOKS 9
  popular p.   BODY 11
  result of pride and p.   LITERATURE 9
  To everybody's p.   WOMEN 27
prejudices it p. a man so   CRITICS 34
  such of the proprietor's p.   NEWSPAPERS 33
premises arguing from different p.   ARGUMENT 19
Presbyterian P. hair   BODY 23
  P. smile   APPEARANCE 18

presence p. of mind in a railway   TRANSPORT 33
present know nothing but the p.   PAST 7
  this is the *p.* Mrs Harris   MARRIAGE 124
  when they aren't p.   GOSSIP 8
presents If it were not for the p.   MARRIAGE 1
presidency lose the p.   SUCCESS 34
  US p. is a Tudor monarchy   POLITICS 17
  wants the p. so much   POWER 2
president American p.   GOVERNMENT 43
  anybody could become P.   AMERICA 11
  any boy may become P.   AMERICA 26
  becoming P.   FAMILY 24
  elected a P., not a Pope   PRESIDENTS 16
  first modern p.   PRESIDENTS 6
  I'm P.   FOOD 14
  than any other P.   GOVERNMENT 28
presidential P. Office   AUTOBIOGRAPHY 12
presidents p., editors, and people   LANGUAGE 17
press as well as for the p.   WRITING 4
  Freedom of the p.   CENSORSHIP 13
  Freedom of the p. in Britain   NEWSPAPERS 33
  god of our idolatry, the p.   JOURNALISM 11
  I'm with you on the free p.   NEWSPAPERS 32
  in the British p.   HYPOCRISY 1
  p. cuttings to prove it   ACTORS 27
  protect the people from the p.   NEWSPAPERS 35
  racket is back in its p.   LOVE 5
  viewed by the p.   JOURNALISM 9
  where the p. is free   CENSORSHIP 10
presumption amused by its p.   ALCOHOL 65
pretender James II, and the Old P.
     LITERATURE 19
pretentious P.? *Moi?*   COMEDY 34
  p. rubbish   CRITICS 1
prettiness characteristic of Victorian p.
     PEOPLE 1
pretty p. can get away   BEHAVIOUR 34
previous no P. Chapters   BOOKS 10
prey quarry, the destined p.   MEN AND WOMEN 44
price I won't put a p. on him   MEN AND WOMEN 16
  p. of everything   CHARACTER 19
  sold at a p.   ART 37
  very heavy p.   MISTAKES 11
prices High p. profit   MONEY 6
pricey p. ancestors   GENERATION GAP 7
prick Get me a p. that can play   MUSIC 14
pride having given up his p.   WRITERS 37
  result of p. and prejudice   LITERATURE 9
priest As a p.   THE CLERGY 7
  great being a p.   THE CLERGY 17
  religion from the p.   THE CLERGY 11
primates African P. Meeting   NAMES 25
prime One's p. is elusive.   YOUTH 9

prose (*cont.*):

pin up my hair with p.	LETTERS 4
p. in ribands	POETRY 14
p. of incomparable grandeur	WRITERS 21
p. run mad	POETRY 21
speaking p. without knowing it	POETRY 20
prospect noblest p.	SCOTLAND 5
prospects affording delightful p.	HOTELS 4
prosper affairs p.	FUTURE 2
prostitute doormat or a p.	WOMEN 78
mistaken for a p.	MISTAKES 17
p. all their powers	LITERATURE 18
protect Heaven will p. a working-girl	POVERTY 19
p. the Government of the day	SECRECY 10
p. the people from the press	NEWSPAPERS 35
p. the writer	BUREAUCRACY 1
protected squirrels, must be p.	LAW 30
protest lady doth p. too much	WOMEN 62
p. against golf	CRICKET 5
Protestant I am the P. whore	RELIGION 26
Irish P.	COUNTRIES 54
like a P. curate	DANCE 12
P., if he wants aid	RELIGION 18
P. with a horse	IRELAND 1
Protestantism contribution of P.	GOD 33
Protestants they were honorary P.	RELIGION 30
proud always p. of the fact	SLEEP 8
Everyone was poor and p.	POVERTY 12
p. to work with the great Gershwin	WORK 14
prove I could p. everything	TRAVEL 23
p. that you don't need it	MONEY 16
to p. it I'm here	COMEDY 10
	COMEDY 25
proverbs Solomon wrote the P.	RELIGION 46
proves p. that he is one himself	PHILOSOPHY 5
providence workings of P.	ARGUMENT 18
provinces peddles in the p.	WIT 50
provocations intolerable p.	GOLF 6
provoker Drink, sir, is a great p.	ALCOHOL 54
prudence effect of p. on rascality	VIRTUE 19
Prussians may be P.	COUNTRIES 19
psalms David wrote the P.	RELIGION 46
psychiatrist Any man who goes to a p.	MEDICINE 14
p. is a man who goes	MEDICINE 34
p.'s couch	MIND 6
psychical For P. Research	MURDER 3
pub funky p. pianist	MUSICIANS 10
retired to the p.	CRITICS 11
pubic p. hair factory	DESCRIPTION 21
public as if I was a p. meeting	ROYALTY 70
describe holding p. office	WORK 1
English p. school	EDUCATION 47
give the p. a rest	HOLIDAYS 7

give the public p.	DEATH 64
in a p. place	BEHAVIOUR 32
It's not a p. conveyance	MARRIAGE 89
one to mislead the p.	POLITICS 7
precedence over p. relations	TECHNOLOGY 6
p. be damned	BUSINESS 20
p. relations	JOURNALISM 16
p. think you are either dead	TELEVISION 11
to p. speaking	SPEECHES 3
to the p. this season	DANCE 6
uncritical buying p.	ADVERTISING 6
went to p. school	EDUCATION 7
publication book p.	BOOKS 11
praised their last p.	WRITERS 2
publicity now called p.	FAME 14
publicly not insult his wife p.	MARRIAGE 123
published before this book is p.	BIOGRAPHY 10
publisher agent to a p.	PUBLISHING 16
Barabbas was a p.	PUBLISHING 8
murdering his p.	PUBLISHING 2
p. has to do is write cheques	PUBLISHING 21
p. who writes is like a cow	PUBLISHING 17
publishers Easier to change p.	PUBLISHING 11
most famous p. in London	PUBLISHING 10
p. and printers	CENSORSHIP 11
p. are untrustworthy	PUBLISHING 20
publishing easier job like p.	PUBLISHING 1
p. business was almost run	PUBLISHING 13
pubs all the p. in Dublin	DEATH 21
pudding plums for the p.	WIT 50
p. of exhaustion	OLD AGE 29
Take away that p.	FOOD 20
puff friends all united to p.	EPITAPHS 23
solemn interposing p.	SMOKING 3
pug O most charming p.	WIT 9
Pulitzer as a P. Prize	JOURNALISM 9
Pulitzers apply for the P.	JOURNALISM 1
pull had to p. him out	PEOPLE 16
pulls p. a lady through	HOPE 5
pulse feeling a woman's p.	WOMEN 68
punch p. another person	WOMEN 43
punctual would always be p.	FILM STARS 17
punishing p. anyone who comes between them	MARRIAGE 117
punishment My fees are sufficient p.	LAW 1
punster inveterate p.	WIT 20
pure has not a p. heart	COOKERY 3
p. as the driven slush	VIRTUE 1
truth is rarely p.	TRUTH 13
purée p. of white kid gloves	FOOD 72
purgatory department of P.	OLD AGE 10
purge p., and leave sack	ARISTOCRACY 18
puritanism P. The haunting fear	RELIGION 42
purple story of a p. man	BIOGRAPHY 7
walk by the colour p.	COLOURS 9

racket gigantic r.   ART 3
    r. is back in its press   LOVE 5
radical I never dared be r. when young
     POLITICAL PARTIES 7
    R. Chic   SOCIETY 27
radicals go to the dogs or the R.   POLITICIANS 39
radio I had the r. on   PEOPLE 28
rages weight of r.   WIT 40
rail Say that she r.   MEN AND WOMEN 42
railings Iron r.   HANDWRITING 5
railway Europe by r. timetables   WAR 28
    takes this r. by surprise   TRANSPORT 10
railways R. and the Church   TRANSPORT 2
rain in the pouring r.   GARDENS 9
    left out in the r.   APPEARANCE 1
    r., it raineth on the just   VIRTUE 4
    R. in Spain   COUNTRIES 38
    r. is destroying his grain   COUNTRY 9
    we knew it was only the r.   WEATHER 19
raised r. by a speculator   FAMILY 40
rambling r., over-inflated   INSULTS 16
Ramsbottom Mr and Mrs R.   PLACES 10
rape as bad as r.   CRIME 23
Raphael sheep painted by R.   PEOPLE 1
rapidly talks more r. than I do
     SELF-KNOWLEDGE 18
    Yes, but not so r.   TIME 3
rapist r. bothers to buy a bottle   SEX 31
rapists play r.   ACTORS 26
rapper influence to your son as a r.   PARENTS 5
rascality effect of prudence on r.   VIRTUE 19
rat r. swimming *towards* a sinking   TRUST 3
    r. up a rope   ACTORS 6
ratio increase in inverse r.   BUREAUCRACY 9
rational only r. position   HEALTH 3
rattiest r. of the lot   GOD 31
ratting Goin' r.   FASHION 12
rattling r. of a stick   ADVERTISING 13
Ravel R. refuses the Legion of Honour
     MUSICIANS 14
ravished about to be r.   ACTORS 37
    would have r. her   SEX 32
rawhide r. suitcase   LOVE 9
razor sliding down the r.-blade   FUTURE 13
    tyranny of the r.   CRICKET 12
reach other beers cannot r.   ALCOHOL 39
react I r. on it at once   WRITERS 23
reaction I can't get no girl r.   SEX 41
read Don't r. much   READING 14
    do *you* r. books *through*   READING 11
    he has r. too widely   QUOTATIONS 17
    I'd not r. Eliot   POETS 14
    I r. part of it   READING 8
    I've never bothered to r. another   LITERATURE 27
    learnt to r. so quickly   CINEMA 9

    neither heard, r., talked   MURDER 13
    never r. a book   CRITICS 34
    Not that I ever r. them   NEWSPAPERS 30
    People don't actually r. newspapers
     NEWSPAPERS 19
    people praise and don't r.   READING 18
    people who can't r.   JOURNALISM 27
    r. and write with unusual speed   WRITERS 14
    r. any good books   COMEDY 14
    r. the book   CRITICS 22
    r. the life   BIOGRAPHY 9
    r. your play   CRITICS 37
    suffered in learning to r.   LITERATURE 38
    to write and r. comes by nature   MEN 15
    we should r. them   READING 13
    When I want to r. a novel   LITERATURE 16
    world doesn't r. its books   READING 12
readable edible and the r.   FOOD 81
reader definitely a great r.   READING 10
    give the r.   AUTOBIOGRAPHY 6
    ideal r. of my novels   READING 3
    r. need not   AUTOBIOGRAPHY 4
    r. of autobiographies   AUTOBIOGRAPHY 17
    R.'s Digest Condensed   FAME 7
    R.'s Digest lost   BOOKS 23
    Tonstant R.   CRITICS 26
readers full of fourth-rate r.   READING 1
    give their r. sleep   POETS 12
    r. in particular   LIBRARIES 11
reading breeding than they are of r.   WEALTH 19
    careful of his r.   CERTAINTY 15
    I prefer r.   READING 17
    modest place in Mr X's *Good R.*   LITERATURE 1
    noise in the r.-room   WOMEN 5
    no time in r.   READING 6
    not worth r.   ROYALTY 12
    of the r. rabble   GOSSIP 9
    r. a French novel   CRITICS 28
    R. a speech with his usual   SPEECHES 17
    r. biographies   BIOGRAPHY 14
    R. isn't an occupation   READING 15
    R. it slower   TECHNOLOGY 18
    r. letters   CENSORSHIP 25
    r. on the beach   HOLIDAYS 10
    Some day I intend r. it   LITERATURE 25
    soul of r.   BOOKS 21
    think other people are r.   WRITERS 31
ready he may not be r. for marriage
     MEN AND WOMEN 46
Reagan mind of Ronald R.   PRESIDENTS 12
Reagans R. intend to say it   SNOBBERY 17
real Be r.   ACTING 7
    confuse the r.-life   ACTORS 29
    r. estate advertisements   AUTOBIOGRAPHY 11

roast learned r.   COOKERY 16
    no politics in boiled and r.   POLITICAL PARTIES 17
    R. Beef, Medium   FOOD 27
    r. beef and rain   ENGLAND 9
roasted r. swans to the public   DANCE 6
rob r. a lady of her fortune   MARRIAGE 55
robbed I'd expect to be r. in Chicago   TOWNS 25
    We was r.   BOXING 8
robbing r. a bank   CRIME 4
robin little r.   COUNTRY 21
robs r. Peter   GOVERNMENT 38
rock cast the first r.   MEN AND WOMEN 27
    dank r. pools   FOOD 45
    dealing in r.'n'roll   HUMAN RACE 10
    R. Journalism   JOURNALISM 27
    subject of r.-salt   BORES 7
Rockefeller rich as R.   WEALTH 13
Rockefellers Where would the R. be today
                          WEALTH 23
rocking horse made r.   LOVE 9
rodeoing R. is about the only sport   SPORTS 18
rogue this r. and whore together   RELIGION 3
rogues couple of r.   ART 8
role perform in a r.   THEATRE 45
    poor r. models   PARENTS 17
roll don't r. over   FAME 2
rolled r. along on wheels   MEN AND WOMEN 18
rollers glanced at her Carmen r.   NAMES 7
roller skates up hill in r.   BORES 2
Rolls being a R.-Royce   CIVIL SERVANTS 1
Roman no R. ever was able to say   SOCIETY 2
    rhyme for r.   WIT 9
    R. Conquest   ENGLAND 28
Roman Catholic is a R.   FRIENDS 6
romance fine r. with no kisses
                   MEN AND WOMEN 12
    lifelong r.   LOVE 48
    Twenty years of r.   MARRIAGE 131
romances torrid r.   CENSORSHIP 1
romantic her penchant For something r.
                   LITERATURE 33
    most r. signature   TITLES 1
    r.—given to dashing about   WEATHER 17
    R.? In your mother's clean   LOVE 41
Rome It's R., it's hot   CINEMA 3
room All I need is r.   HOME 18
    find my way across the r.   PREJUDICE 7
    sitting in the smallest r.   LETTERS 14
Roosevelt Once we had a R.   AMERICA 17
Rooshans may be R.   COUNTRIES 19
Roosian might have been a R.   COUNTRIES 26
rope rat up a r.   ACTORS 6
    see a piece of r.   TRUST 5
    spare a r.   AMERICA 17
Rosalind R. was a gay and giddy   ACTING 30

rose One perfect r.   TRANSPORT 29
    r.-coloured glasses   HOME 3
    r. petal down the Grand Canyon   POETRY 17
    r.-red city   PLACES 16
    r.-red sissy   DESCRIPTION 28
roses I would like my r. to see you
                   MEN AND WOMEN 45
    Wars of the R.   CINEMA 2
rosewater Revolutions are not made with r.
                   POLITICS 5
Rosie Never got R. a ring   MEN AND WOMEN 5
rot it must be all r.   RELIGION 47
    living talked r.   DEATH 6
    R. them for a couple   ART 8
rotational professor of r. medicine   POLITICS 53
Rothschild taken by R. and Baring   MONEY 12
rotted Or simply r. early   MIDDLE AGE 8
rotten good and r.   THEATRE 27
    You r. swines   DEATH 43
rouge too much r.   FASHION 40
round R. up the usual suspects   CRIME 14
roundly r., but hollowly   CONVERSATION 23
routine r. hard to distinguish   WRITING 15
row better than a good row   ARGUMENT 2
Rowe R.'s Rule   BETTING 3
rowed All r. fast   SPORTS 8
royal R. Family feel their myth   ROYALTY 51
    What a R. Academy   PAST 5
royalties twice my usual r.   THEATRE 61
royalty Aren't we due a r. statement
                   PUBLISHING 9
    when you come to R.   ROYALTY 24
rub if you r. up against money   MONEY 21
rubbish all they provide is r.   NEWSPAPERS 22
    powerful heap of r.   LIBRARIES 8
    pretentious r.   CRITICS 1
rude do not think me r.   SEX 35
    r. about my mother   INSULTS 27
    r. to discuss money   MONEY 19
    r. to some of the most famous   PUBLISHING 10
rudeness r. of its people   AMERICA 5
Rudolph R. the Red-Nosed   ANIMALS 26
rug we both were on the r.   SEX 12
rugger nuns in a r. scrum   ARCHITECTURE 12
ruin increasingly to resemble a r.   MARRIAGE 33
    make a woman look like a r.   MARRIAGE 131
ruined r. by literature   LITERATURE 8
Ruislip Gaily into R. Gardens   SOCIETY 4
rule infallible r.   CLASS 31
    r. all afternoon   ALCOHOL 24
    they that r.   GOVERNMENT 4
    unfit to r.   DEMOCRACY 11
ruler R. of the Queen's Navee   LAW 10
rulers all may be R.   ARMED FORCES 10
    r., mostly knaves   HISTORY 2

sardines s. will be thrown · JOURNALISM 7

sashes nice new s. · DEATH 27

Prizes are like s. · AWARDS 1

sat arse upon which everyone has s. · POLITICIANS 14

Satan incarnation of S. · PEOPLE 25

S. finds some mischief · PAST 11

S. made Sydney · TOWNS 1

S. probably wouldn't · GOD 36

satire end of s. · HUMOUR 2

It's hard not to write s. · WIT 15

it was s. · HUMOUR 43

s. is a lesson · WIT 23

S. is a sort of glass · SELF-KNOWLEDGE 23

S. is what closes Saturday · THEATRE 32

S. or sense, alas · INSULTS 35

satiric one s. touch · EPITAPHS 21

satirist bounding past the s. · HUMOUR 11

satisfaction I can't get no s. · SEX 41

satisfied Massey won't be s. · ACTORS 25

S. great success · MUSIC 53

satisfying s. a voracious appetite · LOVE 15

Saturday date on a S. night · SEX 3

on a S. night · HUMOUR 13

Satire is what closes S. night · THEATRE 32

S. morning, although recurring · TRANSPORT 10

sauce pouring tinned s. · COOKERY 5

sausage s. and haddock · COOKERY 22

savage s. nobility · CRITICS 19

untutored s. · MARRIAGE 57

savaged s. by a dead sheep · INSULTS 19

save less democracy to s. · WAR 3

s. all the parts · TECHNOLOGY 4

saved Are you s. · RELIGION 39

s. by being dammed · COUNTRIES 30

saw *I s. you do it* · ACTORS 34

say did not s. them things · CERTAINTY 13

do what I s. · GOVERNMENT 41

I did not s. · CERTAINTY 19

manage to s. what we meant · LANGUAGE 16

nothing to s. · SPEECHES 12

Reagans intend to s. it · SNOBBERY 17

s. of me behind my back · SELF-KNOWLEDGE 29

s. the perfectly correct · BEHAVIOUR 29

s. what you mean · CONVERSATION 5

someone else has got to s. · ARGUMENT 6

way I s. it · FILM STARS 16

you have something to s. · WRITERS 7

saying if something is not worth s. · SONGS 6

s. a good thing · WIT 12

says can't s. aloud · OLD AGE 28

scallywags Women love s. · MEN AND WOMEN 1

scamp I've been a s. · RELIGION 54

scandal never make one's début with a s. · OLD AGE 40

one good s. left · GOSSIP 10

s. is the second breath · AUTOBIOGRAPHY 15

scarlet sins were s. · DEATH 11

scenery God paints the s. · COUNTRY 7

scenes no more behind your s. · THEATRE 25

scent s. on a pocket handkerchief · PRIME MINISTERS 18

sceptical we're s. · CERTAINTY 7

schedule s. is already full · DIPLOMACY 8

schemes s. of political improvement · POLITICS 40

scherzando *S.! ma non troppo ppp* · MUSIC 20

schizo It's so S. · CLASS 30

Schleswig S.-Holstein question · DIPLOMACY 12

scholar s. is the only man of science · SCIENCE 17

scholarship great distraction to s. · SEX 19

indications of s. · EXAMINATIONS 1

school Baby, I went to night s. · MEN AND WOMEN 56

Beauty s. report · EDUCATION 21

been to a good s. · EDUCATION 36

s. without any boots · PRIME MINISTERS 7

this is the S. play · THEATRE 9

vixen when she went to s. · WOMEN 61

woman at my public s. · WOMEN 49

world outside the s. · EDUCATION 18

schoolboy every s. knows · FOOLISHNESS 29

School for Scandal seen the S. in its glory · OLD AGE 25

schoolmaster becoming a s. · CLASS 34

schools We class s. · EDUCATION 45

schoolteacher s. is certainly · EDUCATION 33

Schopenhauer I was reading S. last night · INTELLIGENCE 7

science investigated by s. · WOMEN 19

neither a s. nor an art · ARGUMENT 12

scholar is the only man of s. · SCIENCE 17

S. becomes dangerous · SCIENCE 29

S. is his forte · INSULTS 45

s. was largely conceived · SCIENCE 23

Success is a s. · SUCCESS 37

They're s. and technology · TECHNOLOGY 15

triumph of modern s. · MEDICINE 36

scientific S. family · ECONOMICS 9

validity of the s. method · SCIENCE 26

scientist elderly but distinguished s. · SCIENCE 12

exercise for a research s. · SCIENCE 24

s. were to cut his ear · ART 19

s. who yields anything to theology · SCIENCE 25

s. without industry connections · SCIENCE 27

scientists in the company of s. · SCIENCE 3

S. are rarely to be counted · SCIENCE 22

scissors always end up using s. · TECHNOLOGY 9

larger pair of s. · FASHION 27

senna dutiful boy takes s.-tea CRITICS 21
sense different s. of morality MORALITY 4
Satire or s., alas INSULTS 35
s. and entertainment POLITICIANS 36
s. beneath is rarely found WORDS 24
s. of humour ENGLAND 20
senses should they come to their s.
POLITICIANS 26
sensibilité word equivalent to s. LANGUAGES 18
sensible S. men are all of the same RELIGION 19
sensitively lie to them s. MEN AND WOMEN 32
sensitivity extraordinary s. HYPOCRISY 1
sensual Catholic and s. COUNTRIES 9
sentence end a s. with a climax SPEECHES 8
Every s. he manages LANGUAGE 12
half a s. at a time SMOKING 3
let her husband finish a s. MARRIAGE 94
Marriage isn't a word . . . it's a s. MARRIAGE 126
originator of a good s. QUOTATIONS 6
S. structure is innate LANGUAGE 1
simple declarative s. EPITAPHS 27
sentences Backward ran s. LANGUAGE 8
s. always had verbs LANGUAGE 2
sentencing s. a man CRIME 30
sentimental s. crap of it AMERICA 10
s. value BODY 17
separated so joined that they cannot be s.
MARRIAGE 117
seraglio s. of eunuchs POLITICS 32
serendipity s. means WORDS 3
serial s. killer APPEARANCE 14
s. monogamist TRUST 4
serious joke's a very s. thing HUMOUR 10
more s. than that FOOTBALL 20
s. and the smirk ART 6
s. thing as a joke HUMOUR 30
You cannot be s. TENNIS 7
seriously S., though COMEDY 35
seriousness S. is stupidity FOOLISHNESS 22
sermons S. and soda-water HAPPINESS 4
She can't even hear my s. RELIGION 74
servant answer to the s. problem SCIENCE 23
lookingglass of a s. ART 15
s.'s cut in half DEATH 26
s. to the devil CIVIL SERVANTS 8
topic was the s. problem COUNTRY 3
servants English s. COUNTRIES 6
in the s.' hall CLASS 2
serve s. both God and Mammon GOD 40
service good after-sales s. TENNIS 6
soong the s. dyvyne WOMEN 9
unfit for military s. ARMED FORCES 13
sesquippledan 'S. verboojuice' WIT 48
set he had a complete s. LIBRARIES 7
s. fair PRIDE 1

settled waiting till the children are s. LOVE 49
seven Even the Almighty took s. POLITICS 20
learned in s. years GENERATION GAP 12
lowly air Of S. Dials ARISTOCRACY 7
talk about the s. inches BODY 36
seventh couple of hours every s. day
RELIGION 63
seventy At s., I'm in fine fettle HEALTH 9
Palmerston is now s. PRIME MINISTERS 14
several hear s. times MUSIC 42
severity with its usual s. WEATHER 6
sew s. rings on the new curtains INSULTS 9
sewer trip through a s. CINEMA 33
sex become a s. maniac EXAMINATIONS 2
chance to have s. TELEVISION 19
conceal its s. ANIMALS 34
Continental people have s. life SEX 51
discussing s. CHILDREN 21
haven't had enough s. SATISFACTION 3
her poor feeble s. is bent WOMEN 75
Instant S. SEX 29
Money was exactly like s. MONEY 2
more dangerous than s. FOOD 48
more important then s. SEX 50
never s. in Ireland TELEVISION 7
newspaper prints a s. crime NEWSPAPERS 27
No s., please COMEDY 30
s., smoking dope EDUCATION 10
s. and jewels ART 27
s. business isn't worth SEX 44
S. ever rears its ugly head SEX 13
s. in Hyde Park SPEECHES 13
S. is something I really don't SEX 69
S. was a competitive event SEX 34
[s.] was the most fun SEX 4
s. with someone I love SEX 1
short-legged sex the fair s. MEN AND WOMEN 40
talk on 'S. and Civics' SEX 16
What s. are you going to put TRAVEL 19
When you have money, it's s. MONEY 8
which is the superior s. WOMEN 52
sexes All the s. From Maine to Texas LOVE 20
there are three s. THE CLERGY 22
sexophones s. wailed SEX 40
sexton s. tolled the bell DEATH 30
sexual primary s. activity SEX 79
s. astonishment HEALTH 11
s. frustration FRIENDS 14
S. intercourse began SEX 43
true s. equality MEN AND WOMEN 29
sexually Life is a s. transmitted disease LIFE 1
sexy want you to be here and s. MARRIAGE 116
Seymour Lower S. Street CLASS 26
Shah mention the S. out loud NAMES 3
shake s. The catsup bottle FOOD 2

show (*cont.*):

My s. is the stupidest show	TELEVISION 16
s. is frozen	SONGS 17
s. me where	WORDS 1
Why must the s. go on	THEATRE 13
show-business s. with blood	BOXING 2
shower HANDSTAND IN S.	TELEGRAMS 22
showgirls S. MORE OR LESS THE SAME HEIGHT	
	TELEGRAMS 11
shows All my s. are great	SELF-KNOWLEDGE 10
two s. a day	COOKERY 7
shrieks s. to pitying heav'n	DEATH 55
shrimp as a potted s.	CRITICS 29
shrimps lobster to attendant s.	ROYALTY 50
shrine I found a s.	TOWNS 12
shrink discussed it with his s.	CHOICE 4
s. from acts of hospitality	PARTIES 5
Shropshire brother in S.	ACTING 3
shroud gaiety is a striped s.	WALES 6
shudder you awake with a s. despairing	
	MONEY 12
shunting s. engines were shunting	
	DESCRIPTION 24
shut Whenever you're right, s. up	MARRIAGE 91
shutters keep the s. up	CHARACTER 5
we'd need keep the s. up	SECRECY 7
shy s.—of the Violet persuasion	YOUTH 3
shysters driving the s. out	LAW 33
sick hired to watch the s.	SICKNESS 9
I feel too s. to tell	SICKNESS 24
I'll be s. tonight	CHILDREN 22
little too much like being s.	NATURE 5
Mummy, I'm s. with disgust	SPORTS 5
Pass the s. bag	COMEDY 33
s. enough to call for help	MEDICINE 23
were you not extremely s.	SEX 67
sicker far s. than he	TRAVEL 20
Sidcup If only I could get down to S.	TRAVEL 23
side don't care which s. wins	SPORTS 7
I am on the s. of the angels	RELIGION 17
sides both s. of the paper	EXAMINATIONS 5
everyone changes s.	GENERATION GAP 2
holding on to the s.	CHARACTER 6
said on both s.	ARGUMENT 1
sidestep I never s. skunks	INSULTS 13
sideways walk s. towards them	CRICKET 13
We think s.	IRELAND 7
sight at first s.	FRIENDS 19
sights few more impressive s.	SCOTLAND 1
sign I don't wish to s. my name	LETTERS 16
some clear s.	GOD 2
signalling wildly s.	BODY 9
signature official s.	TITLES 1
one's style is one's s.	LETTERS 16

signed he never s. off	POLITICIANS 5
not yet s. her contract	ACTORS 30
significance song of social s.	POLITICS 65
silence easy step to s.	POLITICS 8
flashes of s.	CONVERSATION 25
Indecency's conspiracy of s.	VIRTUE 18
silent Absolutely s.	SOCIETY 16
'g' is s.	INSULTS 8
God is s.	GOD 3
t is s. as in *Harlow*	INSULTS 4
silicon Had s. been a gas	EXAMINATIONS 6
silk make a s. purse	ANIMALS 32
s. makes the difference	CLASS 14
s. stockings of your actresses	THEATRE 25
worn with a s. hat	FASHION 11
silly getting s.	BIBLE 2
silver Georgian s. goes	POLITICS 46
s. foot in his mouth	PEOPLE 35
s. lining in the sky-ee	WAR 31
s. plate on a coffin	DESCRIPTION 12
thirty pieces of s.	POLITICS 11
simple beautiful and s.	CRIME 20
rarely pure, and never s.	TRUTH 13
S. tastes, you will agree	SATISFACTION 6
What do the s. folk do	ROYALTY 46
simplicity s. of the three per cents	MONEY 23
Simpson with 'is Mrs S.	ROYALTY 67
sin autobiography is a s.	AUTOBIOGRAPHY 14
beauty is only s. deep	APPEARANCE 24
cardinal s. is dullness	CINEMA 4
Excepting Original S.	VIRTUE 5
go away and s. no more	ROYALTY 7
not generally a social s.	HYPOCRISY 6
one unpardonable s.	SUCCESS 2
researches in original s.	SEX 64
s. with Elinor Glyn	SEX 7
sincere wit should be no more s.	WIT 6
sincerity s. is a dangerous thing	VIRTUE 30
Sindh I have s.	WAR 33
sing cannot s., dance	ACTORS 33
die before they s.	DEATH 14
heard no horse s. a song	MUSIC 2
people s. it	SONGS 6
s. my best in this position	SONGS 7
they could s.	PREJUDICE 9
singing in spite of the s.	SONGS 23
single s. and proud of it	MARRIAGE 48
s. entendre	THEATRE 28
s. man in possession	MARRIAGE 8
singles What strenuous s. we played	TENNIS 2
sings instead of bleeding, he s.	SONGS 15
With every word it s.	DESCRIPTION 16
sink s. my boats	MARRIAGE 3

sluicing browsing and s.   FOOD 91
slum swear-word in a rustic s.   LITERATURE 3
slums intimacy of the s.   EDUCATION 47
slurp s., slurp, slurp into the barrels   MONEY 9
slush pure as the driven s.   VIRTUE 1
smacked s. in the mouth   BOXING 9
small as a s. whisky   ALCOHOL 31
     desire s. beer   ALCOHOL 53
     Microbe is so very s.   SCIENCE 4
     pictures that got s.   FILM STARS 3
     schange me s. scheque   MONEY 5
     s. and full of holes   SMOKING 1
     s. of the back   DESCRIPTION 34
     s.-talking world   LANGUAGE 7
smallest s. room of my house   LETTERS 14
smart Don't get s. alecksy   PROGRESS 11
     versus S. Alec   CHOICE 5
smarter many who thought themselves s.
     PRIME MINISTERS 3
smell run after a nasty s.   SPORTS 2
     s. too strong of the lamp   LITERATURE 34
smile Cambridge people rarely s.   PLACES 3
     Colman's s.   ACTORS 16
     faint fleeting s.   CHARACTER 16
     occasions for a s.   DICTIONARIES 6
     Presbyterian s.   APPEARANCE 18
     s. bathed us   DESCRIPTION 5
     s. on the face of the tiger   ANIMALS 4
     You're the s. on the Mona Lisa
     MEN AND WOMEN 39
smirk serious and the s.   ART 6
smith Chuck it, S.   HYPOCRISY 3
     I have a niece called S.   SNOBBERY 13
smog in the grip of a s. attack   SICKNESS 19
smoke horrible Stygian s.   SMOKING 4
smokestack burying your head in a s.
     SICKNESS 19
smut sex crime, it is s.   NEWSPAPERS 27
snake in case I see a s.   ALCOHOL 27
     Once bitten by a s.   TRUST 5
     S. is living yet   ANIMALS 7
     s. likes live rabbits   WRITERS 33
     s. of a poem   POETRY 4
snapper s.-up of unconsidered   CHARACTER 11
snatch s. Bookie Bob   BETTING 12
snatches s. a man from obscurity   THEATRE 44
sneering I was born s.   ARISTOCRACY 6
sneezes when he s.   CHILDREN 9
snigger eunuch and a s.   THE CLERGY 9
snipe shoot s. off him   CHARACTER 9
snobbery if s. died   HUMOUR 41
     S. with Violence   SNOBBERY 4
snobs bad Brits are s.   COUNTRIES 52
snooker s. gives you firm hands   SPORTS 3

snore My lord, you s. so loud   ROYALTY 66
     snorer can't hear himself s.   SLEEP 11
snored Coolidge only s.   GOVERNMENT 28
snoring Whom, s., she disturbs   SICKNESS 9
snow congealed s.   CINEMA 38
     no word for s.   SEX 59
     thick s. on the coolibah trees   WEATHER 2
     wrong kind of s.   WEATHER 27
Snow White I used to be S.   VIRTUE 25
snuff checked up on the s.-boxes   DIPLOMACY 4
     s.-box from an Emperor   AMERICA 6
snug Skugg Lies s.   EPITAPHS 12
so It's s. unfair   COMEDY 24
soap I used your s. two years ago   PRAISE 8
     S. and education   EDUCATION 44
sober different when you're s.   HOME 23
     go to bed s.   ALCOHOL 30
     I've tried him s.   ROYALTY 20
     keep absolutely s.   WEALTH 29
     one-third s.   ALCOHOL 12
     s. in your diet   WOMEN 47
     s. me up   LIBRARIES 6
     tomorrow I shall be s.   INSULTS 12
sobriety perfect s.   ALCOHOL 3
social Boston s. zones   CLASS 15
     not generally a s. sin   HYPOCRISY 6
     she has s. instincts   SOCIETY 10
     song of s. significance   POLITICS 65
socialist I am a S.   POETS 15
     we want a s. world   POLITICS 51
socialists Education with s.   EDUCATION 6
social security s., not girls   SEX 72
society call it 'primitive s.'   PREJUDICE 6
     class-ridden s.   CLASS 22
     disrespectfully of S.   SOCIETY 25
     Indexers, S.   INDEXES 5
     Nescafé s.   SOCIETY 9
     S. did   TELEVISION 15
     S. drives people crazy   ADVERTISING 7
     s. has had a taste   FOOD 61
     s. is wonderfully delightful   SOCIETY 24
     those who govern s.   RELIGION 73
sociological it is a s. study   NEWSPAPERS 27
socks In your shirt and your s.   TRAVEL 13
     s. compelled   FASHION 33
     s. with tangerines   BODY 34
     You still have to wash your s.   SUCCESS 10
Socrates Think they're S.   COUNTRIES 48
Socratic S. method   EDUCATION 30
sod till he got under the s.   ART 10
     under his first s.   EPITAPHS 9
soda Sermons and s.-water   HAPPINESS 4
sodium Of having discovered S.   SCIENCE 5

straw Pat is the last s. NAMES 5
strawberry I'm not a s. SELF-KNOWLEDGE 8
  s. ice-cream DESCRIPTION 31
straws start drawing s. CRICKET 16
street don't do it in the s. SEX 25
  sunny side of the s. WEALTH 13
streets s. are paved CINEMA 39
  S. FLOODED. PLEASE ADVISE TELEGRAMS 3
streetwalking in the s. scene ACTING 23
strength When you've the s. for it ACTING 19
streptococci you figure the s. lurk SICKNESS 14
stretched There was things which he s. TRUTH 11
strictest s. in Europe CENSORSHIP 24
strike s. it out WRITING 12
  week of the garbage s. APPEARANCE 25
  when in doubt, s. it out WRITING 19
string too much s. POETRY 8
striped gaiety is a s. shroud WALES 6
strive need'st not s. DEATH 13
stroke None so fast as s. SPORTS 8
  s. a platitude until it purrs NEWSPAPERS 20
strong two s. men stand ARGUMENT 23
strove little still she s. SEX 24
struck not s. by lightning MARRIAGE 128
  women should be s. regularly MEN AND WOMEN 6
struggling still s. SUCCESS 38
strumpet Enter the s. voluntary SEX 84
Stuart Do you know S. Hampshire BOOKS 20
stubbornness self-righteous s. PEOPLE 22
student for every s. TRANSPORT 37
studies Humour s. HUMOUR 42
studio also in the s. ALCOHOL 17
study Criticism is a s. CRITICS 20
  s. is the last pursuit EDUCATION 11
  s. of mankind is *black* PREJUDICE 15
  s. of wit WIT 38
stuff our s. can get by without it LOVE 1
  too short to s. a mushroom TIME 6
stumbled occasionally s. over the truth TRUTH 4
stump mount the s. and make a speech NATURE 9
stunt Did a s. at the bar PARTIES 2
stunted s. his growth BODY 38
stupid *all* questions were s. SCIENCE 33
  appear s. FOOLISHNESS 32
  as s. as you FOOLISHNESS 3
  interesting . . . but s. COMEDY 39
  s. editors CRITICS 18
  s. man is doing something MORALITY 12
stupidity Seriousness is s. FOOLISHNESS 22
stupidvision It is s. TELEVISION 17
Stygian horrible S. smoke SMOKING 4

style failure may be your s. SUCCESS 9
  make it a matter of s. SOCIETY 23
  one's s. is one's signature LETTERS 16
  taste, and s. BEHAVIOUR 24
subconscious actor's s. ACTORS 22
subject Etiquette, sacred s. BEHAVIOUR 23
  one s. you must stay away from POLITICS 75
  s. might never again be mentioned RELIGION 8
subjects elementary s. EDUCATION 19
  embarked on all five s. CONVERSATION 6
subjunctive s. mood is in its death throes LANGUAGE 13
sublime step is short from the S. TRANSPORT 13
submarines worked with more s. ACTORS 28
subordinate quaint old s. GOD 38
substitute s. for the real thing TOWNS 23
subtle be a little more s. PRAISE 1
subtract don't teach him to s. EDUCATION 25
subtraction two dollars, that's s. MEN AND WOMEN 53
suburbs s. of morality VIRTUE 7
subversive It just had to be s. NAMES 9
succeed How to s. in business SUCCESS 21
  if at first you don't s. FAMILY 15
  If at first you don't s. SUCCESS 9
  SUCCESS 13
  want to s. in politics POLITICS 44
succeeds Nothing s. like excess SUCCESS 36
  s. he is taken over SUCCESS 22
  Whenever a friend s. SUCCESS 33
succès S. *d'estime* WIT 17
success If *A* is a s. in life LIFE 13
  Satisfied great s. MUSIC 53
  S. is a science SUCCESS 37
  S. is the one unpardonable sin SUCCESS 17
  s. that ran out of WIT 17
  S. took me to her bosom SUCCESS 8
successes some of the ampler s. SUCCESS 29
successful s. in your profession CRIME 10
successor publish 'the s.' PUBLISHING 14
suck s. on a boiled sweet SEX 87
sucker Never give a s. BETTING 4
sudden s. cuckoo COUNTRIES 62
sue S. me, sue me LAW 20
suffering man's s. has been lifted POLITICS 51
suffragettes s. were triumphant WOMEN 4
sugar can't rhyme 's.' WORDS 18
  shower you with s. lumps ANIMALS 24
  S. Replacement Therapy FOOD 92
  triumph of s. over diabetes PEOPLE 29
suggest name *not* s. COUNTRIES 2
suicide commit s. GOVERNMENT 42
  committed s. MARRIAGE 10
  it wasn't s. FAMILY 26
  where they commit s. COUNTRIES 4

swelled audience s. to six — POETRY 15
swift To read S. — WRITERS 22
swindles all truly great s. — CRIME 20
swine have offered them 's.' — CENSORSHIP 2
Pearls before s. — INSULTS 33
swines You rotten s. — DEATH 43
swing room enough to s. a cat — POVERTY 21
s. a cat — HOME 13
swinging which would keep s. — DANCE 10
Swiss at a S. bank — GOD 2
operated by the S. — TOWNS 30
switch s. off the lights — NEWSPAPERS 5
switching ultimate sanction of s. off — TELEVISION 6
Switzerland don't like S. — COUNTRIES 63
look upon S. — COUNTRIES 56
swore Our armies s. terribly — WAR 26
swum she had s. the Channel — SOCIETY 12
Sydney felt like an exile in S. — TOWNS 19
Satan made s. — TOWNS 1
[S.] was all London — TOWNS 23
syllable of more than one s. — CINEMA 43
sylph only s. I ever saw — ACTING 11
sylvan nothing much more s. — COUNTRY 17
sympathy s. even as an endangered species — LAW 15
your God-damned s. — LETTERS 17
symptoms hundred good s. — DEATH 54
synod S. of Cooks — COOKERY 11
systems I summed up all s. — WIT 51

t t. is silent, as in *Harlow* — INSULTS 4
table better t. manners — QUOTATIONS 8
get a t. — FAME 12
t. near the floor — FOOD 47
t. next to Michael — CHOICE 16
under the t. with the telephone — WAR 11
tablet keep taking The T. — RELIGION 70
tablets assortment of t. — ALCOHOL 34
tabloids sports pages of the t. — CRICKET 14
taboo repose is t.'d by anxiety — LANGUAGE 9
tail kettle to a dog's t. — WRITERS 26
salmon standing on it's t. — PEOPLE 44
t. that wagged — EPITAPHS 25
t. was a plume — ANIMALS 23
verb chasing its own t. — LANGUAGE 12
tailor coat from the t. — THE CLERGY 11
taint t. of legality — LAW 17
Taj Mahal how the T. must feel — MARRIAGE 13
take I'll t. that one — CHOICE 17
T. him — MEN AND WOMEN 16
T. my wife — COMEDY 38
taken When t., To be well shaken — MEDICINE 9
takes t. less than three days — BASEBALL 12
taketh author t. away — WRITERS 19

taking t. something — GOVERNMENT 46
talcum bit of t. — BODY 26
tale This most tremendous t. — CHRISTMAS 3
talent can't buy t. — FOOTBALL 12
mediocre t. — BOOKS 18
NO REAL T. REQUIRED — TELEGRAMS 11
Pack up your t. — THEATRE 13
t. of a liar — LITERATURE 10
t. of our English nation — ENGLAND 11
talk easy to t. — FOOD 23
English how to t. — CONVERSATION 31
fun of t. — CONVERSATION 10
people don't t. — CONVERSATION 30
People don't t. in Paris — TOWNS 10
rot the dead t. — DEATH 6
t. like a lady — CLASS 27
t. on 'Sex and Civics' — SEX 16
t. out of the mouth — LANGUAGES 6
t. under their feet — PRESIDENTS 14
teach us to t. about — BOOKS 17
things like that to t.about — FASHION 23
talked not being t. about — GOSSIP 14
t. like poor Poll — EPITAPHS 13
t. of me — FOOLISHNESS 8
talking art of t. about oneself — TELEVISION 9
doin' all the t. — CONVERSATION 11
opposite of t. — CONVERSATION 16
stop people t. — DEMOCRACY 3
t. to plants — CONVERSATION 7
t. to Tallulah — CONVERSATION 14
you will still be t. — INSULTS 40
talks Licker t. mighty loud — ALCOHOL 33
person who t. — BORES 3
t. good for a black guy — PREJUDICE 10
t. more rapidly than I do — SELF-KNOWLEDGE 18
t. so fast — SPEECHES 4
tall T. men come down — BOXING 4
Tallulah day away from T. — DESCRIPTION 13
talking to T. — CONVERSATION 14
T. Bankhead barged — ACTORS 4
T. is always skating — ACTORS 7
tambourine play the t. — ACTING 11
tangerines socks with t. — BODY 34
tap I can turn off the t. at will — WRITERS 32
tapeworms editors, and people with t. — LANGUAGE 17
tar T.-baby ain't sayin' — ANIMALS 17
tart t. who has finally married — POLITICIANS 3
tarts t. in him — FOOD 36
Tarzan Me T. — FILMS 13
playing like T. — GOLF 10
task t. is not to be yours — HANDWRITING 9
task force sending a t. — FOOD 84

translation Browning's t.	CRITICS 39	**Trojan** T. 'orses will jump out	DIPLOMACY 2
mistake in the t.	MORALITY 14	**trooping** t. in companies	HUMAN RACE 6
Perhaps we could have a t.	LANGUAGES 15	**trot** Slowed down to a t.	SICKNESS 4
translations T. (like wives)	MARRIAGE 30	**trouble** asking for t.	NAMES 15
transplanted When our organs have been t.		women and care and t.	WOMEN 76
	OLD AGE 23	**troubled** t. with her lonely life	MARRIAGE 98
trap t. in a trap	DANCE 13	**troubles** over all its t.	HOME 16
trapped t. or shot	MEN 9	**trouser** illluminated t.-clip	TECHNOLOGY 12
trashman t. and the policeman	INSULTS 28	three t. suits	FASHION 23
travel Englishman does not t.	ENGLAND 36	**trousers** best t. on	FASHION 18
never t. without	DIARIES 9	steam-engine in t.	PEOPLE 39
rapid and convenient t.	TRAVEL 24	t. so copiously flared	FASHION 5
real way to t.	TRANSPORT 14	**trout** find a t. in the milk	LAW 36
ship would *not* t. due West	TRAVEL 4	**trowel** lay it on with a t.	ROYALTY 24
thirty years of t. together	MARRIAGE 92	reach of a t.	ARCHITECTURE 17
t. broadens the behind	TRAVEL 9	**truck** apologizes to the t.	ENGLAND 21
t. broadens the mind	SEX 77	**truckman** t., the trashman	INSULTS 28
	TRAVEL 5	**true** entirely t.	GOSSIP 13
t. light	BODY 17	might not be t.	CERTAINTY 16
two classes of t.	TRAVEL 1	no matter how t.	PAST 16
Why do the wrong people t.	TRAVEL 6	nothing in the newspapers is ever t.	
travelled which way he t.	PRIME MINISTERS 4		NEWSPAPERS 12
travelling T. Swede	COUNTRIES 13	story because it is t.	TRUTH 8
trawler When seagulls follow a t.	JOURNALISM 7	**truer** nothing's t. than that	TAXES 2
tread t. most neatly	EPITAPHS 1	**trumpets** to the sound of t.	HEAVEN 5
treason [T.], Sire, is a question	TRUST 14	**trust** difficult to t. the Chinese	TRUST 5
t. to his country	TRUST 9	To t. people is a luxury	WEALTH 15
word t. to me means nothing	TRUST 1	t. with anything	POLITICAL PARTIES 18
treated t. me very well	UNIVERSE 6	We shouldn't t. writers	READING 13
treatment scientific t. for all diseases		**trusted** is not to be t.	POWER 2
	MEDICINE 32	t. neither of them as far	TRUST 15
tree barking up the wrong t.	CRITICS 13	t. two persons whom I knew	PEOPLE 27
billboard lovely as a t.	ADVERTISING 11	**truth** anxious to tell the t.	TRUTH 6
cut down a redwood t.	NATURE 9	best policy to speak the t.	TRUTH 7
when we chop a t.	NATURE 3	Blurting out the complete t.	TRUTH 9
trees birds coughing in the t.	NATURE 1	I just tell the t.	TRUTH 10
books, t. and women	POLITICIANS 35	lures the t.	JOURNALISM 23
I think of the poor t.	NEWSPAPERS 22	mainly he told the t.	TRUTH 11
Nice t. are taken for granted	COUNTRY 19	stumbled over the t.	TRUTH 4
T. in the orchard	COUNTRY 5	telling the t.	LIES 11
trembles list of their names, he t.	WAR 30	telling the t. about them	POLITICS 72
trench like t. warfare	PRESIDENTS 12	t. at last	EPITAPHS 15
triangle idea for a new t.	IDEAS 1	t. is always strange	TRUTH 2
trickle T.-down theory	ECONOMICS 4	t. is chimerical	TRUTH 1
tried pick the one I never t.	VIRTUE 26	t. is rarely pure	TRUTH 13
trinity also is a T. man	GOD 10	T. is suppressed	SECRECY 10
hazy about the T.	RELIGION 6	t. may sometimes be disinterred	LAW 26
trip t. through a sewer	CINEMA 33	wedded to the t.	GOVERNMENT 35
triplicate that come in t.	FAMILY 27	**truthful** t. than factual	HUMOUR 31
triste jamais t.	HOPE 6	**try** t. again. Then quit	SUCCESS 13
triumph t. of hope over experience	MARRIAGE 77	t. him afterwards	LAW 24
t. of modern science	MEDICINE 36	**trying** business without really t.	SUCCESS 21
t. of the embalmer's art	PEOPLE 46	I am t. to be	INSULTS 43
trivial diversion of t. men	POLITICS 55	**tsar** T. of all the rushes	CINEMA 41
Nothing t., I hope	SICKNESS 16	**tuba** t. is certainly the most	MUSIC 11

tube toothpaste is out of the t.   POLITICS 35
Tudor do you know *T. Cornwall*   BOOKS 20
  US presidency is a t. monarchy   POLITICS 17
Tuesday If it's T.   TRAVEL 25
  T. simply doesn't count   WORDS 21
tuition Concorde after five minutes' t.
   TECHNOLOGY 11
tummy he'll get a t. ache   FOOD 52
tune I t. my latent song   SONGS 5
  keep thinkin'll turn into a t.   MUSIC 24
tunes I only know two t.   MUSIC 22
tunnel at the end of the t.   BETTING 3
  I have always been pro-t.   TRANSPORT 26
  train going into a t.   HUMOUR 45
Tupperware like living inside T.   WEATHER 4
turbot by way of t.   THE CLERGY 23
  T., Sir   FOOD 85
turd rhyming is nat worth a t.   POETRY 6
turn t. for ten thousand dollars   WEALTH 18
turned anything t. up   HOPE 4
  with the sound t. down   PEOPLE 20
Turner resembled a T. sunset   DESCRIPTION 15
turnstones T. were turning   DESCRIPTION 24
turtle t. Enormously fert'le   ANIMALS 28
  t. lives   ANIMALS 34
Tutankhamun T.'s tomb   COLOURS 1
TV how they look on T.   BROADCASTING 5
  T. —a clever contraption   TELEVISION 1
tweed t. nightgowns   ENGLAND 14
tweet I say 't. tweet'   SONGS 20
twentieth-century t. failure   SUCCESS 6
twenty T. years of romance   MARRIAGE 131
  you're t. minutes   CHARACTER 21
twenty-twenty Hindsight is always t.   PAST 18
twice must do t. as well as men
   MEN AND WOMEN 57
  t. as much as your last   THEATRE 61
twinkle Twinkle, t., little bat   UNIVERSE 5
twins Clara threw the t.   CHILDREN 16
twisted t. imagination   ART 13
two are there t. nine o'clocks   TIME 1
  Audience of T.   THEATRE 60
  Between t. evils   VIRTUE 26
  make only t. people miserable   MARRIAGE 23
  there are t. meanings   WORDS 4
  T. for a woman   MEDICINE 4
  t. men to write one song   SONGS 19
  t. of them   PEOPLE 4
  t. people with a German shepherd   TRAVEL 8
  t. things about   ANIMALS 41
  t. things that will be   ALCOHOL 63
  Why I see *t.*   WIT 36
  you the t. fingers   CHOICE 8

typewriter buy an electric t.   TECHNOLOGY 11
  changing a t. ribbon   WRITING 2
  demented t.   ACTORS 14
  t. full of oyster shells   PLACES 15
typewriters electric t. keep going mmmmmmm
   TECHNOLOGY 3
  million t.   COMPUTERS 5
typewriting t. machine, when played   MUSIC 55
typhoid t. germ magnified   DOGS 3
tyranny t. of the razor   CRICKET 12

ubiquitous by being at any rate u.
   INTELLIGENCE 2
uglier u. a man's legs are   GOLF 12
ugliness u. was destined   APPEARANCE 20
ugly Bessie, you're u.   INSULTS 12
  Frazier is so u.   INSULTS 1
  I was so u.   APPEARANCE 30
  knowing that he is u.   JUDGES 4
  than to be u.   APPEARANCE 29
ulsterior look for the *U. motive*   PREJUDICE 14
Ulysses kiss the hand that wrote U.   WRITERS 18
umble so very 'u.   HYPOCRISY 4
umbrella unjust steals the just's u.   VIRTUE 4
unattractive most u. old thing   OLD AGE 21
unavailable forgiving, and u.   LOVE 32
unawareness u. of the world of ideas   IDEAS 6
unbearable in victory u.   WAR 7
unbeatable In defeat u.   WAR 7
unbends nothing u. the mind   WOMEN 24
unbribed man will do u.   JOURNALISM 26
uncivilized unconquered, and u.   ENGLAND 25
uncle Call U. Teddy   FAMILY 24
  obliged to call him U.   THE CLERGY 1
  U. Bud's pants   DESCRIPTION 30
  u. who lives there   FAMILY 45
uncles wronged u.   FAMILY 56
uncomfortable he is only u.   ENGLAND 30
unconquered kept u.   ENGLAND 25
unconscionable u. time dying   ROYALTY 19
uncool U. people   FASHION 13
undecided five who are u.   BASEBALL 11
under have been u. the host   ALCOHOL 49
  talk u. their feet   PRESIDENTS 14
underachiever he's an u.   GOD 1
undercover queen of u. loves   SECRECY 9
underdeveloped u. the country   WOMEN 23
underdogs among the u.   ENGLAND 40
underestimate u. them   FOOTBALL 18
underestimating u. the intelligence
   INTELLIGENCE 12
undergraduates of the u.   EDUCATION 11
undersexed happy u. celibate   SUCCESS 6
undersized could call the u.   MEN AND WOMEN 40

upstairs u. into the world   CLASS 7
  went u. with Margery   ALCOHOL 4
Urals wind that swept down from the U.
                                                  PLACES 12
urban pretty u. sort of person   COUNTRY 4
urinal always take place in the u.   SECRECY 4
use But what's the u.   WEALTH 10
  not the slightest u.   ROYALTY 71
  u. of my body   BODY 3
  u. rather than ostentation   ROYALTY 40
used It is what it u. to be   SONGS 11
  most u. two-letter word   WORDS 9
  since then I have u. no other   PRAISE 8
useful trying to become u.   GOVERNMENT 47
useless u. when inert   CENSORSHIP 7
usen't u. you to be   FAME 15
uterine u. contractions   HEALTH 7
utopia We rose to bring about U.   IRELAND 3

v spell it with a "V" or a "W"   WORDS 7
vacancy v. at Canterbury   THE CLERGY 4
vacations No extras, no v.   EDUCATION 15
vacuum out from behind the v.   WOMEN 29
  v. is a hell of a lot better   NATURE 11
vain Most people are v.   WRITERS 8
  Pavarotti is not v.   SELF-KNOWLEDGE 27
  You're so v.   SELF-KNOWLEDGE 21
valentine author of this v.   SECRECY 9
valet unnerved by Banquo's v.   ACTING 6
valium baseball on v.   CRICKET 18
value learn the little v. of fortune   WEALTH 30
  v. of nothing   CHARACTER 19
  we v. none   SEX 10
van Follow the v.   HOME 6
Vanbrugh V.'s house of clay   EPITAPHS 10
Van Eyck younger V. was christened Jan
                                               MISTAKES 5
vanilla some v.-flavoured pixie   POLITICS 61
vanished manners have v.   HOME 2
vanity Being an MP feeds your v.   POLITICS 60
varicose Victorian V.   ARCHITECTURE 14
vase v. in the hands of a chimpanzee   WRITERS 42
VAT doing your V. return   TAXES 7
  forty-nine plus V.   MIDDLE AGE 4
vaudeville Terrible V.   TELEVISION 1
veal cold boiled v.   FRIENDS 11
  condemned v.   ACTORS 5
vegetable passion of a v. fashion   ART 9
  v., animal   ARMED FORCES 11
vegetarian Atheist and a V.   POETS 15
veins Scotch blood in her v.   PREJUDICE 2
Venice We open in V.   THEATRE 42
venom pots of oily v.   GOSSIP 7
venomous V. Bead   RELIGION 61
Venus You're the breasts of V.   SEX 8

verb v. chasing its own tail   LANGUAGE 12
  Waiting for the German v.   LANGUAGES 17
verbal risk of v. infection   QUOTATIONS 18
  v. contract   CINEMA 21
  with its own v. music   MUSIC 49
verboojuice 'Sesquippledan v.'   WIT 48
verbosity exuberance of his own v.   INSULTS 14
verbs sentences always had v.   LANGUAGE 2
verge She's always on the v.   SEX 38
verse all that is not v. is prose   POETRY 19
  as polished as my v.   SELF-KNOWLEDGE 13
  I'd as soon write free v.   POETRY 11
  Of all my v.   PRIDE 10
  only with those in v.   LETTERS 4
  Who died to make v. free   POETRY 22
verses Non-navigational V.   MISTAKES 18
versions hundred v. of it   RELIGION 62
vertical v. man   SEX 10
very V. interesting   COMEDY 39
vessel v. with the pestle   WIT 26
vest wears a v.   CHARACTER 14
vestry in the v. after service   SEX 75
vexation Multiplication is v.   SCIENCE 2
viagra theatrical V.   THEATRE 52
vibrator invent a v.   MEN AND WOMEN 13
vicar Evangelical v.   THE CLERGY 16
  I will be the V. of Bray, sir   POLITICIANS 1
vicars v. off the incense   THE CLERGY 27
vice distinction between virtue and v.   VIRTUE 10
  v. and religion   ENGLAND 34
  Well sure that v.   CRIME 7
vicious expect a boy to be v.   EDUCATION 36
victim v. of my own choices   CHOICE 12
victims reformation must have its v.   RELIGION 60
victor my shock-headed v.   LOVE 5
Victorian passed the V. Era   CENSORSHIP 17
  V. age   ECONOMICS 10
  V. Varicose   ARCHITECTURE 14
Victorians in favour of the V.   ARCHITECTURE 17
  V. had not been anxious   HOLIDAYS 12
victory in v. unbearable   WAR 7
view you get a v.   PLACES 4
viewers shouldn't v. be given   BASEBALL 5
vilify v. without being called a racist   WALES 8
villains v. wholly bad   BOOKS 13
villainy natural expression of v.   VIRTUE 22
Vinci They spell it V.   LANGUAGES 22
vine crosses V.   TOWNS 12
vinegar life of v.   MARRIAGE 19
vines advise his client to plant v.
                                           ARCHITECTURE 18
violence extreme v.   FOOTBALL 8
  lead to acts of v.   EDUCATION 49
  Snobbery with V.   SNOBBERY 4
  using v.   CRIME 27

violent usually v. ENGLAND 43
violet of the V. persuasion YOUTH 3
violin v. is wood and catgut FOOTBALL 17
virgin Doris Day before she was a v. SEX 49
Marina, a beautiful v. SEX 71
trouble with a v. SEX 38
virginity just a little more v. ACTING 29
No, no; for my v. SEX 67
virtue Adult v. includes being VIRTUE 13
disguised as a v. HOPE 1
distinction between v. and vice VIRTUE 10
pay to V. HYPOCRISY 2
Self-denial is not a v. VIRTUE 19
what v. is to a lady NEWSPAPERS 31
virtuous because thou art v. MORALITY 11
When men grow v. OLD AGE 32
visit purpose of v. AMERICA 18
vita all aqua, no v. PEOPLE 5
vitality full of v. CRITICS 29
vitamin don't believe in v. pills MEDICINE 8
vitriol sleeve with a bottle of v. PEOPLE 50
vixen She was a v. WOMEN 61
vocabulary It shows a lack of v. LANGUAGE 3
vogue he'd be working for *V.* FASHION 36
totter into v. FASHION 38
voice gorgeous v. ACTORS 19
have no speaking v. DESCRIPTION 16
in that tone of v. INSULTS 38
I see a v. WIT 28
[Joyce] has the most lovely v. PEOPLE 30
search for a v. of his own WRITERS 30
supplicating v. CHOICE 11
voices v. of young people YOUTH 7
volcanoes exhausted v. DESCRIPTION 14
vole passes the questing v. LANGUAGE 18
volubility I'll commend her v.
MEN AND WOMEN 42
volumes exhibited in both these v. WORDS 14
two hundred thousand v. LIBRARIES 8
voluntary Enter the strumpet v. SEX 84
vomit returning to one's own v. DIARIES 6
vote most people v. against DEMOCRACY 1
never v. *for* DEMOCRACY 6
told which way to v. THE CLERGY 12
v. agains me GOVERNMENT 7
v. for the devil DEMOCRACY 18
V. for the man who promises POLITICS 10
v. just as their leaders tell 'em to POLITICS 34
voted v. at my party's call DEMOCRACY 8
voter Every intelligent v. POLITICS 2
voting If v. changed anything POLITICS 43
not the v. that's democracy DEMOCRACY 15
vowels scrabble with all the v. missing
MUSIC 16

vulgar Cocoa is a v. beast FOOD 19
in the least bit v. ACTORS 20
let the v. stuff alone LANGUAGES 5
money-spending always v. MONEY 10
vulgarity V. often cuts ice SNOBBERY 3

w spell it with a "V" or a "W" WORDS 7
Wagner I love W. MUSIC 4
too much w. MUSIC 1
W. has lovely moments MUSIC 43
W.'s music is better MUSIC 37
waistcoat digest its w. FOOD 75
fourth w. button BODY 22
wait DON'T W. TELEGRAMS 21
people who have to w. BEHAVIOUR 21
w. in the car TIME 2
waited w. on hand and foot SATISFACTION 8
waiter good head w. FOOD 32
inattentive w. PLACES 8
nothing but a head-w. DIPLOMACY 17
You can't make a w. see you SUCCESS 4
waiters theologians and w. COUNTRIES 63
w. discussing the menu FOOD 11
waiting of talking is w. CONVERSATION 16
put you on a w. list MEDICINE 15
w. for Godot CERTAINTY 3
w. for speech to finish LANGUAGE 6
W. for the German verb LANGUAGES 17
w. till the children are settled LOVE 49
We've been w. 700 years TIME 5
worth w. for SEX 33
waits endless w. LOVE 24
wake in wedlock w. MARRIAGE 100
you will w. the king ROYALTY 66
Wakefield W. is a bit like Wollongong TOWNS 8
wakes Wordsworth sometimes w. LITERATURE 11
Wales influence of W. WALES 7
W. where the only concession WALES 6
what has he done for W. WALES 1
whole world . . . But for W. WALES 2
walk can w. to work PRESIDENTS 9
good w. spoiled GOLF 11
I can w. WEALTH 4
W. across my swimming pool RELIGION 56
W.! Not bloody likely TRANSPORT 36
w. to the kerb TRANSPORT 1
worship the ground you w. on MARRIAGE 134
walking act of w. round him ART 4
w. backwards for Christmas CHRISTMAS 9
w. the length and breadth TRAVEL 2
walks take them for w. ANIMALS 13
wallpaper of the w. DEATH 74
Wall Street barefoot boy from W. POLITICIANS 21
waltzes w. like a Protestant curate DANCE 12

working besides the one he's w. on | WRITERS 40
Chamberlain loves the w. man | WORK 7
have a w. relationship | GOD 18
Heaven will protect a w.-girl | POVERTY 19
I killin' meself w. | MEN AND WOMEN 33
w. on a case of Scotch | ALCOHOL 9
working-class job all w. parents want | POLITICS 1
workings w. of Providence | ARGUMENT 18
works Greed w. | ECONOMICS 13
world around the w. to count the cats | TRAVEL 28
arranging the w. | TECHNOLOGY 7
makes the w. go round | ALCOHOL 40
not as fast as the w. record | SPORTS 10
small-talking w. | LANGUAGE 7
upstairs into the w. | CLASS 7
w. doesn't read its books | READING 12
w. famous | COUNTRIES 49
w. has treated me | UNIVERSE 6
w. is a comedy | HUMAN RACE 15
w. is disgracefully managed | UNIVERSE 8
w. is full of care | WOMEN 76
w. is your lobster | SUCCESS 15
w. locks up its spoons | ARMED FORCES 27
w. that's better for Rupert | PEOPLE 43
worsening the w. | TELEVISION 12
worm as a crushed w. | MARRIAGE 106
man to a w. | FOOD 7
you have tasted your w. | WIT 42
worry any one he wanted to w. about | MEDICINE 16
worse each party is w. than the other | POLITICS 63
fear of finding something w. | CHILDREN 3
geting steadily w. | HISTORY 18
I don't feel w. | MORALITY 5
If my books had been any w. | LITERATURE 14
worsening w. the world | TELEVISION 12
worst one of the three w. pianists | MUSICIANS 6
w. is yet to come | FUTURE 9
worth not w. going to see | TRAVEL 16
not w. reading | ROYALTY 12
she's w. all she costs you | LOVE 33
what your flattery is w. | PRAISE 6
Worthington Mrs W. | ACTING 8
Regarding yours, dear Mrs W. | LETTERS 5
worthy good old laugh gets w. | THEATRE 26
wotthehell w. archy | HOPE 6
would He w., wouldn't he | LIES 9
wouldn't It's not 'cause I w. | WOMEN 59
wound Shall w. Him worst of all | TRUST 10
wow women you will w. | THEATRE 43
wrap have to w. them round | CENSORSHIP 1

wrapped He w. himself in quotations | QUOTATIONS 11
wrath w. of the police | MUSICIANS 3
wrecker such a w. | ANIMALS 31
wren Sir Christopher W. | ARCHITECTURE 3
wrinkled face was that w. | APPEARANCE 13
wrinklies ageing w. | DRUGS 8
write act much better than you w. | WRITERS 6
can just w. | INSULTS 18
don't also offer to w. it | PUBLISHING 14
glad you'll w. | WRITING 17
had to w. for a living | WRITING 7
He would fain w. a poem | SATISFACTION 5
people who can't w. | JOURNALISM 27
read a novel, I w. one | LITERATURE 16
restraint with which they w. | LITERATURE 12
scarcely w. it | BOOKS 3
They w. about it | LOVE 1
to w. and read comes by nature | MEN 15
Who would w., who had any | WRITERS 1
w. *A Panegyric* | AUTOBIOGRAPHY 13
w. for posterity | FUTURE 6
w. for the fire | WRITING 4
w. like Shakespeare | WRITERS 29
w. no memoirs | AUTOBIOGRAPHY 16
w. on both sides | EXAMINATIONS 5
writer animosity against a w. | WRITERS 48
being both w. and musician | MUSICIANS 19
brilliant w. in the editor's chair | NEWSPAPERS 8
may be a great w. | READING 10
no w. can give | HOME 14
woman and a w. | MARRIAGE 10
working w. | CRITICS 16
w., in the eyes | CINEMA 35
w. for the ages | WRITERS 34
w. is to the real world | WRITERS 24
w.'s fame | FAME 12
w.'s pride in having given up | WRITERS 37
w. that people think | WRITERS 31
w. to eat a whole sheep | WRITERS 27
writers all w. should be in prison | WRITERS 36
full of fourth-rate w. | READING 1
How few w. can prostitute | LITERATURE 18
Merrick liked w. | WRITERS 33
We shouldn't trust w. | READING 13
We w. all act and react | WRITERS 23
writes everybody w. | AUTOBIOGRAPHY 3
publisher who w. is like a cow | PUBLISHING 17
w. with a feather | THEATRE 21
writing give a toss about w. | LITERATURE 37
little point in w. | WRITING 1
Miss Y's *Good W.* | LITERATURE 1
rich from w. | WRITING 14
thought *nothing* of her w. | WRITERS 38
validity in w. | BORES 12

writing (*cont.*):
W., I explained, was mainly WRITING 5
w., like the art of love WRITING 15
w. is on the wall HUMOUR 5
written w. a book BOOKS 8
W. English is now inert WRITING 10
w. in such small print READING 7
wrong as likely to be w. FUTURE 3
called the w. number MISTAKES 27
for the w. word CRITICS 40
gets it w. MISTAKES 8
he is very probably w. SCIENCE 12
he usually gets it all w. POLITICIANS 23
Kings to w. wrong ROYALTY 58
neighbours do w. CRIME 21
not always to be w. SELF-KNOWLEDGE 7
on the w. side of DOGS 4
people will think it w. LAW 21
some ideas so w. IDEAS 8
Whenever you're w., admit it MARRIAGE 91
When women go w. MEN AND WOMEN 55
Why do the w. people travel TRAVEL 6
w. bar or bed MISTAKES 6
w. bits are in CRITICS 14
w. boat at Dover TRAVEL 14
W. but Wromantic DESCRIPTION 29
w. end of a gun SPORTS 37
w. kind of snow WEATHER 27
wrote play wot I w. THEATRE 10
this play the way you w. it THEATRE 15
w., except for money WRITING 13
w. like an angel EPITAPHS 13
Wykehamist rather dirty W. RELIGION 9

yachts echoes the sails of the y. PLACES 15
yaks y. jumping about MUSIC 5
Yale libel on a Y. prom WOMEN 56
Yankee Doodle One of them is 'Y.' MUSIC 22
Yanks Y., through and through AMERICA 9
yawns grave y. for him BORES 17
year last y. in Australia TRAVEL 26
next y. I shall be sixty-two MIDDLE AGE 11
this time of y. WEATHER 11
Was I a good y. ALCOHOL 59
yearns y. so hungrily ACTORS 36
years 10 y. in a boiler suit WOMEN 72
additional dozen y. MEDICINE 22
Every twelve y. MEDICINE 27
Methus'la live nine hundred y. OLD AGE 20
well stricken in y. OLD AGE 41
We've been waiting 700 y. TIME 5

Yeats Y. is becoming so aristocratic SNOBBERY 7
yello y. stripes LIFE 14
yes getting the answer y. BEHAVIOUR 4
sounds like y. DIPLOMACY 14
yet but not y. SEX 11
ying Y. tong iddle I po COMEDY 41
yob eel-and-pie y. SNOBBERY 6
y. ethics FOOTBALL 24
yoghurt between the milk and the y.
WRITERS 39
yolk y. runs down FOOD 23
Yossarian Y.—the very sight of the name
NAMES 9
you Yet I get a kick out of y. MEN AND WOMEN 36
young as y. as ever I did HEALTH 1
as y. as he feels OLD AGE 41
Being y. is not having any money YOUTH 10
denunciation of the y. GENERATION GAP 10
I never dared be radical when y.
POLITICAL PARTIES 7
outrageous y. fellow GENERATION GAP 4
so glad I'm not y. any more OLD AGE 27
too y. to take up golf MIDDLE AGE 1
voices of y. people YOUTH 7
y. can do for the old YOUTH 6
y. have aspirations GENERATION GAP 9
you're too y. ACTING 19
your y. shoulders EDUCATION 43
Youth is wasted on the y. YOUTH 5
younger had a y. brother ACTING 3
Seek y. friends OLD AGE 37
we do not get any y. MIDDLE AGE 11
y. than a twenty-four-year-old girl
MEN AND WOMEN 46
yourself would you fall in love with y. LOVE 30
youth better to waste one's y. YOUTH 1
I have been in a y. hostel YOUTH 11
look after my y. BEHAVIOUR 31
y. is as dull as paint OLD AGE 27
Y. is wasted on the young YOUTH 5
y. of America AMERICA 30
yuppie y. version of bulimia HEALTH 4

Zanzibar count the cats in Z. TRAVEL 28
zeal bigot z. RELIGION 33
not the slightest z. LIFE 23
Zeus Z., the God GOD 27
zip Children and z. fasteners POWER 13
Z.! I was reading Schopenhauer INTELLIGENCE 7
zones We retain our z. erogenous OLD AGE 23
Zuleika Z. on a desert island WOMEN 3